INFORMATION PROCESSING

INFORMATION PROCESSING

FOURTH EDITION

Marilyn Bohl

SCIENCE RESEARCH ASSOCIATES, INC.
Chicago. Henley-on-Thames. Sydney. Toronto
A Subsidiary of IBM

Acquisition Editor	Terry Baransy
Project Editor	Ron Lewton
Copy Editor	Alice Lescalleet
Designer	Judith Olson
Production Assistant	Naomi Takigawa
Illustrators	House of Graphics
Picture Research	Roberta Spieckerman
Chapter Commentary	Lawrence Gold, Ron Lewton

Library of Congress Cataloging in Publication Data

Bohl, Marilyn.
  Information processing.

  Includes index.
  1. Electronic data processing.
  2. Electronic digital computers.
I. Title.
QA76.B58   1984   001.64   83-16508
ISBN 0-574-21445-3

10 9 8 7 6 5 4 3

Preface

As today's computers reach out to a broader base of users and extend into new areas of application, so also does *Information Processing*. This new edition, the fourth, is the result of careful efforts to retain the characteristics that made earlier editions best sellers, yet modify the content to meet current needs. Computers are becoming faster and more powerful— yet, at the same time, smaller and less expensive. They are being used not only in large government and business organizations but also in small firms, in offices, schools, and homes.

This book does not attempt to be encyclopedic. It does not present all there is to know about history, problem solving, programming, business and nonbusiness applications, or social implications. It does present an up-to-date survey of computer hardware and software systems in use today. It does discuss a wide variety of applications. *Information Processing* is designed to help you increase your understanding of computers and of how they affect each of us and our society. Saying this another way, *Information Processing* is designed to help you become computer literate.

Several hundred colleges and universities are using *Information Processing*. Their criticisms and suggestions have been heeded carefully in preparing this revision. As before, I have aimed to keep the book simple and succinct. My intent is to provide a firm, accurate base from which both instructors and students can gain maximum benefits, in line with their educational objectives as well as their personal interests or needs.

Today, more than ever before, almost everyone is a user of computers. Therefore, a major focus of this edition has been to present material with users in mind. As before, Chapters 1 and 2 explore the concept of a data-processing system, with new developments and new applications noted. A unique feature of this edition is a guided, step-by-step, hands-on interaction with the computer. Readers who have access to a computer are encouraged to see how simple communicating with a computer really is.

Chapter 3 explains how data is coded for computer processing. The next two chapters have been updated and reorganized to focus on input, in Chapter 4, and output, in Chapter 5. Magnetic tape is now discussed, together with the wide variety of disk devices and media available for systems of all sizes, in Chapter 6.

Chapters 7 and 8 cover processors and basic operations that computers can perform. Today's tiniest central processing unit—the one-chip microprocessor—is placed in perspective. Chapter 9 is new. For many readers, it may be the high point of the book. In it, the concepts, components, and operations discussed in preceding chapters are folded into a small but meaningful whole—the microcomputer and its uses. In Chapter 10, we extend this discussion to cover larger computers in a similar manner.

Chapter 11, on system analysis and design, is also new. Whether you pursue a career in computing, work in a place that uses computers, or buy one of your own, you must be able to understand user information needs. (The user may be you, but not necessarily.) Chapters 12 and 13 are designed especially for those interested in programming. Structured programming and other program-development methodologies are explained. A balanced treatment of widely used programming languages is provided.

Chapters 14 and 15 deal primarily with system software. New to this edition are brief overviews of CP/M and UNIX, operating systems used widely on computers from numerous manufacturers. The discussion of key database concepts is extended to cover not only management information systems but also decision support systems—what they are and who uses them.

Because the field of data communications is changing rapidly and is, in fact, somewhat in transition, Chapter 16 has been broadly updated. Distributed processing, word processing, electronic mail, voice mail, teleconferencing, and videotex are all discussed with users in mind.

In Chapter 17, we tie together what has preceded by looking directly at what it all means to us as members of a dynamic, changing society. Topics such as robotic systems and artificial intelligence are demystified. Issues of individual privacy and computer crime are discussed. The background you acquire through your study of *Information Processing* will help you deal with society's questions in these areas whenever you are confronted with them.

To assist both instructors and students, a topical outline of chapter content is included at the beginning of each chapter. New to this edition are the groups of full-color photographs and the prose preludes that begin each chapter, to help you see the varying influences of computers on the world around you. Also new to this edition are the brief introductions to the chapter contents, in the opening paragraphs of the chapters. They are designed to alert you to what's ahead. Another new feature of this edition are the brief but complete summaries of key points, found at the ends of the chapters. As in earlier editions, end-of-chapter discussion questions are provided. A comprehensive glossary of terms is combined with the index at the back of the book.

The New Literacy, a telecourse comprising 26 half-hour video lessons about computing, was developed concurrently with the fourth edition of *Information Processing.* Produced under the leadership of the Southern California Consortium for Community College Television, the video lessons are richly visual and employ a full range of techniques to enhance learning—documentary sequences, on-location interviews, demonstration closeups, nationwide filming of real-world uses of computers, and computer animation, to name a few. The content of each video lesson and of the corresponding portion of *Information Processing* were closely coordinated throughout their development. Thus, tutorially, they support each other.

Additional study helps are provided in the *Study Guide* to *Information Processing,* which comes in two editions—one for those who are learning about computing without reference to the telecourse, and another for those who are viewing the video lessons as well as reading the richly illustrated text materials.

Perhaps it is the focus on computer-system fundamentals, with users in mind, that makes *Information Processing* so well suited for a wide variety of courses. It is being used, for example in courses identified by the following titles:

Introduction to Computer-Based Systems
Introduction to Data Processing with BASIC
Introduction to Data Processing with COBOL
Introduction to Computers with FORTRAN
Computer Literacy
Business Data Processing and Business Applications

Some general guidelines for using *Information Processing* in such courses, with supplementary materials when appropriate, are given in the *Instructor's Guide* to *Information Processing.*

To meet the needs of its ever-expanding user base, the fourth edition of *Information Processing* is offered in two versions. The seventeen chapters of text are alike in both versions. One version is language-free. The other version— with BASIC—is intended for instructors and students who want to pursue program-development concepts further.

Sincere thanks are due the hundreds of students, teachers, and reviewers whose comments and suggestions have helped me improve the book through its various editions. I would particularly like to acknowledge the members of *The New Literacy* Advisory Committee who shared their ideas based on the rough draft of the fourth edition manuscript. A special note of appreciation is extended to:

Elvin H. "Al" Campbell, Jr., Golden West College
Wilbur P. Dershimer, Jr., Seminole Community College
Phillip J. Drummond, Queens College of the City University of New York
R. J. Fedrick, El Camino College
Peter L. Irwin, Richland College
Daniel L. Klassen, Information Technology Design Associates, Inc.
Susan Krimm, Los Angeles Pierce College
Victor Langer, Milwaukee Area Technical College
Marjorie M. Leeson, Delta College
Don B. Medley, California State Polytechnic University—Pomona
E. George Smith, Malcolm X College
Carolyn M. Stauffer, Apple Computer, Inc.

I would like to thank Sally Beaty and her staff at the Southern California Consortium for Community College Television, with whom I worked in developing *The New Literacy* telecourse. This project adds the dimensions of sound and motion to *Information Processing.* It permits students to share the knowledge and experience of computer professionals in a vast array of application environments across the country. It gives me an opportunity to reach millions of television viewers who want to learn more about the mysterious devices known as computers.

Every author knows that changes must occur to transform raw manuscript into a published book. I've been through the cycle several times. Even so, I was amazed by the metamorphosis in this transition. The full and vibrant color throughout reflect the incredible research efforts of Roberta Spieckerman and her staff and the outstanding design talent of Judith Olson. The copyediting of Alice Lescalleet and the art rendering of Alex Teshin were performed under deadline pressure and always subject to my insistence upon total accuracy. I will always be grateful to Ron Lewton and Terry Baransy. Ron's total professionalism and dedication to quality were evidenced thoughout the book's development. He led all of us in bringing together a beautifully crafted product. Terry shared with us his vision and his confidence in what could be accomplished. For all these efforts and those of others whose names are unknown to me I offer very special thanks.

Marilyn Bohl

Contents

ix

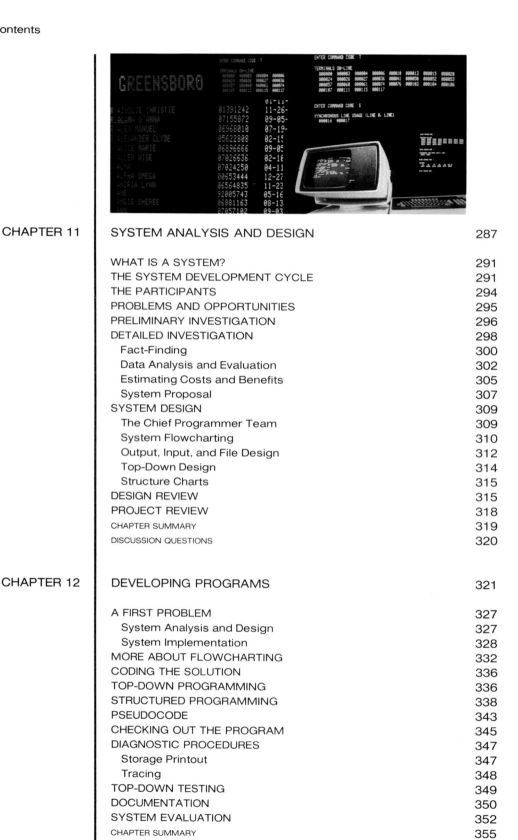

ABOUT THE AUTHOR

A list of Marilyn Bohl's professional activities might make one pause and wonder where she finds the time to pursue all her interests. Marilyn is an extremely dedicated and energetic person, with an impressive string of accomplishments to her credit. She is an award-winning IBM Development Manager in San Jose, California. Positioned at the forefront of technological developments, she is experienced in software design, system and application programming, database concepts, and customer data processing education and documentation. She is the author of eight books on data processing, programming, and related topics, which are widely used by colleges and universities throughout the world. A former teacher, Marilyn is very sympathetic to the needs of educators and she is dedicated to helping students learn more about computers and computer-related careers. In her "spare" time, she is a jogger, a country music fan, and an ardent supporter of the Dallas Cowboys.

COMPUTERS AND THEIR USES

This statue of a warrior comes down to us from antiquity. A product of early Greek civilization, it had aged with the passing of time; but with computer help, much of its beauty and force have been restored.

In ancient days, information was passed down from generation to generation more often by word of mouth or by demonstration than by writing, and a single person could possibly know all that was known by a generation.

By contrast, much of the information of our generation came to us through the written word, and our body of knowledge has grown so much that it would take many lifetimes for one to master it. Accordingly, in these times, most of us specialize in certain fields of knowledge.

Computers themselves have grown out of the trend toward specialization. As individuals and small groups specialized and took over tasks previously shared by an entire community, they had to handle a lot more work and information. They were aided

by technology, at first in the form of hand-operated weaving machines, then automated weaving machines, and now computerized weaving machines. Each step in technology filled a need, until, at last, computers appeared. Where previous forms of technology filled the needs of agricultural or industrial societies, computers fill the information-processing needs of today.

Paradoxically, as individuals have tended toward more narrow specialization, computers have become broader in their applications. Today, a Sperry-Univac computer helps a German company design and manufacture lenses; that same computer can also help the company with order processing and inventory control.

Modern computers are also performing such amazingly diverse tasks as sorting tomatoes in a California cannery, switching calls in a Near Eastern communication system, controlling a robotic device delicate enough to handle a single egg, as well as educating a preschool child, or monitoring production in a Mexican steel mill.

Just as the early weaving machines were a helpful extension of human hands to multiply the output of a single individual, modern computers are an extension of human intellect to multiply the amount of data that can be managed. Used in combination with other technology, today's computers can increase the productivity of the individual far more than any other advance made since the Industrial Revolution.

© Erich Hartmann / Magnum

Courtesy Sperry Corporation

Reproduced with permission of AT&T

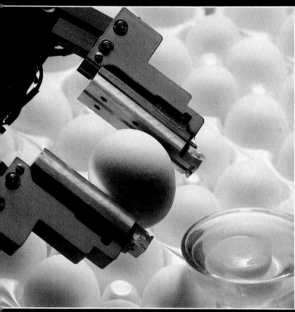

Courtesy Chris Maynard

Courtesy Hewlett-Packard Company

Courtesy Apple Computer, Inc.

1 COMPUTERS AND THEIR USES

Every day you use tools. You need a certain key to unlock your bike padlock or your car door. A telephone puts you in contact with friends across town or across continents. Radio and television help you to learn about what's going on worldwide. This book is a tool to help you learn about computers. Computers may well be the most exciting, most powerful, most versatile tools yet developed.

Just as hammers, pulleys, cranes, and bulldozers extend our physical power, so computers extend our thinking power. Some of you may be "at home" (even literally) with computers; you use them as casually as you use pencil and paper. Others may be awed by computers—what are these fantastic machines everybody is talking about?

In fact, many of us use computers daily without even realizing we are doing so. Microprocessors—the "hearts" of today's smallest computers—are everywhere. Wristwatches, microwave ovens, automatic sprinkling systems, automobile carburetors, and electronic security systems contain them. Slide rules and pocket calculators are giving way to them. You may not be a grand master (or even an expert) at any of the 300 or so video games in common use, but you can probably learn to play most of them without much trouble. Can you imagine blaming a hammer for hitting your thumb? Or an automobile for running a traffic light? Similarly, we can't blame a computer for mixing up class schedules, printing statements for bills that aren't owed, and so on. One purpose of this book is to help you to understand why we must look beyond the computer to determine who or what is at fault when things go wrong.

The phrase *computer literacy* has no single, universally accepted meaning. It means different things to different people. That should not surprise us since even the general term *literacy* has several definitions. We may say that a literate person is one who can read and write, or one who demonstrates a basic ability to communicate. On the other hand, we may consider a literate person to be one who is especially knowledgeable, learned, or well read in a particular field or discipline.

In practice, scientific and technological literacy has come to mean the possession of an in-depth knowledge in a chosen area of science or technology (say, botany, geology, or the electromagnetic spectrum), as well as an understanding of the implications of that science or technology for individuals and for society. In keeping with this practice, we might choose to define *computer literacy* to be the knowledge and understanding one needs to function effectively within a given social role that directly or indirectly involves computers. With computers becoming so prevalent, the need to be computer literate confronts each and every one of us. This book, *Information Processing*, is designed to help you learn more about computers and their implications for you and your role in society. You will not know or understand all about computers when you've completed this book. No one book could contain all the relevant information. Furthermore, new computer information is being created daily. Computer technology is still developing. Computer history is right now in the making. By studying this book, you will become better equipped to participate in this exciting adventure.

In this opening chapter, we look first at data processing, the societal needs that initially gave rise to computers, and the tasks they were designed to perform. We trace some of the technological milestones that have brought us both multimillion-dollar supercomputers and pocket computers that can be ordered from catalogs for less than one hundred dollars. We look at some of the many, diverse ways computers are being used. We summarize briefly why studying about computers makes sense. You're helped to think about employment opportunities directly or indirectly involved with computers. The perspective you gain by studying this chapter will be useful to you throughout your work in this course and in your daily exposure to the many facets of computer application.

A DATA-PROCESSING SYSTEM

Since very early times, humans have searched continuously for efficient ways to obtain information. We want the facts. We want to manipulate those facts to obtain new facts, or results. Once we understand those results, we may decide we need other, related facts or results. We go after them. We manipulate them. Very soon, we become engulfed in a sea of paperwork. Each time we receive a document, we create another one. That document, in turn, leads to the creation of other documents.

As an example, let's consider the paperwork required in a company that manufactures fabrics for the wholesale market. The research scientists in this company work daily to improve the quality of current materials; to develop new fabrics with greater resistance to wear, heat, and chemicals; to find easier ways to produce synthetic materials; and so on. These scientists record the data obtained from their experiments, use the data to make calculations, and summarize their findings in various recommendations and reports.

In the same company, the manufacturing department requires summarized data to control production. What items are needed? What raw materials must be purchased to produce the items? What people and machines are needed to meet current production goals?

The financial department of the company processes data to produce accurate records of the company's financial transactions. Accountants deal with vendors, invoices, purchase orders, shipping orders, customer statements, general ledgers, budgets, variance reports, annual reports, reports to stockholders . . . the list is endless. Together, these documents reflect the total worth and profitability of the company.

Data processing, the modern name for paperwork, is the collecting, processing, and distributing of facts and figures to achieve a desired result. The facts and figures are *data.* This data, together with the equipment (devices) and procedures by which the result is achieved, is part of a data-processing system. The devices vary. In some data-processing operations, all work is done with pencil and paper; in others, the work is done by machines; in still others, people and machines work together. For a given task, the procedures are basically the same. The data may change. That is, the same devices and procedures may be reused with different data. (See Figure 1-1.)

We can treat the terms *data* and *information* as synonyms, or we can distinguish between them by saying that data is raw material gathered from one or more sources, and that information is processed, or "finished," data. Generally, *information* implies data that is organized and meaningful to the person or group receiving it. Since knowledge and decision-making activities are important in many different areas, and at many different levels of detail, one person's information may be another person's data.

DATA PROCESSING IN THE PAST

The efforts leading to today's computers began several hundred years ago. As early as 1642, an 18-year-old Frenchman, Blaise Pascal, developed a mechanical adding machine with rotating gears that contained teeth representing the digits 0 through 9. Carrying was automatic: when a gear was rotated past the tooth representing the digit 9, the next gear to the left rotated one tooth (or digit). Some of you may be familiar with the Pascal programming language in use today. Those who aren't will learn about it later in this book. The language was named for that young Frenchman.

Extending the principle of the adding machine, Gottfried Leibnitz, a German mathematician, devised a calculating machine that multiplied by repeated addition and divided by repeated subtraction. This machine was demonstrated for the first time in 1694. As time went on, more sophisticated mechanical methods of computation either supplemented or replaced manual methods.

In the 1880s, the U.S. Bureau of Census employed Dr. Herman Hollerith to develop a mechanical method of performing a massive data-tabulation task – the processing of census data, which by constitutional provision must occur every 10 years. He developed a device that coded population data as punched holes in

FIGURE 1-1 Data-processing systems vary widely, and may or may not include computers. (*Courtesy* [A] *Raoul Hackel/Stock Boston;* [B] *John Running/Stock, Boston;* [C] *TRW Inc.;* [D] *Magnuson Computer Systems*)

cards. The data that had been recorded in this way was then read, or sensed, by another mechanical device.

The 1890 census was completed in $2\frac{1}{2}$ years, less than a third the time required to complete the 1880 census, despite the fact that the population of the United States had increased from 50 million to 63 million during the decade. Hollerith's punched-card data-processing system made this saving of time possible.

In 1896, Hollerith formed the Tabulating Machine Company to manufacture and sell punched-card equipment. In 1911, merchant-banker Charles R. Flint organized 13 companies into a holding company known as the Computing-Tabulating-Recording Company (C-T-R). Hollerith became C-T-R's chief engineer. In 1914, Flint identified the person he wanted as C-T-R's president: Thomas J. Watson, Sr. Ten years later, C-T-R became International Business Machines Corporation, the well-known IBM.

ENTER THE COMPUTER

Until World War II, data was processed either manually or mechanically. The war created an urgent need for new data-processing methods. People involved in aircraft design, development of military weapons, procurement of supplies, and so on, needed more efficient ways to handle and process information and statistics vital to the war effort. Increased speed and accuracy in computation were essential.

Howard Aiken, a naval lieutenant assigned to Harvard University to find faster ways of processing data, approached Watson. Would IBM, already a leader in business machines, provide the financial and technical assistance needed to develop not simply a faster mechanical calculator, but rather an electromechanical one? Watson agreed. During the early 1940s, a team of Harvard graduate students and IBM engineers worked to build the machine. Known as the *Mark I*, it accepted data on punched cards as input, performed calculations by means of electromagnetic relays that served as on/off switches and mechanical arithmetic counters, and punched the results into cards. The device was "automatic" in that computations were controlled by a prepunched paper tape; no step-by-step human intervention during processing was required. When completed, the Mark I was 51 feet long, 8 feet high, and weighed 5 tons. It could add or subtract two 23-digit numbers in 0.3 second, multiply them in 5.7 seconds, or divide them in 5.3 seconds. The Mark I has been referred to as the first *electromechanical computer*. (See Figure 1-2.)

During the same time frame (early 1940s), technology was also being advanced at other universities. John Atanasoff, a professor at Iowa State College, decided to employ a binary (base two) approach to machine calculations. He and a graduate student, Clifford Berry, succeeded in building the *Atanasoff-Berry Computer (ABC)*, which became operational in 1942. It was specifically designed to solve simultaneous linear equations. Though not widely recognized at the time, this work was key to another step in computer development. The impetus behind that step was the U.S. Army's need for high-speed computation of firing and ballistic tables to guide artillerymen in aiming weapons. Working under a contract between the U.S. Army and the Moore School of Electrical Engineering at the University of Pennsylvania, John W. Mauchly and J. Presper Eckert developed the *ENIAC* (Electronic Numerical Integrator and Calculator). In this machine (as in the ABC), the switching and control functions that had

FIGURE 1-2
Prepunched paper tapes (A) directed operations of the 51-foot, 5-ton Mark I (B), the first electromechanical computer. (*Courtesy Harvard University, Cruft Photo Lab*)

been performed by electromagnetic relays were handled by vacuum tubes. The relatively slow movements of switches were replaced by the swift motions of electrons. Computations could be performed hundreds of times faster. It's said, for example, that the ENIAC could perform in one day the equivalent of 300 days of manual calculations. The ENIAC was a 30-ton, 1500-square-foot monstrosity. More importantly, it was the first *electronic digital computer* put to extended, practical use (in contrast, the ABC was largely a prototyping effort). Though not completed in time to help in the war effort, the ENIAC was used in ballistic research at the U.S. Army's Aberdeen Proving Grounds in Maryland from 1946 to 1955, when it was retired to the Smithsonian Institution.

Europe's first large-scale computing device, the *EDSAC* (Electronic Delay-Storage Automatic Computer), was completed at Cambridge University in 1949. It had, in addition to electronic circuitry, one very significant new characteristic: Both the instructions to control the computer and the data to be operated on were stored in the computer itself. The instructions were arranged in sequential order to form a complete *program*. One instruction in such a program might tell the computer to add, for example, then give the location (also in the computer) of the data to be added. The next instruction might indicate the location where the result of the addition should be stored. Computers in which instructions were stored internally were called *stored-program computers*.

Why was this development significant? In the first computers, machine instructions were programmed on wired control panels, punched cards, or punched paper tapes. Detailed instructions had to be either wired in at the beginning of a job or read into the machine in separate steps as the job progressed. Data read into the computer was processed according to the instructions contained in these preset devices.

It soon became apparent that such techniques limited the performance of the computer. A machine that can calculate faster and more accurately than a human being should not have to depend on a human operator for instructions. Thus, a computer with an *internal storage unit*, or *memory*, for both data and programs was a giant stride forward. It was not dependent on a human operator for instructions; it could process a program in much the same way it processed data and it could perform any number of consecutive operations at its own rate. It could even modify its own instructions if certain developments during processing made modification desirable.

COMMERCIAL USE OF COMPUTERS

The initial opinion of many scientists who developed early computers was that only a few computers would ever be designed and produced. A computer was very large and very expensive. Building one took a lot of effort and a long time. Once built, though, a computer could do many complex calculations at greater speeds and with more accuracy than humans. Unfortunately, few people or groups, it was believed, would have need of its extensive mathematical capabilities.

A *UNIVAC I* computer produced by Sperry Rand was installed at the U.S. Bureau of the Census in 1951. It was the first commercially available (that is, other than one-of-a-kind) computer. (See Figure 1-3.) IBM installed its first commercial computer, an IBM 650, in Boston in 1954. From these beginnings arose the giant computer industry.

BUSINESS DATA PROCESSING

When personnel in business organizations were first exposed to computers, they were impressed and interested—not in the computers' ability to do complex arithmetic, but rather in their ability to do routine business-type tasks. The first business use of a computer occurred at General Electric Appliance Park in Louisville, Kentucky, in 1954. That decade saw the introduction of several medium-size and large computers designed primarily to take over the burdensome clerical chores that beset so many growing companies.

For the most part, the computers of the 1950s and 1960s were similar to earlier computers that had been designed primarily to solve scientific, mathematical,

A

B

FIGURE 1-3
John W. Mauchly and J. Presper Eckert (second and third from left, in A) were on hand when representatives of the U.S. Bureau of Census accepted delivery of a UNIVAC I (shown in both A and B) in 1951. (*Courtesy Sperry Corporation*)

and engineering problems. Some differences were significant, however. In scientific research, most problems involve complex calculations on relatively few items (numerical values). In business operations, the reverse is often true: Vast numbers of items must be operated upon, but the actual calculations are, by comparison, quite simple. The new computers and data-processing systems were designed accordingly.

The early computational devices read input data from punched cards and punched paper tapes. Output was often provided as printed documents. In 1946, a new data-recording medium was introduced: *magnetic tape*. Output information was stored as magnetized spots on the metal surface of the tape. It could be read as input during subsequent processing. To satisfy the information needs of business organizations, however, faster input/output (I/O) devices were required. Since business data processing often involves large volumes of input and output, high-speed I/O was desirable. In 1956, the success of plastic audio tapes inspired computer designers to try a similar approach in developing magnetic tape for computers. Reels of tape that somewhat resembled the reels used in tape recorders were mounted on magnetic-tape units. Data was either read from or recorded on these tapes by the computer. (See Figure 1-4.)

Data could be read from magnetic tape 50 to 75 times faster than it could be read from cards. Reels of magnetic tape required much less storage space than stacks of punched cards. Maintaining data in sequence between processing runs (that is, between executions of a program) was also much easier. Once data was placed on magnetic tape, it remained in its established sequence. In contrast, cards, and therefore data on cards, were more likely to be disarranged, lost, or destroyed.

Because magnetic tape could only be used to store data sequentially, the use of tape had certain data-processing implications. The complete tape had to be rewritten every time a single item or a small group of items was added or changed. Since frequent rewriting of complete tapes was not practical, *batch processing*, the technique of accumulating data in batches before it was put on tape, was developed. This meant that each item of data was only as current as the batch in which it was delivered to the computer. In ordinary operation, hours and sometimes even days might elapse between processing of batches. Furthermore, although tapes could be read faster than cards, the retrieval of information from tapes was often very slow. Unless information was wanted in the same order as the data had been recorded previously, the computer was forced to search

FIGURE 1-4
Magnetic tapes and tape input/output units were developed to ease data-handling tasks and increase I/O speeds for business applications. (*Courtesy IBM Corporation*)

through the tape until it found that information. A great deal of data was read unnecessarily.

Batch processing was very satisfactory for business applications such as weekly payroll and customer billing, but it was not well suited for keeping track of constantly changing inventory or for processing incoming orders from customers. To meet business needs for more responsive processing, rotating *random-access storage* (also called *direct storage*, as opposed to sequential storage) was introduced by Univac in 1955. A *magnetic drum* was used as the data-recording medium. With this new development, the computer was able to go directly to a certain location in a file stored on a drum to write or read data, without having to read all the preceding records in the file. Systems with *transaction-processing* capabilities were developed. Under this approach, data was not collected in batches; instead, it was accepted for processing as it was generated, without preliminary sorting, editing, or holding operations.

A magnetic drum, like the first recording medium used in early phonographs, is large and cylindrical, creating some disadvantages. Only its outer surface can be used for recording data. Because of its size, the drum is not mobile. It cannot be removed from its encasement in the machine unit that holds it.

In 1956, IBM introduced another storage medium based on techniques developed by the recording industry: the platter, or *magnetic disk*. The disk differed from the drum in that both sides of the disk could be used for recording data. Each disk storage unit had a drive on which a stack of magnetically coated rotating disks was mounted. The disks contained numerous tracks, and data could be recorded on, or retrieved from, specific tracks without regard to the order in which it and other data was recorded on the tracks.

The first of these disk storage units, the IBM 305, was developed as part of IBM's RAMAC (*random-access memory accounting machine*) system. It had fifty 24-inch disks, stacked on a vertical spindle like records in an early "jukebox." (See Figure 1-5.) The disks could hold 5 million characters of data—an awesome amount at the time. As we'll see, disk storage densities have doubled about every $2\frac{1}{2}$ years since, leading to today's 5000-fold improvement. Today's storage equivalent of the fifty 24-inch disks of the IBM 305 is a single disk just $5\frac{1}{2}$ inches in diameter.

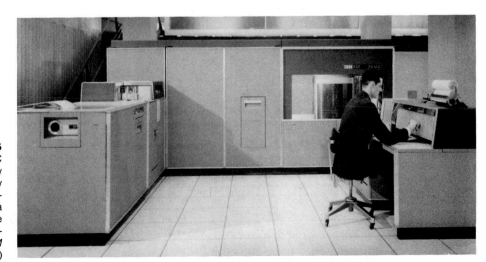

FIGURE 1-5
The disks of IBM's RAMAC system were monstrous by today's standards but they represented a major technological breakthrough: Data stored on them could be read in any order during processing. (*Courtesy IBM Corporation*)

COMPUTER GENERATIONS

Even as new data-recording media and devices were being introduced, continuing developments in electronics and solid-state physics led to newer and better internal components for computers. Like the ABC and other early one-of-a-kind computers, the UNIVAC I and its successors built during the early and mid-1950s had *vacuum tubes* as their basic components. (See Figure 1-6A.) As a group, they are called *first-generation computers.*

In 1947, scientists at Bell Labs invented a tiny, solid-state device called the *transistor* (short for transfer resistor). Made of semiconducting materials, the transistor could act as a switch controlling the ebb and flow of electrons. In the late 1950s, transistors replaced vacuum tubes as the major components of computers. They were much smaller than vacuum tubes, worked much faster, generated far less heat, and were more reliable. Many transistors could be mounted closely together and connected by flat snakelike wires on small plastic cards known as circuit boards. (See Figure 1-6B.) Computers having transistors as basic components are called *second-generation computers.*

New technological advances miniaturized and refined various components of second-generation computers. Electronics manufacturers realized that the circuitry connecting components could be etched into the circuit boards rather than be accomplished by wiring. As many as 664 transistors, diodes, and other components—the equivalent of 64 complete circuits—could be placed on a single silicon chip less than an eighth of an inch square. (See Figure 1-6C.) There was no need for soldering, since all the components on a chip were fused together during the production process. Circuits created in this manner are called *integrated*

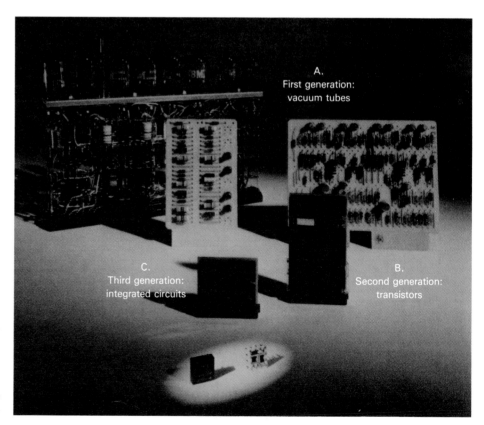

FIGURE 1-6
First-, second-, and third-generation computers were characterized by vacuum tubes (A), transistors (B), and integrated circuits (C), respectively. (*Courtesy IBM Corporation*)

circuits, or *IC's.* Computers having IC's as basic components are called *third-generation computers.*

The change to third-generation computers began in 1963-64, but the major transition occurred in 1965 when IBM began to install its System/360 family of computers. The follow-on computer family, System/370, and large computers produced by other manufacturers in the 1970s incorporated further refinements. Through techniques of *large-scale integration* (*LSI*), designers kept cramming more and more transistors and more and more circuits on a single chip—not to save space, but to save time. Electronic pulses can move through circuitry at the speed of light—186,000 miles per second—but no faster. The shorter the route the pulses must travel, the quicker the processing and the bigger the problem that can be solved. As more logic or memory circuits are placed on a single chip, the cost per circuit decreases. This practice makes it economically feasible to use more circuits and thereby increase computing power, or to offer an equivalent amount of computing power in a much smaller piece of equipment and at a much lower price.

By 1980, the $2.5 million UNIVAC I computer could be duplicated on a single circuit board for less than $500. A set of computations that had cost $1.96 to do when certain System/370 computers were introduced less than a decade earlier could be done for about 30¢. Looking at the UNIVAC I comparison another way, if the same technological improvements had applied to cars, a Ferrari that sold for $28,000 in 1950 would have cost $5.60 in 1980. Pursuing this same idea, a *Time* magazine writer suggested (in a "Machine of the Year" article, January 3, 1983) that a Rolls-Royce might be had today for $2.75 and that it could run 3 million miles on one gallon of gasoline.

In the 1969–71 time frame, another major technological breakthrough occurred, not in chip density but in chip architecture. Prior to that time, the circuits etched in a single chip of silicon could perform very complex functions, but the functions were rigidly fixed as a part of the production process. A chip designed for one purpose could be used only for that purpose, and not for others. In a daring conceptual move, Ted Hoff, a young engineer at Intel, and his associates determined to concentrate the arithmetic and logic circuitry needed for computations on one chip, and to keep that chip (and hence its circuitry) separate from the fixed control and input/output circuitry. The result—a programmable one-chip processing unit, the *microprocessor.* With this versatility, silicon chips became the building blocks of societal enterprise. Microprocessors began to invade everything, from toasters to spacecrafts, from wristwatches to telephone switchboards. In 1975, the first microprocessor-based computer for hobbyists appeared. Known as the MITS Altair 8800, it could be purchased in kit form for $395, then assembled in much the same way as high-fidelity music system components and television sets had been assembled for years. From these humble beginnings have come the Timex Sinclairs, Commodore VIC-20s, TRS-80s, Apple IIs, and other computers now offered as off-the-shelf items at Radio Shacks, ComputerLands, Sears Business Systems Centers, Penney's, and similar stores everywhere.

Annual shipments of microprocessors increased from a few thousand in 1971 to about 200 million, worldwide, in 1981. When the Intel 8080 microprocessor was announced in 1974, it cost about $360. By 1984, it was selling for less than $3.00. Microprocessors have become the "crude oil" of electronics. They're used in computers that book seats on jumbo jets and that help keep the jets from colliding in the air. They count votes, maintain mailing lists, prepare personalized letters to voters, assist in opinion polls, and keep track of candidates' comings and goings. We might say they elect presidents. They control electrical currents that stimulate muscles in otherwise motionless limbs, thereby enabling paralyzed patients to move and even to walk. They're in weapons of war and in systems for peace. They are whatever we choose to make with them.

Technological progress continues, not by magic but by careful study, creativity, innovativeness, and hard work. At Bell Labs, for example, the BELL-MAC-32A microprocessor and the 256,000-cell random-access memory (RAM) chip represent today's leading edge of microelectronics. (See Figure 1-7.) Through *very-large-scale-integration* (*VLSI*) techniques, more than 100,000 transistors are placed on one chip about the size of a thumbnail. In 1981, Hewlett-Packard scientists at the company's Ft. Collins, Colorado, facility achieved a technological breakthrough that allowed them to pack 450,000 transistors on a single quarter-inch-square chip of silicon. Mapping every street of Los Angeles on the head of a pin would be an equivalent feat. In 1982, the chip served as a basic building block in Hewlett-Packard's HP 9000 family of computers. (See Figure 1-8.) By the end of the century, scientists expect to jam

FIGURE 1-7
Through increased miniaturization, scientists at Bell Labs have developed processor chips (top) and memory chips (bottom) that make the face of a watch look big in comparison. (*Courtesy Bell Laboratories*)

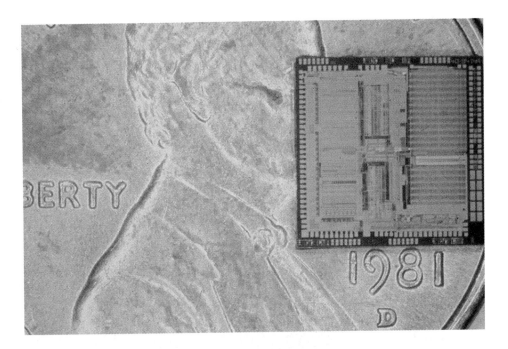

FIGURE 1-8
Hewlett-Packard's 450,000-transistor microprocessor chip (A) is the "heart" of its HP 9000 desktop computer (B). (*Courtesy Hewlett-Packard Company*)

B

more than one million memory cells—1,048,576 to be exact—onto a single chip, a density approaching that of the neurons in the human brain.

In a very real sense, these advancements are significant to each of us. The potential scope of computer use has spread from the realm of large businesses and organizations to the realm of small businesses and even of individual consumers. Having now acquired a basic understanding of how computers came about, let's take a brief look at some of their current uses.

COMPUTERS IN MANUFACTURING

Product planning and control for even relatively simple things means dealing with raw material supply, inventory handling and storage, labor, work center capacity, and accounting, among many other factors. In the early 1960s, computers were first applied by manufacturing firms in the recording and processing of routine financial transactions. Employees received computer-generated paychecks, accounts-payable master files were computerized, and so on. Computerized accounting seemed to work well. Shop foremen were still spending 50 to 75 percent of their time expediting, looking for materials, and in general, "putting out fires." Labor costs were on an ever-accelerating upward spiral. In the 1970s, most if not all manufacturing firms also faced the hard realities of increasing competition. Look what happened to audio equipment, cameras, calculators, and watches, they noted. What can and must we learn from the experiences of the large automakers or from the semiconductor manufacturers? How to increase *productivity* (the rate of finished output per unit of labor input) became, and remains, a major concern at all levels of business management.

The acronomyn *MRP*, meaning *material requirements planning*, has received much attention since the late 1960s. Basically, MRP is a system that relates requirements for assembled (or formulated) products to an end product. It embraces a no-nonsense master production schedule for, say, a year, taking into account level of assembly and time requirements and making prompt adjustments when operations don't work out exactly as planned. Various raw materials, components, and subassemblies from lower levels flow into the system and merge at higher and higher levels to become finished items.

On an automotive, TV, or electronic typewriter assembly line, for example, hundreds of parts and subassemblies from all over the plant or elsewhere must converge in the final assembly area at precisely the right time and place, and in precisely the right sequence. Balancing the line for smooth, efficient production—that is, scheduling the manufacture, test, and movement of all parts and the assignments of workers—is a big job and a recurring one. It is a job that computers can do, while printing out reports that people on the shop floor need in order to manage the operation efficiently.

Today, some firms have moved beyond MRP to what's known as *MRP II*, or *manufacturing resource planning*. Here, all aspects of manufacturing (including not only production but also engineering, marketing, and finance) are tied together through one consistent set of numbers that can be analyzed by managers of all functions, and at all levels, for use in decision making. The numbers are financial numbers, expressed in dollars-and-cents terms, but they are derived directly from ongoing operations. This coordinated management was impossible before MRP II, when what was really happening on the plant floor bore little or no resemblance to the formal paperwork, or to what was supposed to be happening.

No computerization of factory operations can succeed without basic inventory control. In some installations, computer-controlled inventory stocks have been cut as much as 75 percent with no loss of production, simply because production lines operate with "just enough," and computers and personnel know what's on hand and where it's located. (See Figure 1-9.)

Computers can also take an active part in the physical control of manufacturing processes. *Numerical control (NC)* of machine tools was introduced in the late 1950s as a means of guiding a production machine through a complete

FIGURE 1-9
Both the number and location of items in inventory can be displayed on an online terminal in the stock room at any time. (*Courtesy NCR Corporation / Rainbow Natural Foods*)

manufacturing cycle by means of coded instructions recorded on a computer-generated NC tape. Once work has been placed in position on the machine, the coded instructions control the selection of the machine tools, feed rate, spindle speed, coolant setting, and the direction and distance of movements until the work is completed. A high-speed precision drilling machine is a common example of a production machine often controlled by means of an NC tape. This is truly *computer-aided manufacturing (CAM)*.

A step beyond the use of numerical control is the use of *robotic systems*. These are general-purpose programmable machines that can do any of several tasks under stored-program control. Contrary to what you might expect, these systems are not usually built to resemble humans. The resemblance is coincidental. They are built to do work that might otherwise be done by humans, or not done at all. (See Figure 1-10.) Spray painting, spot welding, lifting, assembling, and packaging are some tasks that they accomplish easily, without complaints, coffee breaks, sick days, or vacations. Given the decreasing costs of microprocessors and other electronic circuitry, they are becoming less expensive rather than more costly. As we'll see, this means that small manufacturers as well as big auto, aerospace, and heavy-equipment companies can put them to work.

Small computers are being used increasingly in *process-control* applications. They're found, for example, in paper plants, steel mills, oil refineries, and the like. A process-control computer reads measuring and sampling instruments, checks the readings for conformity to preset limits, relays corrections to adjusting devices as needed, and prints out a continuous record of instrument readings, if desired.

Product testing also lends itself to computerization. Quality-control test times are reduced significantly, yet inspections are completed with new highs in accuracy. Products that are built right the first time need not be recalled or returned for rework after they've been shipped to customers.

COMPUTER-AIDED DESIGN AND ENGINEERING

Without computers, the U.S. space program might never have come about. At the Kennedy Space Center, for example, a highly automated Launch Processing System (LPS) checked and rechecked thousands of bits of data, some as often as

FIGURE 1-10
At RCA's robotics research laboratory, a computer-controlled robotic system assembles simple parts in studies designed to increase automation in manufacturing. (*Courtesy RCA*)

100 times a second, during the 1981–82 Columbia space shuttle launching countdowns. Eight autonomous networks, each comprising up to 40 computers, participated. On board the Columbia were additional computers and associated display equipment. From prelaunch checkout through landing, these computers helped flight crews and controllers to monitor conditions, command and control the orbiter, and obtain information on the status of the Columbia and its missions.

As awesome as these tasks are, the behind-the-scenes preparatory tasks that are basic to space flights are equally awesome. Before a spacecraft travels beyond Earth's gravity, goes into orbit, or starts on a trip to our moon or another planet, and even before it's built, computers are involved. Proposed characteristics of the spacecraft – shape, length, width, weight, exterior coating, power of thrust, and so on – are provided as input to a computer. Through *simulation*, the effects of gravity, thrust angles, weight loss with fuel burnup, and other environmental influences upon the proposed spacecraft are studied. If the spacecraft does not respond as desired, the characteristics can be changed and the simulation rerun. The computer completes within seconds or minutes intricate calculations that would take years to complete manually. The simulations are but one of many techniques of *computer-aided design (CAD)* applied throughout the space program. (See Figure 1-11.)

In like manner, CAD simulations are used by engineers to analyze the designs for bridges, skyscrapers, and other structures. Architects use them to model the traffic flow when designing large office complexes, shopping centers, and airports. Through interactive graphics, they develop detailed floor plans and create human-factored work centers (e.g., in kitchens or in office areas). The color

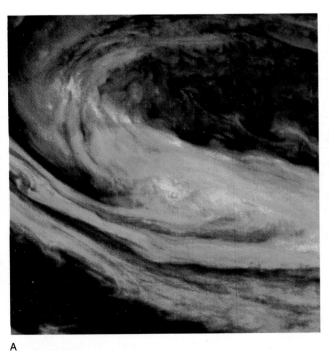

A   B

FIGURE 1-11 Without computers, space trips by the Voyager I, providing pictures such as this one of Jupiter's Great Red Spot (A) might never happened. Scientists at the Johnson Space Center in Houston (B) depend on computers to monitor and direct space activities. (*Courtesy* [A] *Jet Propulsion Laboratory / California Institute of Technology / NASA;* [B] *TRW Inc. / NASA*)

schemes and interior decor for rooms can be chosen from a wide variety of alternatives. Then, both designers and clients can "walk through" the planned buildings and work centers. The computer generates graphics on the display screen, from the perspectives of persons inside the buildings. When everyone is satisfied, architectural blueprints, contractual agreements, and orders for needed materials can be generated as printed output.

Today, major productivity gains are being achieved through combining the techniques of computer-aided design and computer-aided manufacturing in CAD/CAM applications. The data that a designer needs to specify the geometry of a part is also needed to determine how a cutting machine such as a lathe must be operated to shape the part. If all the data is stored in a computer-accessible database, engineering designs can be transferred directly to the manufacturing floor. By 1995, an estimated 190,000 CAD/CAM systems will be installed, doing mechanical design, civil engineering and architectural design, and electronic and electrical design and manufacture. Given what we already know about the microscopic detail required in IC-chip design and manufacture, it should not surprise us to learn that computers are involved. We might say that computers are producing themselves, or perhaps, more accurately, their descendants.

Finally, no discussion of CAD/CAM would be complete without a look at *solids modeling (SM)*. Computer systems with SM capabilities allow designed objects to be viewed either as wire frames or as three-dimensional (3D) solids. Ordinarily hidden lines of the wire frame can be removed—say, to produce illustrations for technical manuals—or analyzed to see how the objects react under stress (simulation again). Sections of a solid model can be cut away to reveal inner subassemblies and components. Bills of material, cost estimates, and inventory control reports can be generated as byproducts. (See Figure 1-12.)

FIGURE 1-12
Solid surfaces can be peeled away (A) or made translucent, complete with shadows (B), in today's advanced CAD/CAM solids modeling systems. (*Courtesy General Electric Research and Development Center*)

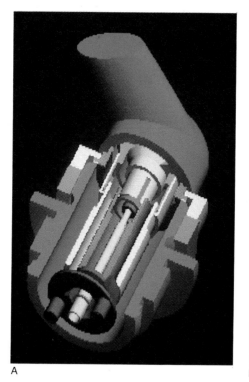

A

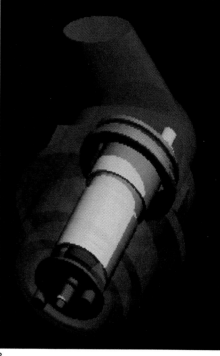

B

COMPUTERS IN MEDICINE

In no area of human life is expert, personal service more essential than it is in medical care. Today, an electrocardiograph system containing a small computer can be wheeled to a patient's bedside. Within minutes, it can record and interpret an electrocardiogram (ECG). The ECG is a graph of the pulses that cause the patient's heart to beat. By interpreting the ECG, the computer helps the attending doctor to locate quickly any damaged or diseased heart areas. Proper treatment can then be prescribed.

At many hospitals, computers are being used to interpret medical X-rays. A CAT (computerized axial tomography) scanner takes many small X-ray views from slightly different positions about a patient's body. A computer combines all the X-ray pictures to form a cross-sectional view of the patient's body on a display screen. Clinical laboratories that must deal with hundreds of chemical blood tests, tissue tests, urine tests, microbiologic tests, and so on, are putting computers to good use. In intensive care units, computers continuously monitor instruments and sensors attached to critically ill patients to detect and report any abnormalities. (See Figure 1-13.)

Another machine containing a small computer, commonly known as a blood cell separator, can accept blood directly from donors or patients. The machine separates the blood into such major components as red cells, white cells, plasma,

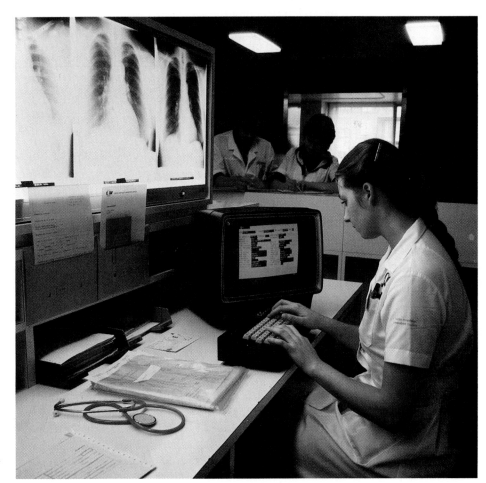

FIGURE 1-13
The staff at Lausanne, Switzerland, uses its Hospital Information System for admission, discharge, and transfer, for outpatient services, as a central locator, a medical records index, for patient accounting, medical record statistics, laboratory procedures, and total patient-care information. (*Courtesy Burroughs Corporation*)

and platelets. Concentrates of the components are used in transfusions to control acute infections, plasma abnormalities, and other disorders. One pint of blood may, in effect, go much further because the separated concentrates can be used exactly as needed. One patient may need only white blood cells; another may need only blood plasma.

Today's doctors, clinics, and hospitals could not get along without computers to help them with administrative paperwork—insurance claims, patient billing, accounts receivable, payroll, inventory control, bed accounting, and the like. In hospital kitchens, menus are planned, food is ordered, and meals are cooked with computer help. From admission to discharge, data about a patient is added continually to the patient's history record. Doctors and nurses can access the patient's record to check the results of tests administered in various laboratories, to determine what drugs have been ordered from the pharmacy (or should be) and when they have been administered (or should be), and so on. By freeing doctors and nurses from much time-consuming, routine clerical work, computers make it possible for the hospital staff to give patients more personal attention.

On an even broader scale, researchers are using computers to analyze thousands of medical records. They're studying the records to isolate causes of illnesses and to find relationships between people's habits or diets and certain diseases. For example, the link between cigarette smoking and lung cancer was proved with computer assistance. Summaries of all medical articles published in the United States, data on more than 1500 drugs, and descriptions of 3500 diseases and disorders are available to physicians who subscribe to AMA/Net, a joint American Medical Association and GTE Telenet effort. An electronic mail service called MED/Mail supports doctor-to-doctor, doctor-to-hospital, and doctor-to-group-of-subscribing-doctors communications throughout the Telenet network.

COMPUTERS AND THE LAW

In the late 1970s, the Bank of America building in Santa Barbara, California, was bombed. Evidence was collected, a suspect was identified, and the case was solved—with the help of a computer.

Among the collected evidence was a ceiling tile from the bank building containing bomb fragments and unburned explosives, a pipe from the suspect's garage, and soil from the suspect's shoes. These were taken to the Treasury Department's Bureau of Alcohol, Tobacco, and Firearms (ATF) Crime Laboratory. There, the material was chemically treated and exposed to radiation from a nuclear reactor. The analysis proved the fragments embedded in the ceiling tile were made up of the same material as the pipe from the suspect's garage. The soil from the suspect's shoes matched the soil around the bank building. These findings were used as evidence in court.

In like manner, computers at the ATF Crime Lab are used frequently to analyze unidentified substances, check swabs from a suspect's hands for components of gunshot residue, determine the types of weapons used in misdeeds, and so on. The facilities are available to any law enforcement agency in the United States as an aid in crimefighting.

The FBI's computer system, known as the National Crime Information Center (NCIC), links 64,000 federal, state, and local law enforcement agencies. It contains millions of records about persons who have been officially accused of crimes. More than 300,000 queries are processed against the NCIC system daily.

Local law enforcement officers may query the system for background information on persons they come in contact with, for example. If the persons have prior arrest records, the NCIC system will supply that background information. (See Figure 1-14.)

In 1982, the New York City Police Department installed a new computer system to simplify and reduce the overwhelming burden of paperwork required to track each suspect, from time of arrest, through the judicial maze of district attorneys and city courts, to final disposition. Suspects are taken from any of the city's 73 precincts to a central booking station in lower Manhattan, where their arrests are entered immediately into the Department's computer system. The current status and data of 300,000 arrest warrants and a list of 8000 so-called "public enemies," or "career" criminals, are available at all times. This capability helps officers to more quickly identify suspects and alerts them when they're dealing with known offenders. Because attorneys can report back on the disposition of cases, police officers can follow up on bookings and create more effective crimefighting strategies.

FIGURE 1-14
Law enforcement officers at Houma, Louisana, and similarly equipped facilities across the country obtain and share computerized information to help insure public safety. (*Courtesy IBM Corporation*)

Our nation's court systems depend heavily on computers. Courtrooms, judges, juries, and cases are scheduled with computer help. Given the vast backlog of cases waiting to be heard at all levels of the judicial hierarchy, and the slow rate at which many of the cases move through that hierarchy, computerized tracking and record-keeping are vital. The rules we live by are an amalgamation of congressional laws and legal precedents established through court rulings. The texts of these laws and case histories are maintained in vast databases. Lawyers often need access to such data in preparing legal documents or advising clients in routine business dealings, as well as in court-related matters. Without computer assistance, the tasks of organizing and storing all this data, and then of finding the data relevant to a particular situation, would be difficult if not impossible.

COMPUTERS IN EDUCATION

"Speak and Spell," said Texas Instruments (TI) in the 1970s as it marketed its Speak and Spell handheld learning aid for youngsters. "An Apple computer and the computer language Logo can teach your child to think," said Apple Computer about 1980. Children's Computer Workshop, an offshoot of Children's Television Workshop (the creators of "Sesame Street"), has developed more than 40 computer games for children. The social and psychological aspects of these home computer games are designed to foster cooperation rather than competition (a criticism often raised against popular arcade video games). Other more obviously tutorial materials such as self-paced arithmetic drill and practice programs are being developed and marketed widely for use with home computers.

With much less fanfare, other firms have been developing educational materials for use with large computers. Perhaps most noteworthy is *PLATO*, an interactive self-paced computer-based training system that runs on Control Data Corporation (CDC) equipment. More than 10,000 hours of *courseware* (computer programs for instructional use) now exist, some of which are proprietary, having been developed by CDC and educational consultants for specific clients. A user organization may install a large CDC computer dedicated to PLATO on its own premises. Others choose to access PLATO courseware via interactive touch-sensitive graphics terminals tied into a CDC-maintained PLATO network. Individuals can study on site at any of more than 100 CDC Learning Centers and Business Centers where PLATO courses are offered. To expand the use of its courseware, CDC and other authorized organizations are developing modified versions of selected courses to run on CDC 110, Apple, IBM, Atari, and TI microcomputers. CDC has also announced a version of PLATO that can be run on large CDC computers without having to dedicate the computers to PLATO use. (See Figure 1-15.)

In what ways are computers helping people to learn? We can group the commonly used approaches within seven general categories:

- Problem solving—The student/user gathers data about a problem, submits the data as input to a computer, and draws conclusions based on the output. For example, the problem may be: How much interest must a family pay on a mortgage loan if the principal is $210,000, the interest rate is 10.5 percent compounded monthly, and equal payments are made on the loan each month for 30 years? In a follow-on problem, the student may vary one or more of the

FIGURE 1-15
Even homework can be fun
when students are guided by
PLATO courseware running
on a microcomputer.
(*Courtesy Texas Instruments
Incorporated*)

numeric values. The results of many such calculations, each done by the computer in a fraction of a second, can be analyzed for better understanding of mortgage borrowing.

- Inquiry—The student/user extracts data from a computerized data bank. For example, brief summaries, or abstracts, of articles from professional journals and extensive bibliographies pointing to research in specific areas are widely available in computerized databases. Use of them can eliminate the need to spend many tedious hours searching manually for required information.

- Simulation—The computer is programmed to simulate, or imitate, real-world situations. In medicine, for example, computers play "patient" roles as students attempt to diagnose illnesses, prescribe medications or self-help, monitor their patients' reactions to prescribed treatments, and thereby lead the patients back to health.

- Computer-managed instruction (CMI)—This courseware tests a student's understanding of a particular subject area, diagnoses weaknesses in that area, prescribes remedial steps, and tracks progress. The subject matter may be a part of the courseware or may be available in another (usually, printed) form.

- Computer-assisted instruction (CAI)—This courseware presents information to the student, asks questions about the material, processes the student's responses, and provides feedback. Usually, the student may study the material at any of several levels. Drill and testing are often included.

- Drill and practice—This self-paced question–response–feedback approach is designed to help a student master basic arithmetic facts or higher mathematics, reading, spelling, vocabulary, grammar, or other subject matter through reinforcement.

- Testing—Data banks of test questions are provided from which all or a subset can be selected by an instructor for a particular test session. This approach is particularly useful for matching, true or false, and multiple-choice testing of many students. The computer checks the responses, keeps track of the correct and incorrect answers, and computes a grade for each student. Validation of test questions, re-evaluation of teaching materials or methodology, and analysis of each student's strengths and weaknesses may be addressed in follow-on activities.

According to U.S. Department of Education surveys, more than 100,000 microcomputers were in use in U.S. public schools in 1982—that's roughly 1 for every 400 students. An additional 30,000 or so terminals provided access to large computer systems. By mid-1983, the number of microcomputers was claimed by some to have already doubled. There are now computer camps for children, and computer camps at which children are instructors. At college and university levels, computers are the hottest thing on campus. Student demands for computing knowledge have led to independent study programs, courses having video components, and cooperative work-study programs. In many of these programs, computers are both the means and the subject of learning. Figure 1-16 suggests some of the reasons why computers and their uses are important to us.

It's not unrealistic to suggest that computers will soon be as basic to student learning as pencils and notebooks. They'll replace the latter in many instances. Computer-education bills "to provide every American student with access to computer training over the next 10 years" have been introduced in Congress. Computer vendors are making their products available to educational institutions at discounts, or even at no cost in some instances. Clarkson College in Potsdam, New York, and Drexel University in Philadelphia were among the first to insist that all incoming students have computers. Joint studies much like the efforts that led to the Mark I and other early computer developments are being undertaken by many businesses and universities. By working together, all benefit.

COMPUTERS IN HOMES

Initially, computers entered our homes under the guise of "smart machines"—as components of microwave ovens, dishwashers, washing machines, driers, cameras, and so on. As mentioned earlier, in 1975 hobbyists who were into assembling electronic gadgetry were offered computers in kit form. Children clamored for the "smart toys" they saw on TV. Then came the video games: Pac-Man, Donkey Kong, and Space Invaders became household words. Parents reluctant to spend hundreds of dollars on a game machine could be persuaded if they saw "educational" value.

About 1980 the floodgates opened. Through technological progress, intensive program development, skillful packaging, aggressive marketing, and volume production, not just smart machines but also programmable computers were within the reach of many households. Today's home computers can be purchased for less than $1000. Some cost less than $100. As you may be well aware, the leaders include: Tandy Radio Shack's TRS-80 Color Computers and Model IIIs, Atari 400s and 800s, Commodore VIC-20s and 64s, and Texas Instruments 99/4As. In 1982 alone, about two million of these computers were sold. Hundreds of thousands of the more expensive Apple IIs and IBM Personal Computers were also purchased for home use. (See Figure 1-17.)

☐ You may decide to pursue a career in the computing field. Since this field is both expanding and changing rapidly, it offers many job opportunities.

☐ Even if you're not working directly in computing, there's a good chance you'll be expected to interact with data-processing personnel, to assess your needs for computing resources, or to use a computer in your on-the-job environment.

☐ When you receive a computer-generated bill for $0.00 three months in a row, you'll be in a better position to discuss this situation with the credit department of the firm responsible. You'll know that human error—not "the #*¢*%! computer"—is at fault.

☐ You may find ways to enrich your personal life—to make your home-environment tasks simpler or less time-consuming, to fill your leisure time with interesting activities—by taking advantage of computer capabilities.

☐ If your video game, microwave oven, or electronic security system goes "kaput," you may be able to fix it.

☐ When your business associates, friends, or kids start talking about computer-related "gee-whiz" situations, you'll be able to hold your own.

☐ When issues of computer crime, individual privacy, protectionism vs free-trade in high-technology areas, and the like are aired via newspapers, magazines, radio, and television, you'll have a background of understanding that you can draw upon. Some legislation has been passed concerning federal data banks, access to individual credit status information, and what constitutes computer crime. Many more bills are pending. What controls should be effected in these areas? As a member of society, you can (and should) help decide.

(You may have other reasons for studying computing. If so, list them below.)

FIGURE 1-16 There are many reasons for studying computing, some of which are listed here. (Add yours at the bottom.)

FIGURE 1-17
Computers in the home often interest parents and children alike, and serve as a focal point for discussion and activity. (*Courtesy Radio Shack, a Division of Tandy Corporation*)

Use of these computers requires programs as well as machines. Many, many programs are available. They're marketed on cartridges and cassettes at widely varying prices. A user may also enter programs into storage from the keyboard and save them on diskettes for reuse.

We've already noted that home computers can be used to play games. They can provide individualized instruction to students of all ages. As familiarity with a system increases, data on household budgets, taxes, car payments, transportation expenses, recipes and menus, tape or record collections, personal libraries, and so on, can be organized, indexed, stored, and retrieved at will. A home computer can chart biorhythms, balance bank accounts, and even control household appliances. It can monitor heat on a room-by-room basis. It can maintain constant surveillance against smoke, fire, intruders, and other dangers. The system can be connected to an ordinary dial or pushbutton telephone so that a call will be placed automatically to a neighbor or to the local fire or police department if an emergency arises.

With the availability of low-cost communication interfaces to home computers has come a new, exciting dimension: the *home information system*. Both cable TV and telephone-based systems are currently testing the market for a wide array of consumer services. For example, Chemical Bank of New York offers Pronto, a home banking system. Balance inquiry, electronic funds transfer, electronic check register, home budgeting, and electronic mail capabilities are invoked via Atari 400 home computers. More than 250 area merchants—major department stores, credit-card companies, utilities, and large landlords—have agreed to accept payments directly from the Pronto system. As another example, armchair computerists who subscribe to The Source, an information utility based in McLean, Virginia, can access about 800 information services. You might choose to (1) get the latest news within minutes after it's filed by UPI correspondents; (2) scan current domestic and international airline schedules, book reservations on flights, rent a car, make hotel reservations, and then check the weather ahead and the best place to eat; or (3) obtain regularly updated reports on stocks, bonds, commodities, futures, options, gold and other precious metals, money markets, mutual funds, foreign exchanges, and U.S. Treasury rates. Subscribers can post classified ads, share ideas, sell or swap merchandise, and transmit simple messages or lengthy reports within minutes to other subscribers the world over—usually at lower costs than long-distance telephone or express mail.

EMPLOYMENT OPPORTUNITIES

The image of a person replaced by a computer is a common one. We see an automated teller machine (ATM) on the outside of a bank, and we know that a computer is now doing a job that was once done by a person. How many human employees would perform consistently, 24 hours a day, always smiling, always ready to respond to customers with the same prompt service? At $150 per month (the bank's operating cost for the ATM), how many of us would want the job?

Looking at computers from another point of view, we see that their use actually creates a wealth of new jobs. In a recent survey, the total data-processing revenue of the top 100 companies in the data-processing industry was shown to be $79.4 billion.* This amount reflects an $11.6 billion increase over the corresponding figure derived in a similar survey just one year earlier. These are the companies that develop and build computers and other equipment; prepare programs to instruct them; provide services such as processing time on a particular computer, use of a particular program, or expertise on how to design and implement a particular application; and sell their products or services to other vendors and to end users. All these companies employ people.

System analysts work with users to understand their information needs. Business planners determine what products or services are required to respond to those needs. Engineers design computers and related equipment. System designers and programmers develop the programs needed to instruct computers. Operations personnel provide the computer system environments required to support product development efforts. Technical writers and other documentation specialists express product details in readily understandable terms. Sales personnel interact with potential customers, assisting them in acquiring and using computer capabilities. Customer service personnel keep installed systems

---

*Archbold, Pamela. "The Datamation 100: Welcome to the Club," *Datamation* 29, 6 (June 1983), 86ff.

operating. Also needed are a manufacturing work force; quality-control personnel; order-processing, shipping, receiving, and inventory-control personnel; and, of course, competent management to coordinate all these computer-related activities. Without computers, these jobs would not exist. The pay is good, and the number and kinds of opportunities are increasing daily.

Many thousands of government departments and agencies, businesses, educational institutions, and other organizations use computers. These organizations also need system analysts, system designers, and programmers. They need operations personnel to run their computers and related equipment; data-entry personnel to prepare computer-readable input; support personnel to maintain existing programs, respond to problems that arise, and so on; a database administration or library staff; output-distribution personnel; data-processing auditors; and managers for all these functions.

As one result of the reductions in computer size and cost, computers have entered small businesses and office environments. Here, firms may not have in-house system design and programming staffs. They do need system analysts and operators. These same persons may also be the system users. Business professionals, administrative specialists, and office workers with some knowledge of data processing often have "a foot in the door" when competing, jobwise, with persons not knowledgeable about computing.

There's room for the entrepreneur in the computing field. The freelance artists of the data-processing industry are the individuals who acquire the education and experience necessary to make it on their own. Some are consultants, specializing, for example, in how to use computers effectively in the insurance industry, or how to use computers to achieve inventory control, or how to design, develop, and install a management information system. Others are contract programmers, developing programs for specific clients on a per-job or per-hour basis.

With the advent of personal computers, self-employment opportunities in the data-processing industry have mushroomed. Some people act as consultants or contract programmers as noted above, but for individual user clients rather than for traditional business, government, and other organizational users. Some, with about $100,000 of front money, have opened computer stores. Some are software publishers, offering computer-related newsletters, magazines, paperbacks, even complete programs as listings or on machine-readable media. Still others are software authors, writing and making available programs for which they receive royalties. People with a "mechanical bent" are designing, manufacturing, and marketing low-cost input/output units or circuitry to be used with computers, or handling equipment service calls for computer stores on a per-call basis.

In 1980, the U.S. labor force numbered about 105 million. By 1990, it's expected to be from 122 to 128 million—a projected increase of from 17 to 22 percent. So says the U.S. Bureau of Labor Statistics in the 1982–83 edition of its *Occupational Outlook Handbook*.* Especially designed to offer vocational guidance, the *Handbook* presents the nature of work today, education and training requirements, and job outlook for about 250 occupations. Figure 1-18 summarizes the

---

*The *Occupational Outlook Handbook* is published every two years by the U.S. Department of Labor, Bureau of Labor Statistics, Division of Occupational Outlook. Its contents are based on more than four decades of intensive research on employment in occupations and industries. It's well written and easy reading.

number of persons employed in occupations solely or in part closely related to computing, as well as the job outlook in those occupations. The category "system analyst" should be understood to include both system analysts and system designers. Not all electrical engineers are working directly with computers, but the job opportunities for those who are should be at least as good as (and probably better than) those of the category as a whole. Technical writers are employed throughout the United States, but the largest concentrations are in the Northeast, Texas, and California. In addition, of course, many people

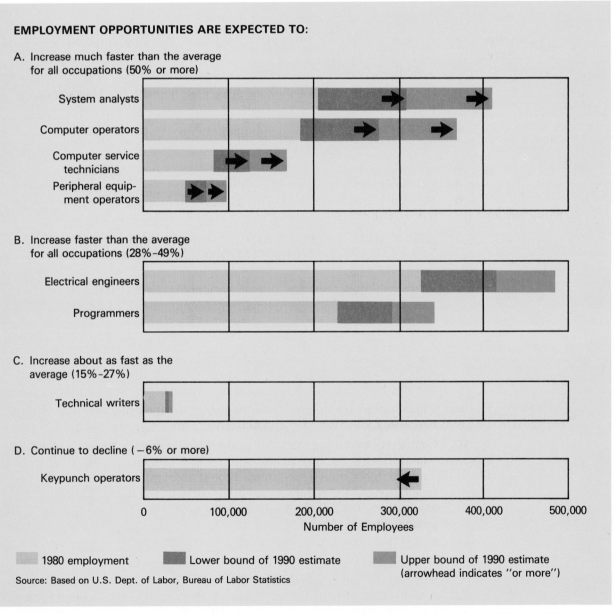

EMPLOYMENT OPPORTUNITIES ARE EXPECTED TO:

A. Increase much faster than the average
   for all occupations (50% or more)

System analysts

Computer operators

Computer service
technicians

Peripheral equip-
ment operators

B. Increase faster than the average
   for all occupations (28%-49%)

Electrical engineers

Programmers

C. Increase about as fast as the
   average (15%-27%)

Technical writers

D. Continue to decline (−6% or more)

Keypunch operators

0   100,000   200,000   300,000   400,000   500,000

Number of Employees

1980 employment   Lower bound of 1990 estimate   Upper bound of 1990 estimate
                                                      (arrowhead indicates "or more")

Source: Based on U.S. Dept. of Labor, Bureau of Labor Statistics

FIGURE 1-18 The number of jobs in computing is large, and it's expected to continue to increase significantly. (*U.S. Department of Labor statistics*)

working in the computing field are not shown on this chart—sales representatives, accountants, and personnel and administrative specialists, to name a few. Well-qualified instructors for data-processing and information-system courses are needed throughout education and industry.

It's been said that the 1960s were the decade of the technician, the 1970s the decade of the programmer, and the 1980s the decade of the end user. Most of us belong to at least one of these groups; some belong to all three. You may or may not decide to pursue a career in the computing field, but whatever you decide, you're sure to find an understanding of data processing helpful. Computers and their uses underlie the present and the future in all aspects of our society.

CHAPTER SUMMARY

1. Computer literacy is the knowledge and understanding one needs to function effectively within a given role that directly or indirectly involves computers.

2. Data processing is the collecting, processing, and distributing of facts and figures to achieve a desired result.

3. Data consists of facts and figures gathered from one or more sources; information is processed, or "finished," data.

4. Mechanical adding machines, calculators, and punched-card data-processing systems were precursors of computers.

5. The Mark I, ABC, ENIAC, and EDSAC were early one-of-a-kind computers. The UNIVAC I was the first commercially available computer.

6. Magnetic tapes, drums, and disks were developed to meet the large-volume, high-speed input/output and storage requirements of business data processing.

7. First-generation computers had vacuum tubes as basic components, second-generation computers had transistors, and third-generation computers were constructed from integrated circuits (IC's).

8. Through techniques of large-scale integration (LSI) and very-large-scale integration (VLSI), the microminiaturization of processor chips and memory chips continues. Most versatile of all are the programmable one-chip processing units known as microprocessors.

9. Computers are being used in large businesses and organizations, in small businesses, and even by individual consumers.

10. Computers are aiding manufacturing in material requirements planning, manufacturing resource planning, inventory control, numerical control of machine tools, robotic systems, process control, and product testing. Simulation, solids modeling, and other computer-aided design techniques are applied in CAD/CAM systems that support the complete cycle of product development.

11. People in medical and legal professions are finding computers increasingly valuable. In education and in the home, computers may well be the most exciting, most powerful, most versatile tools yet developed.

12. A wide range of employment opportunities exists in the computing field. Both the number of persons employed and the number of jobs available are increasing as computer use spreads.

**DISCUSSION
QUESTIONS**

1. What does the phrase *computer literacy* mean to you?

2. Justify the following statement: "The development of modern electrical power, machinery, and techniques of mass production created a need for computers."

3. Distinguish between *data* and *information*. In doing so, give several examples.

4. What advantages were gained by storing instructions as well as data in a computer?

5. What new devices and techniques were developed to meet the needs of business data processing?

6. (a) For what reasons are designers continually trying to pack more circuitry on smaller chips?
   (b) What are some outcomes (or possible outcomes) of these efforts?

7. Select one modern business organization (such as a large construction firm, a telephone company, an automobile manufacturer, or a large discount store), and show how it uses data processing.

8. Describe a situation in which the computer's simulation capabilities may prove to be especially helpful.

9. In what ways do modern hospitals use computers?

10. How do computers help to make individualized instruction possible?

11. Discuss some ways that computers are being used in homes.

12. What employment opportunities involving computers sound interesting to you, and why?

2

THE COMPUTER AS A SYSTEM

The importance of data as a human resource has grown dramatically over recent decades. Most of the world's resources are shrinking, especially in relation to our growing population's need for them. It may well be that data is the only human resource that is growing rather than diminishing. Computers, of course, are helping to make that rapid growth possible and useful.

In both scientific and business efforts of all kinds, the analysis of data helps us learn how best to use our available resources, whether they are the natural resources of our world or the potential profit resources of the marketplace. The analytical orientation of science is commonly seen in our daily lives—in financial forecasting for business, in buying and selling goods and services, and even, by some, as a basis for human relationships.

The process of analyzing data involves, first, accumulating the raw data and then, second, generating new and more organized or refined data on that basis. In reality, although the results of the data processing may be technically "valid," they may not all be useful. Some of the results become the data for further processing, and some of them may be "waste." At the outset of an analysis, it is not always clear what results may be useful and what may be unimportant or irrelevant. Computers are an invaluable aid to humans in making and evaluating those distinctions.

Courtesy IBM Corporation

Courtesy Storage Technology Corporation

Courtesy Hendrix Technologies, Inc.

Courtesy Sperry Corporation

Courtesy IBM Corporation

Computers have made it relatively "easy" to process data quickly and accurately. The visual-display terminal with its typewriterlike keyboard has become a common sight in the workplace. Software—the instructions that tell the computer how to perform the desired tasks—is being developed every day, for more and more purposes. Standard and convenient ways of structuring computer use have been developed to make it possible for almost anyone to learn "computing" with ease and speed. The complexities are now "inside" the computer system—the province of computer designers and other highly trained specialists. "Outside" the computer are the user-friendly interfaces that make its use relatively simple.

In this age when data and information are some of our most important resources, the burden of processing huge amounts of data can be lifted from human shoulders by computer systems. For the most part, what is left are the relatively straightforward tasks of programming what is to be done, entering the data, and letting the computers produce the results. These jobs can be quite sizable, of course, as we shall see in later chapters.

Courtesy Sperry Corporation

Courtesy Honeywell Inc.

Courtesy IBM Corporation

2 | THE COMPUTER AS A SYSTEM

As we saw in Chapter 1, there are many types of data-processing systems. Each of them performs one or more operations on data by means of various devices. When a machine performs most of the required operations, the system is called an *automatic data-processing (ADP) system*. More particularly, when that machine is an electronic digital computer, the system is called an *electronic data-processing (EDP) system* (or, sometimes, simply a *computer system*). If the system is designed and marketed especially for small businesses, it may be further classified as a *small business system*. A computer intended for individual or home use may be called a *personal computer*.

In this chapter, we look first at three basic elements of data processing: input, processing, and output. We discuss how stored programs and microcode are used. You're introduced to the functional units of an EDP system. (This introduction will be expanded in later chapters.) You will read about a typical interaction between a computer and a user. You will see how simple communicating with a computer really is. And you will use the computer to solve a problem.

40

**BASIC
CONCEPTS**

EDP systems vary in cost, size, complexity, speed, and kinds of operations performed. Nonetheless, all data processing involves at least three basic elements:

- The source data, or *input*, entering the system
- The orderly, planned *processing* within the system
- The end result, or *output*, from the system

As a first example, let's consider a familiar situation not involving a computer. Imagine that a utility company is preparing a customer's bill. First, a representative of the company reads the customer's meter, which has recorded all electric usage. (See Figure 2-1.) The previous meter reading (from the end of the last billing period) is available in the company's records. This previous reading is subtracted from the current reading to determine the amount of electricity used during this billing period. An accountant, using established billing rates, calculates how much money the customer owes. Finally, the customer's bill is completed and mailed out.

In this example, the *input* is the previous and current readings of electric usage. The *processing* is the subtraction of one of these numbers from the other, the multiplication of measuring units by billing rates, and the addition of taxes to determine the total bill amount. The *output* is the customer's bill and the company's record of the amount owed. All together, then, these functions constitute a data-processing system.

Now suppose the same operations are performed with computer help. (See Figure 2-2.) The input values are the same. However, in this case, the customer's current meter reading may be keyed into the EDP system from a data-entry device having a televisionlike screen and a typewriterlike keyboard. The previous meter reading may be read into the computer from a magnetic tape where it was stored the previous month. Then the calculations are carried out by the computer. The customer's bill is the output. The current meter reading is stored on another magnetic tape, to be used as the previous meter reading in next month's billing.

We can extend these ideas further to consider typical EDP systems used today in many organizations. The input may consist of any type of data. It may be customer orders received by phone or by mail, the findings of scientific experiments in laboratories, sales figures from branch offices, atmospheric data for weather forecasting, and so on. Employees, suppliers, or customers may prepare the input as a byproduct of other organizational functions or specifically for the job at hand in a separate data-preparation step. The processing is carried out by a pre-established sequence of instructions executed by the computer. The plan of processing is always of human origin. By sorting, classifying, calculating, and other operations, the computer determines results. These results may be used immediately for further processing, or they may be provided as output in the form of printed reports, graphics on visual-display terminals, and even spoken words. (See Figure 2-3.)

**STORED
PROGRAMS**

An EDP system is designed to perform specific kinds of operations. It is directed to perform each operation by an instruction that defines the operation and identifies the data or device needed to carry it out. As noted in Chapter 1, the

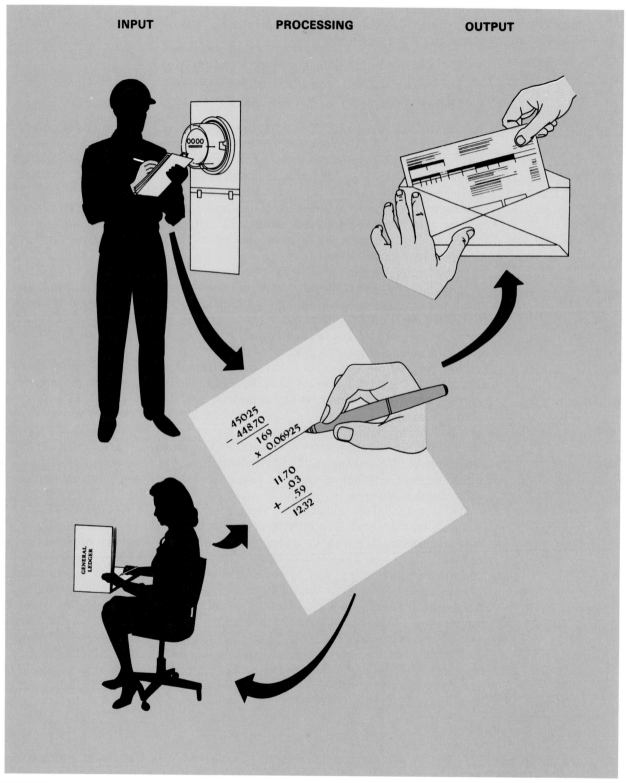

FIGURE 2-1 A utility company may use a manual data-processing system (including input, processing, and output) for billing.

INPUT PROCESSING OUTPUT

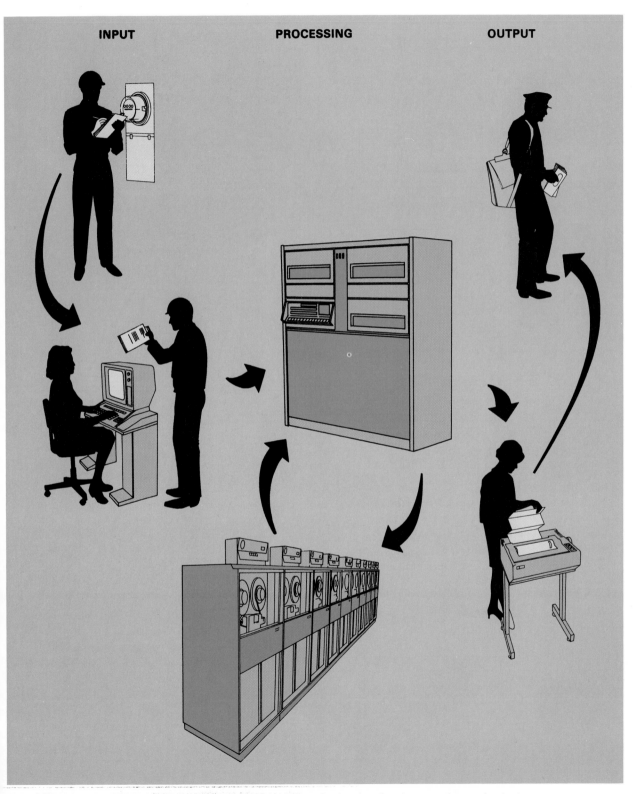

FIGURE 2-2 An electronic data-processing system for billing also involves input, processing, and output.

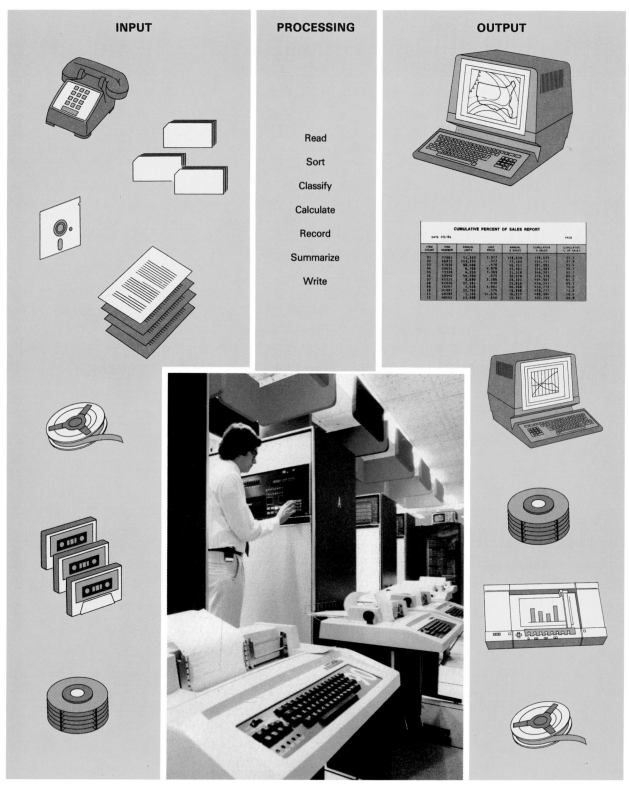

INPUT

PROCESSING

Read

Sort

Classify

Calculate

Record

Summarize

Write

OUTPUT

FIGURE 2-3   A general-purpose EDP system may have a wide range of processing capabilities and include a wide variety of input and output devices. (*Photo courtesy NCR Corporation*)

entire series of instructions required to perform a given task is known as a *program*.

The computer may have the operation of multiplication built into its circuits in much the same way that the ability to multiply is built into a simple pocket calculator. The computer must be directed to multiply by some means, just as the calculator is directed to multiply when a certain key is pressed on its keyboard. There must also be a way to tell the computer where in its internal storage it can find the numbers to multiply.

The relatively simple operation of multiplication implies other activities that precede and follow it. Assume that the multiplicand and the multiplier are read into the computer's internal storage by an input device (for example, a visual-display terminal). The numbers must first have been keyed in by the user at the terminal. Then, after the multiplication has been done, the product must be placed in a specified location in internal storage. From there, it can be written as output or used in other calculations.

In the same manner, any calculating operation involves a number of steps that must be spelled out to the computer: reading, locating numbers in storage, performing the actual calculation, perhaps adjusting the result (for example, by getting rid of unwanted positions to the right of an implied decimal point or rounding to tens or hundreds), placing the result in storage, and writing that result at the appropriate time. A calculation procedure, therefore, is composed of a sequence of individual steps leading to a desired result. As you have learned, the steps are coded as instructions and read (loaded) into the computer as part of a stored program to direct the processing. It is the stored program that makes the computer "automatic." Once the program is loaded and processing is initiated, the stored-program instructions are executed, one after another. No further human intervention is required.

A computer can solve a seemingly infinite variety of problems. To solve a particular problem, one must load a program designed to solve that type of problem into the internal storage unit of the computer. Any of the common input devices can be used to do this, because instructions, like data, can be expressed in machine-readable form. After the data related to the problem has also been loaded into storage, operations can be performed on the data to solve the problem.

The task of writing instructions to direct the operations of a computer is called *programming*. The person who writes the instructions may be called a *programmer*. A simple program written in the BASIC programming language is shown in Figure 2-4. Notice that the program directs the computer to accept a set of five numbers as input. The processing performed under the direction of this program is to first add the five numbers and then divide their sum by 5 to find the average (see line 140). The quotient of the division operation (i.e., the average) is then printed as output. The program user indicates whether or not there are more sets of numbers to process by typing Y (Yes) or N (No) in response to the prompt on line 160. Control is returned to line 120 in order to repeat the input-processing-output steps, or program execution is stopped.

Each programmer or user of an EDP system does not have to write all the instructions necessary to control the system. Computer manufacturers and other firms specializing in program development offer many ready-made programs. These programs are of two types: *system software* and *application software*. System software directs the computer in performing tasks that are basic to

```
100   REM AVERAGE
110   REM FIND THE AVERAGE OF A SET OF FIVE NUMBERS
120   PRINT "ENTER A SET OF 5 NUMBERS"
130   INPUT A, B, C, D, E
140   LET X = (A + B + C + D + E) / 5
150   PRINT "AVERAGE IS "; X
160   PRINT "ANY MORE SETS TO PROCESS? TYPE Y OR N"
170   INPUT R$
180   IF R$ = "Y" THEN 120
190   END
```

FIGURE 2-4
This program tells the computer to find the average of a set of 5 numbers.

proper functioning of the system or are commonly needed by system users. For example, the major control program, also known as the *supervisor, monitor,* or *executive,* controls system resources; it allocates input devices, output devices, and internal storage to specific programs when they are executed. Application software directs the computer in performing specific user-related data-processing tasks. For example, accounts payable programs, payroll processing programs, and programs that help to control inventories are application software. Programs that direct the computer in controlling space flights or auto ignition systems, in helping students learn to spell or read, and in game playing are also in this category.

More than one program may be stored in the computer at any given time. The only limit is the number of storage locations available for both programs and data. Normally, after an application program has been loaded into storage and executed, control of the computer is released to the major control program (also in internal storage). The control program may, in turn, handle inquiries from users at typewriterlike devices, direct any of a number of other input/output units to perform necessary operations, transfer control to another application program, and so forth. The capabilities of any one control program are, of course, determined by its human designers.

MICROCODE With the advent of third-generation computers, computer manufacturers recognized that the distinction between *hardware* (physical components) and *software* (programs) is not simple and straightforward. Although basic operations such as multiplication and division can be built into a computer in the form of permanently wired circuitry (called *hard-wired circuits*), more flexibility is possible if some of the basic operations are controlled by special stored-program instructions sometimes referred to as *firmware* or *microcode.*

Sequences of microcode instructions, called *microprograms,* are provided for some computers by their manufacturers. The microprograms are placed in *read-only memory (ROM)* where they can be interpreted by the computer during processing. Unlike other internal storage, the ROM cannot be occupied or altered by regular stored-program instructions or by data. Such a computer has certain standard features plus the optional capabilities that are wanted or needed.

Through microprogramming, the basic operations of the computer can be tailored to meet the user's data-processing requirements.

Generally, it is to the user's advantage to have system functions controlled by microcode rather than simply by regular stored-program instructions. Because the microcode is in ROM, it cannot be altered accidentally. In effect, the user is protected from himself or herself. Another important advantage is speed of operation. Generally, a function controlled by microcode is executed much faster than it would be if it were controlled by regular stored-program instructions.

Detailed knowledge of computer circuitry is required to write microcode instructions. In practical usage, only computer designers need be familiar with the techniques of microprogramming and of specific microcode. We shall not examine the makeup of any computer to the depth needed for microprogramming, but now you have some understanding of why programs are provided in ROM on some commonly available computers.

FUNCTIONAL UNITS

An EDP system typically consists of four types of functional units: the processor unit, secondary-storage devices, input devices, and output devices. The interrelationships of these units are shown schematically in Figure 2-5.

The Processor Unit

The *central processing unit* (*CPU*) is the computer part of an EDP system. It is the control center of the entire system. As such, it has two parts: an *arithmetic/logic unit* and a *control section*. As we'll see later, these two parts together are sometimes called the *processor* of the EDP system. If both parts are built on a single chip of silicon, we call that chip a *microprocessor*. (The first microprocessor was, of course, the one built by Ted Hoff and associates at Intel, which we learned

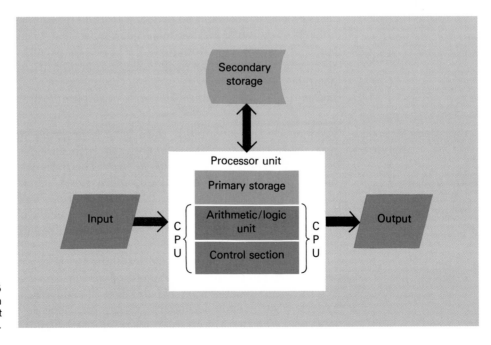

FIGURE 2-5
The functional units of an EDP system interact during processing.

about in Chapter 1.) The *internal storage unit* (also called *memory, primary storage,* or *main storage*) of the EDP system is often housed within the same physical unit as the arithmetic/logic unit and the control section. All three of these units are integrally involved in the computer's internal processing operations. For this reason, the three of them are sometimes referred to collectively as "the CPU." Their physical housing is called the *processor unit.*

The arithmetic/logic unit performs operations such as addition, subtraction, multiplication, and division, as well as moving and comparing data. This unit also has the ability to test conditions encountered during processing and to take action accordingly.

The control section of the CPU directs and coordinates all the operations of the computer system according to conditions set forth by stored programs. It fetches instructions from primary storage and interprets them. It then generates signals and commands that cause other system units to perform certain operations at appropriate times. That is, it controls the input/output units, the arithmetic/logic operations of the CPU, and the transfer of data and instructions to and from storage, within given design limits. It acts as a central nervous system but performs no actual processing operations on data. The processing must be carried out by other system components.

The internal storage unit, or primary storage, is somewhat like an electronic filing cabinet; each "bin," or location, can hold data or instructions. During normal system operation, this unit contains the following:

● All data being held for processing

● Data involved in current processing

● The final result of processing until it is released as output

● Stored-program instructions that control the processing being carried out

Each position, or location, in storage is identified by a particular *address.* Using the addresses, the control section of the CPU can readily locate data and instructions as needed. The primary-storage capacity obviously determines the amount of data and instructions that can be held within the system at any one time. Since primary storage is designed to permit very rapid storing and retrieving, systems that include large amounts of primary storage are often desirable. Because storage is a relatively expensive part of an EDP system, however, the storage capacity in many computer systems is limited.

Secondary-Storage Devices

Frequently, the amount of data that a program must access exceeds the primary-storage capacity available. In such cases, the data is retained on *secondary,* or *auxiliary, storage devices.* The data can be retrieved as needed during system processing (albeit, more slowly than if it were in primary storage). Programs not currently in use are also kept in secondary storage. As mentioned in Chapter 1, various types of devices have been developed to provide storage space. The most common are magnetic-tape units and disk units. (See Figure 2-6.)

Processing restrictions caused by limited primary storage have been somewhat alleviated by the development of *virtual-storage* techniques. In an EDP system with virtual-storage capabilities, the addresses within a program being executed can include secondary-storage locations as well as primary-storage locations. When data or instructions referenced during execution of the program

FIGURE 2-6   Magnetic-tape units and magnetic-disk units are common secondary-storage devices. (*Courtesy Aetna Life and Casualty, Hartford, Conn./Tandem Computers Incorporated*)

are in secondary storage but not in primary storage, the portion of the program that contains them is moved to primary storage immediately. As we shall see, the capacity and design of the storage in a computer system affect the way data is handled and the speed of processing.

Input and Output Devices

As part of its information-handling ability, the data-processing system requires devices that can introduce data into the system and devices that can accept data after it has been processed. These functions are performed by input/output (I/O) devices linked directly to the system. Some typical devices are shown in Figure 2-7.

Before data can be processed by the computer, it must be entered into the computer's storage. As EDP system users, we make the data available to it via an input device. The data may be recorded as punched holes on cards, as magnetized spots along a tape, as characters or drawings on paper, and so on. The data may also be keyed directly into the system (without first having been recorded on an input medium) by means of a direct-input device.

Output is data that has been processed. It may be in a form that humans can understand, or it may be in a form acceptable as input to another machine. For example, an output device such as a printer can display information in a form that is readily understandable to us. A magnetic-tape unit used as an output device records information in a form that is useful only as input for further processing.

The number and types of I/O devices connected to a particular system depend on the design of the system and the kind of processing for which it is used. Some devices are used only for input, some only for output, and some for either. The variety of I/O devices available today seems almost unlimited. As you may have

Magnetic-tape unit. (*Courtesy United Technology*)

Desktop terminal for source-data input and printer for output. (*Courtesy TRW Inc.*)

Bar-code scanner and key-input device.
(*Courtesy MSI Data Corporation*)

Data-entry terminal. (*Courtesy Bell Helicopter Textron, Inc.*)

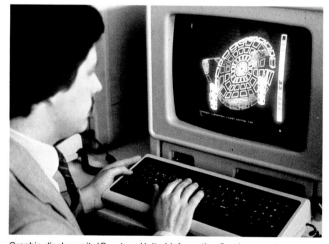

Graphic-display unit. (*Courtesy United Information Services, Inc.*)

Point-of-sale terminal. (*Courtesy American Express Company*)

FIGURE 2-7 Data enters, and information leaves, an EDP system by means of input/output devices.

noticed, magnetic-tape units appear in both Figure 2-6 and Figure 2-7. A magnetic-tape unit may be regarded as both a secondary-storage device and an input or output device.

The System Console

If you watched a TV program or a movie that involved computers in any way in the 1970s, you probably saw lights flashing, tape reels spinning, or cards being fed into a machine—some action to convince you the computer was working. The flashing lights were part of the *console* of the computer system. It contained switches and buttons as well as lights. These lights, switches, and buttons were used by data-processing personnel to control, service, and communicate with the computer. The switches were needed to turn power on or off, to start or stop operations, and to activate or deactivate various devices. The buttons were pressed to set certain conditions or modes. The lights were provided so that data in the system could be represented externally for human verification. (See Figure 2-8.)

In early computer systems, the console as we've just described it often covered the entire front of the physical unit that housed the CPU. A printer-keyboard unit positioned next to the CPU was also needed. System messages signaling error conditions or giving directions to the computer operator—say, to mount a particular tape or to put a certain type of paper on the printer—were printed out on this unit. Conversely, the operator used the keyboard to enter certain information (e.g., the current date) into the system. Programmers and service personnel sometimes entered data or displayed the contents of primary-storage locations by means of the console.

As system software and hardware have become increasingly sophisticated, the system itself has become increasingly capable. Less human intervention is required during processing. Large CPU consoles with external lights, buttons, and switches are no longer needed. A visual-display unit with an attached

FIGURE 2-8
EDP-system consoles containing many lights, switches, and buttons were used to control, service, and communicate with computers in the 1960s and 1970s. (*Courtesy Bell Helicopter Textron, Inc.*)

keyboard is now usually identified as the system console for communication purposes. Another visual-display unit and keyboard may be identified as a maintenance console, for use by service personnel. (See Figure 2-9.)

In today's systems, the contents of storage locations are not represented by lights. They are displayed as numeric values, letters, or words. It's now much easier to find out what's going on inside the system. Operators and service personnel can interact with the system by following simple procedures outlined in the system documentation.

In some systems, there is no CPU console as such. One of the input/output devices connected to the system is designated as the "system console" for purposes of system control and communication. Certain system commands can be entered only from this device. System messages may be directed to this device or to a printer designated as the "system output unit." If you've keyed information into a microcomputer system from the keyboard of the system unit, you've used the system console of the microcomputer system (whether you realized you were doing so or not).

COMMUNICATING WITH THE COMPUTER

Now you have some idea of what a computer system is and what it does. Would you like to see how simple communicating with the computer (and even directing it) really is? In this section, we describe a typical user–computer interaction. If you have access to a microcomputer or to a terminal that is part of a larger computer system, you can interact with your system in much the same way as described here. We'll key in the BASIC program in Figure 2-4, which directs the computer in finding averages. We'll enter sets of data values as input and receive the results of processing as output. Where necessary, your instructor or lab assistant will provide information that is unique to your system. If you do

FIGURE 2-9
As computer systems have become increasingly capable, EDP-system consoles have become smaller because less human intervention is required. (*Courtesy IBM Corporation*)

not have access to a computer, you will still learn much about how to interact with a computer by reading this section.

Signing On   The first step in interacting with the computer is to establish contact with it. If you have access to a microcomputer, you may simply pull up a chair, sit down, and turn on the equipment. (If you can't find the power switch, just ask someone.) Apple II and IBM Personal Computer users must place a diskette containing certain system software in an available disk drive, from where the software is then loaded into storage. Commodore and TRS-80 personal computer systems "come up" with BASIC ready for use.

If you intend to use a terminal to interact with a larger computer system, you may need to connect the terminal to the computer by using telephonelike dial-up facilities. To do this, you'll need to enter the computer's telephone number, listen for a high-pitched tone that tells you the computer is ready to receive input, and then place the telephone handset firmly into the data set or acoustic coupler serving as a connection device. (See Figure 2-10.) After the connection has been established, you'll probably have to enter an *account number* so that the computer knows which account to charge for your use. Most systems also require that you enter a unique *user identification* and *password*. These are checked to insure that you have proper authorization before you are allowed access to the system. Assuming you pass the authorization checks, you simply type in a system command, such as BASIC, to tell the system that you intend to enter and run a BASIC program.

FIGURE 2-10
A user at a terminal may establish a connection to a distant computer by means of an acoustic coupler and ordinary telephone lines. (*Courtesy National Semi-conductor Corporation*)

Entering the Program

Most computer systems provide system messages as prompts to guide you. These messages help you decide what to do next. They also tell you when certain actions within the system have been completed. A representative interactive session is shown as an example in Figure 2-11. The messages generated by the system are differentiated in the example. The user responded to the first prompt by keying in the current date. The user responded to the prompt A> by typing basica. This told the computer to load the Advanced BASIC system software into storage from disk drive A. The second screen header appeared. The user keyed in the BASIC program in Figure 2-4. As we know, that program directs the computer to find the average for a set of five numbers keyed into the system by the user during processing.

Entering a BASIC program is really quite simple. You key in each statement, line by line, pressing the ENTER key or its equivalent after each statement. Whatever you key in will appear on the screen of your terminal or microcomputer as you enter it. An underscore character called the *cursor* moves about on the screen to show your current position as you are keying. If you make a mistake while keying a line, most systems allow you to backspace to the point of the error and rekey the remainder of the line. (See line 150 in Figure 2-11.) If you see you've made an error after you've pressed the ENTER key, you can simply rekey the whole line, line number and all. The computer will replace the erroneous line with the new line.

Of course, merely entering BASIC program statements does not solve a problem. On most systems, you can enter a LIST command to tell the computer to print or display a list of the statements you've entered in storage. Doing this allows you to check all the statements visually to make sure that what you think you entered is actually there. The statements will be listed in ascending line-number order. Remember, if any line is wrong, you can simply rekey it. (See the rekeying of line 160 after the program was listed, in Figure 2-11.) When you've done that, your next step is to tell the computer to execute the program.

On most systems, a RUN command can be entered to tell the computer to execute a program in storage. Enter that command or its equivalent on your system now. You should see the prompt ENTER A SET OF FIVE NUMBERS appear on your screen. If your system supports both uppercase and lowercase letters, the prompt will be displayed as you entered it. A question mark should be displayed at the beginning of the next line. (Lines 120 and 130 of the program cause these actions to occur.) Now you must key in (on the same line) a set of five data values, separated by commas. For this first execution, enter the values 1, 2, 3, 4, 5 as shown in Figure 2-11. Then press the ENTER key again. If you've entered the program and the set of five data values correctly, you should see AVERAGE IS 3 appear on the screen as output. (The extra space between IS and 3 would have been used for a minus sign if the value had been negative.)

Then line 160 of the BASIC program causes the computer to ask whether or not there are more sets of numbers to process. If you type Y following the question mark that appears on the next line and then press the ENTER key, control will return to line 120 of the program. The process we've just described will be repeated, giving you an opportunity to enter another set of five values and have the computer find the average of those values. If you type N following the question mark, control will pass to the END statement in line 190. Program execution will terminate, as in Figure 2-11.

```
Current date is Tue 1-01-1980
Enter new date: 6-30-83  ◄─────────────────┐── User types this
Current Time is  0:00:14.13                │
Enter new time: 00:00:00  ◄────────────────┘

The IBM Personal Computer DOS
Version 2.00 (C)Copyright IBM Corp 1981, 1982, 1983
                                    ──── User's main disk drive, and a prompt for input
A>basica ◄───────────────────────── User requests Advanced BASIC
```

```
The IBM Personal Computer Basic
Version A2.00 Copyright IBM Corp. 1981, 1982, 1983
60865 Bytes free ◄──────────────── Amount of primary storage
                                   available for BASIC
Ok

100 rem average
110 rem find the average of sets of five numbers
120 print "Enter a set of 5 numbers"        ┌─ User notices keying error in
130 input a, b, c, d, e                      │  print and presses DELETE (←) key
140 let x = (a + b + c + d + e) / 5          │  twice to go back to the error
150 prnt←←int "Average is "; x  ◄────────────┘  and rekey the rest of the line
160 print "Any mor sets to process? Type y or n"
170 input r$
180 if r$ = "y" then 120
190 end

list ◄───────────────────────────── User requests a listing of the program
100 REM average
110 REM find the average of sets of five numbers
120 PRINT "Enter a set of 5 numbers"
130 INPUT A, B, C, D, E
140 LET X = (A + B + C + D + E) / 5
150 PRINT "Average is "; X
160 PRINT "Any mor sets to process? Type y or n"
170 INPUT R$
180 IF R$ = "y" THEN 120
190 END                             ┌─ User notices keying error in
Ok                                  │  more  and rekeys the line

160 print "Any more sets to process? Type y or n" ◄──┘
run ◄──────────────────────────── User runs the program
Enter a set of 5 numbers         and responds to the prompts
? 1,2,3,4,5 ◄──────────────────┐
Average is  3                  │
Any more sets to process? Type y or n │
? n ◄──────────────────────────┘
Ok ◄─────────────────────────────── Program execution is complete
```

FIGURE 2-11   An interactive session between a user and a computer is documented by messages and responses that appear on the display screen as interactions occur.

If your interaction with the computer doesn't occur more or less as we've just described, you may have made a mistake—say, in procedure or in keying. The system may have printed a message on the screen to tell you about the mistake. Check the actions you've taken, or consult the system documentation. Correct your mistake and try again. Next, choose another set of five data values. Calculate the average of the set of values manually. Then run the program again, enter the values as input, and see whether or not the computer's result agrees with the average you calculated. If not, you must find the error and try again. In computer jargon, errors are known as *bugs*, and the process of finding errors and correcting them is known as *debugging*. If your program is error-free, there is no need for debugging.

Signing Off　　When you're finished, it's time to sign off the computer system. On some systems, a command such as BYE or OFF is used to disconnect from the computer and terminate the session. In any case, your last step is to turn off your terminal or microcomputer.

Wasn't that simple? You've now entered a program into the storage of a computer system and caused that program to be executed. You've entered input values, which were processed as directed by statements of the program. You've received the results of execution as output. Programs to direct computers in processing payrolls, computing accounts receivable, scheduling airline flights, planning highways, playing chess, and so on, are longer and more complicated than the one we've shown here — but the basic concepts are the same. This is what directing the computer is all about.

CHAPTER SUMMARY

1. All data processing (with or without computer help) involves input, processing, and output.

2. An EDP system is directed to perform operations by a series of instructions known as a *program*.

3. The task of writing instructions to direct the operations of a computer is called *programming*.

4. Programs are of two types: system software and application software. System software directs the computer in performing tasks that are basic to proper functioning of the system or are commonly needed by system users. Application software directs the computer in performing specific user-related tasks.

5. Special stored-program instructions known as *firmware*, or *microcode*, may be placed in read-only memory (ROM) to tailor a computer to the user's data-processing requirements.

6. An EDP system consists of four types of functional units: the processor unit, secondary-storage devices, input devices, and output devices.

7. The processor unit houses the central processing unit, or CPU, and the internal storage unit. The CPU has two parts: an arithmetic/logic unit and a control section. A one-chip CPU is called a *microprocessor*.

8. The internal storage unit, or primary storage, contains all data being held for processing, data being processed, the result of processing, and instructions that control the processing.

9. A console is used by operators and service personnel to control and communicate with a computer system during processing.

10. A representative interaction with a computer may involve signing on to the system, keying in a program, causing that program to be executed, entering data values as input, receiving output, and signing off.

DISCUSSION QUESTIONS

1. What three factors are involved in any data-processing operation?

2. Consider a familiar situation that involves the processing of data (such as checking out at the counter of a supermarket, purchasing a roll of stamps at the post office, checking supplies in a company supply cabinet, or handling a concession stand at a school benefit).
   (a) Explain how the factors given in your answer to Question 1 are involved in the situation.
   (b) Explain how the steps you're describing can be carried out manually. Then suggest what might be done differently with the help of a computer.

3. (a) What are the functions of an instruction in an EDP system?
   (b) What must be done with an instruction before it can do its job effectively?

4. (a) Distinguish between system software and application software.
   (b) Give examples of functions directed by programs of each kind.

5. What is microcode and how is it used?

6. (a) List the four types of functional units of an EDP system.
   (b) Explain each briefly.

7. (a) What are some typical input and output devices of modern computer systems?
   (b) What devices can be used for either input or output?

8. Why is a magnetic-tape unit considered both a secondary-storage device and an input or output device?

9. What is a console and how is it used?

10. If you have access to a computer system, describe how you establish contact with the computer and what you have used "your" computer to accomplish.

11. Refer to Figures 2-4 and 2-11. If you have access to a computer system, enter the program into storage as suggested.
    (a) What actions are caused by the statements on lines 120 and 130?
    (b) If you provide the values 20, 30, 45, 30, and 25 as input, what information should the computer provide as output?
    (c) How do you get the computer to stop?

3

DATA REPRESEN- TATION

Events consist of so much more than we see. Usually, we notice only a few key points about an event, and base our understanding on them. In most cases, this process is adequate to deal with the everyday things in our lives, Today, however, the kinds and amounts of data we have to handle are increasing astronomically. We can no longer be concerned only with our personal lives, or events within our own small worlds; our growing interdependence requires us to respond to events on a planetary or even universal scale. The needs of our times have helped call the computer into existence.

Our technology is based on mathematics, the foundation of measurement. Our sciences use measurement as a basic procedure for investigation. The manipulation of numbers and the discovery of numerical relationships are major occupations of our culture. As our world becomes increasingly complex, the handling of numerical data becomes increasingly unwieldly. Fortunately, computers can make fast work of unwieldly mathematical calculations that might take humans years or even lifetimes to perform with

The space shuttles, for example, will probably soon be accepted as commonplace—yet they represent truly amazing engineering feats when considered in terms of the data involved. During the design process, thousands of items of data were studied to reveal the complex interrelationships of parts and functions. During each flight, again myriad pieces of data must be collected and monitored. Humans alone cannot handle all this data and get results fast enough to direct a flight in progress—but computers can and do!

At the other extreme, computers are used in such procedures as taking the census in many countries. Collecting the census data on the populations of Brazil or Boston, as examples, and then correlating those millions of pieces of data, are achievements that make many others pale by comparison.

Insurance companies use computers to analyze huge amounts of data and set their premiums high enough to make needed profits yet low enough to attract the maximum number of customers. Managing data on hundreds of thousands of policyholders is clearly a formidable task, even with the help of computers.

Air traffic control is an example of a computer-assisted task that requires a constant, "real-time" flow of information.

Courtesy Satellite Business Systems

Courtesy Aetna Life and Casualty, Hartford, Conn.

Courtesy IBM Corporation

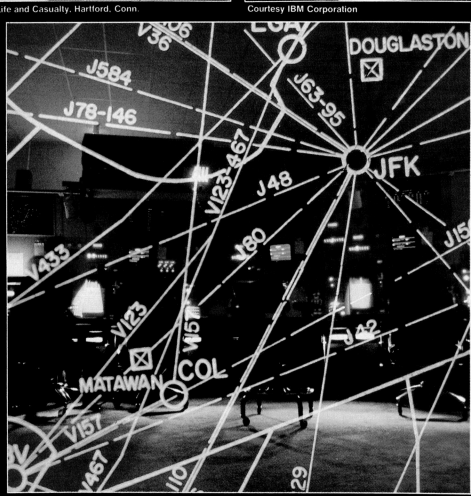

Courtesy Sperry Corporation

The controllers must know the location of air traffic at all times. More planes in the air mean more data to manage. Computers help by predicting where aircraft will be at any given moment, thereby alerting the controllers to potential problems.

Another "real-time" application of computers is in our communication networks. With hundreds of thousands of calls being placed every day, the job of switching and routing them has long since passed the point of manageability by humans alone. Even the electromechanical devices that formerly helped are now being replaced by computerized electronic ones.

Another facet of computer usage in communications involves message transmission itself. This process is becoming digitized, with voice and picture information represented by electronic pulses that can be sent over communication lines. Often many messages are transmitted over one line at the same time, to be decoded at their destinations.

Digitized television broadcasts, beamed via satellite, are received with better clarity than has been possible with older methods. Even if parts of the broadcast signal are lost, the rest of the signal can be used by the computer to fill in the gaps, so that the interference is scarcely noticed. Many sports events are broadcast "live" in this way.

These and many other examples show us that the magnitude of our tasks has grown far beyond our abilities to handle them in strictly human ways. Only with computer help can some of these huge jobs now be managed effectively or affordably.

Courtesy Prime Computer, Inc.

Courtesy GTE

Courtesy Sperry Corporation

Courtesy Intel Corporation

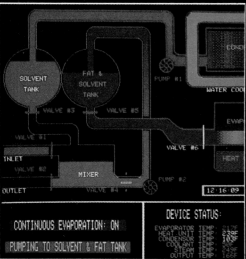

CONTINUOUS EVAPORATION: ON

PUMPING TO SOLVENT & FAT TANK

Courtesy Ramtek Corporation

Courtesy Honeywell Inc.

3 | DATA REPRESENTATION

Symbols convey information. The symbol itself is not information, but it represents information. The printed characters on this page are symbols that convey one meaning to some persons, a different meaning to others, and no meaning at all to persons who do not know how to interpret them. Look at the symbols in Figure 3-1. Which ones are meaningful to you?

Presenting data to a data-processing system is similar in many ways to writing a letter to a friend. The ideas and facts you want to convey must be expressed by symbols your friend can understand. In most cases, that means you use the letters of the English alphabet, numerals, and punctuation marks. You write these symbols in specific sequences to form words, sentences, and paragraphs. The finished letter is sent to your friend, who then reads and interprets the symbols. The symbols are your means of communication.

The symbols that can be read and interpreted by data-processing machines often differ from those used by people. The nature and meaning of the symbols that can be read by a particular machine are determined by the designer of the machine. These symbols, once devised, become the language of the machine. If the machine cannot understand the meaning of our human symbols, they must be converted from our language to the language that the machine is capable of understanding. That language becomes the means of communication between us and the machine.

In this chapter, we look first at how data can be represented when it is provided as input to a computer system. Then we look at how data can be represented within the computer. We discuss some of the common data-representation, or coding, schemes that we as users can understand easily. Then we see how the digits of a binary, octal, or hexadecimal number system can be used as convenient shorthands. As users, we don't have to deal with numerals expressed in these number systems. Programmers seldom do either. Some understanding of them will help you to understand the flexibility that's available with various methods of data representation, however.

INPUT DATA REPRESENTATION

In an electronic data-processing system, data is first entered as input to the system through an input device. When discussing data representation, we can group input devices within three broad categories:

- Direct-input devices, which allow users to enter data without first transcribing it on a data-recording medium
- Devices that accept input data represented in a form that is readable by both humans and machines
- Devices that accept input data represented in a form that can be interpreted by machines but cannot be read easily by humans

We are interested in the methods of data representation here. In the next chapter, we discuss the devices and their uses.

Perhaps the most common input device is a *visual-display unit*. The user enters data from this unit by pressing certain keys on its keyboard. (See Figure 3-2.) Pressing the key for the letter E, for example, causes a particular sequence of electronic pulses to be sent over a transmission medium (usually a wire or cable) to the computer. The sequence of electronic pulses is the internal data representation for the letter E. With this direct-input capability, we as users need not express the letter E in symbolic form before we can enter it into the system. However, the letter E must be expressed symbolically to pass from the input device to the computer.

Have you ever given verbal input to a computer system? *Voice-input units* are doing tasks formerly done by customer service personnel in catalog shopping

FIGURE 3-1
Many kinds of symbols are used to convey information.

FIGURE 3-2
Keying is a way of entering
data directly. (*Courtesy
Tandem Computers
Incorporated*)

and banking services, for example. A voice-input unit is another example of a direct-input device. The user simply speaks into the device, using words of a limited vocabulary that the device is able to recognize. The sounds of the user's voice are converted to discrete sequences of electronic pulses and forwarded as input to the computer. The conversion process is called *digitizing.*

Input devices in the second category above accept data represented by symbols that are meaningful to us, but the symbols must be expressed on a data-recording medium. For example, a *magnetic-ink character reader* can interpret numbers printed with a special type font and an ink containing magnetizable particles on an ordinary check. An *optical character reader* may be able to read and understand letters and numbers printed in any of several type fonts. Some optical character readers can even accept handwritten data. (See Figure 3-3.)

Input devices in the third category accept data in an encoded form that is readily understandable to the devices but not to us. Best known of these is the *card reader.* It accepts data represented symbolically by specific combinations of holes in the columns of punched cards. Since we don't commonly express data as holes in punched cards, we must convert our data to that form in a data-preparation step before we provide it as input to the computer.

The bar code that appears on most items at your supermarket is another example of machine-readable data that is not generally understandable to humans. (See Figure 3-4.) Merchandise tags at department stores also often contain data in bar-code form. The *point-of-sale (POS) terminals* at customer checkout counters are optical readers that can read and understand the bar code.

MARK REPORTING ALPHABETIC GRADES

ETS 6437

SCHOOL NAME
Cogco Jr. High

Marking Period 8 NKPD

| 43728915782 | CODE 2891 | SECTION 57 | COURSE TITLE English | TEACHER L. Smith | ROOM 001 | PERIOD 02 |

STUDENT NAME	OFFICIAL CLASS	STUDENT ID	CLASS ABSENCE	CLASS MARK	EXAM MARK	EXAM TYPE
Alessi, Grace	A1A3	67892	11		76	
Alessi, Thomas	B1B2	56820			100	
Augustyn, Janice	C1C2	24687	2		89	
Belanger, Gerry	D1D2	13573	2		81	
Bucchignano, John	E1E2	15933	20		56	
Callahan, Alan	F2F2	87650	3		91	
Capper, Ed	G1G4	87650			96	
Carney, Donna	H8H9	75614	1		73	
Cook, Harvey L.	I0I8	47597	4		85	
Coolis, Linda	J2J7	37903	1		92	
Darling, Claire	K0K6	06270	4		87	
Dore, Dorothy	L5L3	11502	2		74	
Duncanson, Tony	M8M7	43760			81	
Fields, Nancy	N0N7	89300			87	
Flanigan, Matt	0806	62455	1		100	
Fountain, Barbara	P3P4	67892	5		65	
French, John	Q2Q4	24687	9		62	
Gray, Ffarrington	R1R7	15933	2		93	
Gushue, Edward	S2S3	56820	7		80	
Harrison, Vinny	T9T5	13573	3		76	
Hayter, Henry	U9U2	87650			74	
Insolia, Gerry	V1V3	75614			80	
Johnson, Bill	W2W4	47597			74	

FIGURE 3-3 This reporting form used by a school contains specially printed characters that can be read by both humans and machines. (*Courtesy Cognitronics Corporation*)

Just as there is communication between humans and machines, there is also communication between machines. As we've already mentioned, that communication may be a direct exchange of data in electronic form over wires and cables. Data may also be carried by microwaves. Communication satellites are increasingly involved in long-distance, direct machine-to-machine communications. A computer aboard an orbiting spacecraft may generate data that is transmitted as wave pulses to another computer at Kennedy Space Center, for example.

Alternatively, data to be exchanged between machines may be recorded on a data-recording medium rather than transmitted directly in pulse form. In such cases, the recorded output of one machine or system is used as input to another machine or system. The output may even be used as input to the same machine or system, at another time. For such purposes, we represent data symbolically on magnetic tape, floppy disks, conventional (hard) disks, or other media. Some printers can produce output that is acceptable as input to certain optical readers.

FIGURE 3-4
Bar-code data can be read by machines but is not easily understood by humans. (*Courtesy National Semiconductor Corporation*)

Many credit-card statements are examples; we call them *turnaround documents*. Some day soon, computer systems will probably talk to each other!

In all cases, the data we provide as input to a computer is converted from its input form to electronic pulses. The circuitry of the computer can sense the presence or absence of these pulses. It is this ability of the computer that allows data and instructions to be stored and moved about internally. Let's look now at the structure of the computer's internal storage unit and some common internal data-representation schemes.

DATA REPRESENTATION IN THE COMPUTER

It is easy to understand that there must be a method of representing data on employee time cards, customer sales orders, floppy disks, tapes on reels or in cassettes, and so on. There must also be a method of representing data inside the computer. We've just learned that data is sent to the computer as electronic pulses. But what happens to the pulses? We might suspect that it's one thing to send pulses into the computer but another thing to know what to do with them once they're there.

Binary Components

Consider an ordinary light bulb. At any one time, the light bulb is either on or off. It can be in only one of two possible conditions. We say, therefore, that it operates in a *binary mode*. We refer to the two possible conditions, or settings, as *binary states*.

Computer components operate in the same way. Each component can be in only one of two possible conditions at any given time. We know that electronic pulses are either present or absent. Materials such as the tiny magnetic cores used in the internal storage units of some computers are magnetized in one direction or the opposite. Transistors in the computer's logic or memory circuitry are either conducting or nonconducting. Logic gates planned by the computer designer to act as switches are either open or closed. (See Figure 3-5.)

Representing data in the computer is accomplished by assigning a specific value to each binary component or group of components. This technique is

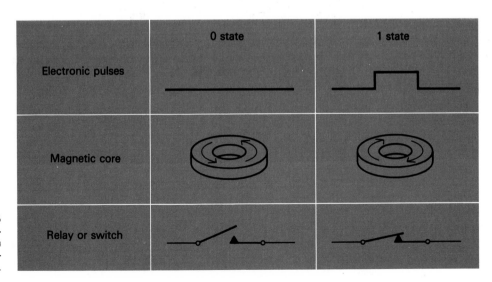

FIGURE 3-5
Each binary-state component in a computer can be in one of two possible conditions at any given time.

illustrated by a simple four-bulb device in Figure 3-6. The bulbs in the device have been assigned decimal values of 1, 2, 4, and 8, from right to left. When a bulb is lighted, it represents the value associated with it. When a bulb is not lighted, it can be ignored. The numeric value represented by this simple device at any time is the sum indicated by the lighted bulbs. Thus, decimal values from 0 through 15 can be represented by this device. With all bulbs off, the value is 0. With all bulbs on, the value is 15.

In Figure 3-6, the decimal value 5 is represented because the 4 and 1 bulbs are on and the 8 and 2 bulbs are off. The bulbs could have been assigned quite different values (for example, 1, 2, 3, and 4, or 10, 100, 1000, and 10,000). The representation scheme is simply a selected code. In a computer, the values that the designer assigns to individual binary components or to groups of components become the code for representing data.

Binary Notation

So far, we have discussed how binary components can be used to represent decimal values—numbers of the familiar decimal (base 10) number system. Now let us consider how a binary method of notation can be used to describe the settings of the binary components.

Binary notation uses only two symbols: 0 and 1. In any position of the notation, the symbol 0 represents the absence of an assigned value and the symbol 1 represents the presence of an assigned value. For example, the data represented in Figure 3-6 can be described in binary notation as 0101. In the coding system we've just defined, the rightmost 1 has a value of 1; the leftmost, a value of 4. Thus, the binary notation, 0101, means 5.

The symbols used in binary notation (0 and 1) are called *bits*, which is a short way of saying *binary digits*. For example, the binary notation 0101 can be described as having a 1 bit in the 1-bit and 4-bit positions, and a 0 bit in the 2-bit and 8-bit positions.

A major point you should understand here is that this binary notation is a general-purpose mechanism for describing the settings of binary components. What the bit pattern—0101, 00000011, 11010101 ... 111, or whatever—means is determined by the coding system that is the basis for the representation.

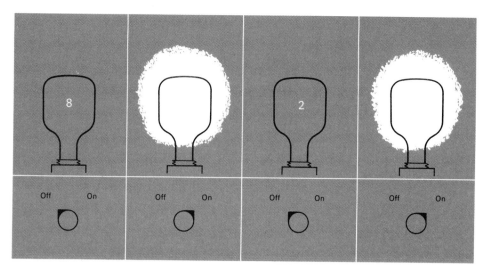

FIGURE 3-6
Groups of binary-state components can represent decimal values.

2^{14}	2^{13}	2^{12}	2^{11}	2^{10}	2^9	2^8	2^7	2^6	2^5	2^4	2^3	2^2	2^1	2^0
16384	8192	4096	2048	1024	512	256	128	64	32	16	8	4	2	1

FIGURE 3-7 The positions in a binary numeral have place values that are powers of 2.

BINARY NUMBER SYSTEM

In some computers, the values associated with binary notation are related directly to the *binary number system*. In such computers, the values of the binary digits (0, 1) are determined by their positions in a multidigit symbol. The multidigit symbol is actually a *binary numeral*. The position values in the numeral are based on the right-to-left progression of powers of 2 (2^0, 2^1, 2^2, 2^3, and so on). Therefore, the rightmost position has a value of 1*; the next position, a value of 2; the next, 4; the next, 8; the next, 16; and so on. (See Figure 3-7.)

In the binary (base 2) number system, then, the binary digit 0 or 1 in a particular position of a binary numeral indicates whether the corresponding power of 2 is absent or present in the quantity being represented. (As in our light-bulb example above, the 1 bit indicates the presence of the value; the 0 bit indicates the absence of the value.) Using this system, the value of the binary numeral 1001 is determined as follows:

$$
\begin{aligned}
1001 &= (1 \times 2^3) + (0 \times 2^2) + (0 \times 2^1) + (1 \times 2^0) \\
&= \quad 8 \quad + \quad 0 \quad + \quad 0 \quad + \quad 1 \\
&= \quad 9
\end{aligned}
$$

Thus, we see that the binary numeral 1001 is equivalent to the decimal numeral 9. The largest value that can be represented by a bit pattern consisting of four binary digits is 1111, which is equivalent to the decimal numeral 15. (See Figure 3-8.)

---

*Any number followed by the exponent 0 has a value of 1.

BINARY	DECIMAL
0000	0
0001	1
0010	2
0011	3
0100	4
0101	5
0110	6
0111	7
1000	8
1001	9
1010	10
1011	11
1100	12
1101	13
1110	14
1111	15

FIGURE 3-8
Equivalent binary and decimal values.

The binary number system is used as a means of representing numeric data values in many modern computer systems. Each storage location in the computer consists of a fixed number of binary components. Each component in a particular storage location can be set to either a 1 state or a 0 state.

As an example, assume there are eight binary components in each storage location. Further assume the components in one location are set to the states 01010111. The leftmost bit is treated as a special indicator, the *sign bit*. Here, 0 tells us the value is positive, that is, greater than zero. (A 1 would have told us it was negative.) The remaining seven bits represent the value. The bits are the binary numeral 1010111. We can determine the decimal equivalent of this binary numeral by using the same approach we used before:

$$
\begin{aligned}
1010111 &= (1 \times 2^6) + (0 \times 2^5) + (1 \times 2^4) + (0 \times 2^3) + (1 \times 2^2) + (1 \times 2^1) + (1 \times 2^0) \\
&= \quad 64 \quad + \quad 0 \quad + \quad 16 \quad + \quad 0 \quad + \quad 4 \quad + \quad 2 \quad + \quad 1 \\
&= \quad 87
\end{aligned}
$$

Thus, we can say that the value stored in this location is the binary equivalent of the decimal numeral 87.

The largest value that can be represented by a bit pattern consisting of seven binary digits is 1111111, equivalent to the decimal number 127. We conclude that, when the binary number system is used for data representation, the largest numeric value that can be represented in the seven available bits of one 8-bit storage location is 127. Computers having 16-bit, 32-bit, and 64-bit storage locations can represent much larger (i.e., longer) binary numerals. Therefore, much larger numeric values can be stored.

EBCDIC We've just seen how the binary number system can be used as a coding scheme to represent numeric values. We've also seen how numeric values in that form can be stored in a computer. But what about nonnumeric data—say, customer names and addresses, product descriptions, titles of books, even all the text of books? And what about the messages that we see on visual-display screens—where do they come from, and how are they stored?

Remember that the settings of the binary components making up a storage location in the computer are simply a bit pattern. A string of bits such as 10111001 may represent a binary number, but it doesn't have to. EDP system designers have also developed other coding systems. One of the most widely used is the *Extended Binary Coded Decimal Interchange Code*, or *EBCDIC* (pronounced eb'-si-dick). This code uses 8-bit code patterns to represent characters. For example, the bit pattern 11000001 represents A; the bit pattern 11000010 represents B; and so on. (See Figure 3-9, the rightmost column.) Since there are 2^8, or 256, possible combinations of eight bits, up to 256 different characters can be represented. This allows for the digits 0 through 9, both uppercase and lowercase letters, and a wide range of punctuation marks and other special characters. It also allows for control characters that are meaningful to certain input/output devices. In Figure 3-9, NUL means null (all zeros), SOH means Start of Heading, STX means Start of Text, and so on. Some bit patterns currently have no assigned meanings; they are available for future assignments.

EBCDIC	BIT PATTERN Zone Digit	EBCDIC	BIT PATTERN Zone Digit	EBCDIC	BIT PATTERN Zone Digit	EBCDIC	BIT PATTERN Zone Digit
NUL	0000 0000	SP	0100 0000		1000 0000	PZ 7/11	1100 0000
SOH	0000 0001		0100 0001	a	1000 0001	A	1100 0001
STX	0000 0010		0100 0010	b	1000 0010	B	1100 0010
ETX	0000 0011		0100 0011	c	1000 0011	C	1100 0011
PF	0000 0100		0100 0100	d	1000 0100	D	1100 0100
HT	0000 0101		0100 0101	e	1000 0101	E	1100 0101
LC	0000 0110		0100 0110	f	1000 0110	F	1100 0110
DEL	0000 0111		0100 0111	g	1000 0111	G	1100 0111
	0000 1000		0100 1000	h	1000 1000	H	1100 1000
RLF	0000 1001		0100 1001	i	1000 1001	I	1100 1001
SMM	0000 1010	¢ [	0100 1010		1000 1010		1100 1010
VT	0000 1011	.	0100 1011		1000 1011		1100 1011
FF	0000 1100	<	0100 1100		1000 1100	∫	1100 1100
CR	0000 1101	(	0100 1101		1000 1101		1100 1101
SO	0000 1110	+	0100 1110		1000 1110	⌐	1100 1110
SI	0000 1111	|	0100 1111		1000 1111		1100 1111
DLE	0001 0000	&	0101 0000		1001 0000	MZ 7/13	1101 0000
DC1	0001 0001		0101 0001	j	1001 0001	J	1101 0001
DC2	0001 0010		0101 0010	k	1001 0010	K	1101 0010
TM	0001 0011		0101 0011	l	1001 0011	L	1101 0011
RES	0001 0100		0101 0100	m	1001 0100	M	1101 0100
NL	0001 0101		0101 0101	n	1001 0101	N	1101 0101
BS	0001 0110		0101 0110	o	1001 0110	O	1101 0110
IL	0001 0111		0101 0111	p	1001 0111	P	1101 0111
CAN	0001 1000		0101 1000	q	1001 1000	Q	1101 1000
EM	0001 1001		0101 1001	r	1001 1001	R	1101 1001
CC	0001 1010	!]	0101 1010		1001 1010		1101 1010
CU1	0001 1011	$	0101 1011		1001 1011		1101 1011
IFS	0001 1100	*	0101 1100		1001 1100		1101 1100
IGS	0001 1101	)	0101 1101		1001 1101		1101 1101
IRS	0001 1110	;	0101 1110		1001 1110		1101 1110
IUS	0001 1111	⌐	0101 1111		1001 1111		1101 1111
DS	0010 0000	-	0110 0000		1010 0000	RM 5/12	1110 0000
SOS	0010 0001	/	0110 0001	—	1010 0001		1110 0001
FS	0010 0010		0110 0010	s	1010 0010	S	1110 0010
	0010 0011		0110 0011	t	1010 0011	T	1110 0011
BYP	0010 0100		0110 0100	u	1010 0100	U	1110 0100
LF	0010 0101		0110 0101	v	1010 0101	V	1110 0101
ETB	0010 0110		0110 0110	w	1010 0110	W	1110 0110
ESC	0010 0111		0110 0111	x	1010 0111	X	1110 0111
	0010 1000		0110 1000	y	1010 1000	Y	1110 1000
	0010 1001		0110 1001	z	1010 1001	Z	1110 1001
SM	0010 1010	7/12	0110 1010		1010 1010		1110 1010
CU2	0010 1011	,	0110 1011		1010 1011		1110 1011
	0010 1100	%	0110 1100		1010 1100	H	1110 1100
ENQ	0010 1101	—	0110 1101		1010 1101		1110 1101
ACK	0010 1110	>	0110 1110		1010 1110		1110 1110
BEL	0010 1111	?	0110 1111		1010 1111		1110 1111
	0011 0000		0111 0000		1011 0000	0	1111 0000
	0011 0001		0111 0001		1011 0001	1	1111 0001
SYN	0011 0010		0111 0010		1011 0010	2	1111 0010
	0011 0011		0111 0011		1011 0011	3	1111 0011
PN	0011 0100		0111 0100		1011 0100	4	1111 0100
RS	0011 0101		0111 0101		1011 0101	5	1111 0101
UC	0011 0110		0111 0110		1011 0110	6	1111 0110
EOT	0011 0111		0111 0111		1011 0111	7	1111 0111
	0011 1000		0111 1000		1011 1000	8	1111 1000
	0011 1001	6/0	0111 1001		1011 1001	9	1111 1001
	0011 1010	:	0111 1010		1011 1010	≠	1111 1010
CU3	0011 1011	#	0111 1011		1011 1011		1111 1011
DC4	0011 1100	@	0111 1100		1011 1100		1111 1100
NAK	0011 1101	'	0111 1101		1011 1101		1111 1101
	0011 1110	=	0111 1110		1011 1110		1111 1110
SUB	0011 1111	"	0111 1111		1011 1111	EO	1111 1111

FIGURE 3-9 EBCDIC character representation.

EBCDIC was initially developed by IBM and is used extensively in medium and large computer systems, both IBM's and similar ones from other manufacturers. As you might expect, each storage location in one of these computers consists of eight binary components. These eight components together are called one *byte*. Each data character read into storage from an input device is stored in one byte. For example, the characters MAR 16 may be keyed in the date field of a sales order, converted to electronic pulses that reflect the EBCDIC bit patterns for these characters, and stored in six bytes of primary storage—as shown in Figure 3-10.

There is no need for you, or system analysts, programmers, or any other users of computers to memorize EBCDIC code patterns. However, some general observations about how the code is constructed are useful. Each 8-bit pattern can be divided into two parts. The leftmost four bits are the zone portion. The remaining (rightmost) four bits are the digit portion. Look again at Figure 3-9. You'll see that the zone portions for lowercase letters (1000, 1001, 1010) and for uppercase letters (1100, 1101, 1110) are assigned systematically. The digit portions for the letters range from 0001 through 1001 within the zone groupings. A zone portion of 1111 is a sure clue to a numeric character in the vast majority of cases. Persons who deal often with EBCDIC learn to recognize quickly the values represented.

ASCII Another widely used data-representation scheme is the *American Standard Code for Information Interchange,* or *ASCII* (pronounced as'-key). This code was developed jointly by equipment manufacturers and users. Their objective was to simplify and standardize machine-to-machine and system-to-system communi-

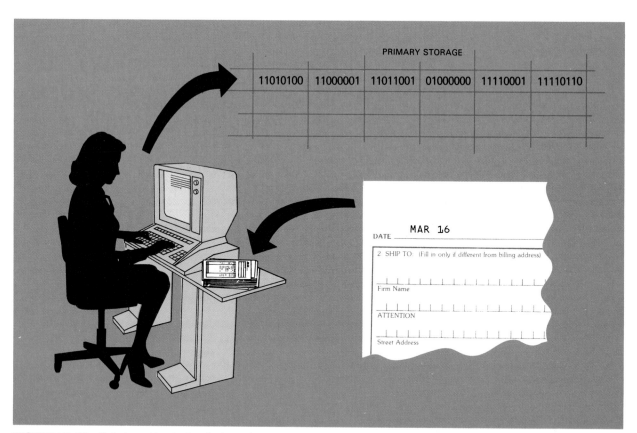

FIGURE 3-10 Data keyed in at a terminal may be converted to electronic pulses and stored internally in EBCDIC form. (*Courtesy TRW Inc.*)

cation. They hoped to allow data to be passed freely between computers and devices produced by the same manufacturer or by different manufacturers.

As Figure 3-11 shows, ASCII is a 7-bit code. Each character is represented by a unique combination of seven binary components. This allows up to 2^7, or 128, different characters to be represented. The pattern 1000001 represents A; 1000010 represents B; and so on.

The use of ASCII is especially common in data communication systems, where data is transmitted long distances over telephone lines, microwaves, or other media. Typewriterlike devices supporting the ASCII character set are often referred to as ASCII terminals. If the computer at the receiving end of the transmission stores data in EBCDIC, the ASCII bit patterns must be converted to EBCDIC before they are placed in primary storage. Manufacturers such as Hewlett-Packard and Prime have developed computers as well as input/output devices that handle ASCII data. Most microcomputer systems also accept, store, process, and write out data in ASCII form.

ASCII has been adopted as a standard by the International Standards Organization and the American National Standards Institute. As the combined use of data-processing equipment and data-communication facilities increases, we can expect the use of ASCII to increase as well.

COMPUTER STORAGE ORGANIZATION Some computers use one character as the basic unit of information storage. They perform operations on individual characters, one at a time. Other computers use a fixed number of binary components in storage as a basic unit. We can think of

ASCII	BIT PATTERN	ASCII	BIT PATTERN	ASCII	BIT PATTERN	ASCII	BIT PATTERN
NUL	0000000	SP	0100000	@	1000000	`	1100000
SOH	0000001	!	0100001	A	1000001	a	1100001
STX	0000010	"	0100010	B	1000010	b	1100010
ETX	0000011	#	0100011	C	1000011	c	1100011
EOT	0000100	$	0100100	D	1000100	d	1100100
ENQ	0000101	%	0100101	E	1000101	e	1100101
ACK	0000110	&	0100110	F	1000110	f	1100110
Bel	0000111	'	0100111	G	1000111	g	1100111
BS	0001000	(	0101000	H	1001000	h	1101000
HT	0001001	)	0101001	I	1001001	i	1101001
LF	0001010	*	0101010	J	1001010	j	1101010
VT	0001011	+	0101011	K	1001011	k	1101011
FF	0001100	,	0101100	L	1001100	l	1101100
CR	0001101	–	0101101	M	1001101	m	1101101
SO	0001110	.	0101110	N	1001110	n	1101110
SI	0001111	/	0101111	O	1001111	o	1101111
DLE	0010000	0	0110000	P	1010000	p	1110000
DC1	0010001	1	0110001	Q	1010001	q	1110001
DC2	0010010	2	0110010	R	1010010	r	1110010
DC3	0010011	3	0110011	S	1010011	s	1110011
DC4	0010100	4	0110100	T	1010100	t	1110100
NCK	0010101	5	0110101	U	1010101	u	1110101
SYN	0010110	6	0110110	V	1010110	v	1110110
ETB	0010111	7	0110111	W	1010111	w	1110111
CAN	0011000	8	0111000	X	1011000	x	1111000
EM	0011001	9	0111001	Y	1011001	y	1111001
SUB	0011010	:	0111010	Z	1011010	z	1111010
ESC	0011011	;	0111011	[	1011011	{	1111011
FS	0011100	<	0111100	\	1011100	|	1111100
GS	0011101	=	0111101	]	1011101	}	1111101
RS	0011110	>	0111110	^	1011110	~	1111110
US	0011111	?	0111111	—	1011111	DEL	1111111

FIGURE 3-11 ASCII character representation.

the binary components as bit positions. The bit positions may be capable of holding multiple characters. Such computers may operate on multiple characters at one time.

Consider IBM 4300-series computers as an example. These computers are especially flexible in that they can use either of two units: a byte, which consists of 8 bit positions as suggested above, or a *word*, which consists of 32 bit positions. Whether an IBM 4300-series computer operates on bytes or words depends on the stored-program instructions that control the operations being carried out.

In general, a computer that operates on bytes operates on 8-bit units. Many computers operate on words, and word sizes vary widely. The earliest microcomputers had 8-bit word sizes. Some microcomputers and minicomputers in common use have 16-bit word sizes. Other popular word sizes are 18, 32, 36, 48, and 64 bits. Some very large computers operate on 128-bit words.

An important point needs to be understood here. (It will come up again later.) When speaking in general terms, we sometimes regard a computer word as the amount of data transferred to or from storage at one time. As we shall see, in this context, in an IBM 4300 computer, the contents of 32 bits may constitute a *fixed-length word;* the contents of several bytes may constitute a *variable-length word.*

The bit positions within a byte or word can be related to positions in a binary numeral. When used in this way, they have place values related to the binary number system. As shown earlier, in Figure 3-8, the decimal values of the positions (from right to left) are 1, 2, 4, 8, 16, 32, 64, and so on. The combinations of 1 bits and 0 bits can also represent data other than a binary numeral. Figure 3-12 shows how the bit positions in one 32-bit word can be used to represent any of three types of data: one 32-bit binary numeral; an 8-digit hexadecimal numeral (explained later in this chapter); or four *alphanumeric characters,* that is, any combination of four alphabetic, numeric, and special characters of the EBCDIC character set.

Obviously, binary numerals greater than 0 and 1 contain more digits than equivalent decimal numerals do. The 32-bit binary numeral in Figure 3-12, for example, is 11100010011110111100010011010001. Its decimal equivalent is 3,799,762,129. Most of us are much more comfortable with the latter. Because binary numerals are usually long and cumbersome, values are frequently expressed in other forms that are more convenient for us to handle. These notations may be used in programming or in printed listings or displays of stored values. They are, in effect, "shorthands" for binary notation. It is to our

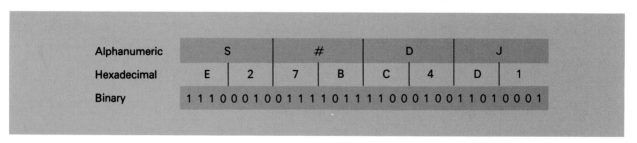

FIGURE 3-12 One 32-bit word may contain data in alphanumeric, hexadecimal, or decimal form.

advantage to understand the notations and to know how to convert values from one form of representation to others.

Decimal-to-Binary Conversion

Suppose that a value expressed as a decimal numeral is to be represented as a binary numeral and stored in the computer. The numeral must be converted from decimal to binary. One approach is to use the *division-multiplication method* of conversion. The procedure is simple:

To convert a decimal whole number (not involving a fraction) from base 10 to any other base, divide that number repeatedly by the value of the base to which the number is being converted. Repeat the division operation until the quotient is 0. The remainders—written in reverse of the order in which they were obtained—form the new equivalent numeral.

This procedure is applied below to convert the decimal numeral 149 to its binary equivalent.

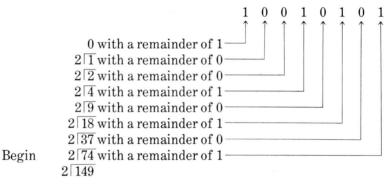

The value expressed by the decimal numeral 149 can thus be expressed by the binary numeral 10010101. Any decimal numeral can be converted to binary the same way. Fortunately, we do not usually have to do this conversion, even when numeric values we enter are to be stored in binary form in the computer. The system performs the conversion for us.

Binary-to-Decimal Conversion

The reverse procedure—converting a binary numeral to decimal—can be done by the use of *expanded notation*. When this approach is used, the position values of the original numeral are written out. For example, 100110 is converted to its decimal equivalent as follows:

$$
\begin{aligned}
100110 &= (1 \times 2^5) + (0 \times 2^4) + (0 \times 2^3) + (1 \times 2^2) + (1 \times 2^1) + (0 \times 2^0) \\
&= \quad 32 \quad + \quad 0 \quad + \quad 0 \quad + \quad 4 \quad + \quad 2 \quad + \quad 0 \\
&= \quad 38
\end{aligned}
$$

Such conversions often occur when numeric values stored in binary form are printed or displayed on a screen. However, if the contents of primary storage are printed or displayed as stored, and you want to understand them, you may have to do the conversion yourself.

OCTAL NUMBER SYSTEM

A common form of shorthand notation used with computers is the *octal number system.* When this shorthand is used, any group of three binary digits can be represented by one octal digit. The base of the octal number system is 8, and it contains eight symbols: 0, 1, 2, 3, 4, 5, 6, and 7. Equivalent binary, octal, and decimal numerals are shown in Figure 3-13.

Consider the octal numeral 14. The position values in an octal numeral are based on the right-to-left progression of powers of 8 (8^0 or 1, 8^1 or 8, 8^2 or 64, and so on). Therefore:

$$
\begin{aligned}
14 &= (1 \times 8^1) + (4 \times 8^0) \\
&= \quad 8 \quad + \quad 4 \\
&= \quad 12
\end{aligned}
$$

Binary-to-Octal Conversion

Remember that three binary digits are represented by one octal digit. Therefore, conversion from binary to octal is simple. For example, 110010.001 (binary) is equivalent to 62.1 (octal):

$$
\begin{array}{ccccc}
110 & 010 & \cdot & 001 \\
\vee & \vee & \cdot & \vee \\
6 & 2 & \cdot & 1
\end{array}
$$

As another example, assume you are using a computer that stores data in 18-bit words. An error occurs somewhere in the system. The values in certain storage locations (words) are converted from binary to octal and displayed on the system console so the error can be found. In particular, the value 110111001011010000 is converted to octal, as shown below:

$$
\begin{array}{cccccc}
110 & 111 & 001 & 011 & 010 & 000 \\
\vee & \vee & \vee & \vee & \vee & \vee \\
6 & 7 & 1 & 3 & 2 & 0
\end{array}
$$

Your responsibility is to determine the meaning of 671320 by referring to system documentation. Chances are it's easier to look up the octal value than it would be to look up the string of 1s and 0s. You may find, for example, that a write operation to a disk could not be completed successfully.

Octal-to-Binary Conversion

The opposite of binary-to-octal conversion—conversion from octal to binary—is also easy. Any one octal digit represents three binary digits. Thus, 731.4 (octal) is equivalent to 111011001.100 (binary), as shown at the top of the next page.

BINARY	OCTAL	DECIMAL
000	0	0
001	1	1
010	2	2
011	3	3
100	4	4
101	5	5
110	6	6
111	7	7

At this point, a carry to the next-higher position of the octal numeral is necessary, since all eight symbols of the number system have been used.

BINARY	OCTAL	DECIMAL
001 000	10	8
001 001	11	9
001 010	12	10
001 011	13	11
001 100	14	12
.	.	.
.	.	.
.	.	.

FIGURE 3-13 Equivalent binary, octal, and decimal values.

$$\begin{array}{cccc} 7 & 3 & 1 & \cdot & 4 \\ \wedge & \wedge & \wedge & \cdot & \wedge \\ 111 & 011 & 001 & \cdot & 100 \end{array}$$

As another example, the octal numeral 632 is equivalent to the binary numeral 110011010:

$$\begin{array}{ccc} 6 & 3 & 2 \\ \wedge & \wedge & \wedge \\ 110 & 011 & 010 \end{array}$$

Now you probably realize why octal notation is a convenient shorthand for binary.

Decimal-to-Octal Conversion

Suppose a decimal value is to be converted to octal for storage in the computer. Decimal-to-octal conversion is much like decimal-to-binary conversion. That is, using the division-multiplication method, we repeatedly divide the decimal numeral by the base of our new numeral (which, in this case, is 8). Our remainders, in reverse order, form the octal equivalent.

Thus, the decimal numeral 151 is converted to the octal numeral 227 as follows:

$$\begin{array}{l} \qquad\qquad\qquad\qquad\qquad 2 \quad 2 \quad 7 \\ 0 \text{ with a remainder of } 2 \longrightarrow \\ 8\,\overline{|\,2} \text{ with a remainder of } 2 \longrightarrow \\ \text{Begin} \quad 8\,\overline{|\,18} \text{ with a remainder of } 7 \longrightarrow \\ \longrightarrow \quad 8\,\overline{|\,151} \end{array}$$

Octal-to-Decimal Conversion

Now suppose an octal numeral is to be converted to decimal. Octal-to-decimal conversion can be accomplished by the same technique that we use for binary-to-decimal conversion. Expanded notation shows the position values (powers of 8) of the octal numeral. For example, 713 (octal) is converted to 459 (decimal) as follows:

$$\begin{array}{rl} 713 = & (7 \times 8^2) + (1 \times 8^1) + (3 \times 8^0) \\ = & 448 \quad + \quad 8 \quad + \quad 3 \\ = & 459 \end{array}$$

HEXADECIMAL NUMBER SYSTEM

A *hexadecimal number system* provides still another convenient shorthand for expressing values represented by binary numerals. Any group of four binary digits can be represented by one digit of a hexadecimal number system. The base of the hexadecimal number system is 16. It uses 16 symbols: the digits 0 through 9 and the letters A through F. Equivalent binary, hexadecimal, and decimal numerals are shown in Figure 3-14.

Consider the hexadecimal numeral 1A6. The position values in a hexadecimal numeral are based on the right-to-left progression of powers of 16 (16^0 or 1, 16^1 or 16, 16^2 or 256, and so on). Therefore:

$$\begin{array}{rl} 1A6 = & (1 \times 16^2) + (10 \times 16^1) + (6 \times 16^0) \\ = & 256 \quad + \quad 160 \quad + \quad 6 \\ = & 422 \end{array}$$

BINARY	HEXADECIMAL	DECIMAL
0000	0	0
0001	1	1
0010	2	2
0011	3	3
0100	4	4
0101	5	5
0110	6	6
0111	7	7
1000	8	8
1001	9	9
1010	A	10
1011	B	11
1100	C	12
1101	D	13
1110	E	14
1111	F	15

FIGURE 3-14
Equivalent binary, hexadecimal, and decimal values.

Binary-to-Hexadecimal Conversion

Recall that IBM 4300-series computers have eight data bits in each byte of primary storage. Each byte can be thought of as containing two hexadecimal digits. Conversion of the bits from binary to hexadecimal is easy. For example, 00110101 (binary) is equivalent to 35 (hexadecimal):

Hexadecimal-to-Binary Conversion

Conversion from hexadecimal to binary is easy, too. Suppose that the content of a 32-bit word in IBM 4300 computer storage were expressed as the hexadecimal numeral 2489C1AA. Since each hexadecimal digit represents the same value as four binary digits, the actual content of the word is as follows:

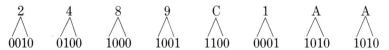

We have determined that the actual content of this computer word is 00100100100010011100000110101010. However, the shorthand notation 2489C1AA is much easier for us to read than the binary digits.

Decimal-to-Hexadecimal Conversion

The division-multiplication method can be used to convert any decimal numeral to hexadecimal. We repeatedly divide the decimal numeral by 16 and use the remainders in reverse order as before. Any remainder greater than 9 must be expressed as a hexadecimal digit.

The decimal numeral 1710 is converted to the hexadecimal numeral 6AE as follows:

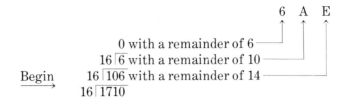

Hexadecimal-to-Decimal Conversion

Hexadecimal-to-decimal conversion can be accomplished by using expanded notation. But because it is difficult to remember or calculate the values of 16^3, 16^4, and so on, hexadecimal–decimal conversion tables are often used.

The following example shows how the table in Figure 3-15 can be used to convert FA9C4D (hexadecimal) to an equivalent decimal numeral. Note that the position (place value) of each hexadecimal digit in the numeral being converted corresponds to the position of the X below a column in the table. In other words, the first (leftmost) digit of FA9C4D—the F—is in the sixth column from the right (X00000). All the values must be added to obtain the final decimal result.

$$
\begin{array}{rrr}
\text{FA9C4D} & \text{F00000} = & 15{,}728{,}640 \\
& \text{A0000} = & 655{,}360 \\
& 9000 = & 36{,}864 \\
& \text{C00} = & 3{,}072 \\
& 40 = & 64 \\
& \text{D} = & \underline{13} \\
& & 16{,}424{,}013
\end{array}
$$

Thus, the hexadecimal numeral FA9C4D is equivalent to the decimal numeral 16,424,013. Other hexadecimal numerals can be converted to decimal in a similar manner.

HEX	DECIMAL							
0	0	0	0	0	0	0	0	0
1	268,435,456	16,777,216	1,048,576	65,536	4,096	256	16	1
2	536,870,912	33,554,432	2,097,152	131,072	8,192	512	32	2
3	805,306,368	50,331,648	3,145,728	196,608	12,288	768	48	3
4	1,073,741,824	67,108,864	4,194,304	262,144	16,384	1,024	64	4
5	1,342,177,280	83,886,080	5,242,880	327,680	20,480	1,280	80	5
6	1,610,612,736	100,663,296	6,291,456	393,216	24,576	1,536	96	6
7	1,879,048,192	117,440,512	7,340,032	458,752	28,672	1,792	112	7
8	2,147,483,648	134,217,728	8,388,608	524,288	32,768	2,048	128	8
9	2,415,919,104	150,994,944	9,437,184	589,824	36,864	2,304	144	9
A	2,684,354,560	167,772,160	10,485,760	655,360	40,960	2,560	160	10
B	2,952,790,016	184,549,376	11,534,336	720,896	45,056	2,816	176	11
C	3,221,225,472	201,326,592	12,582,912	786,432	49,152	3,072	192	12
D	3,489,660,928	218,103,808	13,631,488	851,968	53,248	3,328	208	13
E	3,758,096,384	234,881,024	14,680,064	917,504	57,344	3,584	224	14
F	4,026,531,840	251,658,240	15,728,640	983,040	61,440	3,840	240	15
	X0000000	X000000	X00000	X0000	X000	X00	X0	X

FIGURE 3-15 Hexadecimal–decimal integer conversions.

CHAPTER SUMMARY

1. Symbols convey information. They are our means of communication.

2. The data presented to a data-processing system must be expressed symbolically. The designers of any particular machine determine which symbols it can read and interpret.

3. Data may be entered directly into a computer system without first being recorded on a data-recording medium. Keying and speaking are examples of direct-input technologies.

4. Some input devices accept data represented by symbols that are readable by both humans and machines. The characters printed along the lower edge of an ordinary check are an example.

5. Some input devices accept data represented by symbols that are readable by machines but not by humans. The holes in punched cards and the bar codes on retail items are examples.

6. A computer consists of binary components, each of which can be in one of two possible conditions, or states, at any given time.

7. A binary notation involving only the two symbols 0 and 1 can be used to describe the states, or settings, of binary components. The symbols themselves are called *binary digits*, or *bits*. Groups of bits (bit patterns) are assigned meanings in a particular data-representation scheme, or code, used with a computer.

8. In some computers, the positions in bit patterns are assigned place values of the binary number system. The place values are based on the right-to-left progression of powers of 2.

9. In the Extended Binary Coded Decimal Interchange Code (EBCDIC), unique combinations of 8 bits represent characters.

10. The American Standard Code for Information Interchange (ASCII) is a 7-bit code. Up to 128 different characters can be represented.

11. Some computers operate on one character of data at a time; others operate on multiple characters. The internal storage unit that holds the data may be organized to hold bytes or words.

12. Decimal, octal, and hexadecimal numbers can also be used to represent data values. Any of several methods can be used to convert values from one of these representation schemes to another.

1. Give some examples of symbols and explain what each represents.

2. Give two examples of each of the following:
   (a) direct-input devices
   (b) devices that accept input in forms that are readable by both humans and machines
   (c) devices that accept input in forms that are machine-readable only

3. Describe some ways in which computers communicate with each other.

4. (a) What is a code?
   (b) Why might code standardization be desirable?

5. Why is binary notation a likely choice for expressing values stored in an EDP system?

6. Use the binary number system to represent the following values:
   (a) the number of hours in a day
   (b) the current day of the month
   (c) the difference between 23 and 9

7. Show how the following data items can be represented in EBCDIC:
   (a) 632
   (b) A. J. Rose

8. Show how the following data items can be represented in ASCII:
   (a) #2 CLAMPS
   (b) 999

9. Where, in EDP systems, might you find ASCII used?

10. What are the relationships between bits and bytes, between bits and words, and between bytes and words?

11. Convert the following values as specified:
    (a) 62 (decimal) to binary
    (b) 0101101 (binary) to decimal
    (c) F4A7 (hexadecimal) to binary
    (d) 1011100.11 (binary) to hexadecimal

12. Develop a 3-bit code to represent the vowels, a, e, $\imath$, o, and u. What things must you consider in setting up the code?

4

ENTERING DATA

In the early days of electronic data processing, there were few uses for computers and even fewer methods of data entry. One of the earliest methods, the punched card, is cumbersome by today's standards. Nevertheless, it made possible a vast improvement in information management over non-computerized methods.

Today is still the dawning of the Information Age, and new applications for the computer are increasingly being recognized and developed. Computers are now found in the home, in the supermarket, in the design studio, in industry, and in the laboratory. With such new uses have often come specialized methods of data entry.

In business and industry, computers are used to control manufacturing processes, to monitor supplies, to predict income and expenses, and to maintain records of all kinds of transactions.

Some Japanese manufacturers, for example, are using computers to determine and to maintain exactly the amount of supplies necessary for the manufacturing processes scheduled for each day. Data on supplies received is entered into the computer; supplies are then allocated and distributed, according to computer-generated instructions, to

the plant and to production lines. This use of the computer minimizes the amount of storage space needed and the amount of capital tied up in inventory, permitting increased business flexibility and responsiveness to changing conditions.

In retail business, computers make ordering and keeping track of inventory easier and provide information for effective pricing. Some companies use a computer to keep track of stock at multiple locations across the nation or around the world. All forms of business data can easily be entered into and retrieved from a computer, economizing on file space and on the amount of time needed to get and organize information.

Computers are increasingly being used as a creative tool in much the same way as pen, compass, and T-square are used, but with one major difference—computers are smarter. Aircraft designers, for example, use computers to simulate the flight behavior of different aircraft designs before having their models built. Each design is represented by a mathematical model that is made to interact, by the computer, with mathematical models of forces such as wind resistance, drag, and gravitational effects on the aircraft. These interactions are made visible by computer-generated graphics on a video screen.

Courtesy Mohawk Data Sciences

Courtesy Ralphs Grocery Company

Courtesy Yasu Computer Plant / IBM Corporation

Courtesy Commodore International Limited

Courtesy Harris Corporation

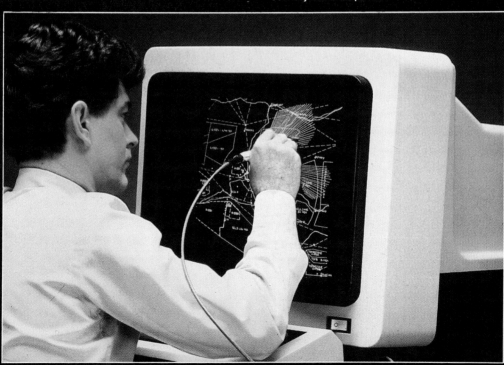

Courtesy CalComp

In the laboratory, electrical engineers use computers in the process of circuit design to simulate circuit behavior, and technicians use them to troubleshoot malfunctioning devices. In troubleshooting, the computer generates a test signal and compares the output signal from the device being tested to a "normal" output signal. Based on the comparison, the computer can then predict the location of the circuit defect in the device.

Some exotic uses of computers are being made by scientists in the field. For example, the University of California sent an archaeological team to Bordeaux, France, to reconstruct the culture that existed there 15,000 to 20,000 years ago. The team used a computer to record and organize data that, without a computer, would have been virtually unmanageable. Minute details about each artifact found were recorded—location, position, dimensions, and other physical characteristics. A computer-simulated map of the site was then generated, showing the artifacts in relation to one another, providing a view of the site that would have been tediously slow to develop manually. Data on artifacts with common characteristics could also be viewed and compared selectively.

A team of biologists used computer assistance to correlate data collected during a survey of plant and animal life in the Northwest Territory of Australia. Oceanographers can use computers to record data on such conditions as temperature, water depth, current speed and direction, and oceanic life, to construct a dynamic model of the oceanic region being studied.

Some of the most appreciated uses of computers will likely turn out to be simple things. How many of us have sat at a street intersection waiting for a red light to change when there was no cross traffic? Some day, our entire road system may be monitored and controlled by computers, increasing the travel-efficiency of all our streets and highways.

As we see, there are many sides to the computer, as many sides as there are forms of information. Different kinds of data often require different input methods and procedures. The usefulness of computers is limited only by the ways in which organizing data can improve the human condition.

Courtesy IBM Corporation

Courtesy Tektronix, Inc.

DATA-PROCESSING METHODS

There are two basic approaches to inputting and processing data with computer help. One is *batch processing;* the other is *transaction processing.* Whether batch or transaction processing is used depends upon the requirements of the application.

In a batch-processing application, data is collected in a group, or *batch,* before it is submitted to the computer. For example, time cards may be collected by Friday noon from the employees in Building 28, grouped by department, and sent as a batch to the Payroll Department. Time cards from the employees in other locations of the firm may be collected, grouped, and forwarded similarly. The data from all the batches may be put together in one large batch that serves as input to weekly payroll processing.

In a transaction-processing application, data is not collected in batches. Instead, data is entered into the computer system for immediate processing whenever the activity that creates the data occurs. For example, customer requests for reservations on airline flights are *transactions* that generate one-by-one inputs to an airline reservations system. The requests may be submitted at any time, via telephone, at airport service desks, and so on. Each individual request must be handled promptly. In many cases, an airline attendant keys in the transaction data (flight number, date, number of reservations wanted, and other information) from a visual-display terminal. The data is processed immediately. A confirmation that the reservation has been made, or a message indicating that it cannot be made, is sent back to the airline attendant. A transaction-processing system that not only allows users to enter transaction data as it is generated but also provides immediate feedback to those users supports *interactive,* or *conversational, processing.*

Batch processing of input data usually involves gathering and transcribing data from *source documents* onto a data-recording medium that is acceptable as EDP-system input. The source documents may be invoices, sales slips, or simple listings on paper. The transcription step is usually a keying operation. For many years, the most common approach was to key the data onto punched cards. However, the disadvantages of card processing—slow input rates, susceptibility to operator error, excessive card handling, and so forth—have long been recognized. Skyrocketing labor charges for data preparation, the need to keep pace with rapidly increasing amounts of data, and the requirements for fast system response (shorter *turnaround time*) led to a search for alternatives. Today, key-to-tape, key-to-disk, or key-to-diskette devices may be used. Magnetic-ink character-recognition devices and optical character-recognition devices reflect still further advances in the preparation of batch input. As we'll see, these devices help to ease the data-preparation task by capturing data in a machine-readable form at its source (the place where it is generated). This technique is known as *source data automation.* It is being used increasingly in business data processing.

A device that has both a televisionlike screen and a typewriterlike keyboard is by far the most popular means of entering transaction data. The data is entered either by keying or by using a light pen to select values from among various data choices displayed on the screen. (See Figure 4-1.) The list of choices is called (appropriately) a *menu.* Alternatively, the user may be guided, step-by-step, by messages, or prompts, that appear on the screen. Of course, this kind of device has output as well as input capabilities. We'll direct our attention to its use for input here, and discuss output considerations in the next chapter.

FIGURE 4-1
Instead of keying, this user
selects data to be entered by
pressing a light pen against
that data on the display screen.
(*Courtesy IBM Corporation*)

Source data automation is "the name of the game" in transaction processing. Chances are you see examples of source data automation whenever you visit a local supermarket. Clerks responsible for stocking or inventory control commonly check shelves and record their findings on handheld terminals. Other clerks use wand readers or optical scanners to enter sales data at checkout counters. If you've used an automated teller machine (ATM) to make a deposit or withdraw funds from a bank account, you've entered transaction data yourself. Can you think of other examples?

PUNCHED-CARD INPUT

A card reader is used to provide punched-card data as input to an EDP system. The card reader feeds cards through a reading unit that converts the data into electronic form. The reading unit may contain either brushes or photoelectric cells.

In a *brush reader*, cards are moved mechanically from the card hopper through the read-feed unit and under the reading brushes. The reading brushes sense the presence or absence of holes in each column of each card. The data on the cards is then converted to electronic pulses. The pulses are detected by the card-reader circuitry and stored as data. After cards are read, they are moved from the read-feed unit and placed in the card stacker in the same sequence in which they were fed into the reader.

A *photoelectric reader* performs the same functions as a brush reader; the difference between the devices is the method used to sense punched holes. When a photoelectric reader is used, each punched card is passed over a light source.

Light passing through holes in the card activates photoelectric cells. This causes pulses to be generated. There is one cell for each column of the card.

A photoelectric reader is inherently more reliable than a brush reader because its reading mechanism is less prone to damage than are metal read brushes. It is also better equipped to read columns in which the punched holes are slightly out of position.

Data Representation

The most common type of punched card is the Hollerith, or IBM, card. It contains 12 horizontal rows and 80 vertical columns. Data is represented (coded) by the presence or absence of small rectangular holes in specific locations in the columns. The method of data representation generally used with these cards is called *Hollerith code*. Each character in this code is represented by a unique combination of punched holes in one card column. The Hollerith code characters represented in the card columns in Figure 4-2 are printed directly above the appropriate columns at the top of the card. These characters are shown on the card for our convenience. They are not read by the card reader; it looks only at the combinations of holes.

An 80-column punched card is often called a *unit record*, because the data on the card is read or punched as an 80-column unit of information. Actually, the data to be entered may occupy only a part of a card, or it may occupy several cards. When more than one card is needed, continuity between cards is established by punches that identify the continuation cards.

Data Preparation

Data is punched into 80-column cards in either of two ways—*offline* or *online*. In the vast majority of offline operations, a human operator, using a machine called

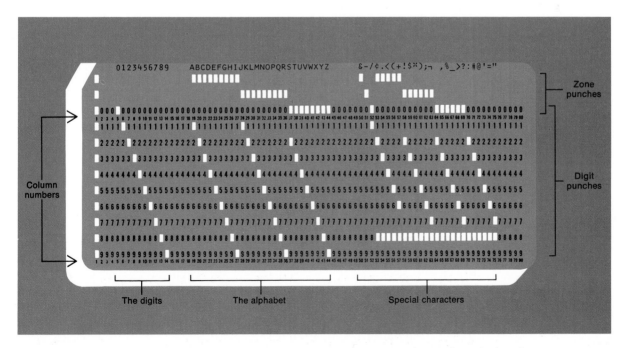

FIGURE 4-2 Hollerith code appears as unique combinations of holes in the columns of punched cards.

FIGURE 4-3
Keypunching is one "tried and true" way of entering data. (*Courtesy California State University, Long Beach*)

a *keypunch*, transcribes the data from source documents to the punched cards. (See Figure 4-3.) The keyboard of a keypunch is similar to that of a typewriter. The accuracy of the punched cards is then checked in a rekeying operation on another machine known as a *verifier*. Any incorrectly coded cards are removed from the batch of input that is being prepared. The data they were to contain is keypunched again into new cards.

Finally, the correctly punched cards are placed in the hopper of a card-reading machine that is attached (online) to the processor of an EDP system. The data punched into the cards is entered into the EDP system via this machine. The Hollerith code characters could be transcribed and stored as 0 bits and 1 bits (corresponding to the punched and unpunched positions in a column) in the computer's internal storage. However, representing each character by a 12-bit code would require a significant amount of that storage. For this reason, input data in Hollerith code is converted to a code such as EBCDIC or ASCII before it is stored internally. This conversion is performed automatically by the control unit of the card reader as data is read from the card.

In an online data-preparation operation, the punching of holes into 80-column cards is controlled by the computer, rather than by a human operator. Electronic pulses are transmitted from the computer to a *card punch*. It interprets the pulses and causes holes to be punched in specific locations on previously unpunched cards. These newly punched cards can then be read by other machines or (if a *card read-punch unit* is available) by another part of the same machine. Thus, the punched card is both a useful input medium that provides a means of transferring data from an original source document to machine-readable form, and a versatile output medium that can be used to exchange data between machines. Once the cards are punched, it matters little whether a human operator using a keypunch or the computer and a card punch did the punching.

A noteworthy feature of some card readers is the capability to read columns of data preprinted on the punched cards or marked on the cards with an ordinary pencil. In effect, the card reader serves as an optical-mark page reader, each "page" being a punched card. Marked fields and punched fields can appear on a single card and can be read in one pass through the device. This means, for example, that basic data such as customer names and account numbers can be punched into cards mailed out as notices of payments due. The amounts can be coded manually with little effort when the notices and payments are returned by the customers.

PUNCHED PAPER TAPE

Like punched cards, punched paper tape predates computers. For many years, it served as a primary input medium to message-sending devices (teletypewriters, for example). The data to be transmitted was punched into the tape, read by the message-sending device, and converted to electrical signals for transmission. At the message destination, a duplicate paper tape was produced by a message-receiving device. With the advent of computers and computer-input devices that could read data punched into paper tape, the data on tape could also be read into a computer for processing.

Not uncommonly, paper-tape input was produced as a byproduct of routine clerical procedures. For example, a paper tape was punched while an operator typed invoices to be mailed to customers. The paper tape containing the invoice data was used to update the company's internal accounting records.

A paper tape produced as output from a computer system was often used as input to machine tools used in production and manufacturing processes. The tape-driven tools were called numerical control (NC) machines. We discussed such machines under "Computers in Manufacturing" in Chapter 1. Today, more flexible robotic systems are replacing machines controlled by prepunched tapes in many applications.

KEY-TO-TAPE

The concept of *key-to-tape* was introduced in 1965 when Mohawk Data Sciences Corporation marketed a data recorder as a single-unit replacement for two punched-card devices: the keypunch and the verifier. The data recorder consisted of a keyboard for entering data, a small memory to hold data while it was being checked for accuracy, and magnetic recording hardware to write the data on tape. After data had been keyed on the tape, the tape was rewound and the same device was used to verify it.

In 1968 Honeywell became the first major computer manufacturer to compete with Mohawk Data Sciences for key-to-tape business. Soon many other companies entered the field. Two different configurations were offered to users: standalone and key-to-central tape.

Standalone devices were initially the most common. Each device of this type is self-contained with its own magnetic-tape unit built into the data-entry station. Standalone devices take either of two forms:

- Keypunch-replacement devices have keypunchlike keyboards and are usually located in a centralized data-preparation area where they replace keypunches on a one-for-one basis. These devices may have visual-display screens that permit operators to view data being entered or verified. The devices record the data on magnetic tapes wound on reels, in cartridges, or in cassettes. The reels, cartridges, or cassettes from all operators are pooled onto a single standard half-inch magnetic tape. This tape is provided as batch input to a computer for processing.

- Typewriterlike devices may be used wherever data is created. In most cases, a typist without special training can create machine-readable data as a byproduct of routine office activities. In effect, the operator simultaneously produces printed output and records data on tape. Each device includes a standard electric typewriter and a magnetic-tape cassette or cartridge recorder. It may include a telephone-type transmitter that relays the keyed data to a central cartridge or cassette reader for verification. The user must carry out a pooling process to transfer the data from the small cassette or cartridge tapes to standard half-inch magnetic tape for computer processing.

Key-to-central-tape devices, or clustered key-to-tape devices, were introduced in 1968. Each cluster consists of several keyboard work stations, a multiplexer device for control of the keyboards (accepting input from one, then another, and so on, while any number of operators are keying continually), and one or two magnetic-tape units. (See Figure 4-4.) Such a configuration is intended primarily for batch applications where large quantities of the same kind of data are keyed. For such uses, this configuration tends to be less expensive than one involving standalone keypunch-replacement devices because the recording hardware is centralized. The pooling of the keyed data onto a single magnetic tape happens as part of the initial keying activity.

The introduction of key-to-tape devices was a major breakthrough in data-recording technology. It marked the first significant departure from use of punched cards as the initial data-recording medium for computer input. The early key-to-tape devices stored from 200 to 800 characters on a single inch of tape. In contrast, to store 800 characters on punched cards, at least 10 cards were required. Data could be read from magnetic tape much faster than from cards. Whereas cards were bulky and difficult to store, magnetic tapes could be transported and stored easily. When the data stored on a tape was no longer needed, the tape could be reused to store other data.

Both standalone and clustered key-to-tape devices have evolved into complete data-preparation systems. Generally, a small computer system (called, appropriately, a *minicomputer*) is involved. The key-to-tape data is not initially keyed into the minicomputer; it is, however, "preprocessed" (edited and validated) by the minicomputer before it is sent to the user's main computer system. This helps to free the user's large-computer resources for more complex or higher-priority processing.

Key-to-tape devices are not in widespread use at this time, primarily because of further advances in data-recording technology. By demonstrating that magnetic media could be used successfully as the primary means of entering data, they laid the groundwork for the key-to-disk and key-to-diskette developments that followed.

FIGURE 4-4
Many operators can transcribe data simultaneously in a clustered key-to-tape environment. (*Courtesy Sperry Corporation*)

KEY-TO-DISK The *key-to-disk*, or *shared processor*, concept was introduced by Computer Machine Corporation in 1968. It was especially important because it constituted a step toward direct input of data (even for large-volume processing).

When a key-to-disk system is used, the data keyed by each operator goes immediately to a minicomputer. It is edited and validated as it is entered by stored-program instructions in the minicomputer. If an error is detected, the responsible operator is notified, and the error can be corrected right away.

A typical key-to-disk configuration consists of from 8 to 64 work stations. (See

Figure 4-5.) Each work station has both a keyboard and a visual-display screen. All the stations are linked to a minicomputer (the "shared processor"). It stores the keyed data temporarily on magnetic disk. Additional data stored previously can be combined with the keyed data under stored-program control. For example, operators may key in customer numbers and amounts of orders. A stored program may direct the minicomputer to read each customer number as it is entered, retrieve the corresponding customer name and address from a file on disk, and place that data following the customer number in the batch input that is being created. Less keying by operators and less verifying of newly keyed data are required. When the data entry has been completed, the data on disk is written as final output to a standard half-inch magnetic tape that can be used as batch input to a main computer.

When key-to-disk devices are used, no main-computer edit run is needed. These devices offer increased speed and efficiency in data preparation because all data goes directly through the minicomputer. There is no need to pool data from a number of standalone key-to-tape units or to transfer it physically (on an intermediate magnetic tape) to a special minicomputer for editing and validation before forwarding it to the main computer.

FIGURE 4-5 Operators work at devices with keyboards and visual-display screens in a key-to-disk data-entry environment. (*Courtesy Dynabyte Business Computers*)

KEY-TO-DISKETTE Newer, and increasingly popular, are key-to-diskette data-entry systems. In such a system, flexible (floppy) disks, or diskettes, are substituted for the single, conventional (hard) disk and ancillary tape of a key-to-disk system. Each operator inserts a diskette into a slot in the disk drive of his or her data-entry unit and then enters data via a keyboard that is also part of the device.

The first key-to-diskette data-entry unit was a standalone device, the IBM 3741 Data Station. This unit was introduced in 1972 as a replacement for punched-card devices, to speed batch input. It could be used to key more than 242,000 characters of user data—the equivalent of more than 3000 punched cards—on a single diskette. One or more of these diskettes could hold all the input for a weekly payroll, inventory control, or order-processing run.

Today, some standalone key-to-diskette units are treated much like typewriters. (See Figure 4-6.) The recording of data on diskettes is a byproduct of routine office procedures. Operators are secretaries or administrative specialists rather than data-entry personnel. For example, the function being performed (from the operator's point of view) may be the preparation of a business letter. The format and content of the letter may be such that most of it can be copied from a general letter form already available. The operator need only modify that general letter form (in storage) to suit the particular business need. She or he then causes the modified letter to be printed on paper and written to diskette. The diskette copy of the letter is the company's record of the correspondence.

The preparation of a business letter as just described is a typical *word-processing* activity. We'll say much more about word processing later. The important point to note here is that this kind of key-to-diskette device is a multi-function unit; it handles both word processing and data processing.

Users with large data-processing workloads may set up clustered key-to-diskette configurations. Like standalone key-to-diskette units, the role of clustered units has often expanded beyond that of data entry. Some are used for word-processing functions. Some are supported by system software that allows business application programs to be executed. Off-the-shelf software for common business operations such as accounts payable, accounts receivable, and payroll is available from well-known vendors.

Multiple standalone key-to-diskette units imply full redundancy, so that data-entry functions can proceed even if one unit "goes down." Further, there is flexibility in the placement of the devices. Vendors of clustered devices emphasize lower per-unit costs with as few as two or three operators, better control, more powerful processing capabilities, and the ability to expand without duplicating everything. A system printer, for example, can be shared by many units to provide hard copy if desired.

In both the standalone and clustered key-to-diskette approaches, the initial medium of interchange between the key-to-diskette devices and the main computer was magnetic tape. The contents of diskettes were transcribed to tape for entry into the main computer. Now, diskette input/output units that can read the contents of diskettes directly into large computers are available. An operator places the diskettes into the input hopper of such a unit. Under stored-program control, the diskettes are moved, one at a time, from the input hopper to the drive spindle of the unit. When the contents of a diskette have been read, it is removed automatically from the spindle and the next diskette is moved to the spindle. This capability allows uninterrupted processing.

FIGURE 4-6
A standalone key-to-diskette
system may be used for both
data-processing and word-
processing functions.
(*Courtesy BASF Systems
Corporation*)

**DATA-ENTRY
CONSIDERATIONS**

Key-to-tape, disk, and diskette devices operate electronically, with very little noise. Because these devices are not mechanical, operators are able to achieve higher data-transcription rates than are common with keypunches. Errors can be corrected simply by backspacing and rekeying correct data over incorrect data. Erroneous characters are erased magnetically. Most devices have automatic features (tab stops, formats, instructions displayed on the screen, and so on) to assist operators. All these operator-oriented features help achieve a major objective of today's business managers: increasing productivity.

Data entry is a labor-intensive task. Equipment costs are decreasing, but labor costs are increasing. The volume of data that users want to process with computer help is increasing. This means that the volume of data that must be entered into computers is increasing also. Many organizations are adopting incentive plans as well as new equipment and procedures, in efforts to increase productivity. Monetary bonuses are given to employees who achieve keying rates above an established standard. Pleasant surroundings, flextime work scheduling (allowing operators to choose their own working hours, within specified ranges), and showing operators how their work relates to the rest of the organization are important.

We can expect a continuing push by many data-processing managers to move the responsibility for data entry out to user departments. User managers (rather than the data-processing managers) must then budget for data-entry costs. Many persons see this trend to distributed data entry as a first step to distributed data processing.

MAGNETIC-INK CHARACTER RECOGNITION

Have you written a personal check recently? Or have you received your processed checks and a monthly statement showing which of the checks you've written found their way back to your bank during the past accounting period? Did you notice the stylized characters printed at the bottom of each check before you used it? Did you notice that the amount for which you wrote each check was also recorded in the same stylized characters at the bottom of the check when it was returned to you? Figure 4-7 shows an example of a personal check that has been processed.

Magnetic-Ink Characters

Magnetic-ink character recognition (MICR) was adopted by the American Bankers Association (ABA) in the late 1950s as a way to meet an urgent need of the banking industry: the need to process an ever-increasing volume of checks with speed and accuracy. The number of checks that had to be handled daily was already a problem. Check volumes in the millions were anticipated in the not-too-distant future.

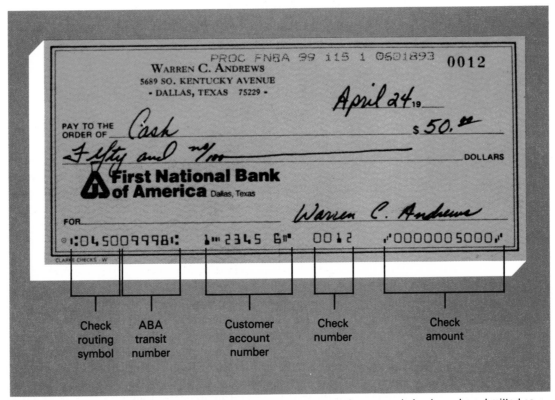

FIGURE 4-7   The magnetic-ink characters inscribed at the bottom of a personal check can be submitted as input to a computer. (*Courtesy Recognition Equipment Incorporated*)

FIGURE 4-8 The E13B type font serves as a standard character set for MICR processing. (*Photo courtesy NCR Corporation*)

In common practice, a check may be written on an account at one bank (its home bank), initially cashed at another bank, and then handled by one or more Federal Reserve banks before it is finally returned to its home bank and then to its originator. The need not only for speed but also for standardization in MICR processing soon became apparent. In 1960 the ABA agreed on the *E13B type font* as a MICR standard character set. This font was chosen primarily because it is easily readable by humans as well as by machines. The set consists of 14 characters: the digits 0 through 9 and four control characters. (See Figure 4-8.)

Data Preparation Blank checks are originally supplied with certain identifying information printed on each check in MICR characters. The information includes both the account number of the customer and the unique bank number assigned to the bank location handling that customer's account. (Look again at Figure 4-7.) The characters appear to be printed in ordinary black ink but the ink contains finely ground particles of iron oxide.

When a check is first cashed or deposited at a bank, personnel at the bank receiving the check must insure that the amount for which the check was written is encoded on the check in MICR characters. (See Figure 4-9.) A keyboard-type device called a *magnetic character inscriber* is used to do this encoding. All the checks received by the bank are handled similarly. Then the checks are read by a *magnetic character reader/sorter*, which first magnetizes the characters and then reads them electronically. The checks are physically sorted by bank number so that they can be returned to their home banks. At each home bank, they are again read by a magnetic character reader/sorter. This time they are sorted into account-number sequence so that they can be returned to customers with monthly banking statements.

Another output of the reader/sorter consists of the bank numbers, account numbers, and amounts of the checks, converted to a machine-readable form acceptable as input to a computer system. This output may be forwarded immediately to the computer, or it may be stored on tape for later processing. This data is used in preparing the monthly banking statements.

An important labor-saving feature of the MICR approach is that data need not be transcribed from a source document to a special input form before it can be processed. The customer's check is the input form. A second point to notice is that only the amount of the check and whether it is to be debited or credited to a customer account must be recorded after the check is received at a bank.

The ability of the reader/sorter to physically arrange the checks is another important labor-saving feature. The lengths, widths, and thicknesses of checks containing MICR characters can vary. MICR devices are also highly tolerant of smudges and wrinkles. Human involvement, which is both costly and error-

FIGURE 4-9
Banking personnel encode the amounts for which checks are written as MICR characters in preparation for further processing. (*Courtesy NCR Corporation*)

prone (whether we like to admit it or not), is minimized. Without MICR or similar automated data-entry and handling procedures, it is unlikely that the banking industry could process annually the more than 80 billion checks that it now handles. The "bottom-line" benefit achievable through MICR is increased productivity.

OPTICAL CHARACTER RECOGNITION

Data recorded on paper in optically readable symbols can be provided as input to some computer systems. The symbols can take any of a wide variety of forms: marks; bars; numbers, letters, and special characters of certain type fonts; and ordinary handwriting. You deal with many optically readable symbols daily without even realizing it. The letters and words you are reading now are "optically readable" by you and by some computer input devices.

Because optical character recognition (OCR) devices offer such a wide range of capability, the use of OCR to enter both batch and transaction data is increasing. We look at those capabilities here and again under "Remote Terminals" later in this chapter.

Optical Marks

Optical marks are the simplest form of optical data. An ordinary pencil or pen is used to make the marks in predetermined locations on source documents. After the source documents have been marked, they become input to an *optical mark reader (OMR)*. It uses a light beam to scan the sheets and generates electrical signals to represent the data. The signals are forwarded to the computer for processing.

Multiple-choice test score sheets, forms used in surveys, and questionnaires are common examples of optical-mark source documents. (See Figure 4-10.) Optical-mark data may also be used for order writing, inventory control, insurance policy rating, payroll, and so forth. The source documents must be designed and manufactured carefully; unless they are people-proof (that is, can be understood and completed easily), users may not mark them correctly. Because optical marks, like the magnetic-ink characters described earlier, do not have to be converted by an operator to a computer-acceptable form, they increase the speed with which data can be handled by an EDP system. In today's "hurry-up" world, speed is a key requirement of many applications.

Bar Codes

A second type of OCR device is the *bar-code,* or *line-code, reader.* It senses vertical bars, or lines, that are machine-printed on tags or merchandise. The widths of the bars and the distances between them represent data.

You are probably familiar with at least one bar code: the *Universal Product Code (UPC)* that appears on many consumer products to facilitate checkout at retail stores. The code for each product is a unique combination of ten pairs of vertical bars. The bars are read, or sensed, by a handheld reader or a fixed scanner. (See Figure 4-11.) This data is converted to electrical signals and forwarded to a computer for processing. Given only this data as input, the computer can determine what the product is, find its price from price lists in storage, and print out the name and the price of the product on a customer receipt. The computer also maintains inventory records of the products sold and thus helps store personnel keep merchandise in stock. The initial processing of

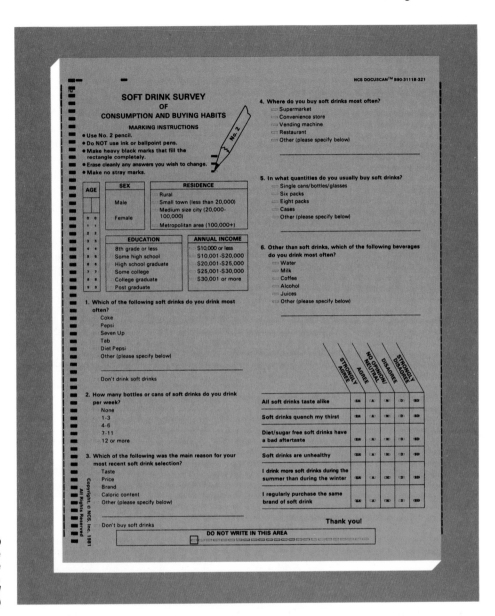

FIGURE 4-10
Survey responses are made as optical marks that can be read as input to a computer. (*Courtesy National Computer Systems*)

the customer's purchase is an example of transaction processing. Maintaining inventory records may be done as a part of this processing. Alternatively, the inventory data may be accumulated for subsequent batch input to an inventory-control program that is run at a convenient time. Notice also that it's much easier to change the price of a product by changing one stored price in the computer than by restamping the price on a large, already-shelved supply of the product.

Bar-code data is also used for entering credit-card data and for automatic routing of mail. Many manufacturers use bar-code tags to track work in process and to control parts inventories. The tags on finished goods are read ("wanded") in the shipping department so that the goods being shipped can be matched against previously stored records of the orders being filled. In this way, short shipment losses are reduced or eliminated. Customer satisfaction is likely to improve because better service is provided.

Optical Characters Consider the cents-off discount coupons included in the food section of your newspaper or in some of your magazines. Billions of these coupons are distributed annually. Consumers are hauling them back to supermarkets in record numbers. Have you ever wondered how the discounts are reconciled? One answer is: with the help of computers and OCR devices.

Large coupon clearinghouses are located in the United States and Mexico. Thanks to OCR reader/sorter capabilities, more than 35,000 of the coupons can be sorted, counted, and validated in one hour. Product manufacturers are achieving total coupon control. The OCR reader/sorters can also print a variety of related management, marketing, and accounting reports.

Some *optical character readers* (or *reader/sorters*) can read characters printed in any of a wide variety of type fonts. This capability has led to the use of OCR in word processing. The characters on each page of text are scanned, represented as electronic pulses, and stored. There is no need for skilled typists to key in all the data. They can use their special skills to edit the stored text, make required content changes, and produce final documents. Some users achieve a doubling or tripling of productivity. (See Figure 4-12.)

Not all optical character readers can read a variety of type fonts. To help insure that OCR data acceptable to most if not all readers will be generated, the *OCR-A type font* was adopted as a standard by the American National Standards

FIGURE 4-11
An optical scanner reads bar-code data at a super-market checkout. (*Courtesy Ralphs Grocery Company*)

FIGURE 4-12 Less keying has to be done when data that has been typed previously can be read as input by an OCR scanner. *(Courtesy Hendrix Technologies, Inc.)*

Institute. (See Figure 4-13.) The OCR-A characters can be printed on source documents by any of several common machines—computer printers, adding machines, cash registers, and typewriters, for example. The presence of OCR-A characters on any hard copy is a clue—though not proof—that the data is intended to be processed with computer help.

Handwritten Data Even greater versatility is available through the use of OCR devices that can read ordinary handwriting as well as machine-printed characters. (See Figure 4-14.) Because handwriting is a basic form of recording, handwritten documents are common. For example, handwritten credit-card receipts may be used as direct input to an accounts-receivable application.

ABCDEFGHIJKLMN
OPQRSTUVWXYZ ,.
$/*-1234567890

FIGURE 4-13
Characters printed in the OCR-A type font can serve as input to most optical character readers.

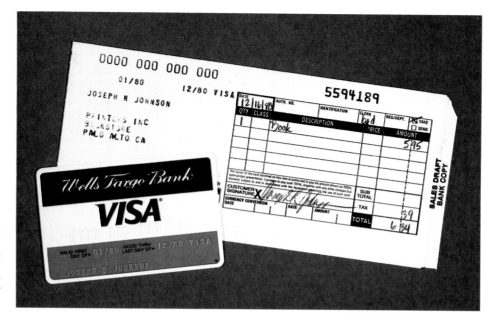

FIGURE 4-14
Credit-card receipts contain both handwritten and printed characters that can be read by OCR devices. (*Courtesy Wells Fargo Bank and Printers Inc. Bookstore*)

When an OCR device that can read handwriting is available, letters and numbers can be written using an ordinary pen or pencil, then entered directly into the computer (without any keying). To help insure that the handwritten characters will be machine-readable, boxes for the characters may be preprinted on the source documents as guides to the writers. (Look again at Figure 4-14.) Figure 4-15 gives some additional guidelines. You may want to refer to this "handwriting" as "handprinting," for clarity.

REMOTE TERMINALS

It is often desirable to provide data to a computer, or to get information from it, at a location away from the central computer facility. The location may be a different part of the same building, in the same vicinity, across the state, or across oceans and continents. It may be a nurses' station in a large hospital, a

RULE	CORRECT	INCORRECT
1. Write big characters.	0 2 8 3 4	0 2 8 3 4
2. Close loops.	0 6 8 9	0 6 8 9
3. Use simple shapes.	0 2 3 7 5	0 2 3 7 5
4. Do not link characters.	0 0 8 8 1	0 0 8 8 1
5. Connect lines.	4 5 T	4 5 T
6. Block print.	C S T X Z	C S T X Z

FIGURE 4-15
Following these basic guidelines helps to insure that handwritten data can be read as input to a computer.

school library, the shop floor of an automobile plant, or an executive office on the twelfth floor of a large office building in midtown Manhattan. We use *remote terminals* to do the providing or getting.

A remote terminal installed for convenient access by a busy executive, highway patrol officer, supermarket checkout clerk, or student is, in fact, one component of a geographically distributed communication network known as a *data communication system*. (We will look at such systems in more detail in Chapter 16.) A wide variety of such terminals are available. Their number, types, and uses are increasing daily. In this section, we direct most of our attention to remote terminals used for data entry. As you'll see, many of these terminals can also perform other functions.

When selecting a remote terminal, a user must first decide whether the application needs are best served by a terminal that is dumb, smart, or intelligent. A *dumb terminal* is totally dependent on the computer to which it is connected. It provides for online data entry or information output, but that's all. A *smart terminal* has certain editing capabilities as well. For example, a stored data definition may specify that only numeric values are acceptable as input for number of units sold and price per unit. The data keyed in by the terminal user is checked by hard-wired circuits to insure that only digits are entered. Some smart terminals have small storage areas (buffers) where data can be stored and modified before it goes to the central computer. This means that the terminal user can check to be sure the data is correct (and fix it if it isn't). An *intelligent terminal* is user-programmable. It contains not only a storage area but also a microprocessor. The terminal can be programmed to communicate with and instruct the user who is entering data. It can also do some processing of the data (sorting, summarizing, checking both input and computed values for reasonableness, and so on). In some systems, personal computers such as Apple IIs are being used as intelligent terminals.

Special-Purpose Terminals

Many remote terminals are special-purpose devices. That is, they are designed to meet particular needs. For example, in retail operations, devices known as *point-of-sale* (POS) *terminals* are used to capture data at the point of sale. (See Figure 4-16.) A POS terminal may include a keyboard for data entry, a lighted display on which the price is flashed, a printer that provides a receipt for the customer, and a cash drawer. Some POS terminals have wand readers that can be passed over tags or labels on grocery items, containers, and other merchandise to read and record product data.

Remote terminals such as the alphanumeric keyboard/display unit in Figure 4-17A have been developed for use by tellers in banks, savings and loans, and other financial institutions. The tellers can process deposit and withdrawal transactions, post passbooks, and print checks or receipts at their individual locations. Automated teller machines (ATM's) like the one in Figure 4-17B enable customers to withdraw cash from personal accounts, inquire about account balances, and take care of other business without teller assistance.

Data-Collection Devices

In manufacturing and in distribution, remote terminals are often used as data-collection devices. The terminals must be sturdy—able to withstand the dust, temperature, humidity, and vibrations of shop floors, factory production lines, or warehouses. They must be accessible and easy to use. Many are wall-

FIGURE 4-16
A point-of-sale (POS) terminal captures data at the store. (*Courtesy IBM Corporation*)

mounted. (See Figure 4-18.) Desktop data-collection devices that accept keyed input are also common. As the term *data-collection device* implies, most remote terminals of this type are used to gather data for input to batch-processing applications.

Voice Input An increasing amount of work is being done to develop terminals with voice-input capabilities. Such terminals have tremendous potential in applications such as parts management and quality control where hands and/or eyes are otherwise occupied. Assembly workers can speak the part numbers of components they're assembling. A quality control inspector wearing a small microphone can follow a checklist on a televisionlike screen and orally describe the physical characteristics of components, subassemblies, or finished products. The voice input is transmitted directly to a computer. It can update stock status, determine the immediate disposition of defective items, and provide timely, accurate reports for management. (See Figure 4-19.) Personnel at United Parcel Service (UPS) distribution centers can speak destination codes into wireless microphones as parcels are unloaded at arrival docks. Each destination code becomes a command to a conveyor system that distributes a particular parcel to the proper outgoing truck. Remote order entry by sales representatives is another important voice-input application that saves both time and money. Several banks, too, are using voice input to support pay-by-phone operations.

Most voice-input units can accept data (sounds) from locally connected microphones or from remote sources via telephones. Some are speaker-independent. They can understand any user. Others must be trained by each user to recognize his or her voice. The training involves repeating from 10 to 15 times each "word" (sound of 2 seconds or less duration) the system will be expected to recognize. At present, the tradeoffs for speaker independence are a small vocabulary and a big price. Voice-input units are available with vocabularies ranging from 16 to as many as 900 words.

Generally, voice-input units cannot as yet recognize continuous speech. Pauses of varying lengths are required between words. Computer recognition of human speech has not come easily. No one ever says a word exactly the same way twice. However, voice-recognition research is continuing. Advocates of voice input estimate that two-thirds of the Fortune 500 companies are using spoken data entry, at least in pilot programs. Recognition accuracies of better than 99 percent are being achieved. (In contrast, the accuracy of keypunching operations seldom ranges above 95 percent.) Increased worker productivity and significant cost savings are being realized.

Portable Terminals Computer power at your fingertips, anytime, anywhere—sound attractive? Whether you're on the road and want access to the latest home-office competitive sales data, or at home and want to avoid the early morning rush-hour commute,

A   B

FIGURE 4-17 Teller terminals (A) and automated teller machines (B) are used to interact with computers in many banking applications. (*Courtesy* [A] *IBM Corporation;* [B] *NCR Corporation*)

FIGURE 4-18
A wall-mounted data-collection device helps keep track of work in process in job environments. (*Courtesy NCR Corporation*)

FIGURE 4-19
An inspector whose hands are busy enters data by speaking into a voice-input device. (*Courtesy Interstate Electronics Corporation, a Figgie International Company*)

that computer power can be an important productivity booster. It's available through *portable terminals.*

Today the most popular portable terminals resemble office typewriters. Data is entered by keying; output is printed on standard $8\frac{1}{2}'' \times 11''$ plain paper or on a silver-coated thermal paper by means of a heat process. Some have small (5- or 7-inch) TV-like displays. Most have built-in acoustic couplers that can be used to establish computer connections via ordinary telephone lines. The terminals range in weight from about 11 to 23 pounds. It's not uncommon to see a business-person boarding an airplane with a case that holds a portable terminal.

Sales personnel are major users of portables. Putting the power of the computer behind a sales pitch—even if you're not selling a computer-based service—can greatly enhance your credibility. The customer sees you're "with it"; presumably your product is, too. Furthermore, the sales discussion can be customized. Variables such as local labor rates, fuel prices, interest rates, and length of payback can be dealt with. A hard copy of the sales data can be left with the customer for later perusal.

Portable terminals equipped with internal storage units capable of holding several thousand characters of text are especially useful to persons whose jobs involve data gathering—poll takers, meter readers, news reporters, and the like. (See Figure 4-20.) Those with nonvolatile internal storage units do not lose their stored data when shut off. A user of one of these terminals can enter data throughout the day, then dial the central computer location via an ordinary telephone to transmit that data during evening hours.

FIGURE 4-20
A meter reader uses a portable terminal to enter data. (*Courtesy Sarasota Automation Inc.*)

FIGURE 4-21
The telephonelike keypad of a handheld terminal, coupled with ordinary telephone lines, allows convenient data entry from almost anywhere. (*Courtesy Interface Technology, Inc.*)

Handheld Terminals

Even more portable than the portables are *handheld terminals*. These units may weigh from 4 ounces to 3 pounds. Many resemble electronic calculators. Some are Touch-Tone devices with keypads like those of familiar telephones. (See Figure 4-21.) These terminals permit remote data entry and access to Touch-Tone-activated systems from any telephone (provided, of course, the user enters the access information required to pass authorization checks).

Handheld terminals with OCR wand readers are used to monitor on-the-shelf inventories at stores. The wand readers can be passed over machine-readable tags posted on the edges of the shelves. Products whose tags are wanded may be listed on a printout for management attention or reordered automatically.

At some hospitals, nurses use handheld terminals as electronic scratchpads. They "download" small amounts of patient-related data from a central computer to the terminals before making their rounds to patient bedsides. During the rounds, they use, update, or add to this data. When a nurse completes her rounds, she transmits the data in her terminal back to the central computer. It gets re-included in the hospital's patient database, and can be referred to by doctors caring for the patients and by other hospital personnel.

Persons who spend much of their time in planes, on trains, or in trucks or automobiles often put handheld terminals to good use. A plane trip across the United States or abroad occupies some time. Busy executives can formulate preliminary business plans, make notes for a speech, or record trip expenses while they are in flight. The terminals with communication capabilities allow travelers to key in or say messages that can be sent to home office staffs from distant locations.

Some day, many of us may consider handheld terminals to be indispensable parts of our daily lives. We've become accustomed to checks, credit cards, and pocket calculators. We'd be lost without telephones. Handheld terminals put computing power at our fingertips and will go wherever we want to take them.

**CHAPTER
SUMMARY**

1. In a batch-processing application, data is collected in a group, or batch, before it is submitted as input to a computer. In a transaction-processing application, data is entered into a computer for immediate processing as user activities occur.

2. Capturing data in a machine-readable form at the place where it is generated is called source data automation.

3. A card-reading device converts data represented as combinations of holes in the columns of punched cards into electronic pulses. The most common method of punched-card data representation is Hollerith code.

4. Key-to-tape devices were a major data-recording breakthrough. They made possible the first significant departure from use of punched cards as the initial data-recording medium for computer input.

5. Key-to-disk and key-to-diskette devices are being used increasingly for data entry. Because these devices are electronic, they operate faster and with less noise than keypunches. Data-entry errors can be corrected by rekeying.

6. Magnetic-ink character-recognition (MICR) devices help the banking industry to process an ever-increasing volume of checks with speed and accuracy.

7. Optical character-recognition (OCR) devices can read data in many forms. The optically readable symbols may be marks; bars; numbers, letters, and special characters of certain type fonts; or ordinary handwriting.

8. Remote terminals allow data to be entered at locations away from a central computer facility. They may be classified broadly as dumb, smart, or intelligent.

9. Special-purpose remote terminals are designed to meet particular user needs. Point-of-sale (POS) terminals and teller machines are examples.

10. Data-collection devices in a wide variety of user environments gather data for input to batch-processing applications.

11. Voice-input units are especially useful in applications where hands and/or eyes are otherwise occupied.

12. Portable terminals resembling office typewriters with memories are especially useful to persons whose jobs involve data gathering.

13. Handheld terminals weighing from 4 ounces to 3 pounds are used for data entry in retail stores, hospitals, planes, trains, trucks, and autos—in short, wherever users of these terminals want to enter data.

1. Distinguish between batch-processing systems and transaction-processing systems. In doing so, give one or more examples of each.

2. What is source data automation, and what advantages does it offer?

3. Assume that data is to be entered into an EDP system on punched cards. Show how the Hollerith coding system can be used to represent the following data in the appropriate fields (card columns) on one 80-column card. Alphabetic or alphanumeric (combinations of alphabetic and numeric) fields are punched left-justified; that is, with the leftmost characters filled and any unused positions at the right. Fields containing only numeric data are punched right-justified.

Card columns	Data
1–5	1742A
6–20	Dolan, Jane
70–73	40.0
74–76	0.05

4. (a) Why is data in Hollerith code converted to another code before being placed in storage?
   (b) When and how does the conversion take place?

5. Explain how the use and environment of keypunch-replacement key-to-tape devices differ from those of typewriterlike key-to-tape devices.

6. Argue for or against standalone key-to-diskette devices versus clustered key-to-diskette devices.

7. What advantages does key-to-diskette data entry offer over punched-card data entry?

8. What data-representation scheme was developed primarily to aid the banking industry, and how does it do so?

9. Describe some common business situations in which optical recognition of symbols is useful.

10. List some guidelines for preparing handwritten computer input.

11. Describe some user applications for which voice-input capabilities are especially suitable.

12. Choose one type of remote terminal. Discuss its features and some of the ways it might be used. In what situations have you encountered, or might you expect to encounter, the device?

5

OBTAINING INFOR- MATION

A great deal of the data that we process comes to us in abstract, often mathematical, terms. It is often much easier to understand such data when it can be seen in pictorial or graphic form. Computers have the ability to produce pictures from abstract data.

At the Domglas bottle-manufacturing plant in Canada, workers visually inspect the finished products as they come off the manufacturing line on a conveyor. Their inspection is the final step in a process that may have started on a computer-graphics terminal, where a designer was able to plan and test many aspects of the bottle's future existence before it was made. The computer gives the designer the power to manipulate both major aspects and minute details of the product in advance of its actual manufacture.

Courtesy IBM Corporation

Courtesy Phototheque, National Film Board of Canada

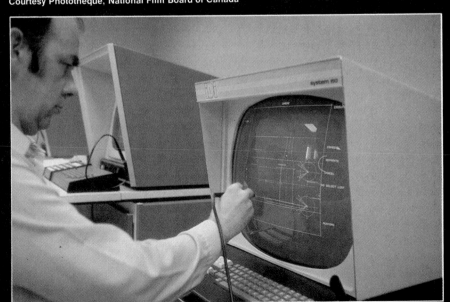

An area in which graphic display of data can be especially useful is in architectural design. A building plan can be entered into the computer as measurements or mathematical data; the output from the computer can be a three-dimensional representation of that plan in full color. Walls can be cut away to reveal views of the inside areas. The floor plans of large buildings can be worked out by these same techniques, saving hours and hours of labor. Many architects are using this process instead of trial-and-error visualizing and paper-and-pencil drafting.

Oy Esso AB of Helsinki, Finland, has installed computers to help with depot management, distribution, and inventory control of its oil and petrochemical products. Visual representation of budget or expenditure information can help, too, with many kinds of management decisions vital to the success of the business.

Sometimes a picture can be worth much more than the often-cited "thousands words." In some situations, it might be impossible to communicate in anything else except pictures or, in our sense, computer-made graphic images. At Pratt-Whitney computer graphics can give information on what is happening inside a turbofan engine that is in the design and testing stages. Heat distribution within the engine can be shown, for example. It would be impossible to obtain or communicate this data without computer assistance. Engineers studying the data can plan adjustments and improvements for maximum engine efficiency.

Courtesy CalComp

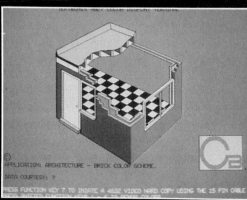

Courtesy Ramtek Corporation

Courtesy Ramtek Corporation

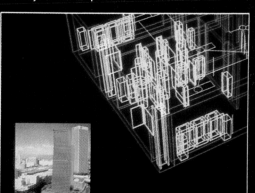

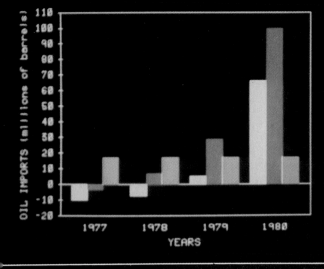

Courtesy Megatek Corporation, San Diego, California

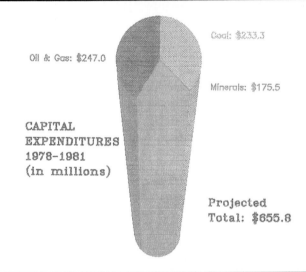

Oil & Gas: $247.0

Coal: $233.3

Minerals: $175.5

CAPITAL
EXPENDITURES
1978-1981
(in millions)

Projected
Total: $655.8

Courtesy Datapoint Corporation

Courtesy Sperry Corporation

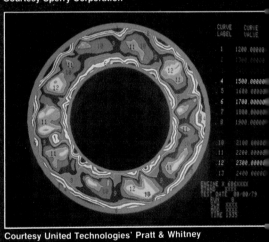

CURVE LABEL	CURVE VALUE
1	1200.00000
2	1700.00000
4	1500.00000
5	1600.00000
6	1700.00000
7	1800.00000
8	1900.00000
10	2100.00000
11	2200.00000
12	2300.00000
13	2400.00000

ENGINE X 686XXXX

TEST DATE 00/00/79

TIME 1935

Courtesy United Technologies' Pratt & Whitney

Words as well as graphic images, of course, still have their place in our world. Much of our formal education comes through printed words in books, and computers are often involved in their production. Computers may be involved in creating the actual type fonts used in typesetting, as well as in storing and manipulating the text itself. The text for this book, as a matter of fact, was first keyed into a word processor for editing and updating. The floppy disks that contained the final version of the text were used to drive the typesetting equipment that created the characters you are reading right now. (Computers were also very much involved in reproducing, by digitizing, the color photographs that accompany this text.)

Some of the newest typesetting devices are creating images by lasers, making precise characters in almost unlimited sizes. This technique is an important use of computer-guided laser imaging. As type characters are enlarged by ordinary photographic methods, minute flaws may become unpleasantly noticeable—but not so with laser imaging.

You may have heard about computer enhancement of photographs in other contexts. Computers can use digitized data to fill in loss of detail that comes with ordinary enlargement. This process provides the high-resolution detail of pictures taken from thousands of miles out in space—yet another example of images created by the computer from basic numerical data.

We can see how computers have the ability to make abstract data into more concrete, and therefore more understandable, graphic information. These images may be readily changeable, as on a display terminal, or relatively fixed, as on a paper "hard copy."

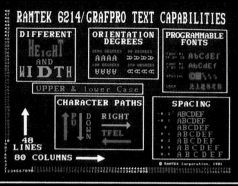
Courtesy Ramtek Corporation

Courtesy Xerox Corporation

5 | OBTAINING INFORMATION

PRINTED OUTPUT
IMPACT PRINTERS
NONIMPACT PRINTERS
PLOTTERS
VISUAL-DISPLAY OUTPUT
VOICE OUTPUT
MICROFILM/MICROFICHE

We know that data in a wide variety of forms can be provided as input to a computer system. The data is then processed. The results of processing—information—are usually written as output. From a user's point of view, the computer system itself is only as good as the output it provides.

Look at Figure 5-1. Suppose you were asked to select, from this figure, an example of output generated by a computer system. Which would you choose?

In fact, all the items in Figure 5-1 are examples of computer output. Computers can produce printed reports. They can also produce paychecks, invoices, and sales slips. They can print memos and letters addressed to named recipients. Some can produce bar graphs, line drawings, and pictures. The information may be written in one color (usually green or black) or in many colors. Because printed forms of output are relatively permanent, we call them *hard copy*.

On the other hand, *soft-copy* forms of output have a more audiovisual aspect. For example, if the user's information needs are best satisfied by a quick look at the results of computations displayed on a televisionlike screen, the computer can be directed to write its output on a visual-display unit. Some units can display graphs and line drawings in any of a wide variety of colors. Some can generate sequences of images at very fast rates; we perceive the sequences as animated cartoons, filmstrips of natural phenomena, and so on. Even personal computers can be programmed to speak verbal responses, to "beep," or to play the latest hit tunes. If programmed to converse in a foreign language, their French or Spanish (for example) may be better than that of their users (in this case, their listeners).

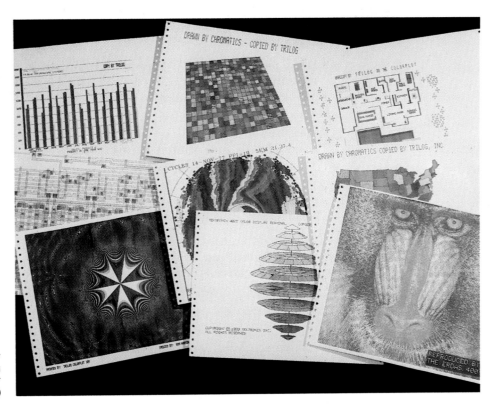

FIGURE 5-1
Output in an amazing variety of forms and colors is being produced with computer help. (*Courtesy Trilog, Inc.*)

The output capabilities of a particular computer system are determined in large part by the software that directs it, and also by the types and features of its output devices. This chapter is about output devices. Since printed output has been and remains the most common form of output, we look first at printers. Then we discuss plotters. Visual-display units are especially popular where ongoing direct interaction with computers is required. We'll see how even the display screen itself can be used for input as well as output. Next, we consider voice output. Finally, we look at the unique advantages of computer output microfilm (COM) media and devices.

PRINTED OUTPUT   Printing devices provide permanent, human-readable records of information. A printer receives the information in the form of electronic pulses from the EDP system. It converts the pulses to a form that we can understand. Nearly every EDP system includes some type of printing device; most have several of them. The variety of printing devices seems almost as widespread as their use.

In selecting a printer, the user installation must look at its printing requirements: Is the large volume of printing to be done a major concern, say to satisfy the business reporting requirements of many intracompany departments? Is each printed output unique, or are multiple copies required? Are fixed-format forms, such as orders to be completed, a common requirement? Is the print quality acceptable if the output is merely readable? Or is high-quality printing required for, say, final copies of user manuals to be distributed to customers, or intercompany letters, statements to stockholders, and the like?

Printers are classified in several ways. The first distinction relates to how much information is printed:

- *Serial printers* print one character of information at a time; their speeds are measured in terms of *characters per second* (*cps*) or *characters per minute* (*cpm*); speeds up to 900 cps are possible with some models.

- *Line printers* print one line of information at a time; their speeds are measured in terms of *lines per minute* (*lpm*); speeds up to 3800 lpm are achieved with some printers of this type.

- *Page printers* print complete pages, one-up or two-up (side-by-side) across the printer paper; their speeds are measured in terms of lines per minute or *pages per minute* (*ppm*); speeds up to 21,000 lpm are possible under certain conditions with some models.

The great differences in possible speeds are in large part due to the technology that is used in printing. And herein is a second kind of distinction, based on the way that information is printed. There are two categories:

- *Impact printers* form images when electronic pulses activate printing elements that are pressed against an inked ribbon and form an image on paper.

- *Nonimpact printers* use thermal (heat), chemical, electrical, and/or optical techniques to form images.

In general, nonimpact printers are much faster than impact printers, primarily because there is less physical movement of parts. A speed of 3800 lpm is very fast for an impact printer, but speeds of up to 21,000 lpm are offered with several nonimpact printers. Of course, we should understand that these speeds are rated maximums. In actual practice, speeds vary depending on the amount of blank space on the printout, the number of lines per inch, and other factors.

A third method of distinction is based on how the printer forms characters—*solid* or *dot matrix*. All the characters you see in this book are solid characters. Indeed, the reproduction masters for some books are created as computer output. Figure 5-2 shows examples of dot-matrix characters printed at various densities. In general, the more dots used to form characters, the better the character resolution (and hence the better the print quality). Through recent technological advances, high-quality optical bar-code symbols and OCR characters intended for subsequent input to OCR devices can be produced as dot-matrix output.

Impact printers use either solid characters or dot-matrix characters. Nonimpact printers use only matrix techniques. Look again at Figure 5-1; you may detect some additional examples of dot-matrix output.

IMPACT PRINTERS

Some serial printers and some line printers are included in the impact printer category. Printers of this kind have been with us for some time. In the early 1950s, users were more or less forced to accept low-quality printing, wavy print lines, almost illegible carbon copies, and restricted page layouts. The very slow speeds of online printing operations encumbered computer operations and led to offline techniques. The most common of these was to write information onto magnetic tape and then transfer the content of the tape to paper in a subsequent step.

other ticketing systems used in
prior Olympics games, at method
used by various sporting organi
zations now, and at general bus
ness applications before decidi
on the IBM system.
    "We also felt it necessary to
be able to print tickets to ord

Draft quality

other ticketing systems used in
prior Olympics games, at method
used by various sporting organi
zations now, and at general bus
ness applications before decidi
on the IBM system.
    "We also felt it necessary to
be able to print tickets to ord

Memo quality

other ticketing systems used in
prior Olympics games, at method
used by various sporting organi
zations now, and at general bus
ness applications before decidi
on the IBM system.
    "We also felt it necessary to
be able to print tickets to ord

Letter quality

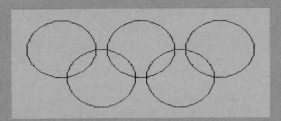

Graphics

FIGURE 5-2 Some printers can print dot-matrix characters at various densities, allowing users to trade over-all printing speed for higher quality for selected types of output.

The introduction of the IBM 1403 printer in 1959 brought a fourfold increase in speed (600 lpm), improved quality, and less restricted format. Its printing mechanism is an interchangeable print chain like that shown in Figure 5-3A. Like other *chain printers*, it is an electromechanical line printer using engraved type. Character sets comprising alphabetic, numeric, and special characters are assembled in the chain. The more copies of the set on the chain, the faster the speed of printing. As the chain travels horizontally, a comparison is made between the character of type in front of each print hammer and the character that is to print in that position of the print line. When the desired character of type is in position to print, the hammer for that position is fired to force the paper and ribbon against the type, thus printing the character.

The 1403 worked so well for so long that it served throughout the 1960s as the de facto standard for printers. Some are still in use. Subsequent chain and *train printers* developed in recent years are capable of printing 2000, 3000, or even 3800 132-character lpm when a standard 48-character set is used. To understand these speeds, you can think of 3800 lpm as 57 pages of $11'' \times 14\frac{7}{8}''$ computer printout. Larger character sets are offered as options. (A *print chain* differs from a *print train* in that the character slugs on the chain are linked together rather than placed on a track. With the print train, individual characters on the chain as well as the entire chain can be changed. (See Figure 5-3B.)

Besides chain/train printers, the impact line printer group includes drum printers, belt printers, and band printers. Of these, drum printers are the oldest.

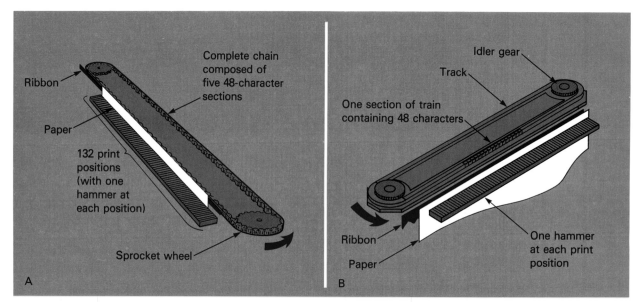

FIGURE 5-3 A chain printer uses an interchangeable print chain (A) composed of linked character slugs. A train printer uses a track (B) containing individual character slugs of a user-selected character set.

A *drum printer* prints with a metal cylinder that has bands of characters engraved on its surface. (See Figure 5-4A.) If the printer is to print 132-character lines, the drum must have 132 bands. Each band must contain every character in the character set that is being used. During printing, the drum revolves, moving the characters (for example, the row of R's) past print hammers. It makes one revolution for each line of print. As the appropriate character on the drum passes a particular print position, the print hammer at that position strikes the paper against an inked ribbon, which simultaneously presses against the character on the drum.

Drums are inherently more reliable than chains or trains. By design, they have fewer independently movable parts. Some drum printers can print up to 2000 lpm (with from 120 to 144 positions per line). However, the drum printer has one very serious drawback: It lacks flexibility due to its fixed character set. Other user considerations are that the print hammers may require frequent adjustments to maintain horizontal alignment of the characters printed on a line, and the drum may have to be replaced because of wear. Most manufacturers are phasing out their drum printers in favor of printers based on other technologies.

Belt printers are similar to chain/train printers in operation. The interchangeable print chain or train is replaced by a metal belt. Like the chain/train printer, a belt printer's speed varies depending on the size of the character set. Typical maximum speeds are 400 lpm using a 48-character set, 300 lpm using a 64-character set, and 230 lpm using a 94-character set. Thus, in contrast to recent chain/train printers, belt printers are relatively slow-speed printing devices. They are also less costly. Many users of medium-size and small computers willingly trade high speed for lower cost.

The *band printer* was a major innovation for slow-speed line printing. It offered a 30 to 35 percent reduction in cost over comparable drum printers and belt printers. Whereas the drum printer uses a vertical font, the band printer

A   B

FIGURE 5-4 A vertically moving print drum (A) contains a complete character set for each position on the print line. A horizontally moving print band (B) can be changed easily by the user to print different styles of output. (*Courtesy Dataproducts Corporation*)

uses a horizontal font. (See Figure 5-4B.) Horizontal spacing problems between characters are less noticeable than the wavy print lines inherent in drum printing. The horizontal band motion insures straight lines of printed output. A major operational benefit of band printing is flexibility. Print bands are as easy to change as the interchangeable print elements of office typewriters. The use of stainless steel alloys for the bands significantly improved their resistance to wear or damage.

To users of small and medium-size computer systems, band printers operating at speeds of 300 to 700 lpm may be very acceptable. (The processors, disk drives, and other system equipment are also likely to be slower than those of larger systems.) As above, these users willingly trade speed for high print quality at relatively low cost.

At the slow-speed end of solid-character impact printers are remote terminals that provide printed output. Initially, the most widely used of these terminals were *teleprinters*. They had communication capabilities and produced hard-copy output. The most common teleprinters were those produced by Teletype Corporation. These devices were relatively inexpensive, easy to operate, and readily available. Furthermore, they could be linked to a central computer facility from geographically distributed locations via established communication networks (say, installed telephone facilities).

As user demands for hard-copy terminals increased, several vendors developed printers or printer-keyboard devices that could be operated remotely. New devices seem to be announced daily. IBM features a replaceable *"golf ball"* print element in its Selectric typewriter terminals. An operator can change type fonts rapidly by snapping out an existing element and replacing it with a different one. (See Figure 5-5.) Other teleprinter terminals use a flat disk with petal-like projections called a *"daisywheel."* (See Figure 5-6.) Still others use a cup, or *"thimble,"* with fingerlike projections. At the end of each projection is an embossed character. Printing can be done in either direction. Paper can be fed either up or down. Character and line spacings are variable. The manufacturers of these terminals emphasize their flexibility and print quality. Many terminals are used for both data-processing and word-processing applications.

Teleprinter terminals are typically available in three basic configurations. Because these configurations are often referred to in news articles, sales literature, and so on, without explanation, you should become familiar with them. They are:

- *Receive-only* (*RO*), which includes only a printer
- *Keyboard send/receive* (*KSR*), which includes a keyboard and printer
- *Automatic send/receive* (*ASR*), which includes a keyboard, printer, and storage device

The receive-only teleprinter terminal in Figure 5-6A is controlled by commands issued from a stored program in the computer. The keyboard send/receive terminal in Figure 5-6B allows commands, data, and programs to be entered by the user. Two-way communication between the computer and the user is provided.

FIGURE 5-5
Changing the character set on a printer may involve simply replacing the golf-ball print element of a typewriter-like terminal. (*Reproduced with permission of AT&T*)

Wire-matrix (also called *dot-matrix*) *printers* are an increasingly common alternative to solid-character printing devices. These printers were first developed to overcome the apparent speed limitations of early solid-character impact serial printers. Users were willing to trade some print quality for substantially increased print speeds. They were also attracted by the lower costs of these devices.

In a wire-matrix printer, each character is printed by a vertical set of wires that is pushed forward against an inked ribbon, and the ribbon against the paper, as the print mechanism moves across the print line. (See Figure 5-7.) One line of dots is printed at a time. The number of wires in the set determines the density of the dot matrix. Both 5×7 and 7×9 dot-matrix characters are common. Speeds of up to 560 lpm are available with some impact printers of this kind. Some can print at any of three user-selected densities and speeds. Higher densities mean slower printing speeds but higher-quality output.

Some wire-matrix printers can produce multiple-color output. This means, for example, that both colored graphs and paragraphs of printed text can be included in a computer-generated business report. Some provide expanded character sets with special or larger fonts for additional flexibility.

NONIMPACT PRINTERS Throughout the computer industry, one trend is unmistakable: User demands for nonimpact printers are increasing. Whereas nonimpact printers accounted for about 10 percent of total printer shipments in 1980, they may well account for 40 percent by 1990.

A

B

FIGURE 5-6 Daisywheels are used as print elements on many receive-only (A) and keyboard send/receive (B) teleprinter terminals. (*Courtesy Qume Corporation, a subsidiary of ITT;* [A, B] *Dataproducts Corporation*)

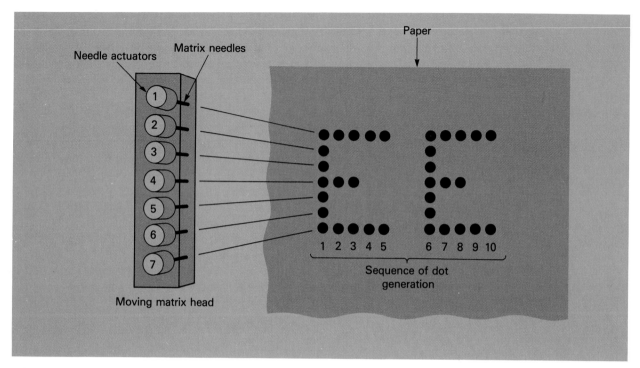

FIGURE 5-7 The letter E is printed as a 5 × 7 dot-matrix character by some wire-matrix printing mechanisms. (*Courtesy Dataproducts Corporation*)

As noted earlier, nonimpact printers are faster because they have fewer moving parts than impact printers. For the same reason, they tend to be more reliable and quieter in operation. To managers whose basic business operations are dependent on computer-generated hard copy (invoices, paychecks, scheduling reports, and the like), reliable printers are essential. To users who work near to their small business computer systems or to remote printers (say, in office environments), quiet printers are essential. Initially, the print quality of nonimpact printer output was not as good as that of commonly available impact printers. However, that is no longer the case in many instances.

Several nonimpact printing technologies have been developed. Because these technologies differ significantly, the nonimpact printers also differ. Nonimpact serial, line, and page printers ranging in price from $300 to more than $300,000 are available.

At the slow-speed serial end of the nonimpact group, *thermal printers* are common. Dot-matrix characters are formed by heating selected elements of a print head as it moves across a special heat-sensitive paper. Usually silver coated, the paper turns black wherever heat is applied. The print quality of the dot-matrix characters is generally acceptable for low-volume, routine business applications. Unfortunately, the special paper is expensive and the printing on the paper tends to fade with time. Nevertheless, the relatively low costs of thermal printers have attracted many users. You'll find these printers attached to Apple III microcomputers as well as on large systems. Many lightweight Texas Instruments' Silent 700-series terminals include thermal printers that operate in virtual silence, producing hard copy at a 30-cps rate. (See Figure 5-8.)

FIGURE 5-8
Low-cost thermal printers are common on portable terminals and in microcomputer systems. (*Courtesy Texas Instruments Incorporated*)

Serial and line printers using *ink-jet technology* shoot a stream of charged ink from a nozzle; the ink is deflected by plates to produce dot-matrix characters. (See Figure 5-9.) Print quality is achieved through use of many dots—500 as opposed to 35, 63, or thereabouts in comparable wire-matrix or thermal printers. Other advantages are the ability to print with multiple type fonts (changeable electronically) and suitability for use with ordinary paper. Ink-jet printers that provide multiple-color output are also available.

You can expect to find ink-jet printers used offline (independently of computers) for word-processing functions and as terminals. Typical print speeds range from 30 to 92 cps. Some ink-jet printers can print several thousand lines per minute, but they cost far more than their slow-speed counterparts.

An *electrostatic printer* forms an image by means of charged pins or wires that supply a charge in the desired pattern to a nonconducting paper. The paper passes through a solution ("toner") containing ink particles of opposite charge. The particles adhere to the charged area of the paper and melt when exposed to high heat, thus forming the image. Graphical images as well as characters can be produced since the dots can be positioned to form pictures. However, the paper costs several times more than ordinary paper. Typical electrostatic printers operate at speeds of from 275 to 3600 lpm. At the top of this group is Honeywell's Page Printing System. Models capable of printing up to 18,000 lpm are available.

The Xerox 1200, introduced in 1973, was the world's first *xerographic* (also called *electrophotographic*) *page printer*. The 1200 can be operated online with a medium-size computer, or offline to print information written earlier to magnetic tape as output of EDP-system processing. It uses a process similar to

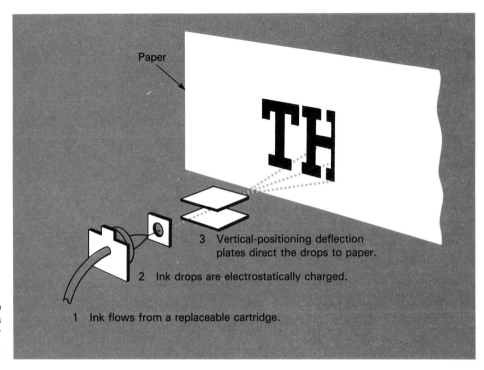

3 Vertical-positioning deflection plates direct the drops to paper.

2 Ink drops are electrostatically charged.

1 Ink flows from a replaceable cartridge.

FIGURE 5-9
Ink-jet printing mechanisms can project many densely positioned dots on paper, producing high-quality output.

that first used in Xerox office copiers to print at a rate of 4000 lpm. Users soon learned to appreciate the distinct character images produced on letter-sized ($8\frac{1}{2}'' \times 11''$) paper rather than as traditional ($11'' \times 14\frac{7}{8}''$) computer printouts.

In 1977, Xerox announced the first of its follow-on products: the 9700 Electronic Printing System. (See Figure 5-10.) In the 9700 a *laser* (rather than an ordinary directed light and lens) forms character images with pinpoint accuracy on a rotating, coated drum. The dot-matrix resolution is equivalent to 90,000 dots per square inch. Forms, including company logos, signatures, vertical and horizontal lines for tables and charts, and so on, can be stored and then imaged electronically together with variable data. This feature eliminates the need for forms overlays or preprinted forms.

FIGURE 5-10 Very fast nonimpact printers handle high-volume printing requirements at large in-house reproduction departments, computer centers, and publishing houses. (*Courtesy Xerox Corporation*)

Like the 1200, the 9700 operates either online or offline. It prints on one or both sides of standard $8\frac{1}{2}'' \times 11''$ paper at a rate of 2 pages per second—up to 18,000 lpm. Two-sided printing is especially useful for inventory listings, catalogs, directories, manuals, and the like. It also offers savings in paper, filing, storage, and mailing costs.

Priced at $300,000 to $400,000, the 9700 is a top-of-the-line printer suitable for large computer centers and large publishing houses. Subsequent printers—the 8700, 5700, and 2700—print at 70 ppm, 45 ppm, and 12 ppm, respectively. The 8700 is aimed at computer centers, commercial printing operations, and in-house reproduction departments printing 200,000 to 700,000 pages a month. The 5700 brought laser printing into office environments. In just seconds, it can send documents to other printers around the country over ordinary phone lines. Each recipient of a letter or report can receive an original-quality document addressed directly to him or her. The 2700 offers multiple type fonts, multiple type sizes, vertical or horizontal printing, and high-quality imaging capabilities much like those of its larger counterparts at a cost of less than $20,000.

The IBM 3800 and 6670, Datagraphix 9800, Sperry Univac 0777, and Siemens NDJ-2 are other printers using laser and electrophotographic technologies. Credit-card and utility statements, insurance policies, brokerage portfolio information, and direct-mail sales and campaign literature, as well as business, governmental, and stockholder reports, are examples of common output.

PLOTTERS A plotter is an output device that converts tabulated numerical data into graphic form. (See Figure 5-11.) Bar charts and line graphs, work-flow charts of manufacturing projects, organization charts, engineering drawings, and maps are some of the many forms of data that can be displayed on a plotter. Most offer gray-scale halftones, which we might commonly refer to as *shading*. With some plotters, 4-, 6-, or 8-color output is provided. All can be used to produce user-oriented, easy-to-understand output.

FIGURE 5-11
A drum plotter can produce engineering drawings, architectural layouts, topological maps, and other large graphic output items. (*Courtesy Calcomp*)

Plotters have been available since the early days of computers. They have been used in aircraft and automotive design, architectural layouts, topological surveys, and similar complex drafting jobs. Like printers, plotters are getting faster, smaller, less expensive, and smarter. The recent boom in CAD/CAM (computer-aided design/computer-aided manufacturing) has encouraged equipment vendors and software firms to develop and market complete CAD/CAM systems with plotters as basic components. These systems are widely used in tool design, computer printed-circuit-board design, and end-user product design. They allow for reiteration of design and feedback procedures between engineering and manufacturing groups during product development. As suggested above, it is now also possible and practical to use plotters to prepare graphic representations of business data.

Plotters are of two basic types: pen and electrostatic. Pen plotters may be drum, flatbed, or beltbed devices.

In a *drum plotter*, recording is achieved by incremental movements of a pen on a paper surface (y-axis) and/or movements of the paper under the pen (x-axis). (See Figure 5-12.) The vertical (x-axis) plotting motion is achieved by rotation of the pin-feed drum. The drum and the pen carriage are bidirectional; that is, the paper moves up or down, and the pen moves left or right. When both move at once, diagonal lines are produced. Commonly available plotters accommodate ballpoint, liquid-roller, fiber-tip, and nylon-tip pens in a wide variety of colors. If 4-, 6-, or 8-color drawings are to be produced, then 4, 6, or 8 pens of different colors can be mounted on the pen carriage. For high-quality output, drafting pens are used.

A *flatbed plotter* is basically an electromechanical drafting table. Computer-controlled motors move a pen along x and y axes to produce a graph or schematic on stationary paper. Some flatbed plotters produce $8\frac{1}{2}'' \times 11''$ output. Large flatbed plotters can produce drawings up to 5 or 6 feet in width. The output medium may be report-grade (bond) paper. Vellum is suitable for reproduction. Acetate or Mylar film is especially useful when dimensional stability is required.

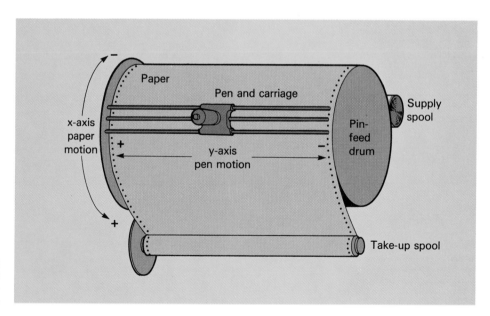

FIGURE 5-12
Both the pen and the paper move to produce drum-plotter output.

Another advantage of the flatbed plotter is that the user can observe the output as it develops. (See Figure 5-13.)

A *beltbed plotter* has a vertical plotting surface. It operates much like a drum, but provides the flat plotting surface of a flatbed plotter. Like a drum, it moves the paper under the pen as well as the pen over the paper. Like a flatbed plotter, however, it plots on cut sheets of paper rather than on a continuous roll.

Electrostatic plotters work the same way as electrostatic printers. In fact, some vendors refer to their products as *printer/plotters*. Usually, dielectrically coated paper is moved past a row of tiny pen-shaped styli that generate charged dot-matrix patterns in response to electrical signals. The paper is then exposed to a liquid solution (toner), which produces visible output.

Compared to the pen type, electrostatic plotters are very fast. They are limited only by the speed of the paper movement. Stated print speeds can be misleading, however. They do not take into account the time required to form the data for printing. For complex drawings, this time may be considerable.

As computer usage expands, so does the use of both pen and electrostatic plotters. However, electrostatic plotters seem to be gaining faster in popularity. From a user's point of view, pen plotters have one major disadvantage: Additional time is required if any alphanumeric characters are to be included on the output. This is not true of electrostatic plotters. They have a simultaneous print/plot feature that permits the overlay of plot data and characters on the same print area.

Another consideration when using plotters is that extensive software is often required to generate the lines or dots that compose the output drawings. For this reason, specific plotting routines provided by the vendor, or the ease with which such routines can be created, should be evaluated carefully when selecting a plotter. As mentioned above, some firms are developing complete systems that include both the hardware and the software required for specific applications.

FIGURE 5-13
Flatbed plotters with many capabilities are available for large computer systems as well as for microcomputers. (*Courtesy Houston Instrument Division of Bausch & Lomb*)

VISUAL-DISPLAY OUTPUT

No matter where you look these days—large computer center, engineering design shop, word-processing center, business office, stock room, or shop floor—you're apt to see a device that looks much like an ordinary television set. The data-recording medium in most of these devices is a *cathode-ray tube* (*CRT*), similar in design and function to a television picture tube.

Most of the devices have keyboards and provide both output and input capabilities. We call them *CRT's*, *visual-display units* (*VDU's*), or *visual-display terminals* (*VDT's*).

The time needed to analyze information displayed on a CRT screen is likely to be significantly less than would be required to analyze the same information in a computer-generated statistical report. (A picture *is* worth a thousand words.) The response to a management inquiry, a question for the student to answer in a carefully planned course of computer-assisted instruction (CAI), or a plot of a mathematical relation can be shown in a readily understandable way. (See Figure 5-14.) Furthermore, many applications today are designed to offer "HELP" screens. If the user does not understand what is displayed on an initial screen, or wants additional detail, pressing a specified key on the keyboard will cause a backup (nested) screen containing additional information to be displayed.

Depending on the capabilities of the particular device, CRT's provide visual output in any of several forms:

- Alphanumeric (displays containing letters, numerals, and/or special characters)
- Graphic (bar graphs, histograms, line drawings, line graphs, pie charts, and so on)
- Combinations of alphanumeric and graphic output

FIGURE 5-14
Output displayed on the screen of a monochrome visual-display unit is suitable for many applications. (*Courtesy IBM Corporation*)

Initially, all CRT's were monochrome displays. They showed light characters on a dark background or dark characters on a light background. (Look again at Figure 5-14.) Today CRT's that display output in 4, 8, or even 64 colors are available. (See Figure 5-15.) Ask yourself: "Do I learn more from material printed in several colors than from conventional black-and-white printing?" Your answer is probably "Yes." Now ask yourself: "Would I pay several dollars to have a telephone directory printed in eight colors?" Your answer is probably "No." For many applications, color enhances output; for others, it is not needed. As yet, color displays cost much more than comparable monochrome displays. In today's economy, whether or not that cost should be incurred is a tradeoff that organizations, departments, and individuals must make on the basis of their requirements.

According to several recent surveys, CRT's are most frequently used for:

- Interactive data entry and information retrieval
- Computer program development
- System operation (i.e., as the EDP-system console)
- Word processing/text editing
- Intercompany messages
- Business graphics (sales trends, budget vs actuals, etc.)

Visual-display units are by far the most common output device of microcomputer systems. They are fast, quiet, and often cost less than printers. Some are video monitors (color or black and white) made especially for microcomputer systems. Others are color TV receivers; a special hookup allows output to be directed to a user's home television set.

FIGURE 5-15
CRT's with color and graphics capabilities provide readily understandable, visually pleasing output.
(*Courtesy Genisco Computers Corp.*)

When a visual-display unit serves as a remote terminal, the transfer of data from primary storage to the device, or vice versa, can occur at speeds ranging from 250 to 10,000 characters per second. An entire record of information can be displayed almost instantly. In contrast, most teleprinter terminals are serial printers. They must type each record one character at a time. If the visual-display unit has graphic capabilities, then charts, graphs, and line drawings as well as character data can be displayed. Such terminals are especially appreciated in areas where computer-generated statistical reports were previously analyzed and plotted manually.

With some visual-display units, the user can draw lines on the screen by pointing at the desired endpoints of the lines. The locations of the endpoints are made known by a light-sensitive cell in a small device called a *light pen*. In other visual-display units, data can be entered via a *sense probe* that activates sensitive points on the face of the screen. Visual-display units with *touch-sensitive screens* are a more recent development. These devices are useful, for example, in entering patient data for hospital information systems, preparing claim data and new policy data at insurance companies, and modifying circuit diagrams in research and development laboratories. (See Figure 5-16.)

In this book, we often use the acronym *CRT* interchangeably with the term *visual-display unit*. Most persons in industry do also. Be aware, however, that not all visual-display units use cathode-ray tubes as the data-recording medium. Vendors' product literature may refer to "raster scan" visual-display units. Such units do use CRT's, but the vendors are trying to convince you that their devices provide very high-quality images. To understand that message, you need to know a little more about imaging techniques.

FIGURE 5-16
Touch-sensitive screens are a convenient means of entering data for processing. (*Courtesy Four-Phase Systems, Inc.*)

Devices described as using storage tubes, raster refresh, or raster/random scan technology are actually CRT displays. Storage-tube technology uses an electron beam to draw an image on the screen. The screen is electrically charged to hold the image there. This technology can provide complex, dense pictures with no flicker, but color is not usually available.

In raster refresh and raster/random scan units, the images on the CRT must constantly be reproduced to avoid flickering. A raster refresh unit operates in much the same way as a television set. The screen image is held in digital form in internal storage. The digital data is used to project (or not project) light, point by point, line by line, on the screen until it is filled. Then the projection process is repeated, starting again at the top. Two advantages of raster refresh units are the availability of color and the relatively low cost. The main disadvantage is limited point density, and hence limited resolution capability.

Raster/random scan technology is used for top-of-the-line graphics terminals. Data is generated in an x-y format that can be plotted. An a-z component can be added to produce three-dimensional views. The main advantage of this technology is high resolution. Disadvantages are the high cost and the large amount of storage required for the positioning data.

Non-CRT displays use plasma (gaseous displays), light-emitting diodes (LED's), or liquid crystals (liquid-crystal displays, or LCD's). Of these, plasma displays have received greatest attention. A plasma display has three touching sheets of glass. The middle sheet has tiny, gas-filled holes. The outside sheets contain electrical conducting strips that activate the gas and cause it to glow at specific points. These displays are brighter than CRT's; they are not subject to flickering, and they can provide high resolution. As yet, however, they are significantly more expensive than comparable CRT devices.

An early objection to visual-display output was that no permanent record of the data displayed on the screen was produced. To meet this need, some vendors have developed compatible hard-copy units that can print out whatever appears on the screen. Similarly, some plotters have CRT's attached so that users can preview plots before committing them to hard-copy form. Display-before-print capabilities are useful in many applications. (See Figure 5-17.)

VOICE OUTPUT   Next time you put a coin into a pay phone and dial a long-distance call, listen carefully. The voice that tells you how much more money to deposit for the call may belong to a computer. The computer may also keep track of the coins you deposit and the time you talk. If a problem develops with the phone equipment, the computer may alert technicians that the phone is in need of repair.

As another example, suppose you enter an elevator. A voice says, "Second floor; this elevator will leave soon." You see no one. Again, the voice may belong to a computer.

An intelligible voicelike signal, or *audio response*, is a suitable form of output for limited-volume, formalized messages in many EDP systems. (See Figure 5-18.) In the banking industry, a talking computer may inform tellers or customers of account balances. Stock quotations, airline flight schedules, the current time, and weather conditions may be provided by computers as spoken output. A sales representative may submit a product order by calling the computer and then entering order data from a Touch-Tone telephone or similar terminal. The computer at the other end of the phone line may restate the order

FIGURE 5-17 Some computer systems can produce the same output in both hard-copy and soft-copy forms. (*Courtesy General Electric Research and Development Center*)

FIGURE 5-18 Intelligible voicelike responses can help handicapped persons use computers effectively. (*Courtesy University of Pennsylvania Handicapped Training Center*)

for instant verification. It may prompt the representative to enter additional data. It may then verify price and availability.

The data-recording medium, the output device, and even the computer system may not be obvious to voice-output users. In some systems, each word or phrase that may be spoken by the computer is prerecorded on a series of sound tracks. Digital output from the computer acts as a selector of the sounds to be played. The sounds then go through an amplifier and telephone or loudspeaker arrangement. Played in a controlled order, the recordings form the "spoken" responses. In other systems, the voice-output devices are voice synthesizers. A mathematical model of the human throat formulates the spoken output.

The techniques of voice processing are software-intensive. They involve lots of processing and lots of data. The computer instructions are often stored and executed as microcode, provided on a silicon chip by the vendor. The data (vocabulary or library of sounds) may be stored in the computer or in a voice-output terminal. The prices of voice-output terminals range from $2000 to more than $50,000.

Research and development efforts in voice output are continuing. These efforts are directed primarily at increasing the practical limits of computer vocabularies and the quality of voice output. A computer that tells the time of day may need to say only "The time is . . .," followed by a couple of numbers. A computer that trains pilots via simulated airplane flights may need to speak many words, in many sequences. Similarly, a voice coming from an EDP-system console that says, "Printer number four is jammed," need not speak eloquently. On an assembly line where the computer system reads bar codes on parts moving down the line and directs workers accordingly, a pleasant voice is essential; otherwise, fatigue and frustration are likely. The ultimate test of voice quality is transparency: Do at least 80 percent of uncued listeners fail to detect the voice as that of a computer?

**MICROFILM/
MICROFICHE**

A *microfilm* is a photographic image, on a reduced scale, of information that might otherwise be handled in a printed form. Generally, it appears as a continuous roll, containing about 2000 frames—each of which may hold the equivalent of one printed page. A *microfiche* is a cardlike film medium. One 4″ × 6″ microfiche at 48× reduction can hold the equivalent of 270 pages of printed matter. The weight of 100 microfiches is 14 ounces; printed pages of the same data weigh about 200 pounds.

Computer output microfilm (COM) consists of photographic images produced in miniature with the aid of a computer. This term is also used to refer in general to the techniques and equipment used to combine micrographic technologies with work done by computers. We use the term in an inclusive way here to mean both products and processes.

Consider the volume of printed matter generated in our society—both with the computer's help and without it. COM is a satisfactory substitute in many cases. For example, a firm may print a letter acknowledging a customer's order. This letter is mailed to the customer. The file copy of this letter and other details relevant to the same order are stored on microfiche. These microfiches are distributed to the credit department, accounting, inventory scheduling, manufacturing, distant branch warehouses, and shipping.

In some EDP systems, computer output to be microfilmed is written directly onto magnetic tape at the user installation. Then, a special photocopier/reducer is used to produce a microfilm copy of the information on the tape. Generally, this step is done by another firm that specializes in photography.

In other systems, computer output to be microfilmed is displayed on a CRT. The CRT is exposed to microfilm. The result is a microfilm copy of the output in one of two forms: a roll of film or a microfiche. (See Figure 5-19.)

FIGURE 5-19
A representative COM configuration includes an online microfiche recorder (left) and a microfiche duplicator with collating carousel (right). (*Courtesy Datagraphix/Ralston Purina*)

COM was proposed as a cost-saving alternative to printed reports for a number of years before it gained much acceptance. The need to process the film chemically (usually at another facility) tended to limit its use. To overcome this drawback, printers employing a laser-imaging system to print computer output directly onto dry, heat-processed microfilm were developed. In many aspects, these devices are like other high-speed nonimpact printers. With them the need for a darkroom, a special processing machine, plumbing, and processing chemicals is eliminated. Some can operate online as well as independently. Some can write output on either paper or film.

The primary advantage of COM as a data-recording medium is that it can hold vast amounts of data (including graphics) compactly and safely. The $48\times$ reduction (270 pages per fiche) mentioned above and $42\times$ reduction (207 pages per fiche) are possible with CRT COM technologies. With laser imaging, $60\times$, $72\times$, and $96\times$ reductions are also possible. Using current prices (which vary with geographic location and the grade of paper purchased), we can expect a 1000-page report printed on three-part computer paper to cost about $30. The same amount of information can be written on four microfiches at a cost of about $1. If additional copies of the report are needed, the savings become even greater. Each paper copy costs about as much as the first one. A duplicate microfiche costs about 25¢.

Another advantage of COM is lower storage cost. Some users find that the cost of storing microfilm is about 1/45th the cost of storing an equivalent volume of paper. Experienced COM users often state that COM printouts require only 2 percent of the space otherwise required for paper reports.

Because microfilm is compact and lightweight, distributing a report on microfilm is faster and less expensive than distributing computer printouts. Microfiches can be sent in envelopes to users through regular mail channels. Unlike printouts, they need not be loaded into boxes which are then wheeled on carts to user distribution areas. Assume six copies of a 1000-page report weighing about 70 pounds are to be sent to other locations. Further assume United Parcel Service (UPS) is used. The delivery cost is about $9. Equivalent microfilm can be sent for about $1.50. A 200-page report printed on $11'' \times 14\frac{7}{8}''$ computer paper weighs about 3 pounds and costs from $3 to $4 to mail first class within the continental United States. The same report contained on one microfiche can be mailed at the cost of a single stamp.

An early disadvantage of microfilm was the inability to use a computer to retrieve microfilmed data. A first step in solving this problem was a computer-generated index indicating the proper microfilm roll or microfiche and the right frame. Mechanical devices and humans retrieved and processed the data. Now *computer input microfilm* (*CIM*) technologies are gaining recognition. Initial impetus in this area was generated by the use of minicomputers in COM equipment as a means of giving that equipment more capabilities. If minicomputers can process microfilm, why can't all computers? The requirement here was for vendor development of I/O devices that could read the contents of microfilm directly into the computer. Eastman Kodak's IMT-150 microimage retrieval terminal announced in 1978 is an example.

Today, computers and attached micrographics terminals are being used for both batch and transaction processing. At the Internal Revenue Service, an intelligent micrographics terminal can find a single wage report in seconds, bypassing millions of others stored on microfilm. Personnel at Warren County,

Ohio, use online retrieval of microfilmed deeds and other documents to speed land transfers and conduct title searches. California's Sonoma State University manages thousands of student documents with the help of a large computer and online micrographics terminals. Many organizations are finding that COM is a major aid to office automation.

CHAPTER SUMMARY

1. Computer systems with attached printing devices can produce many printed, hard-copy forms of output. Those with output devices such as visual-display units and voice-output units can produce less permanent, soft-copy output. A system may include either or both kinds of devices.

2. Printers may be classified as serial (character), line, and page printers, according to how much information is printed in one output operation.

3. Printers may also be classified as either impact or nonimpact. The former are dependent on the physical movement of print elements; the latter print by thermal (heat), chemical, electrical, and/or optical techniques.

4. Some printers form solid characters. Others print dots at various densities to form dot-matrix characters.

5. Early impact printers had chains, trains, and drums as printing mechanisms. Whereas a print chain or train can be changed, allowing different character sets to be used, a drum provides only one fixed character set.

6. Belt and band printers are gaining widespread acceptance on medium-size and small computer systems. Low-cost wire-matrix printers and printers with golf balls, daisywheels, or thimbles as print elements are common on microcomputers.

7. Thermal printers and most ink-jet printers are at the low end of the nonimpact printer category. Electrostatic, xerographic, and laser printers print from 12 to 120 pages a minute and cost from a few thousand to hundreds of thousands of dollars.

8. Plotters convert tabulated data into graphic form. Initially, pen plotters of drum, flatbed, or beltbed types were common. Very fast electrostatic plotters are gaining in popularity.

9. Visual-display units record output on cathode-ray tubes (CRT's) in monochrome or multiple colors. Light pens, sense probes, and touch-sensitive screens allow input as well as output operations to be done with these devices.

10. Audio responses are suitable for some banking, sales ordering, and user inquiry applications where limited-volume, formalized messages are required as output.

11. Major technological advances are occurring in computer output microfilm (COM) products and processes. Users are achieving significant savings in material, storage, distribution, and labor costs.

1. What outputs of computer systems do you use in your daily life?

2. (a) What is meant by the term *hard copy*?
   (b) When might this kind of copy be desirable?

3. Distinguish between serial, line, and page printers.

4. (a) What are the two broad categories of printing methods?
   (b) What are some advantages of each of the methods that you named?
   (c) Describe some printers that use each of these methods.

5. Discuss some of the tradeoffs that printer-shopping users may make. In doing so, suggest situations where the various tradeoffs may be good ones from the users' points of view.

6. Point out some user situations where plotter output would be especially useful.

7. Distinguish among the kinds of plotters available, showing how users may choose among them.

8. Select one type of plotter and build an argument to convince the manager of a particular business (also of your choice) to buy it.

9. Suggest some user applications for which visual output is appropriate.

10. What options are available to users who want hard copies of visual-display output?

11. (a) Suggest some applications for which audio output is especially suitable.
    (b) What are its advantages and limitations?

12. Assume that you are the manager of a large discount store with access to a centralized EDP system. Give arguments to justify the use of microfilm at your facility.

6

STORING DATA

We have come a long way as a civilization. One concern that has been with us since the beginning is the concern for self-preservation. Out of that concern has come an increasing urge to preserve our resources. In these times, one resource we seek to preserve above all others is our knowledge. The techniques for obtaining, interpreting, and storing data have become critical to our further progress as a technical civilization.

Our data-storage techniques have moved toward compactness and greater speed. These trends are perhaps nowhere more evident than in the appearance of the silicon chip, which represents a huge leap forward when compared to any earlier data-storage medium.

The earliest machine-readable data-storage media were made of paper: punched tape and punched cards. An "antique" form of punched paper tape stored the musical instructions used by the mechanism of a

player piano several generations ago . . . long before the invention of the computer. Later, the Teletype, the TWX, and other devices used punched paper tape to store data and machine-readable instructions.

Today, the two most common media for storage of data are magnetic tape and magnetic disk. Both are far more compact and faster to process than paper tape or card. Both come in a wide variety of formats.

On punched card or tape, the patterns of the holes represent the data; on magnetic media, the data is represented by the patterns of tiny magnetized spots. In both cases, patterns of holes or spots on the storage medium *are* the data characters. When these media are used to store machine-readable instructions, the functioning of the system is controlled by the patterns of the holes or magnetized spots.

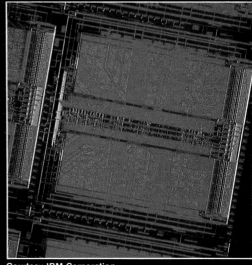

Courtesy IBM Corporation

Courtesy IBM Corporation

Courtesy Harvard University, Cruft Photo Lab

Courtesy Nashua Computer Products

For today's applications with relatively small storage requirements, a commonly used storage medium is the floppy disk. This medium can serve many small-business purposes. It is compact, but stores enough data to be useful to Eben Whitcomb, the owner-operator of a large wind-jammer-cruise business based in Connecticut. He uses a computer to keep track of schedules, book-ings, maintenance, and accounting information. Some of his data appears in more than one of these categories but access to all the data is both con-venient and economical.

Large businesses often have very demanding data-storage needs. Companies doing batch processing or maintaining large amounts of historical data may find magnetic tape to be the most appro-priate storage medium for some of their applications. A large computerized can-nery, for example, is using magnetic tape to store both inventory and accounting information. Magnetic tape can hold large amounts of data in relatively little space and at relatively low cost.

Magnetic disk is well suited for interactive data processing that involves many individual transac-tions. Some disk-storage systems have multiple drives per disk-storage unit, and multiple disks are mounted on each drive. Such systems offer both rapid, direct retrieval of individual records and online storage capacity for very large numbers of records.

Where still larger amounts of data are con-tinuously being stored and retrieved, many disk drives may be used by a single system all at one time. Entire rooms may be de-voted to row upon row of disk-storage devices.

Businesses that collect large amounts of data on past transactions can hold the data on magnetic tape in long-term "data archives" or tape libraries. When specific data rec-ords are needed again, the contents of the tape can be transferred to a direct-access medium such as magnetic disk, from which single data records can be quickly retrieved without having to read through every record in sequence.

Just as paper has largely been supplanted by magnetic media, even newer technologies are being developed today. Some mass-storage de-vices are using an optical-disk technology in which a laser encodes and reads the data.

Data can be stored in many forms and on many media. The medium that should be chosen is usually determined by the amount of data to be stored, by how it is to be organized, and by how frequently the system needs access to it. Since we continue to generate, process, and store data at an ever-increasing pace, the search for better data-storage media will con-tinue. We must protect our data resource—because we don't know when we'll need it to produce information.

Courtesy Eben N. Whitcomb and 3M

Courtesy Robert Scully and 3M

Courtesy Applicon, a Division of Schlumberger Technology Corporation

Courtesy Sperry Corporation

Courtesy Honeywell Inc.

Courtesy Dialog Information Services, Inc., Palo Alto, California

Courtesy Boeing Computer Services Company

Courtesy Memorex Corporation

Courtesy RCA

Courtesy Motorola Inc.

6 STORING DATA

When we make notes to ourselves on the backs of envelopes, we are storing data. Check stubs, sales slips, and duplicate tax forms are common data-storage devices. Businesses store large volumes of valuable data in customer account records, general ledgers, and large filing cabinets. When a business elects to use a computer system, most of this data is stored in a form that is accessible to the computer.

A variety of techniques have been developed to store both programs and data in modern computer systems. We look at some of the techniques in this chapter. A variety of storage media—the EDP-system counterparts of check stubs, filing cabinets, and so on—have also been developed. Some of the media are used extensively for entering data into a computer system and for transferring data between systems, as well as for data storage. We've already discussed these briefly, but we see them in broader perspective here.

When you've completed this chapter, you'll understand how large amounts of programs and data can be stored in a computer system. You'll also understand how we can access the programs and data, once they're stored. We look first at primary-storage concepts and technologies. Then we discuss secondary-storage concepts and devices. Finally, we consider mass storage systems, which perform a library function.

As you study this material there may be times when you think you're being told more than you'll ever want to know about computer storage. Today's computer users sometimes feel the same way, and sometimes feel just the opposite. If you have a computer or are thinking about getting one, you're likely to find that determining how much storage and what types of storage you need is a major challenge. If you're employed by an organization that uses computers, you're likely to be asked to work with data administrators to estimate your data-storage requirements for computerized applications. This chapter is designed to increase your awareness of storage problems and to help you understand options that may need to be considered in answering such questions.

STORAGE CLASSIFICATIONS

Storage in an EDP system is classified as either of two types:

- *Primary storage*, the *internal storage unit*,
  also called *main storage* or *memory*
- *Secondary storage*, also called *auxiliary storage*

Primary storage is sometimes considered to be part of the central processing unit (CPU) of a computer system. It's always positioned near or with the computer's control section and arithmetic/logic unit. Secondary storage is often provided by magnetic-tape or disk storage devices connected by cabling to the processor unit. (See Figure 6-1.) In a microcomputer system, secondary storage may be provided via diskettes that can be inserted in small disk drives packaged neatly with other system components in a desktop configuration. (See Figure 6-2.)

Storage technologies have come a long way since the days of the 30-ton, 1500-square-foot ENIAC. Twenty-five years ago, one million characters of data could be stored on magnetic surfaces that together equaled the size of a double bed. Today, one million characters fit on a surface the size of a postage stamp. Twenty-five years hence, they may fit on a point the size of a grain of salt. No single storage medium satisfies all EDP-system storage requirements. There are fast, expensive internal memories for calculations. There are slower, less expensive secondary-storage devices for large-volume storage. There is a very significant gap between them in terms of speed and cost.

PRIMARY STORAGE

The term *primary storage* is used to designate the internal storage unit of a computer system. During processing, primary storage accepts data from an input device, exchanges data with and supplies instructions to the CPU, and sends the results of processing to an output device. (See Figure 6-3.) Its capacity

FIGURE 6-1
An EDP system includes both primary and secondary storage. (*Courtesy Honeywell Inc.*)

FIGURE 6-2
Most microcomputer users find that removable diskettes are handy for secondary storage of programs and data. (*Courtesy 3M*)

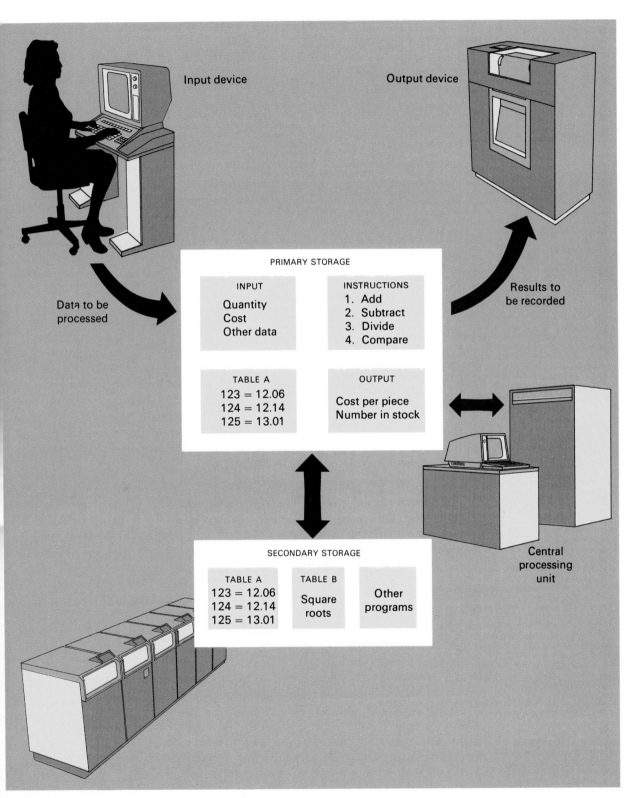

FIGURE 6-3   Data and instructions are transferred to and from primary storage many times during processing.

must be sufficient to retain both a usable amount of data and the instructions needed to process it.

Consider IBM System/370, 303X, 308X, and 4300-series computers as representative of modern data-processing equipment. In these computers, primary storage consists of the following:

- Primary data storage (also called real storage), which varies in capacity; it can contain from 65,536 to more than 64 million characters on some models.

- Control storage, which often contains special built-in microprograms that are invoked to carry out certain system functions.

- Local storage, which consists of high-speed working areas (registers) used for certain arithmetic operations, comparisons, and other types of processing.

The System/370 Model 145 was the first of these computers to have a reloadable control storage. Model 145 users are supplied with small prewritten disk cartridges containing the System/370 basic instruction set, plus the instructions for optional system features that the users select. Because this reloadable control storage is read-only storage, the instructions that it contains can be interpreted and executed. They cannot be changed, however.

If you've read or heard about personal computers or small business computers, you've probably come across phrases such as "from 16,384 to 262,144 characters of RAM" and "40,960 characters of ROM." The *RAM*, or *random-access memory*, is primary data storage. It can hold user programs and data. The programs and data actually stored in RAM may change many times during processing. The *ROM*, or *read-only memory*, is control storage. It holds programs and data supplied by the vendor. They are essential to proper functioning of the system and cannot be changed by users. As you may recall, we discussed the advantages of ROM earlier. (See "Microcode" in Chapter 2.)

STORAGE CAPACITY

In daily conversation, we often speak of the capacity of an object—say, a shopping cart, a swimming pool, or a football stadium. We express that capacity in terms of number of items, cubic feet, gallons, people, or whatever unit is appropriate. In each case, the capacity is a measure of how much the object can hold.

In like manner, we speak of the capacity of a computer's internal storage unit. The capacity is a measure of the amount of programs and data the unit can hold. We may express that capacity in terms of *K*. One K is either 1000 or 1024, depending on which manufacturer is using it. Further, it may mean 1000 or 1024 bits, 8-bit bytes, or words of lengths 8, 16, 32, or 60, and so on. The capacity of some large internal storage units may also be described in terms of *M*. Thus, 1M means 1 megabyte, 2M means 2 megabytes, and so on. Each *megabyte* is equal to 1024×1024 8-bit bytes, or 1,048,576 storage locations. (That is, 1M = 1024K, where 1K = one *kilobyte*, or 1024 bytes.)

Some computers have internal storage units as small as 32K, where *32K* means 32,000 16-bit words. Other computers have up to 8192K, where *8192K* means 8,388,608 8-bit bytes. Still others have less capacity, more capacity, or capacity that is somewhere between these two examples. So you see that when discussing specific amounts of storage we must be careful to understand the unit of measure that is being applied.

In the past, typical business computers had from 32K to 256K bytes of primary storage. Computers with 512K bytes of primary storage were considered to have very large memories. That picture has changed. Today, even a microcomputer may have 512K bytes of primary storage. Advances in technology have brought about significant reductions in the physical size of internal storage units and in storage costs. Even a 32-megabyte storage unit (plus its associated circuitry) is little bigger than an ordinary kitchen cabinet. In 1976, 1 million characters of memory cost about $170,000. By 1979, the cost had dropped to $15,000. That's a 90 percent reduction in less than three years. Obviously, the less expensive memory is, the greater the amount of memory that users can afford.

STORAGE ADDRESSES AND ACCESSING

In Chapter 2, we pointed out that the internal storage unit of a computer resembles an electronic filing cabinet. The internal storage unit can also be compared to a group of numbered mailboxes in a post office. (See Figure 6-4.) Each post office box is identified and located by a number. In the same way, storage is divided into locations, each of which has an assigned address and holds a specific unit of data. Depending on the system, the unit of data may be a character, a digit, the contents of a byte, or a word. To write data to a location or to read data from it, the address of the location must be known.

When data is written to a particular location, it replaces the previous contents of that location. The previous contents are no longer available to us. Thus, the "write" operation is a *destructive* operation.

When data is read from a location, the contents of the location are not altered. In contrast to the mailboxes discussed above, which are empty when their contents are removed, storage locations from which data is retrieved (read) are not empty. Once written into storage, data may be read many times. Thus, the "read" operation is *nondestructive*. In effect, a duplicate copy of the stored data is made available each time a read occurs. The stored data is destroyed only when it is replaced by new data.

To appreciate the importance of the nondestructive read capability, imagine that you are adding individual test scores for many students. As you do so, you write the total score for each student on a scratch pad for subsequent grand totaling, analysis, and computation of averages. Now suppose each total is

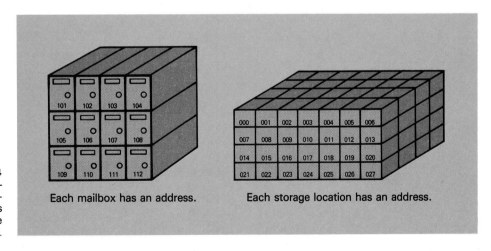

FIGURE 6-4
When writing data to or reading data from a primary-storage location, the address of that location must be specified.

Each mailbox has an address.   Each storage location has an address.

erased the first time you read it from the scratch pad. You may be able to complete one calculation using the totals. Any subsequent calculations using the (erased) totals will be difficult!

ACCESS TIMES AND CYCLE TIMES

The time the computer takes to locate and transfer data to or from storage is called *access time*. It varies for different storage media and devices. The time the computer takes to get ready to process the next request is called *cycle time*. It is uniform for each computer but varies from one kind of computer to another.

Because several storage media and devices are used within a computer system, we must be concerned about the access times of all of them. How fast can data be located and transferred? It makes little sense to attach an expensive, high-speed printer to a microcomputer. Conversely, it does little good to have a very-high-speed internal storage unit if the over-all system spends much of its time waiting for data transfers to and from slower-speed disk storage devices.

Internal data transfers are accomplished by electronic circuitry. Therefore, they are fast. The access times of the internal storage units of microcomputers and minicomputers are measured in millionths of a second, or *microseconds*. The access times of the internal storage units of large computers are measured in billionths of a second, or *nanoseconds*. So are cycle times. To appreciate how short such intervals of time are, consider a spaceship traveling at 100,000 miles per hour. In one microsecond, the spaceship would travel about $1\frac{3}{4}$ inches. In one nanosecond, it would travel about 1/1000th of $1\frac{3}{4}$ inches.

To increase the over-all speed of internal data transfers, computer system designers are continually trying to decrease the distances that the data must travel. That's why miniaturization is such an important consideration in memory development.

CORE STORAGE: HISTORICAL PERSPECTIVE

The internal storage units of most computers developed in the 1960s and 1970s were made of magnetic cores. Each core is a tiny ring of ferromagnetic material, a few hundredths of an inch in diameter. The core is pressed from a mixture of ferric oxide powder and other materials. Then it is baked in an oven. Its compact size is a decided advantage in a computer component. Another important advantage of the core is that it can be easily magnetized in a few microseconds. It retains that magnetism until it is deliberately changed.

Cores can be placed on a wire like beads on a string and then magnetized by sending a strong electrical current through the wire. The direction of the current determines the magnetic state, or polarity, of each core. The magnetic state of each core can be changed by reversing the direction of the current through the wire.

In core storage, the two possible states of a magnetic core are used to represent 0 and 1, plus and minus, positive and negative, on and off—conditions that are basic to a binary method of storing data. Because any specified location in storage must be instantly accessible, the cores are arranged so that any combination of ones (1s) and zeros (0s) representing a character can be written magnetically or read back when needed. (To review how data is represented in storage, look back at Chapter 3.)

To make possible the selection of an individual core in storage for reading or writing, two wires are run through each core at right angles to each other. (See Figure 6-5.) When half the current needed to magnetize a core is sent through each wire, only that core—the one at the intersection of the wires—is magnetized. No other core on either wire is affected. Generally, many cores are strung on one screen, or plane, of wires. Nevertheless, any one core in the screen can be selected for writing or reading without affecting any other core.

The flow of current through the wires is not constant; it is sent through each wire as an electrical pulse. When the direction of the pulse is changed, the state of the magnetic core is changed. This change induces a current in a *sense wire* that also runs through the center of the core. The pulse through this wire can be tested to determine whether the core contained a 1. Only one sense wire is needed for an entire plane of cores, because only one core at a time in any plane is tested for its magnetic state. The wire is therefore strung through all cores in the plane.

Data that is read from core storage is not destroyed because the computer automatically re-stores any data it reads. The process of reading a core that is set to 1 resets the core to 0. To retain the 1 bits, and therefore the data representation, the computer tries to write back 1 bits in all locations that it reads. A pulse in the *inhibit wire* (a fourth wire) suppresses writing in cores that previously contained 0s. The inhibit pulse in effect cancels out the writing pulse in one of the two wires used to magnetize the core. Like the sense wire, the inhibit wire also runs through every core in a plane. If it were not for the restoration of the 1 state in cores that were set to 1, the process of reading would be destructive. As we've seen, that could be disastrous.

Core technology has just about reached its physical limits. To make the cores more compact, and reading and writing faster, the diameters of both the cores and the wires over which they were strung have been reduced to a few

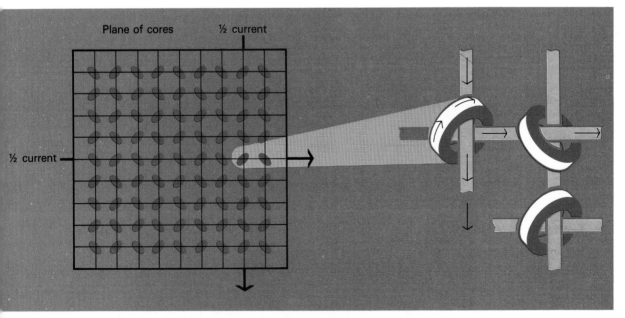

FIGURE 6-5 Tiny cores threaded on wires can be magnetized to represent and store data.

thousandths of an inch. They cannot be made much smaller. Although core-storage costs have dropped significantly as a result of improved manufacturing processes, little room is left for further improvement or cost reduction. Thus, cores today are giving way to other technologies.

SEMICONDUCTOR MONOLITHIC STORAGE

The primary storage of most recently developed computers consists of microminiature integrated circuits (IC's). They are designed to store data in addressable locations called *bit cells*. Each bit cell contains electrical components (storage capacitors, transistors, resistors, and so on). These components are capable of being in one of two states: conducting a current or not conducting a current. Therefore, the two states can be used to represent 0 and 1, plus and minus, positive and negative, on and off—just as with the two states of magnetic cores described above.

Since any specified location in primary storage must be instantly accessible, the bit cells are arranged so that any combination of 1s and 0s representing a character can be electronically written into or read from storage when needed. Other electronic circuits are used to locate the desired bit cells as x-y intersections on an imaginary grid (again, much like the magnetic cores discussed above). Even though magnetic-core memories have similar random-access capabilities, the acronym *RAM* has been commonly accepted to mean semiconductor random-access storage.

In a complicated manufacturing process, all of these electrical components are built into a single chip of semiconductor material. These chips make up the computer's internal storage unit, and also its control section and arithmetic/logic unit. They are called "monolithic" because each chip forms an indivisible building block of storage. Even the earliest silicon chips, only a little bigger than one magnetic core, could hold the equivalent of thousands of bit settings. (See Figure 6-6.) The size of a bit cell is incredible—30 of them lined up side by side are about as wide as a human hair!

We noted in Chapter 1 that electrical pulses can travel through circuitry at the speed of light but no faster. The more densely that electrical components are

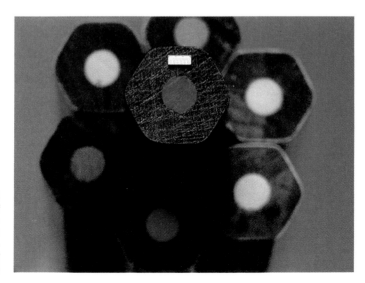

FIGURE 6-6
Compared to the ends of pencils, this chip looks tiny—yet it contributes to the high reliability of satellite communications. (*Courtesy NEC America Inc.*)

packed on a chip, the shorter the distances that pulses must travel, and the faster the computer's internal operating speed. For the same reason, designers are packing the chips themselves as densely as possible.

Intel Corporation introduced the first 1K chip back in 1971. (Here, *1K* means 1024 bits.) This was followed by the 4K chip in 1973. In 1977, 16K chips became available. In 1978, IBM announced several products containing 64K chips. In 1982, 64K chips only 62 percent the size of the original 64K chips were introduced. Slightly larger chips providing 128K or 256K of memory were also available.

Three kinds of semiconductor memories are available. They are bipolar, dynamic metal-oxide-semiconductor (MOS), and static MOS.

Bipolar storage is fast, but it has not yet achieved the packing densities per chip (and hence the lower costs) of MOS RAM's. It also consumes more power than equivalent storage made from either kind of MOS RAM.

Dynamic MOS RAM's require their contents to be "refreshed" periodically. Logic within the memory circuits or in the CPU checks each bit cell periodically to make sure that it is still strong enough to be read. Additional circuits are needed to make sure that the refreshing operations don't interfere with normal read and write operations.

Static MOS RAM's do not need to be refreshed. Even so, static RAM technology requires more on-chip components per bit cell than dynamic RAM technology does. It is easier to design with static RAM chips. They are most likely to be used in the internal storage units of minicomputers and microcomputers, since their higher per-chip cost is less important where small storage units are required.

Besides increased speed and reduced size, semiconductor monolithic storage offers the advantage of a truly nondestructive read. There is no need to write back data after it is read. Hence, the potential exists for shorter computer cycle times. Semiconductor storage is also easier to maintain than magnetic-core storage if an equipment malfunction occurs. Established diagnostic techniques for circuit analysis can be applied. However, unlike core storage, the semiconductor monolithic storage commonly used in computers is dependent on an uninterrupted power supply. Since the storage elements are circuits, a pulse is required to maintain their contents. Therefore, a loss of power is a loss of stored data and instructions. Such semiconductor monolithic storage is said to be *volatile*.

In contrast to core technology, semiconductor storage technology is in its infancy. Much of its potential is still undefined. The silicon chips can be designed and processed in a variety of ways. Because costs are likely to be reduced further as production becomes more mechanized, we can expect use of semiconductor storage to further increase.

BUBBLE MEMORIES

A "bubble" is actually a cylinder-shaped magnetic domain contained in a thin, crystalline magnetic film. Many of these microscopic bubbles appear, disappear, and move around on the film under the control of a separate conductor (magnetic field) mounted close to the film. The bubbles have a polarization opposite to that of the magnetic film on which they are contained. The presence of a bubble represents a 1; the absence of a bubble represents a 0. Again we see the binary form of representation so prevalent in electronic data processing.

Bubble memories are similar to core storage. They differ from semiconductor storage in that they are magnetic. This means that bubble memories are not volatile; they retain their contents even if the power supply is removed. Another important point about bubble memories is that they are a combination of random-access and sequential devices. It is possible to access randomly a block of data, but then the contents of the block must be read sequentially—a consequence of the shift-register construction used in their design. (See Figure 6-7.)

The first patent for a bubble memory was filed back in the middle 1960s, when researchers at AT&T's Bell Labs disclosed their work with magnetic bubble storage and pointed to garnet as a viable storage medium. In March 1977, Texas Instruments announced the first commercial bubble memory: a 1-inch-square chip that could hold 92K bits of data. A number of these chips were incorporated within their Silent 700-series Model 765, a 17-pound portable terminal. (See Figure 6-8.) The bubble memory allowed a user to enter data into the terminal throughout the day, then dial a central computer via an ordinary telephone to transmit the stored data later (say at night, when rates are lower). Prior to the introduction of the Model 765, portable data terminals could only be operated online (connected to the computer, under its control, and in direct communication with it).

As recently as yearend 1980, enthusiasm for bubble memories was still running high. However, by yearend 1982, three of the leaders in bubble-memory development—Rockwell International, Texas Instruments, and National Semiconductor—had terminated their development efforts. Throughout the industry, questions were rampant: Why? Were bubble memories to be or not to be? Were we at the end of a rainbow?

Stated simply, despite extensive efforts, bubble memories had not proved to be price-competitive against alternative products designed to provide large-volume storage. The technologies of dynamic RAM's and $5\frac{1}{2}$-inch disks (see below) had developed much faster. Both could provide equivalent storage capacity at a fifth of the cost or even less.

Although Texas Instruments has stopped working on bubble memories, the company has declared that its portable terminal "will continue as a product." Bubble memories are used by AT&T to store the data needed to tell you that "all circuits are busy, please call later." AT&T is also looking at emergency telephone

FIGURE 6-7
By design, bubble memory allows an individual block of data to be accessed randomly, then read sequentially until specific items are found. (*Courtesy IBM Corporation*)

switching systems for places where a temporary service is required, such as at major business meetings at remote sites or at large multiple-vendor exhibits and conferences.

Still other firms are looking at bubble memories as alternatives to the punched paper tapes used to direct numerically controlled machine tools. Bubbles are also being tested for use in storing oil and gas production data at wellheads. Experiments now underway to monitor home water or gas meters via statistics recorded in bubble memories and accessed via telephone lines may save much time and money expended by human meter readers.

In all these instances, the ruggedness and durability of bubble memories are important advantages. These characteristics are also important for portable terminals, not only in business but also in military applications. There is a future for bubble memories, but it is much more modest than once thought. Intel, Motorola, Bell Labs, and IBM (which make bubble memories primarily for their own use), as well as Hitachi and Fujitsu of Japan, are still involved.

FIGURE 6-8
A user can key data into the bubble memory of a portable terminal as events occur, then transmit that data to a computer when convenient. (*Courtesy Texas Instruments Incorporated/General Automotive Parts*)

ADD-ON MEMORIES

The term *add-on memory* is used to refer to an additional amount of primary storage acquired by a user installation to supplement the amount of primary storage initially obtained for a computer. Currently, most of these memories are designed for IBM computers. They are also usable with similar, interchangeable computers produced by other manufacturers – Amdahl's 470 V7 and V8, Four Phase System's 311 and 312, and National Advanced System's 7000 and 9000, for example. (These computers are said to be plug-compatible; their manufacturers are called *plug-compatible manufacturers*, or *PCM's*.) Add-on memories are also available for other widely used computers manufactured by firms such as National Cash Register (NCR) and Digital Equipment Corporation (DEC).

Why does a user installation need add-on memory? For any of several reasons. Perhaps the amount of work the user wants to accomplish has increased significantly since a particular computer was installed. Additional primary storage is needed to increase the number of jobs that can be processed concurrently or to decrease the time needed for certain large, complex jobs. Perhaps the kind of work that could be done is curtailed by the amount of primary storage available. For example, the system may not be able to process transactions entered by users at remote terminals. Perhaps the user is unable to obtain the amount of memory wanted or ordered from the computer manufacturer when the computer itself is installed. And so on.

Add-on memory may be acquired from the computer manufacturer or from another firm that specializes in add-on memories. Prominent firms within the latter group include Ampex, Cambridge Memories, Control Data, Dataram, Intel, and Mostek. (Such firms are also called PCM's, since they supply hardware that can be used with – is plug-compatible with – the hardware of another manufacturer.) The add-on memory is housed in a boxlike unit. The memory has its own power supply and is connected via cables to its host processor. Some PCM's offer special speed enhancements that actually enable a computer to perform faster (taking advantage of shorter access and cycle times possible with the add-on memory). Add-on memories from PCM's may sell for 40 percent less than equivalent amounts of memory from the computer manufacturers.

Three kinds of semiconductor add-on memories are available: bipolar, static MOS RAM, and dynamic MOS RAM. As noted earlier, bipolar is more costly and consumes more power than MOS RAM. Dynamic RAM is slower than static RAM because it has to be refreshed, but it is easier to build (and hence less expensive). The serviceability features of add-on memory units and the technical support provided by their vendors should be evaluated carefully by users who are considering memory alternatives.

ADD-IN MEMORIES

Unlike add-on memory, which is a physically separate component, *add-in memory* is plugged directly into the backplane, or bus, of a processor. For example, from 64K to 256K bytes of addressable primary storage may be included on a single board that plugs into an IBM 303X processor. Add-in memories are also available for microcomputers and small business computer systems. (See Figure 6-9.)

Add-in memories offer many of the advantages provided by add-on memories. Moreover, there is no need for connecting cables, interface logic, and redundant circuitry and power supplies. An add-in memory does not take up additional desk

FIGURE 6-9
A memory expansion board can be acquired to increase the primary-storage capacity of a small business computer system. (*Courtesy Datapoint Corporation*)

or floor space in the home, office, or central facility where the computer is installed. It may supplement or replace the internal storage unit of that computer.

Add-on memories have been around for some time. Add-in memories are a more recent development. In industry, the term *add-on memory* is sometimes used inclusively to refer to both types.

SECONDARY STORAGE

Some data-processing operations require more data than can be held in primary storage at one time. In such cases, primary storage is augmented by secondary, or auxiliary, storage.

For example, assume an automotive parts distributor maintains records for a warehouse inventory of 25,000 parts. Each part is identified by a 10-character number. Each part is stocked at one or more of 15 warehouse locations. At any time, some quantity of each part may (or may not) be available at each location. Other important facts about each part are the wholesale price per unit, whether volume discounts are available, the lead time required for reordering, and so on. Each of these facts about the part is an *item*. The complete set of items about one part is a *record*. The complete set of records for all parts is a *file*. (See Figure 6-10.)

Obviously, we don't want to keep the whole file in primary storage, just to be able to respond to one dealer's inquiry as to the closest warehouse with at least 20 fan belts of a particular type. Nor do we want to worry about whether or not the whole file will fit in primary storage each time the firm decides to stock a new type of part. So we create a machine-readable file, but we keep it in a secondary-storage device. Then, whenever an inquiry is received from a dealer, a stored program can access the file in secondary storage, read in the record for the part to be dealt with, and supply the needed information as output. When a new part is stocked, another stored program can add a new record to the file.

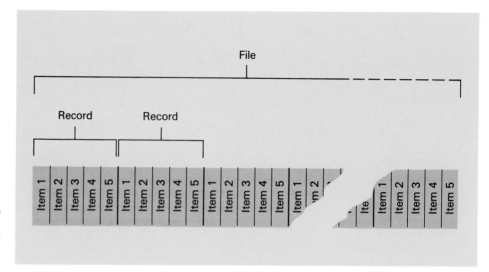

FIGURE 6-10
Data is commonly organized by grouping related items into a record and related records into a file.

In like manner, data files and programs not in use are kept in secondary storage in many EDP systems. From there, they can be transferred to primary storage when needed for processing. The secondary storage may be either of two types:

● *Sequential:* magnetic-tape, punched-card, and other devices that hold files which must be read in sequence from the beginning in order to read or write a desired record.

● *Direct:* magnetic-disk units and other direct-access storage devices (DASD's) that give immediate access to individual records; there is no need to read from the beginning of a file to find a desired record.

Secondary-storage devices extend the storage capability of a computer system beyond that of primary storage by providing large-capacity, lower-cost, slower-speed, but accessible storage. A computer installation may use both sequential and direct-access storage devices.

STORAGE AND DATA-PROCESSING METHODS

The two types of secondary storage—sequential and direct—correspond directly to the two primary methods of handling data: *sequential,* or *batch, processing* and *direct processing.* The user's needs determine which method of processing should be used. The method of processing, in turn, determines the type of secondary storage required.

Sequential Processing

In sequential processing, data is collected and stored in batches before being forwarded to the computer as input. Examples of data that may be handled in this manner are issues and receipts from inventory, accounts receivable, accounts payable, and employee work hours for payroll. These data records are called *transaction,* or *detail, records.* They form a *transaction* (or *detail*) *file.* The records in the file are arranged sequentially (sorted) according to part number, name, or some similar entry that is common to all of them. The portion of a record containing the entry or entries that determine the record's position in the file is called its *control field*, or *key*. All records in the file are positioned according to a predetermined sequence. The entries in the control fields of the various records are used to maintain the sequence.

For most applications, certain calculations must be performed on data items recorded in other fields of the transaction records. Additionally, most application processing also involves the updating of items within the company's *master records* (records of previous business activities) stored sequentially in *master files*. Therefore, both transaction and master records must be provided as input to a particular processing run. Furthermore, the sequence of the transaction records and the sequence of the master records must be the same. (See Figure 6-11.)

The outputs of a sequential processing run may include customer statements, employee paychecks, printed reports, or similar hard-copy information to be routed directly to users. A revised (updated, or new) master file is also part of the output; it will be used as input the next time the application is scheduled for processing. We call it a *turnaround file*. The old master file is generally kept for a fixed period as a backup file.

Sequential master files are often stored on magnetic tapes. They can also be stored on magnetic disks. As you'll soon see, there are many kinds of tape and disk devices.

Direct Processing

To appreciate the advantages of direct processing, think about searching for an entry in a large unabridged dictionary. Suppose you wanted to look up a particular word in that dictionary. How long would it take you to find it?

If you had to start reading from the beginning of the dictionary to find the word, you could expect to read, on the average, half the dictionary before you found it. Obviously, a much quicker approach is to look at the first letter of the word, go to that portion of the dictionary, look at succeeding letters of the word, and so on, until the exact word is found. Actually, it takes most people about 12 seconds to find a word in such a dictionary.

If the dictionary were stored on magnetic tape, which can only be read sequentially, the complete dictionary could be read in less than one minute. Note, however, that about half that time would be required to find any one word. (Even 30 seconds is a long time in electronic data processing.) In contrast, if the dictionary were stored using a direct method of organization on magnetic disk, the address of the location in which the desired word was stored would be available in the system. The word could be found instantaneously.

In direct processing, data is not collected in batches before it is processed. Usually, transaction records (transactions, for short) are forwarded to the computer as they occur. (See Figure 6-12.) The input device is online. Only the master records needed to supply data for, or receive data from, the transactions are actually read into primary storage during a run. Each of these records is located directly by means of its storage address. There is no need to read the other records in the master file.

Direct processing, like sequential processing, may produce several types of output. Frequently, one output is in the form of responses to the users entering transactions. Another may be a printed summary report of situations needing immediate attention, such as stock that must be recorded or bills that are due.

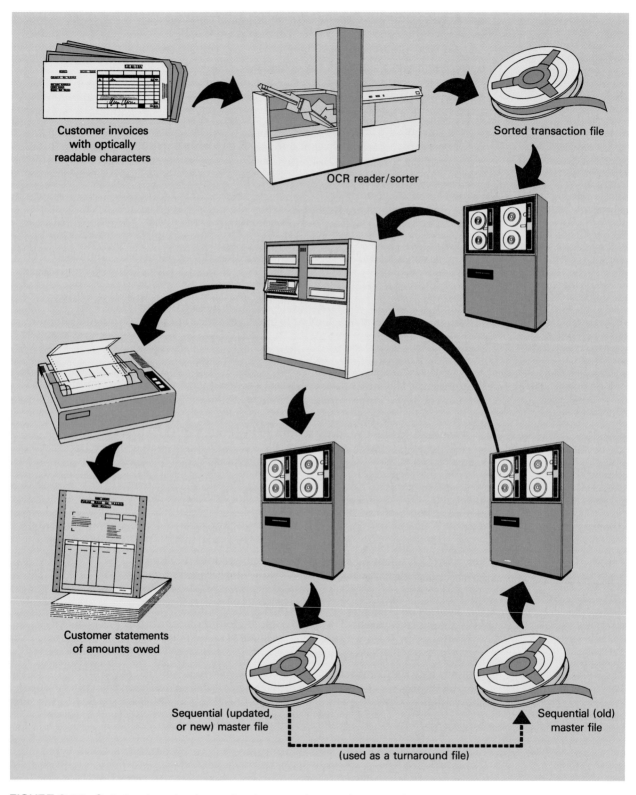

Customer invoices
with optically
readable characters

OCR reader/sorter

Sorted transaction file

Customer statements
of amounts owed

Sequential (updated,
or new) master file

Sequential (old)
master file

(used as a turnaround file)

FIGURE 6-11 Sorted customer invoices and customer master records serve as input to this sequential-processing application.

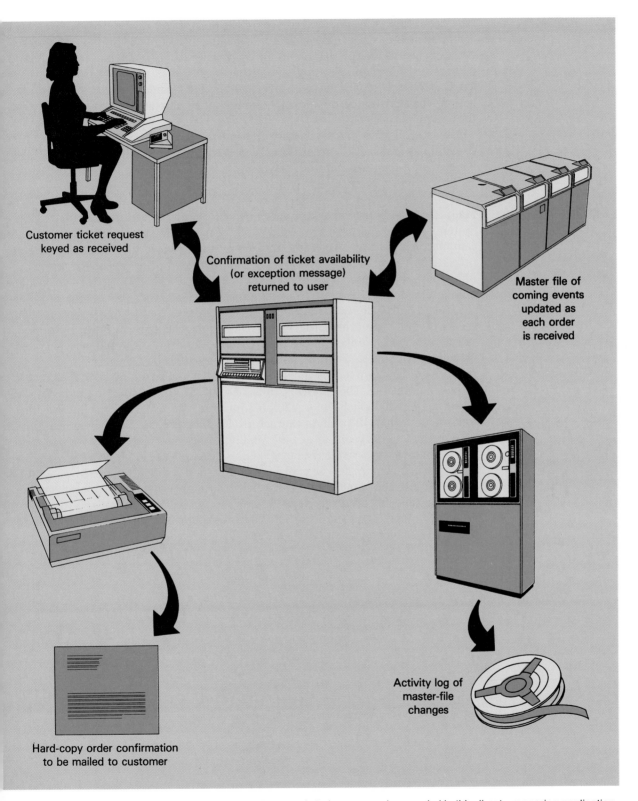

Customer ticket request
keyed as received

Confirmation of ticket availability
(or exception message)
returned to user

Master file of
coming events
updated as
each order
is received

Activity log of
master-file
changes

Hard-copy order confirmation
to be mailed to customer

FIGURE 6-12 Customer ticket requests cause master records to be accessed as needed in this direct-processing application.

Another output is the updated records of the master file. In updating records, the complete master file is not rewritten. Unchanged records remain as they were; updated records are rewritten in their original locations in the master file. When new records are added, they are either positioned appropriately between existing records or placed in an overflow area set aside for that purpose. An activity log showing before and after images of changed records may be written for backup purposes.

A master file on a DASD is current, as of the last transaction, and ready for processing. Transaction records to be processed against the file need not be batched, and they need not be sorted into a particular order before processing.

MAGNETIC TAPE Magnetic tape is an important secondary-storage medium in many computer systems. It may be used extensively for storing the intermediate results of computations during processing and for retaining large files of data between processing runs. In the latter case, the tape serves as a data-transfer or input/output medium as well as a storage medium. The data written as output onto a tape is read as input from the tape during another processing run. For example, a daily sales totals tape may be written as output by one program, then read as input by another program that arranges the sales in order by region, calculates average sales per region, checks for large discrepancies between actuals and quotas, and prints management-oriented sales reports.

Magnetic tape is often wound on individual reels. A reel may be 6, 7, $8\frac{1}{2}$, or $10\frac{1}{2}$ inches in diameter. The tape length is 200, 600, 1200, or 2400 feet accordingly. Most tapes are half-inch wide. A full $10\frac{1}{2}$-inch reel weighs about 4 pounds. It may contain more than 120 million characters (120 megabytes). This amount of data is equivalent to that contained on 1.5 million fully punched cards. Yet one tape reel of this size may cost less than $20. (See Figure 6-13.)

Magnetic tape may also be packaged in dust-resistant cartridges or cassettes. The cartridge-contained tape is threaded automatically when placed on the magnetic-tape unit that reads the data on the tape. A tape cassette is like those used on common tape recorders. Both tape cartridges and tape cassettes are used widely, especially on small EDP systems. They are compact, relatively inexpensive, and help to protect tapes from dust, humidity, temperature fluctuations,

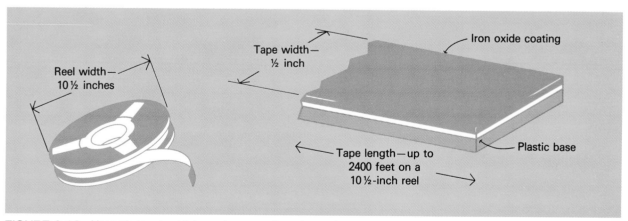

FIGURE 6-13 Magnetic tape is widely used as secondary storage in medium-size and large computer systems.

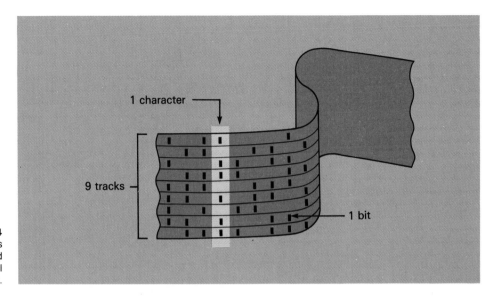

FIGURE 6-14
Individual data characters are stored as magnetized areas (bits) across parallel tracks or 9-track tape.

and other environmental factors that could destroy the tape contents or cause read or write errors during processing.

Data Representation

Data is recorded on magnetic tape as magnetized spots called *bits*. The bits are positioned in parallel channels, or *tracks*, that run the length of the tape. The bits representing a particular character are aligned vertically in rows across the tracks. (See Figure 6-14.) The spacing between the rows is generated automatically during the write operation. It varies with the *tape density*, that is, the number of characters written per inch. A common density is 1600 characters per inch (cpi). Tapes that hold 6250 cpi are being used increasingly. From the user's point of view, a higher density offers several advantages. More data can be stored on a given length of tape. The data can be written or read with greater effective speed since less tape motion is required.

As Figure 6-14 suggests, magnetic tapes in common use today are 9-track tapes. Data is written on these tapes using any one of several coding schemes. Usually, EBCDIC or ASCII is used. (We discussed both of these coding schemes in Chapter 3.) In any row on the tape, eight of the nine tracks are used for the bit combinations that represent a particular letter, number, or special character. The ninth track is used for error-checking purposes.

Writing on and Reading from Magnetic Tape

Data is written to or read from magnetic tape by a magnetic-tape unit. The unit may be about 6 feet high, or it may be table height. It houses a tape drive. When a tape is to be written on or its contents read, an operator mounts it on the drive vertically or horizontally as appropriate. An installation that uses magnetic tape usually has banks of several magnetic-tape units. (See Figure 6-15.)

A magnetic-tape unit reads or writes data as the tape moves past a read/write head. The tape is always in motion during reading and writing. It moves, for example, at speeds such as 25, 50, 75, 125, or 200 inches per second, depending on the unit. In addition, tapes can be rewound, backspaced, and skipped ahead

FIGURE 6-15
Magnetic-tape units are
included in many users' computer systems. (*Reproduced
with permission of AT&T*)

under control of a stored program. Rewind speeds are as high as 640 inches per second with some units. (Rewinding a full 2400-foot reel takes only 45 seconds.) Some tape units also have the ability to read backward. If a tape unit normally moves the tape from left to right to read, it moves the tape from right to left to read backward.

On magnetic tape, writing is destructive; when new data is written, old data is destroyed. Reading is nondestructive; the same data can be read again and again. If the application needs warrant, the data recorded on a tape can be retained indefinitely. The data can also be erased by the magnetic-tape unit and the tape reused for other data.

An application program cannot cause a record to be written to a tape, then read from that tape, then read again, then written to it, and so on (repetitively and at random) during a single processing run. At any given time, a tape is "opened" either for input or for output (but not both). Remember, records can only be written or read sequentially from magnetic tape. Each record (except the first one) is written or read after the one before it.

For magnetic-tape units, the major performance considerations are the speed at which tape is moved past the read/write head and the tape density (cpi). Both considerations affect the rate at which characters can be written or read. If a tape moves at 200 inches per second, and data is written on the tape at 6250 cpi, then up to 200×6250, or 1.25 million, characters can be transferred from the tape in one second. In common usage, however, the theoretical maximum and the effective maximum are not the same. Let's see why.

Assume a weekly payroll program is run as one step in calculating employee wages and printing paychecks. The program needs access to data recorded in the company's employee master file: year-to-date (YTD) gross pay, YTD federal income tax withheld, YTD social security (FICA) withheld, and so on. Assume the file is stored on magnetic tape at 6250 cpi.

In this application, the records on the master file are not simply read into primary storage as fast as possible. Instead, individual blocks consisting of one or more employee records are read into primary storage as needed during processing. This means that the magnetic-tape unit operates in a start/stop fashion. Short areas of blank space (*interblock gaps*, or *IBG's*) are left between consecutive blocks on the tape (see Figure 6-16). They allow time for the tape to get up to the speed required for reading or writing (or to come to a stop after reading or writing has occurred). Tape drives that operate in this manner are called *start/stop tape drives.*

During the past few years, much time and money have been spent developing disk storage technologies and devices. Some persons have begun to assume that disks will totally replace tapes; they say "tape is on the way out." That's not likely. Many application programs and much system software are designed and coded to process data stored on magnetic-tape files. Tape drives are reliable and well-standardized. Tapes are compact, lightweight, and readily transportable (even mailable). Because tape drives are standardized, a tape created as output on one computer system can be read as input on another computer system—even a system produced by a different manufacturer. Low-cost tapes on reels, in cartridges, or in cassettes are readily available for computers of all sizes.

Instead of making tapes obsolete, disk developments have led to tape developments. Disk storage devices offer many advantages to users, but they also have disadvantages. One is apt to be cost. To insure that data is not lost if a disk becomes damaged, if a disk storage drive malfunctions, or if a program or procedural error causes data to be overwritten unintentionally, users must make backup copies of disk files. To store the data a second time on another disk or to retain data on disk for historical purposes may be prohibitively expensive. An alternative available to users is to store the backup or historical copy of data on quarter-inch or half-inch tape. The writing (copying) of the data to tape and the subsequent reading (if necessary) are done by a *streaming tape drive.* As the

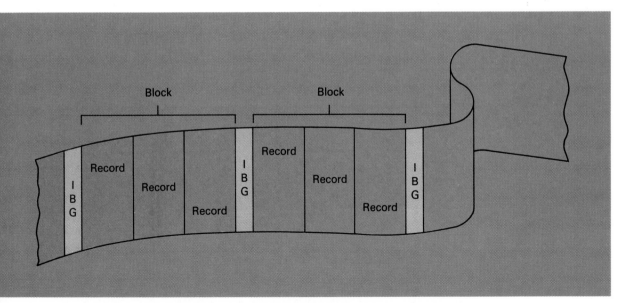

FIGURE 6-16   During processing, blocks of three records each are read from this employee master file.

word *streaming* suggests, this type of drive does not write or read data as blocks of records. The program that directs the computer to read or write the data does not deal with the data in a meaningful way. Instead, the data is simply written to tape as a continuous stream, or flow. It can be read back into storage and rewritten (re-stored) to disk in like manner.

Streaming tapes that can hold 10 or 20 megabytes of data are designed to meet the needs of small system users. Tapes that can hold from 200 to 350 megabytes of data are intended for large system users. These streaming drives are less expensive than comparable start/stop drives because they need not contain the costly electromechanical components needed for frequent tape starting and stopping operations. Some disk storage vendors are including a cartridge-type tape backup unit within the physical unit that houses the disk drive it is intended to support. (See Figure 6-17.) This packaging is especially attractive to users installing systems in environments where compactness and good looks count.

MAGNETIC DISK   In 1956, just 10 years after the invention of the stored-program computer, IBM introduced the magnetic-disk technology that helped to spin the world rapidly into the Computer Age. As mentioned in Chapter 1, the IBM 350 magnetic-disk file of its 305 RAMAC system was a huge creation, but it was also the first use of disks as a means of storing computer-readable data for subsequent use—an approach that has not yet been supplanted.

A magnetic-disk storage unit looks simple enough. It's a box or a group of boxes. Inside each box is at least one disk storage drive. A certain number of read/write heads are part of the drive. One of the heads writes data to, or reads data from, a magnetic disk that spins beneath it. This means that one or more magnetic disks are also inside the box. They resemble phonograph records, but they are really storehouses for programs and data.

FIGURE 6-17
Backing up important data files on disk is easy when the files can be copied onto tapes in removable tape cartridges in the same device. (*Courtesy Datapoint Corporation*)

Because there are so many kinds of disk storage units, we're going to discuss them from a user's point of view: What kinds of storage needs does each satisfy? Before doing so, we look briefly at how data is represented on disk. We also look at how reading and writing are accomplished.

Data Representation

A conventional (hard, or rigid) disk is a thin metal platter. The platter is coated on both sides with a magnetic recording material such as iron oxide. Data is stored as magnetized areas in tracks that form concentric circles on the surface of the disk. (See Figure 6-18.) The combination of bits that represents a particular character is not spread across several tracks (as is the case with magnetic tape). Instead all the bits representing one character are written serially, one after another, on a selected track. The bits representing the next character (assuming there is another one in the data record) are written immediately following it, on the same track. Remember, however, that data records are not necessarily stored sequentially on a magnetic disk. They may be, but they don't have to be. Individual storage locations on the disk surface have assigned storage addresses. If necessary, individual records can be written to, or read from, these storage locations directly—without writing or reading any records that immediately precede or follow the desired record on the disk surface.

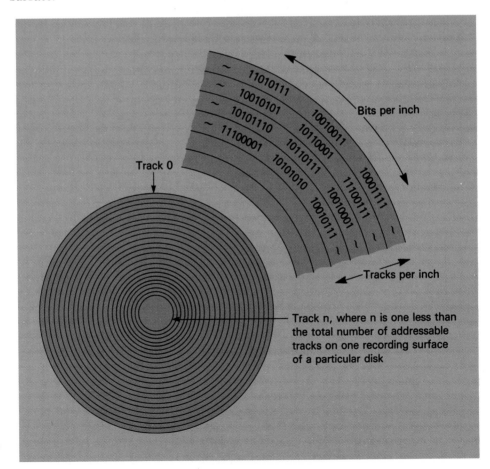

FIGURE 6-18
Data is stored as adjacent magnetized areas (bits) in concentric circles, or tracks, on the surface of a magnetic disk.

Note in Figure 6-18 that our comparison of a disk to a phonograph record is not perfect. The tracks on a disk are independent. They do not form a continuous spiral like the groove in a phonograph record. The same amount of data can be recorded on each track, even though the tracks near the center of the disk are smaller. The bits on these inner tracks are simply packed together more closely. As with magnetic tape, any of several coding schemes may be used for data representation. Again, EBCDIC and ASCII are common.

A flexible (soft, or floppy) disk, also called a *diskette*, is made of a soft Mylar plastic. The surface of the disk is coated with iron oxide. The coated disk is then packaged in a paper or plastic envelope. When the disk is to be used, the entire envelope is inserted into a disk storage unit. (See Figure 6-19.) The disk rotates inside the protective covering. The read/write head of the disk drive reads or writes the data when the disk surface is exposed to it through the slot in the covering. As on hard disks, the data is recorded in concentric circles, or tracks. In general, the storage capacities of flexible disks are lower than those of hard disks. Both the bits per inch and the tracks per inch are fewer. Flexible disks also cost less. They are designed to meet different data-storage needs than are met by high-volume hard-disk storage units.

Writing on and Reading from Magnetic Disk

When data is to be written to or read from magnetic disk, the disk storage drive must be powered on. The disk (or disks) in the unit must be rotating at the speed required for writing or reading. Data can be read from a disk repeatedly. When data is written on a disk, it replaces any data previously recorded on the same area of the disk surface.

Figure 6-20 shows the comb-type access mechanism and disk pack of a common disk storage unit. To operate on a particular track of a recording surface, the access mechanism is moved horizontally on a line to or from the center of the disk

FIGURE 6-19
The user selects a diskette and inserts it into a drive slot to make a particular program or data file available to the computer during processing. (*Courtesy NCR Corporation*)

FIGURE 6-20
Many disk drives have comb-
type access mechanisms
with read/write heads that
move above the recording
surfaces of disks to read or
write data. (*Courtesy Sperry
Corporation*)

pack. All the read/write heads are moved at once, even though only one is used at
a time. The access mechanism may, for example, be positioned over the 70th
track on each recording surface. Together, all the tracks below the read/write
heads at that position make up the 70th *cylinder* of the disk pack.

Now suppose that data has to be read from another track on one of the
recording surfaces. The access mechanism must be moved to position the
read/write heads above that track. This movement is called *head positioning*.
Naturally, the time required to move the access mechanism depends upon the
distance it must be moved.

After the access mechanism has been positioned, the head that is going to read
or write data is switched on. This *head switching* is simply activating an
electrical current, so the time required is negligible.

Finally, the disk-pack rotation positions the particular data to be read beneath
the activated read/write head. The time required for this movement is called
rotational delay, or *latency*. How long it takes is determined in part by the
rotational speed of the disk. Current rotational speeds range from 5 to 1000
revolutions per second, depending on the design of the particular unit. An
average of one-half revolution is used in estimating the time required for
rotational delay, because, in reality, one complete rotation, part of a rotation, or
no rotation (if the activated read/write head is positioned directly over the area
that contains the desired data) may be required.

After rotational delay, the record can be read or written. The time required for
data transfer (reading or writing data) is based on the length of the record
transferred and the transfer rate of the disk storage drive.

Actually, it is difficult for humans to comprehend the speed at which reading or
writing from disks takes place. All the actions we have just mentioned—access-
mechanism movement, head switching, rotational delay, and data transfer—

may be required to read data. The total time required for all these actions is referred to as the *access time* of the disk storage unit. Access times range widely—say, from 150 to 275 thousandths of a second (*milliseconds*) on floppy disk drives and from 20 to 175 milliseconds on other drives.

Floppy Disk Drives   Eight-inch flexible disks (diskettes) were developed by IBM in the early 1970s—not as a secondary-storage medium for small computer systems but as an inexpensive means of providing programming for its large computers. (For the discussion of small prewritten disk cartridges whose contents were read into reloadable control storage, see "Primary Storage" earlier in this chapter.) Another early use of flexible diskettes was in data entry. As we saw in Chapter 4, even an early 8-inch diskette could hold 242,000 data characters—the equivalent of more than 3000 punched cards. Today, data can be stored on both sides of double-sided diskettes. Data can be recorded at twice the density per track on double-density diskettes. Such 8-inch diskettes are the favored data-storage medium on numerous data-entry systems, word-processing systems, and micro-computer systems. The storage capacities of these diskettes range from 256,000 to 1,500,000 characters. The most commonly used ones hold about 500,000 characters, the rough equivalent of about 250 typed pages.

In 1976, Shugart Associates introduced what was to become the workhorse of desktop computers and personal computers: the $5\frac{1}{4}$-inch flexible disk unit, commonly known as the *mini-floppy*. Today, double-sided $5\frac{1}{4}$-inch diskettes hold about 250,000 characters. More expensive, top-of-the-line $5\frac{1}{4}$-inch diskettes can hold 1,000,000 characters.

The advantages of flexible disks include ease of handling, ease of storage, and portability. The disks are often used on distributed computer systems—in offices, laboratories, shop rooms, and the like. When not in use, the disks can be locked in secure cabinets, thereby protecting the data from both accidental and intentional harm or misuse. Since the drives are standardized, the disks are readily available from numerous vendors. A disk written as output of one system can be read as input on another. Furthermore, the disks are relatively inexpensive and reusable. Most vendors offer volume discounts when the diskettes are purchased in quantities.

The limitations of floppy disk drives are inherent in the technology on which they are based. As with magnetic tape, the head that reads or writes data on the disk actually rides on the recording surface during reading or writing. This causes friction and wear and limits the disk's rotation speed to about 300 revolutions per minute. The Mylar plastic disk itself expands and contracts with changes in temperature and humidity. Therefore, the tracks on the disk must be far enough apart to allow for changes in dimension. This limits the amount of data that can be stored.

Looking at things from an operational point of view, flexible disks can become a user nightmare. Many small businesses soon find that their data-storage requirements exceed their data-storage space. Up to a dozen flexible disks may be needed to store the records of, say, 500 customers in an accounts-receivable master file. Most businesses also have inventory records, purchase-order records, sales records, vendor records, employee records, and so forth. (See Figure 6-21.) A system may have two floppy disk drives, but each drive can hold only one disk at a time. The computer may be constantly flashing instructions to the user to

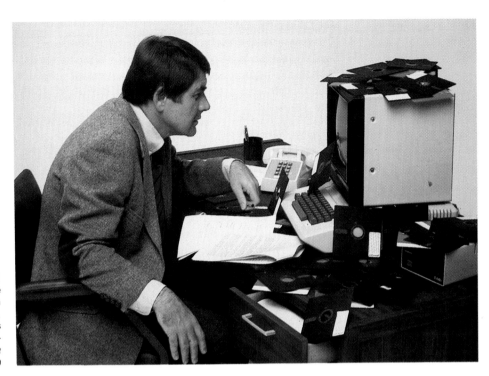

FIGURE 6-21
Diskettes are great, but if the user's needs for program and data storage expand, keeping track of what's where can be a major undertaking. (*Courtesy Corona Data Systems*)

replace the disk on the current input drive. Handy-dandy dust-tight storage cabinets for flexible disks are sold by many vendors. But what does the user do when there are no more desktops to put them on (or cabinet space, or floor space)? Flexible disks are an important storage medium, but demands for ever greater storage capacities have led to further developments.

Winchester Disk Drives

Does the term *Winchester* bring a picture to your mind? Strangely enough, the term does indeed refer to the Old West's famous Winchester 30-30 rifle. An early prototype disk storage unit contained two drives. Each drive could hold 30 megabytes of data. The product code name "Winchester" was a natural consequence.

In 1973, IBM introduced the first Winchester drive, known as the IBM 3340 Direct-Access Storage Facility. The drive uses 14-inch disks made of highly polished aluminum and covered with a thin coating of iron oxide. Not only the disk but also the vertical shaft, access mechanism, and read/write heads of the disk storage drive are enclosed in a removable sealed cartridge. This approach eliminates head-to-disk alignment problems and reduces the exposure of recording surfaces to airborne contaminants. It also satisfies a primary objective of the design—high reliability.

Unlike the read/write heads in floppy disk units, the heads of a Winchester drive do not touch disk surfaces when reading or writing. As the disks spin up to speed, the heads literally take off and "fly" a few thousandths of an inch above the disks on a cushion of air created by the disks' spinning motion. The disks can spin at 3600 revolutions per minute. When the disk rotation slows, the heads "land" on the disk surfaces. The lubrication on the disks prevents damage to the head, disks, or data. More bits can be written on a track and less space is required between tracks than on comparable conventional disk storage units or on flexible disk drives. Recently announced Winchester drives with several enclosed 14-inch disks can hold up to 330 megabytes of data. On units like the 3340, the sealed cartridges are removable. On other units, the cartridges are fixed (i.e., they cannot be removed).

Shugart Associates announced the first mini-Winchester, which uses 8-inch disks, in 1979. Disk storage units of this type are best suited for use with minicomputers and other small and medium-size computers. Today, mini-Winchesters with storage capacities ranging up to 85 megabytes are available from many vendors. Some of the units have removable cartridges. Others have permanently mounted disks encased together with other components in a boxlike structure. (See Figure 6-22.)

The micro-Winchester, which uses $5\frac{1}{4}$-inch disks, was introduced by Seagate Technology in late 1980. Here at last was a disk storage unit that addressed the online data storage needs of small business users. The unit may be packaged with other components of a computer system, or it may be obtained later.

Even the simplest $5\frac{1}{4}$-inch Winchester disks can hold about 2,500,000 characters, the rough equivalent of about 1250 typed pages. A drive with four of these disks provides up to 10 megabytes of online storage. From a cost point of view, such a Winchester drive may cost three times as much as a drive that holds one 8-inch flexible disk, but it may provide 20 times as much space for data. Backup copies of the data are usually retained on flexible disks or on tapes written and read by streaming tape drives. As on the 14-inch and mini-Winchesters described above, the disks on a micro-Winchester drive may be encased in the unit or packaged in a sealed cartridge that is removable.

FIGURE 6-22
A 14-inch Winchester drive (left) is designed for large system users; an 8-inch drive (right) is suitable for medium-size and small system environments. (*Courtesy Kennedy Company*)

Conventional Disk Drives

As mentioned earlier, IBM's 305 RAMAC was the first system to have a disk storage unit. It housed the first conventional disk drive, as we are using the term here. The 24-inch disks of the IBM 305 and subsequent drives gave way to 14-inch disks in the IBM 1311, marketed in 1962. Thereafter, 14-inch disks became the standard of the computer industry. Comb-like access mechanisms like the one in Figure 6-20 were used to access the disks. As on Winchester drives, the read/write heads float slightly above the disk surfaces. On some units, the disks are fixed; they cannot be removed from the drives. Other units have removable disk packs. An operator can remove such a pack from the drive on which it is mounted and put another pack in its place. This feature allows different data to be made available as input to the computer or provides online storage space on which output can be written during processing.

Surveys of medium-size and large computer users show that their requirements for online storage are growing at rates of 45 percent to 60 percent per year. Manufacturers are investing much time and money in responding to these requirements. Their objectives are to allow more data to be stored in less space and to help users get at that data faster. Through technological advancements, the storage capacities and access times of disk storage units have been improved dramatically. Disk storage units with maximum storage capacities ranging from 400 to 635 megabytes are common. A large computer installation may have several hundreds of these units. As with magnetic tape, in actual usage some storage space is used for gaps between consecutive blocks of records. Space is also used for track addresses, record keys, and other information needed to complete direct read and write operations. The increased benefits to users are obvious. IBM's top-of-the-line disk storage unit, the IBM 3380 Direct-Access Storage Device (DASD), has a maximum capacity of 2,520,975,600 characters (2520 megabytes; also expressed as 2.52 billion bytes, or *gigabytes*). That's the rough equivalent of about 374,330 typed pages—a stack of paper 132 feet high! In the 1960s, it cost $130 to store one million characters of data on disk. Today, the cost is less than $1.

To provide very fast access to critical or often-used data, some disk storage units are designed with fixed read/write heads over a few tracks on each disk surface. (Here, *fixed* means unmovable and describes the heads; it does not mean nonremovable, as when describing the disks above.) When accessing data on these tracks, there is no need for access-mechanism movement. Because there must be one head for each track (rather than one head that moves from track to track on each surface), this design tends to increase the over-all cost of the disk storage unit. The access-time/cost tradeoff is one that users are willing to make for some applications.

When disk manufacturers increase the number of bits that can be stored per inch and the number of tracks per inch on a disk, they are providing a basis for faster access times as well as for increased storage capacities. A statement made early in the chapter about the speed of internal data transfer applies here also: The shorter the distance that data must travel, the faster the data transfer can be accomplished. Access times of disk storage units are measured in milliseconds rather than in microseconds or nanoseconds (as is the case with internal storage units). That's because the movement of physical parts is involved, rather than simply the motion of electrons. The over-all efficiency of a computer system depends on the performance characteristics and frequency of interactions of all its components.

MASS STORAGE   Through technological advancements, primary-storage components with increasingly higher densities have been developed. These developments have led to EDP systems with large primary-storage capacities. The larger the amount of primary storage available, the greater the number of tasks that can be accomplished within the system. This increased capacity in turn leads to increased requirements for online storage so that programs and data will be available to the CPU whenever they are needed during processing.

One obvious alternative is to keep all programs and data in primary storage, but we have seen that this approach is not feasible as yet. A second alternative is to keep all programs and data in online storage devices. DASD's seem preferable, because we can access directly any program or data file in a DASD. Like main storage, however, DASD's are expensive. Further, they take up lots of space in a computer rooom. A reel of magnetic tape costs significantly less than a comparable area on a magnetic disk, but data on magnetic tape can only be accessed sequentially. Many magnetic-tape units (or repeated mounting and demounting of tape reels by operators) are required to make programs and data consistently available when needed during processing.

A third alternative is feasible at some large computer installations. (It is really a variation of the second alternative above.) Vast amounts of programs and/or data are stored on magnetic tape. The mounting and demounting of tapes is under system—not operator—control, however. When needed, a program or data is read onto a magnetic disk for subsequent transfer to the CPU. With some systems, the data can be read from the tape directly into the CPU, but at a slower rate, of course. The hardware and the software that together make such operations possible are called a *mass storage system*, or *MSS*.

Three products based on this alternative are the IBM 3850 Mass Storage System, Control Data's 38500, and Masstor's M860. They provide up to 472, 16, and 440 gigabytes of online storage, respectively. We can look briefly at the 3850 to understand how these systems work. The same approach is used by all.

Data and programs are stored within the 3850 on fist-sized data cartridges. (See Figure 6-23.) Each cartridge contains a spool of magnetic tape about 3 inches wide and 770 inches long. Data is written on the tape in the same format as it is written on disk packs used with IBM 3330 disk storage drives. Each cartridge can hold up to 50 megabytes of data. All cartridges under control of the system are physically within the 3851 Mass Storage Facility of the 3850. Within the 3851, the data cartridges are stored in a honeycomb-like arrangement of cells. There can be two 3851s in the system. Each can contain up to 4720 cartridges. Hence, up to 472 gigabytes ($2 \times 4720 \times 50$ million $= 472$ billion bytes) of online storage are provided for.

When a program calls for a certain file or portion of a file, one of two cartridge accessors of a 3851 retrieves the needed cartridge from its cell and mounts it at a read/write station. The cartridge is opened, and the contents of the tape are transferred to a disk pack on a 3330 disk storage drive for immediate use. This process is called *staging*. When the data is no longer needed for processing, and the space on the disk pack is needed for another file, any new or updated data is written back onto the cartridge. The cartridge is returned to its home storage cell in the 3851. This process is called *destaging*.

These mass storage systems provide relatively inexpensive storage (from 0.00002¢ per bit to 0.00026¢ per bit). Of course, not all users need them or can afford the total mass storage system cost (from $500,000 upward). A large

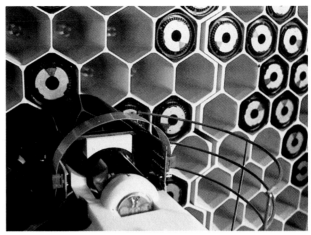

FIGURE 6-23 MSS data cartridges are retrieved from honeycomb-like cells and their contents copied onto disks as needed during processing. (*Courtesy IBM Corporation*)

insurance company may need to keep the records of millions of policyholders up-to-date and available for reference. A large bank must be able to access data about long-term and short-term loans, credit-card accounts, savings plans, time deposits, and so on – all of which can be kept on the MSS. (In contrast, data about checking and savings accounts that must be referred to daily should probably not be kept on the MSS.) Government agencies and computer service companies that sell processing time, do processing for other firms, or make large collections of data available for reference via nationwide communication networks are potential users of MSS. Compactness, elimination of manual handling, data security through password-protection programming, and protection from physical hazards such as water, fire, and fumes – in addition to storage economy – are among the advantages provided.

CHAPTER SUMMARY

1. An EDP system has both primary and secondary storage.

2. Primary storage is provided in the internal storage unit. While the storage capacities of these units are increasing, their physical sizes and costs are decreasing significantly.

3. The internal storage units of computers developed in the 1960s and 1970s were made of magnetic cores. The two possible states of each core were used in binary methods of storing data.

4. Today's computers have semiconductor monolithic memories consisting of integrated circuit (IC) chips. Microminiature bit cells on the chips contain electrical components whose conducting and nonconducting states are used to represent data.

5. Bubble memories are not price-competitive for large-volume storage, but their ruggedness and durability make them especially suitable for portable terminals and for some business and military applications.

6. Add-on and add-in memories are acquired by some users to supplement the primary storage initially obtained for their computers.

7. Secondary storage may be either sequential or direct. Sequential, or batch, processing and direct processing, respectively, are used to process the stored data.

8. Magnetic tape is an important secondary-storage medium. Data is recorded (written) as magnetized spots on the tape and read sequentially as many times as needed by start/stop or streaming tape drives.

9. Magnetic disks can provide either sequential or direct storage. The data is recorded in concentric circles, or tracks, on the surface of a disk by a read/write head of the disk drive.

10. Flexible, or floppy, disks are made of a soft Mylar plastic. Their speeds and capacities are limited, but they offer ease of handling, ease of storage, and portability.

11. Not only the disks but also the vertical shaft, access mechanism, and read/write heads of a Winchester drive are enclosed in a removable sealed cartridge or encased in a boxlike structure. A Winchester drive offers greater storage capacity than can be provided on floppy disks, and has high reliability.

12. Conventional, or hard, disk storage units satisfy medium-size and large computer users' ever-growing requirements for online storage. A mass storage system, or MSS, may provide additional safe, economical online storage at very large computer installations.

DISCUSSION QUESTIONS

1. Distinguish between primary storage and secondary storage.

2. Why is storage capacity so important in a computer system?

3. Distinguish between destructive and nondestructive operations. Give examples of each.

4. What characteristics of magnetic cores make them especially suitable for use as primary-storage components?

5. Compare the capabilities and structure of semiconductor monolithic circuitry with magnetic-core technology.

6. For what uses is bubble memory especially appropriate, and why?

7. Give at least three reasons why a user installation may decide to acquire add-on memory.

8. Describe how the data of a restaurant, public library, or educational facility might be organized into items, records, and files.

9. Would you use sequential or direct processing for the following data-processing applications? Justify your answers.
    (a) Printing of employee payroll checks
    (b) Maintaining up-to-date control of inventory
    (c) Preparation of monthly budget report
    (d) Responding to management inquiry about current vs budgeted expense

(e) Solving a mathematical equation submitted from a terminal

(f) Calculating and printing customer statements

(g) Updating an accounts-receivable file

10. Compare and contrast the use of tape with the use of disk as a secondary-storage medium.

11. Why might a user installation have both magnetic-tape and magnetic-disk drives?

12. What actions that occur during reading and writing of data on a magnetic disk have a bearing on access time?

13. (a) What are the distinguishing characteristics of Winchester drives?
    (b) Describe user situations where Winchester drives may be appropriate.

14. (a) Show how a mass storage system works.
    (b) What advantages does this approach offer?

7

PROCESSING DATA

No one would deny that the pace of human life has accelerated, particularly in our Western culture. It is also clear that the complexity of our lives has grown rapidly in recent decades. There are simply more things to do—more things that *can* be done as well as more things that *must* be done. Some of these are opportunities for more enjoyment in life; others are requirements for the safety, progress, or even continuation of life. Some of these tasks are so time-consuming, so demanding, or so boring that humans no longer can or want to perform them. Microprocessors come to our rescue!

Microprocessors can supplement and sharpen our powers of observation and our abilities to control interactions otherwise beyond our senses. They can monitor microfine tolerances and highly precise processes—even those used in their own manufacture.

Microprocessors connected to sensing devices are being used to test the efficiency of newer, energy-saving light bulbs being developed by General Electric. On a grander scale, the Westinghouse Electrical Energy Management System conserves energy by monitoring demands, scheduling, and setting priorities for large industrial operations.

Microprocessors are also being used, in conjunction with lasers and video terminals, in precision machining of parts. They can be used to control devices measuring events that occur in picoseconds. A computer-aided scanning electron microscope can help save lives in the testing and manufacture of pharmaceutical products.

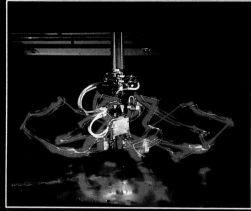

Courtesy IBM Corporation

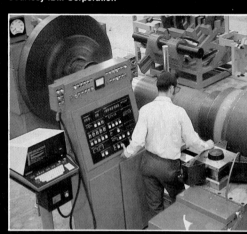

Courtesy Westinghouse Electric Corporation

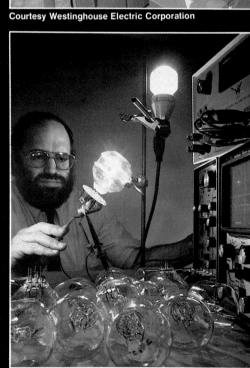

Courtesy General Electric
Research and Development Center

Courtesy Westinghouse Electric Corporation

Courtesy General Electric Research and Development Center

Courtesy Lawrence Berkeley Laboratory

Courtesy Burroughs Wellcome, Research Triangle Park, N.C.

A magnetometer on the ground at the Cerro Prieto geothermal field in Mexico can measure small fluctuations in the earth's magnetic field; it can also be used in exploring for oil, gas, and valuable mineral deposits.

Future engineers and other students can be taught about computer graphics with the help of the dome-covered "Terrapin" device, directed via microprocessors. Weather maps can be drawn with "inhuman" precision by microprocessor-guided devices. The maps, of course, are based on data collected and interpreted with computer assistance.

Marine navigation can be made simpler and safer through training, and microprocessors can make that training much more effective. Computer-simulated "live-action" graphics can portray various conditions and situations for hands-on training. The trainee can get immediate simulated feedback on decisions made and actions taken at the helm.

Some of the most unsuspected or unnoticed uses of microprocessors occur around us in everyday life. Many bowling alleys, for instance, have electronic game-monitoring devices that allow everyone to follow the action without that disliked scorekeeping duty. Some of our home appliances, such as microwave ovens, contain microprocessors to control temperatures and cooking times . . . maybe allowing for an extra game at the bowling alley!

Courtesy Lawrence Berkeley Laboratory

Courtesy Sperry Corporation

© Ellis Herwig/Stock, Boston

Courtesy Genisco Computers Corp.

Courtesy Texas Instruments Incorporated

Courtesy Motorola Inc.

Courtesy Motorola Inc.

7 | PROCESSING DATA

The computer is the most significant new product of the twentieth century. It is not a luxury; it is a necessity. By the year 2001, nearly everyone will have not just one, but several. There may be only one comparable product—the automobile.

In its early years, the automobile was a technological mystery to most people. Carburetors, fuel pumps, distributors, and the like were magical components of that mystery. Starting a car, changing gears, and steering were remarkable feats attempted only by the daring! Yet, today, in many countries, nearly everyone of high school age or above knows how to drive a car. Many know how to fix or rebuild one.

So it is with computers. In their early years, the mid-1940s through the mid-1960s, computers were a rarity, known only to a few researchers, scientists, and educators. In the 1970s, as people became more aware of them, they were greeted, not with joy, but with doubt, fear, and resentment. Even while some people were trying to decide whether or not computers should be allowed to impact society, computers became an indispensable part of society. About 1978, when computers such as Radio Shack's TRS-80 and the Apple II arrived on the scene, they moved into our homes, schoolrooms, and offices.

The computer is a tool. You need not be afraid of it. You need not even be in awe of it. You *can* learn to use it and communicate with it.

How much do you need to know about an automobile in order to drive it? Well, you need to know where to get the key to the car. You need to know where the ignition is. You need to know how to steer the car, where the brakes are and how to use them, and how to stop the car's engine at the end of your trip. If you drive at night, you need to know how to turn the lights on, when and how to switch them to low beam (or high beam), and how to turn them off. You'd better learn how to use the windshield wipers, in case of rain or snow.

Do you have to know about mufflers, tailpipes, crankshafts, and fuel pumps? Are you an expert on intake manifolds, cooling systems, and engine blocks? Probably not.

On the other hand, suppose the car you are driving just doesn't have any pickup. Or suppose it starts to sputter when you're driving 55 miles per hour along a four-lane highway. It may help you to know that the car runs on unleaded gas (not regular, not diesel). There are times when you need to know what grade of oil should be used. You can probably avoid a labor bill if you know how to change the oil yourself. If you know something about how the car works, and about its parts, you may save yourself some unneeded repair costs. You need not panic at the first sign of a problem.

So it is with computers. As was pointed out in Chapter 1, many of you who are reading this book have probably used computers many times without even realizing it. You may know how to play video games on computers. You may know how to key in simple requests for information from a typewriterlike keyboard and receive that information back on a televisionlike screen. You may even know how to write or run computer programs.

Now, suppose you are keying in simple requests for information and the computer fails to respond to your requests. (It just "sits there.") Or suppose the computer prints out a message that you can't understand. Or suppose the computer responds, but only after you've had time to read the paper or go to the refrigerator for a snack.

Suppose you've got a job to do and you're wondering whether or not the computer can help you. Or you've decided to buy a computer but you don't know whether to buy one that costs $500, or $5000, or $50,000. Or your boss thinks his firm should make more use of computers and he asks your advice. In the very near future, such situations will be commonplace. For some, they are already.

So far, we've taken a look at what computers can do. We know how data is entered into the computer and how information is obtained from it. We know about both primary and secondary storage. Now we're ready to learn about processors. In this book, you'll *not* learn about AND gates, OR gates, combinatorial logic, gate arrays, and so forth. That level of detail is best left to computer designers (just as we leave some details of our cars to engineers and other specialists at GM, Ford, or Toyota). You will learn something about how a computer works. You'll be introduced to the internal organization, or *architecture,* of processors and microprocessors (which are, after all, just small processors). When you've completed this chapter and the next one, you'll know how stored-program instructions are acted on by a computer. You'll know about the basic operations that a computer can perform under the direction of those instructions during processing.

THE PROCESSOR The processor (central processing unit, or CPU) of an EDP system controls and supervises the entire EDP system. It also performs arithmetic and logic operations on data. It has two major parts: a control section and an arithmetic/logic unit. As explained in Chapter 2, the computer's internal storage unit, or memory, is often packaged together with these components in a physical housing called the *processor unit*. You do not generally see the processor, but you do see the processor unit. To help you appreciate what's inside even the simplest computers, an Apple II with its cover removed is shown in Figure 7-1. Its processor is a microprocessor, mounted on the main, or "mother," board of the processor unit. Interfaces to input/output units that can be used with the Apple II are provided.

The processor of a large computer may be built as several circuit boards grouped within a boxlike structure, or frame (hence, the nickname *mainframe*). In a minicomputer, the processor may be constructed on a single processor

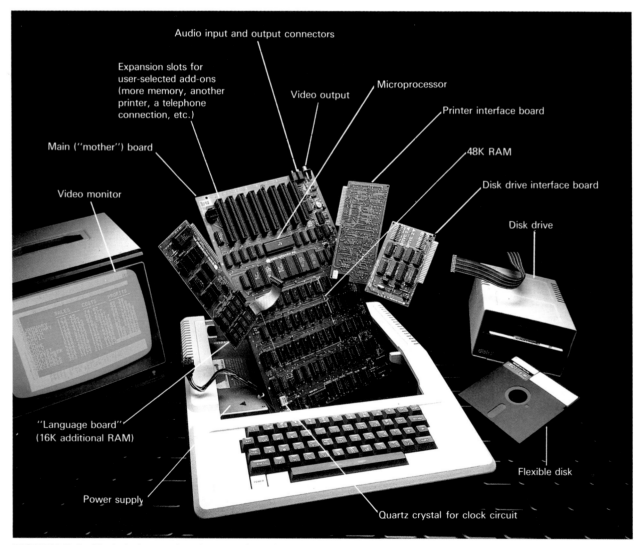

FIGURE 7-1 Much design, engineering, manufacturing, and packaging expertise goes into building a computer. (*Photo* © *Jonathan Goell 1982, 1983*)

circuit board. In a *microcomputer*, the processor is a microprocessor, contained on a single chip of silicon. This chip may be mounted together with memory, input, and output chips on a single circuit board. There may be other boards in the system (as in Figure 7-1), or the one board may hold all the chips required.

As we might expect, the processor of even a very small computer system is made up of many hardware components. Some of them are shown schematically in Figure 7-2. Each component has a specific function. It carries out that function

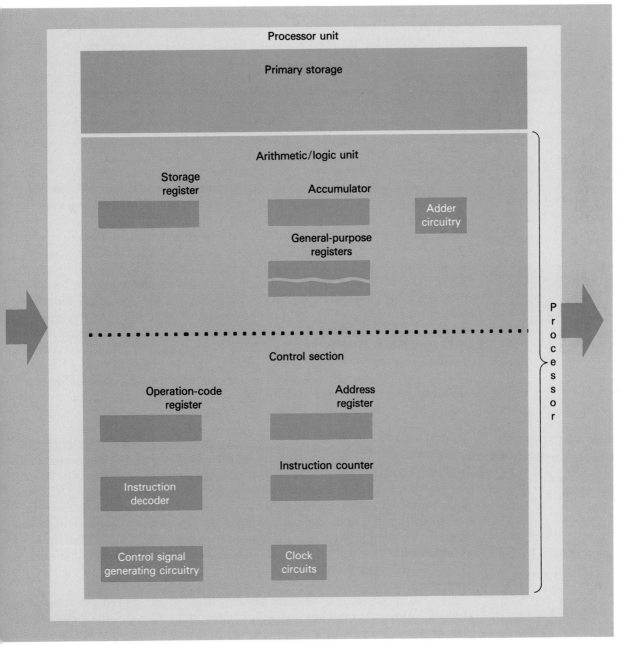

FIGURE 7-2 The processor unit contains many components that perform specific functions during processing.

during the execution of stored-program instructions. We cannot describe all the interrelationships of these components in this book, nor do we want to. The architectural details of one computer may differ in many ways from those of another. A general discussion will help us understand how any computer works. This will in turn remove some of the mystery that often seems to surround them.

Microprocessors are like other processors in some ways. They have many of the same types of components, carry out many of the same operations, have access times and cycle times, and so on. They also share a common ancestry with other processors. What we say here is general and applies in large part to all processors. Some specific details for microprocessors are given later in this chapter.

THE CONTROL SECTION

Perhaps the best way to describe the control section of a processor is with a simple analogy. In many ways, the control section of a processor can be compared to a telephone exchange system. The telephone exchange contains all the equipment necessary to connect the telephones it services. The control section contains all the mechanisms necessary to transfer data from one part of the system to another.

The telephone exchange controls the instruments that carry sound pulses from one phone to another, ring the phones, connect and disconnect circuits, and so on. The electronic path that permits calls between one telephone and another is set up by the appropriate controls in the exchange itself.

The processor control section directs and coordinates all EDP-system operations. It governs input/output devices, entry and retrieval of data from storage, and routing of data between storage and the arithmetic/logic unit. For example, the control section may start or stop an I/O device, turn a binary component on or off, rewind a tape reel, or initiate a calculation. In some computers, a part of the control section consists of read-only storage that contains microcode to control circuits that perform operations designated by stored-program instructions. (Recall "Microcode" in Chapter 2.) Sometimes the control section also contains *emulator circuits*. These circuits enable the computer to execute stored-program instructions written for another computer. In effect, one computer is directed to emulate another.

THE ARITHMETIC/ LOGIC UNIT

The arithmetic/logic unit contains the circuitry necessary to perform arithmetic and logical operations. The arithmetic circuitry calculates, shifts numbers, sets the algebraic signs of results, rounds numbers, compares algebraically (taking the sign bit into account), and so on. Sometimes these operations are performed on numeric values stored internally as binary numbers. In other cases, each digit of a numeric value to be operated on may be represented by a particular bit pattern. (To review data-representation schemes, see Chapter 3.) In some systems, the meaning of a particular bit pattern in storage depends not only on the hardware design of the computer but also on the type of arithmetic instructions being carried out.

The usual practice is to classify all arithmetic/logic operations other than addition, subtraction, multiplication, division, and shifts as logical operations. The most basic and widely used operations are comparisons and tests. We mentioned arithmetic (algebraic) comparisons above. They are performed only on numeric data. Logical comparisons may be performed bit-by-bit or character-by-character; no bit position is recognized as a sign-bit position. They may be performed on alphanumeric, character, or numeric data (but numeric data items are not treated as signed values). Tests may be applied to determine whether a value is positive, negative, or zero. Most computers can also test the states of indicators and switches, for example, to insure that the combination of bits in a particular location has been recognized as valid for the data-representation scheme in use. (If not, the system is alerted to an apparent error.) In general, the logic circuitry of the processor performs a decision-making function. When certain conditions are present, it changes the sequence of instruction execution.

Less common logical operations are editing functions and masking operations. Examples of the former, performed on numeric output data, include providing a leading dollar sign, changing leading zeros to blanks, inserting commas and decimal points, and converting algebraic signs to special symbol combinations such as *CR* for credit and *DB* for debit. A mask usually acts as a selective screen, permitting operations to be done on only a part of an addressable unit of data. For example, a mask may be 00001111. The common rule is that a 1 bit permits the data or operation to reach through the mask, but a 0 is like a closed door shutting off action or resulting in a replacement by zeros.

REGISTERS Registers are devices capable of receiving information, holding it, and transferring it very quickly. (See Figure 7-3.) They are designed primarily for temporary storage. (The term *temporary storage* is used here to designate information that is stored only for the length of time required to execute one instruction.) As Figure 7-3 suggests, registers have bit positions just as primary-storage locations have. They are a part of the processor, but they are not considered a part of primary storage and are not included when discussing storage capacity. Each register receives information in the form of electrical-pulse representations. It releases that information in the same form when directed to do so by control circuitry.

Note the references to an 8-bit data bus in Figure 7-3. As the word *bus* suggests, a *data bus* is simply a means by which data can travel about within the computer system. It consists of a set of wires, or lines, grouped in a particular way to form a data path between system components. If a system has 8-bit registers, it usually has an 8-bit (8-line) data bus. This allows all the bits that are to be stored in a particular register to travel together to that register and arrive at the same time. The bit width of the data bus of a particular computer is an indicator of the amount of information immediately accessible to the processor in one instruction execution. It is a very concrete measure of the power of the machine.

Certain registers perform very specific functions. An *accumulator* accumulates results. A *storage register* contains information taken from or being sent to storage. An *address register* holds the address of a location in storage or the address of a device. An *operation-code register* holds the operation-code portion of an instruction being executed.

If you read about processors in other literature, it may help you to know some synonyms. Storage registers are sometimes called *input/output buffers* or *data registers*. Address registers are sometimes called *address buffers* or *data counters*. Operation-code registers are sometimes called *instruction registers*.

A. The register is "empty." (It probably contains data but that data is no longer needed.)

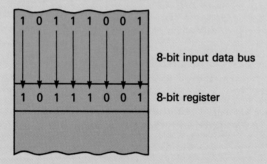

| 1 | 0 | 0 | 1 | 1 | 0 | 0 | 0 | 8-bit register

B. Data is transferred to the register as electrical pulses.

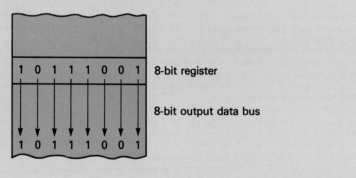

C. Data is transferred from the register as electrical pulses. (Since the transfer-out, or read, is nondestructive, the register contents remain unchanged.)

FIGURE 7-3 Data in the form of electrical pulses is transferred to and from registers very quickly during processing.

Some registers are *general-purpose registers,* or simply *general registers.* As their name implies, they can be used for any of several functions. Processors in common use contain 1, 2, 4, 8, or 16 of these registers. Remember that an important advantage of registers is that they provide for very fast access to data. Therefore, they also provide the potential for getting work done quickly. For this reason, most computers are designed so that at least some of these registers are available for use by programmers. The registers have assigned numbers. Programs that are part of the system software developed for a particular computer system often contain instructions that refer directly to the registers, either by their assigned numbers or by symbolic labels that have been equated to the assigned numbers. Because there are a limited number of these registers, and because their correct use is vital to proper functioning of the system, great care is required on the part of programmers who write instructions referring to them.

On some systems, no registers serve strictly as accumulators. Any of the general-purpose registers can be used to perform accumulation functions.

How big is a register? Each register is designed to hold one unit of information at a time. If the computer's internal storage unit is constructed to deal with 8-bit bytes or words, then the processor registers used in data transfers are also constructed to hold 8-bit units of data. If the computer's internal storage unit holds 16-bit words, then its registers are constructed to hold 16-bit words; and so on.

During most processing, operations involving registers are completed quickly and effectively. Data moves in and out of registers, and between registers, at nanosecond or microsecond speeds (depending on the processor). In some situations the data to be stored in a register will not fit in that register. Extra, or overflow, positions in the register are used to detect such situations.

For purposes of illustration, assume that three registers are being used in an arithmetic operation. (See Figure 7-4.) Further assume that the registers are designed to hold 11-digit decimal numerals. An overflow condition exists when two 11-digit numerals are added, and their sum is a 12-digit numeral. For example, in Figure 7-4, register 1 holds one numeral, and register 2 holds another. Their sum is placed in register 3 where an overflow condition is indicated by the presence of data in the overflow position. This particular position, or a special status flag set by the hardware, can be tested by stored-program instructions. In some instances, a warning message is generated. If the user application or system processing that is being done cannot tolerate or recover from this overflow condition, the processing may be terminated.

Sometimes registers are used to shift data. Shifting can be either to the right or to the left within a register and, in some cases, between registers. Figure 7-5 shows the shifting of register contents three positions to the right. Vacated

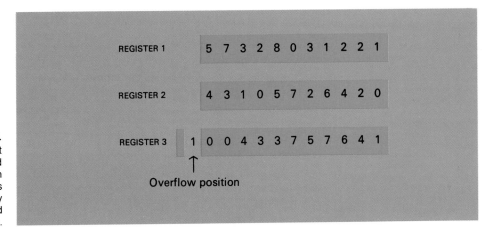

FIGURE 7-4
When a register cannot contain the value transferred to it, an overflow condition occurs. This condition is detected automatically by hardware or must be tested for by software.

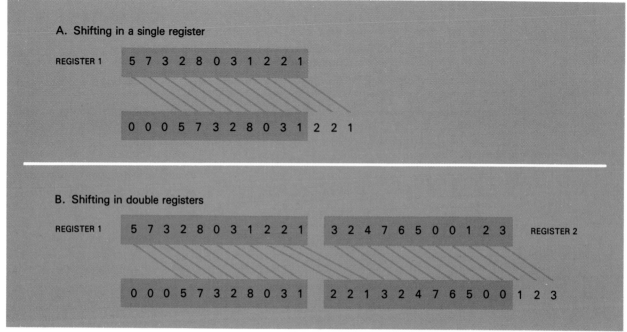

FIGURE 7-5 During processing, data can be shifted within a register or between registers.

positions are filled with zeros, and digits shifted beyond the rightmost position in the register are lost. In part A of this illustration, a single register is used for shifting. In part B, two single registers are treated as one double register and used together in one shift operation.

INSTRUCTION COUNTER

A fundamental assumption of computer architecture is that the instructions of any program being executed are stored in consecutive memory locations. This assumption allows the use of a very simple mechanism to keep track of the next instruction to be executed. The mechanism is a special register known as the *instruction counter*. (In other literature, it may be referred to as the *instruction address register, program counter, control register*, or *sequence control register*.) Every processor has one.

When a stored program is to be executed, the instruction counter holds the primary-storage address of the first instruction of that program. While the first instruction is being executed, the instruction counter is automatically set to the address of the next instruction. This process continues throughout execution of the program.

ADDERS

The adder circuitry of a processor receives data from two or more sources, performs addition, and places the result in a location that can be referred to by stored-program instructions. Adder circuitry varies in complexity, depending upon how the data is represented internally and upon the way the arithmetic operations are carried out.

Figure 7-6A shows a serial, or 1-digit, adder. In a computer having this type of adder, the two digits in the rightmost positions of the numbers to be added are added first and the rightmost digit of the result is stored. If there is a carry in this result, it is held by a delay device and then added to the result of the addition of the next-rightmost (next-higher-order) digits in the numbers being added. The process continues from right to left until all the digits in the numbers have been summed.

Figure 7-6B shows two positions of a parallel adder. It involves a more complex type of adder circuitry. The number of adder positions varies. The circuitry at all

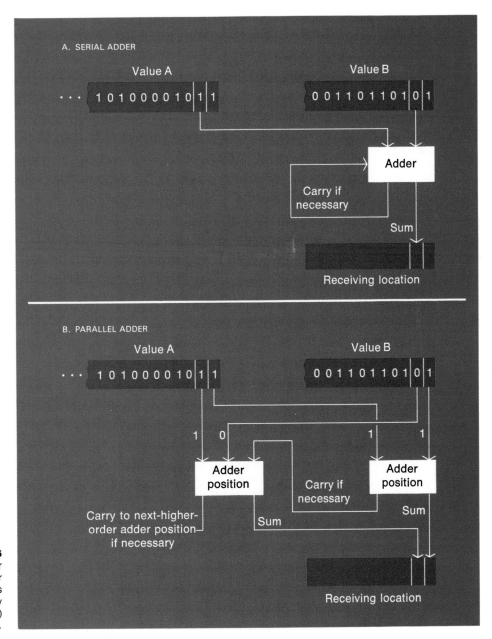

FIGURE 7-6
A computer may have either serial or parallel adder circuitry, and performs arithmetic operations serially (A) or in parallel (B) accordingly.

adder positions operates simultaneously, forming tentative sums and then sending carries (if any) forward to the next positions to the left. If additional carries result from adding these carries, they are forwarded, and so on. (We say more about serial and parallel operations later in this chapter.)

STORED-PROGRAM INSTRUCTIONS

Before we discuss how registers, the instruction counter, and adder circuitry perform their functions, we need to say more about stored-program instructions. Each instruction is a unit of specific information that is loaded into primary storage. This unit of information is interpreted by the control section of the processor as an operation to be performed. If data is involved, the instruction directs the computer to the data. If some device (for example, a printer) is to be controlled, the instruction specifies the device and the required operation.

Instructions may change the condition of an indicator, copy data from one location in storage into another, add 1 to the contents of an accumulator, and so on. In some cases, an instruction specifies the storage address of the next instruction to be executed. The specification may be predetermined and unalterable, or it may depend on the result of some machine or data indication. With such an instruction, it is possible to alter the sequence in which other instructions or blocks of instructions are executed.

Stored-program instructions must, of course, be represented in machine-readable code. In some computers, instructions are fixed in length. Each instruction is one word long. That means each instruction is 8 bits, or 16 bits, or whatever, in length (depending on the computer's architecture). In other computers, instructions are made of a variable number of characters; their lengths vary. In still other computers, instructions may be any of several fixed lengths. For example, each instruction may be one halfword, one full word, or one full word plus one halfword in length, depending upon what information has to be given about the operation it describes.

For our current purposes, let us assume that each instruction is 32 bits in length. (See Figure 7-7.) The 12 leftmost bits of the instruction make up the *operation-code field*. The remaining 20 bits make up the *operand field*.

FIGURE 7-7
A 32-bit instruction format allows many details about a required operation to be specified in a single machine-language instruction.

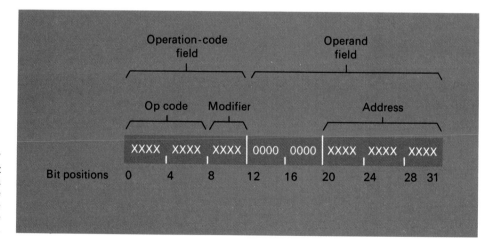

The 8 leftmost bits of the operation-code field contain the *operation code,* or *op code.* These bits tell the computer what operation is to be performed. The computer may be directed to add, subtract, compare, move data, and so on. The remaining 4 bits of the operation-code field contain a *modifier.* For example, a bit setting of 0010 in positions 8 through 11 of an add instruction may tell the computer to place the result of the add operation in register 2.

The operand field of a machine-language instruction tells the computer where to find or store data to be processed, the address of the device needed for the specified operation, or where to find the next instruction to be executed when that instruction is not simply the next sequential instruction. For our current purposes, the rightmost 12 bits of this field contain a *primary-storage address.* The remaining positions of the word are assumed to contain zeros.

Figure 7-8 shows a machine-language instruction represented in hexadecimal notation, a convenient shorthand for binary. The op code of the instruction (5A) tells the computer to add an amount to a value in an accumulator. The modifier (2) indicates that the accumulator—already containing one of the values to be added and into which the sum will be placed automatically—is register 2. The address (628) tells the computer that the second value to be added is in primary-storage location 628. Now let's see how the computer executes such an instruction.

INSTRUCTION EXECUTION

The computer time required to perform one specific machine operation is called a *machine cycle.* The number of machine cycles required to execute one stored-program instruction depends on the kind of instruction. Sometimes several machine operations must take place.

All computer operations take place in fixed intervals of time. These intervals are measured by regular pulses of an electronic clock. In some computers, the pulses occur at frequencies as high as 20 million or more per second. As we've explained elsewhere, computer time measurements are expressed in terms of milliseconds, microseconds, and nanoseconds. It is difficult to imagine how infinitesimally short these intervals of time are. For example, the blink of an eye takes about one-tenth of a second, or 100 milliseconds. A microsecond is one-thousandth of a millisecond. A nanosecond is one-thousandth of a microsecond. There are as many nanoseconds in one second as there are seconds in 30 years!

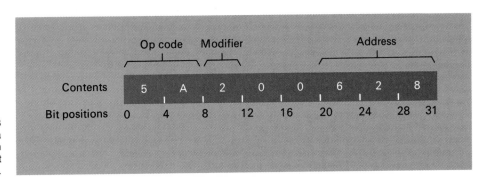

FIGURE 7-8
Hexadecimal notation is a convenient shorthand form of representing the bit settings of an instruction.

I-Time   The first machine cycle involved in executing an instruction is called an *instruction cycle*. The time required to complete this cycle is called *instruction time,* or *I-time*. I-time is not under the control of the stored-program instruction. The actions during I-time are built into the control section circuitry. They are the same for each instruction and require a uniform amount of time.

I-time begins when the instruction to be executed is moved from primary storage to the storage register. The instruction is located and "moved" in the following manner. Control circuits decode the address in the instruction counter and send electrical pulses to storage to "read" (fetch) the instruction. The bit settings that make up the instruction are then converted to pulses to accomplish the move. The operation-code field of the instruction is routed to the operation-code register. The address portion of the operand field is routed to the address register. An *instruction decoder* interprets the op code and sets the circuit paths necessary to execute the instruction. The circuits may, for example, activate the "reading" of relevant bit cells in the primary-storage location pointed to by the address register and the bringing of the data (in the form of pulses) into the arithmetic/logic unit. The data flow that occurs during I-time is highlighted in Figure 7-9.

The location of the next instruction to be executed is also determined at this time. The instruction counter is set automatically to the address of this instruction.

Although instructions are stored in consecutive locations, they do not *have* to be executed in the sequence in which they are stored. Certain instructions cause the computer to branch to another instruction. The op code of an instruction of this type indicates that the next instruction in sequence is not to be executed; the address in the operand field identifies the location of the instruction to be executed instead. The instruction counter is set to this address.

Some instructions cause the computer to *branch unconditionally;* that is, it must go to the instruction that is specified by the address in the operand field. Other instructions cause the computer to *branch conditionally;* that is, the computer must examine conditions elsewhere in the system and select the address of the next instruction to be executed accordingly. An instruction may say, in effect: "Look at the sign of the quantity in the accumulator. If the sign is minus, take the next instruction from location 5000; if the sign is plus, proceed to the next instruction in sequence." The sign is checked by computer circuitry when this instruction is executed. The instruction counter is then set automatically either to location 5000 or to the address of the next instruction.

E-Time   I-time is followed by *execution time,* or *E-time*. During E-time, the operation itself is performed. Several machine cycles may be required.

Since this is E-time, the storage register and the accumulator are under control of the operation-code register, which contains 5A2. (See Figure 7-10.) As we have seen, this op code and modifier tell the computer circuitry to add the contents of a specified storage location to the value already in register 2, which, of course, is the accumulator. First, the contents of the location specified by the address in the address register (628) are moved from primary storage to the storage register. Then, the contents of the storage register and the accumulator are placed in the adder circuitry, their values are added, and the sum is returned to the accumulator.

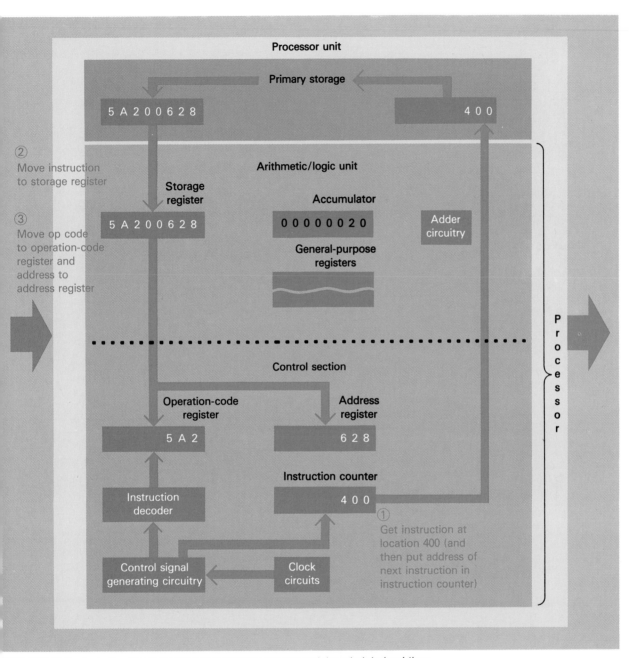

FIGURE 7-9   An instruction is fetched from primary storage and decoded during I-time.

According to Figure 7-10, the original value moved from primary-storage location 628 to the storage register during the depicted E-time is 00003364. The original value in the accumulator is 00000020. These values are combined in the adder. Their sum, 00003384, will be in the accumulator at the end of E-time.

The only distinction between instructions and data in storage is related to the time they are forwarded to the processor. If machine-readable code is brought to

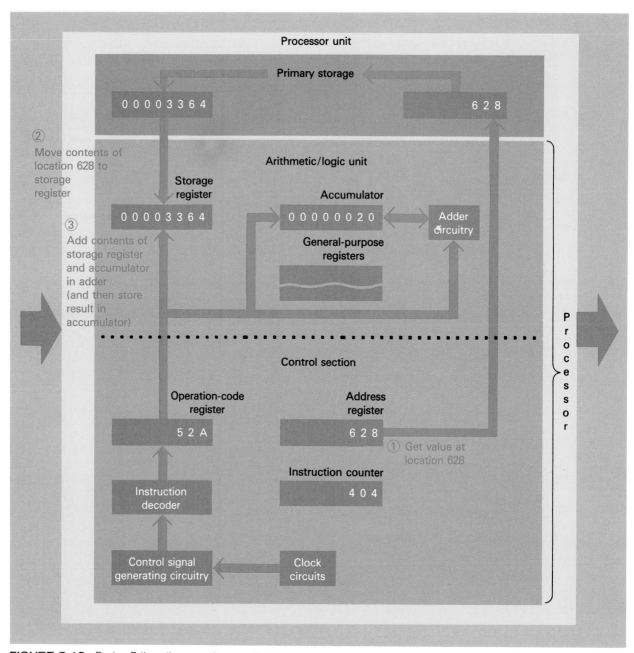

FIGURE 7-10 During E-time, the operation specified in an instruction is carried out.

the processor during an instruction cycle, it is interpreted as an instruction. If it is brought in during any other cycle, it is assumed to be data.

If instructions are supplied as data, the computer can operate on them. As we'll see in Chapters 11 through 13, this capability is extremely important to persons writing instructions to be executed by the computer. The computer can also be programmed to alter its own instructions according to conditions encountered during processing.

SERIAL AND PARALLEL OPERATIONS

Computers and parts of computers are classified as either serial or parallel, depending on whether only a single action or multiple actions can occur at a time. Let's see how this applies in arithmetic operations. Essentially, all arithmetic is performed by addition. In a serial processor, numerals are added one position at a time. (This is the way we add numbers when using pencil and paper.) Whenever a number must be carried, it is retained temporarily and then added to the sum of the next-higher-order position. The time required for the operation depends on the number of digits to be added. Serial addition of two numerals is shown in Figure 7-11. (Recall also the serial adder shown in Figure 7-6A.)

In a parallel processor, all positions of the numerals to be processed, including carries, are added in one step. The number of digits to be added does not significantly affect the amount of time required to do the addition. Figure 7-12 shows parallel addition. (We looked at parallel adder circuitry in Figure 7-6B.)

In these days, when computers are becoming smaller and smaller, it's easy to overlook the fact that computers are also becoming more powerful. Capabilities for parallel operation are behind much of this power. In Figure 7-3, we saw a data bus that is 8 bits wide. That means 8 bits can move in parallel along the bus. Some computers have data buses that are eight 8-bit bytes in width. That means 8 bytes of data can move in parallel. The amount of work that can be accomplished within the system in a given amount of time differs accordingly.

FIXED-LENGTH AND VARIABLE-LENGTH OPERATIONS

We have learned that data is stored as binary digits, or bits. The binary digits can be interpreted as a binary number that represents a numeric value. A certain number of binary digits, usually 7 or 8, can also represent a character; the character may be a letter, a numeral, or a special symbol such as the ampersand (&) or the dollar sign ($).

In some computers, a single character can be referred to by stating the address of the location in which it is stored. Machines whose circuitry is designed to process data serially as single characters are said to be *character-addressable*. When a character-addressable computer is instructed to read from a specific location, it reads any number of succeeding locations or characters, depending on the particular instruction or on a code that is provided. In effect, the computer operates on *variable-length words*.

In other computers, each address refers to a fixed number of locations

	1ST STEP	2ND STEP	3RD STEP	4TH STEP
Addend	1234	1234	1234	1234
Augend	2459	2459	2459	2459
Carry	1	1		
Sum	3	93	693	3693

FIGURE 7-11 Serial addition occurs as a multiple-step operation.

Addend	00564213
Augend	00000824
Carry	1
Sum	00565037

FIGURE 7-12 Parallel addition is a one-step operation, in which the bits in all positions of a value are added simultaneously.

containing a fixed number of binary digits. Each group of digits is treated as a single unit of data—a *fixed-length word*. The choice of word size is one aspect of the computer's architecture. That choice is designed into the computer. Internal processing operations are performed in parallel, as we've just described. Storage locations, accumulators, and other registers are designed to accommodate words. Such computers are said to be *word-addressable* and operate on fixed-length words.

Variable-length operations offer advantages in data-handling flexibility. Fixed-length operations usually offer greater speed. Some computers are designed to perform either kind of operation. In such computers, the type of operation performed depends upon the stored-program instruction controlling the operation.

MICRO-PROCESSORS

Even though microprocessors are just small processors, it's appropriate to spend some time looking at them specifically. Their use is widespread. They are being incorporated not only in computers but also in other machines, educational tools, household equipment, toys, and so on. Their potential is tremendous.

The first microprocessor, unveiled in 1971, contained 2250 transistors in an area barely $1/6 \times 1/8$ inch in size. In computational power, it almost matched the monstrous 1500-square-foot ENIAC completed just 25 years earlier. Known as the Intel 4004, the microprocessor was designed to handle 4 binary digits, or bits, at a time. It was followed a few months later by an 8-bit microprocessor, the Intel 8008.

Like the processor of a large computer system, a microprocessor performs certain well-defined processing functions. Its tasks are to (1) receive data in the form of binary digits from an input mechanism, (2) store the data for later processing, (3) perform arithmetic and logical operations on the data in accordance with previously stored instructions, and (4) deliver the results through an output mechanism.

Figure 7-13 shows the basic components of a typical microprocessor. The *decode and control unit* interprets the instructions of the stored program. The *arithmetic/logic unit* (*ALU*) performs arithmetic and logical operations. The *registers* provide readily accessible storage for data that is being manipulated. One of these, the *accumulator*, is one source of data for arithmetic and logical operations performed by the ALU and the immediate destination of all its results. The *address buffers* supply the address of the location from which the next instruction is to be fetched, and the address of the location from which a data item is to be read or in which it is to be written. The *input/output buffers* are used in reading instructions or data into the microprocessor and in writing them out. The data and instructions travel along the *data bus*. Control signals are carried by the *control bus*. The *timing circuitry* synchronizes the operations of all components.

Thus, we see a basic similarity between the components of this microprocessor and those of the processor described earlier in this chapter. We did not label or even show many specific buses in Figures 7-9 and 7-10 because we wanted to avoid unnecessary complexity. However, you can assume that on most mainframe processors, the functional components that have to interact are connected point-to-point by separate buses. They don't have to share buses. This freedom

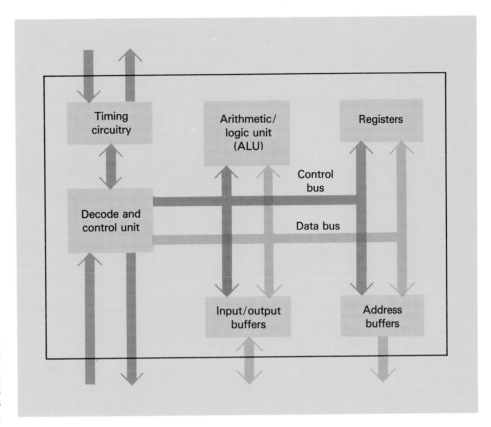

FIGURE 7-13
The bus architecture of a microprocessor allows data, instructions, and control signals to move among its internal components during processing.

allows several bit patterns in the form of electrical pulses—representing data, addresses, operation codes, and so on—to move simultaneously within the system. In contrast, this microprocessor has only one control bus (for control signals) and one data bus (for all else). Some microprocessors have three buses: one for control signals, one for data, and one for addresses. In either case, the requirement to share buses tends to limit operations within the system. Extremely fast over-all speeds are not always necessary. Remember, even microprocessor speeds are much faster than the speeds of devices that require movements of physical components rather than transfers of electrical pulses. More than 4 million such transfers may occur in one second on a microprocessor.

Microprocessors are usually classified on the basis of their word size, reflected as the number of bit positions in registers. There are four common types: 4-bit, 8-bit, 16-bit, and bit-slice (of which there are two subtypes, 2-bit and 4-bit). Bit-slice microprocessors are usually equipped to execute certain primitive operations (microinstructions) very rapidly. These microinstructions are combined to form microprograms, which are stored in a read-only memory associated with the microprocessor. (To review microprogramming, see "Microcode" in Chapter 2.) A microprocessor, together with appropriate memory units for instructions and data, interfaces for input and output, and a master electronic clock to control system timing, forms a complete microcomputer.

Today, about a hundred companies are manufacturing microprocessor chips. The chips range in price from $1 to $1000. The manufacturers may—and often do—incorporate their chips into products they produce and market. Alternatively, they may sell the chips to other firms known as *original equipment manufacturers* (*OEM's*), who in turn incorporate the chips into their own products. A major significance of microprocessor chips is that they serve as standard building blocks of the electronics industry. By taking advantage of existing, proven chip designs, companies can achieve significant increases in the efficiency of their engineering and manufacturing efforts. (Consider, for example, the inefficiency that would exist in the housing industry if each contractor had to design individually every nail or plank instead of using standard 6-penny nails and 2-by-4 boards.)

The standard microprocessor chip designs are assigned unique numbers for identification purposes. For example, we referred to the first two Intel-developed chips as the 4004 and the 8008. Other common early designs were the Intel 8080, Zilog Z80, Motorola 6800, and MOS Technology 6502. Slight variations of these designs, sometimes known as *customized chips*, are the 8080A and the 6502A. The Intel 8086, Zilog Z8001, and Motorola 68000 are faster, more powerful, 16-bit microprocessor chips developed about 1980.

Because a microprocessor is so small and relatively inexpensive, it can be incorporated into almost any device whose usability is improved by some "intelligence" (thinking power). Early examples include handheld calculators, video games, pinball machines, vending machines, sewing machines, microwave ovens, gas pumps, and traffic signals.

Today, microprocessors are used in many products *and* in the tools used to produce those products. Take again, for example, automobiles. Microprocessor-based analyzers are extensively used for vibration studies in development labs. Microprocessor-controlled robotic systems are increasingly common on assembly lines. Most new cars have microprocessors that adjust their spark timings, mix air and fuel, and fine-tune their emission control equipment. (See Figure 7-14.) Digital speedometers, bar-chart fuel gauges, and illuminated message centers, interfaced with microprocessors throughout the cars, provide driving information. (See Figure 7-15.) Some models are equipped with voice synthesizers enabling them to tell drivers when fuel is low or parts are malfunctioning.

Hughes Aircraft incorporates Motorola 68000 microprocessors into its medical imaging systems. The microprocessors process X-ray or ultrasound data to produce detailed images of internal organs. The systems can even do digital image enhancement (the process that is used to improve detail in space photographs).

Microprocessors are used widely in offices and other business environments. For example, a microprocessor within an electronic typewriter interprets signals from the keyboard and sends pulses to electromagnets that control printing. The intelligent terminals discussed in Chapter 4 contain microprocessors. Sophisticated visual-display units, printers, and plotters also contain microprocessors that initiate and control many device functions.

A wide variety of computer programs have been developed to control the operations of the 8080, Z80, and 6502 microprocessor chips mentioned above. Vendors who build microcomputers based on these chips can assure potential buyers that extensive software for their microcomputers is available. Programs for the 68000 microprocessor chip, and related microcomputers, are becoming increasingly common. We'll find out more about both microprocessors and microcomputers in Chapter 9.

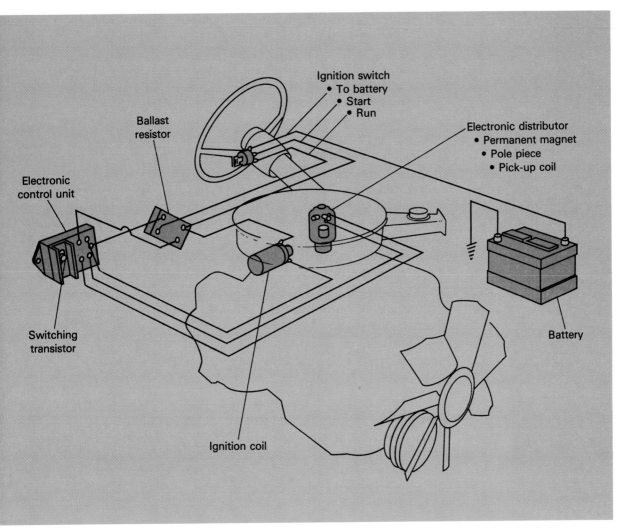

FIGURE 7-14 Not just computers but also automobile ignition systems and other common devices are controlled by microprocessors. (*Courtesy Chrysler Corporation*)

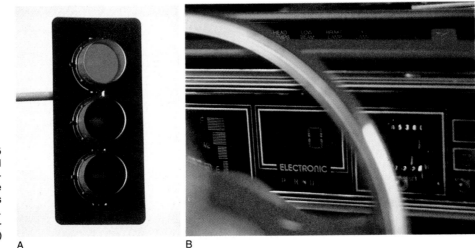

FIGURE 7-15
Microprocessors control traffic lights at busy intersections (A) and provide timely, accurate indicators of car performance (B). (*Courtesy* [A] *Intel Corporation;* [B] *Motorola Inc.*)

A   B

CHAPTER SUMMARY

1. The term *computer architecture* refers to the internal organization of a computer.

2. The processor of an EDP system consists of a control section and an arithmetic/logic unit. It may be housed in a boxlike structure, constructed on a single circuit board, or contained on a single silicon chip (in which case it's called a *microprocessor*).

3. The control section of a processor directs and coordinates all EDP-system operations; the arithmetic/logic unit contains the circuitry needed to perform arithmetic and logical operations.

4. Registers are small internal devices that receive information as electrical pulses, hold that information, and then release it very quickly when directed to do so. Registers such as the accumulator, storage register, address register, and operation-code register perform specific functions; general-purpose registers may be used for any of several functions.

5. An instruction counter keeps track of the next instruction to be executed. That instruction is normally the next instruction in primary storage.

6. A stored-program instruction may have any of several formats. The common 32-bit format includes a 12-bit operation-code field and a 20-bit operand field.

7. During I-time, an instruction is fetched from primary storage and interpreted to set up the circuit paths necessary to execute it.

8. During E-time, the operation specified in an instruction is performed.

9. Computer operations may be carried out serially or in parallel, depending on the architecture of the computer.

10. Some computers have character-addressable storage and operate on variable-length words. Others have word-addressable storage and operate on fixed-length words.

11. Microprocessors are classified on the basis of their word size. Standard microprocessor chip designs allow microprocessors to serve as basic building blocks in a wide variety of products and in the tools used to produce those products.

DISCUSSION QUESTIONS

1. Distinguish between the processor and the processor unit of a computer system.

2. (a) Identify the two major parts of a processor.
   (b) Discuss the functions of each major part.

3. (a) How are registers and primary-storage locations similar?
   (b) What is the primary advantage of registers?
   (c) Discuss the functions of registers.

4. (a) Name the two parts of a stored-program instruction.
   (b) What is the function of each part?

5. Assume that the following operation codes are available for use with a particular computer:

Operation code	Meaning
58	Load accumulator
5A	Add to accumulator
5B	Subtract from accumulator
50	Store
47	Branch

   Further assume that this computer is directed by 32-bit instructions like the one in Figure 7-7. Using binary notation, show how an instruction causing the computer to add the contents of location 34A to the accumulator, which is register 2, would be stored in one computer word.

6. Refer to Question 5. Express the same instruction in hexadecimal notation.

7. Using the same 32-bit instruction set, write a sequence of three instructions directing the computer to load the contents of storage location 608 in the accumulator, subtract the contents of storage location C44 from this value, and store the result, automatically placed in the accumulator, in location FB4. Use either binary or hexadecimal notation.

8. Distinguish between I-time and E-time.

9. Support or refute the following statement: "Parallel operations are apt to be faster than serial operations."

10. Compare variable-length operations with fixed-length operations. Discuss differences in execution and in effect.

11. (a) What is a microprocessor?
    (b) Compare and contrast it with the processor of a large computer system.

12. What are some uses of microprocessors?

8

COMPUTER OPERATIONS

The ability of computers to process data quickly and in large quantities can greatly aid human decision-making. Time is often a critical ingredient in a decision: A correct decision made too late may no longer be "correct." Many of today's decisions, whether in business or personal situations, involve many complex and variable factors. Some of the factors may even be unintelligible without a great deal of calculation or interpretation. When good information is needed in a hurry, computers are invaluable.

The New York Stock Exchange suggests situations that constantly call for clear and current information. Transactions at the Exchange are monitored and recorded via computers. Many brokerage firms have direct computer links to the floor of the Exchange. These links provide minute-by-minute information. With large sums of money at stake, the timing of buy and sell decisions is often critical. The computers cannot tell which stocks to buy or sell, but they can offer information to form the basis for good decisions.

Long-range trends frequently enter into financial decisions, too. At a London bank, for example

officials track the results of their investment decisions and develop long-range financial plans to take into account changing trends. They may see such trends in the data that computers have analyzed for them.

Individuals also use computer technology in making sound financial decisions. It is often said that the biggest financial decision an individual makes concerns buying a home. Such a purchase usually involves assuming the burden of a long-term loan or mortgage. Can the buyer afford the monthly payments? The technology built into a programmable calculator can give a quick answer to the question. It can also help with a myriad other related questions and decisions— square footage, carpeting, insurance, commuting expense, and so forth.

On a national or global scale, some of our most important decisions may involve natural resources. Where can we find more of what we need? The Landsat satellite can help us find answers to this kind of question. Electronic instrumentation aboard the Landsat, for example, can give us clues about the location of water for agriculature. Gathering this data from traditional aircraft or from land-based positions would be very slow and difficult, if not impossible. Data gathered by the satellite's instruments, however, when converted into pictorial or graphic form by computers, becomes readily accessible and useful.

Courtesy Eagle Computer

© 1983 Dick Luria Photography, Inc., New York

Courtesy Sperry Corporation

Courtesy Hewlett-Packard Company

Courtesy Ramtek Corporation

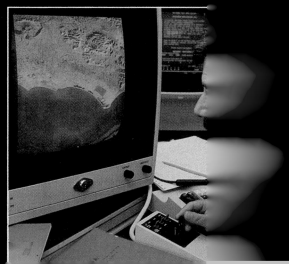

When resources such as coal and ores are found, they must be transported to where they can be used. The products that result from their use must also be transported to their buyers and users. Railroads often provide the needed transportation. Varying shipping schedules and load demands on railroads require precise routing of trains and knowledge of available equipment. Computers can keep track of the data involved, and help make the thousands of decisions that are needed daily. Computers can also perform the actual switching that routes trains to the right tracks at the right times. All these decision-making processes were once totally dependent on humans, but now the heavy responsibilities have been at least partly lifted from our shoulders.

Today's demand for increased precision in industrial design makes it necessary to take into account more and more factors. Whether in testing a truck's suspension system or an aspect of its engine performance, computer-handled data helps designers and engineers make good decisions. Factors to be studied may include not only the efficiency of the product itself, but also the efficiency of the manufacturing process that creates it. Computers can also simulate and predict strengths or weaknesses of various design options. Finally, of course, computers analyze expenses and expected profits to help in the making of sound business choices.

We will see in a later chapter how computers enter into the creative and artistic processes. The composing of music, for example, may require several separate decisions for every note! Writing music by hand is a painfully slow process, especially when compared to the computerized keyboard that Herbie Hancock now uses. It would appear that any kind of decision can be made more effectively with the clever use of a computer.

Courtesy Sperry Corporation

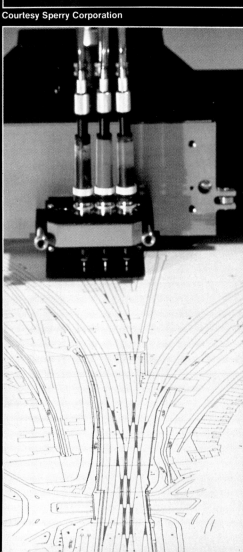

Courtesy TRW Inc.

Courtesy Boeing Computer Services Company

Courtesy Sperry Corporation

© David Burnett/Contact

8 | COMPUTER OPERATIONS

As pointed out frequently in this book, a computer is a tool we can use for many purposes. Under the direction of stored-program instructions, the computer accepts data as input, processes that data, and provides the results of processing as output. The data may be entered from any of several input devices. The results of processing may be written to any of several output devices. The processor may be the MOS Technology 6502 microprocessor chip used in an Apple II microcomputer or the 800-million-operations-per-second processor used in a CRAY 1 supercomputer.

Whether a computer system is small or large, in completing the input–process–output cycle, the computer itself performs certain basic operations. Some are input/output (I/O) operations, some are arithmetic operations, and some are logical operations. In this chapter, we take a closer look at these operations. Much of what you read here is common across systems. Where there are significant differences between small and large systems, those differences are pointed out. When you've completed this chapter, you'll have a better understanding of computer operations, including how a computer solves problems.

READING AND WRITING WITH MICRO- PROCESSORS

As we've said, small and large computer systems are alike in many ways. Nonetheless, it's also intuitively obvious that there must be ways in which microcomputers are simpler. After all, some microcomputer systems can be purchased for $1000 or less. Large computer systems are likely to cost 100 times that much. Since a microcomputer can't do anything with data until it gets the data, we'll start by discussing how getting data, or *reading*, occurs. Putting information out, or *writing*, is in many respects the converse of reading. We'll discuss that also.

The I/O devices on a microcomputer system usually include a keyboard for input and a CRT for output. Assume you're keying data into such a system. Though you may not consciously think about it, whatever you key in will be transferred to the microprocessor *only* when a stored-program instruction in the microprocessor's memory directs it to read input from the device at which you are keying.

If you are keying data in response to messages displayed on the CRT, a stored program containing both write and read instructions is being executed. The write instructions direct the microprocessor to write messages as output to the CRT. The read instructions direct the microprocessor to read whatever is keyed as input from the keyboard. (See Figure 8-1.)

Remember our discussion of buses in Chapter 7. To transfer data between the processor and an I/O device, an *I/O bus* is used. As stated before, the bus is a collection of lines along which electrical pulses can travel. One particular I/O bus

FIGURE 8-1
Stored-program read instructions direct the processor of a microcomputer system to accept keyed data values as input; stored-program write instructions direct it to display messages on the screen as output. (*Courtesy Radio Shack, a Division of Tandy Corporation*)

that you may have heard mentioned in discussions of microcomputers is called the *S-100 bus*. It's a collection of 100 lines. Standard usages for subsets of these lines have been agreed upon by several manufacturers of EDP-system components. By standardizing bus line usage, the manufacturers can design circuit boards and then use those boards in a variety of processors and devices that communicate with one another over the S-100 bus.

Back to our example. The keyboard device from which you are keying data may convert each keystroke to an 8-bit representation of the character you keyed. (See Figure 8-2A.) It forwards those 8 bits to be transmitted in parallel along the I/O bus to an *I/O port*. As the term *port* implies, the I/O port is simply an 8-bit connection between the microprocessor and the outside world. It and other I/O ports are created via a commonly used integrated circuit chip known as the *PIO*, or *programmable input/output chip*. The PIO also provides an 8-bit storage area, or *buffer*, for each I/O port. Data can be kept temporarily in these buffers. This temporary storage allows the microprocessor to read input and write output somewhat independently of the sending and receiving devices.

Some I/O devices are designed to send or receive data serially. As you might expect, when data is transferred serially, the bits of an 8-bit representation follow one another along the I/O bus. (See Figure 8-2B.) One common example of such a device is the Teletype, which has a typewriterlike keyboard for input and a relatively slow-speed printer for output. To provide for connection of serial I/O devices to a microprocessor, a *UART*, or *universal asynchronous receiver transmitter chip*, is often employed. We'll say more about "asynchronous" later. For now, you should understand that the UART can receive an 8-bit parallel representation from the microprocessor and send that representation serially along the I/O bus to the output device. Conversely, it can accept bits transmitted serially along the I/O bus from an input device and convert them to a single 8-bit representation for the microprocessor.

In addition to requiring either a PIO or a UART, most I/O devices require interface logic. This logic is contained on the main "mother" board of the system or on an interface board included within the system to provide for connection to the I/O bus and hence to the microprocessor.

If an input device has some "smarts" of its own, it may be able to send commands and status information as well as data characters to the microprocessor. Similarly, a smart or intelligent CRT may be able to respond to commands sent to it by the microprocessor. To support these devices requires command decoding. This logic is contained on a more sophisticated board called a *controller board*, or *controller*. Controllers are also required when data, commands, and status information are to be transferred between the microprocessor and disk drives or tape drives. We usually think of disk and tape units as storage devices. Since they receive data from and send data to the processor unit, they are also I/O devices.

As a user who is entering input or receiving output, you may not be aware of I/O buses, PIO or UART chips, and boards. However, if you are deciding what microprocessor, printer, or disk drive to buy, or wondering what can be used with what, you must find out the interface capabilities of each piece of hardware. This means you'll have to study the product documentation or talk with persons who are familiar with the devices you're considering. Interface logic is not fully standardized. To provide for both your current and future needs, you must choose carefully.

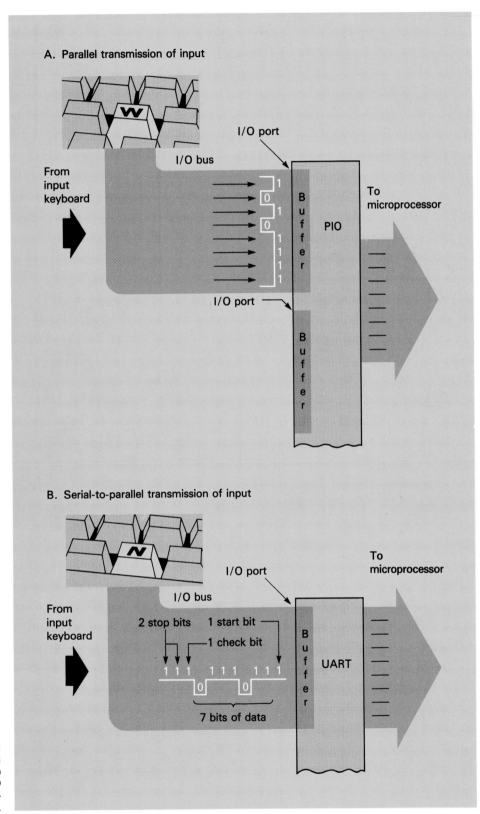

A. Parallel transmission of input

I/O port

I/O bus

From input keyboard

To microprocessor

Buffer

PIO

I/O port

Buffer

B. Serial-to-parallel transmission of input

I/O port

I/O bus

From input keyboard

2 stop bits   1 start bit

1 check bit

1 1 1   1 1 1   1 1 1
      0   0

7 bits of data

To microprocessor

Buffer

UART

FIGURE 8-2
Data may be transmitted in parallel (A) or serially (B) along an I/O bus to an I/O port and, from there, in parallel, to a microprocessor.

MAINFRAME INPUT/OUTPUT

In a system where data is read from one input device, where processing is done under the direction of one stored program, and where results are written to one output device, the interactions within the system are relatively straightforward. In analyzing these interactions, we've acquired a basic understanding of how reading and writing occur. Systems designed to process the ever-increasing workloads of most users today are not that simple, however. Most users have spent lots of money in acquiring and installing both hardware and software. Because they have so much processing to do, they want to get lots of work out of all their system components. If the computer doesn't get the work done, who will?

We know that data and instructions move about within the processor unit of a computer system in the form of electrical pulses. These movements, say between two registers, or between a register and a primary-storage location, are called *internal data transfers*. (An instruction being moved is, in fact, treated like data.) The transfers occur at very fast rates.

We also know that data and instructions move between the processor unit and input devices, output devices, and secondary-storage devices. These movements are called *external data transfers*. We know that page or line printers operate at faster rates than character printers, that data is transferred much faster from some disk drives than from others, and so on. Because some kind of physical movement of the hardware is involved, all external data transfers are slower than internal transfers.

To help accommodate the vast disparities in speed, particularly on large mainframe systems, computer designers have developed *I/O channels*. *Control units* that perform functions similar to those of controllers (and indeed, that may even be called *controllers*) are also included in these systems. (See Figure 8-3.) Data buffering and asynchronous or synchronous data transfers are techniques developed to further enhance system performance. All these design considerations are discussed briefly below.

INPUT/OUTPUT CHANNELS

Bus architectures that provide for internal and external data transfers much as described above are not unique to microcomputer systems. Digital Equipment Corporation's PDP-11 and VAX minicomputers and Data General's ECLIPSE-series minicomputers are examples of larger systems that employ bus architectures. However, many large systems, including those of IBM and IBM-compatible mainframes, employ an I/O channel architecture. As the terminology implies, an I/O channel is like an I/O bus in that it provides a path for data transfer to or from an I/O device.

Physically, an I/O channel may be a standalone unit with its own logical circuitry and storage. Alternatively, it may be integrated within the processor unit (as in Figure 8-3). The types of channels available in an EDP system vary but they perform similar functions. Each channel is like a small computer in many ways. It executes the commands of a channel program, just as the processor executes the instructions of a stored program. By relieving the processor of the task of communicating directly with devices, the channel makes it possible for read, write, and internal processing operations to occur at the same time. The primary responsibility of a channel is to direct I/O operations.

The I/O channels that can be included in a particular system configuration may be of one or more of the following types: selector, byte multiplexer, and

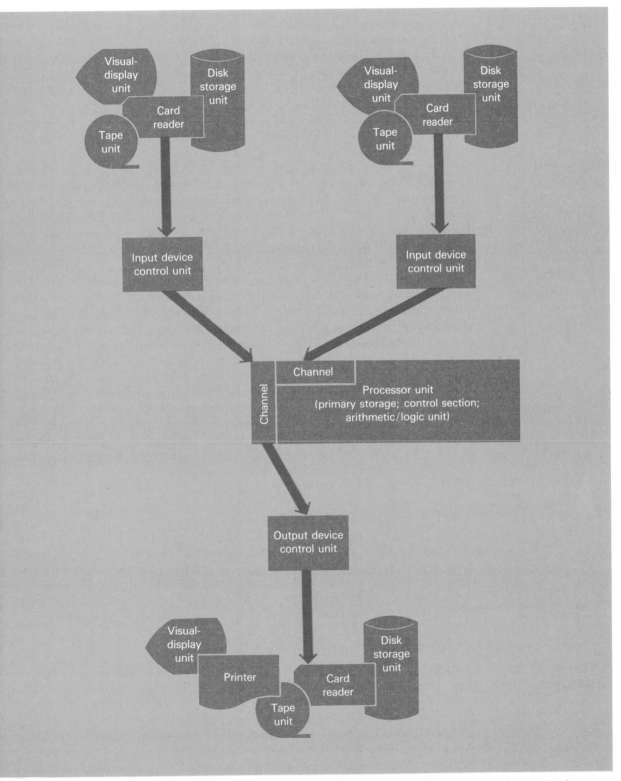

FIGURE 8-3 Input/output devices, control units, and channels provide paths for data entry and information exit in a large computer system.

block multiplexer. A *selector channel* transmits, in one operation, all the data in one record from an input device to primary storage, or all the data in one area of primary storage to an output device. This type of transfer is called, appropriately, *burst mode.* Because selector channels operate in this manner, they are usually attached to the control units of devices that transfer data at high speeds, such as very fast printing devices. They can also handle slow-speed devices. Only one device can be transmitting data at any given time. (See Figure 8-4A.)

A *byte multiplexer channel* may operate in burst mode, but it more commonly operates in *byte mode.* In byte mode, the single data path of the channel can be shared by many slow-speed devices (such as card readers, serial printers, and remote terminals) operating concurrently; the channel receives and sends data from and to the devices on demand. Only one byte of data is transferred to or from primary storage in one operation. Obviously, several operations are required to transfer all the data from one record or one area of storage. Generally, several slow-speed devices and their control units are attached to one byte multiplexer channel at any one time. The channel can accept or receive data from one device, then another, and so on. (See Figure 8-4B.)

A *block multiplexer channel* has advantages of both selector and byte multiplexer channels. It can simultaneously handle many high-speed devices. When operating in *selector mode,* it permits the interleaving (multiplexing) of channel programs for high-speed devices in such a way that channel programs can be initiated sooner and channels can be freed earlier than would be possible with selector channels. The byte and block multiplexer channels differ primarily in that block multiplexer channels can operate with much faster devices, and they transfer larger quantities of data per transmission. These quantities are referred to as *blocks.* They may include a number of records.

When an I/O operation is to be performed, the processor identifies the appropriate channel by referring to a table in primary storage. The processor then forwards the storage location of the first command in the channel program to the channel. Then the processor is free to continue its processing. The channel carries out its own program, transferring data to or from primary storage independently.

Just as the processor is free to continue executing its program once it has given an instruction to start a channel program, so a channel is free to execute other commands as soon as it has told a particular control unit what to do and what device to do it with. For example, it may tell a control unit to start a transfer-in (read) operation from a particular disk drive. Thus, a channel is constantly juggling various I/O operations to make the most efficient use of time, not only by overlapping inputs and outputs but also by doing so without tying up the processor.

CONTROL UNITS   Just as the control section of a processor governs the processor's operations, a control unit governs the activity of each I/O device. Sometimes the control unit is built into the device. Sometimes it is separate and may be used to govern any of several devices. Some control units control a particular type of device, such as disk storage units. Others can control several different types of devices, for example, visual-display units and serial printers. Sometimes intelligent terminals are designed for use as control units. They may be called *controllers, intelligent controllers,* or *storage controllers.*

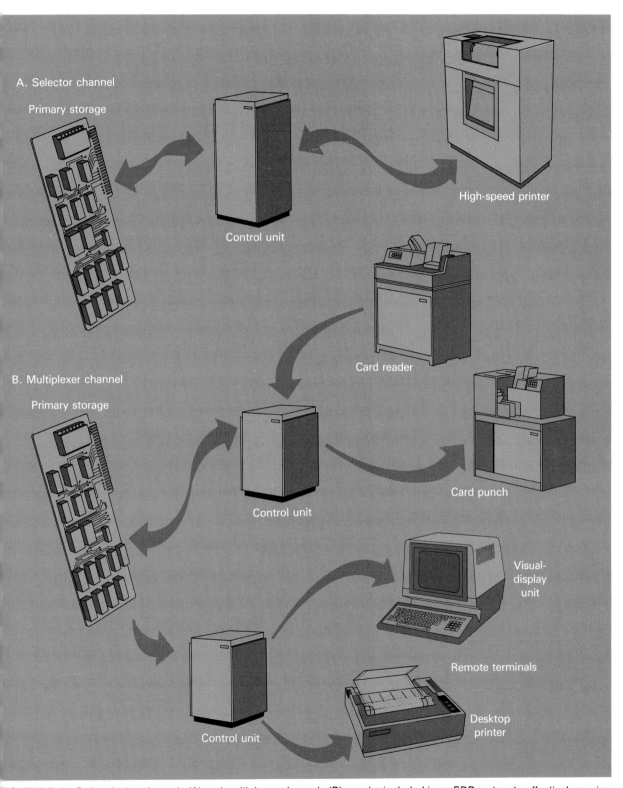

A. Selector channel

Primary storage

Control unit

High-speed printer

Card reader

B. Multiplexer channel

Primary storage

Control unit

Card punch

Visual-display unit

Remote terminals

Control unit

Desktop printer

FIGURE 8-4 Both selector channels (A) and multiplexer channels (B) may be included in an EDP system to effectively service both high-speed and slow-speed devices.

As explained above, a control unit receives commands from a channel. It decodes each command and initiates operation of the required device. The control unit is also responsible for any required code conversion during read or write operations. Checking the validity of data is another of its important functions. Data buffering, as explained below, is often a control-unit function, too.

If several similar devices are governed by one control unit, two additional functions are required: (1) determining priority of servicing, and (2) signaling device identification when requesting service for an input device or routing output to a particular output device.

DATA BUFFERING

We've come a long way since Chapter 2, where we first observed that all data processing involves at least three basic elements: input, processing, and output. Each element takes a specific amount of time. The usefulness of an EDP system is often directly related to the speed at which it can complete a given user task. Ideally, the configuration and speeds of the various I/O devices should be such that the main processor is always working at full capacity. The efficiency of any system, therefore, depends heavily on the extent to which input, internal processing, and output operations can be *overlapped*, or allowed to occur simultaneously.

When input occurs, a specific unit of data is entered into primary storage under the direction of a stored program. Multiple outputs may be developed from a single input. Conversely, several inputs may result in one output. Chart A in Figure 8-5 shows the basic time relationship between input, processing, and output with no overlap of operations. In this system, internal processing operations are suspended during read and write operations. Inefficiency is obvious, because much of the available processor time is wasted.

Charts B and C in Figure 8-5 show possible time relationships between input, processing, and output when data buffering is used. As these charts suggest, more work can be accomplished in a given period of time when operations are done simultaneously.

In one type of buffered system, data to be read as input is first collected in an external buffer. Usually, this buffer is in the control unit associated with a particular input device. When the contents of the buffer are actually transferred to primary storage, the transfer takes only a fraction of the time that would otherwise be required to read the data directly from the input device. While the data is being collected in the buffer, internal processing operations can occur.

Likewise, external buffering can be used on output. The results of processing are transferred from storage to the external buffer at high speed. The output device is then directed to write out the contents of the buffer. The processor is free to continue with other work while the writing occurs.

Note that if the same buffer is used for both input and output (for example, in one control unit governing two required disk drives), reading and writing cannot occur at the same time. (This case is shown in Figure 8-5B.) If several buffered control units are included in a system, reading, writing, and internal processing can all occur simultaneously (Figure 8-5C). The system components can be filling one buffer, processing data in primary storage, and writing out the contents of another buffer all at the same time.

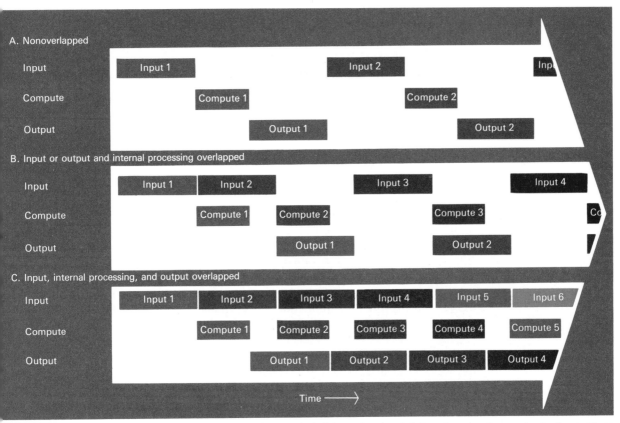

A. Nonoverlapped

Input	Input 1	Input 2	Inp
Compute	Compute 1	Compute 2	
Output	Output 1	Output 2	

B. Input or output and internal processing overlapped

Input	Input 1	Input 2	Input 3	Input 4
Compute	Compute 1	Compute 2	Compute 3	Cc
Output	Output 1	Output 2	

C. Input, internal processing, and output overlapped

Input	Input 1	Input 2	Input 3	Input 4	Input 5	Input 6
Compute	Compute 1	Compute 2	Compute 3	Compute 4	Compute 5
Output	Output 1	Output 2	Output 3	Output 4

Time ⟶

FIGURE 8-5 More work can be accomplished in a given period of time when input, internal processing, and output operations are done simultaneously.

The type of system we've just described is called an *external* buffered system because the buffers are outside of primary storage. Another type of buffered system uses *internal* buffering. In this case, a portion of primary storage serves as the major buffer area. Data is transmitted to and from primary storage in words or in fixed groups of characters. Transmission is interspersed automatically with computation. Because the time required for the transmission of a single word or group of words is relatively insignificant, this approach gives the effect of overlapping internal processing with both reading and writing.

The commonly stated advantage of internal buffering over external buffering is that the amount of data handled is restricted only by practical considerations of storage usage. When external buffering is used, the amount of data handled at any time is limited by the capacity of the buffer involved. The size of the buffer is fixed when the hardware is designed.

You should understand that data buffering is a technique often used on microcomputer, minicomputer, and mainframe systems. Though it may seem that storage constraints (and therefore buffer-size constraints) are more apt to be encountered on small systems than on large ones, that is not necessarily the case. Large systems must often handle large user workloads. Much system software as well as several application programs may occupy primary-storage locations. If many I/O devices are used, many buffers may be needed. It is also true that buffers are usually much larger on large systems than they are on small systems. In IBM 303X and 308X environments, 4K buffers are not uncommon. On microcomputer systems, buffers may be restricted to one word or one byte in size. Those used for I/O to and from screens, keyboards, or printers may be large enough to hold the contents of one full visual-display screen or of a single screen or print line.

SYNCHRONOUS AND ASYNCHRONOUS OPERATIONS

An EDP system in which actions of I/O devices are permitted to occur only at fixed points in a program and only in a sequence established by the program is described as having *synchronous operations*. As an example, assume a user wants to key in data from a visual-display unit. The keying activity may cause an indicator to be set automatically by hardware. Let's suppose a particular bit in storage is set to 1. The setting of the bit does not cause a read operation to occur immediately, however. At fixed intervals, the processor is directed to test that bit position. It also tests the bit positions reserved for other I/O devices on the system. This technique is called *polling*. When the visual-display unit's turn comes, and its bit is found to be set, the input operation is allowed to occur. Since internal processing operations occur very rapidly, it may seem to the user that the data keyed in is read immediately. That is not the case. All activities within the system are rigidly controlled by the hardware and/or by stored programs.

Other EDP systems perform *asynchronous operations*. Such systems are designed to permit the automatic interruption of processing whenever the need for some kind of I/O activity arises. The input or output device signals the processor by means of an *interrupt* when it is ready to read or to write. The interrupt means, in effect: "My particular job is done. As soon as convenient, use the data I have given you [if it was an input operation] or give me any additional information you have [if it was an output operation]." The signal may be the setting of a bit as above, but in this case, the bit has an immediate effect. As soon as the processor finishes whatever instruction it is executing, it accepts the data as input or transmits the information as output.

The effect of overlapped reading, writing, and computing operations can be achieved with either synchronous or asynchronous operations. Generally, synchronous requires greater attention to timing considerations on the part of persons who write programs to run on the system; asynchronous is possible only when certain features are present in the system hardware. EDP systems that accept simultaneous direct input from many users and must provide immediate responses to all of them are often dependent on asynchronous processing and interrupt capabilities.

CALCULATING

Once data has been read into the EDP system, calculation can begin. Any computer is capable of performing addition, subtraction, multiplication, and division; these operations may be either built into the machine or controlled by a stored program. For most commercial applications, these operations are adequate. Many intricate scientific problems can also be solved by elementary arithmetic. Some systems can perform additional, specialized operations to solve very complex mathematical problems.

In even the simplest arithmetic operation, at least two factors are involved: multiplier and multiplicand, divisor and dividend, and so on. The factors are operated on by the arithmetic portion of the arithmetic/logic unit of the computer to produce a result, such as a product or quotient. In every calculation, therefore, at least two storage locations are needed. Both quantities may be in primary storage, or one quantity may be in primary storage and the other in a register. When both quantities are in registers, calculating speeds are especially fast.

As a first example, assume that an arithmetic operation involving one factor in storage and another in a register is to be carried out on a large computer system or by a microprocessor. Initially, both factors must be read into primary storage or be available in registers as the results of prior operations. In general, we cannot assume that either factor is already in primary storage or in a register. Let's use a read instruction to make both factors available to the computer for processing. (See Figure 8-6, step 1.) Next, before calculation can take place, an instruction must be executed to transfer one of the factors to a

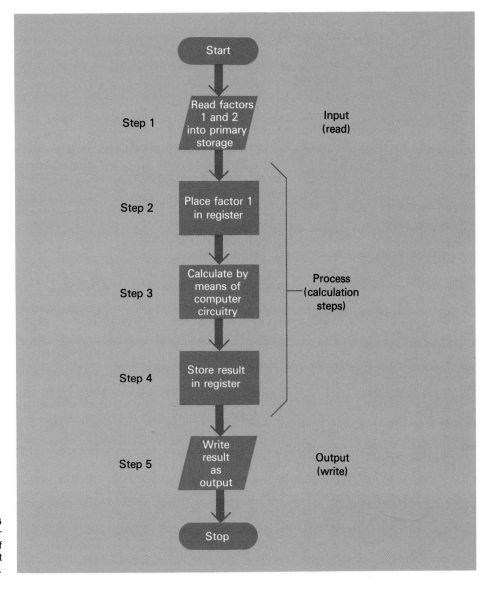

FIGURE 8-6
Calculation operations occur during the process part of the input–process–output cycle.

specific register (step 2). At the same time, this register is cleared of any previous factor or result that may have been there. The register is either explicitly specified in the instruction or implied, say, by the operation code of the instruction or by the action of a preceding instruction. The method of register selection depends on the instruction and on the computer being used. In our case, the preceding instruction was simply read into primary storage; it's unlikely that action would imply what register to use in a subsequent internal data transfer.

The actual calculation is performed under the control of another instruction (step 3). The operation-code field of this instruction specifies the arithmetic operation to be performed. The operand field specifies the location of the second factor. The computer acts upon the two factors, one in the register and one in primary storage, and stores the result in either place, as directed. In our example, the result is placed in the register (step 4). To see what the result is, we write it as output (step 5).

Now look at Figure 8-6 as a whole. It is a *program flowchart* for a complete input-process-output cycle. Step 1, the read, is input; steps 2 through 5, the calculation, are process; step 5, the write, is output. Note the parallelogram-shaped *input/output symbol* (⬦) used to represent input and output operations. Note the rectangular *process symbol* (⬜) used to represent process steps. The oval-shaped symbols (⬭) are called *terminal symbols;* they mark the beginning and end of all the operations that are to occur, and hence the beginning and end of the program flowchart.

Now let's consider a more complex sequence of calculations. Our purpose here is to help you think about all the operations the computer must do just to complete an often-required routine task, for example, calculating an employee's "take-home pay." You should assume that read and write operations occur as required, but we'll focus our attention on the calculations that must be accomplished. (See Figure 8-7.)

In the calculation sequence, the number of hours worked is placed in a register and multiplied by the hourly rate to determine earnings. Piecework and bonus amounts are added to earnings to develop a total regular earnings amount. Total regular earnings are divided by hours to produce an average hourly rate. This rate is multiplied by 1.5 times overtime hours to produce overtime earnings. Total gross pay is then calculated. Taxes are computed using the calculated gross pay. Year-to-date payroll data is accumulated using the amounts that were calculated. Certain intermediate results of calculations, namely the tax amounts and a total of all other deductions, are used in calculating net pay. The net pay figure is the amount the employee actually sees on his paycheck, or on his bank statement if a direct banking option is available and he has elected to use it.

As this example demonstrates, any number of calculations can take place on several factors in one series of instructions. That is, a factor may be placed in a register and multiplied. Other factors may be added to or subtracted from the product. The result can then be divided by another factor. Other add and subtract operations can be performed on the quotient. The same register or other registers may be used. The sequence of operations can take place as rapidly as the computer can execute the required steps. Intermediate results can be stored in specified locations at any time. Some results must be so stored if they are to be used again later. The result of a calculation involving one or more factors already in registers may be stored back into one of the registers. This result overlays the

FIGURE 8-7
A computer can perform long
sequences of calculation operations under stored-progran
control. There is no need for
human intervention between
each step to tell it to do the next
one (as is commonly required
when the same operations are
done with a calculator, for
example). The calculation
operations needed to accomplish a routine business task
that's important to many of us—
calculating an employee's take-
home pay—are shown on this
portion of a program flowchart.
Each step is represented by a
process symbol because
calculation operations are
internal processing operations.
When this sequence of operations has been completed, the
values that have been computed
can be written as output.
(*Photo courtesy Bunker-Ramo
Information Systems*)

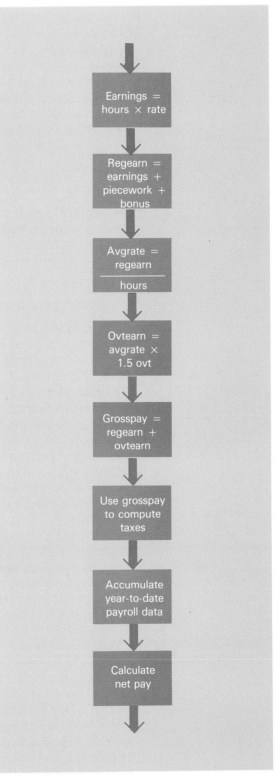

factor that was there. If it hasn't been saved (by storing it elsewhere), it's no longer available to the computer.

The contents of registers can be shifted (as described under "Registers" in Chapter 7) to adjust, lengthen, or shorten the results of calculations. If the dropped digits are simply ignored, we say the results are *truncated*. For example, 134.893 may be truncated to 134.89. Alternatively, a result may be *rounded* by an addition operation before shifting is done. As an example, assume the decimal value 565.846 is to be rounded to have only two digits to the right of the decimal point so that it looks like an ordinary dollars-and-cents value. In rounding, we add 5 to the leftmost position to be dropped, before shifting. Thus:

565.846
+.005
565.851, which is then shifted and becomes 565.85

On the other hand, if the value 451.973 is to be rounded to two decimal places, the same technique is used, but the rightmost retained digit is not increased by 1 (because the leftmost dropped digit is not 5 or greater). That is:

451.973
+.005
451.978, which is then shifted and becomes 451.97

The numerical values we're using here are examples of *fixed-point data*—numerical data items with digits on each side of a point, such as 25.00 or 3.8. The point is not actually placed in storage. More important, the computer is not even aware of it. It sees only 2500 or 38. Instructions in the stored program must tell the computer where to place the point when a result is provided as output. (As we will see below, instructions of this kind may not be necessary when the computer is directed to perform floating-point operations.)

All calculations must take into account the algebraic signs of factors in storage locations and registers. Consequently, a computer is designed so that it has the ability to store and recognize the sign of a factor. As suggested in Chapter 3, if primary storage is made up of words of a fixed length, one position of each word is designated as a *sign-bit position*. Whenever a numerical value is stored in binary form in one of these words, the sign-bit position is used for the sign. A 0 bit in this position indicates a positive value; a 1 bit indicates a negative value. Registers also have a special sign position or a sign indicator. The sign of a result, as well as its numerical value, can be determined by calculation.

In most computers, when fixed-length arithmetic operations are used, the sign of a result is stored in the leftmost bit position of the word containing the result. (See Figure 8-8.) The numerical value is stored in binary form, right-justified, in the remaining bit positions.

Positive numbers not in binary form are converted to binary and stored in the computer in the same way that they are written. The sign bit of each number is zero. Any unused positions following the sign bit and not needed for the binary numeral are filled with zeros. A number that is stored in the way in which it is written is said to be stored in *true form*.

In a few computers, negative numbers are also stored in true form. In others, however, negative numbers are stored in *complement form*. The sign bit of each number is 1, and the rightmost bit positions of the computer word contain the *two's complement* of the original number.

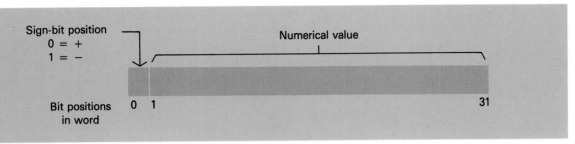

FIGURE 8-8 A sign bit and a 31-digit binary numeral may be stored in one 32-bit computer word.

Mathematically, the two's complement of a negative number is the difference between the absolute value of that number and the next-higher-order power of 2. We find the two's complement by converting the original number to binary (if it is not already in that form) and then doing a binary subtraction. The absolute value of the binary numeral is subtracted from the next-higher-order power of 2. For example, the negative decimal numeral -5 is equivalent to the negative binary numeral -101. The two's complement of -101 is computed as follows:

$$
\begin{array}{r}
1000 \\
-\ 101 \\
\hline
011
\end{array}
\qquad \text{which can be shown in detail as} \qquad
\begin{array}{r}
0\ 1\ 1 \\
1^1 0^1 0^1 0 \\
-\quad 1\ 0\ 1 \\
\hline
0\ 1\ 1
\end{array}
$$

A simpler but somewhat mechanical way to find the two's complement can be summarized as follows: *To find the two's complement of a negative binary numeral, invert all the bits of the numeral and add 1 to the result.* In our case, we apply this rule as follows:

$$
-101 \qquad \text{inverted, becomes} \qquad
\begin{array}{r}
010 \\
+1 \\
\hline
011
\end{array}
$$

With each method, we have shown the two's complement to be 011. As stated above, this result is stored in the rightmost bit positions of the computer word reserved for it. Any unused positions following the sign bit and not needed for the two's complement are filled with ones.

Since we have not studied binary arithmetic in this book, the details of the binary subtraction above are shown for those who wish to follow it. In practice, the two's complement is formed automatically by computer circuitry, so a programmer or other user need not be concerned with it when setting up calculations. However, if it becomes necessary to examine the contents of primary storage to find out why certain errors have occurred, it may be helpful to know whether negative numbers are stored in true or complement form.

Two familiar arithmetic rules for handling signed numbers are applied in computer calculations:

- To add numbers with *like signs*, find the sum of the values and give it the same sign.

- To add numbers with *unlike signs*, find the difference between the values and give it the sign of the one that is larger in absolute value.

A few simple problems using decimal numbers will illustrate that these rules apply to both addition and subtraction. Some examples are:

Add like signs	*Subtract like signs*

```
   Add like signs              Subtract like signs

      + 5                  + 10            + 10
   +                    −         becomes +
      + 3                  + 3             − 3
   ─────                ─────           ─────
      + 8                                  + 7


   Add unlike signs            Subtract unlike signs

      − 13                 + 5             + 5
   +                    −         becomes +
      +  8                 − 1             + 1
   ─────                ─────           ─────
      −  5                                 + 6
```

You have probably noticed that in this book a processor is described as having adder circuitry. We have not said that a processor has subtracter circuitry. Now that you know about two's complements, it's appropriate to point out that most computers perform subtraction by doing addition. They add the two's complement of the value to be subtracted instead of subtracting that value.

In a multiplication operation, if the signs of the factors are the same, the result is positive. If the signs are not the same, the result is negative. In most computers, a zero result is always negative.

In a division operation, if the signs of the factors are the same, the quotient is positive. If the signs are not the same, the quotient is negative. In most computers, the sign of the remainder is the sign of the dividend. These rules apply even if the quotient or remainder is zero.

The length of one computer word and the minimum and maximum values that can be stored and processed depend on the design of the computer. The exact rules governing the placement of factors during calculations and the placement of results vary somewhat from system to system. In all cases, if a result of calculations performed on fixed-point data may exceed the capacity of the storage location or register to be used for it, the programmer must provide for the possibility of overflow. He or she may arrange data to produce partial results and then combine the partial results, or totals. Alternatively, he or she may use *scaling* so that very large or very small values can be handled conveniently. When scaling is used with decimal values, each value is represented as a decimal fraction multiplied by a power of 10. The power of 10 is the scale factor, remembered by the programmer. For example, $80000 = 8 \times 10^4$. Another alternative that may be available is the use of instructions that govern floating-point operations, as described below.

FLOATING-POINT OPERATIONS

Mathematicians and scientists often use logarithms to simplify mathematical operations involving very large numbers or very small fractions. For the same reason, computers are often designed so that floating-point operations can be performed if necessary. As the term *floating point* implies, the point in a very large number or a very small fraction may be moved to facilitate calculations. If you have some understanding of floating-point operations, you'll be better able to decide whether or not they're appropriate for your particular application. On some systems, use of floating-point operations occurs automatically if very large or very small numbers must be dealt with. On other systems, floating-point operations are used only if instructions are written to invoke them.

We've pointed out before that a computer's primary storage and its registers are designed to handle specific units of data, for example, 8-bit bytes, 8-bit words, 16-bit words, or 32-bit words. If numerical values are stored in binary form in 8-bit bytes or words, the acceptable range of values extends from -128 through $+127$. (See Figure 8-9.) Clearly, if the computer can only handle values in that range, its applicability to real-world problems is limited. A 16-bit word length eases the situation somewhat; the acceptable range of values extends from $-32,768$ through $+32,767$. Even that's not enough for many common situations. Furthermore, the user may be unable to forecast in advance exactly what range of values must be provided for. In all these cases, use of floating-point numerals rather than binary integer values may be advisable.

Floating-Point Notation

As a first step in understanding floating-point operations, let's look at how a familiar decimal value can be expressed in floating-point form. The first numeral in the leftmost column of Figure 8-10 is the decimal numeral 271.55. This value can also be represented as a decimal fraction multiplied by a power of 10. The alternate way of writing the value is shown in the center column of this figure. In a very simple third step, this value can be rewritten in floating-point notation as shown in the third column. Thus, 271.55 becomes $.27155 \times 10^3$, which becomes .27155E + 3. In this example, .27155 is the *fraction;* 3 is the *exponent.* Because the fraction represents a value between .1 and 1.0, the floating-point numeral is said to be in *normal form.*

Both the exponent and the fraction of a floating-point numeral can be either positive or negative. The sign of the fraction is the sign of the original value. The sign of the exponent depends on whether the value of the original numeral is greater or less than 0.1, ignoring its sign. If the original value is greater than 0.1, the exponent is positive. (For examples, see the first, third, and fourth numerals in Figure 8-10.) If the original value is less than 0.1, the exponent is negative. (The second numeral in Figure 8-10 has a negative exponent.) An unsigned exponent or fraction is assumed to be positive. Floating-point notation is obviously so named because it is possible to "float" the point by adjusting the exponent appropriately.

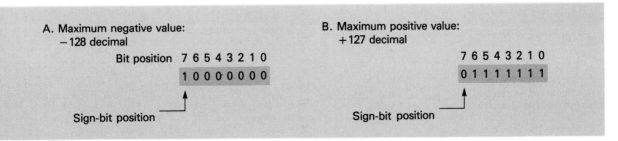

FIGURE 8-9 A value in the range from -128 to $+127$ can be stored in one 8-bit storage location.

DECIMAL NUMERAL	REPRESENTATION AS DECIMAL FRACTION × POWER OF 10	FLOATING-POINT NOTATION
271.55	$.27155 \times 10^3$	$.27155E + 3$
.0789	$.789 \times 10^{-1}$	$.789E - 1$
−123760000	$-.12376 \times 10^9$	$-.12376E + 9$
84499.3	$.844993 \times 10^5$	$.844993E + 5$

FIGURE 8-10
Decimal numerals and floating-point notation are ways of representing numerical values.

Floating-Point Representation

Now let's see how floating-point numerals are represented in computer storage. Some computers use decimal floating-point; others use hexadecimal or binary. The techniques are the same; only the base (10, 16, 2) changes. Since IBM's large computers systems are widely used, let us consider how these computers store floating-point numerals.

Within primary storage and in registers, the hexadecimal number system is used for floating-point operations. A hexadecimal floating-point numeral is expressed in the same way as a decimal floating-point numeral except that digits of the hexadecimal number system are used. Some examples are shown in Figure 8-11.

Floating-point operations are fixed-length operations. Each floating-point numeral is stored in one or two computer words. Each word is 32 bits in length. The sign of the hexadecimal floating-point numeral is represented by a 0 if it is a plus sign, or by a 1 if it is a minus sign. The sign digit is placed in the leftmost bit position of the word as shown in Figure 8-12.

The value that represents the exponent of the hexadecimal floating-point numeral is placed in the 1st through 7th bit positions of the computer word. These 7 bits can hold values that are equivalent to decimal values ranging from −64 to +63. However, to avoid carrying the sign of the exponent in the computer, a technique called *excess-64 arithmetic* has been developed. A value of 64 is added to the exponent of each floating-point numeral. Thus, exponents ranging from −64 to +63 are converted to positive numbers that range from 0 to 127. For example, the exponent −3 becomes +61. In computer terminology, +61 is called the *characteristic* of the number −3.

The 8th through 31st bit positions of the computer word contain the fraction of the hexadecimal floating-point numeral. This fraction can be up to six

HEXADECIMAL NUMERAL	REPRESENTATION AS HEXADECIMAL FRACTION × POWER OF 16	FLOATING-POINT NOTATION
1A5.3	$.1A53 \times 16^3$	$.1A53E + 3$
3CB92100	$.3CB921 \times 16^8$	$.3CB921E + 8$
−77.D45E	$-.77D45E \times 16^2$	$-.77D45EE + 2$
.0000B15	$.B15 \times 16^{-4}$	$.B15E - 4$

FIGURE 8-11
Numerical values can be represented as hexadecimal numerals and in hexadecimal floating-point notation.

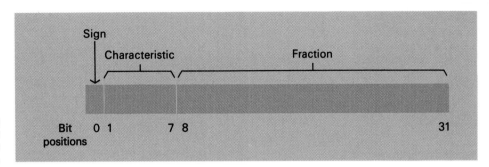

FIGURE 8-12
A hexadecimal floating-point value can be stored in one 32-bit computer word.

hexadecimal digits in length and can represent a value that is equivalent to a six-digit decimal numeral. A floating-point numeral stored in one computer word is said to be stored with *short precision*. (See Figure 8-13A.)

If more than six digits are required to represent a value, the floating-point numeral can be stored in two consecutive words treated as one long word—that is, one *doubleword*. (See Figure 8-13B.) In this case, the numeral is said to be stored with *long precision*. As in short precision, the sign and the characteristic occupy the leftmost 8 bits of the area. The remaining bits are reserved for the fraction. Therefore, it is possible to store a 14-digit hexadecimal numeral, which can represent a value that is equivalent to a 15-digit decimal numeral. This can be a very large number or a very small fraction, depending on the value of the exponent.

Advantages and Disadvantages of Floating-Point Operations

As pointed out, floating-point operations are fixed-length operations. Data is manipulated very rapidly in parallel. Very large numbers and very small fractions can be represented in only one computer word or doubleword.

Furthermore, when data is handled as floating-point data, the computer assumes responsibility for keeping track of the point in each numerical value. For example, as arithmetic operations are performed, the points may be floated to the right or left to convert all numerals involved in the operation to the same power. All numerals must have the same number of places to the right of the point. This process is similar to changing fractions with different denominators into fractions with a common denominator.

In contrast, the numerical data that we, as humans, deal with most frequently is expressed—not in floating-point notation—but simply as, say, 48, .33, and so on. As mentioned earlier in this chapter, such numerals are called *fixed-point data*. If the numerals are read into computer storage, instructions in the program must keep track of the positions of all points and direct the computer to place the data in storage and provide output accordingly.

Thus, floating-point operations offer advantages of speed, ease of working with very large and very small numbers, precision, and point handling. In scientific applications that involve numerous calculations and deal with very large or very small values, these advantages are often important. The calculations will be performed rapidly, and the computer will keep track of points. In many business applications, however, calculations are comparatively few and relatively simple. Extreme speed is not vitally significant. Numerals used in business applications seldom have more than two places to the right of the

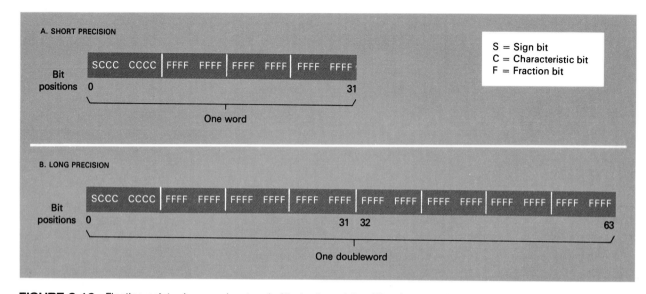

FIGURE 8-13 Floating-point values can be stored with short precision (A) or long precision (B) in one computer word or one doubleword, respectively.

decimal point. They are rarely either extremely large or extremely small. With care, instructions can be written to handle them accurately.

The user who works with large volumes of input and output data must be concerned with how that data is represented on I/O devices. This user is usually willing to sacrifice high degrees of precision in order to deal with familiar decimal numerals. Numbers expressed as familiar decimal numerals can be converted to floating-point by the computer. If they are, time for conversion operations is required. Furthermore, in some EDP systems, not all decimal numerals can be represented accurately in internal floating-point form. A series of calculations performed as floating-point operations on values initially expressed in dollars-and-cents form may not yield the same results as the same calculations performed manually. Such discrepancies, though small, are often intolerable in the business environment. Thus, any speed gained in calculation is offset by loss of time in conversion and by possible inaccuracy. Remember, conversion is required for both input and output.

Floating-point operations are not available on all computer systems. Most systems that support floating-point operations require both special instructions and special hardware. In some cases, the hardware can be obtained as a feature, but only at an additional cost. In other cases, the hardware is a standard no-cost option. In any case, whether or not floating-point operations should be used is best determined by analyzing the user's needs.

SELECTION AND LOOPING

The sequence in which a stored-program computer executes its instructions is determined in one of two ways: Either the instructions are executed in the consecutive order in which they are stored, or the operand of one instruction indicates the location of the next one. If all instructions had to be executed in consecutive order as stored, the computer could operate only in a fixed pattern. It would have no ability to deal with exceptions to the single established procedure or to choose from among alternatives on the basis of conditions encountered during processing. Further, without some way of resetting the computer to re-execute a given series of instructions, a complete program would have to be written, stored, and executed for every data record to be processed.

Consider the program flowchart in Figure 8-14. The steps on the flowchart show how to cause the computer to prepare an invoice for one customer. During one execution of the program corresponding to this flowchart, the computer reads one customer order as input, computes one amount owed, and writes one invoice as output.

Now suppose we want the computer to write an invoice for the customer only if the amount owed exceeds $5.00. A modified version of the program flowchart is shown in Figure 8-15. Note the *decision symbol* (◇) following the computation step. An instruction must be included in the program at this point to cause the computer to examine the amount owed. If the amount owed is greater than $5.00, the computer selects the "Yes" path from the decision-making step. If the amount owed is $5.00 or less, it selects the "No" path instead.

We see here an example of the computer's logical decision-making capabilities. It can select either of two instruction sequences, depending on the value it has computed for a data item. This selection capability is helpful in many situations. For example, the computer can examine a student's total points earned and select or not select an instruction sequence to add the student's name

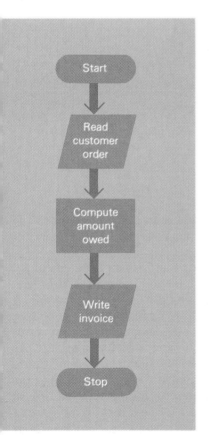

FIGURE 8-14 One customer invoice is prepared in one input–process–output cycle. (*Photo courtesy Honeywell Inc.*)

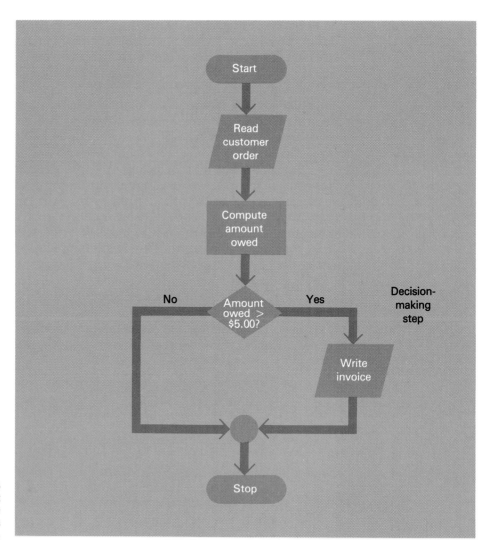

FIGURE 8-15
To determine whether or not
the customer owes more
than $5.00 requires a
decision-making step.

to an honors list. It can examine the current balance in a customer's checking account and select or not select an instruction sequence to print a notice that the account is overdrawn.

Now suppose we want the computer to prepare an invoice for a customer, irrespective of amount owed, as in our original problem (Figure 8-14). However, we want the computer to prepare invoices for many customers, not just one. A convenient way to do this would be to reuse the steps on the program flowchart, multiple times. We can do so. That is, we can direct the computer to repeat one or more steps that it has already done. It can execute and re-execute instructions during processing. Again, we need a logical decision-making step. (See Figure 8-16.) An instruction must be included following the write step to make the computer check to see if it has processed all orders. If it has not, it must branch back up to the read step. In effect, a *program loop* is formed. If the computer has processed all orders, it must execute the next instruction in sequence (as it normally would if there were no decision-making step). In our example, it

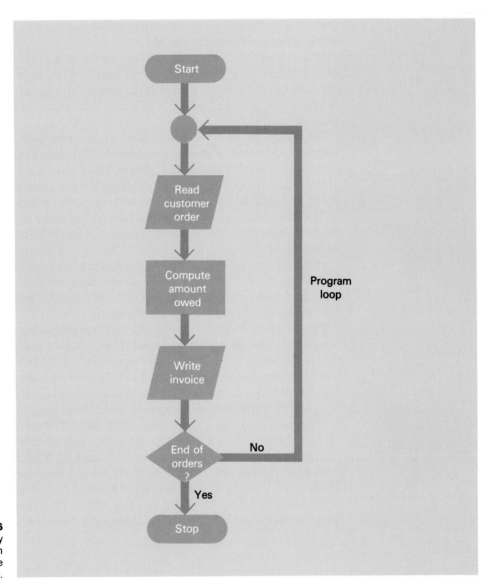

FIGURE 8-16
To prepare invoices for many
customers, the steps within
a program loop must be
re-executed many times.

reaches the end of the program. Each time the computer executes the decision-
making step, whether or not the program loop is re-executed depends on
whether or not all orders have been processed.

It's probably safe to assume that computers would be used in problem solving
even if they didn't have looping capabilities. Writing programs to direct them,
however, would be a never-ending job. Writing one sequence of instructions to
tell the computer how to process an insurance claim may be challenging, for
example. Writing 9999 sequences of instructions just like the first sequence,
simply because 9999 more claims have to be processed, would be something else!

COMPARING The ability of a computer to make decisions on the basis of program logic often
depends on its ability to perform *compare* operations. Through such operations,

the computer is able to determine whether two data items are equal, or whether one is lower or higher than another.

The comparison operators, as expressed in mathematics and in many programming languages, are shown in Figure 8-17. You are probably familiar with them. Note that "equal to" is the converse of "not equal to"; "greater than" is the converse of "less than or equal to"; and "less than" is the converse of "greater than or equal to."

Internally, the computer may carry out several processing steps to perform a compare operation. For example, consider "greater than." First, the computer's compare circuitry tests for the "greater than" condition between two data items. If the condition exists, a particular bit position in storage is set to 1. Then, the bit position (often called a *condition code*) is tested by other circuitry. If the bit is set to 1, a transfer to an alternate instruction sequence occurs. If the bit is not set, the next instruction in sequence is executed (as if the compare operation had not occurred).

In some computers, all these operations are performed automatically (by hardware) in response to a single stored-program conditional transfer instruction. In others, a sequence of instructions must be included in the program to specifically direct each operation required.

The simplest compare operations involve comparing an input data item or a computed value to a previously established value that does not change (i.e., a *constant*). We saw this kind of a comparison in Figure 8-15. A computed amount owed is compared to the constant $5.00. The comparison is a test for the "greater than" condition. If the amount owed is greater than $5.00, the test condition is satisfied. A transfer to the alternate instruction sequence then occurs.

Now look again at Figure 8-16. How do you suppose we state the question "End of orders?" in a way the computer can understand? In fact, the more general question we might ask ourselves here is: Whenever the computer has to read and process more than one data record, how can it tell when it's done? Obviously, this kind of logic is needed for many applications.

In planning this program or any other program, a system analyst or programmer must meet with the users whose needs are being addressed. What

OPERATOR	CONDITION (MEANING)
=	Equal to
>	Greater than
<	Less than
≠ or < >	Not equal to
≥ or > =	Greater than or equal to
≤ or < =	Less than or equal to

FIGURE 8-17
The compare operations performed by a computer are much like those we do in daily activities.

data will be provided as input? What information is required as output? When a program is being created to process batch input, an approach that is often mutually agreed upon is to have the user submit a count of the number of data records in a special control record that precedes the batch. Generally, the count is available anyhow as a *control total*. Such control totals are established as a part of normal data-processing procedures in order to help insure that no data is lost during either manual or computer handling of the data.

Figure 8-18 shows the slight modifications that must be made to the flowchart in Figure 8-16 to describe more specifically the end-of-input logic. As suggested, a user-supplied count of the data records (customer orders, in this case) is assumed to be the first input. This count is read and stored in the primary-storage location represented by the variable LIMIT. Another variable, N, is set to an initial value of 0. This initialization step is represented by the *preparation symbol* ($\bigcirc$) on the program flowchart. The comment in the *annotation symbol* ($\square$) tells us that N will be used as a counter during loop processing. Both LIMIT and N are called *variables* because they do not have fixed values when program execution begins. Their values are assigned during processing and may be changed any number of times.

As each customer order is read and processed, the computer increases N by 1. Then, at the decision-making step, the current value of N is compared to the value of LIMIT. The comparison is a test for the "equal to" condition. If this tested-for condition does not exist, the program loop is re-executed. If the condition does exist (i.e., N = LIMIT), the program loop is exited. Program execution is terminated because all customer orders have been processed.

Compare operations are also used to check the sequence of input records. We may write a program to arrange, or sort, input records in some desired order for processing. The comparison of a control field in one record with a control field in another also enables the computer to handle input records from a number of associated sequential files during one processing run. The only requirement is that all the records in the files to be processed must be arranged in the same sequence. We saw examples of this kind of program logic when discussing the sequential processing of transactions and master records under "Storage and Data-Processing Methods" in Chapter 6.

It may seem obvious to you that 16 is greater than 10, -5 is equal to -5, and 400 is less than 890. What if we need to compare other than numerical values? For example, we may want the computer to alphabetize a list of manager names on an intracompany memo distribution list. We may want the computer to create an index for a book, supply manual, or mail-order catalog. In doing so, it must be able to order, or rank, the names or indexed items.

The basis for all such compare operations is built into computer circuitry. However, computers do not all use the same method of ranking because they do not all store values in the same way internally. Generally, the digits 0 through 9 are arranged in their normal ascending sequence, with 9 assumed to be the highest. In the same manner, Z is assumed to be the highest letter of the alphabet. To the computer, then, the numeral 162 is higher in sequence than the numeral 149. The name Jones is higher than the name Harris. Special characters such as / and @ may also be ranked. In some computers, special characters are lowest in sequence, followed by letters of the alphabet and numerals, in that order. (See Figure 8-19.) This sequence is referred to as the *collating sequence* of the computer.

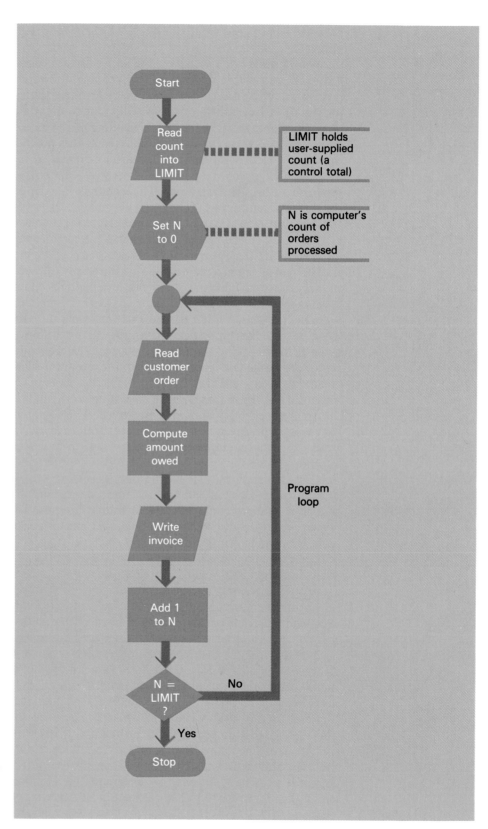

FIGURE 8-18
When more than one data
record must be processed,
end-of-input logic
is required.

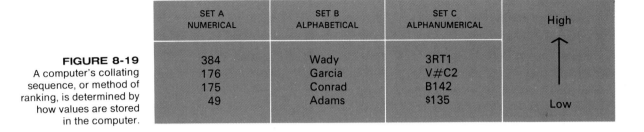

	SET A NUMERICAL	SET B ALPHABETICAL	SET C ALPHANUMERICAL	High
	384	Wady	3RT1	↑
	176	Garcia	V#C2	
	175	Conrad	B142	
	49	Adams	$135	Low

FIGURE 8-19
A computer's collating sequence, or method of ranking, is determined by how values are stored in the computer.

Look back at Figures 3-9 and 3-11 in Chapter 3. These figures show the bit patterns for EBCDIC and ASCII characters, respectively. Both sets of characters are listed in ascending sequence. This shows you how values represented in EBCDIC or ASCII will be ordered by the computer. Then look again at Figure 8-19. Notice that the values in set C are arranged as in EBCDIC collating sequence, but not as they would be if ordered in ASCII sequence. In ASCII, letters are higher than digits.

One additional point needs to be made with respect to the computer's compare capabilities. It can only compare values of compatible data types. Ideally, if one value involved in a compare operation is stored internally in binary form, the other value is stored in that form also. Similarly, if one value is stored in EBCDIC, the other should be also. Some computer systems allow a binary value to be compared to an EBCDIC value if the latter consists only of digits. Internally, the computer converts the EBCDIC value to an equivalent binary value before the compare operation is performed. Other computer systems do not allow EBCDIC (or ASCII) values to be compared to anything other than EBCDIC (or ASCII) values. If an illegal comparison is attempted, an error is declared.

We said earlier that some numerical values expressed initially in decimal form cannot be represented exactly in floating-point form. The computer can convert values from one of these forms to the other, but small inaccuracies may be introduced. In a sequence of calculations, these inaccuracies may get larger. Therefore, floating-point values that would be equal were it not for the introduced error may not compare equally.

For this reason, it's wise not to direct the computer to test for the "equal to" condition between two floating-point values. As an example, assume both DIST1 and DIST2 represent floating-point values, two distances in space calculated by the computer. A test expressed as ABS(DIST1 − DIST2) = .005 may give a truer indication of whether the values are "approximately equal" than a test for the condition DIST1 = DIST2, which is almost sure to fail (be answered "No"). Here *ABS* is a programming-language keyword for the absolute-value function. It directs the computer to find the difference between two values and ignore the sign of the result. Some programming languages support an "approximately equal" comparison operator. In general, this particular operator is implemented by means of software rather than hardware. If it is not implemented as hard-wired circuitry, several machine-language instructions may have to be executed to accomplish it. That means an "approximately equal" comparison may take longer than other compare operations.

CHAPTER SUMMARY

1. During a microcomputer read operation, data travels from an input device along an I/O bus to an I/O port on a PIO or UART chip, then via interface logic and (in some systems) a controller to the microprocessor. The converse occurs during a write operation.

2. Many large systems have an I/O channel (rather than bus) architecture. The channels execute commands (of channel programs) to direct I/O operations, control units, and devices. By doing so, they free the main processor for other work.

3. A system may use either external or internal data buffering to overlap read, internal processing, and write operations. This overlap capability increases the amount of work that can be done in a given period of time.

4. A synchronous system allows I/O operations to occur only at fixed points in a program and in a sequence established by the program. An asynchronous system responds to automatic interrupts whenever read or write operations are to occur.

5. Sequences of calculation operations may be performed on numerical values in registers or primary-storage locations. The values may be represented as fixed-point binary data items, stored in either true or complement form.

6. Calculations may be performed on numerical values stored in floating-point form. Speed of processing, ease of handling very large and very small numbers, precision, and point handling are potential advantages of floating-point operations.

7. The computer's logical decision-making capabilities allow it to select either of two instruction sequences or to loop back and re-execute instructions during processing.

8. Compare operations are basic to decision making. Whether numbers, letters, or special characters are highest in collating sequence depends on the way the values are stored in the computer.

9. Program flowcharts are a convenient way of describing the operations that are to occur during program execution. The input/output, process, terminal, decision, preparation, and annotation symbols are used to represent steps to be carried out.

DISCUSSION QUESTIONS

1. What happens inside a microcomputer system when a user interacts with the system by means of its keyboard and CRT?

2. (a) What is an S-100 bus?
   (b) What advantages does it offer to manufacturers and to users?

3. (a) Why are channels often included in large computer systems?
   (b) Describe three types of channels that may be used in them.

4. (a) What are some of the functions of an I/O control unit?
   (b) Would you expect the number of control units in an EDP system to be less than, equal to, or greater than the number of I/O devices? Why?

5. (a) What are the benefits of data buffering?
   (b) Describe a system in which buffering can be accomplished.

6. Explain the difference between synchronous and asynchronous operations.

7. Suppose a sales representative's weekly earnings, based in part on a fixed salary and in part on a commission (computed as a fixed percentage of sales), are to be calculated by a computer. Describe the series of calculations required, using either narrative paragraphs or flowcharting.

8. How can a computer that has only adder circuitry carry out subtraction operations?

9. (a) Contrast the use of fixed-point data with the use of floating-point data.
   (b) When might either be preferred?

10. Suggest steps in the processing of a student's loan application where the computer's selection capability may be required.

11. What is the purpose of a program loop?

12. Suppose the rainfall amounts for seven days are to be read (one at a time) as input, added to an accumulator, and then used in a calculation step to determine the average daily rainfall. Use either narrative paragraphs or flowcharting to explain how the computer's looping capability can be used to set up the logic required.

13. (a) What do selection and looping have in common?
    (b) What computer operations, even more basic than selection and looping, are prerequisites to these capabilities?

14. Refer to Figures 3-9 and 3-11. How does the collating sequence of EBCDIC differ from that of ASCII?

9
MICRO-COMPUTERS IN USE

The rapid concentration of computing power in smaller and less expensive computers gave birth to the microcomputer, also often called a *personal* computer, *home* computer, or *desktop* computer. New uses for these computers are appearing almost every day.

Ingenious owners and managers of small businesses immediately found many applications for their personal computers. Luthier's Mercantile, makers of parts for guitars and other stringed instruments, uses a microcomputer for accounting, word processing, maintaining a mailing list, and other office-management tasks. Roger Luthier said of his micro: "It's been running for a year and a half, six days a week. . . . We never even needed to kick it or anything!"

A desktop computer may also be used to control simple automated manufacturing processes and to keep track of production and shipments, as in a meat-packing plant. When a computer takes over these jobs, both space-saving and time-saving benefits immediately appear. More importantly, human resources can be freed to think and plan rather than do boring, mechanical tasks.

Some computers are so portable yet so complete that they can be used almost anywhere and at any time. They may have self-contained disk drives, display screens, and power packs. Such portability can be very handy for anyone from a writer in seclusion to a business person frequently away from the home office. By using a modem, or a computer-telephone interface, it is easily possible to communicate with other system users or computers elsewhere. A traveler may input data or reports via the portable keyboard or may access important messages waiting at the other end. Hard copies of the messages may be made by the portable computer's printer. The salesperson in the field can get immediate inventory information from the database back at the home office, and tell the customer when to expect delivery of the order.

Many banks now have after-hours, computerized bank-by-telephone services. A customer uses a home computer, connected via modem and communication line, to communicate with the bank's computer to determine the status of an account. In such uses, authorization codes are always required to protect confidential information.

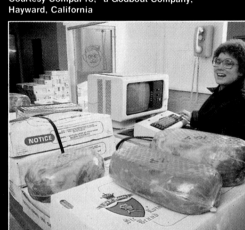

Courtesy CompuPro,° a Godbout Company, Hayward, California

© 1979 Michael Alexander

Courtesy Eagle Computer

© 1984 Nita Winter, Courtesy Photo & Sound Co., San Francisco

Courtesy Radio Shack, a Division of Tandy Corporation

Courtesy Epson America, Inc.

When portability and small size are important factors in a situation, users may rely on note-book-size computers, small enough to fit easily into a briefcase and be taken on a business trip or even a vacation. A handheld computer can be especially convenient when the user must be able to move around freely while using it. This degree of portability might be very useful, for example, in checking inventory or preparing bulky merchandise for shipment.

Handheld computers are also being used to monitor the progress of athletes in training. Data can be easily recorded and analyzed for both individuals and groups. Nike, Inc., maker of running shoes and athletic equipment, has over 1000 "wear-testers" entered in its database. In a recent wear-testing race, the computer could assign handicaps so all the runners had an equal chance of winning. Data about the performance of the shoes was also collected, of course, to help improve the Nike product.

A fascinating use of microcomputers is being made by Dr. John Lilly, who is doing research in dolphin communication! He uses a computerized device called a *digitalker* to convert human speech into ultra-high-frequency sound pulses that dolphins can hear under the water. Sounds made by the dolphins are picked up by underwater microphones and fed into receivers, helping to compile a vocabulary of the dolphins' sonic codes. Dr. Lilly and his researchers hope to establish two-way "conversations" with the dolphins.

Microcomputers have their most "personal" uses in the home. More and more individuals and families are finding them helpful with budgets and investments, as educational aids, and for unique entertainment. The software needed for these uses is growing constantly. One especially creative use for home computers is "cookbook networking." Favorite recipes entered into a database can be shared by all participants in the group.

As an analogy in the kitchen context, one might think of the recipe as software, food ingredients as data, and the stove and utensils as hardware!

Courtesy Commodore International Limited

Courtesy Epson America, Inc.

Courtesy Motorola Inc.

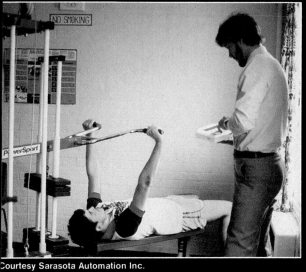

Courtesy Sarasota Automation Inc.

Courtesy Nike Sport Research Laboratory, Nike Incorporated

Courtesy Steve Castillo, Marine World/Africa USA

Courtesy Epson America, Inc.

Courtesy Radio Shack, a Division of Tandy Corporation

Courtesy Apple Computer, Inc.

9 | MICROCOMPUTERS IN USE

SYSTEM COMPONENTS
HANDHELD COMPUTERS
OTHER PORTABLES
HOME COMPUTERS
PERSONAL COMPUTERS
DESKTOP COMPUTERS
APPLICATIONS
SELECTING A MICROCOMPUTER
PRODUCT INFORMATION

Just a few short years ago, computers were a total unknown. Many people alive today were born before computers had even been invented. When computers did arrive on the scene (in the late 1940s and 1950s, remember), few people were aware of them. In the 1970s, many of the people who had heard at least something about computers regarded them as awesome, ugly, electronic giants.

Today computers are everywhere. If you read *Business Week, Time, TV Guide*, or the local newspaper, you see ads for computers. On TV, business computers are advertised during tennis matches and between plays in football games. Computers can be ordered by mail or carried home in shopping bags. You can hold a computer in your hand or put one in your pocket.

Of course, there are still some very fast, very powerful computers that cost thousands of dollars to rent and millions of dollars to buy. There may always be. There are some very demanding user needs—structural, chemical, and mechanical analyses, control of electric utility power systems, generation of high-resolution graphics for film animation, and the like—that only these computers can satisfy. There are also computers that cost $100 or less. These computers can be used for many of the tasks for which calculators have been used for years: simple arithmetic, adding up bills, figuring taxes, scientific and engineering equations, and the like. They can also operate on letters, words, and paragraphs of text as well as on numbers. They can be directed by stored-program instructions instead of by keying. They can play games, make music, and talk. Indeed, their potential may be limited only by our human imagination. (See Figure 9-1.)

Given such a wide range of computers, how can we talk about them? A common approach is to group computers into three broad categories:

FIGURE 9-1
Children of all ages are finding that computers can be both entertaining and thought-provoking. Programs that direct computers in game playing are available from many sources. (*Courtesy Apple Computer, Inc.*)

microcomputers, minicomputers, and *mainframes.* We've used these terms in this book. Each has a general meaning to us. When we try to distinguish between the groups, however, the boundary lines get fuzzy.

Some people classify computers as micros, minis, or mainframes on the basis of cost. They say, for example: a micro is any computer that sells for $5000 or less; a mini sells for $50,0000 or less in a common configuration; and a mainframe is any computer or family of computers more costly than those. You can buy a lot more computer hardware for $5000 now than you could buy even a year ago. Thus, even if we accept cost as a classifier, the boundaries are moving.

Some suggest that technology provides the best way to classify computers. They consider word sizes, processing speeds, or storage capacities. Initially, micros were 8-bit machines and minis were 16-bit machines. Now there are both 8-bit and 16-bit micros, and there are both 16-bit and 32-bit minis. The speeds of today's minicomputers equal or exceed the speeds of mainframes of a few years ago. A memory size that is typical of minis today may be typical of micros within a year or two. Again, the important point is that the boundaries are moving.

From a user (or potential user) point of view, cost may not be the most critical factor when selecting a computer system. Likewise, some users may not be ready to talk about word sizes, processing speeds, or storage capacities. What many users want to know are answers to questions such as: "Can I use the computer to keep track of who owes what?" "If I buy a computer, will it help me do my taxes?" "If our firm buys or leases a computer, how much faster can we get our bills out?" "How can a computer help us manage our inventory?"

Though microcomputers were not first on the computer scene, they are the simplest in many ways. They are also the computers you are most likely to have already encountered. Therefore, we are going to direct our attention to microcomputers in this chapter. We look first at their basic components. This discussion is at a general level. It prepares you for the discussions of some widely used microcomputer systems that follow. We look at some of the ways in which microcomputers are used. Then we suggest factors to consider when selecting a microcomputer system, and ways to find out what's available.

SYSTEM COMPONENTS

As we saw in earlier chapters, a microprocessor is the central processing unit of a computer scaled down to fit on one silicon chip. It is a member of the family of LSI or VLSI circuit chips reflecting the present state of miniaturization efforts that began with the development of transistors as an alternative to vacuum tubes in computers of the late 1940s. (See Figure 9-2.) Suppose we add chips to provide timing, control memory for instructions, read/write memory for use as temporary storage, and interfaces for input and output. In so doing, we assemble a complete computer on a single circuit board. We call the assembly a *microcomputer*.

Microcomputers are usually classified according to the word size of their microprocessor. Their performance is judged by the richness of their instruction set, by the bit efficiency of their programs (the number of bits that need to be stored to implement a given set of tasks), and by the speed with which they execute their programs. The performance level of a microcomputer is an important consideration when identifying applications for it.

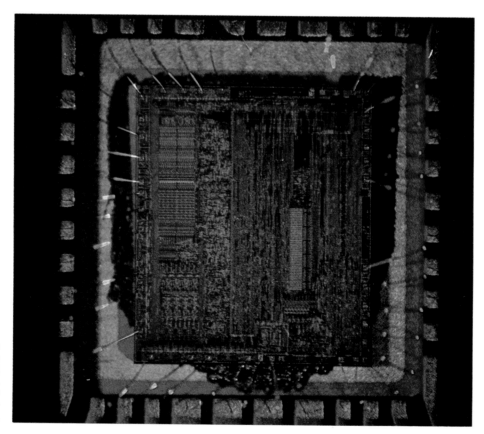

FIGURE 9-2
This microprocessor chip serves as a basic building block in microcomputers and other microprocessor-controlled devices. (*Courtesy National Semiconductor Corporation*)

Microcomputer memories are generally made of semiconductors, fabricated on silicon chips by the same technology that is used to make microprocessor chips. The control memory that holds instructions and fixed (unchanging, or permanent) data such as rate tables is *read-only memory (ROM)*. Its contents cannot be altered during processing. Furthermore, ROM is nonvolatile; the retention of its contents is not dependent on a constant supply of power. The read/write memory that provides for temporary storage of data while the microcomputer is operating is called *random-access memory (RAM)*. As we learned in Chapter 6, most semiconductor RAM is volatile. Its contents are lost when the power supply is shut off. Microcomputers for certain specialized applications may use only ROM (if the registers of the microprocessor provide all the temporary storage needed). Other microcomputers may have only RAM, with a battery backup to maintain memory contents if required.

Microcomputer systems have I/O devices, just as larger systems do. At a minimum, there's a keyboard for data entry. Some systems have visual-display units. Others have interface boards that allow them to be attached to TV sets. The variety of I/O devices available for use with micros is increasing daily.

In some microcomputer systems, cassette tapes serve as secondary storage. Other systems allow programs and data to be read from, and written to, flexible disks. Some systems support hard-disk drives.

The software components of a microcomputer system are the programs that direct its operations. There would be far fewer users of microcomputers if each user had to write all the programs needed to make his or her machine work. Even game-playing is possible only if a program to direct the computer in playing its part is available in ROM or can be loaded into RAM from a cartridge or cassette tape or disk device. Fortunately, a wide variety of both system software and application software has been developed. Most of the programs sell for $10 to $50.

The operating procedures for one microcomputer system differ from those for another. We described some simple procedures in Chapter 2 when we discussed how to enter and run a BASIC program on a microcomputer. The procedures to be used with a particular system are generally described in the system documentation supplied with it. They must be known and followed by system users.

HANDHELD COMPUTERS

The smallest microcomputers for individual use are *handheld computers*. They range in weight from about 6 ounces to 4 pounds. The smallest are pocket computers; the largest look much like 3-ring notebooks.

Radio Shack's TRS-80 PC-1 Pocket Computer, the first handheld computer to be introduced in the United States, is shown in Figure 9-3. It has a typewriter-like arrangement of alphabetic keys; a 20-key section for numeric input, arithmetic functions, and editing; and a screen on which 24 7×5 dot-matrix characters can be displayed. Users can operate the PC-1 as a calculator. They can use an optional cassette interface to read BASIC programs into the PC-1's 1.9K RAM from cassette tapes. They can also key in BASIC programs. In its first year, 1980, the PC-1 sold for $249.

In 1982 Radio Shack announced the TRS-80 PC-2. In 1983 the TRS-80 PC-3 and PC-4 were offered at $99.95 and $69.95 respectively. The PC-4 allows up to 10 short programs to be retained in memory and run selectively by pressing certain

FIGURE 9-3
The TRS-80 PC-1 Pocket Computer weighs only 6 ounces and is powered by four easy-to-replace, long-life batteries. When introduced in 1980, it opened new doors to American consumers. (*TRS-80 is a trademark of Radio Shack Division of Tandy Corporation*)

keys. A 1K plug-in RAM module, cassette interface, and 5×7 dot-matrix printer expand its capabilities.

Also available in 1983 was the TRS-80 Model 100, a notebook-size model with computing capabilities similar to those of many desktop micros. Up to 32K of RAM, a full-size typewriterlike keyboard, a display that holds up to eight 40-character lines, and interfaces to other I/O devices are provided.

To many computer-shoppers and computer-watchers, it seemed that much progress had been made in just three short years. Since hundreds of thousands of circuits can now be packed on one tiny chip of silicon, the functions available with today's handheld computers are determined by what users want and are willing to pay for, not by size. Other pocket computers competing for consumer attention are the Sharp PC-1250 and PC-1500, Texas Instruments' CC-40, and the Panasonic Link. Hewlett-Packard's 2.2-pound HP-75 is perhaps the best-known higher-priced handheld model. (See Figure 9-4.) The Epson HX-20 is another popular 4-pound, notebook-size computer.

OTHER PORTABLES

Next in size above the handheld micros are the briefcase portables and the more bulky "transportables." The weights of computers in these categories range up to 30 pounds. Like their smaller counterparts, they are powered by batteries, not via electrical outlets. Their prices generally range from $500 to $5000.

FIGURE 9-4
An HP-75 portable computer helps a busy traveler make productive use of inflight time, taking advantage of available software in areas such as math, engineering, statistics, finance, and management planning. (*Courtesy Hewlett-Packard Company*)

The Osborne 1, based on the 8-bit Z80A microprocessor, was the first briefcase portable. Its compact carrying case houses 64K of RAM, two flexible disk drives (storage space for about 60 pages of typed, double-spaced text), and a 5-inch (diagonal measure) display that can hold up to 24 52-character lines. The Teleram T-3000-1 and T-3000-2, Grid Systems' Compass, and the Sharp PC-5000 are other briefcase portables. The go-anywhere, work-anywhere convenience of these portables, complemented by larger storage capacities, a rich array of software, and standard interfaces for a wide variety of I/O devices, makes them attractive to many business users. (See Figure 9-5.) Some of the higher-priced models have not only battery-powered RAM but also nonvolatile bubble memories similar to those provided with some portable terminals. On those models, both programs and data can be retained indefinitely.

Typical transportables have at least 128K of RAM, 9-inch display screens, one or two flexible disk drives, and a letter-quality printer. Some are based on 16-bit microprocessors. Many of them are designed to be IBM-PC-compatible so that software developed for the IBM PC (discussed below) will also run on them. Examples are the Kaypro II, Compaq Computer, Columbia Data Product's VP, Computer Devices' Dot, and Osborne's Executive.

Though only about 2000 of these larger portables existed in 1982, some enthusiasts argue that by 1987 from 750,000 to 1 million will be in use. Other industry watchers warn that portables may be well received by users who want to carry their computers from place to place but will never attain the status of conventional desktop models (even if they offer functional equivalence).

A   B

FIGURE 9-5 Grid Systems' 10-pound Compass computer is designed for busy executives who want the option of taking some of their work with them (A). Its amber display and 57-character keyboard are designed for ease of use (B). ([A] © *David Burnett/ Contact;* [B] *courtesy Grid Systems Corporation*)

HOME COMPUTERS

In broadest terms, a *home computer* is obviously any computer used in a home. Analysts who want to talk more specifically of this area often define a home computer as a computer with more capabilities than user-oriented handheld computers but selling for under $1000 in a basic configuration. The early leader here was Warner Communications' Atari Division. Atari capitalized on its strength in video games to develop and market Atari 400 and Atari 800 micros. (Few people today have not tried their hands at Pac-Man, Asteroids, Space Invaders, or Video Checkers.) Other leading home computers are the Timex Sinclair, Commodore's VIC-20, Texas Instruments' 99/4A, and Radio Shack's TRS-80 Color Computer. In this section we focus on home computers marketed primarily for nonbusiness uses. We expand this discussion in the next section to include home computers also used for business purposes.

"What can I get for $1000 or less?" That's a question you and many others may be asking. One answer is: "With respect to home computers, usually more than you could a year ago." A Radio Shack TRS-80 Color Computer standard configuration includes an 8-bit microprocessor, 16K of memory, and a 53-key keyboard. It does not include a display. However, the unit can be attached to any home TV set and that can be used as a display. (See Figure 9-6.) Users willing to pay more can acquire more memory, add a couple of flexible-disk drives for secondary storage, and attach a line printer. The Color Computer features instant-load Program Paks and can be programmed in BASIC. It gets its power supply from an ordinary electrical outlet rather than from batteries.

Home computers are now marketed widely—visit Sears, J. C. Penney, K-Mart, Bloomingdale's, Marshall Field & Co., or Radio Shack, for starters. Customers often buy their computers for one purpose, say, playing video games or teaching math or spelling to their children. Later they start using the machines for other

FIGURE 9-6
The TRS-80 Color Computer may be an appropriate choice for a family that enjoys video games but also wants a system that can be used for household, business, and educational tasks. (*TRS-80 is a trademark of Radio Shack Division of Tandy Corporation*)

tasks—budgeting, correspondence, and so on. Until recently, the lack of software to support household tasks was a serious constraint. Vendors realizing this have poured millions of dollars into the development of such software. Programs to assist in home management are increasingly available.

How many U.S. homes today are without telephones? What the telephone is to home communications, the home computer may be to home information. The latest news, stock market quotations, and cataloged information on a wide variety of consumer-oriented topics are already available to home computer users in some areas. You may shop for groceries, select a lamp, pay your bills, or hire a gardener without ever leaving your family room. Some researchers suggest that computers will be in 95 percent of U.S. homes by 1990.

PERSONAL COMPUTERS

A pocket computer is a personal computer. A home computer is a personal computer. However, much more powerful, much more expandable computer systems are also included in the personal computer category. What, then, is a personal computer? It's a tool for a person. It's a computer so simple and easy to operate that you can learn to use it by yourself. You can use it at home or away from home, at work, at school, and at play.

Two primary questions are facing vendors of these computers:

- Which user-oriented capabilities can and should we package in a personal computer system, and yet price that system in a range that individual users can afford?

- Which user-oriented capabilities can and should we package in a system that can be marketed as a productivity tool for the individual user, and yet price that system in a range acceptable to both large and small businesses and other organizations?

A potential buyer of a personal computer system — whether for personal use or for an organization — faces another dilemma:

- How can I choose one system from among the vast array of systems and options available?

The initial vendors of personal computers were not the established computer manufacturers. In 1975, the first personal computers were marketed as ready-to-assemble kits for hobbyists. Resistors, capacitors, RAM, ROM, and microprocessor chips, a teletype interface, timing crystal, and voltage regulator had to be soldered onto a small printed circuit board. I/O units had to be acquired or assembled similarly. Then came the rather awesome task of writing programs in a machine-oriented programming language to make the system work.

We've come a long way in a short time! In 1976 Commodore Business Machines announced the first ready-to-use, fully assembled microcomputer. Known as the PET (Personal Electronic Transactor), it had a 9-inch black-and-white display screen, a 73-key calculator-style keyboard, from 4K to 32K of RAM, and a built-in tape cassette recorder/storage unit for programs and data. This PET computer was Commodore's first entry into the computer field. By 1982 Commodore had installed 200,000 desktop computer systems outside of the continental United States. A strong marketing program was under way to increase the number of Commodore systems in U.S. home, education, and business environments. Today, its low-end system, the VIC-20 home computer mentioned above, is widely used. The Commodore 64 and PET Professional Computer are also popular. (See Figure 9-7.)

Tandy Corporation's first venture into the microcomputer field was the TRS-80 Level I, a 4K RAM machine with an 8-bit Z80 microprocessor that could be programmed in minimal BASIC. This machine was soon renamed the Model I and enhanced with add-on memory kits and a (confusingly named) Level II BASIC. An expansion interface could be purchased to allow attachment of a printer and a $5\frac{1}{4}$-inch flexible-disk drive. In 1980 Tandy announced the TRS-80 Model III as a replacement for the TRS-80 Model I. (See Figure 9-8.) Like the Model I, the Model III is an 8-bit machine and supports Level II BASIC. Tandy's Radio Shack Division estimates that about 80 percent of the software developed for the Model I can be run without change on the Model III. In 1983 Tandy announced a further upgrade of this line of computers, the TRS-80 Model 4.

Meanwhile, the TRS-80 Model II introduced in 1979 and subsequent models known as the TRS-80 Model 12 and TRS-80 Model 16 are marketed as another line of computers intended primarily as multipurpose work stations for business. These computers are based on the 8-bit Z80A microprocessor. To take advantage of the software available for these computers, not only flexible-disk drives but

FIGURE 9-7 Today's students are learning about computers and studying traditional subjects with the help of computers in many classrooms and laboratories. (*Courtesy Commodore International Limited*)

FIGURE 9-8 The TRS-80 Model III is intended for beginners and pros alike—easy to use, hard to outgrow, and supported by a wealth of ready-to-run programs. (*TRS-80 is a trademark of Radio Shack Division of Tandy Corporation*)

also hard-disk units are commonly included in system configurations. Programs can be written in COBOL and FORTRAN as well as in BASIC. Application packages for accounting, inventory control, word processing, management planning, and other business functions are marketed widely. The Model 16 is somewhat unique in that it also includes a 16-bit Motorola 68000 microprocessor. Organizations can acquire Microsoft's XENIX operating system to use the Model 16 in a multiple-user environment. More than 500,000 of these computers have been sold through Tandy's Radio Shack stores.

Before 1977-78, an *apple* was something to eat—a fruit, red or green in color, produced on a tree. Today there are still apples—but there are also Apples. An *Apple* is a personal computer—a machine, usually beige in color, produced by Apple Computer, Inc.

The first Apple, strangely called the *Apple II*, was a 12-pound desktop unit. It had a standard 52-key typewriterlike keyboard, a game I/O connector that allowed the use of paddles (joysticks) for interactive control, a speaker, and expansion slots for up to eight I/O devices. A built-in video interface allowed the attachment of a visual-display unit. The screen could be programmed to display (1) 24 lines of up to 40 uppercase characters each, (2) color graphics (40 horizontal by 48 vertical dots per location, 15 colors), or (3) high-resolution graphics (280 horizontal by 192 vertical dots, 4 colors: black, white, violet, and green). This versatility made the Apple II suitable for a wide range of applications.

Internally, the Apple II had an 8-bit 6502 microprocessor and from 4K to 48K (later, 64K) of RAM. Apple's Integer BASIC and Resident Monitor, a system control program, were supplied as system software in 8K of ROM. Other programs were available on cassettes. Thanks to a strong product and aggressive, timely marketing, Apple sales mushroomed. Apples appeared in homes, education environments, and business offices. People were soon talking about Logo, a language that helps students learn how to perceive things, how to think, via experimentation. PILOT, another language, helps teachers to write lessons for their classes. Later versions of the Apple II, known as *Apple II Plus* and *Apple IIe*, are software-compatible with the initial Apple II and incorporate many niceties—a full ASCII keyboard supporting both upper- and lowercase letters, a screen width of 80 characters, 64K of RAM expandable to 128K, and so on. An estimated 20,000 to 30,000 of these units are being sold monthly. More programs are available for this machine than for any other computer—some 16,000 in all. There are also more user groups, more plug-in expansion units, and more I/O devices for it.

In May 1980, Apple III was announced. (See Figure 9-9.) Like the Apple II, it has an 8-bit 6502 microprocessor, but the chip design has been modified to increase its speed. Additional circuitry allows it to run somewhat like a 16-bit machine. In contrast to the Apple II, the Apple III is aimed primarily at offices. One built-in $5\frac{1}{4}$-inch flexible-disk drive and up to three add-on drives can be used with the Apple III. Each of these drives can hold up to 140,000 characters. That's 250 average-length business letters, a mailing list of 950 names and addresses, or a complete business report. In November 1980, Apple announced its ProFile Personal Mass Storage, a hard-disk system that holds up to 5 million characters. That's 2400 typewritten pages, 30,000 names and addresses, or probably all the files of a small business.

FIGURE 9-9
Apple III micros are serving as aids to decision makers at many business locations.
(*Courtesy Apple Computer, Inc.*)

In the eyes of many, Apple Computer "entered the big time" on January 19, 1983, when it introduced the Apple Lisa (*local integrated software architecture*), a 16-bit desktop microcomputer intended for use in offices throughout the world. User-friendliness is emphasized by features such as a palm-size pointer, known as a *mouse*, that the user simply moves across the desktop to control an arrow on the screen. By positioning the arrow at the word *Print* and then pressing the button on the mouse, for example, an executive can cause a copy of a memo intended for him or her to be printed (without ever touching the keyboard). The screen can be divided into four parts, or *windows*, so that the user can look at a memo while writing a response to it, compare budgeted amounts in one file with year-to-date expenses just calculated by a program in storage, and so on. Perhaps most significant is Apple's integrated approach to software. Programs for text editing, electronic filing, financial or spreadsheet analysis, communications, and graphics are included in the purchase price of the system and designed so that data can easily be shared among them.

Though IBM, Digital Equipment Corporation (DEC), Hewlett-Packard, NCR, Honeywell, and other leading computer manufacturers had developed desktop business computer systems in the 1970s, they had not marketed computers for home use. Today that's changed. IBM announced its first entry into this field, the IBM Personal Computer, or PC, in 1981. Based on a 16-bit 8088 microprocessor, it has from 16K to 256K (and, more recently, an additional 256K) of RAM and 40K of ROM. Up to 25 lines of 80 characters each can be shown on the optional IBM monochrome (green on black) display. The user's TV set or a color display can be attached through an adapter. An 80-cps dot-matrix printer and up to two built-in $5\frac{1}{4}$-inch flexible-disk drives were initially offered as options. Thanks to widespread TV advertising, IBM PC's and Charlie-Chaplin-like characters became frequent visitors in many households.

In 1983, IBM announced the IBM PC XT, an expanded version of the PC having 128K of RAM, one 320K flexible-disk drive, and one 10-megabyte hard-disk drive in a basic configuration. (See Figure 9-10.) The system is aimed

FIGURE 9-10
The 83-key typewriterlike keyboard and numeric keypad of an IBM PC XT are cable-connected to the processor unit for flexibility in positioning—an ease-of-use feature in many environments. (*Courtesy IBM Corporation*)

primarily at small and medium-size businesses or business units, and at professionals. Because several operating systems are supported on these IBM PC's, and because very widespread usage of them is anticipated, a large amount of application software for them already exists or is under development. As mentioned earlier, numerous vendors are marketing IBM-PC-compatible systems with hopes that their systems will be purchased by organizations that already have some PC's or instead of them.

In 1982, DEC announced its Rainbow 100 personal computer, a compact, modular system that uses a two-processor, bus architecture to run either 8-bit or 16-bit application programs. (See Figure 9-11.) At that time, DEC also announced its DECmate II personal computer aimed primarily at office management. (We'll say more later about considerations of office management, word processing, electronic mail, and office automation.) A third product, the Professional 350, uses the same processor as DEC's well-known PDP-11 minicomputers (discussed in Chapter 10). This is its top-of-the-line personal computer and contains provisions for adding a 5-megabyte Winchester disk drive. By offering a wide range of system capabilities, DEC hopes to attract a wide community of users.

DESKTOP COMPUTERS Many microcomputer systems are developed *for use by* individuals, but not *marketed to* individuals. Instead, they are marketed to persons acting on behalf of a business or other organization. The organization pays the bill. The microcomputer is used in the office, at a desk in the Shipping Department, by the analysts in the Finance Department, and so on. Of course, "personal computers" are also used in these ways, but the computers we are talking about here are not called personal computers by their vendors. They are usually called *desktop* computers or *office* computers.

FIGURE 9-11
DEC's Rainbow 100 personal computer is a general-purpose system housing two processors for maximum flexibility. (*Courtesy Tymshare, Inc.*)

Today's desktop computers may be either 8-bit or 16-bit machines. A few 32-bit desktop units have been announced but they are not yet available widely. Generally, each desktop computer has a typewriterlike keyboard, a visual-display unit, and one or two flexible-disk drives. The screen of the unit may be a clue to its intended use. General-purpose machines are much like the personal computers we discussed above; their screens typically display up to 25 80-character lines. (See Figure 9-12A.) Application programs to support routine business operations are often provided.

Some desktop computers have very-high-resolution graphic displays. Increasingly, information can be shown on the screens in any of several colors. Extensive engineering or business graphics software is marketed to provide the logic needed to create, modify, enlarge, and highlight screen images. (See Figure 9-12B.)

Still other desktop computers are intended primarily for office administrative tasks—the preparation and editing of documents to be printed later in hard-copy form or sent as electronic messages. The screens of these computers are often large enough to hold the contents of an $8\frac{1}{2}'' \times 11''$ printed page. (See Figure 9-12C.) Software to assist in entering, correcting, formatting, filing, retrieving, and printing is needed. Text data in the form of lists, memos, reports, and other traditional office paperwork is created and processed with computer help.

APPLICATIONS   The microcomputer systems discussed above are but a small sampling of the rapidly expanding field of microcomputers and related products. Already, microcomputer unit sales have outstripped the unit sales of minicomputers and mainframes. The gap between computers designed for personal use and computers designed for business is rapidly closing. Some vendors are marketing their latest products as "personal business computers." "What can I do with such a computer?" asks the skeptic. Again, a firm warning: You have to have more than just a computer. You have to have a system—complete with not just hardware, but also software, user documentation, and training aids. Fortunately, the systems are becoming more "user friendly." (That's an industry term that describes how easy it is to understand and use a system.) The computer asks you questions or prompts you via a menu. Most systems have a programmed HELP facility invokable via a special function key. The left column in Figure 9-13 is a starter list of the many ways microcomputers are being used in homes today. What additional uses do you know of?

Some microcomputer systems operate as standalone units for small businesses. They're capable of handling payroll, inventory control, accounts receivable, billing, and other common business applications. An attorney who has access to a microcomputer can file data on complete cases, then retrieve that data in seconds. A doctor or dentist can keep patient and supply records up to date. Small contractors and instant-printing shops can quickly compile bids for jobs. A personnel agency can maintain its database of positions and applications. Current 64K microcomputer systems can handle applications involving, say, one master file (customer, inventory, or whatever) of 200,000 to 300,000 characters stored on a diskette and one application program of about 30,000 characters (in its original form, a few hundred program statements) resident in primary storage. A starter list of business uses of computers is given at the right in Figure 9-13.

A

B

FIGURE 9-12
Desktop computers can be
tailored, both by hardware
design and by software, to
meet application needs.
(*Courtesy* [A] *Zenith Data
Systems;* [B] *Calcomp;*
[C] *IBM Corporation*)   C

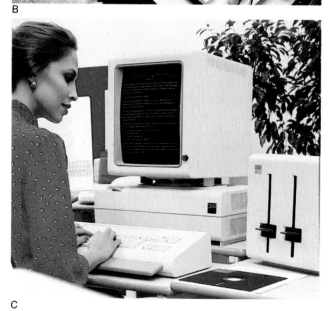

HOME	BUSINESS
Playing games	Accounts receivable
Composing or playing music	Accounts payable
Drawing	General ledger
Learning math, spelling, other subjects	Payroll
Solving problems (calculations of all kinds)	Personnel
Indexing manually maintained files	Benefits
(phonograph records, hobbies, etc.)	
	Order processing
Budgeting/financial planning	Billing/invoicing
Keeping track of expenses (actuals)	Sales analysis
Record-keeping for tax purposes	
Completing tax returns	Inventory control
Playing the stock market	Material requirements planning
Simulating actions, to anticipate results	Project costing
	Human resource planning
Mailing lists, address labels	Purchasing
Personal correspondence	Receiving
Form letters	Computer-aided design/computer-aided
Filling out forms	manufacturing (CAD/CAM)
Writing, editing, filing, and printing reports,	
other text materials	Financial planning
Creating illustrations/artwork	Capital budgeting
	Fixed-assets accounting
Receiving and placing phone calls	Depreciation
Security (alarm systems)	Completing quarterly government,
Controlling lights, appliances	stockholder reports
	Completing tax returns
Planning vacations, trips	Forecasting
Catalog of daily activities	Modeling
Maintaining a "tickler" file	Management reporting
Shopping lists	
Recipes and meal planning	Electronic filing
Buying/sales analysis	Electronic mail
	Word processing

FIGURE 9-13
"What can I do with a
computer?" (Starter lists—
add your own ideas.)

One major business use of microcomputers—known as *word* or *text processing*—received its initial impetus not from the EDP community but from the area of business administration. Because of the unique aspects and increasing importance of word processing, we will discuss it in some detail in Chapter 16.

Microcomputers are not just for microbusinesses. Some very large corporations are buying them by the hundreds. Here, a very important characteristic of the microcomputers is their flexibility. A busy executive can use the microcomputer as a standalone tool to plot financial trends, obtain answers to "what if" questions, or keep track, through a daily calendar, of where to be when. The executive can key in memos or simple messages and then zip them electronically, by means of communication links, to colleagues and subordinates. If access to corporate databases or sophisticated programs is needed, the microcomputer can serve as a terminal to a mainframe computer system. Incoming customer orders can be keyed as input to the mainframe from remote sales offices, for example. Programs in the mainframe can access the company's master inventory file to determine how the order should be filled.

Microcomputers were initially used in industrial automation. In product development laboratories and on shop floors, microcomputers still perform data acquisition, measurement, and control in ways that greatly simplify product testing and control of manufacturing processes. In rugged environments such as on ships and airplanes, or in remote unattended locations such as offshore oil-well platforms, microcomputers monitor physical conditions such as pressures and temperatures, and control equipment and processes accordingly. Microcomputers are also the basis for robotic devices capable of factory assembly operations formerly too complex for mechanization. Powerful microcomputers are helping to bring down the prices of computer-aided design and computer-aided manufacturing (CAD/CAM) systems to ranges that even small engineering and machine shops can afford. At the front end of the product development cycle (i.e., design), on the production line, and in shipping and distribution, microcomputers are making big contributions to productivity.

SELECTING A MICROCOMPUTER

Some time, you may have to shop for a microcomputer. You may want it for yourself, for your home or your own business, or for a large organization by whom you're employed. We've mentioned several factors you should consider as you shop.

One is cost. From just what's been said here, it should be clear that you can spend from less than a hundred dollars to several thousand for a micro. What do you really need?

Hardware is a second factor. Again, we noted earlier that microcomputers differ in word size, processing speed, and storage capacity. Perhaps more important is the fact that you're not just buying a microcomputer—you're buying a microcomputer system. You must consider not just the processor but also I/O and secondary-storage devices. If you just want to keep track of inventory, a low-cost dot-matrix printer that can produce reports for internal use may be adequate. If you want to prepare executive memos or personal correspondence, a letter-quality printer may be a better choice. If you are buying a microcomputer for home use only, two flexible-disk drives may provide all the secondary-storage capacity you need. For business use, you're likely to find that a hard-disk drive is necessary, or soon will be.

That leads us to another point: When shopping for a computer, you can't just think of the present. You must also think of the future. A system with 64K of RAM may meet your current data-processing needs very well. Can you attach additional memory modules later, when you want to do more?

Never underestimate the importance of software. Many enthusiastic owners of computers have received rude awakenings: "I bought this computer to handle the weekly payroll and customer billings. I can't make it do either!" A first step here is to find out what programs are available for use with the systems you're considering. Will they accept your data as input? Will they produce the kind of output you want? If the system supports a well-known operating system such as CP/M, a number of application programs that run in that environment may be available. Therefore, the number of programs you have to choose from may be quite large.

A second step concerning software is to find out how easy (or hard) it is to write new programs for the systems you're considering. What programming languages can be used on each system? Equally important, how easy (or hard) is each system to use?

Often the main factor determining how easy it is to use a system is not the system itself, but rather the documentation available for it. As mentioned earlier, some systems provide a programmed HELP facility. The printed documentation that tells how to use the system must be understandable and complete as well as accurate.

Finally, don't overlook reliability and maintenance considerations. Today's organizations depend on their computer systems to carry out basic business operations. They can't afford to have their systems inoperable ("down") for even short periods of time. When a failure does occur, service personnel must be readily available to find the cause of the failure. Repairs or replacement parts must be readily obtainable. If you are buying a computer for home use, you want it to work. A "problem" may be a hardware error, a software bug, or a procedural mistake on your part. You need someone who can assist you. It's frustrating to have to put the whole system back in your car and return it to the store. It's even more frustrating to have to mail an apparently failing part across the country, and wait weeks for word on what's wrong or even to hear whether or not the part arrived at its destination.

International Resource Development, a leading research firm, predicts that, just among small businesses, the number of microcomputers in use will rise from less than 2 million in 1982 to almost 34 million by 1990. Large organizations are expected to have 9.1 million microcomputers by yearend 1992, up from 383,000 at yearend 1982. (Here, "large organizations" means companies and government agencies employing 100 or more persons.) Even today, 50 percent of microcomputer purchases from computer retail stores are made by Fortune 500 companies. A typical microcomputer system (not just the microcomputer itself) sells for about $4000. In a few years, it is likely to cost less than half that much.

PRODUCT INFORMATION

As a prospective buyer or user of a microcomputer system, how can you find out more about them? Today, you can shop for, and purchase, the items of your choice in any of several ways. Radio Shack with its 400 computer centers, over 8700 consumer electronics outlets worldwide, and a catalog circulation of nine million is well positioned to reach a vast consumer base. (See Figure 9-14.) Franchises are growing by leaps and bounds. There are now over 2000 computer stores, and more are coming. As mentioned earlier, large retailers are moving into the computer sales arena. The first computer trade mart was opened in Chicago in January 1981. Again, more are coming. The established computer manufacturers are selling their microcomputer products through their own sales forces and through independent sales organizations, distributors, and retail outlets.

Computer stores and computer business centers provide a nonthreatening environment in which anyone can learn about computers. They not only stock hardware and software for immediate purchase, but also demonstrate systems, assist in configuration planning (so that you can be sure the pieces you select will work together as a system), and give application assistance. The only "dumb" question is the one you want the answer to, but don't ask. Most of the stores

FIGURE 9-14
Computer browsers and serious shoppers gain insights and product information from store employees, in-store materials, or other customers at any of more than 400 Radio Shack computer stores. (*Courtesy Radio Shack, a Division of Tandy Corporation*)

carry a wide variety of personal computing magazines. *Byte, PC, Personal Computing, Creative Computing,* and *Dr. Dobb's Journal* are leading examples. Some carry introductory books on computing, microprocessors, programming, specific programming languages, and the like. Many product vendors provide high-quality tutorial and reference materials.

Computer clubs and user groups are springing up everywhere. Some have been formed under the sponsorship of specific vendors or computer stores. Others are just neighborhood enthusiasts who have computer interests in common. You can find out about them through your friends or through people you meet while computer shopping.

Today, there are microcomputer shows just as there are national computer conferences for vendors and users of mainframes. At these shows, you can see the latest equipment in action, talk to the vendors, and obtain a wealth of product-related literature. The schedules for these shows are published widely. Attend one. You'll meet many interesting people and learn a lot about computers.

CHAPTER SUMMARY

1. A wide range of computers exists. They can be grouped into the categories of microcomputers, minicomputers, and mainframes, but the boundary lines between these groups are not clear and are continually moving.

2. A microcomputer consists of a microprocessor together with chips to provide timing circuitry, control memory for instructions, read/write memory for use as temporary storage, and interfaces for input and output.

3. Both system and application software are needed to direct a microcomputer system. The operating procedures for the system must be known and followed by system users.

4. The smallest microcomputers for individual use are handheld computers. They have been available in the United States since 1980 and range from pocket-size to notebook-size.

5. Above the handheld micros in size are briefcase portables and more bulky transportables. Some weigh up to 30 pounds. Like handheld micros, they are powered by batteries.

6. A home computer can be defined as a computer with more capabilities than user-oriented handheld computers but selling for under $1000 in a basic configuration. Some are marketed primarily for nonbusiness uses but others are also employed for business purposes.

7. The first personal computers were marketed in 1975 as ready-to-assemble kits for hobbyists. In 1976 Commodore Business Machines announced its PET, the first ready-to-use, fully assembled microcomputer.

8. Tandy Corporation's Radio Shack Division and Apple Computer were early vendors of personal computers. Both have continued to expand their product lines, offering personal computers that can be used as work stations in businesses as well as in home and education environments.

9. IBM, DEC, Hewlett-Packard, NCR, Honeywell, and other leading computer manufacturers now also market machines they call *personal computers*. Some are used in homes. Others are used by individuals in businesses.

10. Desktop, or office, computers can be defined as microcomputers developed for use by individuals but not marketed to individuals by vendors.

11. When shopping for a microcomputer, not only cost but also hardware, software, documentation, reliability, and maintenance should be considered. The system must meet the needs of its users.

12. Microcomputer product information is available from a wide variety of sources. Among them are computer stores, personal computing magazines, books, vendor publications, computer clubs, user groups, and microcomputer shows.

DISCUSSION QUESTIONS

1. Support or refute the following statement: "An electronic calculator is really a small computer."

2. (a) What are some factors we can use to categorize computers?
   (b) What makes classification difficult?

3. Describe the hardware components of a microcomputer system.

4. Support or refute the following statement: "Software is less necessary on a microcomputer system than on a large computer."

5. Show how the terms *handheld computer*, *home computer*, and *personal computer*, as used in this chapter, are related.

6. Identify at least six vendors of microcomputers.

7. Choose one of the vendors you named in response to Question 6. Discuss the microcomputer products offered by this vendor. In doing so, point out factors that users should consider in making a choice.

8. Distinguish between Logo and PILOT. If you've had experiences with either, discuss them.

9. Refer to Figure 9-12. Suggest applications for which each microcomputer system shown in the illustration is apt to be best suited.

10. Suggest factors that either a college student or a business executive should consider when shopping for a microcomputer.

11. What are some ways that persons in your locality can find out about microcomputers?

12. Discuss, in detail, one application of microcomputers with which you have come in contact. What's good or bad about it? How might it be improved?

10

MINIS, MAIN-FRAMES, AND MONSTERS

One of the primary differences between microcomputers and their larger counterparts, minicomputers and mainframes, lies in versatility. The central processing unit (CPU) of the microcomputer is involved in all data processing. In a larger computer system, many functions may be performed by other devices within the system that have some "intelligence" or "processing power" of their own. This arrangement frees the mini or mainframe CPU for other tasks while the specialized devices are doing their own jobs. This giving-over of some responsibilities to the other parts of the system may be compared to what happens when a human has mastered a task. In first learning to do the task, a great deal of mental concentration is required of the human. When a microcomputer is used for a task, the CPU is constantly needed. After the human has mastered the task, the whole body has learned it and the hands, for example, may perform without total direction from the brain (somewhat "automatically"). When

some devices of a mini-computer or mainframe system can function independently of the CPU, less CPU time is needed for certain tasks. This capability enables a large computer system to process more data faster than a microcomputer system can. As a result, the larger and more sophisticated computers are more powerful than micro-computers, and greater demands can be placed on them.

One of the valuable uses of minicomputers is in special education. A minicomputer can serve as a tool assisting teachers of hearing-deficient children—even pre-schoolers. The computer can have a vast library of sounds and images in its internal storage unit. These sounds and images can be instantaneously displayed on command as part of the teaching process.

Courtesy NEC

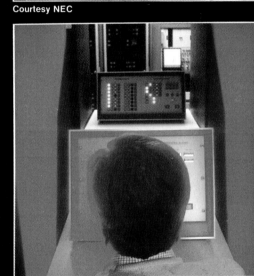

Courtesy RCA

Courtesy Ramtek Corporation

Minicomputers and mainframes can perform an endless variety of functions for every imaginable kind of business. The Royal Dutch Shell Group, for example, uses the abilities of mainframes to handle many tasks involved in the storage and shipment of its petroleum products throughout Europe. Data from hundreds of sources may be coming and going at the same time.

A newspaper chain in Pennsylvania uses computerized entry of text for its classified advertising. The huge amount of data represented by this task was once painstakingly managed by hand, and changes in placement and content called for hours of labor on the part of many people. Now, not only is time saved, but also advertisers can check their ads on a visual-display terminal in advance of actual typesetting and printing.

As businesses become larger, the versatility of computers becomes increasingly important to them. In tire manufacturing and selling, for example, a single mainframe computer may be used to monitor available raw materials, to control manufacturing and testing processes, and to track inventory of finished products. Data may come to the computer from any number of terminals throughout the plants, offices, and warehouses.

An instance where computer speed makes a critical difference involves the cataloging of data that can be used to identify known criminals. In the Bronx, New York, a computerized law-enforcement system called C.A.T.C.H. can rapidly sift through thousands of criminal records in search of a suspect that fits a certain description. When a match is found, that individual's "mug shots" and history are displayed.

All our state governments must maintain large databases concerning motor vehicles, their owners, and their drivers. Data about the transfer of vehicles, persons granted licenses and driving infractions, can be maintained and constantly updated with the help of large computers. These operations may involve millions of records. Some computer systems even supply electronic photographic identification of individuals. The next time you get your picture taken at the DMV, remember that—and smile!

One of the most demanding uses of computers is in producing realistic imagery. (You will see some amazing examples of "computer art" at the beginning of Chapter 13.) The computer must handle data for every position on the screen, and one image can easily involve millions of these items. A "monster" computer such as the Cray 1 has the stupendous data-handling capacity needed for this kind of task. The Cray 1 itself can be seen here on a C-shaped platform in a red-carpeted room. Below it can be seen its own self-created portrait!

Courtesy Sperry Corporation

Courtesy IBM Corporation

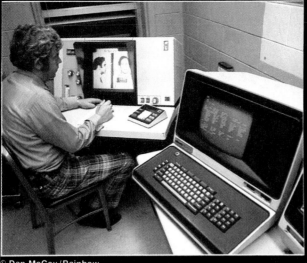

© Dan McCoy/Rainbow

Courtesy Mohawk Data Sciences

Courtesy Boeing Computer Services Company

Courtesy Ramtek Corporation

10 | MINIS, MAINFRAMES AND MONSTERS

MINICOMPUTERS
    Product Developments
    Minicomputer Applications
    Marketing
FULL-SCALE COMPUTERS
    Small Computers
    Medium-Size Computers
    Large Computers
SUPERCOMPUTERS AND THEIR USES

In Chapter 9 we discussed microcomputer systems. We looked at their characteristics and at their uses. Now we're ready to discuss larger computer systems. In this chapter we look at minicomputer systems, full-scale computers (mainframes), and supercomputers ("monsters"). We also look at what they can do.

MINICOMPUTERS

Somewhere between the ever-expanding field of full-scale computer systems and that of calculators, microcomputers, and conventional office machines is the portion of the user community whose data-processing needs are best served by minicomputers. There is no universally accepted definition of the term *minicomputer*. Some say, "A minicomputer is a marketing phenomenon." Others say, "A minicomputer is any machine its manufacturers decide to call one." Such statements acknowledge the fact that when minicomputers first became available (about 1960), the trend in computers was to bigger, faster machines. Yet, there were significant numbers of potential users for whom such computers were out of reach. Once the attention of these users had been drawn to "minicomputers"—smaller, slower pieces of equipment that could nevertheless satisfy their data-processing needs on a cost-effective basis—the total number of computer users began to increase dramatically.

    Let us recognize that a machine referred to as a minicomputer by some firms or users may look very much like a machine called a microcomputer by others. In general, minicomputers have faster internal processing speeds and larger memories than microcomputers. Some have bus architectures in common with microcomputers, but the buses are less likely to be shared among all components. One bus may link the processor with input devices, another may link the memory with input devices, and so on. This means that input, processing, and output operations are less likely to be delayed while waiting for data transfers to be completed. Minicomputers are also likely to support a larger number and greater variety of I/O devices. On the other hand, they also take up more space, use more energy, and cost more than microcomputers.

In a somewhat analogous fashion, a machine referred to as a minicomputer by some firms or users may be labeled a small computer by others. In general, minicomputers are word-addressable computers with fewer registers, smaller word sizes, smaller internal storage units, and slower internal processing speeds than mainframes. Their I/O devices tend to be slower than the I/O devices of full-scale computer systems. The low-end model of a particular mainframe computer family often has capabilities comparable to those found on minis. Low-end models of mainframe families are seldom (if ever) called minicomputers, however.

From the user's point of view, minicomputers were welcomed onto the computer scene because they could meet particular needs at significantly lower costs than could large computer systems. "Limited functionality" is not a constraint if the user does not need functions beyond the limit. Another important advantage was that minicomputers were easier to install and operate. Typically, they imposed fewer environmental restrictions. Before minicomputers came along, installing a computer system was a mammoth undertaking. Special air conditioning, special power supplies, raised flooring to allow for cables, and lots of floor space were needed. Minicomputers require floor space, but less of it. They can function in most users' ordinary operating environments.

According to recent surveys, the average primary storage size of today's minicomputers is 383,000 8-bit bytes (or a roughly equivalent number of 8-bit to 32-bit words). That's more memory than a typical mainframe system had in the first half of the 1970s. An average of 143 million 8-bit bytes (143 megabytes) of secondary storage is available on disk or tape. Basic systems can be purchased for $50,000 or less. A fully configured minicomputer system that meets multiple user needs is likely to cost about $90,000. A 32-bit minicomputer system (the *"supermini"* or *"megamini"*) may cost $300,000.

Product Developments

The first entrant in the minicomputer field was Digital Equipment Corporation (DEC). DEC introduced a forerunner, its basic PDP-1 machine, in 1959 at a cost of $120,000. (*PDP* is an acronym for Programmed Data Processor.) The PDP-8, a 12-bit machine introduced in 1965, is generally recognized as the first true minicomputer. It was designed primarily for use in laboratory instrumentation. A unit with 4K of primary storage was priced at $18,000.

Note that the date of the first mini precedes the date of the first micro by about 10 years. Minis arrived in 1965; micros, about 1975. The significance of this time difference is reflected in the early minicomputer developments we're discussing here.

Over the years, DEC has not relinquished its lead position in minicomputers. Its big seller, the PDP-11 series of minicomputers, was introduced in 1970. The

16-bit-word parallel-logic processor, 8 general-purpose registers, and from 4K to 28K words of magnetic-core storage of a PDP-11/05, for example, were housed in a processor unit that weighed about 50 pounds. Like other units of its time, the PDP-11/05 could be packaged in a desktop cabinet or mounted in a standard 19-inch rack. The desktop cabinet held only the processor unit. The standard rack looked like a floor-to-ceiling storage locker and accommodated the input, control, output display, output buffer, and output power modules, and the power supply as well. Today's widely used members of this 16-bit-word family include the PDP-11 Models 23, 34, 44, and 70. They differ primarily in processor speeds, primary-storage capacities, number and types of I/O devices supplied, and costs. (See Figure 10-1.)

In October 1977, DEC announced its VAX-11/780 computer system. This announcement was heralded widely. Here at last was the first 32-bit-word-length computer offered by DEC, traditionally a minicomputer manufacturer. (See Figure 10-2.) Because the VAX-11/780 can handle 32 bits at once, it is potentially more powerful and faster than DEC's PDP-11 16-bit minis or any other smaller-word-length machines. The longer word length also means that stored-program instructions can contain more bits representing addresses. In fact, up to 2 million bytes of primary storage can be addressed directly by the VAX-11/780. It has 16 32-bit general-purpose registers, 32 interrupt priority levels (16 for hardware and 16 for software), and a very fast 8K memory buffer, or *cache*, that yields memory access times measured in nanoseconds. In addition to its own instruction set, the VAX-11/780 can execute almost all of the PDP-11 instruction set in compatibility mode. User application programs initially written for PDP-11 computers can run on the VAX-11/780 with little or no modification.

FIGURE 10-1
Colleges such as Cal State, Los Angeles, use DEC PDP-11 minicomputers for a wide variety of administrative tasks and educational purposes. (*Courtesy California State University, Los Angeles*)

DEC describes the VAX-11/780 as a multiple-user, multiple-language, interactive computer system with extensive batch- and transaction-processing capabilities. Yet, at announcement, a basic VAX-11/780 system with 256K of primary storage could be purchased for about $130,000, then upgraded by adding more storage, faster I/O devices, and so on, as the user's data-processing needs dictated.

Since 1977, DEC has unveiled three additional members of its VAX-11 family: a slightly less powerful VAX-11/750; the VAX-11/782, which combines two VAX-11/780 processors, for computation-intensive applications; and the VAX-11/730, an entry-level system, designed to make 32-bit computing power available at department levels in organizations. With the addition of the VAX-11/730, DEC broadened this product line, or *family*, and positioned it to be a strong competitor against IBM's 4300 series. (The 4300s are generally classified as mainframes; we discuss them later.) Prices ranged from $50,000 to $500,000.

Other leaders in the minicomputer field include:

- Data General, with its ENTERPRISE 1000, NOVA, microNOVA, ECLIPSE, and CS (Commercial Systems) families
- Hewlett-Packard, with its HP 1000 and HP 3000 series
- IBM, with its Series 1, System/34, System/36, and System/38 computer systems
- Prime Computer, with its 50 series
- Honeywell Information Systems, with its Level 6 and DPS 6 product lines
- Wang Laboratories, with its VS and 2200 systems

FIGURE 10-2
Minicomputers like this DEC VAX-11/780 are widely used for continuous, high-volume processing at research, government, and military locations, at universities, and at manufacturing, banking, and other business facilities. (*Courtesy Digital Equipment Corporation*)

This list does not include all the manufacturers of minicomputers. It does not even include all the systems that may be called minicomputers produced by these manufacturers. Its purpose is to alert you to some of the better-known systems, so that you will have some idea of "where they fit." Systems with 8-, 16-, and 32-bit architectures are on the list. Some—the HP 3000 Models 44 and 64, Data General's ECLIPSE MV/8000 and MV/10000, and so on—are very powerful. You can obtain product literature to find out more about all these systems or watch them in action to determine the needs they are best equipped to satisfy.

Minicomputer Applications

Early applications of minicomputers included instrumentation systems production test systems, process monitoring and control, and data acquisition and reduction. In process monitoring and control, for example, an operator reads the process-control program into the minicomputer via a tape reader. Parameters such as heat, pressure, flow rate, valve settings, and motor speeds of machines on the production line can be checked by the minicomputer. If adjustments are needed, the minicomputer can make them happen. (We say they are done "automatically.") The finished product may be a mixture of components—for example, fertilizer, insecticide, or synthetic cloth from which tents, gloves, or clothes are to be made. In such cases, the minicomputer can control the mixing process to insure that the required percentages are maintained for the various components. On production lines where mechanized parts are being assembled, the minicomputer can insure that the required lubricants are present, the right amounts of force are applied in the right places in stress testing, and so on. As discussed in Chapter 1, the use of computer-controlled robotic systems in manufacturing is receiving much attention now. You should realize that minicomputers have been playing important roles in industrial automation— albeit less dramatically—for nearly 20 years. About half the minicomputers purchased these days are used in what are regarded as traditional minicomputer applications as we've just described them. (See Figure 10-3).

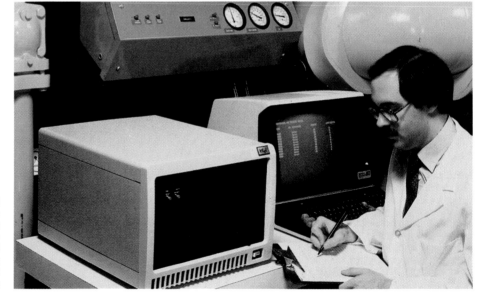

FIGURE 10-3
Through minicomputer-controlled processes such as testing, inspection, monitoring, and control, industrial automation is becoming a reality. (*Courtesy Intel Corporation*)

An important characteristic of the applications for which minicomputers were first used is that they could be accomplished without a lot of software. The minicomputer manufacturers did not spend time and money to provide several high-level programming languages, system software to control several concurrently executing programs, user-friendly interfaces, and so on. It was not until such features and many ready-to-run application programs had been developed that the second major use of minicomputers really began to take hold. That was the use of minicomputers as *small business systems.* The small business, the payroll or finance department of a large business, or similar group that purchases a minicomputer doesn't buy it just to have a mini. No, the mini is bought to do the payroll, process accounts receivable, and so on. These users do not have large, full-time programming staffs. Therefore, they need ready-to-run application programs (*application packages,* or *canned software*). Thanks to some of the minicomputer manufacturers and a number of independent software development firms, such packages are now available. (See Figure 10-4.)

A second prerequisite to the increasingly widespread use of minicomputers for basic business applications was the availability of lower-cost secondary-storage and I/O devices that could be attached to these minicomputers. Why should a small business user pay $70,000 to $100,000 for a high-speed (say, 2000-lpm) printer if a 360-lpm printer will do? Some of the needed devices have been developed by the minicomputer manufacturers themselves. For example, DEC has established a well-known line of hard-copy terminals known as *DECwriters* for use with its minicomputers. Other devices have been developed by firms that specialize in the development of secondary-storage and I/O devices for use on other firms' minicomputers. As mentioned earlier, in Chapter 6, these firms are called *plug-compatible manufacturers,* or *PCM's.* Some devices pro-

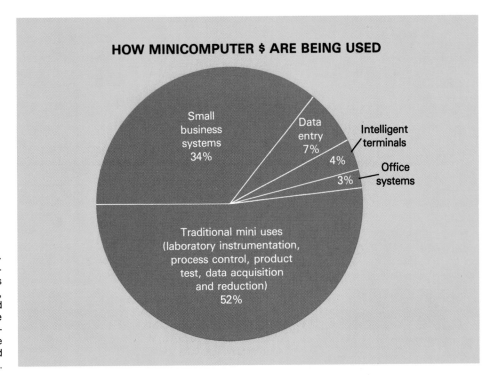

FIGURE 10-4
About half of today's spending for minicomputers goes for industrial applications, but minicomputer-based small business systems are a strong second, and minicomputer-based office systems have emerged as a new growth area.

duced by Control Data for use with IBM's Series 1 minicomputers are shown as examples in Figure 10-5.

You should understand that a "small business system" may be either a microcomputer system or a minicomputer system. How does a user decide which to get? Again, on the basis of requirements. If a large number of simultaneous users must be serviced interactively, if the system response time to those users is critical, and if a significant amount of primary storage is needed for programs and data to make the system perform well, a minicomputer is probably the right choice. If the user's needs are likely to outgrow a micro, then starting with a mini may be advisable.

Given adequate processing speed, devices, and software, there are three types of application areas for which small business systems are especially suitable. The first area includes *data-intense applications*, characterized by heavy data flow, much paper shuffling, and highly repetitive functions. Examples include payroll, accounts receivable, accounts payable, general ledger, billing, and inventory control. Often, when such applications are automated, a standalone small business computer is used.

The second application area is *functional applications*, the bread-and-butter operations relating to the "real" business of a firm. These applications cover client/customer/supplier interfaces. Examples are order processing, production

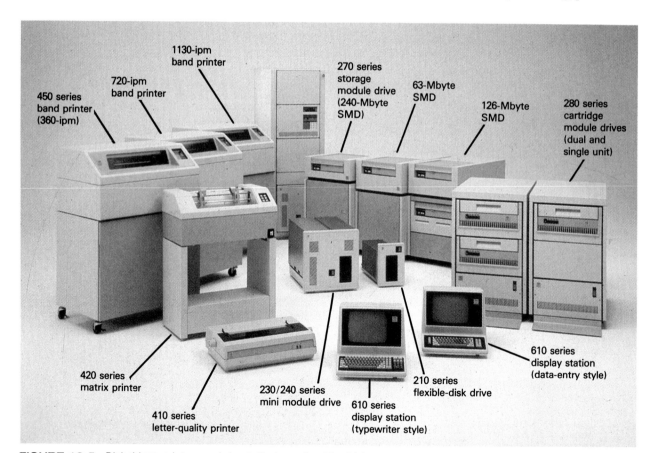

FIGURE 10-5 Disk drives, printers, and visual-display units with widely varying capabilities are available to meet the diverse needs of minicomputer users. (*Courtesy Control Data Corporation*)

scheduling, fare ticketing, credit authorization, and management reporting. Generally, small business computers supporting these applications must have interactive processing capabilities.

The third application area is *database applications*, characterized by the integration of data and the sharing of information among multiple applications. Whereas database processing was once thought to be possible only on large EDP systems, numerous small business computer manufacturers now offer data management software. For example, Hewlett-Packard offers IMAGE, a database management system, across several of its product lines. IMAGE provides for file and database sharing, integrated network database structures, and database inquiry facilities for ad hoc database access and update.

Look back at Figure 10-4. In addition to the traditional mini systems and those marketed as small business computers, 7 percent of the mini users' dollars are being spent on minis for use in data entry. We discussed this use of minis in key-to-tape, disk, and diskette data-entry systems in Chapter 4. The minicomputer performs tasks such as user verification, input validation, preliminary editing, and data conversion. The system may need to support a large number of terminal users performing the data-entry function. (See Figure 10-6.)

A minicomputer may provide the "intelligence" of an intelligent terminal. As we've suggested, microprocessors are assuming this role, so the need for minis

FIGURE 10-6
Some minicomputer systems are designed to support simultaneously a number of interactive users. Each user enters data and receives responses independently. (*Courtesy Wang Laboratories, Inc.*)

here is diminishing. However, if the user wants to distribute a significant amount of the data-processing (as well as the data-entry) functions required in a system, the power of a minicomputer may be needed. The spreading of computer power out to users at distant locations is called *distributed data processing*, or simply *distributed processing*. Since not only data-processing but also data-communication capabilities are needed, we'll discuss distributed processing in greater detail later (in Chapter 16).

Finally, an area of minicomputer use whose potential is just beginning to be realized is that of *office systems*. The minicomputer system becomes a piece of office furniture, as much a part of the office as typewriters, desks, and telephones have been for years. The hardware capabilities for this kind of use have existed for some time. The constraints have been primarily in software and in the vendors' lack of understanding of the users' needs and thinking. Because the office is a relatively "untouched" area so far as automation is concerned, the potential for increased efficiency and productivity gains is enormous. We'll say more about these systems in Chapter 16.

Marketing In general, minicomputers are marketed in any of three ways:

- Directly to end users, by the minicomputer manufacturers.

- To *original equipment manufacturers* (*OEM's*), who purchase the minis from the manufacturers and then package them together with their own hardware or software.

- To *system houses*, who go a step beyond OEM's by developing complete application systems, often specializing in a particular functional area or in a particular industry. For example, one system house may develop and market systems especially for firms that are involved in distribution activities; another may offer systems that do all the tasks required by insurance companies.

As mentioned earlier, in the minicomputer field, software development lagged far behind hardware development at the outset. Many independent software-consultant and software-development firms have been established to provide assistance to users of minis. We call these firms *third parties*. They play an important role in the industry.

Microcomputer systems based on 16-bit microprocessors are becoming more and more available. Extensive software to support them is already available or under development by numerous vendors. Many are widely marketed through many distribution channels. The 16-bit microcomputer systems also tend to cost less than conventional 16-bit minicomputer systems. In a very real sense, therefore, mini sales are being crowded by micros.

At the same time, however, leading minicomputer vendors are developing increasingly powerful 16-bit or 32-bit minicomputers (the superminis mentioned earlier). Since the vendors are aiming to protect their current user base as well as to attract new business, compatibility between their new and old systems is usually provided. End users, OEM's, and system houses that have significant investments in software and training but want to accomplish more with computer help than their current hardware allows are eager to take advantage of the additional capabilities of the superminis in many instances. We can expect superminis to represent an increasingly large portion of the installed minicomputers in years to come.

FULL-SCALE COMPUTERS

During the first 20 years of recorded computer history (1946–65), only a few computers existed. There were even fewer computer manufacturers. Each manufacturer offered one or two computer product lines, or families. In general, each family had a high-end model, one or more medium (in-between) models, and a low-end model. All computer models, across all families, were grouped into three general categories: large, medium-size, and small. Though no hard-and-fast definitions were established, there was general agreement on the category where each computer belonged.

Some questions arose when minicomputers arrived. Another computer category was established: the minicomputer. After all, minicomputers were minis — considerably smaller than small, so another category was warranted. Furthermore, minicomputers were made by minicomputer manufacturers. Other computers were made by different manufacturers. When we wanted to talk about large, medium, and small computers (as distinct from minis), we called them "mainframes." In turn, we called their manufacturers "mainframe manufacturers."

Now all that's changed. As we've just seen, the machines produced by minicomputer manufacturers are growing in storage capacity, types and quantities of I/O devices supported, and so on. Their capabilities often overlap those of mainframes. Indeed, mainframe manufacturers are building machines that are (or could be) classified as minis.

Be aware as we discuss mainframes that we are not discussing an exclusive grouping of computers above the minicomputer category. Much of what's said here applies to 32-bit (and even some 16-bit) minis. Such machines are called superminis or megaminis for good reasons.

Today, it's not easy to distinguish between small, medium-size, and large computer systems. Their capabilities, sizes, and costs frequently overlap. The classifications are most clear-cut when applied to the products of a single manufacturer or to a single product line. For example, Burroughs' B1955 and B2900 systems are small computers. Its B5900 systems are medium-size computers. Its B7800 and B7900 systems are large computers. Similarly, IBM's System/370 Model 115 is a small computer. The Models 138 and 148 are medium-size computers. The Models 158 and 168 are large computers. IBM's follow-on computers, the 303X and 308X series, are even larger.

Representative computers from several mainframe manufacturers are discussed below. We look at some typical systems in each of the categories and at some applications for which they are commonly used.

Small Computers

A small computer is typically a word-addressable machine with a primary-storage capacity of from 64K bytes to 4 megabytes. Its processor has a 16-, 18-, 24-, or 32-bit word size. Its machine cycle time ranges from about 225 nanoseconds to 100 nanoseconds. Looking at this characteristic from a more user-oriented point of view, a processor with a 225-nanosecond cycle time may perform about 200,000 instructions per second. A machine with a 100-nanosecond cycle time may perform about 420,000 instructions per second. In data-processing jargon, these instruction rates are often expressed as .2 *million instructions per second* (*MIPS*) and .42 MIPS, respectively. We mention these characteristics of small computers at the outset to alert you to the fact that mainframe users are likely to be very concerned about the performance of their machines. Their "bottom-line" question is: Within a given amount of time, how much work can be done?

Of course, the over-all performance of a computer system depends on more than just processor word size and internal processing speed. Even small computer systems are likely to support from 2 to 20, 40, or even more secondary-storage devices and I/O devices. The speeds of these devices are likely to be faster than the speeds of devices commonly used with minis and micros. Some small systems employ bus architectures. Others employ channels and high-speed I/O buffers (caches) to help insure that all components of the system are used as efficiently as possible.

Initially, small computer systems were offered by their manufacturers as replacements for punched-card data-processing systems. As we might expect, therefore, they were card-oriented. The user's data was punched into cards to be read as input. Even master-file items – for example, employee year-to-date payroll figures or inventory reorder quantities – were stored as punched-card records. The most common form of output was the regularly scheduled, printed business report. These small computer systems were well suited for low-volume batch-processing applications. In general, they offered faster, more efficient data processing at a lower cost than manual or electromechanical punched-card systems.

The Burroughs B1700, announced in June 1972, was the first small computer with an operating system able to support *multiprogramming*. With this capability, two or more programs can be in primary storage and run concurrently. The Burroughs B1700 was also the first small computer to support virtual storage (a capability we discussed briefly in Chapter 2 and will look at again in Chapter 14). Systems with these capabilities are usually able to support direct processing of transaction data as well as sequential, or batch, processing.

The V-8535 II, a typical small computer system, is offered by National Cash Register (NCR) as the low-end model in its NCR V-8500 II series. (See Figure 10-7.) The V-8535 II has a 32-bit processor with a machine cycle time of 112 nanoseconds. It can have up to 1 megabyte of primary storage. NCR's VRX (Virtual Storage Executive) operating system software is supported on this processor and on six medium-size and large models of the V-8500 II series. This approach helps to insure that users can acquire additional computing capabilities within this product line when their needs dictate.

Many other manufacturers make small computers. Among them are Burroughs, Sperry Rand's Univac division, Hewlett-Packard, DEC, Honeywell, and IBM. Generally, these computers are designed to handle transactions (say, customer orders) entered by users as well as batch input. Those purchased by small businesses, small agencies or institutions, and similar groups usually function as standalone systems. They may accept input from remote terminals as well as from nearby typewriterlike devices or visual-display units. They do not communicate with other computer systems. In larger organizations, small computers may themselves function as remote terminals. Data entry and some processing are done locally (at the user's site). The results of that processing and/or job requests are forwarded as input to other small computers or to a large central computer. In effect, distributed processing is carried out.

FIGURE 10-7
Accounts payable, accounts receivable, and other basic business data-processing tasks are frequently handled well by small computers. (Courtesy NCR Corporation)

Medium-Size Computers

Medium-size computer systems provide faster internal processing speeds and larger storage capacities than small computer systems. They can support high-speed I/O devices. Several disk drives can be used to provide online access to large data files as required for direct-processing applications. Multiple tape drives can be used for sequential-processing applications or to provide backup copies of data stored on disks for recovery purposes. Most systems support local card readers, other data-entry devices, visual-display units, and printers. They also support a wide variety of remote terminals for input and output.

System software developed for medium-size computer systems generally supports both multiprogramming and virtual storage. This means that many programs can be run concurrently. Some of them may be batch jobs—for example, a payroll program, a billing program, or a program that prints a list of overdue accounts. In addition, engineers may use the system to do electrical circuit design and structural analyses. Sales personnel may key in inquiries about the current status of customer orders. A fairly sophisticated management information system (MIS) can be implemented on medium-size computers with database-processing capabilities.

Medium-size computer systems are very flexible; they can be expanded to meet the needs of users. For example, a publishing firm may purchase or lease a system with 256K of primary storage, 4 visual-display units, 8 online disk drives, a 55-cps daisywheel printer for letter-quality output, and an 1130-lpm band printer for high-volume printed output. As the data-processing needs of the business increase, additional storage modules (in increments of 32K or 64K), some remote data-entry devices, more disk drives, and a plotter may be added.

The wide ranges in rental and purchase prices for medium-size systems are in part a reflection of this expandability.

Honeywell's DPS 7 computers are a family of medium-size computer systems that illustrate well this concept of expandability. Announced in late 1981, the systems provide a growth path for users of the firm's Series 200/2000, Level 62, and Level 64 computers. All systems are *field-upgradable*, which means a user can install one of the low-end models of the family, then add additional hardware and software as needed. The Model 35 is an entry-level system. It supports up to 5 local I/O devices and 15 communication lines. The high-end Model 65 supports up to 10 local I/O devices and 271 communication lines. Extensive system software is available to assist users in moving to distributed processing. (See Figure 10-8.)

Few announcements have caused more excitement among computer users than IBM's introduction of its 4300 series of small and medium-size computers. Here at last (late 1979) were the first IBM mainframes designed to be used outside a central computer room. Since the processors were compact and did not need special cooling, they could be used in remote sales offices, plants, and warehouses. IBM's System/370 system control programs (and therefore users' application programs written for use on System/370 machines) could be run on

Model	MIPS	Primary Storage (Mbytes)	Disk Storage (Gbytes)	Local I/O Devices	Communication Lines
35	.24	1–2	.8	5	15
45	.38	1–4	10	5	143
55	.45	2–4	15	10	143
65	.72	2–4	20.8	10	271

FIGURE 10-8 Like other mainframes, Honeywell Information Systems' DPS 7 series is a family of machines, designed to meet a wide range of needs and to allow users to upgrade to larger machines when advisable. (*Courtesy Honeywell Inc.*)

the 4300 series. New system software, most notably DOS/VSE (Disk Operating System/Virtual Storage Extended), was also available. Additional communication software was provided to enable the 4300s to act as host computers to a number of remote terminals or be easily hooked up with other computers.

When first introduced, a 4331 computer with 512K bytes of primary storage cost $65,000. A comparable System/370 Model 115 with only 64K bytes of primary storage cost $78,000. In addition, the 4331 has up to 4 times the instruction execution rate of the Model 115. Stated simply, that's 8 times the primary storage and 4 times the performance at about 80 percent of the cost. A 4341 with 2 times the primary storage and 3.2 times the performance of a comparable System/370 Model 138 cost $15,400 less than its predecessor ($245,000 vs $260,400). Furthermore, incremental memory was priced at a new low of $15,000 per megabyte. Comparable prices ranged up to $75,000 and even $110,000 per megabyte on other machines. The price for instruction execution for one second was about 28¢ on the 4300 processors, as compared to $1.45 to $1.70 on the older System/370 models.

Since 1979, IBM has continued to expand the 4300 series. It now includes both smaller and larger models. All are still within the small and medium-size computer ranges. In addition, several plug-compatible manufacturers (PCM's) now offer plug-compatible mainframes designed to compete directly with the 4300 series. The software developed by IBM and other firms for use on the 4300s can be run unchanged on these machines. The PCM's hope to provide more performance at comparable or lower costs, with shorter lead times on deliveries of orders. Because the PCM's are in some respects "second-round developers," they can turn out products with much less engineering and programming expense than would otherwise be possible. Users who are unwilling to undertake massive conversion efforts to allow their existing application programs and data to be used on non-IBM machines may consider alternative hardware that supports IBM software if the price and timing are right.

Large Computers

Many of today's medium-size and large corporations, government agencies, and service organizations depend on large computer systems to get their work done. A large computer system may involve one large computer and many I/O and secondary-storage devices. It may involve several large computers operating in a complementary fashion. The computers may all be in one large central location, or they may be at widely separated locations, joined by communication facilities.

To be considered large-scale, a computer must have operating speeds measured in nanoseconds and a primary-storage capacity of at least 4 million characters. Expandability to 16, 32, or even 64 million characters is possible with some systems. The primary storage may be structured as independent memory banks, allowing several simultaneous data transfers to or from storage. Hundreds of online secondary-storage devices may be supported. Hundreds or even thousands of online terminals may provide for user inputting of data to the system and obtaining of information from it.

Large-computer users acquire computer systems to handle the same kinds of applications that medium-size computers handle. In most instances, however, much greater volumes of data are processed. In addition, these systems can provide complex modeling, or *simulation*, of complete business operations—the

environment in which a business operates, the anticipated performance requirements on newly designed products or constructs (e.g., bridges), or manned space flights. A large computer system can even simulate itself or other computer systems in operation—for example, to determine the optimum or maximum number of online terminal users that can be serviced during peak times.

A large computer is well suited for design and engineering work because its speed enables it to do mathematical calculations that are not practical on other computers. The research and development processing necessary for the creation of new products can be done on a large computer system that is also used for basic business data processing.

Applications requiring large databases can be handled effectively only when large-computer capabilities are available. For example, the New York Stock Exchange uses the tremendous processing potential of large computers to handle the data generated by daily sales of 90 million or more shares of stock. Federal Express, the Memphis-based air-express company, depends on its large computers to support more than 800 agents answering more than 60,000 phone calls each day. Not simply the paperwork but also the actual customer materials—more than 160,000 packages per day—are accepted, transported, and delivered with computer help. To insure service commitments are met, Federal Express maintains its own fleet of planes—again, with computer help. Vast numbers of terminals, including small computers, minis, and micros at remote locations, can be connected to a central large-computer complex, thus forming a communication network. Jobs that are too large for the smaller computers can be forwarded to the large-computer complex, and the results can be sent back to the remote locations. An organization's corporate files and integrated databases can be maintained at the central location and shared by authorized users via the communication network.

IBM's System/370 Models 115 through 168 were mentioned earlier in this chapter. In March 1977, IBM enhanced the high end of this line by introducing its 3033 processor. In October of the same year, two somewhat smaller (but still large) processors, the 3031 and 3032, were introduced. Still later, *attached processor* (*AP*) and *multiprocessor* (*MP*) versions of some models were made available.

In these systems and similar ones, an attached processor shares I/O channels and primary storage with the main processor. (See Figure 10-10A.) Both processors are governed by one system control program that balances the workload between them to achieve high productivity. Each processor in an MP configuration has its own I/O channels, primary storage, power supply, cooling unit, and system console. (See Figure 10-10B.) Together, the processors may provide from 60 to 80 percent greater throughput than a single main processor (called a *uniprocessor*, for clarification) can provide. Perhaps equally important,

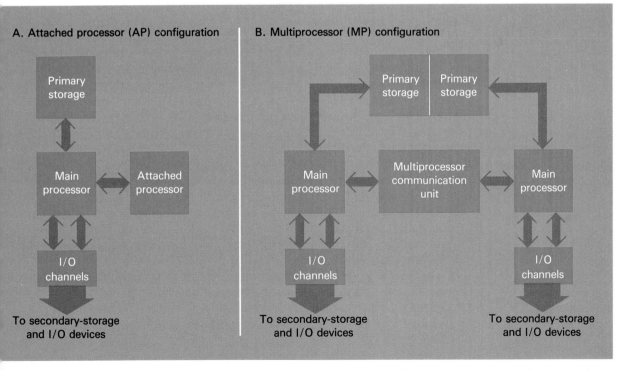

FIGURE 10-10 A large computer may consist of two or more processors designed to work together to complete processing tasks quickly and correctly.

FIGURE 10-11
Large computers, hundreds of disk drives, and thousands of remote terminals directed by extensive system and application software help banks, insurance companies, and other large businesses carry out daily activities with relatively little involvement of information system personnel. (*Courtesy IBM Corporation*)

the system can be reconfigured to allow one of the processors to function independently if the other processor must be removed from service for testing or maintenance. This capability helps to insure high system availability, a major requirement in online processing environments.

In 1981, IBM continued its evolution of power and performance in large systems by introducing the 308X family of mainframes. (See Figure 10-11.) The first member of this family was the 3081. It has two processors, referred to collectively as one *dyadic processor*. The two processors share one primary storage, either 16, 24, 32, or 48 megabytes in size. They run under one system control program. However, each processor has its own 32K-byte high-speed buffer and its own channels. This helps to maximize the amount of work that can be accomplished.

In 1982, IBM announced the 3084, its most powerful computer to date. The 3084 has four processors, up to 64 megabytes of primary storage, and up to 48 channels. It is a 26 MIPS machine that can be partitioned to function as two independent computers (each having two processors) if desired.

Like models of many computer families of the 1980s, all 308X models are field-upgradable. This means that users can move to bigger machines when their data-processing needs dictate.

In late 1981, IBM moved to protect users' return on investment (ROI) and yet offer additional computing capabilities to 308X users. It did so by announcing an extended architecture (XA) version of its high-end operating system: MVS/XA. Under the MVS/XA operating system, either 24 bits (as in earlier systems) or 31 bits of each 308X computer word can be used in primary-storage addressing. With 24-bit addressing, system and application programs can access 2^{24}, or *16 million*, bytes of instructions and data per address space. With 31-bit addressing, up to 2^{31}, or *2 billion*, bytes of instructions and data can be accessed. The more programs and data that can be in storage at one time, the faster the data can be processed. This principle is being applied to meet the needs of large organizations that have many jobs to be done and very large volumes of data.

Not surprisingly, PCM's are developing large plug-compatible mainframes to be used with the extensive system and application software base that exists for other vendors' large mainframes. The leaders in this area are Amdahl, with its IBM-compatible 470 and 580 series, and National Advanced Systems, with its Fūjitsu, are actively marketing large mainframes. Assuming that current trends continue, by 1985 a typical large-scale installation will include 23 MIPS of processing power (housed in one or more computers), 29 megabytes of primary storage, and 91.4 gigabytes of secondary storage. Such a system may process more than 220,000 transactions each day, execute more than 2500 batch jobs, and interact with 300 or more simultaneous users at terminals.

Other mainframe manufacturers are also investing vast amounts of resources in both large-computer hardware and large-computer software development. For example, Control Data Corporation (CDC) offers the Cyber 170 series, 700 series, and series-800 mainframes. These are 60-bit-word computers with powerful internal processing capabilities designed for computer-aided design/computer-aided manufacturing, energy management, meteorology (weather forecasting), mining, oil-industry applications, and the like. Plato, CDC's computer-based education system, can be run under CDC's Network Operating System (NOS) Version 2 on series-800 machines together with other user applications. Previously, Plato required a computer dedicated to its use.

SUPER-COMPUTERS AND THEIR USES

Clearly, computers are not one-of-a-kind machines (though even their most enthusiastic supporters may have assumed so in the 1940s). There are, however, computers whose vast size, capabilities, and costs make them suitable only for certain kinds of users—national laboratories, research labs, weather centers, large airlines, oil companies, utility companies, automotive firms, film animation studios, computer service organizations, and the like. Such users require vast amounts of data to be processed, and thousands or even millions of computations to be done per second. Computers such as we have discussed thus far cannot handle such tremendous tasks within the time constraints imposed. Cray Research and CDC are developing supercomputers to meet these user needs. Hitachi and Fujitsu introduced their first supercomputers in 1982.

The first CRAY 1 supercomputer was shipped by Cray Research in 1976. As the term *supercomputer* implies, the CRAY 1 is super in several ways. Physically, it is a cylindrical machine 9 feet in diameter at its base and 6.5 feet high. It weighs 10,500 pounds. That's twice as much as an IBM System/370 Model 168 and 400 times as much as an Apple III. More important, the CRAY 1 can add two 64-bit words in parallel in just one machine cycle, and yet that machine cycle takes only 12.5 nanoseconds. It has a theoretical MIPS rate of 80. In actual practice, a 20 to 60 MIPS rate is experienced on typical jobs. For comparison, the CRAY 1 is described as having the power of 15 System/370 Model 168s.

A second supercomputer model, the CRAY 1S, was offered about 1980. Oil companies such as Arco Petroleum Company have installed CRAY 1S machines to do reservoir modeling. Assume computer simulation enables one of these

FIGURE 10-12
Nuclear weapons and super-sonic aircraft design, oil reservoir simulation, weather forecasting, and space and fusion energy research are being done with the help of supercomputers like this CRAY X-MP at government facilities, universities, and privately owned corpora-tions. (*Courtesy Cray Research Inc.*)

companies to improve the productivity of a $100-billion oil field by 2 percent. The difference in yield from this one oil field may very well offset the cost of the CRAY 1S. In late 1982, Cray announced that it intended to reduce the price of the Model 1S by about 50 percent (to between $4 million and $7 million) by using semiconductors instead of magnetic cores for primary storage. The lower-priced model is called the CRAY 1M.

In May 1982, Cray Research announced the CRAY X-MP. (See Figure 10-12.) It has two CRAY-1-type processors linked together. They share either 2 or 4 million 64-bit words of primary storage. Each processor has four parallel memory-access ports; therefore, eight references to primary storage can occur simultaneously. The machine cycle time is 9.5 nanoseconds—25 percent faster than the incredibly fast CRAY 1. A solid-state device (SSD) provides an additional 64, 128, or 256 megabytes of online secondary storage. The storage is available to either processor via a 1250-megabytes-per-second I/O channel. Large data sets generated and accessed repetitively by application programs can be placed on the SSD. Temporary storage for system programs is also provided by this device.

The CRAY X-MP is software-compatible with the CRAY 1S. It is expected to offer up to 5 times as much throughput as a CRAY 1S at about twice the cost. The CRAY X-MP sells for between $9 million and $11 million. The SSD, a practical necessity for most applications, ranges in price from $1.5 million to $3.5 million, depending on the amount of storage required.

Control Data Corporation has been active in supercomputer development for more than 20 years. In fact, Seymour Cray, the founder of Cray Research, worked at CDC during the 1960s and early 1970s. The firm's CDC 6600 (1964),

CDC 7600 (1968), STAR-100 (1974), and Cyber 203 (1979) were predecessors of its newest offering: the Cyber 205. The first Cyber 205 was installed at the United Kingdom Weather Center in Bracknell, England, in 1981. Among its major characteristics are:

- Up to 800 million floating-point operations per second achieved through parallel array, or vector, processing
- Up to 50 million instructions per second (our familiar MIPS) achieved through single-item, or scalar, processing
- Up to 4 million 64-bit words of primary storage
- Up to 2 trillion (2×10^{12}) 64-bit words of addressable virtual storage
- Up to 16 I/O ports with a total I/O rate of 3.2 billion (3.2×10^9) bits per second

Both CDC and Cray Research say it takes from 9 to 12 months to build a supercomputer. By mid-1983, 18 Cyber 205s had been installed. Cray is now installing 12 to 18 machines each year. By yearend 1982, it had installed 50. When Cray shipped its first machine in 1976, the total potential user base was considered to be about 100. Today, the number of organizations that might reasonably be expected to acquire supercomputers is projected by some to be 400. We can all benefit. For example, in 1982 the National Weather Service in Washington, D.C., decided to acquire a Cyber 205 to speed weather forecasting. It acts as a collection point for climate information from 335 service offices. Information from the observation stations at these service offices is supplemented by information from the military services, from fishermen, and from the Federal Aviation Administration. Numerical models of the atmosphere are created with computer help and used to produce a new forecast every 12 hours.

Digital Productions, a special effects studio based in Los Angeles, placed an order for the first CRAY X-MP in 1982. Even at that time, the firm was busy planning special computer graphics for the movie "Starfighter," to be produced on a leased CRAY 1S. Photographically realistic computer animation well beyond that of Disney's movie "Tron" was their ultimate objective. Imagine it if you can!

CHAPTER SUMMARY

1. Minicomputers were introduced in 1965 as smaller, slower machines than mainframes that could satisfy many user needs on a cost-effective basis. They were also easier to install and operate.

2. Minicomputers are being used in industrial automation, small business systems, data-entry systems, and office systems, and as intelligent terminals.

3. Full-scale computers, or mainframes, can be categorized as small, medium-size, or large. A manufacturer may offer one or more product lines that include models in all three categories.

4. Small computers are typically word-addressable machines with from 64K to 4 megabytes of primary storage. Initially, they were offered as replacements for punched-card systems and were well suited for low-volume batch-processing applications. Today's small computers can also handle transaction data entered by users at remote terminals or nearby I/O devices.

5. Medium-size computer systems can support a wide variety of secondary-storage and I/O devices. Batch jobs and interactive applicatons can be done concurrently. As users' needs increase, their systems can be expanded to handle them.

6. Large-scale computer systems involving one or more large processors can support hundreds of online secondary-storage devices and hundreds or even thousands of online terminals. Simulation, design and engineering work, and applications requiring large databases can be handled effectively when large-computer capabilities are available.

7. Cray Research and Control Data Corporation are developing supercomputers to meet the needs of national laboratories, university research labs, weather centers, large airlines, oil companies, computer service organizations, and the like. These supercomputers can handle vast amounts of data and do thousands or even millions of computations per second to meet demanding needs within the time constraints imposed.

DISCUSSION QUESTIONS

1. What makes a minicomputer a minicomputer?

2. What advantages do minicomputers offer over full-scale computers?

3. Discuss prerequisites for the use of minicomputers as small business systems.

4. What products and/or services are offered to minicomputer users by (a) OEM's, (b) system houses, and (c) other third parties?

5. (a) Describe a typical small computer system.
   (b) Identify some user applications for which the system you've described is well suited.
   (c) Identify some requirements that cannot be satisfied by the system you've described.

6. (a) How do medium-size computer systems differ from small computer systems?
   (b) Suggest situations where these differences may be important.

7. Describe some needs that can be satisfied only by large computer capabilities.

8. Distinguish between the following: uniprocessor, attached processor, multiprocessor, dyadic processor.

9. Why is field upgradability important from a user's point of view?

10. Why is compatibility important from a user's point of view?

11. (a) What are PCM's?
    (b) Discuss their potential impact on the data-processing community.

12. Who uses supercomputers? For what? Why?

11

SYSTEM ANALYSIS AND DESIGN

When you want to know if something is appropriate, look for signs of its invisibility! The surest signal that something is working correctly is that it seems very ordinary.

The use of computers for recording reservations at the beautiful Hyatt Regency Hotel in Dallas seems perfectly expected and ordinary in today's world. What may not be realized, however, is that computers may also be in use to manage restaurant supplies, laundry, air-conditioning and heating, elevators, and other "invisible" services. What better way to keep track of constantly changing conditions than by computers?

One might stop at a lobby boutique in the hotel to sample a perfume by Guerlain of Paris. Would the scent reveal that one of the world's largest perfume makers depends heavily on computers in its manufacture? Guerlain uses computers for many accounting and management functions, too.

© 1981 Peter Menzel

A chain of high-fashion clothing stores in Paris relies on computers to manage an inventory of over six million items. A total of 35 terminals in eight stores communicate with a computerized central warehouse to handle ordering and supplying garments. Customers undoubtedly appreciate the huge selection and prompt service.

Some people say change is best when it goes unnoticed. At the Towle Manufacturing Company, a 300-year tradition in silver craftmanship is now supported by computer-controlled production, inventory maintenance, and distribution.

The opera and the circus may not have many obvious things in common, but they are alike in many uses of their computers. Aside from the expected applications for reservations and ticketing, both groups schedule their bookings far in advance and have complex transportation needs that must be carefully managed. Both also use computers for handling lighting and sound equipment, and both must monitor and order various supplies.

Sometimes computers can be used to restore things to their "ordinary" states. The U.S. Capitol dome in Washington is one of 15 buildings being restored with the help of computers. The computers are being used not only in project management of materials and labor, but also in reconstructing the original appearance of the buildings.

In Taiwan, a project under way at the Asian Vegetable Research and Development Center is improving the quality and quantity of locally grown food crops. Scientists from 10 nations are using computer time donated by IBM to analyze the nutritional value and "growability" of various strains of fruits and vegetables.

In Houston, Texas, the Union Equity Coop Exchange uses a computer to keep track of the amounts and destinations of grain shipments. Sorting and grinding the grain can also be controlled by computers. Who would think of so much computer involvement in an ordinary bag of flour or a loaf of bread?

In Los Angeles County, there are approximately 700 firefighting vehicles, 2200 uniformed firefighters, and 130 fire stations. Optimum coordination of all these resources is handled by computers, providing quick and effective response to emergencies.

To those who would otherwise have to deal with the complexities of all these situations, computer assistance has provided extraordinary benefits. To most of us, however, that assistance is invisible in these "ordinary" situations.

Courtesy Sperry Corporation

Courtesy Sperry Corporation

© Dan McCoy/Rainbow

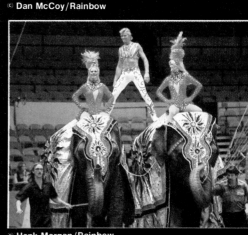

© Hank Morgan/Rainbow

11 | SYSTEM ANALYSIS AND DESIGN

Suppose you're driving a car in downtown Chicago. You're not quite sure how you got there, but you know that's not where you want to be. You have tickets to a Chicago Bears game at Wrigley Field, or you're due at your aunt's home in Evanston in an hour. How do you get there? Aha—there's a map in the glove compartment. But it's a map of Detroit. It won't help you decide whether to go straight, turn left, or turn right when the traffic signal changes.

Take another example. You've been searching some time for new floor mats for your car. Now, you come upon some quite accidentally while shopping for a bike light. The mats look acceptable. "How much are they?" you ask. The salesclerk tells you they come in brown, red, and beige. "How much are they?" you ask. The salesclerk tells you they stay in place well. "How much are they?" you ask. The salesclerk tells you they resist heat, tar, oil, and even strong chemicals. The mats may be great, but you leave the store without them.

Now consider a third example. You've just received an attractive, colorful brochure. There's a photo of Spanish dancers on the front.

Inside, there are photos of old missions. You see the words *Mexico* and *Old Mexico*. Looks interesting! Unfortunately, the major portion of the brochure is written in Spanish, and you can read only English.

What can we conclude from these three examples? For starters: (1) Information is of little or no value if it doesn't meet the user's need; (2) an answer is likely to be ignored if it fails to address the question it's supposed to answer; and (3) information that is not understandable to the user is not usable information.

Notice that none of these examples involves a computer. The observations we've just made, however, apply to computerized situations as well as to non-computerized ones.

A computer is useful only if it's put to work on the right task. It may do a job in 10 microseconds, but if nobody wants the job done, who cares? It may be ready to accept sales data as input from remote terminals, but if the data-entry procedures aren't understandable, or don't exist, how can anyone provide the data to it? It may produce a 20-page inventory report, but if the report doesn't tell stock clerks, shipping personnel, or managers what they need to know, who gains? If the needed information is there, but it's buried on page 17, who finds it?

A computer is more expensive than many of the tools that an individual or organization acquires, but it is a need-satisfying machine. Many users can benefit from its help. The major objectives of performing system analysis and design are to understand fully user problems or information needs, and to plan how the computer can be used in addressing them (if, indeed, the computer can or should be used). An individual or an organization cannot afford to fail in meeting these objectives. The tasks of system analysis and design are crucial to the successful use of computers. These tasks are the subject of this chapter.

WHAT IS A SYSTEM?

The term *system* is not an unusual one; you probably hear or speak the term daily. Each of us depends directly on one continuously functioning system; it's a biological system: our human body. Our cars have ignition systems. When we attend classes, teach courses, or work in the Dean's office, we're part of an educational system. To talk to friends across town, in a nearby state, or across continents, we use a telephone system. Businesses have accounting systems, payroll systems, inventory control systems, and so on. Again, notice that some of these systems do not involve computers at all. Others may or may not. A system is simply a group of interrelated elements that work together to perform a specific task. (See Figure 11-1.)

In Chapter 1, we looked at several examples of data-processing systems. In Chapter 2, we looked more closely at electronic data-processing (EDP) systems, or systems that involve computers. The business systems we just mentioned are, of course, data-processing systems. Increasingly, these systems are based on EDP. It's important to understand that (1) each system consists of *interrelated elements*, (2) the elements *work together*, and (3) the elements share a common objective: *to perform a specific task or function.*

THE SYSTEM DEVELOPMENT CYCLE

In this chapter, we direct our attention first to the over-all task of system development. You can assume that the system under development is a data-processing system. The steps of system development are referred to collectively

FIGURE 11-1 Systems differ widely, but they all have one characteristic in common: Each system involves a group of inter-related elements working together. (*Courtesy* [A] *Owen Franken / Stock, Boston;* [B] *Magnuson Computer Systems;* [C] *Burroughs Corporation;* [D] *AT&T*)

by various names: the system development cycle, the system life cycle, the system development life cycle, and so on.

Figure 11-2 shows one way we can group the steps of the system development cycle into phases. No hard-and-fast rules determine how many phases there are, nor how many steps make up each phase. Some groups establish four phases, as shown here. Others define 10 or 20 phases. Some define 10, 20, or more steps in each of the phases. The only purpose of viewing system development in this way is to set up a general framework within which we can proceed. Our ultimate objective is to achieve project control. We can agree upon the amount of time to be allocated to each phase. At the completion of each phase, we can check our progress. Some important questions to be asked at each checkpoint are:

- How far along are we, compared to where we're supposed to be?
- Has all the work that should be done in this phase really been completed?
- Should we proceed to the next phase?

In broadest terms, *system analysis* is the study of an existing task or function in order to understand that task or function and to find ways to better accomplish it. *System design* is the creation of a detailed plan to accomplish improvements. *System implementation* is the enactment of the plan. *System evaluation* is a review of the system that's been developed to determine how well it meets its objectives.

At any step in system development, we may discover previously unidentified problems. For example, at the checkpoint following system design, a plant manager may see that he needs quarterly reports of absence and overtime by product or by function as well as by department. While doing the detailed design of department variance reports, a programmer may discover that travel data not currently being collected must be recorded in each department's operating expense file. Making even minor changes without considering what has been done previously can cause errors or have unanticipated effects elsewhere. Therefore, as Figure 11-2 shows, a return to the system analysis phase may occur at any point in the system development cycle.

The last phase in the system development cycle—evaluation—often leads to follow-up actions. Few if any systems are "finished" when this phase is

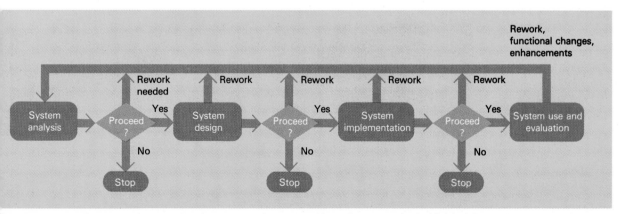

FIGURE 11-2 The steps of system development can be grouped into phases, each of which is followed by a checkpoint; together they form a system development cycle.

completed. The need for corrections, a desire for improvements, and new requirements often lead to another round of system development.

THE PARTICIPANTS

Several persons or groups may take part in system development. The user may be an individual, industrial department, manufacturing plant, distribution center, small business, or whatever, that has a problem or an opportunity to be investigated. Putting this another way, the user is the client for whom system development is done. User personnel are the only ones who know what they (and the systems of which they are a part) really do. They are the only ones who really know their requirements. Therefore, they must participate in system development. They can best perform the quality-control function because they have a self-serving interest that things be done right. After all, if a new or changed system results, they are the ones who will have to live with it. (See Figure 11-3.)

Information system personnel are consultants or contractors to the user in system development. They may be members of an in-house information system staff. They may be hired from outside the organization. Sometimes the initial steps of system development are done by in-house analysts but products or services needed later are obtained from outside sources. In any case, the information system personnel apply their specialized knowledge to the system development efforts. They also make recommendations. Final decision making is a user responsibility; it should not be delegated.

FIGURE 11-3
System development is a joint undertaking in which users and information system personnel work together. (*Courtesy General Electric and Comshare Inc.*)

Usually, the information system personnel who participate in system analysis and design are called system analysts, system designers, or programmer/analysts. A *system analyst* works with the user to understand the problem or opportunity being investigated. He or she documents findings, develops alternatives, and presents a system proposal to user management. The analyst may be a member of a user department rather than of an information system group. This arrangement makes it easier for the analyst to acquire a good understanding of the user's work and work environment.

If some or all of a system is developed in-house, a *system designer* creates a detailed plan, or specification, for the system. This specification translates the *what* of the system into the *how*. Not uncommonly, system analysts do both system analysis and system design. There may be no one who holds a position specifically designated as that of system designer.

Small firms often employ one or more *programmer/analysts*. They may be full-time employees of the firm, or they may be hired on a contract basis. These persons have system analysis, system design, and programming responsibilities.

As the system development activity proceeds, outside groups, such as vendors of hardware and software being considered, may have to be contacted. In-house system support groups, such as data-processing operations personnel or financial analysts and accountants, may need to be involved. User and information system management must be kept fully informed of progress and problems.

Finally, we should consider the one-person situation, the individual who has purchased or is contemplating purchasing a microcomputer for business, home, or personal use. Obviously, this individual is the user. Such a user may seek analysis and design help. The needed software may be purchased, or a contract programmer or an independent software firm may be paid to develop it. A few brave, data-processing-knowledgeable, or optimistic individuals may take on all the responsibilities of system development alone.

The purpose of this chapter is not to teach you to be a system analyst or system designer. Its purpose is not even to teach you how to do system analysis or system design. You can't learn those skills by reading one chapter of a book. The purpose of this chapter is to help you understand what system analysis and design are, and why they are important. Many people can benefit by learning some of the tools and techniques used by system analysts. Administrators, accountants, auditors, and users of computer-based systems need to understand how their roles relate to that of the analyst. Managers need to understand the steps involved in determining how to make the best use of computers within their organizations.

PROBLEMS AND OPPORTUNITIES

Usually, the impetus for system development activity comes from the user community. The manager of a large supermarket may become concerned because the lines of customers awaiting checkout are too long (how can we speed up the checkout process?) or too short (how can we attract more customers on weekdays?). A regional sales manager may complain because the sales-by-salesperson reports he receives are incomplete or too slow in coming. Legislated changes in depreciation allowances may represent opportunities for tax savings. A large wholesale distributor may perceive that additional revenues could be generated through short hauls if only better records of scheduled long hauls and of truck repair and maintenance activities were available.

Sometimes the impetus for system development activity comes from the data-processing or information system staff. For example, a system analyst may learn of optical-character-recognition (OCR) equipment that appears to offer major opportunities for productivity increases in sales order entry. Do the potential benefits of the productivity increases outweigh the equipment and training costs that would be incurred? If a high-speed laser printer were acquired, how much faster could customer bills be produced and readied for mailing? What effect would the faster billing capabilities have on the over-all length of time before payments were received? How would these changes affect the over-all cash position of the company?

In today's environments, individuals and organizations alike are faced with increasing costs and limited resources. Both problems and opportunities must be prioritized. These initial requests for system development activity need not be highly formalized, but the use of a simple, standardized form like the one in Figure 11-4 is advantageous to users and to the information system staff. All boxes above the double line must be filled in. With this documentation, unnecessary delays due to insufficient information or misunderstandings are less apt to occur. The submitted design change requests are hard evidence of perceived system development requirements. They can be categorized and filed for individual tracking, reporting, and reference purposes. Some requests will be rejected. Others will be deferred. Others will be assigned to system analysts for preliminary investigation. A target resolution date, prerequisite to approval by user and information system management, will be established at that time.

Even a personal computer user may wish to create and use simple forms to record ideas for system development. Ideas noted on forms can be pursued when time and opportunity permit. Unnoted ideas may be forgotten.

PRELIMINARY INVESTIGATION

The next step in system analysis is the preliminary investigation. If the term *preliminary investigation* seems somewhat awesome, replace it with the simple phrase *initial look*. That's what we're talking about here. The analyst decides whether the problem or opportunity that has been identified warrants further analysis. In effect, the analyst conducts a brief *feasibility study* of the proposed project.

In taking this initial look, the analyst works primarily through personal interviews. A major purpose of the investigation is to insure that the true nature and scope of the problem or opportunity are understood. Managers should not speak for subordinates, and subordinates should not speak for managers. In talking with managers, for example, the analyst may find that not just the sales-by-salesperson report but rather all the sales reports are incomplete and late. In talking with sales personnel in the field, the analyst may learn that the results of daily sales activities are to be phoned in by 10 P.M. each evening. Maybe that's not happening. Maybe the calls are being made, but at times when the sales data is not complete. In talking with the home-office staff, the analyst may find that the data recorded during the calls is hard to understand later. The volume of data to be entered may exceed that which the data-entry staff can handle. Internal, programmed input validation procedures may be inadequate or totally lacking.

One outcome of the feasibility study should be a determination of the scope of the problem. For example, the investigation may show a weak link between the

DESIGN CHANGE REQUEST	DCR No.	Assigned to	

System/Program/Function to be Changed	Usability	Severity	
	Yes No	1 2 3 4	

Reason for Change	Type of Change
	Add Delete
	Change Error

Change Description

Originator	Date Opened	Dept./Bldg.	Phone Extension

Interfaces Affected/Impact

Reviews/Inspections Needed	DR2	DR3	I0	I1	I2

Related Documentation

Test Requirements

Approvals   Date

FIGURE 11-4   A simple design change request form can serve as a reminder of the documentation needed when making a request for system development.

sales force and the home office. If the problem is a broad one, all user activities and procedures associated with providing input may need to be addressed. Selected programs within the sales reporting system may need to be reviewed (and then rewritten or changed). If the scope of the problem is even broader, it may require an analysis of all managers' requirements for sales information, and of all existing or new systems that may be needed to provide this information.

In most cases, the analyst supplements interview findings by simple observations of how user activities are currently being done. He or she may also examine existing user documents. Both techniques will be applied in greater depth later if a decision is made to proceed to the next step of analysis, a detailed investigation.

At the conclusion of the initial look, the analyst prepares a brief *feasibility report*. The report lists:

- The problem or opportunity that triggered this preliminary investigation
- The time period of the investigation, the persons or groups consulted, and the name and position of the analyst
- The true nature and scope of the problem as determined by the analyst's findings
- A brief summary of the alternatives (possibly none!) that may satisfy the user's needs within budget and time constraints, together with rough estimates of the costs and benefits of each and a note of any technical challenges
- A recommendation on the feasibility of pursuing the project and, if the recommendation is positive, a further recommendation on how to proceed

Both the feasibility study and the feasibility report should be as short as possible. For most projects, the feasibility study should take less than one month. (If the feasibility report can be completed at the outset, no feasibility study as such is required.) The feasibility report should be a one-page or two-page document. The analyst should meet with user and information system management to supplement this written report with an oral report and to respond to any questions. At the conclusion of the meeting, one of three decisions should be made: drop the project, shelve the project temporarily, or proceed with a detailed investigation.

DETAILED INVESTIGATION

The information gathered during the preliminary investigation is the jumping-off point for the detailed investigation. This step is similar to the preceding one in that it focuses initially on the nature and scope of the problem or opportunity being investigated. Some of the same investigating techniques may be used. However, this investigation is a more rigorous, more in-depth analysis. Its output includes not only a summary of what is being done but also a comprehensive statement of what ought to be done and a firm direction as to how it should be done.

Whereas the feasibility study may have been largely the responsibility of one analyst, unless the scope of the problem or opportunity is very small, a project team is now formed. Both information system personnel and user personnel must be members of the team. The temptation to plunge immediately into fact-finding will be strong, but this temptation must be resisted. Specific objectives for the detailed investigation must be formulated, agreed upon, and documented. The specific tasks needed to achieve the objectives must be identified and assigned. A timetable reflecting all tasks should be charted in a form visible to all team members. (See, for example, Figure 11-5.) In a large project, several levels of detailed planning (and several levels of charts) may be required.

If the detailed investigation will take several weeks or months, interim checkpoints should be established. At these checkpoints, progress on specific tasks should be assessed both subjectively and quantitatively. For example, one analyst may report the need to spend two more days studying what data is recorded on sales orders and why. Another analyst may report that 10 of 13 shipping clerks have been interviewed on schedule. For any tasks that are behind schedule, catch-up actions must be identified. Otherwise, some replanning is required.

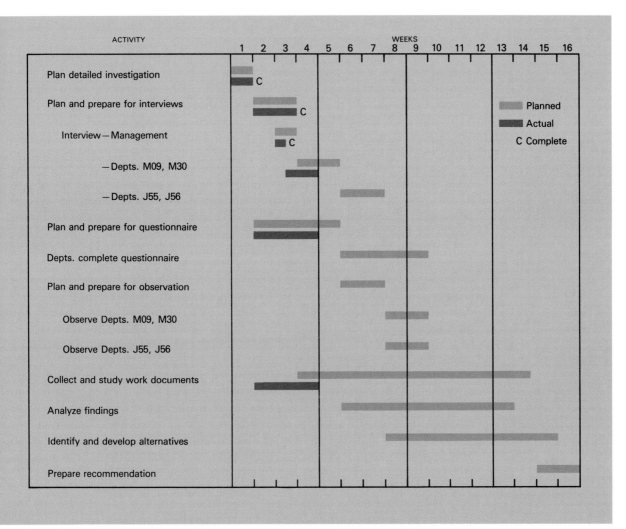

FIGURE 11-5 Both the planned and actual progress on tasks of a detailed investigation are shown on this Gantt chart.

The existence of a problem or an opportunity indicates that there is at least a perceived difference between what is and what ought to be. To fully understand this difference, the project team conducts the detailed investigation as a four-part process: fact-finding, data analysis and evaluation, estimating costs and benefits, and preparation of a system proposal.

Fact-Finding   During fact-finding, analysts direct their attention to the user and to all aspects of the activities within the scope of the matter being investigated. How many people key in order data? How long does keying an order take? Are there peak order periods during the day, week, or month? Is work checked? If so, how? Is the keying activity centralized or done at various locations? What are the working conditions (temperature, light, noise, furniture, and so on)?

Notice that these questions are alike in one very important way: They get at the facts. An analyst may gain valuable insights during fact-finding, but objectivity should be maintained throughout the investigating and recording processes. By maintaining objectivity, the analyst is better able to separate what's being done in what way because of habit or tradition from what's being done in what way because of actual requirements.

The methods commonly used in fact-finding are interviews, questionnaires, observations of work, and studies of user documents. Full chapters and even complete books are available that discuss each of these methods. As you might expect, each method has its advantages and disadvantages.

Interviews must be well-planned in advance. Each participant should know the objectives of the interview beforehand and prepare for it. If an analyst doesn't understand a point that comes up in the interview, he or she can pursue the question right there. Persons are sometimes willing or eager to express orally information that they are unwilling to put in writing. Another advantage of interviews is that they provide opportunities for information system personnel to meet and establish rapport with users. The users learn of their own role in the system development activity.

A questionnaire is a useful technique for obtaining the same kind of information from a large number of users. It may be the only practical method of obtaining information from users at several geographically distant locations of a large decentralized organization. The questions themselves may be either open-ended or fixed-format. (See Figure 11-6.) For best results, both the questionnaire and the questions on it should be short. Users should be told in advance that it's coming. A deadline for return of the questionnaire must be stated clearly in a cover memo.

In most if not all companies, there's a difference between the formal organization (as shown on an organization chart) and the informal organization (who knows whom, who contacts whom to get work done). Differences also exist between the documented standards and procedures for work activities and how work is actually done on a day-to-day basis. Therefore, some facts can be learned only by observation. Some observations are made incidentally. For example, while waiting to interview an administration manager, an analyst may see five employees standing in line to use a single copying machine. This observation may have significance later. Some observations are intense studies of, for example, what causes a manufactured part to be classified as defective, and how the defects are found (or not found) by quality-control inspectors. Under

A. An open-ended questionnaire poses questions to be answered.

Example:

What written documents do you refer to in doing your work?

DOCUMENT   REASON FOR USE

_____   _____

_____   _____

_____   _____

(Etc.)   (Etc.)

B. A fixed-format questionnaire presents either a statement or a question and a limited number of fixed responses from which the respondent chooses.

Example:

I have all the information needed to do my job.

☐   ☐   ☐   ☐   ☐
Strongly   Agree   No   Disagree   Strongly
agree   opinion   disagree

FIGURE 11-6 Open-ended (A) or fixed-format (B) questionnaires can be used to obtain information when many users must be contacted during fact-finding.

systematic activity sampling, observations are made at random and the persons being observed are not told in advance when they will be observed. In general, observations are made to determine (1) the work flow, (2) who does each task and how, and (3) the physical arrangement of the work area. Users should know that observations are being made and why, even though they may not be told exactly when they will be observed.

Many of today's organizations are buried in paperwork. Analysts who attempt to review the user's written documentation may be in similar danger. Copies of existing standards, written procedures, and operating manuals should be obtained. Before studying them, the analyst should determine whether and how each is currently used. Formal reports produced by the existing systems may contain important information about the organization. Factors such as the number of copies made, who receives copies, and where and how long copies are kept may be informative. Existing, completed forms used in day-to-day operations should be analyzed. (In contrast, a study of blank forms may be misleading. Some forms or portions of forms may never be used.) In some organizations, the managers at all levels produce monthly highlight reports. Finally, the day-to-day memos and other correspondence used for communication throughout the organization are important fact-finding indicators.

Data Analysis and Evaluation

As facts are collected, they must be recorded, organized, and evaluated. Notes taken during interviews, responses to questionnaires, charts of user duties constructed by the analysts or by the users themselves, and minutes of meetings must be studied and indexed. The information system personnel begin to extract, from this wealth of data, the significant factors that help them identify the user's system requirements.

One recording technique that is gaining popularity is the use of *data flow diagrams (DFD's)*. As Figure 11-7 indicates, a DFD is a simple picture of what's occurring in a portion of the user's existing system or organization. Each box is a "source" or "sink," a point at which data enters or leaves. Each circle (also called a *bubble*) is a process performed on the data that flows into it. The numbers within the bubbles are reference numbers; they do not show the sequence of the processes. The parallel lines represent files, or collections of data retained for reference. The lines with arrows show the directions of data flow. If the process depicted by a bubble is actually made up of several subprocesses, the DFD may be "leveled." This means that another DFD is created to show in greater detail what is going on within that particular bubble, or process. In Figure 11-7, bubbles 8 and 9 are likely candidates for expansion.

Through creation and study of these DFD's and of related information collected during the fact-finding (user's descriptions of the processes, details of file contents, volume of workload, frequency of events, and so on), the analyst begins making judgments about the virtues and shortcomings of present operations. The analyst may detect, among other things:

- Task duplication
- Task overlap
- Task inconsistencies
- Tasks that aren't being done but should be
- Uneven workload distribution
- Unnecessary delays
- Frequent backtracking
- Lack of task information
- Inadequate tools
- Insufficient task controls

Armed with the results of such analyses, the analyst is ready to develop and evaluate alternatives. At this point, the wise analyst reviews the agreed-upon objectives for the system development activity. The analyst must also review all constraints. No user has unlimited resources. Any recommended changes in staffing, operational (non-computer-related) tools and facilities, and/or EDP-system components must be in line with the user's budgets or ability to acquire additional funds as needed. The time available for development may be a serious constraint. For example, application programs to comply with new government

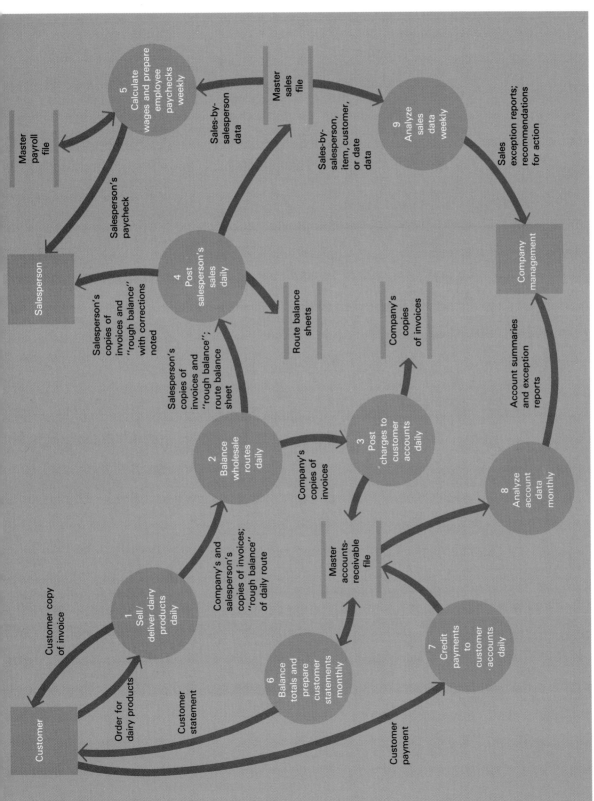

FIGURE 11-7 Dairy deliveries to customers lead to the processes documented on this data flow diagram for wholesale-routes account processing.

reporting requirements may have to be ready for production use by January 1 of a given year.

Systems have many components. Even the simplest one may pose many alternatives. There is little likelihood of finding any one solution to a problem or response to an opportunity that is ideal in all respects. The likelihood that there is only one right solution, or that there is no solution, is small. An accepted approach is to define several alternatives and to show the relative advantages and disadvantages of each. There is no merit in pursuing a dozen or more alternatives. Usually, the set that satisfies the user's needs within the constraints is small. The project team should continuously review each proposed alternative from the standpoints of technical, economic, and administrative feasibility.

Remember that information system personnel are consultants or contractors in system development. An analyst should not try to tell users what they *must* do. Rather, the analyst's job is to outline what can be done, at what expense, and with what potential impact. If, in the eyes of the project team, one alternative is clearly superior, that alternative should be explored in greater detail. However, the final decision as to which alternative is "best" should be made by management and by the users who will live with the system.

The scope of this evaluation-of-alternatives step varies widely. If the user has no computer system, and at least one of the proposed alternatives is computer-based, equipment vendors may have to be contacted. This step also applies if significant changes or additions to an existing computer system are required. The workload of the existing system and of each proposed system should be projected three to five years into the future. Expandability should be an important criterion when reviewing alternatives.

Details of system design should be left to the system design phase, but major architectural directions must be decided upon—for example, whether sequential processing or direct processing of transactions is warranted, whether database-processing capabilities are needed, and what data entry or data processing should be done by users at remote locations via distributed-processing facilities. These system characteristics are stated as part of the initial programming functional specification (IPFS) for the project.

The possibility that the needed software already exists in package form should be investigated. The use of such packages offers many advantages: Fewer in-house development resources are needed, the costs and time needed for development are easier to estimate and control, and so on. Where existing user programs can be used, or can be adapted to the user's newly recognized or changed needs, they should be. There's no merit in "starting over" just to start over.

If a new system is to be implemented, the user will almost certainly be confronted with the task of data conversion. For each alternative, the project team must weigh any technical difficulties in this conversion, whether or not data conversion aids can be obtained, and the cost and time required for the conversion.

Whether a data-processing system is manual or automated, users follow certain procedures in preparing input, providing that input to processing, and using output. For each alternative, therefore, established procedures may have to be modified, or new ones created. Users who come in direct contact with the system will have to be trained to use it. Users who indirectly provide input to or receive output from the system will need to be informed of the new or changed system's characteristics and capabilities.

Estimating Costs and Benefits

In evaluating alternatives, and before presenting a system proposal to user management, the project team must assess the costs and benefits of each alternative to be presented. Both costs and benefits can be categorized in various ways. A first major cost distinction is between:

- One-time, nonrecurring costs associated with the remaining phases of system development
- Ongoing operational costs

At the end of the detailed design step, experienced analysts can estimate the costs for the system design phase with reasonable confidence. However, estimates of costs for the subsequent phases of system development and for the day-to-day operations of the resultant system are educated guesses at best. They must be recognized as such and estimated again later when more is known about the project.

Some costs and benefits are *tangible;* they can be identified and measured easily. Others are *intangible;* their value is hard to quantify in dollars and cents. Examples of both are given in Figure 11-8.

From another point of view, some costs and benefits are *direct;* they are readily attributable to a specific individual, group, or department. Others are *indirect;* they are not incurred as a direct result of user activity, but are allocated to users on a prorated basis. (In Figure 11-8, the examples of tangible and intangible costs and benefits are further categorized as direct or indirect.)

Whether or not both tangible and intangible costs, or both direct and indirect costs, should be included in system development estimates is a decision for information system personnel and the user. The important point is that all parties involved must know and follow the policy agreed upon.

Obviously, detailed cost data could consume many pages of a system proposal or many charts of a presentation to management. Techniques for "netting out" the estimated costs and benefits can be used to provide meaningful summary information. One of these is called *break-even analysis.* The technique is a familiar one often applied in traditional accounting, but it is applied somewhat differently at this step in system development. Costs are not compared to revenues (benefits). Instead, the costs of each alternative being proposed are compared to the costs of the user's existing system. To make the comparison, the costs of the systems are graphed, over time. (See Figure 11-9.) The point at which the cost lines on the graph intersect is the break-even point. The period in which the proposed system has a higher cost is called the *investment period;* the period in which the proposed system has a lower cost is called the *period of return.*

The break-even analysis tells when the costs of a proposed system and of the user's existing system will be equal. It does not tell when the user's initial investment for the proposed system will be recovered as a result of its greater economy. To determine this date, the analyst uses another technique from accounting: calculation of the *payback period.* The system's payback period can be calculated in several ways. Two examples are shown in Figure 11-10. Part A of the figure considers only costs; that is, any benefits are ignored. The costs of the

COSTS/BENEFITS CLASSIFICATION	EDP RESOURCE	EXAMPLES OF NATURE OF COST OR BENEFIT
Tangible, direct	Processor, memory, I/O devices, secondary-storage devices	Purchase, lease, or rental fees, hardware maintenance contracts
	System software, application packages	Permanent license (one-time fee), periodic license (monthly charge), software maintenance contracts
	Tapes, diskettes, paper, other supplies	Purchase ($10–$15 per tape, $2–$7 per diskette, 1¢ per sheet, etc.)
	In-house staff, consultants, contractors, part-time help	Salaries, benefits, recruiting, hiring fees, hourly rates, taxes
Tangible, indirect	The computer system as an entity	Faster billing cycle (bills out 2 days earlier, e.g.), better control of inventory (only a 2-week supply), better control of cash (maximum use of cash discounts at minimum cost)
	In-house training programs, EDP general and administrative (G & A) costs and benefits, other cost-center costs (security, cleaning, etc.) and benefits (environmental control)	Allocated charges based on square feet, number of employees, number of departments, direct expense
Intangible, direct	Equipment availability (uptime), durability, expandability, flexibility (e.g., stock paper and preprinted forms)	Mean time between failures (MTBF), time to repair, field upgradability, latest technology
	Software ease of use, flexibility, correctness, extendibility	Mean time between failures (MTBF), hard-copy and online soft-copy documentation, languages supported, internal design
Intangible, indirect	The computer system as an entity	Corporate image derived from application of latest technology, opportunity costs and benefits (direct consumer to system interface, access to industry data banks, etc.)
	Other cost-center costs and benefits, G & A costs and benefits	

FIGURE 11-8 The costs and benefits of a proposed system alternative may be classified as either tangible or intangible, and as direct or indirect.

proposed system are subtracted from the costs of the user's existing system on a yearly basis. When the difference between these costs becomes a positive value (during the fourth year, in our example), the user has begun to receive a return.

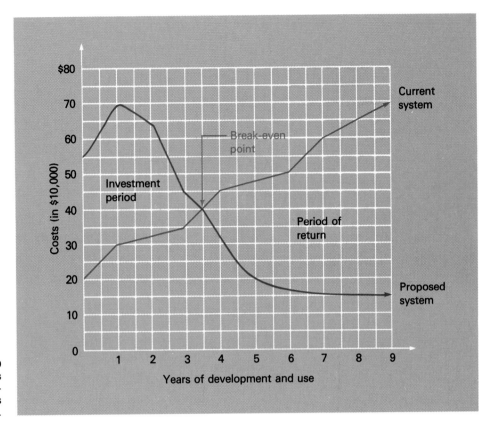

FIGURE 11-9
The break-even point for this proposed system occurs during the fourth year of its development and use.

When the total of the positive difference values outweighs the total of the negative difference values, the user has recovered his initial investment.

Figure 11-10B shows how the payback period is calculated, taking into account a major benefit expected from the proposed system: $1000 per month, or $12,000 per year, through improved inventory control. By the end of the fourth year, the user will have recovered his initial investment and be $3000 "to the good." When a major benefit is expected from a proposed system, this way of calculating the payback period may provide better information for management decision making than any way that looks only at costs.

System Proposal

Having done its homework well, the project team now presents the results of its findings in a *system proposal*. In a sense, what the feasibility report is to the preliminary investigation, the system proposal is to the detailed investigation. However, the system proposal is a more formal document. If and when the system proposal is accepted, it becomes a contractual agreement between information system personnel and the user for the remaining phases of the system development cycle.

A system proposal has no standard format. Generally, it begins with a brief summary of the problem or opportunity that initiated the system development activity. The over-all objectives of the proposed system are clearly stated, thus insuring that information system personnel and the user are fully "in tune" (or clearing up any questions immediately if they are not).

A. Calculating the payback period, on the basis of costs

Investment recovered:
−$58,000 outweighed
by +$74,000

	YEAR					
	1	2	3	4	5	6
Current system cost	$30,000	33,000	35,000	45,000	47,000	51,000
Proposed system cost	$70,000	43,000	43,000	32,000	20,000	17,000
Investment (−)/Return (+)	−$40,000	−10,000	−8,000	+13,000	+27,000	+34,000

B. Calculating the payback period, considering costs and benefits

	YEAR					
	1	2	3	4	5	6
Current system cost	$30,000	33,000	35,000	45,000	47,000	51,000
Proposed system cost	$70,000	43,000	43,000	32,000	20,000	17,000
Investment (−)/Return (+)	−$40,000	−10,000	−8,000	+13,000	+27,000	+34,000
Savings through reduction in inventory	$12,000	12,000	12,000	12,000	12,000	12,000
	−$28,000	+2,000	+4,000	+25,000	+39,000	+46,000

Investment recovered:
−$28,000 outweighed
by +$31,000

FIGURE 11-10 The payback period for a proposed system may be calculated on the basis of costs alone (A); if significant benefits are anticipated (B), both costs and benefits should be taken into account.

The system alternative that the project team prefers is presented in detail. Its estimated costs and benefits, an outline of work, and a schedule for its completion are included. Other alternatives that were seriously considered by the team and that warrant management attention are presented also. The proposal concludes with a clear recommendation to management as to how to proceed.

The presentation of the system proposal marks another major checkpoint in the system development cycle. Therefore, the first question to be addressed by management is: Should the system development activity proceed? (An alternative stated by the project team, and even its recommendation, may be to terminate the activity, based on a full understanding of the expected costs and benefits.) If the decision is made to go ahead, the recommendation of the project team may be accepted as is, or accepted with changes. The requested changes should be reflected in the system proposal before it is finalized. Once the document is approved, it becomes the baseline for the system design phase that follows.

Before we leave this topic, it's appropriate to point out once again that the steps of the system development cycle do not apply exclusively to large organizations or large-system users. A doctor, lawyer, tax accountant, small business owner, educator, student, or family may recognize a problem or an opportunity that perhaps can be addressed with computer help. Such users (or potential users) need to understand their requirements just as much as large-system users do. Whether or not a computer-based solution is appropriate can only be determined by investigation. Our discussion here can serve as a general guideline for the investigation. The "project team" may be the user, or the user with help obtained as the investigation proceeds, or the user and one or more specialists (system analysts) employed to lead the effort.

SYSTEM DESIGN

An artist sketches an office building to be constructed; an architect creates a blueprint; and bricklayers, carpenters, electricians, and others skilled in their trades "make it all happen." Similarly, system analysts set the direction for system development; system designers lay out a detailed plan; and programmers, testers, technical writers, and other support personnel implement the plan. An electrician cannot (and should not) work from an artist's rendition. A programmer cannot (and should not) code from the initial programming functional specification or the system proposal. Putting it simply: *a system must be designed.*

The Chief Programmer Team

Some or all members of the project team should continue to work on the project during the system design phase. The term *chief programmer team* is often used to refer to the group of information system specialists put in place to carry out the remaining phases of the system development cycle.

The nucleus of a chief programmer team consists of a chief programmer, a backup programmer, and a programming librarian. (See Figure 11-11.) Additional designers, programmers, and technicians are added to the team as needed, depending on the size and scope of the project. Many of them may be specialists.

FIGURE 11-11
The members of a chief programmer team work together to plan and carry out system design activities.
(*Courtesy Bell Helicopter Textron, Inc.*)

For example, one designer may have an in-depth knowledge of the operating-system interfaces to be used by the system under development. Another may be an expert on the characteristics and capabilities of input and output devices. Generally, a team of from 5 to 11 members is advisable.

The chief programmer may be a lead system analyst, system designer, or programmer (as categorized by formal job description). He or she is a technical manager to whom all team members report directly. He or she designs the main-line, or control, portion of the system and defines the portions to be designed by other team members. The chief programmer also reviews the work of other team members, oversees the development and integration of all parts of the system, arranges for additional team members when necessary, and keeps management informed of the project status.

The backup programmer is involved in every aspect of the system and participates in all important decision making. He or she may carry out special assignments (for example, investigating alternative approaches to functional recovery of the system), thereby allowing the chief programmer to concentrate on the main line of development.

The programming librarian maintains the records of the project in a *development support library* (*DSL*). These records are kept in both an internal (machine-readable) form and an external (human-readable) form. Examples of internal records are the job-control statements needed to execute the portions of the system under development, the machine-readable versions of all programs, and test data. Examples of external records are current program listings, historical journals (archives) of all replaced listings, and the results of all test runs. As these examples indicate, the DSL is established at this point in system development (in some cases, even sooner) and is expanded throughout the cycle.

System Flowcharting

Still working from the point of view of the user's requirements, the chief programmer team focuses its initial attention on three basic elements:

- The output that must be provided by the system
- The source data, or input, that the user will provide to the system
- The processing needed to produce the output, given the input

Notice that these are the three basic elements of any data-processing system, as we first recognized them back in Chapter 2.

A tried and true method of depicting these system elements is to construct one or more *system flowcharts*. Each system flowchart is a graphic representation of the procedures involved in converting data from input media to data in output form. The emphasis is on the media used and the processing or data flow. Little is shown about how the processing will be accomplished. A complete program that will later be designed in detail is often represented by one symbol on a system flowchart.

A typical system flowchart is shown in Figure 11-12. This flowchart describes an online transaction-processing system that automates certain banking functions. Each *process symbol* (☐) represents a computer program. Each *display symbol* (◯) represents an online printer-keyboard or visual-display unit. In this example, the online units are teller terminals that are part of user work stations at bank locations. The *magnetic-disk symbol* (⬡) represents

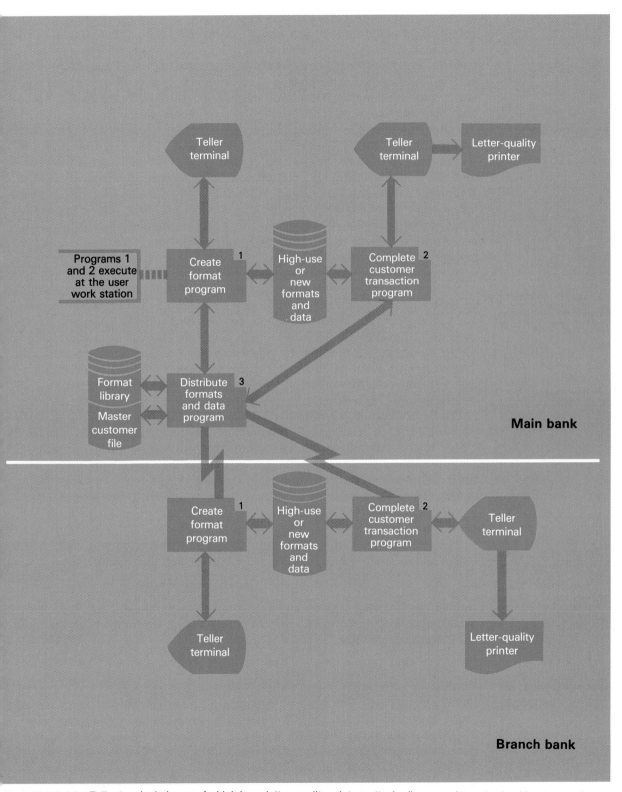

IGURE 11-12 Teller terminals (some of which have letter-quality printers attached) are used to enter banking transactions the system described by this system flowchart.

online magnetic-disk storage. Each *document symbol* (⬡) represents a printer. Its operation is initiated by the user and controlled by a program executed by the microprocessor in the user work station to which it is attached. The *annotation symbol* (⬡) is used to provide comments. The *flowlines* (——) indicate direction of flow. The *communication symbols* (⤳) indicate that some of the user work stations are at branch bank locations, connected to the host computer at the main bank via communication facilities.

System flowcharts serve as a summary page, or index, from which many work efforts proceed. During the system design phase, it's not likely that hardware will be designed. However, if a new system is being installed, or if additional disk storage units, terminals, printers, connecting cables, and so on, are needed, equipment orders must be placed. We cannot tell from the system flowchart exactly how many user work stations are at the main bank, how many branch banks are to be on the system when it first becomes operational, or how many user work stations are to be installed at each branch bank. That detail is planned and recorded elsewhere. We *can* tell where each type of component fits in the system and the general flow of work among them.

Notice that three application programs are included in the system. A bank officer (i.e., user) at a teller terminal can select a stored display-screen format—for opening an individual retirement account or acquiring a money market certificate, for example. The officer can complete the transaction by simply filling in blanks on the screen under direction of the Complete Customer Transaction program executed by the microprocessor, without even involving the host computer. The officer can print hard copies of all transactions on the nearby printer if desired.

The Create Format program is also loaded into the internal storage unit of a user work station and executed by its microprocessor at the request of a bank officer. It allows the officer to create new display-screen or printer formats and to test them interactively before forwarding them to the central computer facility for inclusion in a shared format library. The texts for preformatted letters—for example, reminders of savings certificates due for maturity—can be created and stored, customized for a particular usage via a display-screen format, and then printed for mailing.

A large library of stored formats and relatively permanent data about existing customers (that may be useful in completing forms) is kept on high-speed disk storage devices at the host computer location. The Distribute Formats and Data program is executed by the host computer to receive, store, retrieve, and/or send formats and data to/from user work stations, on request. Thus, the bulk of the formats and data within the system are kept at the main bank's central computer facility.

Output, Input, and File Design

To insure that the user's requirements are satisfied, much care and attention must be given during the system design phase to the contents and formats of all required system outputs. Exactly what printed reports are needed, how often, and what should be on them? Should a particular report be sequenced by work item, due date, or person responsible? If an interactive system is being designed, display-screen formats must be created and tested. (See Figure 11-13.) There are many system design aids—for example, printer spacing charts and display-screen layout forms—that designers can use to sketch mockups for user review.

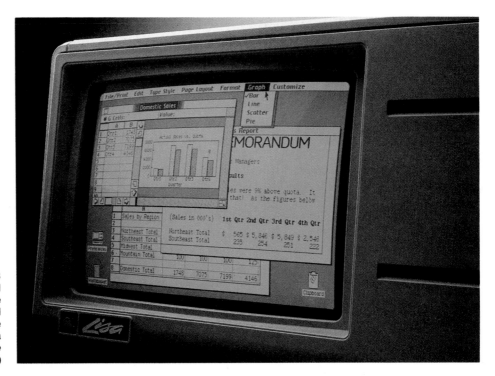

FIGURE 11-13
Much careful analysis and design work goes into the creation of user-oriented display formats like those shown on this Apple Lisa screen. (*Courtesy Apple Computer, Inc.*)

Samples of the outputs and demonstrations of the interactive sessions should be provided for user review as early as possible.

Each data item provided as input and each item of information produced as output is a data element. During the system design phase, a *data element dictionary* should be set up, in a machine-readable form. Whenever a designer identifies a new data item to be provided as input or produced as output, the name and description of the item should be added to the data element dictionary. Keeping the dictionary current helps to insure that the same data item isn't unknowingly handled by several programs in the system, with a different name or definition each time. It also helps to insure that when the output of one program is to be provided as input to another program, the designers of both programs define the data correctly.

Once the data element dictionary is set up, the internal files and/or databases within the system can be designed. The formats of user data records within the system's transaction and master files should be described on record layout forms. Designing sequential files that will meet the needs of several user application programs is a challenge. Designing files that can be accessed directly in ways that provide fast responses to user inquiries, or designing user databases, is an even bigger challenge. We'll say more about these tasks in Chapter 15.

If the decision has been made to purchase or lease the required software (rather than develop it in-house), acquisition processes for the software must be initiated now, just as for the hardware. Contracts have to be worked out and approved. In these cases, detailed program design, coding, and testing are not necessary. But system design still is.

Take, for example, our banking system discussed above. Let's assume that up to 10 user work stations and 3 application programs (plus any required system software) are to be purchased and installed as the first part of what may someday be a very comprehensive banking system. General-purpose display-screen and printer formats are provided by the vendor as a starter set for the format library. Do the display-screen formats allow bank officers to enter all the data that this particular bank needs when opening new accounts? If not, can the provided formats be modified? If not, then additional formats must be designed (and created) before the system becomes operational. Other parts of the system that must be designed include the physical layouts of the work station areas, user training sessions, formats and contents of any user documentation needed by bank officers or by in-house personnel who will support the system, and backup and security procedures for all system components.

The system flowchart, the descriptions of the formats and contents of the system inputs and outputs and of related files, and other user-oriented (external, or functional) characteristics of the system are collected in a final programming functional specification (FPFS) for the project.

Top-Down Design

The chief-programmer-team method of organization is implemented most effectively when another system development methodology is also practiced: top-down development. In its broadest sense, *top-down development* is an all-inclusive term. It covers top-down design, top-down programming, and top-down testing. The top-down design approach applies to the system as a whole as well as to individual programs within the system. Therefore, top-down design begins at the system design phase of the system development cycle.

Top-down design is often referred to by other names—structured design, composite design, and so on. We can also describe it as "functional decomposition." When doing top-down design, we look first at the major function to be accomplished by the system. Next we look at the subfunctions of that major function. Then we look at their subfunctions, and so on. At each level of the design, only the issues relevant to that level are considered, and those issues are formulated precisely. We continue in this way until we are satisfied that we fully understand both the scope and the details of our problem-solving method (solution algorithm).

Suppose, for example, that we are to design a system to automate weekly payroll processing at a construction firm. We can't accomplish this task just by finding out what has to be on an employee paycheck, making sure the data needed to provide that paycheck information is on the employee time card, and then designing, coding, and testing a weekly payroll program. It's not that simple.

Think, for example, of the "relatively permanent" employee payroll data that needs to be stored and kept current—name, department, job code, pay rate, number of dependents, United Way deduction, and so on. Think about the department budget-versus-actual reports that have to reflect what's being paid out in salaries. Think about government reporting requirements (quarterly employee withholding, W-2 forms, and more). Think about the necessity of providing an audit trail and of printing the weekly paychecks. Some firms establish arrangements with local banks whereby employees' net earnings can be credited directly to their bank accounts each week (without intermediate paper shuffling). Perhaps this capability, too, is to be provided in the system we are designing.

The data flow diagrams constructed during the detailed investigation step of system analysis can be referred to at this time, to help insure that all functions and subfunctions of weekly payroll processing are provided for. If the system we are designing differs significantly from the user's existing system, we may decide to construct data flow diagrams to describe the new system as well. The diagrams will be useful to us in design and can serve as additional system documentation later, when other information system personnel and users need to be told about the new system.

Structure Charts We've already seen that system flowcharts are a way of describing the input/output media and work flow of a system. They deal with the hardware, software, and data components of a computer system in a very general fashion. To concentrate in more detail on the internal, logical relationships within the software, we construct one or more *tree diagrams*, or *structure charts*. A first, high-level structure chart might in the extreme case show only one software component—say, Compute Weekly Payroll—at the beginning of the system design step. As designers understand more and more about the system they are designing, additional levels are added to the structure chart. (See, for example, Figure 11-14.)

As the example shows, a structure chart consists of blocks and of lines connecting those blocks. The top block of the treelike structure represents the over-all function of the system as an entity. The lower levels of the tree represent finer breakdowns of that function. A structure chart has no required or minimum number of levels. In fact, one branch of the structure may have several more levels than others. The blocks at the lowest level of each branch may be broken down further on succeeding structure charts. The Create Required Reports block in Figure 11-14 is a likely candidate for expansion.

A major advantage of structure charts is that they help designers to create a well-structured plan for a system. Eventually, each block on the set of structure charts becomes the basis for a program module. Each program module is a relatively small, highly independent segment of coding that performs one or a very small number of functions. It may be a complete program, or it may be combined with other modules to form a complete program. Every module on the structure chart is called into execution by the module above it. After it is finished executing, it returns control of the computer system to the module that called it. When this approach is used, systems and programs are not "bowls of spaghetti" as they are likely to be when the design task is approached without a well-thought-out methodology. The logical structure of the system practically jumps off the structure chart pages. It's available for all to see and understand. Like the system flowchart, the set of structure charts is a reference point from which many parallel work efforts can proceed.

DESIGN REVIEW Not uncommonly, system developers and users alike share certain major concerns: the all-too-often high frequency of errors, or bugs, in system components; the difficulty in isolating, identifying, and correcting those bugs; and the care required to avoid creating new bugs when correcting existing ones. The more programs a software supplier or user installation develops, for example, the greater the resources required to maintain and correct them—that is, to

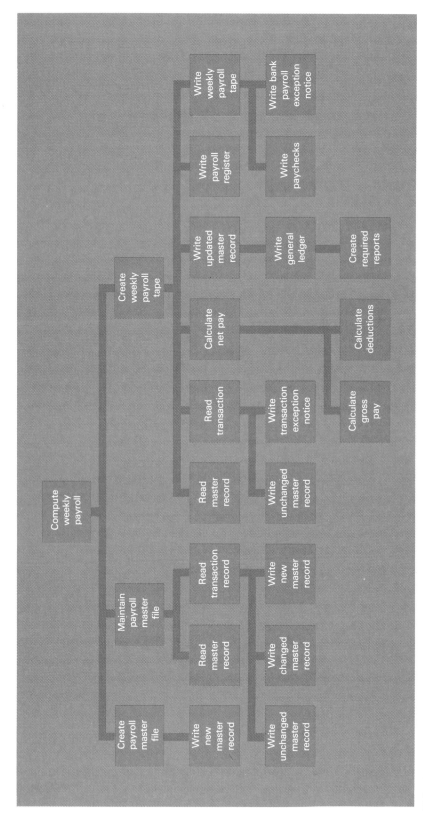

FIGURE 11-14 Up to four function levels are documented on this structure chart for a weekly payroll system.

support the programs in actual use. System development appears to be an error-prone activity.

Though such concerns do indeed appear to be valid, some computer professionals and users are increasingly asking why. Isn't it better to write a program correctly the first time than to patch it later? Certainly it's much less expensive in terms of both time and money to keep errors out of a system to start with than to redesign and reimplement it later just because users are dissatisfied or because the system just plain won't work. The emphasis on careful planning, well-thought-out design, and clear, concise documentation is a direct reflection of efforts to do just that. To further insure that planning, design, and implementation are error-free, formalized techniques have been developed to detect and remove, as early as possible, any defects that do creep in.

As discussed earlier, system verification begins at the problem definition step. The detailed investigation does not proceed until both users and information system personnel review and accept the description of the problem as stated in the feasibility report. System design does not begin until the system proposal is reviewed and accepted. After these steps have been accomplished, then it's time to verify the final programming function specification and the high-level internal software design reflected on the structure charts.

It's important to understand the types of errors that must be detected and removed at this point. The errors are *not* obvious ones like the computer's being directed to add when it should be directed to subtract. Not at all! Rather, the errors are system deficiencies. To detect such errors, we ask questions such as:

- Will the system as designed meet the user's requirements? (Are the right hard-copy reports being produced? Do they contain the right information? Are they formatted for maximum usability? Is graphic output being provided when it should be? Are the formats and contents of visual-display screens planned with users in mind?)

- Will the system as designed accept the user's data as input? Does it validate the input appropriately? Are error procedures planned, and are they easy to understand in cases where users must be involved?

- Does the system provide adequate security for the organization's data resource? Are the definitions of all required data files and/or databases complete? Are the methods of organizing and processing the data appropriate for the user's application?

- Have all system hardware and software requirements been identified and provided for?

- Have user procedures, training, and documentation requirements been taken into account?

- Is the system flexible? Can it be changed when the user's requirements change?

- Is the system serviceable? Is it maintainable? Are backup and recovery procedures included in the system definition? Are the procedures easy to understand and reasonable?

Under one approach to verification of this level of design, the design documentation is distributed to selected reviewers. Each reviewer is asked to study the design and respond within an established time period, noting any changes, additions, or deletions required. This approach is known as an *informal design review.*

Under a more formal approach, the design documentation and problem-log forms are made available to from 6 to 8 people who serve as members of a review team. The review team must include both users and information system personnel. After a specified preparation period, these reviewers meet with the chief programmer or a lead designer and a moderator to conduct one type of *structured walkthrough* known as a *formal design review.*

Each reviewer is expected to have studied the design documentation and is asked to comment on its completeness, accuracy, and general quality. Then a reader (usually the designer) "walks" the group through each part of the documentation, covering any points raised by the review team. The moderator controls the session, making sure that reviewers are heard, clarifying points where necessary, maintaining the emphasis on error detection rather than error correction, preventing reviewers from getting bogged down on any particular topic, and so on. The moderator is responsible for the documentation of the session and of the errors encountered. The moderator's summary report is an action plan for the designer and a communication vehicle for the team. Not until all points of concern noted on the summary report are resolved can the system design step of system development be considered complete.

PROJECT REVIEW Completion of the system design and resolution of any problems raised during the design review are prerequisites to a system design checkpoint review of the project with both user management and information system management.

User management must formally agree that the system that's been designed will meet the user's needs. Both user and information system management must re-evaluate an updated costs-versus-benefits analysis. Information system management must verify that the system implementation plans and schedules are in place and reasonable.

Regardless of whether the system development activity involves a large chief programmer team or is a one-person project, both the system design review and this project review are mandatory. For example, a small business owner who contracts the development of an accounts receivable system to an independent software firm should insure that both reviews are called for in the contractual agreement and that they are carried out. Otherwise, the system that is developed may be a technological masterpiece but fail to meet the owner's needs, costs may balloon unknowingly, and so on. It's the owner's (client's) responsibility as well as the contractor's to insure that these things do not happen. (See Figure 11-15.)

Given the go-ahead at the project review, system implementation can begin. The activities that occur during system implementation and evaluation are described in the next chapter.

FIGURE 11-15
A detailed project review is essential to the success of a system being developed for a small business owner, just as it is for one being developed for a large organization. (*Courtesy Tymshare, Inc.*)

CHAPTER SUMMARY

1. A system is a group of interrelated elements that work together to perform a specific task or function.

2. The system development cycle provides a general framework within which phases and checkpoints can be established and tracked to achieve project control.

3. Both user and information system personnel must participate in system development. Outside groups and in-house system support groups may need to be involved as work proceeds. Simple design change request forms can be used to record ideas for system development.

4. A brief feasibility study may be initiated to decide whether or not an identified problem or an opportunity warrants further investigation.

5. If a decision is made to proceed with system development, a project team is formed to do a detailed investigation. This work involves fact-finding, data analysis and evaluation, estimating costs and benefits, and preparation of a system proposal.

6. Data flow diagrams are a simple way of showing what's occurring in a user's existing system or organization. They may also be used to describe a new system that's being developed.

7. The costs and benefits of a proposed system alternative may be classified as either intangible or tangible, and as direct or indirect. Techniques such as break-even analysis and calculation of the payback period can be used in estimating such costs and benefits.

8. System design is often the responsibility of a chief programmer team. The records of the project are kept in a development support library accessible to all team members.

9. System flowcharts, a data element dictionary, and structure charts are other system design tools. The latter are especially useful when a top-down approach to design is used.

10. At the completion of system design, user and information system management conduct a project review to determine whether or not system implementation should proceed.

11. To help insure that system planning, design, and implementation are error-free, formalized techniques to detect and remove defects are applied throughout the system development cycle. Either informal or formal reviews of the design documentation may be carried out at this point in the cycle.

DISCUSSION QUESTIONS

1. (a) What is a system?
   (b) Choose a system that does not involve computers. Show how it fits the definition you just gave above.
   (c) Choose a computer-based system. Show how it fits the definition you gave in response to (a) above.

2. What is the system development cycle?

3. Support or refute the following statement: "It should not be necessary to return to a preceding phase of system development once that phase has been completed."

4. Distinguish between system evaluation, system analysis, system implementation, and system design.

5. Assume you are a system analyst with responsibility for conducting a feasibility study with respect to the following problem statement: "We need to know, on a week-to-week basis, how each salesperson is doing against plan." How would you go about conducting the study?

6. Discuss the advantages and disadvantages of various fact-finding techniques. Suggest situations where each is appropriate.

7. Discuss the contents and use of data flow diagrams.

8. Why is the consideration of several alternatives a wise (or unwise) approach when doing system analysis?

9. Discuss the purpose and contents of a system proposal.

10. Distinguish between system flowcharts and structure charts with respect to contents and use.

11. Support or refute the following statement: "A detailed plan and checkpoints are more necessary in a large system development effort than in a small one."

12. Explain, by example, a top-down approach to system design.

12
DEVEL-OPING PROGRAMS

Computers, in general, like human beings, in general, are all made of pretty much the same materials. How well and how fast a human being does a job is largely determined by how organized he or she is. How efficiently a computer does its job is largely determined by how organized its programming is. Just as human beings can learn to do different jobs, so can computers. The program often makes the difference.

A computer can be programmed to produce a design for data cartridge tapes, for example. The same computer, given the needed programming and sufficient storage, can be used to help design an automatic call-routing selection pattern used by a telephone company.

This is as true for personal computers as it is for mainframes. The San Francisco Exploratorium, a science-fair-like exhibit that allows visitors to play with exotic technology, uses Apple II+ computers in three of its displays.

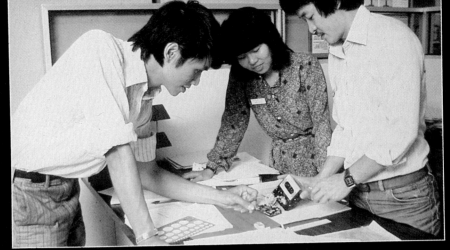

Courtesy Hewlett-Packard Company

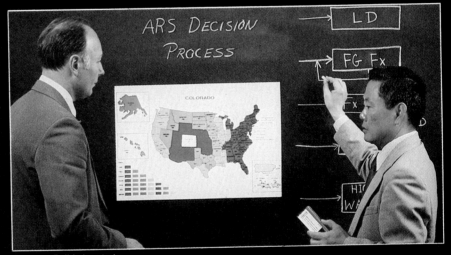

Courtesy Bell Laboratories

designed by artist Paul de Marinis, visitors can play touch-sensitive electric guitars hooked up to the computer and various devices. The computer co-ordinates the input from the guitars so that all of them play in the same key, regardless of the notes each visitor happens to be playing. The other devices cause the visitors to play in coordinated rhythm and allow them to modify the kinds of sounds the guitars produce.

In the "Survival of the Fittest" display, the same kind of computer simulates the population growth of two different species oc-cupying the same habitat. Visitors can enter different growth rates for each species, and computer graphics are used to dis-play their growth. At a cer-tain point of population growth, the computer shows one species crowd-ing out the other.

The "Recollections" exhibit, designed by artist Ed Tannenbaum, again uses the same kind of computer but creates colored projections of body movement. A visitor stands in front of a black-and-white video camera, which projects a silhouette of that person on a screen. As the visitor moves, the computer creates stop-action images of the per-son, each in a different color. Four different stop-action modes are available.

can be programmed to perform many different functions. Nederlandse Gasunie, for example, uses a Sperry Univac 1100 computer to control natural gas distribution. A water treatment plant in Sabesa, Brazil, uses a Sperry Univac 1100 for engineering purposes and in its financial operations. A Sperry Univac 1100 was also used to make the cal-culations necessary to build a dam over which a highway was constructed.

© Exploratorium, photographer Susan Swartzenberg

© Exploratorium, photographer Susan Swartzenberg

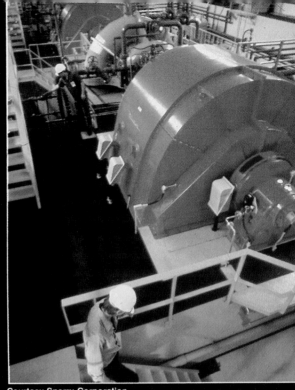

Just as the same computer can be programmed to do different jobs, different kinds of computers can be programmed to do the same kind of job. Whereas one kind of computer can be used to design a Boeing 767, another kind of computer can be used in the design of an automobile. Though the objects being designed are different, the *process* of designing them with computer aid may be the same. Their programming may be the only thing the two computer systems have in common.

Courtesy Boeing Computer Services Company

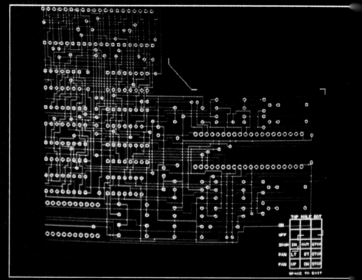

Courtesy Megatek Corporation, San Diego, California

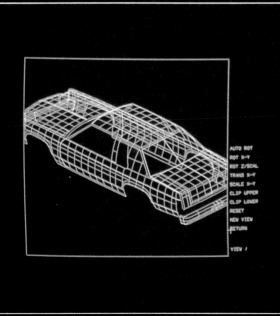

AUTO ROT
ROT X-Y
ROT Z/SCAL
TRANS X-Y
SCALE X-Y
CLIP UPPER
CLIP LOWER
RESET
NEV VIEW
RETURN

VIEW /

12 | DEVELOPING PROGRAMS

In this chapter, we continue our study of how to use the computer as a tool in problem solving. The computer may be a pocket computer purchased for $100 from a mail-order house or discount retailer. It may be a $4 billion supercomputer capable of doing 800 million operations per second. It may be a more conventional computer somewhere between these two extremes in both cost and capabilities. As we've said before, the same general approach to problem solving applies in all cases.

Let's review the phases of system development as we defined them earlier, in Chapter 11:

- System analysis—understand the user's requirements; identify and describe ways of responding to those requirements; select the alternative that's best for this situation.

- System design—define in detail the output that must be provided by the system and the input that will be provided to the system; plan for the hardware, software, data conversion (if any), procedures, training, and documentation.

- System implementation — acquire and install any hardware that is needed; acquire or develop the needed software; create user data files and/or databases; institute required procedures; train personnel who will use the system, its input, or its output; complete the system documentation.
- System evaluation — review the system after it is implemented to determine whether or not it meets the user's requirements; develop plans to follow up on problems.

In Chapter 11, we directed our attention to tools and techniques of system analysis and design. In this chapter, we discuss system implementation and evaluation.

A FIRST PROBLEM

Let's start with a simple problem — one we can follow all the way to completion. In doing so, we'll get a better understanding of the steps in system development. Then we'll be ready to look more closely at the tools and techniques that are used widely in system implementation.

System Analysis and Design

How many times have you read in a newspaper that a nearby furniture store is offering 30 to 80 percent discounts on all merchandise in a going-out-of-business sale, and wished you had a handy way of calculating exactly what certain items would cost? What will your (or your daughter's) school supplies cost if you take advantage of a back-to-school sale, with discounts ranging from 10 to 50 percent? If you buy a set of tires while Sears is offering its 10-percent-off sale, what will the tires really cost?

A close look at these questions shows that they have common elements. We could solve each problem individually, but it's to our advantage to develop a general-purpose solution plan, or *algorithm*, that can be used to solve all these and similar problems. We now restate the questions in a general-purpose fashion as a problem to be solved:

Given the original price and the discount for each of one or more items, determine the total cost of the group of items.

We can solve this problem in any of several ways. Among them are: (1) ask a salesclerk to figure the total cost for us; (2) use a pencil and paper to determine the cost ourselves based on our knowledge of arithmetic; (3) use a calculator — one that has the capability to store intermediate totals; otherwise, it's back to pencil and paper for some of the work; (4) use a pocket computer we take with us to the store; or (5) get the prices for the items we're considering from the newspaper, sales catalog, a visit to the store, or a phone call, and direct the computer on our desk at home to calculate the total cost for us.

Given these alternatives, it's not likely we'll decide to purchase the hardware needed for alternatives 3, 4, or 5 just to solve this problem. Let's assume a TRS-80 Model II computer is available to us. Then, let's select alternative 5.

The output that must be provided by our system is the total cost of the items considered for purchase. The inputs to the system are the original price and discount for each item. Since we may decide to buy several items of the same type, let's say that the desired quantity of each item should also be entered as input. (Otherwise, if we want to buy four tires, for example, we'll have to key in the price and discount for the tires four times.) The system must accept the input values as they are keyed in from the TRS-80 keyboard. It must display the output on the TRS-80 visual-display screen.

If we shopped at a nearby Radio Shack, we could probably find a TRS-80 software package that accepts keyed data values for quantity, price, and discount as input and displays a computed total cost as output. In fact, any applicable package we found would probably do much more. Since our problem is relatively simple, let's decide to develop the solution in-house instead; that is, let's design, code, test, and document the software ourselves. The system flowchart for the system is very straightforward. (See Figure 12-1.) As in Chapter 11, we use the display symbol to represent an online visual-display unit. We use the *manual-input symbol* (⌷) to emphasize that input data values are keyed in from an online keyboard. Given the TRS-80 Model II and the system software provided with it, we need only design, code, test, and document one application program.

System Implementation

Believe it or not, we've just completed the system analysis and design for the system we're developing. We're ready to tackle the first step of system implementation. That means we're ready to plan the detailed logic within the application program. Realizing again that one picture is worth a thousand words, we construct a program flowchart that shows the processing required. (See Figure 12-2.)

Program flowcharts and the symbols on them are not new to us. We referred to several program flowcharts when discussing computer operations in Chapter 8. On this flowchart, we first tell the computer to set to 0 the primary-storage location to be used to accumulate the total cost. Then we tell the computer to execute the statements within a program loop. It accepts the quantity, original price, and discount for one type of item as input (note the input/output symbol within the program loop). Then it multiplies those values to determine the cost for this part of the purchase. It adds that cost to the accumulation of total cost. If all items have not yet been processed, the test at the decision-making step causes the computer to branch back to the start of the program loop. The program loop is re-executed until there are no more items. At this point the loop is exited. A sales tax of 6 percent is computed and added to the accumulated total cost. The

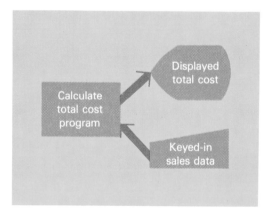

FIGURE 12-1
Sales data is entered as input from an online keyboard and total cost is displayed as output on a CRT in the Compute Total Cost system described on this system flowchart.

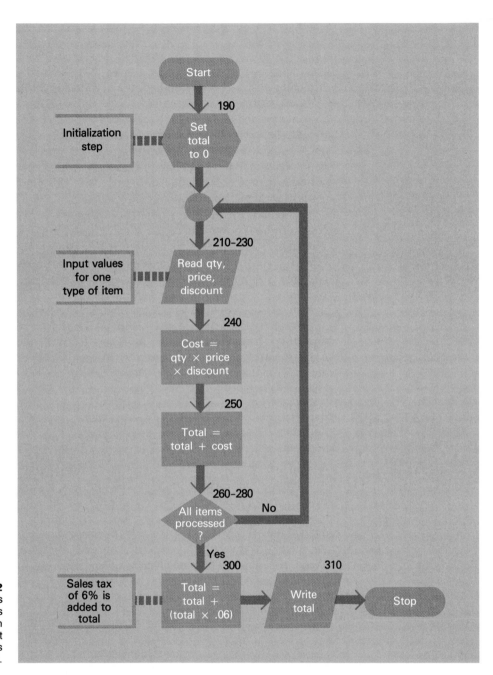

FIGURE 12-2
A program loop to read sales
data and compute cost is
executed repeatedly within
the Calculate Total Cost
program described by this
program flowchart.

result of this addition—the final calculation of total cost—is written as output. Processing is then terminated.

To meet a key system development objective stated in Chapter 11—namely, to detect and remove as soon as possible any errors (bugs) that creep in—it's appropriate at this time to check our solution algorithm as depicted on the program flowchart. Perhaps the best way to do this is to: (1) create a set of test data to be entered as input; (2) figure out what output the computer should provide, given the set of test data as input; and (3) manually step through the program logic shown on the flowchart, assuming the test data is provided as input. For example, assuming the test data shown in Figure 12-3A is provided as input, the total cost calculated in Figure 12-3B should be provided as output.

This approach to program checkout is called *simulation* or *desk checking.* In effect, we simulate, or pretend to be, the computer. If the output of the simulation matches the output we figure out beforehand, we can proceed with the next step of system implementation. That is, we can express the solution algorithm in a programming language. If the outputs do not match, we must find all errors, correct them, and repeat the simulation. We create other sets of test data and expected results, and continue in this manner until we're confident our solution algorithm is error-free. You may be wondering why we place so much emphasis on program quality at this point. The reason is simple: No amount of good coding can repair the damage done by poor design.

Most application programs used with TRS-80 computers are initially written in BASIC. As we saw in Chapter 2, BASIC is an easy-to-use programming language. It's an appropriate choice here, whether we consider ourselves programmers or simply users who are writing an application program. A BASIC program that corresponds to the flowchart in Figure 12-2 is given in Figure 12-4.

As we learned earlier, each line in a BASIC program begins with a line number. The lines that contain the letters REM are remark statements. These statements provide documentation about the program for us and for others who want to use the program. The REM statements have no effect whatsoever on the processing carried out by the computer during program execution. Thus, the REM statements have no corresponding symbols on the program flowchart.

Since we have already discussed the program logic, and the program is well documented, you can probably read and understand the other BASIC statements without any trouble. As an aid to understanding, most programmers place the line numbers of statements represented by the symbols on a program flowchart at the upper right of the symbols. (Look again at Figure 12-2.) The line numbers serve as *cross-references* between the program flowchart and the program. By adding cross-references to the flowchart, we make it easier for others (and for ourselves, later) to follow the logic of the program.

As shown by this example, there is no need for a one-to-one correspondence between the symbols on a flowchart and the statements in a program. The level of detail required on a flowchart is determined by several factors. Among them

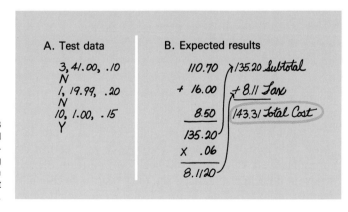

FIGURE 12-3
Both the data to be provided as input (A) and the expected results of processing (B) should be planned in advance when checking out a program.

```
100 REM TOTCOST. CALCULATE TOTAL COST
110 REM SALES TAX OF 6% (.06) IS ASSUMED (LINE 300)
120 REM T IS COMPUTED TOTAL COST OF ALL ITEMS
130 REM Q IS QUANTITY FOR AN ITEM
140 REM P IS ORIGINAL PRICE FOR AN ITEM
150 REM D IS DISCOUNT FOR AN ITEM
160 REM C IS COMPUTED COST FOR DESIRED QTY OF AN ITEM
170 REM R$ IS USER'S RESPONSE, Y OR N
180 REM INITIALIZATION
190 LET T = 0.00
200 REM BEGIN PROGRAM LOOP
210 PRINT "ENTER QUANTITY, PRICE (XX.XX), AND "
220 PRINT "DISCOUNT (.XX) FOR AN ITEM"
230 INPUT Q, P, D
240 LET C = Q * P * (1 - D)
250 LET T = T + C
260 PRINT "ALL ITEMS PROCESSED? ENTER Y OR N"
270 INPUT R$
280 IF R$ = "N" THEN 210
290 REM END PROGRAM LOOP
300 LET T = T + (T * .06)
310 PRINT "TOTAL COST IS $"; T
320 END
```

FIGURE 12-4
The Calculate Total Cost program initially expressed in flowchart form can be written in BASIC to direct the computer.

are: (1) how much the programmer needs to chart to come up with the program logic or to provide a guide that can be used during coding and testing, and (2) how difficult the program logic is, and therefore how much help others may need to understand the program.

Now we are ready to key in the program. When we're done keying, we desk-check what we've entered, just as we desk-checked the logic on the program flowchart. Then we tell the computer to execute the program. When the prompt,

ENTER QUANTITY, PRICE (XX.XX), AND
DISCOUNT (.XX) FOR AN ITEM

appears on the display screen, we key in our first three test data values: 3, 41.00, .10. In response to the next prompt, we key in N. Hopefully, processing continues much like the simulated processing we've just completed. After we key in Y, we should receive the following output:

TOTAL COST IS $ 143.31

If this output doesn't appear on the display screen, there's a problem somewhere. We must find out what's causing the problem and correct it. If, in making corrections, we decide to change the program logic, we must go back to the detailed planning step. If appropriate, we must change the program flowchart. Then we must change the program.

Since the program we've developed is a general-purpose one, it can handle a wide variety of data as input. As a reminder to ourselves, and for the benefit of others who want to use the program, we've noted on line 110 that the constant .06 is used as the sales tax on line 300. This technique is a good one—it helps to insure that if a sales tax value other than .06 applies, we'll remember to change the constant on line 300 accordingly. After we're confident that the program as coded is error-free, we key in a system command to save it under the name

TOTCOST, which we've also noted in a comment (see line 100). This causes the program to be saved in secondary storage (most likely, a $5\frac{1}{4}$-inch floppy disk). We can load it back into primary storage from the disk whenever we want to reuse it.

The program flowchart, the test data and expected results, and the REM statements in the program itself serve as the system/program documentation. As we've just noted, the program is kept in secondary storage. The test data and expected results may be kept there also. The flowchart and any other pertinent information about the program should be filed in a hard-copy library.

Learning the mechanics of programming – how to write instructions to the computer, or how to enter them into computer storage – is no more difficult than learning to use any other tool. The challenging part is understanding the problem to be solved so thoroughly that we can teach an extremely simple, literally minded servant (the computer) to solve it. Programmers are sometimes described as part authors, part tinkerers. When you've completed this chapter you won't be a programmer, but you'll have a good idea of what programming is all about.

MORE ABOUT FLOWCHARTING

Since flowcharting is widely used in system development, it's to our benefit to discuss this design aid further. By now, you should be aware that there are two different kinds of flowcharts. A *system flowchart* shows the flow of data through all parts of a system. A *program flowchart* shows what takes place within one particular program in the system. A system flowchart is usually constructed by a system analyst or system designer during the detailed investigation step of system analysis. Program flowcharts are usually constructed by the programmers responsible for system implementation.*

To encourage uniformity in system and program flowcharting, the American National Standards Institute (ANSI) and its international counterpart, the International Standards Organization (ISO), have approved flowcharting standards. The symbols shown in Figure 12-5 comply with these standards. By using a standardized set of flowcharting symbols, we make it easier for others to understand our flowcharts.

Since standards for flowcharting exist, a logical next step is for some person or group to develop tools that make it easy for system designers and programmers to follow the standards. Several computer manufacturers and other firms specializing in data-processing media have done exactly that. Few programmers would be without a *flowcharting template.* (See Figure 12-6.) The template is a plastic or metallic card containing cutout system and program flowcharting symbols as patterns. The symbols can readily be drawn on flowcharts. As a guide in positioning the symbols, the programmer uses a *flowcharting worksheet.* Each $11'' \times 16\frac{1}{2}''$ worksheet provides an arrangement of 50 blocks with alphabetic and numeric coordinates. Ten horizontal rows are lettered from top (A) to bottom (K). Five vertical rows are numbered 1 through 5 from left to right. Together, these identifiers serve as coordinates (for example, A1 or D2) that can be referred to within *connector symbols* ((A-1)→, →(D-2)). They are especially useful when

---

*A complete explanation of system flowcharts, program flowcharts, flowcharting symbols, and their use is given in Bohl, *Flowcharting Techniques* (Chicago: Science Research Associates, Inc., 1971).

PROGRAM FLOWCHART SYMBOLS

SYMBOL	REPRESENTS
	PROCESS One or more instructions that perform a processing function.
	INPUT/OUTPUT Any input/output function (making data available for processing, recording information, tape positioning, etc.).
	DECISION A decision-making step; used to document a point in the program where a branch to an alternate path is possible.
	PREPARATION An instruction or group of instructions that changes the program for initialization, control, or cleanup.
	PREDEFINED PROCESS One or more operations not detailed on the particular set of flowcharts.
	TERMINAL The beginning, end, or a point of interruption in a program.
	CONNECTOR An entry from, or an exit to, a point on the program flowchart.
	OFFPAGE CONNECTOR A connector used instead of the connector symbol to designate entry to or exit from a page.
< > ∨ ∧	**FLOW DIRECTION** The direction of processing or data flow.

SYSTEM FLOWCHART SYMBOLS

SYMBOL	REPRESENTS	SYMBOL	REPRESENTS
	PROCESS A major processing function.		**INPUT/OUTPUT** Any type of medium or data.
	PUNCHED CARD All varieties of punched cards.		**PUNCHED TAPE** Any type of punched continuous medium.
	DOCUMENT Hard-copy documents and reports of all varieties.		**DISPLAY** Any kind of transitory data not in hard-copy form or intermediate output data used to control processing; usually output displayed by means of online printer-keyboards, visual-display units, etc.
	OFFLINE STORAGE		**ONLINE STORAGE**
	MAGNETIC TAPE		**MAGNETIC DISK**
	MANUAL INPUT Data entered manually by means of an online device.		**KEYING OPERATION** An operation using a key-driven device.
	MANUAL OPERATION A process performed manually or using equipment that operates at the speed of a user.		**AUXILIARY OPERATION** A process using equipment not under direct control of the main computer and not limited to the speed of a user.
< > ∨ ∧	**FLOW DIRECTION** The direction of processing or data flow.		**COMMUNICATION LINK** The transmission of data from one location to another via a communication medium such as wires, cables, or satellites.

SUPPLEMENTARY SYMBOL FOR SYSTEM AND PROGRAM FLOWCHARTS

SYMBOL	REPRESENTS
	ANNOTATION Additional explanation or comments.

FIGURE 12-5 Standardized sets of symbols exist (and should be used) for both systems and program flowcharting.

FIGURE 12-6
A programmer's "tool kit"
often includes flowcharting
worksheets and a flowcharting template. (*Courtesy
Radio Shack, a Division of
Tandy Corporation*)

a flowchart extends over several worksheets. The worksheets are printed in light-blue ink so that the block outlines do not appear on photographic copies.

The normal direction of flow on a flowcharting worksheet is from top to bottom and from left to right. If the direction of flow of any flowline is not normal, an arrowhead must be used on the flowline ($\leftarrow$, $\uparrow$). If the direction of flow is normal, arrowheads can be used for clarity, but they are not required.

When a top-down approach to design is used, either of two flowcharting techniques may be used advantageously. One involves the use of the *predefined-process symbol* ( ). The programmer uses this symbol to refer to a sequence of operations defined in detail elsewhere, but not on this particular set of flowcharts. For example, the Validate Input routine referred to in Figure 12-7 may be a general-purpose routine available in an online program library that is loaded into primary storage and executed at this point in the execution of the program or module described on this flowchart.

Another flowcharting technique that facilitates top-down design is the *striping convention*. This technique does not involve the use of a particular flowcharting symbol. Rather, a stripe can be placed across any flowcharting symbol to indicate that a more detailed description of the function represented by the symbol is provided elsewhere on the same set of flowcharts. For example, Figure 12-8 indicates that the Read Master routine is described, beginning at block A3 on page 4 of this set of flowcharts.

Even when a flowcharting template and flowcharting worksheets are used, a programmer's "first cut" at a program flowchart is not likely to be the final version of the flowchart. Remember, flowcharting is a design technique that

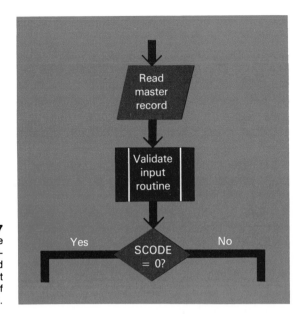

helps us to lay out the logic of a program with care. No programmer creates a flowchart just to create a flowchart. The pictorial representation of program logic is a valuable guide not only during coding but also during testing. The design reflected on the flowchart can be reviewed and interpreted by other information system personnel and by users. When the system or program is released for production use, the flowchart becomes a key part of the documentation package. It can be referred to later if program modifications are needed. It must be kept up to date so that it is an accurate representation of the program logic at all times.

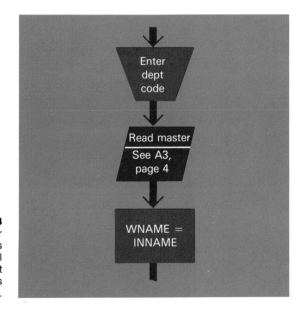

CODING THE SOLUTION

Once the programmer is satisfied that all processing steps have been identified and all alternatives and exceptions provided for, he or she codes the program. If the programming language to be used was not selected earlier, it must be selected now. Program code can be written at different levels, ranging from machine language to a high-level programming language. So far, we've used BASIC, but there are literally hundreds of languages to choose from. Those that are most widely used are discussed in Chapter 13.

If the program design is well thought out and reviewed before coding begins, the coding task should be very straightforward. Nonetheless, it's a very detailed, meticulous job. Whatever the programming language, certain coding rules must be followed exactly. Otherwise, the program will not work as intended. If you've tried your hand at coding, you already know this. That's why special care in design and coding is not a "nice to have" – it's a requirement.

If a one-program system is being implemented, a programmer may work independently with little attention, help, or hindrance from others. Contract programmers, users who are writing programs for their own use, and employees of small organizations may form one-person teams. There are significant opportunities for individuals who can develop applications for businesses they know – say, fast-food restaurants, hardware stores, or pharmacies. On the other hand, teamwork in programming is becoming increasingly important, especially in large organizations and in organizations developing software for resale or for use where a data-processing service is offered. (See Figure 12-9.) Therefore, it's also important for us to look at how detailed design and coding are likely to be done by a chief programmer team in a top-down development environment.

TOP-DOWN PROGRAMMING

Top-down programming involves implementing a system or program in accordance with the top-down design specified for it. As we saw in Chapter 11, that design is commonly reflected on one or more structure charts. Each programmer assumes responsibility for specific modules on the structure charts. Indeed, the

FIGURE 12-9
The saying "two heads are better than one" often holds true when programmers are developing a system for widespread use. (*Courtesy Datapoint Corporation*)

system commands or job-control statements needed to run the system or program may be implemented first. This sequence helps to insure that all required I/O and storage devices have been identified (and will be available when needed). The job-control statements also show the symbolic names of data sets to be referred to in the program coding. (We will learn more about job-control statements in Chapter 14.)

The top function (module) of the system is designed next. This module contains the primary control logic. It serves as a basic skeleton, or main-line path. It contains module names, where appropriate, referring to code that will be written later.

The simplest form of top-down development suggests that all design should be completed before any coding is done. Then the code for the top module is written, then the code for the next lower level, then for the next lower level after that, and so forth. An alternative approach suggests that we should both design and code the top level before any further design is done. The second level should be designed and coded, then the third, and so on. Obviously, this means that some programmers will be writing code at a point in time when the over-all design is not yet complete. (See Figure 12-10A.)

Most computer professionals acknowledge that there is no one correct way to do top-down programming. In practice, top-down development does not imply that all modules at a certain level must be complete before proceeding to the next level. It does imply, however, that any selected path on a structure chart for the program or system must be implemented from top to bottom. For example, we may decide to write all modules related to input functions first. (See Figure 12-10B.) This approach permits all other modules that process the input data to operate on actual problem-related data, even in a test environment.

When a modular approach is used, one question often arises: How big (or how small) should a module be? There are no absolute guidelines. Some computer

FIGURE 12-10
Under one approach to top-down programming (A), all modules at a given level are coded and tested before any modules at a lower level; under another approach (B), all modules in a particular path are coded and tested in a level-by-level fashion, then all the modules in another path, and so on.

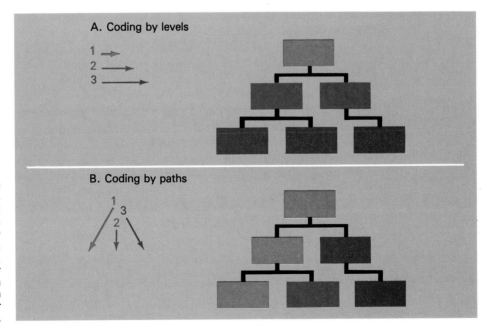

A. Coding by levels

B. Coding by paths

professionals argue that a module may be any size up to that which fits in 4096 bytes (or 512 words, or 1024 words) of primary storage (depending on the computer on which the system or program is to run). Others suggest that a module may be defined as the amount of code that one programmer can write and test during one month — say, from 200 to 300 statements. Still others suggest that each module should be printable as one page of a program listing or displayable on one screen of a visual-display unit. This constraint limits each module to 60 lines of coding or less.

In some cases, several very simple functions may be included in one module. For example, short segments of coding for functions at a low level may be incorporated in the module at the next higher level. If a function requires 100 or more lines of coding, there is a good possibility that subfunctions should be identified.

The most important point to be understood here is that size is no guarantee of modularity. The size of a program module should ultimately be determined by its function.

STRUCTURED PROGRAMMING

A top-down, modular approach to system development is carried to its ultimate level in *structured programming*. Structured-programming techniques can be viewed as the pulling together, or synthesizing, of ideas of top-down design and modularity and the concrete representation of them in the actual program code. Like these other techniques, structured programming is a direct result of attempts to achieve certain objectives:

- Emphasize the importance of well-thought-out program design
- Increase programmer productivity
- Reduce program complexity
- Facilitate program debugging and maintenance
- Encourage error-free coding

No one person "invented" structured programming. A few people have, however, contributed significantly to its development. As early as 1965, Professor E. W. Dijkstra of The Netherlands suggested that the GOTO (or GO TO) construct could be eliminated from programming languages.[*] In 1968, in his now-famous "GOTO letter," he tried to show that programs written using a definite structuring technique were easier to write, read, and debug, and were more likely to be correct. The theoretical framework for structured programming is usually traced to a paper by C. Bohm and G. Jacopini that was initially published in Italian, then republished in English in the May 1966 *Communications of the ACM*.[†] Their "structure theorem" is a mathematical proof that any solution algorithm can be expressed using only three basic building blocks: a process box, a binary decision mechanism, usually referred to as an if-then-else, and a loop mechanism. (See Figure 12-11.)

---

[*]E. W. Dijkstra, "GOTO Statement Considered Harmful," Letter to the Editor, *Communications of the ACM* 11,3 (March 1968), pp. 147-48.
[†]C. Bohm and G. Jacopini, "Flow Diagrams, Turing Machines and Languages with Only Two Formation Rules," *Communications of the ACM* 9,5 (May 1966), pp. 366-71.

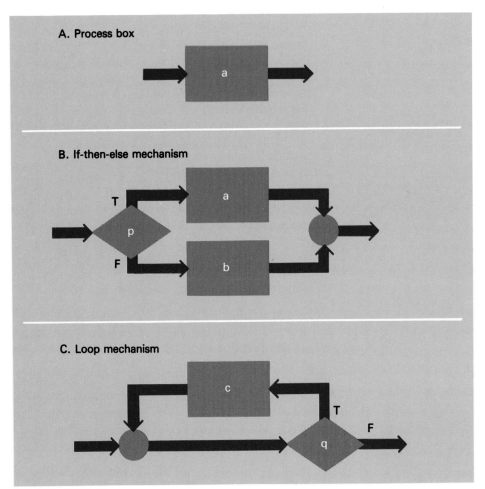

A. Process box

B. If-then-else mechanism

C. Loop mechanism

FIGURE 12-11
The three basic patterns of structured programming are all that's needed to plan the solution to any problem that the computer can be used to solve.

Note that each of the structures in Figure 12-11 is characterized by a single point of entrance and a single point of exit. The process box may be thought of as a single statement or as a properly combined sequence of statements having only one entry and one exit. The if-then-else mechanism indicates that a test is made during execution and the outcome determines which of two alternative paths is followed. The loop mechanism indicates that a test is made and, depending on the outcome, either an immediate exit from the loop occurs or a set of one or more statements is executed and then the test is made again. The fact that the constructs in Figure 12-11B and C have only one entry and one exit is significant: They can themselves be thought of as process boxes.

From this framework, the basic patterns of structured programming have evolved:

- *SIMPLE SEQUENCE.* Statements are executed in the order in which they appear, with control passing unconditionally from one statement to the next. This pattern is so simple that it hardly needs mentioning, but it is necessary for the construction of a program. A problem is solved by executing certain steps in a certain order — an algorithm in program form.

- *IFTHENELSE: IF p THEN a ELSE b.* The condition p is tested. If p is true, statement a is executed and statement b is skipped. If p is false, statement a is skipped but statement b is executed. Control passes to the next statement. This is, of course, the if-then-else mechanism of Figure 12-11B. Note that each "statement" may be a single statement. It may also be a simple sequence of statements combined in some fashion to form a basic pattern that can be treated as a single statement. The connector symbol is used as a collector in Figure 12-11B to emphasize that the IFTHENELSE pattern has only one entry and one exit. When used as a collector, this symbol always has two flowlines entering and one flowline exiting.

- *DOWHILE: DO c WHILE q.* The condition q is tested. If q is true, the statement c is executed and control returns to the test of q. If q is false, then c is skipped and control passes to the next statement. This is the loop mechanism of Figure 12-11C. We have here a leading-decision loop: The test occurs immediately upon entering the loop. What follows is executed only if the tested condition is true. Therefore, the complete loop may never be executed. If the test condition is false, an exit from the loop occurs immediately following the test.

To avoid possible confusion, we should consider another control structure at this point—a loop that must be executed at least once. This control structure is really a combination of SIMPLE SEQUENCE and DOWHILE. It is known as the *DOUNTIL control structure.* (See Figure 12-12.)

Figure 12-12A shows the logic we want to set up. It says: "Do d once, then test for the condition *not* q (indicated by q with a line over it, or q̄). Continue to DO d WHILE the condition q̄ is true." Notice that when the condition q̄ is false, we have not q̄—and, therefore, q! If you find this negative logic confusing, don't be discouraged. That's precisely why programmers often abandon the logic in

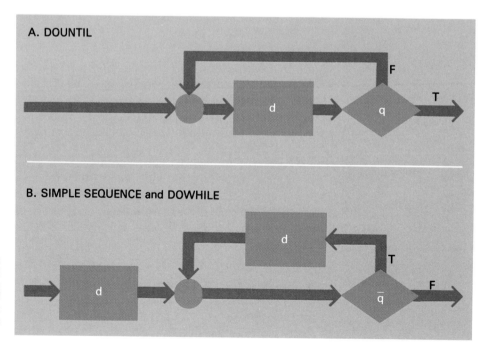

A. DOUNTIL

B. SIMPLE SEQUENCE and DOWHILE

FIGURE 12-12
The DOUNTIL control structure (A) provides a convenient way of expressing the logic of a SIMPLE SEQUENCE and a DOWHILE (B).

Figure 12-12A in favor of the equivalent DOUNTIL control structure in Figure 12-12B. It says: "DO d UNTIL the condition q is true."

When using this logic in an ordinary situation, we might say, for example, for Figure 12-12A: "Walk one block. Continue to walk *while* you are not too tired to do so." Putting it another way for Figure 12-12B, we might say: "After you have walked one block, continue to walk *until* you are too tired to do so."

Note that the test in a DOUNTIL control structure occurs at the end of the loop—that is, after all other processing within the loop has occurred. Therefore, DOUNTIL can be described as a trailing-decision loop. Here, then, is the fundamental difference between DOUNTIL and DOWHILE. To reinforce your understanding of these concepts, look back at the program logic flowcharted in Figure 12-2. What kind of a program loop do you see? The test for loop termination occurs at the end of the loop. The loop is re-executed if the tested-for condition does not exist, that is, until the tested-for condition does exist. This is the logic of DOUNTIL.

Another common control structure is the *CASE control structure*. CASE is really a generalization of the IFTHENELSE pattern, extending it from a two-valued to a multi-valued operation. The logic shown in Figure 12-13A is equivalent to that in Figure 12-13B. Note that the ELSE "statement" of the leftmost IFTHENELSE pattern in Figure 12-13A is, in fact, another IFTHEN-ELSE, which contains another IFTHENELSE. We say that the IFTHENELSE patterns are *nested*. Note also, however, that the over-all construct still has only one entry point and one exit point. So does its equivalent—the CASE control structure in Figure 12-13B.

The concept of nested control structures can be applied repetitively to build one inclusive control structure—a complete program. In other words, a program that is itself composed of only the basic patterns of structured programming, when combined in ways such as we have introduced here, can be thought of as a single structure. A program having only one entry point and one exit point, and having a path from entry to exit for every contained control structure, is called a *proper program*.

The reverse of this building block concept is also possible. We start with a single process box and break that box into a lower level of structures. Next we break some or all of these structures into a still lower level of structures, and so on. We continue until we have reached the level of atomic (basic building block) structures: single statements, if-then-else mechanisms, and leading-decision loops—our SIMPLE SEQUENCE, IFTHENELSE, and DOWHILE. This is precisely the top-down approach that we discussed above.

When a programmer uses only the basic patterns of structured programming, the resulting program can be read from top to bottom, just as we read a page in a book. Careful indenting of certain lines of coding to make the block structure of the program obvious to the reader is another recommended technique. Comments should be used to further clarify the program logic, wherever advisable.*

Sometimes, structured programming is referred to as GOTO-less programming. What this really means is that the programmer does not make frequent use of GOTO statements that cause branches from one part of a program to

---

*A basic explanation of the structured-programming control structures, and how to design well-structured programs, is given in Bohl, *Tools for Structured Design* (Chicago: Science Research Associates, Inc., 1978).

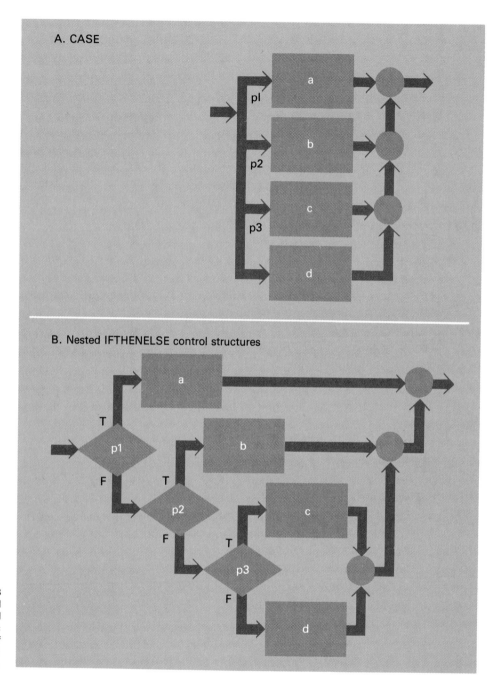

FIGURE 12-13
A single CASE control
structure (A) can be used
to express the logic
of a sequence of
nested IFTHENELSE
patterns (B).

another. Excessive use of GOTO statements tends to obscure the program logic, to hide it from those who must understand what the program does and how it does it (say, for testing or for changing or adding functions at a later time). Certainly, reading straight through a number of short, well-structured program modules is preferable to reading the first 10 pages of a program listing, then reading page 35, then turning back to page 20, and so on. However, to present the elimination of GOTO's as the whole point of structured programming is getting the matter backwards. When the three basic patterns of structured programming are used correctly, there should be little or no need for GOTO's.

Programmers are currently writing structured programs in existing programming languages. Unfortunately, programming-language statements directly analogous to the second and third basic structured-programming patterns are not available in every language. A well-structured program can be written in an assembler language, particularly if a powerful macro facility (which can generate many instructions from one statement that the programmer writes) is available. Of the high-level programming languages in widespread use, PL/I and Pascal are the most suitable for structured programming. In some high-level languages, the use of GOTO statements is necessary to build selection and loop patterns. The definitions of some languages are being extended to include statements that facilitate structured programming.

Not all programmers today are using structured-programming techniques. Those who do may not use them 100 percent of the time. Nevertheless, some computer professionals claim that these techniques can help to establish programming as a science instead of a craft. Hardware designers have known for years that logic circuits can be made from a few basic building blocks (resistors, capacitors, and so on). Programs can be made from basic building blocks of code in a similar fashion.

PSEUDOCODE Figure 12-14 shows the logic for a basic read-and-print program. It reads individual records as input and writes them, unchanged, as output. Such a program is often very helpful at a user installation. For example, data recorded initially on employee time cards may be copied to magnetic tape in a read-and-print run before the main computer run in which calculations are done. Since the data can be read from tape much faster than it can be read from cards, this method minimizes the time needed (in one stretch) for the main computer run. The tape also provides for much more compact storage of the data for backup and recovery or for archiving purposes.

The form of logic representation on the left in Figure 12-14 is familiar to us. We can easily follow this program flowchart. We see here another means of detecting end of input. The logic assumes that a record containing only 9s has been placed as the last record in the input file as a special, or dummy, record indicating end of file. When that record is encountered, program execution is terminated.

The program in Figure 12-14 meets the structured programming criterion of containing only basic control structures. You should be able to detect several examples of SIMPLE SEQUENCE and one DOWHILE. The "statement" within the DOWHILE loop comprises a SIMPLE SEQUENCE of two processing steps: write and read. Since the program contains only one entry point and one exit point, it is a proper program.

Notice the correspondence between the program flowchart and the paragraph of text at the right in Figure 12-14. The text is an informal method of expressing program logic, usually known as *pseudocode*. The pseudocode presents the logic in an easy-to-read, top-to-bottom fashion. For emphasis and clarity, the key words of the DOWHILE pattern (DOWHILE and ENDDO) are written in uppercase letters. The lines describing functions within the DOWHILE pattern are indented two spaces to point out that they are within the DOWHILE.

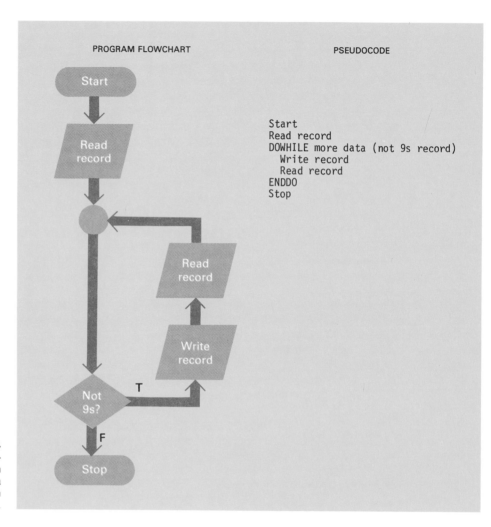

PROGRAM FLOWCHART   PSEUDOCODE

```
Start
Read record
DOWHILE more data (not 9s record)
   Write record
   Read record
ENDDO
Stop
```

FIGURE 12-14
The logic of a well-structured Copy program can be expressed on a program flowchart or in psuedocode.

Pseudocode is an especially convenient tool when designing structured programs. For example, a programmer can draw a flowchart for a program that is structured or for one that isn't. When the flowchart is finished, the programmer may have a difficult time trying to verify whether the resultant program will be structured or not! Not so with pseudocode. The programmer either uses or does not use the patterns available in pseudocode.

The logic of the basic patterns of structured programming, and within DOUNTIL and CASE, is expressed in pseudocode in Figure 12-15. The indentions shown in these forms are a recommendation, not a requirement. (Remember, pseudocode is an informal language, not a programming language. An important advantage of pseudocode over programming languages in the design stage is that it does not enforce coding rules as programming languages do. Because of its similarity to many commonly used programming languages, however, the transition from the design stage to the coding stage is straightforward.)

Another important advantage of pseudocode is that it can be entered readily into the computer from a typewriterlike terminal. If the pseudocode is included

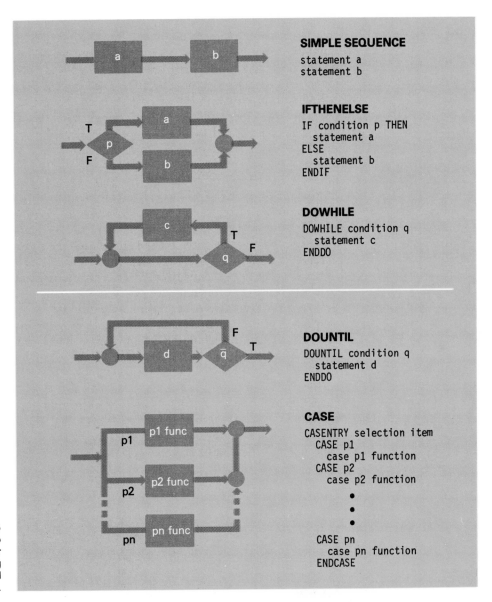

SIMPLE SEQUENCE

```
statement a
statement b
```

IFTHENELSE

```
IF condition p THEN
    statement a
ELSE
    statement b
ENDIF
```

DOWHILE

```
DOWHILE condition q
    statement c
ENDDO
```

DOUNTIL

```
DOUNTIL condition q
    statement d
ENDDO
```

CASE

```
CASENTRY selection item
    CASE p1
        case p1 function
    CASE p2
        case p2 function
            •
            •
            •
    CASE pn
        case pn function
ENDCASE
```

FIGURE 12-15
Programmers may elect to use either flowcharting or pseudocode when planning the logic of a well-structured program.

as comments in program coding or retained on a separate but readily accessible computer file, it can be updated easily with computer help whenever the program logic is changed. Including the pseudocode as comments also helps to insure that it is available when required.

CHECKING OUT THE PROGRAM

Whether we like it or not, a program is seldom executed successfully the first time it is run. Even the simplest programs contain errors, and even experienced programmers make mistakes. It is said that a program that runs correctly the first time is as rare as a hole-in-one on the golf course! As computer programs become increasingly complex, more and more of the programmer's time is spent in program checkout—debugging and testing each new or modified program.

Debugging is the task of finding program errors (bugs) and correcting them so that the program runs properly. *Testing* consists of running the program with input data that simulates, or is a representative sample of, the actual data that will be processed by the program. The care exercised in debugging and testing (or the lack of care) significantly affects the success of the program.

Errors in programming may be either clerical or logical. Most *clerical errors* occur in the coding and keying stages of program development. A programmer may spell a key word incorrectly, or use a variable that has not been defined. The programmer or a data-entry operator may key in the wrong character, omit part of a statement, or place entries in the wrong positions on a line. *Logical errors* are often harder to detect. They occur because the programmer does not thoroughly understand a phase of the problem to be solved, fails to account for certain situations that may (and do) arise during processing, misinterprets some steps in the problem-solving method to be coded, and so on. Both clerical and logical errors must be detected and eliminated from the program.

Earlier in this chapter, we discussed desk checking as a means of detecting errors in the program logic reflected on a program flowchart and in the program coding after it had been entered into computer storage. A few hours of programmer time spent in this manner can prevent needless waste of both programmer and computer time later. If the program logic won't work on paper, it won't work in the computer. In some ways, debugging is like solving a puzzle or doing detective work. The "culprit" is the error in the programmer's own thinking about the problem to be solved.

Going beyond individual effort, some programmers prefer to work in teams, checking their own programs and the programs of others in *informal code inspections*. A programmer who is familiar with a program may unconsciously read into it logic that is not there. Often a fresh viewpoint is more objective, and thus more effective. (See Figure 12-16.)

FIGURE 12-16
Some programmers work in pairs, trading their program listings and performing informal code inspections in order to find errors as early as possible. (*Courtesy Tandem Computers Incorporated*)

In a chief-programmer-team environment, structured walkthroughs, which in this case are *formal code inspections*, may be carried out. Program listings and problem-report forms are distributed to selected inspectors in much the same way as for structured walkthroughs of system design as discussed in Chapter 11. A reader (usually the programmer) leads the inspectors through the code. It is checked not only for errors in what the programmer intended to do, but also against the previously verified design documentation. The moderator presides.

As mentioned earlier, a program may be written in any of several programming languages. COBOL, FORTRAN, and BASIC are especially common choices. The program must be translated into machine language (1s and 0s, remember) before it can control computer operations. The *language-processor program* that does the translation examines the program statements to verify that they have been coded correctly. It assists the programmer by finding some kinds of mistakes. For example, a language-processor program can detect an attempt to perform fixed-point arithmetic on floating-point data or the reverse, an illegal use of certain words or characters, or a missing left or right parenthesis. If errors are detected during translation, a list of error messages, or *diagnostics*, is produced. The list helps to identify the causes of any remaining errors. After the errors have been corrected, the program is again read into the computer to be translated. If errors persist, further corrections are made and the program submitted again. This procedure continues until an error-free run is achieved. Even then the programmer cannot assume that the program is error-free. (It may contain logical errors that are not detectable by the language-processor program.) In any event, additional checkout is required.

The purpose of testing is to verify that a program consistently produces correct or expected results. To test all conditions that could arise during processing may be next to impossible. However, careful construction of a test matrix can help to increase the effectiveness of the testing process. Along the top of the matrix (column headings) the programmer lists all the functions the program can perform. On the left side of the matrix (row headings) are listed the test cases required. (See Figure 12-17.) Each test case (the basis for a test run) should test only one or a very few functions. These are clearly identified by placing check marks or X's in the matrix. If additional conditions to be tested are identified during the testing process itself, they should be added to the test matrix. If the matrix is in a computer-readable form, it can be easily modified.

DIAGNOSTIC PROCEDURES

If a program does not always produce correct results and the errors are difficult to detect, the programmer may elect to use one or more diagnostic procedures. The diagnostic procedures vary according to the language in which the program is coded, what area of the program the programmer thinks might contain errors, how extensive the errors might be, and so on. Storage printouts and tracing are two diagnostic techniques that may be useful.

Storage Printout

If a program fails to work correctly, the programmer can run a *dump program*. Such a program prints out selected portions of primary storage. Usually, it shows all or part of the program being tested and the data on which it is to operate. The contents of registers and the settings of indicators and switches at the time of the dump are also printed. The programmer analyzes this output to determine

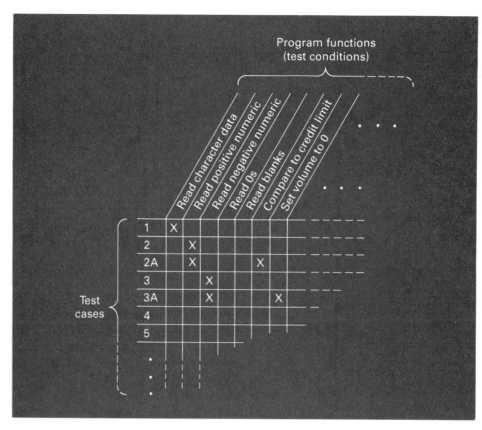

FIGURE 12-17
This test matrix provides a concise summary of the program functions to be exercised by test cases 1, 2, 2A, and so on, during program checkout.

what's happening during program execution. It's a painstaking job. A portion of a storage printout provided by one type of dump program is shown in Figure 12-18. The lines of printing preceded by *GR* show the contents of general registers. Each succeeding line represents the contents of primary-storage locations, beginning with the location named by the address printed at the start of the line. As you have probably noticed, this dump shows the contents of registers and primary storage in hexadecimal notation. Eight-character groupings represent the contents of 32-bit words. From the printout, the programmer can determine whether or not the correct data and instructions have been stored in the appropriate locations. If errors are detected, the programmer can examine related parts of the program to discover why the errors occurred.

Tracing Although a visual check of a storage printout is sometimes a desirable technique, it may not always be the best one. This is especially true when the program is written in a language like COBOL, FORTRAN, or BASIC. Because the programmer who uses these languages is not usually concerned with the exact storage locations of instructions or data, a trace is often a more efficient check than a dump. A program to perform the trace function is usually available to the programmer. The programmer can interpret the output of a *trace program* faster and easier than analyzing a storage printout.

A tracing technique does exactly what its name implies: It traces the steps followed during the execution of a program. In doing so, it prints out

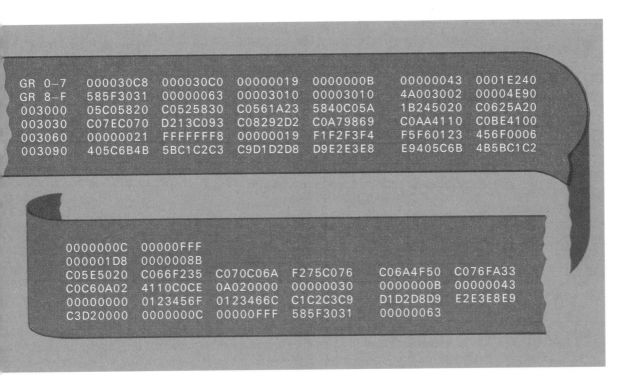

GR 0-7	000030C8	000030C0	00000019	0000000B	00000043	0001E240
GR 8-F	585F3031	00000063	00003010	00003010	4A003002	00004E90
003000	05C05820	C0525830	C0561A23	5840C05A	1B245020	C0625A20
003030	C07EC070	D213C093	C08292D2	C0A79869	C0AA4110	C0BE4100
003060	00000021	FFFFFFF8	00000019	F1F2F3F4	F5F60123	456F0006
003090	405C6B4B	5BC1C2C3	C9D1D2D8	D9E2E3E8	E9405C6B	4B5BC1C2

0000000C	00000FFF				
000001D8	0000008B				
C05E5020	C066F235	C070C06A	F275C076	C06A4F50	C076FA33
C0C60A02	4110C0CE	0A020000	00000030	0000000B	00000043
00000000	0123456F	0123466C	C1C2C3C9	D1D2D8D9	E2E3E8E9
C3D20000	0000000C	00000FFF	585F3031	00000063	

FIGURE 12-18   The contents of 32-bit general registers and primary-storage locations are represented in hexadecimal notation on this storage printout.

information for the programmer. This information may include the location and machine-language code of an instruction being executed. It may also include the contents of involved registers and the values of selected variables after the operation controlled by the instruction has been completed.

Because the printer is a relatively slow-speed output device, the printing of a complete trace—the execution of each instruction in a program—generally takes too much time. For this reason, the tracing technique is usually modified so that only the contents of selected storage locations or registers are printed and only at specific times. With this variation, a "snapshot" of a particular part of a program under a particular processing condition is obtained. For example, the trace and resultant printing may be specified to occur only when the program executes a branch instruction. A series of snapshots is produced, showing each branch instruction that is executed. As a group, the snapshots show the paths followed during program execution. From these the programmer can usually discover when, where, or why errors are occurring.

TOP-DOWN TESTING

Top-down programming facilitates top-down testing. In effect, design, coding, and testing (or simply coding and testing, if the design is completed first) proceed in parallel. The purest approach to top-down development suggests that testing of the top module should begin as soon as it is coded. In practice, programmers usually find that at least one or two modules at a lower level must be designed and coded before any nontrivial testing can be done.

Implementation of top-down testing requires that dummy routines, called *program stubs*, be created for modules that are referred to by name in modules under test but not yet coded. We noted, for example, that the main-line path contains module names referring to code to be written later. By inserting program stubs with the same names into the program library, the programmer can test this main-line path while design and coding of the lower-level modules are being completed.

A program stub is a substitute for a module. As such, it does not perform the actual functions of the module. It does, however, provide sufficiently similar input/output behavior to make the module that references it believe that it does. In most cases, a program stub also provides a program trace. For example, it may be advisable to include a statement causing CALLED NET PAY MODULE to be printed as output in a dummy routine. Such a printout can be very helpful for debugging purposes.

Each program stub is eventually replaced by the module for which it serves as a placeholder. That new module is included in the next combining of the parts of the program or system under development. At any point, the coding already in existence provides a framework within which a newly coded module can be executed. Through the staged integration procedure, the requirement for test time is distributed throughout system development. The need for very large amounts of test time near the end of the project is thus avoided. Errors are generally easier to detect because the suspect areas of code are more readily identifiable. There is no need to undertake the awesome task of trying to mold a large number of separately coded and tested modules into a workable system at the end of the development effort.

The extent of testing may depend on the amount of testing time available. A predetermined schedule and a promised system-availability date may have to be maintained. The recipient of information to be produced by the system may be willing to forgo complete testing because the information is desperately needed. In addition, little money may be available for testing. Often, the degree of testing is determined by balancing its cost against the penalties of acting on incorrect information.

Unfortunately, many user organizations and software development firms have learned the hard way that the consequences of inadequate testing may be very severe. It's one thing not to receive on time an expected report of last week's sales in region 2. It's another thing to have to shut down an entire production line or distribution center because a computer can't produce the required production schedule or shipping orders. Computer manufacturers and software development firms are being sued for hundreds of thousands of dollars because of clients' claims that their systems were not ready for production use within reasonable time frames, did not perform as specified in contractual agreements, or failed during critical business periods. Can we afford to test systems thoroughly? We can't afford not to.

DOCUMENTATION

Documentation is a term with at least two meanings:

1. The act of recording evidence about an activity.
2. The recorded evidence of what has been done, is being done, or is going to be done on a project.

Complete, accurate, and timely documentation of a program or system is as essential to effective use of the program or system as the actual coding itself.

The long-range success (or failure) of the system development effort is dependent on high-quality documentation.

When the steps of system development are carried out as they should be, documentation is not an unwelcome burden imposed as a project nears completion. Instead, both the act of documentation and the result of it are an integral part of the system development cycle. Documentation standards should be established early and procedures enforced to insure initial high quality and to provide for continuous maintenance and updating. The availability of readily usable forms helps to minimize the time required to prepare documentation. These forms provide guidelines leading to complete coverage of the particular aspects of the project being documented, as well as to easier reading and understanding on the part of involved personnel. Such forms may have been designed for preceding projects, or they may be obtained from external sources. They can also be designed by selected team members at the time that documentation standards are established.

In most development efforts, documentation must be developed for the system as a whole *and* for each program within it. As suggested earlier, a development support library should be set up at the user installation. It serves as a receptacle and a retrieval mechanism for all project documentation. Trained personnel can assist system analysts and programmers both in creating high-quality documentation and in distributing or retrieving it at appropriate times. (See Figure 12-19.)

FIGURE 12-19
Long after a system becomes operational, both user and information system personnel need access to system documentation when questions arise. (*Courtesy IBM Corporation*)

To discuss the content and format of all the documentation that may be created during a system development effort is far beyond the scope of this book. Figure 12-20 provides an overview of the types of documentation usually required. Some of the types of documentation are familiar to us. In Chapter 11, we mentioned the need for a set of functional specifications outlining the system requirements. These specifications tell *what* the system under development is supposed to accomplish. They also help to insure that the system under development will solve the problem that it is supposed to solve.

The functional specifications are supported by lower-level, more technical specifications that tell *how* a system or program will perform the functions identified for it. Structure charts, program flowcharts, and pseudocode are commonly used for this purpose. These types of documentation are the basis for accurate communication of information among developers. They are essential when changes or corrections must be made to the system at a later time.

Still other types of documentation must be created for the computer operator who will monitor the system during execution. If users at terminals will interact with the system, some documentation may have to be tailored to their special needs. The complete documentation package provides a visible, understandable trail for management personnel with over-all responsibility for the project and/or for development as a whole. It can also be used by auditors to verify that company policies and procedures are being carried out. To protect a company's computerized assets, to prevent disruption of critical business operations when the unexpected occurs, to satisfy ever-increasing demands for government reporting, to keep stockholders informed, and so on, high-quality documentation is an absolute requirement.

At some user installations, current hard (printed) copies of all human-readable documents are maintained in a central computer library for reference and checkout. At other installations, the current copies are kept on disk or tape. In that form, the documentation can be scanned by people who need it—generally, by calling for particular documents to be displayed on the screen of a visual-display unit. At still other installations, most documentation is kept on rolls of microfilm or on microfiche for storage and retrieval purposes. In such environments, printed copies are made available only in special cases. (See Figure 12-21.)

SYSTEM EVALUATION

Whether or not system evaluation tasks are included in the plan for system development, system evaluation occurs. A data-entry operator who keys in daily quality-inspection data may find the data-entry procedures very cumbersome when large volumes of similar data must be keyed. The sales manager for petrochemicals may become increasingly frustrated because, although sales-by-item totals are interesting, sales-by-territory totals would give him a better fix on what he suspects is the real sales problem. A computer sort run expected to complete within an hour may actually be taking longer—so much longer that the overnight batch jobs are not getting done until 8 or 9 in the morning. Two months after the new system is operational, one of the organization's leading customers may complain that a large back order for fire-deterrent chemicals still has not been received. Upon investigation, a member of the information system staff may find that no back orders for chemicals of any kind exist on the system's back-order master file.

Feasibility Report

System Proposal

Functional Specifications
    System flowchart
    Input/output descriptions
        (printer spacing charts, display-screen layouts, etc.)
    File descriptions
        (record layouts, etc.)
Samples of inputs and outputs

Data Element Dictionary

Logic Specifications
    Structure charts   Nassi-Schneiderman charts
    Program flowcharts   Warnier-Orr diagrams
    Pseudocode   Decision tables
    HIPO diagrams   Decision trees

Program Listings

Documentation of Structured Walkthroughs
    For formal design reviews
        (participants' problem logs, moderator's summary report)
    For formal code inspections
        (participants' problem reports, moderator's summary report)

Computer-Assisted Testing Information
    Test plan
    Test matrices
    Test case descriptions
    Test data and expected results
    Actual results of test runs

Operational Information
    Keying instructions
    Job-control statements
    Run instructions
    Output distribution instructions
    Backup and recovery procedures

User Documentation
    System narrative
        (general information, user's guides, reference manuals)
    Input specifications and instructions
    Output descriptions and distribution
    Education and training materials

Maintenance Information
    Design change requests (DCR's)
    Program change log

Technical References
    Hardware specifications
    Specifications for vendor-supplied software
    Other vendor-supplied documentation

FIGURE 12-20
The documentation created throughout system development should be kept in a development support library where it is available to all who need it.

FIGURE 12-21
As in many computer-using organizations, the central computer facility at Lawrence Livermore Laboratory is a hub of busy activity. (*Courtesy Lawrence Livermore National Laboratory*)

Because system implementation is such a major undertaking, most organizations convert to a new system gradually. For example, the inventory-control programs may be implemented first, then the program to generate purchase orders when stock is depleted, then the program to generate work orders for stock-room employees, and so on. In another approach, the petrochemicals group may get aboard the system first; then the fabrics and finishes group; then the paints and resins group; and so on. When a staged approach to implementation is employed, planned system evaluation tasks can be carried out while the use of the system is still somewhat limited.

The most rigid system evaluation is a well-defined user acceptance test. This test is an extension of the system testing we discussed earlier, but now users performing their routine job responsibilities are directly involved. The system will not be declared ready for production use until the user (client) and the contractor (in-house information system management or an outside development firm) agree that it is performing according to specifications and/or that satisfactory plans are in place for all discrepancies.

Formal machine-based user acceptance testing can and should be complemented by user discussions of their perceptions of the system in operation. Systematic observations of how the system is performing, whether or not the outputs of the system are being used, and so on, should be made. The over-all objective of these efforts is to determine whether or not the system is meeting the user needs that it is supposed to satisfy. A second consideration is whether or not it operates within stated budget and performance limits. The findings of system evaluation should be reported to both the users and information system management. Plans should be put in place to follow up on problems.

If a program that is error-free on its first run is rare, a system that is all-things-to-all-users when first implemented is even rarer. (To attempt to achieve such an objective is unrealistic and likely to be fatal—system implementation may never occur.) Design change request forms can be used to document proposed functional additions, deletions, and changes; errors that must be corrected; and usability enhancements. As before, these requests can be prioritized and acted on accordingly.

Ongoing support of an installed system is a necessity from both operational and development points of view. While some refer to ongoing development support as *system maintenance*, others argue that this work should be viewed and carried out as *system development*. Certainly, care in system analysis, design, and implementation is no less critical when making changes to a system on which an organization's business depends than when initially developing a system. Complete, accurate system documentation is a necessity. If the system was implemented by in-house staff, the changes will be made by in-house staff. If the system was implemented by another firm, either in-house staff must learn the system or ongoing support must be provided under a service contract.

CHAPTER SUMMARY

1. The steps of system development can be grouped within four phases: system analysis, system design, system implementation, and system evaluation.

2. System implementation often begins with program flowcharting, a pictorial method of planning the detailed logic within an application program. The logic shown on the flowchart should then be desk-checked to detect and remove any errors as early as possible.

3. The program flowchart serves as a guide during program coding. The line numbers of program statements can be placed by the flowcharting symbols to serve as cross-references between the flowchart and the program.

4. Structured programming is the application of ideas of top-down design and modularity at the coding level; only three basic patterns—SIMPLE SEQUENCE, IFTHENELSE, and DOWHILE—are used in a well-structured program.

5. Two commonly used combinations of basic patterns are the DOUNTIL and CASE control structures. DOUNTIL is the same as a SIMPLE SEQUENCE followed by a DOWHILE; CASE is the same as a sequence of nested IFTHENELSE's.

6. Pseudocode is an informal method of expressing program logic in an easy-to-read, top-to-bottom fashion that is especially convenient when planning a structured program.

7. Errors in a program may be either clerical or logical. Desk checking, informal code inspections, and formal code inspections can be carried out to detect and remove these errors as soon as possible.

8. The language-processor program that translates the program statements into machine language can assist the programmer by finding some kinds of errors. If errors are detected during the translation, a list of error messages, or diagnostics, is provided as output.

9. Dump and trace programs are additional tools that a programmer may use if a program fails to work correctly and the error causing the failure cannot be found.

10. Top-down, modular programming facilitates top-down testing. Program stubs are created as substitutes for modules that are not yet coded, then replaced by the modules when they are coded and ready for testing in the system environment.

11. Complete, accurate, and timely documentation about a program or system is as essential to effective use of the program or system as the actual coding itself. When system development is carried out properly, the act of creating the documentation and the end results are an integral part of the system development cycle.

DISCUSSION QUESTIONS

1. (a) Name two types of flowcharts.
   (b) Compare the two types, noting similarities and differences.

2. Construct a system flowchart for the following problem:

   There are 26 students in a class. Each student is identified by a student number. His or her name, number, and term grade are to be printed on individual grade cards.

   The computer is to be used to calculate each student's term grade. Eight test and classroom-assignment scores are to be used for this purpose. The scores (ranging from 0 through 100), plus the number and name of each student, are to be keyed as input from an online visual-display unit during processing. If a student's term grade is above 90, the name and number are also to be printed on an Honors List. This list is to be written on magnetic tape and transcribed later to a printed report. Processing is to be completed when all student data has been processed.

3. Repeat Question 2, but now construct a program flowchart showing the logic needed to solve the problem. In doing so, be sure to plan a well-structured program.

4. Explain desk checking—what, why, when, how, and by whom it is used.

5. Describe two flowcharting aids usually available to system designers and programmers.

6. Show how top-down programming and program modularity relate to one another.

7. Give five arguments for the use of structured programming.

8. (a) What is pseudocode?
   (b) When, how, and why is it used?

9. Compare and contrast informal and formal code inspections.

10. How does a language-processor program help the programmer?

11. (a) List the types of documentation needed during the various stages of system development.
    (b) By whom is each type of documentation created?
    (c) By whom is it used?

12. Why should system evaluation be planned for, since it will occur anyway?

13 PROGRAM-MING LANGUAGES

Language communicates experience. It does so by translating events into symbols: words. Words trigger memories in us, and they also signal us to certain kinds of action.

Computer languages do the same thing for computers as human languages do for humans. There are high-level languages, whose words may have specialized and extensive meanings, like human jargon; and there are low-level languages, whose words have simple and basic meanings, like the words "and," "or," and "not."

The kind of task the computer is to perform determines the programming languages that can be used. Different languages are designed to serve different purposes.

One language might be designed for maintaining inventory records or for recording shelf-stocking transactions. Another, lower-level language might be used to control an automated shop machine making parts of many shapes and sizes. Different applications require different types of computer operations. Certain operations can be expressed more easily in some languages than they can in others.

© Laurence M. Gartel 1982

© Dan McCoy / Rainbow

Courtesy Xerox Corporation

The importance of having the right programming language can be seen in the experience of choreographer and educator Bella Lewitzky. She wanted to find the symbols for a language of dance that could be programmed into a computer. "I wanted to investigate what the computer could do for dance," she said. "What I realized was that finding the symbols or language of dance to program into the machine was still quite difficult." Eventually, she went to her company members to create a human computer, with herself as the programmer. In this case, her choreography instructions might be considered software, and the dancers, the hardware. Due to the lack of a verbal language of dance that could be input to a computer, much of the creative process had to be left up to the dancers; human creativity had to do what the computer could not do.

In another effort at integrating computers and dance, choreographer Betsy Erickson and visual performance artist Darryl Sapien created "Pixellage" for the San Francisco Ballet. They followed in the footsteps of "Ballet Mécanique," a much earlier work.

Good form is important when it comes to art. Where graphics are concerned, form is often beyond the ability of words to define adequately, just as it is with dance. The job of a programming language, here, might be to provide an "electronic palette" of basic colors, to accept and store data from a light pen, and to manipulate the color, size, and position of images on a video-display screen.

Courtesy Lewitzky Dance Foundation

© Lloyd Englert/San Francisco Ballet

"Broad Sweep"/© 1981 Darcy Gerberg

© Laurence M. Gartel 1982

Sometimes, the uniqueness of the task and the speed at which it must be performed require programming in assembly language. In the case of the American Heart Association's Cardio-Pulmonary Resuscitation (CPR) course, an Apple II microcomputer was programmed in assembly language to coordinate a video-disk player, a light pen, a specially designed random-access audio player, and a training manikin equipped with sensors. This system monitors the trainee's actions on the manikin and selects, from 700 responses stored on video disk, the right one to instruct the trainee. The result is a system that can train a person better and more quickly than a human instructor can.

Even inexperienced users can create computer graphics using Logo, a simple programming language. In a computer graphics contest for members of the Young People's Logo Association, one of the live-action computer creations was a space-shuttle countdown, complete with liftoff!

Good form is also important in athletics. The process of computerized sports profile analysis can make it easier to study an athlete's form in action. The coach marks the location of the athlete's joints in a series of stop-action photographs. The computer then connects the joints with segments representing feet, calves, thighs, hips, torso, arms, and head; then, it overlays each succeeding photo, showing movement through space.

Another use of computers to show position in space is Nearfield Acoustical Holography. Microphones are placed in a gridwork pattern, 16 by 16, to pick up sounds from a guitar mounted at the center of the grid. The computer-generated image shows both the relative loudness and the relative position of the two sound sources (presumably, two different strings of the guitar being plucked). For special applications such as these, the right computer language must be used in order for the computer to do its job efficiently.

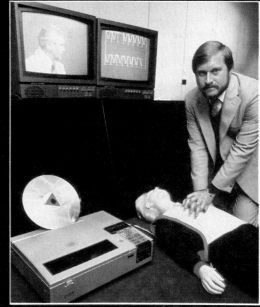

Courtesy American Heart Association/Bob Lukeman photo

Courtesy Texas Instruments Incorporated

Courtesy Young People's Logo Association

© Dan McCoy/Rainbow

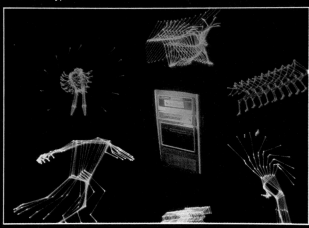

© Dan McCoy/Rainbow

Courtesy Scott Johnson/Pennsylvania State University

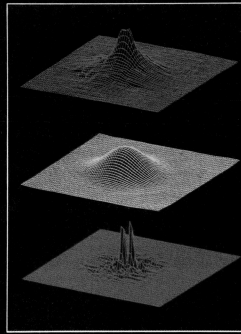

Courtesy Julian D. Maynard, Department
of Physics/Pennsylvania State University

Other computer applications look at language from a different angle. One application involves a machine that electronically reads a book aloud. The machine must recognize the printed words and select the output signals to form those words, which are then input to a speaking device.

The need to communicate with a computer using human language can sometimes be a special problem, especially if you're Japanese! The Japanese language is made up of words, written not as arrangements of letters, but as single "word-pictures," or ideograms. For this reason, a special Kanji keyboard must be used to enter computer input expressed in Kanji. It has far more keys than a common typewriterlike keyboard. A look at the keyboard shows how the structure of a language has a lot to do with the process of using it.

Because each computer language has its own unique structure, each one is best suited for certain uses. Although any of several languages might "work" for a given application, the advantages and disadvantages of each must be weighed in choosing which one to use. For optimum efficiency, the structure of the language chosen must be the one most fit for the function the computer is to perform.

© Dan McCoy / Rainbow

Courtesy George G. Dunbar / IBM Corporation

13 | PROGRAMMING LANGUAGES

We marvel today at what computers can do. Even in the 1950s, their abilities to solve complex equations for chemists and to get weekly paychecks out on time were impressive. By the 1960s they reserved seats on airline flights and predicted who the next president would be. In the 1970s they designed airplanes, bridges, and highways, and controlled manned space flights. Now, they are optimizing gasoline usage in automobiles, sending spacecraft toward other planets, and directing life-maintaining equipment in hospitals. Their abilities are limited only by our imagination.

We know, however, that a computer by itself has no power at all. Whether it is big enough to fill a room or small enough to fit in your pocket, it can do nothing unless it's directed step by step. The power that directs the computer lies in a program.

We learned earlier that a stored program is a sequence of machine-language instructions in the computer's internal storage unit that guides it in carrying out basic operations. The basic operations are simple actions such as adding, subtracting, moving, comparing, reading, and writing. In fact, these "simple" operations are even more basic— they are flows of pulses between the capacitors, resistors, and other two-state components that make up the computer.

In somewhat the same way as a computer responds to electrical pulses, our muscles respond to nerve pulses. Imagine how difficult it would be if, to move an arm or leg, we had to think through and express that movement in terms of nerve pulses. Suppose that our friends could only accompany us to the latest movie if we spelled out, in terms of nerve pulses, the actions they needed to take to get there. Fortunately, we can just say something like, "Take the Camden Avenue turnoff," or, "Wait where you are—we'll pick you up." Once again, there's more than one way to solve the problem. The way need only be communicated and then carried out.

A similar communication capability exists in programming. To fully appreciate this capability, we look first at what it takes to communicate with a computer in its own machine language—the language that directly affects the flow, presence, or absence of electrical pulses. Then we look at the next level of programming languages, those commonly known as *assembler languages*. You'll see that it's more convenient to communicate with a computer by means of languages at a still higher level. BASIC, the language we used for the Calculate Total Cost program in Chapter 12, is one example. Finally, some computer systems accept statements of a *generator language*. User-oriented display support is often provided with the language to help the user-programmer write a complete program by responding to simple prompts on a visual-display screen. In some cases the user-programmer may not even realize that he or she is programming!

Strictly speaking, a programming language is not software. The language is a set of carefully chosen symbols with well-defined meanings, plus a set of rules that users must follow when writing programs in that language. The software is the language-processor program that translates the programming-language statements into machine-language instructions that direct the computer.

You may be surprised to learn that more than 300 programming languages have been developed. An obvious question is: Why so many? An analogy here is: Why are there so many kinds of shoes? Few of us would care to wear 3-inch heels to go hiking, or cowboy boots to go on a job interview, or open-toed sandals to walk across a college campus when it's 10 degrees below zero. Each kind of shoe is best suited to a particular need. So it is with programming languages. In this chapter, we direct our attention to the programming languages in widespread use: COBOL, FORTRAN, PL/I, BASIC, Pascal, APL, and RPG. We look briefly at other languages you may encounter. Our emphasis is not on language rules. Rather, we explore the major characteristics of the languages and the applications for which they are best suited.

Some of you may have used statements of a query language to interact with computer systems. Such a language allows users to communicate with a computer using words and phrases that are much like ordinary English. This interactive query capability is important, but query languages are not programming languages as we discuss them here. We shall discuss interactive query capabilities in later chapters.

MACHINE LANGUAGE

To review what a computer's machine language is, let's assume first that we must communicate with a computer using its machine language. We saw in Chapter 7 that a computer with a 32-bit architecture may be directed by instructions that are 32 bits in length. To cause such a computer to add two values we might write:

```
01011000001000001011000000101010
01011010001000001011000000110010
01010000001000001011000000110110
```
32-bit machine-language instructions

In the first instruction above, we tell the computer to load a particular data item into a particular register. In the second, we tell it to add another data item to that value. In the third, we tell it to store the result. When writing these instructions, we must know exactly where the two data items will be located in storage and where to store the result. We must know the bit patterns (op codes) for the load, add, and store operations needed. Assuming we know this information, we must write it and key it into storage correctly.

Obviously, creating a complete program in this machine language would be both tedious and time-consuming. After a time, all the strings of 1s and 0s would begin to look alike. We would almost certainly write or key in some 1s where there should be 0s and some 0s where there should be 1s.

Some of you may be thinking that writing machine-language instructions for an 8-bit microcomputer might not be so bad. Let's see. Below are the instructions needed to direct an 8-bit 6502 microprocessor (as used in an Apple II, for example) to add two numbers and store the result:

```
10101001 ⎤
00110000 ⎥
00011000 ⎥
01101001 ⎬   Machine-language instructions for an 8-bit microprocessor
00100010 ⎥
10001101 ⎥
00000010 ⎥
01100000 ⎦
```

These patterns are only 8 bits in length, but there are 8 patterns (not 3, as you may have expected). It's not obvious that writing a correct program in this second machine language would be much easier than writing one in the first machine language above.

It's only fair to note that some computers can convert values written in hexadecimal notation to equivalent binary numbers. This means that we could write instructions in hexadecimal rather than binary. Hard-wired circuitry or a machine-language program in the computer's read-only memory would convert the hexadecimal digits to binary for us. For example, we might write

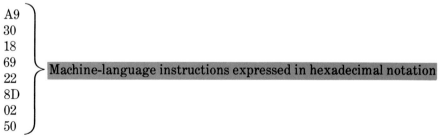

```
A9 ⎤
30 ⎥
18 ⎥
69 ⎬   Machine-language instructions expressed in hexadecimal notation
22 ⎥
8D ⎥
02 ⎥
50 ⎦
```

instead of the 8-bit patterns above. An incorrect digit would be easier to detect, and keying the program into storage would be less tedious and error-prone. However, we would still have to know the exact op codes for operations and the exact storage locations for data.

There are other considerations, too. Since machine-language instructions contain the exact bit patterns (op codes) for machine operations, they can be used only on computers whose operations are defined in exactly that way. That is, A9 may mean Load to one computer but Compare to another. We cannot simply write a program for whatever computer is available and expect it to run with little or no change on another computer. Since the instructions contain exact storage addresses, we have to understand how the internal storage unit of our particular computer is organized and accessed. How would you like to modify a machine-language program initially written by someone else to, say, cause the computer to read employee addresses as well as employee names as input? How long would it take you to find a bug in 300 or more lines of 1s and 0s within a machine-language accounts-receivable program?

Programmers and programming time, computers and computing time, and correctly functioning programs are all valuable resources. In most businesses and other organizations today, increased productivity through more efficient use of resources is critical. Clearly, machine-language programming is not the key to increased productivity in the use of computers.

ASSEMBLER LANGUAGES

Because of the obvious difficulties involved in writing, keying in, and testing machine-language programs, symbolic programming languages have been developed. These languages permit the programmer to use convenient symbols, or *mnemonics* (memory aids), when writing a program. Op codes written as mnemonics are easier to remember and interpret than op codes written as binary or hexadecimal digits. A can stand for Add, L for Load, B for Branch, and so on.

Furthermore, a programmer who codes in a symbolic language need not know or remember the exact storage locations of data and instructions. He or she can simply select a name, or *label*, for an instruction or a data item, and then use that label to refer to the instruction or data item. For example, NAME can stand for employee name, PARTNO for part number, and RATE for hourly wage. As noted earlier, the labels for data items are commonly called *variables* because the values of the data items may be changed many times during processing.

The first commonly used symbolic languages were called *assembler languages*. Like a machine language, an assembler language is a relatively low-level, machine-oriented language. The programmer does not have to write instructions in binary or hexadecimal, but must still be very conscious of the architecture of the computer that will execute the instructions. To understand why, consider the instructions below. They tell the computer to add two values and store the result, as did our machine-language instructions above.

```
ADDROUT   L    2,DATA1 ⎫
          A    2,DATA2 ⎬   Assembler-language instructions
          ST   2,SCORE ⎭
          .
          .
          .
DATA1     DS   F  ⎫
DATA2     DS   F  ⎬   Assembler-language data definitions
SCORE     DS   F  ⎭
```

The current contents of the primary-storage locations reserved for variable DATA1 are loaded into register 2 by means of the Load (L) instruction. The current contents of DATA2 are added to this value by means of the Add (A) instruction. Their sum is stored in SCORE by means of the Store (ST) instruction.

In order to write just these few instructions, the programmer had to know the following:

● That the computer has a register that can be used in addition operations and that can be referred to by the numeral 2
● That a value can be placed in a register by means of a load operation
● That the result of an add operation involving a register is placed back into the same register
● That the result can be saved by storing it in another primary-storage location

This example also shows that an assembler-language programmer cannot make up and use labels without first defining them. The label for an instruction is defined by placing it in the label field (the leftmost positions) of the instruction that it is to identify. The labels for data items are really the labels for primary-storage locations reserved for the data items. The programmer must tell the computer to set aside certain primary-storage locations for all the data items used in a program. Furthermore, the programmer must tell what type of data each item is and how much storage should be reserved for it. In our example, the programmer used three Define Storage (DS) instructions containing F as an operand. These instructions tell the computer to reserve one full word of storage for each of three numeric values to be stored as binary numbers. The programmer had to determine beforehand that one full word would hold the binary equivalent of any value that might be read as input for DATA1 or DATA2, and of any value that might be computed as their sum. He or she had to be sure that the mnemonics L, A, and ST represent machine operations that can be performed on full-word binary values.

In general, each type of computer has its own assembler language. Assembler-language programming is possible with a computer only if a language-processor program known as an *assembler program* (*assembler*, for short) has been developed and is available for the computer. The assembler program accepts the assembler-language statements coded by the programmer as input and translates them into machine-language instructions that can be executed by the computer. The steps necessary from time of problem analysis to time of output are summarized in Figure 13-1.

First, the problem is analyzed in terms of the user's needs. Then it is analyzed in terms of the computer's capabilities. The programmer expresses the needed operations in assembler language, thereby creating a *source program*. The source program is then keyed onto cards, tape, or disk, or entered directly into the computer from a terminal.

An assembler program designed to operate on assembler-language programs is then loaded into primary storage. It serves as the stored program during an *assembly run*. The source program is the input data for the run. The assembler-language instructions arc translated into machine-language instructions.

The assembly run produces two outputs. One output is an *object program*. It comprises the machine-language instructions created during the assembly run. The second output is an *assembly listing*. It shows both the assembler-language coding and the machine-language instructions created from that coding. The assembly listing often provides other valuable information for the programmer.

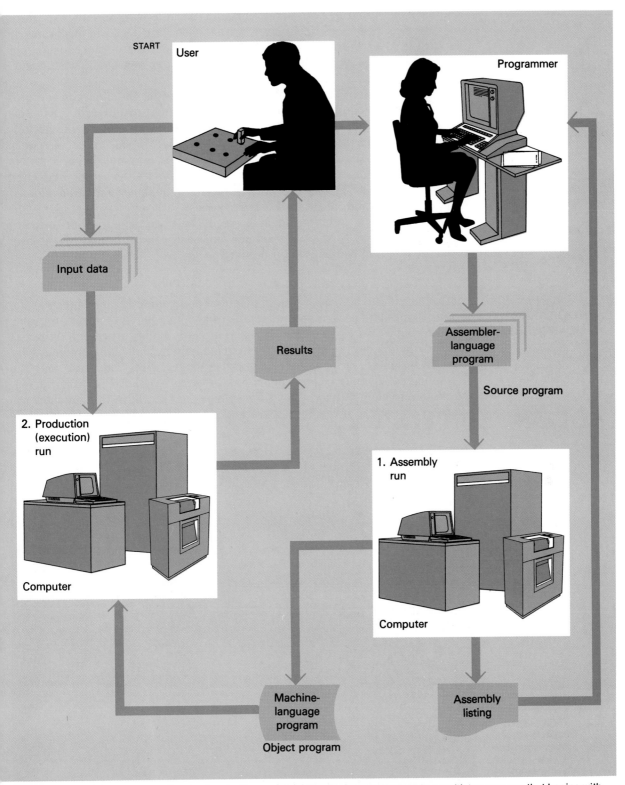

FIGURE 13-1 Creating, assembling, and executing an assembler-language program is a multistep process that begins with user requirements and ends with user-oriented results that satisfy those requirements.

Most assembler programs can detect certain types of coding and keying errors, generally classified as clerical errors (recall "Checking Out the Program" in Chapter 12). All errors must be corrected. Then the source program can again be provided as input to an assembly run, with hope that no new errors will appear. (See Figure 13-2.)

After an error-free assembly run has been achieved, the object program is loaded into primary storage. It serves as the stored program during a *production run*. As noted in Chapter 12, the programmer cannot assume that a successfully translated program is correct. The assembler program can detect errors in *syntax* (that is, in the way instructions are coded). It may not detect errors in logic. For this reason, test data should be processed before the actual production data is provided as input. The output results should be compared against predetermined, valid results. If errors persist, storage printouts may be requested or tracing techniques may be used. Not until the output of test runs appears satisfactory to the programmer and has been confirmed by the user should the program be released for production use.

HIGH-LEVEL PROGRAMMING LANGUAGES

Another significant step in the development of programming languages was the design of high-level programming languages and language-processor programs (also referred to as language translators, compilers, and interpreters). Whereas assembler languages are machine-oriented languages, high-level languages are procedure-oriented or problem-oriented languages. Both the user and the programmer (they may be one person—a *user-programmer*) direct their attention to the problem at hand. The programmer does not have to know how the computer will perform required operations. If multiplication is to be done, for

FIGURE 13-2
Programmers who are developing system programs for widespread use often write assembler-language programs. (*Courtesy Honeywell Inc.*)

example, the programmer need only be concerned with what value is multiplied by what value and what the result is. He or she does not have to place either value in a certain register or set up a special area for temporary storage of the result. The term *high-level programming language* is appropriate because the programmer is removed a considerable distance from concerns related to the machine itself.

One statement in a high-level programming language is often used to create several machine-language instructions. For example, consider the following statement written in FORTRAN, a widely used high-level programming language:

$$AVCST = TOTPR/QTY$$

This one simple statement causes the computer to divide total price (TOTPR) by quantity (QTY) to determine the average cost and then store this result in AVCST. In contrast, several machine-language or assembler-language instructions would be needed to designate the same operations. The total price would have to be loaded into a particular primary-storage location or register; the quantity would have to be positioned properly; division would have to be performed; and the result would have to be stored.

The fact that one high-level-language statement corresponds to several machine-language instructions is important for at least two reasons. First, it reduces the time and effort needed for programming because fewer lines of coding are needed to designate a sequence of processing steps. Second, it cuts down on the likelihood of errors. The sequences of instructions inserted to replace high-level-language statements are pretested, correct routines. Some of these sequences are so complex that the programmer would be apt to make errors if he or she attempted to code them. However, when the programmer uses high-level-language statements, he or she need only check to make sure that the statements are written correctly. Then it can be assumed that the inserted sequences are error-free.

Some assembler languages include macro-instruction capabilities. They permit several machine-language instructions to be generated from a special type of assembler-language instruction known as a *macro instruction*. Such instructions are especially useful for input/output programming. For example, the programmer can write a single GET macro instruction to cause a pretested sequence of machine-language instructions for obtaining data to be inserted at that point in the program. In general, however, a one-for-one correspondence is typical between assembler-language instructions and machine-language instructions created from them.

High-level programming languages are less rigid than low-level programming languages; the programmer has much more freedom in writing a program. Such a language is said to be *free-form*. Generally, the source-program statements do not have to be written in exactly prescribed positions on coding lines.

A high-level language is to a large extent *machine-independent*. To appreciate this characteristic, suppose that you are the manager of an organization or of an information system department. Because of an increased workload, or because a system development effort now underway requires capabilities that your present computer system does not have, a new system has been selected. The relationship between the old and the new systems may be either of the following:

- The new system is completely different and will not accept the machine-language programs run on the old system.
- The new system will accept the machine-language programs run on the old system, but the programs were not designed to take advantage of the new system's special capabilities and features.

In the first case, all existing programs will have to be rewritten if they are to run on the new system. In the second case, you may choose not to rewrite them, but your organization may be little better off than it was before.

If, however, the programs used in the old system were written in a high-level language, your staff may be able to take those programs, in their source-program form, and submit them as input to a language-processor program designed for the new system. This program will make use of the new system's features and develop, for each source program, an object program in the new system's machine language. It is only fair to note that some modifications to the source programs may be necessary. Such modifications will be much less than the work required to rewrite programs, however.

Some high-level languages, such as COBOL and FORTRAN, can be used to write source programs for execution on computers made by different manufacturers. Therefore, a programmer who knows one of these languages will not necessarily have to learn another programming language if a new machine is installed or the programmer changes jobs. For example, a program written in COBOL can be executed on any one of several computers as long as a COBOL compiler program written in the machine language of that particular computer is available to translate COBOL statements into machine language. In contrast, as we learned earlier, machine-language and assembler-language programs written for a particular computer (or family of computers) cannot generally be executed on other computers.

Since the 1960s, organizations such as the American National Standards Institute (ANSI) and the International Standards Organization (ISO) have worked to develop standards for high-level programming languages. These efforts have resulted in very detailed guidelines, or language definitions, that language-processor designers are encouraged to follow. The major objectives of standardization are to create greater uniformity in implementation of a particular language and to determine what modifications or extensions to the language are required. Ease of programmer training and interchangeability of programs are direct user benefits that can be achieved widely only through standardization.

Like an assembler-language program, a high-level-language program must be translated to a machine-language form before it can be executed. The language-processor program that performs the translation may be either a compiler or an interpreter.

A *compiler program* is like an assembler in that it translates each statement of a source program into equivalent machine-language instructions. It creates an object program in primary storage, which can then be executed immediately or saved in secondary storage for execution at a later time. A second output of the *compilation run* is a *source-program listing* that shows the programmer's source statements as they were provided as input to the compiler. (See Figure 13-3.) Unlike an assembly listing, however, a source-program listing does not display the machine-language instructions of the object program. Since a high-level-language programmer does not direct the computer in machine-oriented terms,

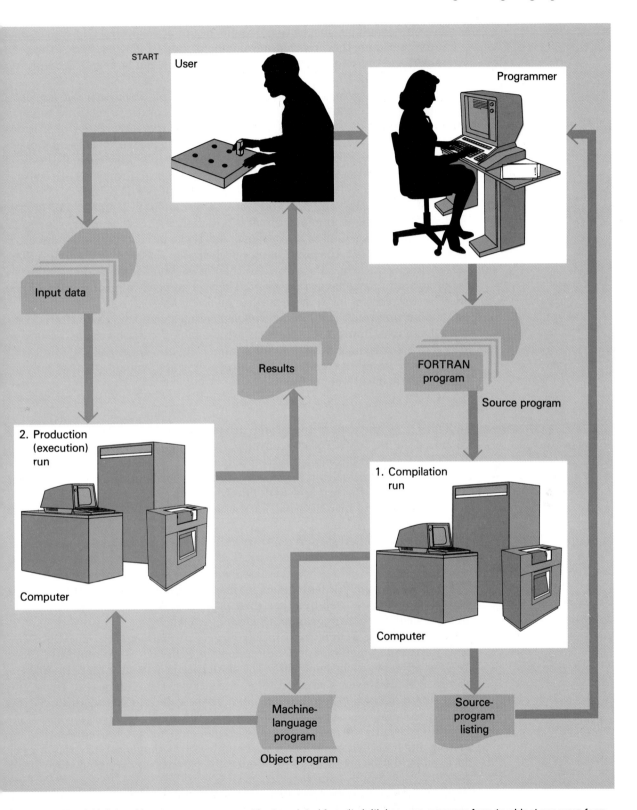

START

User

Programmer

Input data

Results

FORTRAN program

Source program

2. Production (execution) run

1. Compilation run

Computer

Computer

Machine-language program

Object program

Source-program listing

IGURE 13-3 A high-level-language program must be translated from its initial source-program form to object-program form efore it can be loaded into primary storage to direct the computer.

the machine-language instructions would be of little interest or value. The similarity between the program-development steps followed when using an assembler, and those followed when using a compiler, can be seen by comparing Figures 13-3 and 13-1.

An *interpreter program* reads the statements of a source program on a statement-by-statement basis. It determines the operations required to carry out each statement and causes the computer to perform those operations immediately. The interpreter does not create a sequence of machine-language instructions that can be saved and executed again at a later time. To reuse a program, the programmer must save it in source-program form and then cause it to be translated as well as executed again whenever reuse is required.

In many environments, an interpreter program is a valuable tool during program development. It allows direct interaction with the computer system as translation and execution of a program occur. If the interpreter detects an error in a source statement, the programmer is alerted to the error immediately. The programmer can correct the error and then cause translation and execution of the program to continue at that point. There is no need to resubmit the entire program for translation as there is when an assembler or a compiler is used.

Compiler programs have been developed for all common high-level programming languages. Interpreter programs are available for those most often used in interactive environments. If you are a microcomputer user, you may find that both a BASIC compiler and a BASIC interpreter are available for use on your system. The same is true for Pascal.

FORTRAN

FORTRAN is the oldest high-level programming language. A group was organized in the mid-1950s to develop the language. Programs written in FORTRAN were first compiled successfully in 1957. Since that time, FORTRAN compilers have been written for most computers. The language is clearly a "big hit." Members of the original FORTRAN design group met at IBM's Santa Teresa Laboratory, in California, in the summer of 1982 to celebrate FORTRAN's 25th anniversary.

The name FORTRAN is derived from FORmula TRANslator. At the time the language was developed, most computer users were engineers, scientists, and mathematicians. FORTRAN was created with their needs in mind. It works well for research and analytical problems in science, engineering, and business. It is simple enough to be used by other than professional programmers to express problem solutions in a programming-language form.

The language of FORTRAN consists largely of mathematical notation. The rules for forming mathematical expressions in FORTRAN are similar to those for forming expressions in algebra. The similarity is evident in the examples in Figure 13-4. However, there are some exceptions. For example, to cause the value stored in location A to be multiplied by the value stored in location B, the FORTRAN programmer cannot write AB; the multiply operator must be specified explicitly so A*B is required. Exponents cannot be represented by writing numerals half a line above base numbers (3^5); they must be written with the exponentiation operator (3**5). Generally, parentheses are used more often in FORTRAN than in common mathematics.

One-letter symbols are shown in Figure 13-4 to emphasize the similarities between FORTRAN and common mathematics. Usually, the programmer can

ALGEBRAIC EXPRESSION	FORTRAN EQUIVALENT
$X = A + \dfrac{B}{C} - D$	$X = A + B/C - D$
$X = \dfrac{A + B}{C - D}$	$X = (A + B)/(C - D)$
$C = X \times Y^Z$	$C = X*Y**Z$
$C = (X \times Y)^Z$	$C = (X*Y)**Z$
$C = \dfrac{L}{M} \times N$	$C = L/M*N$
$C = \dfrac{L}{MN}$	$C = L/(M*N)$

FIGURE 13-4
The FORTRAN language is similar to common mathematics, with minimal changes that allow all values to be written on the coding line.

use more meaningful names. For example, RATE can stand for an applicable discount rate. A name that stands for a single data item in this way is called a *single*, or *simple*, *variable*. Other names can be used to represent groups of similar data items, known as *arrays*. Such names are called *array variables*. To refer to particular elements of an array, the programmer uses *subscripts*. Thus, if TEMPS is a four-element array, correct references to its elements are TEMPS(1), TEMPS(2), TEMPS(3), and TEMPS(4). Because these names are meaningful, they serve well as documentation for other people who must read and understand the program or modify it at a later time.

The basic element in a FORTRAN program is the *statement*. The types of statements commonly included in a FORTRAN program are summarized in Figure 13-5. There are many ways these and other kinds of statements can be used. For many user applications, however, relatively simple statements of the types shown in Figure 13-5 are sufficient.

In 1962 ANSI took on the task of standardizing the FORTRAN language. Out of this effort, in 1966, came two standard versions: FORTRAN and a subset of FORTRAN called Basic FORTRAN. An enhanced definition of the language known as FORTRAN 77 was accepted as a standard in the late 1970s (ANSI standard X3.9). This standard is now widely implemented. It provides support of character data, a block IF statement for use in structured programming, and internal files (held in primary storage throughout processing, thereby avoiding time-consuming I/O to secondary-storage devices).

Although designed originally for mathematical problem solving, FORTRAN is often used to write business application programs. Because certain I/O operations and certain operations on nonnumeric data cannot be expressed in FORTRAN, it is not particularly well suited for problems involving file maintenance, editing of data, or production of documents. Whether or not FORTRAN should be selected as the programming language for a particular

CLASSIFICATION	EXAMPLE	PURPOSE
Assignment	PAY = HOURS * RATE RESULT = 1.5 * (BASE/3.) LOGVAR = LAST.GT.FIRST	To perform some arithmetic or logical operation, storing a result in a location identified by a variable name
Input/Output	READ (5,100) A, B, C WRITE (6,250) SUM, PROD	To read data from an input device or write information to an output device
Specification	100 FORMAT (2F3.1,F4.2) 250 FORMAT (I6,F5.2)	To describe the data being transferred to or from an input/output device
Control	GO TO 300 IF (LIM.NE.20) GO TO 60 STOP	To direct the flow of control during processing

FIGURE 13-5
A few basic types of statements are included in most FORTRAN programs.

program should be determined largely by the kinds of operations required. When numerous complex arithmetic calculations are necessary, FORTRAN is generally appropriate. Of course, a FORTRAN compiler must be available to translate the programmer's source statements into machine-readable code.

COBOL The initial direction for the development of a COmmon Business-Oriented Language (COBOL) was set in May 1959 in a meeting at the Pentagon. Attending the meeting were representatives of the federal government, computer manufacturers, and the user community. At that time, available high-level programming languages were strongly identified with a single manufacturer. The meeting participants agreed that a language developed independently for use on many manufacturers' computers was required. As the name COBOL implies, it was to be a common language; it was also to be a language designed primarily for writing business application programs.

COBOL looks much like English. In fact, a primary objective of the designers of COBOL was that it should be meaningful to even the casual reader. Their success in meeting this objective is demonstrated by the COBOL coding in Figure 13-6.

The structure of COBOL is comparable to that of a book. The basic element of a COBOL program is the *sentence* (the COBOL counterpart to the statement in FORTRAN). The next level in the structural hierarchy is the *paragraph*. Paragraphs are followed by *sections* and *divisions,* in order as named.

There are four divisions in a COBOL program: Identification, Environment, Data, and Procedure. The *Identification division* identifies the program. At a minimum, the program must be assigned a name. Information such as the writer of the program, the date it was written, the date it was compiled, and security requirements can also be included.

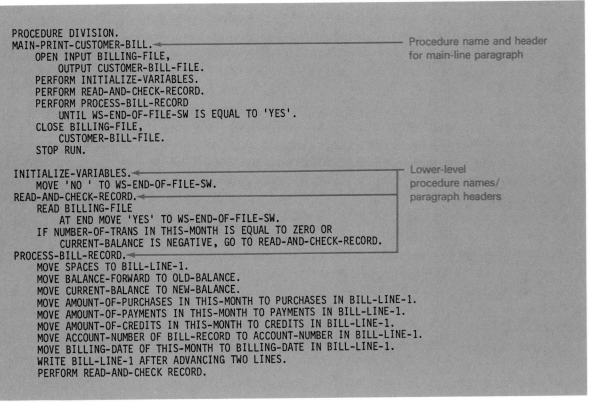

```
PROCEDURE DIVISION.
MAIN-PRINT-CUSTOMER-BILL.◄─────────────────────────────────
    OPEN INPUT BILLING-FILE,
        OUTPUT CUSTOMER-BILL-FILE.
    PERFORM INITIALIZE-VARIABLES.
    PERFORM READ-AND-CHECK-RECORD.
    PERFORM PROCESS-BILL-RECORD
        UNTIL WS-END-OF-FILE-SW IS EQUAL TO 'YES'.
    CLOSE BILLING-FILE,
        CUSTOMER-BILL-FILE.
    STOP RUN.

INITIALIZE-VARIABLES.◄────────────────────────────────
    MOVE 'NO ' TO WS-END-OF-FILE-SW.
READ-AND-CHECK-RECORD.◄───────────────────────────────
    READ BILLING-FILE
        AT END MOVE 'YES' TO WS-END-OF-FILE-SW.
    IF NUMBER-OF-TRANS IN THIS-MONTH IS EQUAL TO ZERO OR
        CURRENT-BALANCE IS NEGATIVE, GO TO READ-AND-CHECK-RECORD.
PROCESS-BILL-RECORD.◄─
    MOVE SPACES TO BILL-LINE-1.
    MOVE BALANCE-FORWARD TO OLD-BALANCE.
    MOVE CURRENT-BALANCE TO NEW-BALANCE.
    MOVE AMOUNT-OF-PURCHASES IN THIS-MONTH TO PURCHASES IN BILL-LINE-1.
    MOVE AMOUNT-OF-PAYMENTS IN THIS-MONTH TO PAYMENTS IN BILL-LINE-1.
    MOVE AMOUNT-OF-CREDITS IN THIS-MONTH TO CREDITS IN BILL-LINE-1.
    MOVE ACCOUNT-NUMBER OF BILL-RECORD TO ACCOUNT-NUMBER IN BILL-LINE-1.
    MOVE BILLING-DATE OF THIS-MONTH TO BILLING-DATE IN BILL-LINE-1.
    WRITE BILL-LINE-1 AFTER ADVANCING TWO LINES.
    PERFORM READ-AND-CHECK RECORD.
```

Procedure name and header for main-line paragraph

Lower-level procedure names/ paragraph headers

FIGURE 13-6 The Procedure division of this COBOL program directs the computer to read customer records and use the data they contain to write customer bills.

The *Environment division* describes the type of computer that will compile the program and the type that will execute it. It relates files to be used by the program to specific I/O devices. In effect, it is the link between the machine-independent divisions of the program and the equipment used. If a COBOL program initially written for one computer system is to be compiled and executed on a different computer system, the Environment division of the program is most susceptible to change.

The *Data division* describes all data to be processed by the program. This includes not only input and output files and the items within the files but also data items developed and processed internally. The number of characters, types of characters, decimal-point locations, and the like, must be specified. Important features of COBOL are the ability to process alphabetic or alphanumeric as well as numeric data, and to perform a wide variety of file I/O operations on sequential, indexed, and direct files.

The *Procedure division* contains the program logic. It tells the processing steps to be performed during program execution and the order in which the computer is to perform them. As noted at the top of Figure 13-6, this example shows the Procedure division of a COBOL program. The COBOL sentences control processing within a common business application: printing customer bills. COBOL PERFORM verbs in the main-line, or control, paragraph (MAIN-PRINT-CUSTOMER-BILL) cause control to be transferred to (and then returned from) lower-level processing paragraphs. Thus, we see that COBOL is well suited to top-down, modular program development. Each paragraph can, in many respects, be treated as a program module. The basic patterns of structured programming are easy to code within these modules. The advantages of structured programming are important when writing large business application programs—programs that are likely to be used for several years and that will have to be changed to meet users' changing requirements.

Other important advantages of COBOL are that it employs the vocabulary of the business world and that it tends to be self-documenting. Few explanatory comments are needed. However, COBOL is not designed for the inexperienced user who wants to write programs. It assumes an understanding of processing concepts and imposes some rather inflexible coding disciplines. Few programmers attempt to write COBOL programs without the aid of COBOL coding forms that provide positioning guidelines (A margin, B margin, etc., as defined in COBOL). The language is more difficult to learn than, say, FORTRAN, but easier to use than a machine-oriented programming language.

The federal government has continued to play an important part in encouraging widespread use of COBOL. The ANS COBOL standard was first established in 1968. Efforts to further define and enhance the language have led to continuing work in standardization. The current ANS COBOL standard (X3.23) was approved in 1974. COBOL implementations that conform to this standard are said to support ANS COBOL 74. Some users expect approval of a new ANS COBOL standard by the mid-1980s. However, the draft initially proposed contained some new reserved words and did not contain some language features of the existing standard. If new compilers enforced these changes, many existing COBOL programs would not compile properly. From some users' points of view, existing software libraries worth millions of dollars would thus be in jeopardy. These users have strongly objected to the draft. A revised draft of the proposed standard, offered in mid-1983, reflected changes in response to these users' comments.

The objective of making COBOL as English-like as possible has led to some disadvantages. COBOL programs tend to be long and wordy. (We showed only one page of a program in Figure 13-6. If we had shown all divisions of the program, Figure 13-6 would have been much longer. Not uncommonly, the source-program listing of a COBOL program extends for 20 or more pages.) A large COBOL compiler program is needed to handle all the COBOL source statements with many options and in various formats that can be provided as input. Large amounts of primary storage are required for the COBOL compiler instructions and data areas. As a result, COBOL compilers that will run on minis and micros are not as readily available as those for large machines. Nevertheless, COBOL is by far the favored language for business applications.

PL/I   As noted above, FORTRAN was designed primarily for scientific problem solving. COBOL was developed for business, or commercial, programming. For a while, this distinction was valid. A similar distinction existed in hardware. Now, however, computer systems are designed and used for a broad range of activities. The business programmer may be confronted by long or difficult series of computations in statistical forecasting, operations research, and so on. The scientific programmer needs a language to simplify the task of submitting problems and to sort and edit the data that provides solutions to these problems.

More and more, computer installations are handling both scientific and business programming needs.

For these reasons, Programming Language I (PL/I) was conceived. In 1963, representatives from SHARE and GUIDE,* together with IBM, set out to develop PL/I as a general-purpose programming language. It was to be used by programmers at all levels for all types of tasks. IBM released the first generally available PL/I compiler in 1966. It was designed for use on IBM's System/360 computers.

Some general characteristics and features of PL/I are shown in Figure 13-7. Part A shows a complete mortgage-processing program. The program is only eight lines in length, yet it directs the computer in performing many operations. The PL/I compiler replaces each PL/I source statement by a sequence of detailed instructions that tell the computer how the operations are to be done. The same mortgage-processing program is written on only two coding lines in Figure 13-7B. For ease of reading and maintenance, this style of coding is not generally advisable. However, for our current purposes, it emphasizes the free-form coding flexibility available to PL/I users.

You can probably understand the program in Figure 13-7A with little difficulty. Values for mortgage number, old balance, current payment, and interest rate for a particular customer (mortgagee) are read into primary storage. The interest due is calculated by multiplying old balance by interest rate, and then dividing by 12 because monthly payments are being made. The result, or interest, is subtracted from the current payment to see how much is being repaid against the principal. This amount is subtracted from the old balance to determine the new balance of the loan. The mortgage number, old balance, and calculated amounts are provided as output. Then control is transferred back to the beginning of the program to do the same calculations for another mortgagee. When all customer data has been processed, implementation-defined end-of-file processing occurs.

In PL/I, as in FORTRAN, addition and other arithmetic operations can be specified by the standard operators $+$, $-$, $/$, $*$, and $**$. A simple PL/I statement is:

$$INCOME = DIVIDENDS + INCOME;$$

This statement differs from a similar FORTRAN statement only in the presence of the semicolon. In PL/I, the semicolon serves as a statement terminator. Because the semicolon is recognized as a terminator, coding like that shown in Figure 13-7B is allowed. Part of a statement or many statements can be written on a single coding line.

Addition can also be specified by a PL/I statement that looks like COBOL, say:

$$SUM = ADD (DIVIDENDS, INCOME, 8, 2);$$

---

*Both SHARE and GUIDE are international organizations of IBM computer users. SHARE was formed in 1955; its membership includes a broad cross section of the computing industry—industrial, government, and university computing installations in both scientific and business data-processing environments. GUIDE, organized in 1956, originally restricted its scope of interest to commercially oriented users, but has broadened its activities to include all types of users. A major purpose of both groups is to foster the development and dissemination of information of mutual interest and value. Project meetings, workshops, lectures, and similar programs are conducted regularly. Meeting notes, research, the results of user experiences, ideas, and comments are made available through numerous publications.

A. A well-formatted PL/I mortgage-processing program

```
1  MORTGAGE:  PROCEDURE  OPTIONS  (MAIN);
2  NEXTCARD:  GET DATA (MORNO, OBAL, PAYM, RATE);
3           CHARGE = OBAL × RATE / 12;
4           PRINPAID = PAYM - CHARGE;
5           BALANCE = OBAL - PRINPAID;
6           PUT DATA (MORNO, OBAL, CHARGE, PRINPAID, BALANCE);
7           GO TO NEXTCARD;
8  END MORTGAGE;
```

B. An alternate free-form coding style available to PL/I users

```
1  MORT:PROCEDURE OPTIONS(MAIN);S:GET DATA(M,Z,B,Y);X=Z×Y/12;A=B-X;
2  C=Z-A;PUT DATA(M,Z,X,A,C);GO TO S;END MORT;
```

FIGURE 13-7   A program to compute the current interest charge, current payment, and remaining balance on a loan can be written in PL/I using either a formatted (A) or free-form (B) style of coding.

This statement directs the computer to add the value of DIVIDENDS to INCOME and put the result in SUM, which is an eight-position field having two positions to the right of a decimal point. ADD, MULTIPLY, DIVIDE, TAN (find the tangent), TRUNC (truncate), LOG (find the logarithm), and ABS (determine absolute value) are a few of the *built-in functions* available in PL/I. The programmer need only specify the function by name and provide input values to cause a required operation to be performed. The function names are key words, but unlike COBOL, PL/I key words are not reserved words. The programmer can use them for other purposes, too.

The basic element of a PL/I program is the *statement*. Statements are combined into larger elements called *groups* and *blocks*. A group is headed by a DO statement. A block may be either a begin block or a procedure (headed by a BEGIN or PROCEDURE statement, respectively). It can be included in or called by other blocks to form a complete PL/I program. Use of the block concept permits symbolic names to be known in only certain parts of a program, or to have one meaning in one part of a program and another meaning in other parts of the program. Storage can be reserved for a variable when control is transferred to a block. It can be freed when control is passed from the block. This support of the block concept helps to make PL/I especially suitable for structured programming.

Because PL/I is designed as a general-purpose language to meet all programming needs, it is both extensive and sophisticated. So that beginning programmers as well as experienced ones can use the language, it is defined in a modular fashion. Beginners need to learn only those language features that satisfy their immediate programming requirements. Experienced programmers can use advanced features of the language to solve complex problems. In most programming situations in which alternatives exist, the PL/I compiler makes certain assumptions (called *defaults*) if no choice is stated by the programmer. In each case, the default is the alternative most often required. Because of the default concept, less coding is required on the part of the programmer. Indeed, the programmer may not even know all possible alternatives, or that alternatives exist in some programming situations.

Users who are well versed in a language such as FORTRAN or COBOL are often reluctant to learn a new programming language. Many FORTRAN and COBOL programs already existed when PL/I was introduced, and users of the programs have tended to stick with these languages, even in subsequent revisions of the programs. Like COBOL compilers, PL/I compilers tend to be large and sophisticated; they require lots of primary storage. Therefore, the full PL/I language is not generally available on small computer systems.

A full PL/I standard (X3.53) was approved by ANSI in 1976. A second standard covering a general-purpose subset of PL/I (X3.74) was approved in 1981. Digital Research, a leader in software development, supports this subset as the primary (but not only) language for developing application programs to run under its CP/M operating system. Since CP/M is widely used on microcomputer systems, Digital Research's support of the PL/I subset has led to increased awareness of it. (We'll say more about CP/M in the next chapter.)

Some extremely powerful features of PL/I are not currently available in other common high-level programming languages. For this reason, PL/I is used extensively by some large organizations (McAuto, DuPont, and Standard Oil of California, for example) for major system and business application programming. (See Figure 13-8.)

BASIC BASIC was originally created in the 1960s for use with the computer system at Dartmouth College. As its name (from Beginners' All-purpose Symbolic

FIGURE 13-8
Firms such as McAuto, which provide computer services to many organizations nationwide, often choose PL/I as the programming language for business applications. (*Courtesy Mohawk Data Sciences*)

Instruction Code) implies, it was intended to be an easy-to-learn programming language that students could use to solve simple problems in many subject areas. Within a few hours, a novice programmer (who may not have considered himself or herself a programmer, but rather an engineer, researcher, or whatever) could write and execute programs of modest complexity. At that time, the system at Dartmouth was unique in that it offered a capability now often taken for granted: Users at geographically distributed terminals could interact with the computer at what appeared to be the same time. (The system was based on the concept of time sharing, which we'll learn about in Chapter 14.) BASIC was designed primarily for use in interactive (conversational) computing environments.

As the availability and use of systems with interactive capabilities increased, so did that of BASIC. When microcomputers such as the TRS-80, Apple, and IBM PC arrived on the scene, the potential for increased use of BASIC arrived also. It's safe to say that this potential has been realized. The number of BASIC users now exceeds one million. Hundreds more are being introduced to BASIC daily. To many of these user-programmers, the terms *BASIC* and *programming* are synonymous.

Figure 13-9 shows a BASIC program to convert temperatures recorded in Fahrenheit to Celsius. Since we've seen BASIC programs before (in Chapters 2 and 12), you can probably follow it easily. Each statement is entered on a separate line, identified by a unique line number. When line-number increments other than 1 are used (10, in this example), it is easy to insert statements within existing sequences. It is also easy to delete and replace statements by referring to line numbers.

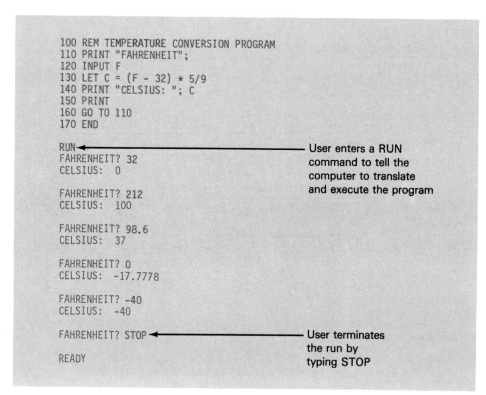

FIGURE 13-9
This BASIC program directs the computer to stop and wait until a user provides a Fahrenheit value as input, then provide the corresponding Celsius value as output.

```
100 REM TEMPERATURE CONVERSION PROGRAM
110 PRINT "FAHRENHEIT";
120 INPUT F
130 LET C = (F - 32) * 5/9
140 PRINT "CELSIUS: "; C
150 PRINT
160 GO TO 110
170 END

RUN
FAHRENHEIT? 32
CELSIUS:  0

FAHRENHEIT? 212
CELSIUS:  100

FAHRENHEIT? 98.6
CELSIUS:  37

FAHRENHEIT? 0
CELSIUS:  -17.7778

FAHRENHEIT? -40
CELSIUS:  -40

FAHRENHEIT? STOP

READY
```

User enters a RUN command to tell the computer to translate and execute the program

User terminates the run by typing STOP

To cause a BASIC program that's been entered into computer storage to be translated and executed, the user enters a RUN command (or its equivalent). Four types of BASIC statements that control processing operations will be encountered during the execution of the program in Figure 13-8. The PRINT "FAHRENHEIT"; statement (statement 110) causes the word FAHRENHEIT to be printed on the terminal. The INPUT F statement causes the computer to print out a question mark and then pause until a value for F is entered from the terminal. Then computation proceeds. The LET statement indicates that a symbol written on the left side of an equal sign (in this case, C) is to be given the value represented by the expression on the right (here (F − 32)*5/9). The word CELSIUS, followed by a colon, and the computed value for C are printed by the second PRINT statement.

The effect of the statement containing only the key word PRINT is to skip one print line. The GO TO statement causes an unconditional branch to statement 110. This sequence of processing steps is repeated as long as input is provided. Since there is no provision for stopping program execution in the program itself, the user must terminate the run by keying in STOP.

As we saw earlier, the REM statement is used to provide remarks for documentation purposes. The END statement in BASIC is similar to the END statement in FORTRAN or PL/I. It tells the language-processor program that this is the last statement coded by the user-programmer.

In many respects, the operators and operations of BASIC are similar to those of FORTRAN. Their arithmetic capabilities are similar. In BASIC as initially defined, a symbolic name that represents numeric data can be a single letter or a letter followed by a digit. Some implementations permit the use of a single letter followed by a dollar sign to represent character (alphabetic or alphanumeric) data. In either case, the values represented may be single data items or arrays. Some FORTRAN programmers are moving to BASIC to take advantage of its especially convenient matrix-handling capabilities. These capabilities simplify work with tables defined as two-dimensional arrays.

On some systems, BASIC programs can be submitted for translation and execution just like COBOL, FORTRAN, or PL/I programs (review Figure 13-3), as well as entered interactively. Of course, such programs should not contain INPUT statements. LET statements as well as READ statements that access data items listed in DATA statements are alternative ways of providing data to be processed. Many implementations include extensions to BASIC that also provide file-processing capabilities. With these extensions, BASIC programs can be written to create, read, and update user data files.

A BASIC standard covering a minimal subset of the BASIC language (X3.60) was approved by ANSI in 1978. Unfortunately, the standard was somewhat late in coming and includes only a small subset of the language supported by most BASIC language processors. The popularity of the language and user demands for additional features have led to a patchwork quilt of manufacturer-dependent BASIC's, extended BASIC's, business BASIC's, and so on. A user who wants his or her programs to be usable on numerous computer systems (i.e., to be portable) is well advised to check whether or not certain language features are common across BASIC language processors, rather than take advantage of them simply because they are convenient and available on the system being used. At this writing, an enhanced BASIC standard has been made available for public comment. Even after such a standard is approved, conformance will be a while in coming.

PASCAL As with BASIC, the initial impetus for the development of Pascal came from the educational community. Professor Niklaus Wirth of Zurich, Switzerland, undertook the design of Pascal in the late 1960s with two principal objectives in mind:

- To create a language suitable to teach programming as a systematic discipline (not a hit-and-miss art) based on certain fundamental concepts clearly and naturally reflected by the language
- To provide for implementations of the language that are both reliable and efficient on available computers

Though many other programming languages already existed, Wirth argued that their features and concepts too often could not be explained logically. He named his new language "Pascal" in honor of Blaise Pascal, a brilliant French philosopher and mathematician of the 17th century. By age 18, Pascal had developed the first mechanical adding machine. By age 31, he had established the fundamental precepts of both probability theory and integral calculus. A first Pascal compiler was operational in 1970. It ran on Control Data Corporation's CDC 6000-series computers.

Initially, little attention was paid to Wirth or to Pascal. The "software crisis" of the late 1960s and early 1970s, however, caused both business professionals and educators to take a hard look at the new language. Pascal had at least one characteristic that warranted attention: It was well suited to the construction of modular, well-structured programs.

Kenneth Bowles, an instructor at the University of California at San Diego, recognized that one factor needed for increased use of Pascal was the ability to run Pascal programs on many different computers. Since microcomputers were cheapest and readily obtainable, Pascal implementations for microcomputers seemed especially desirable.

Bowles and his students developed a "pseudocompiler" that generated a form of pseudocode (*P-code*) rather than machine-language instructions (native code, or *N-code*). This P-code is a set of instructions that cannot be executed directly by any computer. Creating a P-code machine simulator, or interpreter, that runs on a real computer for the purpose of analyzing the P-code and triggering the right actions by that computer is a relatively simple task, however. Pascal pseudocompiler and P-code interpreter implementations (known collectively as UCSD Pascal compilers) are now available for TRS-80, Apple, and other microcomputer families. Pascal is also available on a wide variety of larger systems. The capabilities of the language are such that Pascal programs may be run as batch jobs or keyed in and run interactively by terminal users.

Figure 13-10 shows a complete Pascal program. Its function is to determine whether or not an integer value entered as input by a terminal or microcomputer user is a prime number, divisible only by itself and 1. Like all Pascal programs, this program has a heading and a body, or block. The first part of the body contains a declaration of every user-chosen symbolic name. Here, N (the name for the value entered as input) and TRIALDIV (a trial divisor value computed during execution) are declared to be integers. NODIV (no divisor) is declared to be a Boolean value; it can take on either of two values: TRUE or FALSE.

Within the statement part of the program body, a FOR statement sets up a counter-controlled program loop. An IF statement nested within the loop causes a test to be made. To understand this test, you need to know that Pascal provides

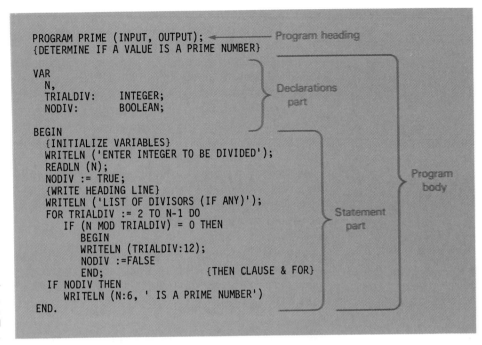

```
PROGRAM PRIME (INPUT, OUTPUT);  ◄────── Program heading
{DETERMINE IF A VALUE IS A PRIME NUMBER}

VAR
  N,
  TRIALDIV:    INTEGER;                        Declarations
  NODIV:       BOOLEAN;                         part

BEGIN
  {INITIALIZE VARIABLES}
  WRITELN ('ENTER INTEGER TO BE DIVIDED');
  READLN (N);
  NODIV := TRUE;
  {WRITE HEADING LINE}
  WRITELN ('LIST OF DIVISORS (IF ANY)');
  FOR TRIALDIV := 2 TO N-1 DO                   Statement
    IF (N MOD TRIALDIV) = 0 THEN                part
      BEGIN
      WRITELN (TRIALDIV:12);
      NODIV :=FALSE
      END;                    {THEN CLAUSE & FOR}
  IF NODIV THEN
    WRITELN (N:6, ' IS A PRIME NUMBER')
END.
```

Program body

FIGURE 13-10
Whether or not an integer value is a prime number can be determined easily with the help of the computer and this Pascal program.

not only the common arithmetic operators but also two operators designed especially for integer division operations: DIV and MOD. DIV returns the quotient of integer division, and MOD returns the remainder, if there is any. In this particular test, if the value entered for N by the user can be divided evenly by some trial divisor, the value of N MOD TRIALDIV is equal to 0. This causes the value of the trial divisor to be written as output and NODIV to be set to FALSE. If there is no trial divisor that divides N evenly, NODIV is never set to FALSE. The IF statement following the program loop causes NODIV to be tested for a value of TRUE. If NODIV has a value of TRUE, the user receives a message saying the value entered as input is a prime number.

Notice that both bracketed comments and indentions can be used in a Pascal program to clarify the program logic. The up-front declaration of meaningful names also helps. The Pascal language was designed with user-programmers in mind. Pascal programs can be so designed also.

In September 1981 the Institute of Electrical and Electronic Engineers (IEEE) Standards Board agreed upon a Pascal standard. At that time, a joint ANSI/IEEE Standards Committee was (and still is) also considering Pascal standardization. Pascal's suitability for application programming—as opposed to system programming and education—remains in dispute by some. They argue that Pascal's I/O capabilities are inconvenient to use and inadequate for the extensive I/O requirements of typical business application programs. Many Pascal implementations include language extensions that, together with the rapidly increasing use of micros, are stimulating the increased use of Pascal.

APL Like BASIC and Pascal, APL (A Programming Language) is well suited for interactive problem solving. Specifications for the language first appeared in Kenneth E. Iverson's book *A Programming Language* (1962). Initially known as

Iverson's language, APL was designed to permit users to specify complex algorithms succinctly. It is interesting to note, however, that the language was developed to solve immediate real-world problems – not necessarily mathematical ones. A subset of Iverson's language was implemented at IBM's T. J. Watson Research Center in 1966. Since 1970, IBM has offered an APL language processor as a program product. Several vendors (including IBM) now offer access to APL for interactive problem solving via communication network facilities.

APL data is either numeric or character. A significant feature of APL (and a marked contrast to Pascal) is that variables are not declared to be either of these types. Any variable may be assigned data of either type during program execution; its current content determines its type. The primary data structure is the array, and a powerful set of operators is available for manipulating arrays. (See Figure 13-11.) IBM's APL2 compiler, announced in 1982, allows users to store both numeric and character data in a single array and to define additional operators.

Any APL statement without the assignment operator $\leftarrow$ is interpreted as beginning with ☐ $\leftarrow$ It causes output. Thus, the numbers at the left in Figure 13-11 are results that appear at the user's terminal. Similarly, a statement such

	STATEMENT	FUNCTION
	A $\leftarrow$ 1 3 5 7	Assigns 4-component list, or vector, to A
16	$+/A$	Performs addition reduction over A
7	$\lceil /A$	Finds the maximum value in A
4	ρA	Interrogates the shape of A (a vector, or one-dimensional array, of length 4)
1 2 3 4 5 6	$i6$	Generates a vector of consecutive integers from 1 through the argument (6 in this case)
	C $\leftarrow i6$	As above, but assigns the results as a vector to C
1 2 3 4 5 6	3 2 ρ C	Creates a 3 × 2 matrix, or two-dimensional array, from the vector C
→23		Transfers to statement 23
→3 2 1 × 7 6 5		Transfers to statement 21
→5 + (y ≥ 10) + (y ≥ 12)		Transfers to statement 5 if y < 10, to 6 if 10 ≤ y < 12, or to 7 if y ≥ 12

FIGURE 13-11
APL data-manipulation and branching operators can be used to direct the computer in performing both simple and complex functions.

Note: The shaded values at the left are written as output when the statements opposite them are executed during processing.

as $C \leftarrow 40 \times \square$ requests that the number by which 40 is to be multiplied be provided as input. The computer system stops and waits for user action at the terminal.

Each statement in an APL program is identified by a line number. Hence, integers can be used to refer to statements for purposes of branching. (See the last three statements in Figure 13-11.) If the result of an evaluation made to determine a branch destination is an array, the first element of the array is taken as the line number. Range specifications can be used, as in the last example in Figure 13-11, to provide branching alternatives.

The strong points of APL are (1) its dynamic features for specifying types and shapes of data, and (2) its few basic operations that, in combination, provide many functions. Since APL includes a wealth of operators defined to operate on arrays of data, there is no need for many of the iteration and control operations commonly found in programs written in the other high-level languages we have discussed.

To use APL effectively, the user needs a keyboard that contains most or all of the characters in the rather large and unusual APL character set. Initially, this equipment requirement was a serious drawback. However, relatively low-cost terminals and interactive systems capable of handling many different type fonts (including the APL character set) are now available. These options, plus the availability of APL via nationwide communication networks and the enthusiasm of APL supporters, are leading to its increased use.

RPG The Report Program Generator (RPG) language was initially designed by IBM in the middle and late 1960s to duplicate the logic of punched-card equipment. Thus, minicomputers and small computer systems that used punched-card input, or that were initially acquired as replacements for punched-card data-processing systems, were often controlled primarily by programs coded in RPG. In the 1970s IBM announced an enhanced version of the RPG language, known as RPG II. RPG II compilers are now offered by many computer manufacturers for many different machines. All RPG implementations are similar, but the language is not yet standardized. RPG programs written for one computer system may not run on others. In 1979, IBM announced a further enhanced version of the language for use with its System/38 computer systems. Known as RPG III, the newer version provides database-processing capabilities.

As its name implies, the RPG language was originally designed to generate programs that produce business-oriented, printed reports as output. Initially, all reports were provided in hard-copy (paper) form. Some enhanced RPG II compilers also support the interactive design of display-screen formats for output. The success of RPG development efforts is evidenced by the fact that many organizations today rely heavily on information produced with the aid of RPG compilers.

RPG is also used for operations other than report writing. Company records stored as data in EDP-system master files on cards, tape, or disk must be updated frequently. New data must be added or old data deleted to keep such files current. These operations are called *file maintenance*. RPG can readily be used to perform them. Today, some of the most common uses of RPG are file updating for accounts receivable, accounts payable, general ledger, and inventory status. Other applications include sales analysis, distribution planning, and budgeting.

A programmer coding an RPG program does not write statements that represent sequential steps to be followed during processing. Instead, the programmer completes a series of descriptions, known as *specifications*. Commonly available RPG II compilers accept and process four basic types of specifications and two additional ones that may be needed in special situations. (See Figure 13-12.) Not all specifications are required for any one program. Even when needed, a particular specification may consist of only a few lines of coding.

Examples of two of the RPG forms are shown, in part, in Figure 13-13. As you can see, specific entries must be written in specific columns. RPG does not provide free-form coding, but English-like names and operators (see SUB on the calculation specifications) can be used. Some RPG II compilers can generate machine-language code for 30 or more different operations. These operations include add, subtract, multiply, divide, table lookup, compare, move, branch, and exit to a subroutine.

Although RPG offers significant potential for many types of applications, it is generally most useful for simple problems requiring printed reports as output. Applications should be straightforward, without complex logic, many loops, or complicated use of files. RPG is especially valuable for minicomputers and small computers because, unlike languages such as COBOL and PL/I, it does not impose large storage requirements.

GENERATOR LANGUAGES

RPG is usually thought of as a high-level programming language that can be used to generate useful output, but it is not usually thought of as a language that generates programs. However, in a sense, it does. There are other languages, known as *generator languages*, that do just that. The output of a generator-language-processor program (*application generator*, for short) is a user application program. Usually, the program consists of COBOL or BASIC source

SPECIFICATION FORM	USE
File description	Identifies each file as input and/or output and associates the file with an I/O device
Input	Describes the types of records in each input file and the locations of specific data fields in the file
Calculation	Specifies the operations to be performed, data to be used, characteristics of results, and tests to be made on results
Output format	Identifies the information to be written as output and describes its location on the data-recording medium
File extension	Is needed to provide additional information when chaining, tables, and/or direct files are to be used
Line counter	Is needed to specify line control when information is written to tape or disk for subsequent printing

FIGURE 13-12
An RPG program is created by completing specifications, the functions of which are indicated by their titles, in accord with user requirements.

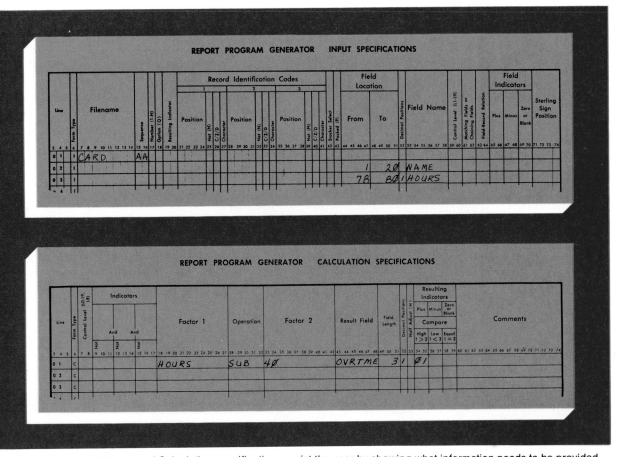

IGURE 13-13 RPG Input and Calculation specifications assist the user by showing what information needs to be provided
the computer.

statements. The program can be run, saved in secondary storage, and modified if
necessary — just like any other in-house-developed COBOL or BASIC program.

Application generators are based on the concept that about 50 percent of a
typical application program has already been written, somewhere, as part of
another application program. If a programmer has access to a library containing
reusable already-coded routines, application programs that he or she may be
asked to write are already half complete.

Though the validity of using thousands of lines of code (KLOC) as a measure of
programmer productivity is often debated, the need to get programs up and
running correctly as fast as possible is a common, well-understood objective.
Advocates of generator languages insist that even experienced programmers
can generate code much more quickly with an application generator than when
using traditional programming methods. One generator-language statement
may cause several reusable routines to be inserted in a program that is being
constructed. Why write 400 COBOL statements when four generator-language
statements will do the job? (See Figure 13-14.) The library routines are pretested
and error-free. Since the routines are standardized, a program written by one
programmer can be understood, tested, and maintained by others. In most cases,
the program is also portable; it can be used on various manufacturers' computers.

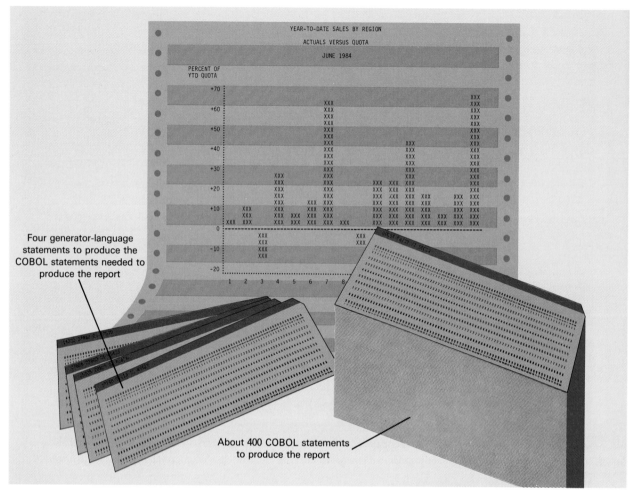

FIGURE 13-14 Generator languages help to increase productivity by making it easier for user-programmers to tell the computer what needs to be done; four generator-language statements take much less time to write than 400 COBOL statements.

Initially, application generators were large, expensive software products. They were designed to ease the workload of large, overburdened information system staffs. Now, micro-based program generators are appearing. For example, DEC offers a COBOL program generator for use with its VT180, Rainbow 100, DECmate II, and Professional 300 personal computers. It is said to allow programmers to produce more than 5000 lines of COBOL code per day. Data General offers BusiGEN, a business BASIC program generator. Programmers are freed to spend their time on system analysis and design, and on coding and checkout of user-unique, nonstandard routines. Users who are not trained programmers can interact with computers directly to get their jobs done. They need not wait until the jobs rise to the top of the priority list in the information system department. Several human communication steps—each providing opportunities for misinterpretation of requirements—are eliminated. Application generators are not substitutes for system analysis and design. They are, however, in many respects, easy-to-use front-ends that shorten the time needed for detailed program design and coding. Automated office environments may arrive faster, for example, in organizations where office personnel have access to application generators that they can use to tell computers directly about office work that needs to be done.

DA, C, AND FORTH

Since literally hundreds of programming languages exist, it's impossible for us to discuss all of them. If you've been around computers for a while, you've probably heard of many of them. Current trade publications are most likely to refer to those we've discussed and a few others. The others are:

- *Ada*–A Pascal-like language developed in the late 1970s and early 1980s in response to the U.S. Department of Defense demand for a new standardized programming language for use in embedded computer systems. The competitive language design efforts that resulted in Ada received much attention. However, standard-conforming Ada compilers tend to be large and are not yet available for some computers. Ada's future as a general-purpose programming language remains in doubt.

- *C*–A lower-level language than PL/I or Pascal developed at Bell Labs as part of the UNIX operating system. At present, C is used mainly for system programming. It is most likely to be available on DEC computer systems, but as use of UNIX spreads, C will also. It is, in many respects, a machine-independent assembler language.

- *FORTH*–A low-level, compact language and operating system developed in the mid-1970s for use on micros. FORTH is unique in that its syntax is reverse Polish Notation (2 2 +, rather than 2 + 2). A user-programmer enters "words," uses these words to define new words tailored to the problem at hand, and then applies the extended language to solve the problem. Instead of simply assigning data items to variables, the user-programmer has to keep track of where the data items are in a first-in, first-out (FIFO) stack in memory. FORTH is sometimes characterized as a good language for good programmers.

Less well known are the special-purpose programming languages. Examples are SNOBOL (for string processing), LISP (for list processing), and SIMSCRIPT (for simulation). These languages were developed and used on large computer systems long before microcomputers became common. Logo (for students) and PILOT (for teachers) are examples of special-purpose languages supported on microcomputers.

SELECTING A LANGUAGE

How does one choose, from among the myriad of programming languages available, the language that's most appropriate for a particular system development effort?

Let's back up a bit. The first phase of the system development cycle is system analysis. The second phase is system design. In most cases, after the user requirements are understood, alternative solutions can be identified. Today, most if not all user organizations are confronted by resource constraints. The programming talent, time, and money needed for in-house system development are likely to be in short supply. Therefore, if application packages that meet or nearly meet the user requirements are available, they should be considered.

Perhaps a nearly-meets-requirements package can be customized to do the job. There's no merit in writing a new program if an acceptable one already exists. However, if detailed program design, coding, and checkout are to be undertaken for the system under development, then the selection of a programming language is a real consideration.

Usually, one assembler program is provided by the computer manufacturer for each particular family of computers. Programs can be written for the computers in the assembler language that the assembler program is designed to translate. Theoretically, any number of high-level-language processors can be written for any computer. It follows that any computer can be controlled by programs initially coded in any of several high-level programming languages, depending on the language processors available on the particular hardware configuration.

In deciding which programming language to use, then, some specific questions should be asked. Which programming languages are available? What knowledge do the assigned programmers or user-programmers have of those languages? What types of problems are the various languages designed for? These and other language selection considerations are summarized in Figure 13-15. The relative importance of the selection criteria varies, depending on the situation.

As we've seen, FORTRAN is well suited for problems involving mathematical computations. COBOL was designed with business applications in mind. BASIC was designed to provide immediate, straightforward answers to simple problems. Like BASIC, Pascal and APL can be used interactively or for batch-processing applications. Pascal, PL/I, and assembler languages are likely choices for system programming.

- Language availability

- Language knowledge of assigned programmers or user-programmers

- Suitability of the language to the particular problem or application

- Ease of learning the language

- Ease of language use for coding and for debugging; over-all program development time

- Understandability of the language and of source programs; self-documentation; ease of program maintenance

- Language standardization; program transportability

- Speed of source-program translation by the language processor; language-processor storage requirements

- Efficiency of resultant object programs in terms of number of instructions, execution speed, and storage requirements

FIGURE 13-15
Many factors must be considered when choosing the language that's most appropriate for a system development effort.

The assembler language of a computer, though more difficult to work with than high-level programming languages, can be used to express all the operations that the computer is capable of performing. If fast execution and/or minimal use of storage by the resultant object program are of primary importance, use of an assembler language may be advisable. Since programming talent and program-development time are increasingly viewed as resources that must be optimized, the trend in programming is toward increased use of high-level languages.

CHAPTER SUMMARY

1. Machine-language instructions are strings of 1s and 0s, containing the exact bit patterns for machine operations and the exact storage addresses of locations where data values are (or will be) stored.

2. Assembler languages allow the use of mnemonics such as A, L, and B as op codes and of labels such as NAME to refer to instructions and data items.

3. An assembler program translates assembler-language statements (a source program) into machine-language instructions (an object program) during an assembly run. The object program can then be loaded into primary storage to serve as the stored program during a production run.

4. High-level programming languages are procedure-oriented or problem-oriented languages. A language-processor program (compiler or interpreter) translates the high-level-language statements into machine-language form.

5. FORTRAN, the oldest high-level programming language, is well suited for research and analytical problems in science, engineering, and business.

6. COBOL was developed in the late 1950s and 1960s primarily as a common language for writing business application programs usable on many manufacturers' computers.

7. PL/I was created as a general-purpose language to be used by programmers at all levels for all types of tasks.

8. BASIC was created at Dartmouth College as an easy-to-learn programming language that students could use to solve simple problems in many subject areas. It is well suited to interactive (conversational) use.

9. Pascal was developed as a tool for teaching programming as a systematic discipline and is well suited to modular, structured programming.

10. APL's strong points are its dynamic features for data typing and shaping and its wealth of operators that provide many functions.

11. An RPG user completes specifications, which are then used to direct the computer in producing business-oriented printed reports.

12. Application generators process generator-language statements to produce application programs, thereby shortening the time needed for detailed program design and coding and freeing user-programmers to spend more time on system analysis and design.

13. Ada, C, and FORTH are three more of the hundreds of programming languages that have been developed. The language that's most appropriate for a particular system development effort must be chosen from this wide range of options.

1. Give reasons why programmers today are not writing machine-language programs.

2. (a) Explain the terms *low-level programming languages* and *high-level programming languages*.
   (b) Give examples of each.

3. Distinguish between the following: (a) source program, (b) compiler program, (c) assembler program, (d) object program, and (e) interpreter program.

4. Discuss some general characteristics of high-level programming languages.

5. (a) Why is FORTRAN an appropriate name for that programming language?
   (b) For what types of applications is FORTRAN generally preferred?

6. COBOL provides for four different areas of programmer coding responsibility. Name the divisions of a COBOL program that reflect these areas and describe the function of each division.

7. (a) What happens when an INPUT statement in a BASIC program is executed?
   (b) What does your response to part (a) indicate about the typical BASIC programming environment?

8. Why is a language such as PL/I useful?

9. (a) What is the function of the Pascal program in Figure 13-10?
   (b) Explain how each variable in the program is used.
   (c) Check your understanding of the program by creating a program flowchart or writing pseudocode to explain the program logic.
   (d) Verify the correctness of the algorithm you created in response to (c) by desk-checking it. Given the data value 29 as input, what information should be provided as output? Is it? If not, where are the errors?
   (e) Repeat (d), but use 117 as input; then use 61. Which of the data values you've processed are prime numbers?

10. Give some significant characteristics of APL.

11. Describe at least two types of applications that can be coded as RPG programs.

12. How can generator languages help to improve user productivity?

OPERATING SYSTEMS

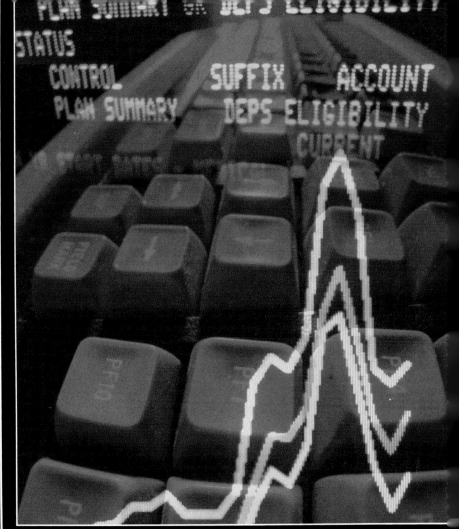

Courtesy Aetna Life and Casualty, Hartford, Conn.

Very often, we concentrate on the parts of things without seeing the whole picture. The value of individual parts is the role they play in an entire *system*. However, computers are more than just another part of a system; they are an *enhancement* of the systems of which they are a part.

Most computers can do many different kinds of tasks at one time. This is especially true in time-sharing where many users with diverse data-processing needs buy time on the same computer network. Each user may be completely unaware that others are using the network at the same time but for different purposes; the users see only their parts of the picture. The terminals they are using might be part of Tymshare, Inc.'s Tymnet network. For them, that network is operating as an integral part of their own businesses. Thus, if we look at the whole picture, we see that Tymshare and its user businesses are not only separate businesses, but also part of a large communication network, a system for information

One use of computers as an enhancement of an existing system is in the airline industry. One part of the picture we usually see is the ticket counter. A terminal at the ticket counter tells the airline representative what flights are going to our destination and which seats are available on each flight. What we usually don't see is the system of computerized baggage handling. Considering the millions of pieces of luggage handled every year, it's a technological miracle that most of them reach their intended destinations at all—a miracle made possible by computerized baggage handling. Both ticketing and baggage handling are areas of the industry whose efficiency has been improved with computers. In the case of ticketing, each representative's terminal gives him or her the whole picture as far as seating availability is concerned. In the case of baggage handling, a computer coordinates baggage routing at the airport terminal. Obviously, ticketing and baggage routing existed before computers, but computers have enabled the airlines to accomplish both with improved speed and efficiency.

Computers can be an integrating factor within businesses, as well. The Cummins Engine Company uses an NCR Data Pathing System for time-and-attendance reporting, shop-floor data collection, material-requirements planning, maintenance scheduling, and inventory control. Better-coordinated workings within a business enable it to operate more efficiently. Workloads can be distributed and capital outlays reduced.

Courtesy Sperry Corporation

ufacturers use computers to aid customers in making upholstery selections, as well as for controlling inventory and purchasing.

Using computers to better integrate internal company operations in these ways also helps to improve working relationships with other companies. Businesses whose efficiency has been enhanced by computers may also work better together as a system of businesses.

A wheat cooperative serving 56,000 farmers in Alberta, Canada, uses a network of IBM computers installed at more than 120 grain elevators for daily inventory and sales accounting. Farmers use the system to get current information on wheat prices.

Computers can be used to coordinate shipping of the wheat, by truck, to the flour mills and bakeries, who may use computers to maintain inventory and accounting information and to control their operations. The supermarket chains to which the bakeries sell may use computers to maintain their own inventory and accounting information, and to validate checks issued by customers as payment at checkout counters. Excessive inventory and, hence, waste, can be avoided, thus allowing the firms to reduce their overhead and their prices.

Courtesy IBM Corporation

14 | OPERATING SYSTEMS

Software—the part of a computer system that makes a computer different from other machines; software—the component of a computer system whereby the system can be directed to do useful work; software—where the action is in today's computing environments.

As we've seen again and again throughout this book, the capabilities of computers are expanding at fantastic rates. The importance of these capabilities to us and to others depends on the use that is made of them. William C. Norris, as chairman and chief executive officer of Control Data Corporation, has said: "The easy things in the computer field have been done. It is much simpler to develop computers than to apply them effectively."

The "applying" (that is, use and control) of a computer system is achieved primarily through software. We saw in Chapter 2 that the software may be either of two types: system programs and application programs. In this chapter, we direct most of our attention to system programs. In particular, we discuss the characteristics and capabilities of operating systems. Because operating system software is such an integral part of any computing environment (even that of a micro), every computer user needs some understanding of it.

To appreciate where we are today, it's helpful to know where we've been. Therefore, after a brief overview of both system and application software, we discuss how and why operating systems came about. We trace the evolution of major system capabilities: batch processing, online direct-access processing, multiprogramming, multiprocessing, real-time processing, time sharing, virtual storage, and virtual machines. Then we discuss portable operating systems. To help you relate the discussions of system capabilities to EDP systems in current use, specific operating systems are mentioned as examples.

SYSTEM AND APPLICATION SOFTWARE

System software directs the computer in performing tasks that are basic to proper functioning of the system or commonly needed by system users. It follows naturally that all systems have system software. However, some systems have more system software than others. The system software of one computer system may differ in many ways from that of another.

For discussion purposes, we can group system programs within three broad categories. Some or all of the programs may be available on the particular computer systems to which you have access. (See Figure 14-1.)

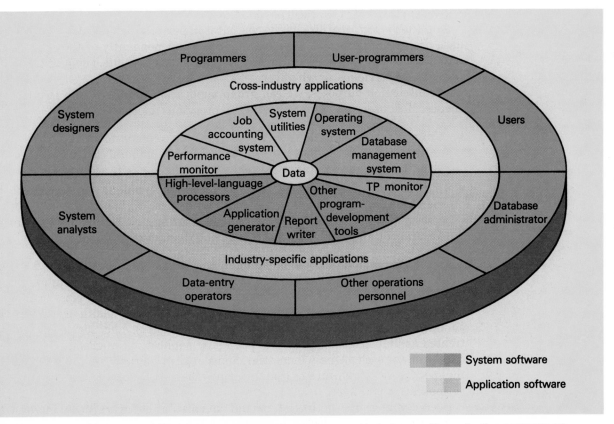

FIGURE 14-1 A diverse set of system software and both cross-industry and industry-specific application programs are needed to tell the computer how to convert data into useful information.

- *System operation*—software that manages the resources of a computer system during program execution. Examples are operating systems, database management systems, and communication (also called *teleprocessing* or *TP*) monitors.
- *System utilization*—software that manages or assists users in managing the system operation. Examples are system utility programs, job accounting systems, and performance monitors.
- *System implementation*—software that assists users in preparing programs for execution. Examples are assemblers, high-level-language processors, application generators, report writers, dump programs, trace programs, symbolic debuggers, and other program-development tools.

Traditionally, system programs have been written in low-level programming languages. A detailed knowledge of the EDP-system hardware is needed to write such programs. Therefore, personnel at user installations do not normally attempt to write them. Instead, most system programs are obtained from external sources such as (1) the computer manufacturer, (2) a software development firm that specializes in writing system programs, (3) a service company that develops or markets programs for multiple use, or (4) any combination of these sources. Some system programs are now being written in high-level languages, but that does not mean that users are now commonly writing their own system software. The system design expertise and development resources needed for such efforts are still beyond those available at most user installations.

Application software directs the computer in performing specific user-related data-processing tasks. The *application* exists independently of the computer; it's simply a job to be done—administering employee benefits, keeping track of investment portfolios, or whatever.

For discussion purposes, we can group application programs into two broad classes. Most user installations have some programs in each class.

- *Cross-industry*—programs that perform tasks common to many industries, organizations, or user groups. Examples are general ledger, financial planning (modeling), statistical analysis, and fixed-assets accounting.
- *Industry-specific*—programs that perform tasks unique to a particular industry, organization, or user group. Examples are bill-of-materials processing (discrete hard-goods manufacturing), claims management (insurance), and mortgage loan accounting (banking and finance).

To help you understand the meaning of the term *industry* as it is used here, some representative examples of industrial systems are shown in Figure 14-2. That transportation, communications, and retailing are industry classifications may come as no surprise to you. That medicine and health care, public administration (local, state, and federal government), and services can be treated as industries is not as obvious. Many application programs have been developed for each of these industries. Some of the programs are known only to the specific user organizations that developed them. Others are marketed widely as application packages.

User demands for both system and application software have increased significantly over the past 5 to 10 years. The most obvious reason for this increased demand is the overwhelming increase in the number of computer users. The EDP-system user base now includes multinational corporations,

NCR Corporation/Brown Palace Hotel

NCR Corporation

IBM Corporation

TRW Inc.

Xerox Corporation

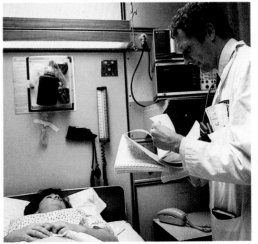

U.S. Dept. Health and Human Services

FIGURE 14-2 Users in many industries are being helped by computers under the direction of specialized application programs.

one-person households, and everything in between. Substantial improvements in hardware price/performance ratios have lowered entry-level costs and opened new application areas. A new generation of managers is (by both education and training) more aware of the types of applications that can be addressed with computer help. Confronted by determined business competitors and unfavorable economic climates in many instances, these managers are eager to capitalize on the advantages that computer processing offers. Families and individuals who have acquired computers are similarly eager to make the most of their investments.

Before 1970, EDP systems were developed and marketed as all-inclusive packages encompassing hardware, software, education, and maintenance services. Since that time, however, most computer manufacturers have adopted a policy of *separate pricing*. The major system control program (SCP) and some basic system utility programs may be supplied with the main processor. Other software components must be purchased or secured under a contractual agreement (license) from the computer manufacturer or a software vendor, or be developed in-house by the user installation. Certain hardware components (magnetic-tape units, disk storage units, and so on), as well as education and maintenance services, are obtained in a similar manner. The total cost of the system is the sum of the costs of all these items.

EARLY HISTORY OF SYSTEM SOFTWARE

Just as computer hardware has evolved through several distinct generations, system software has similarly evolved. (See Figure 14-3.) We can relate the two, but they do not proceed in a lock-step fashion. Nor can we say that the beginnings and endings of system software generations are clear-cut. We cannot assume that one generation has completely ended at the time the next generation begins. Many computers today run under the control of fourth-generation software. Fifth-generation software is being installed or is yet in development. Some users are operating at earlier levels.

Recall that first-generation computers were huge, card-oriented machines with vacuum tubes as basic components. Their operations were controlled by stored programs, but they had no operating systems. Programs were initially coded in machine language. Later, basic assembler programs, utility programs such as basic loaders, and sort routines were made available to system users.

In practice, computers of this period were used as one-department machines. A single department or division of an organization controlled all machine usage. Since the primary-storage capacity of a first-generation computer was small (even though the machine was large), only one program occupied primary storage at a time. The computer operator loaded that program into storage, readied the input and output devices it needed, and started the processor by pressing a START button on the system console. After the program had been executed, the operator repeated this procedure for the next progam. Thus, both setup time and breakdown time were required between jobs. Each job was a standalone application.

Computers of the mid-1950s still used vacuum tubes as basic components, but they were supported by a richer array of system software. All programs ready for execution were assigned identification numbers, or program ID's. They were stored in object-program form on magnetic tape. Each program was preceded by an identification record containing its program ID. A small control program

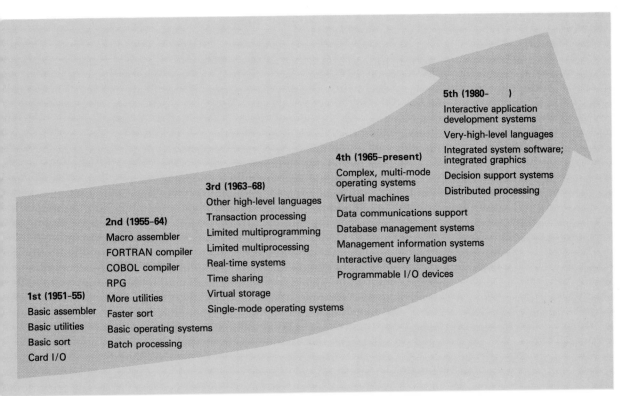

FIGURE 14-3 System software has evolved through several "generations," each having greater capabilities than the ones before it.

known as a *monitor* was loaded into primary storage. (See Figure 14-4.) It accepted as input a single card containing one program ID. The card was punched beforehand by the programmer or the computer operator. The monitor searched the magnetic tape until it found a matching program ID. Once the match was found, the monitor read (loaded) the corresponding object program into storage, beginning at a known, fixed location. After the entire program had been loaded, a branch instruction in the monitor program caused control to be transferred to that location (that is, the first instruction of the loaded program). The loaded program was then executed.

Eventually, more sophisticated monitors and more automated load procedures were developed. The monitor program remained in primary storage at all times, say in the first 1000 locations. All programs were written so they could be read into storage, beginning at a location above those needed for the monitor. The last instruction in every program was a branch back to the monitor. One program besides the monitor was present (resident) in primary storage at a time.

With this procedure, of course, the operator still had to perform many tasks: putting cards into the card reader, mounting and demounting tapes, making sure the printer had paper, and so on. Programmers began to include instructions to operators in their programs. During execution, these messages were printed out on a printer or on the system console. A PAUSE instruction was included in each program to make the computer "wait" until the necessary setup tasks had been completed. Then the operator restarted the system by pressing a

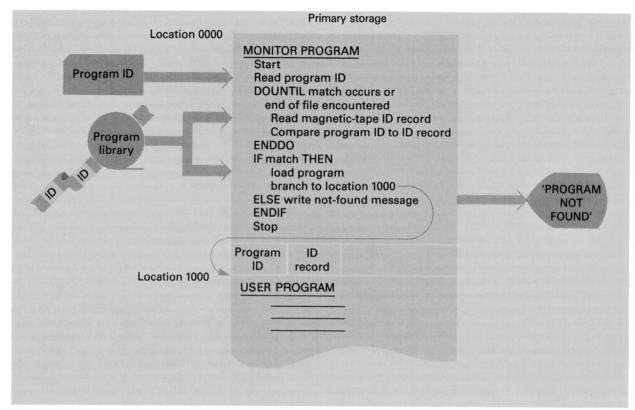

FIGURE 14-4 Early monitor programs were designed to find and load programs from magnetic tape into primary storage to direct subsequent processing.

button on the console. Needless to say, these messages were not uniform. They were often missing or incomplete. Still, too much operator intervention (and too much nonproductive time) was required.

The earliest types of operating systems were developed to alleviate this problem. These systems could handle the transition from job to job. The sequence of job executions was determined beforehand. While one job was running, an operator could mount magnetic tapes, or position cards in the card reader, or whatever, as needed for the next job. With proper scheduling, there was no longer a need to stop the computer between jobs. The operating system checked to see whether or not the I/O devices needed by a program were ready for execution. If they were, execution proceeded immediately. (Note the words *operator* and *operating* — now we have some insight into why the term *operating system* came into use.) From the user's point of view, an operating system was, and is today, an integrated set of system programs whose major function is the control of EDP-system resources. (See Figure 14-5.) By allocating specific resources to specific, independent jobs, the operating system helps to insure that the EDP system as a whole operates efficiently and effectively. The amount of useful work that can be accomplished within a given amount of time (i.e., the system throughput) is determined accordingly.

When an operating system is installed, a human operator no longer acts as intermediary between the user and the computer system. Another means of

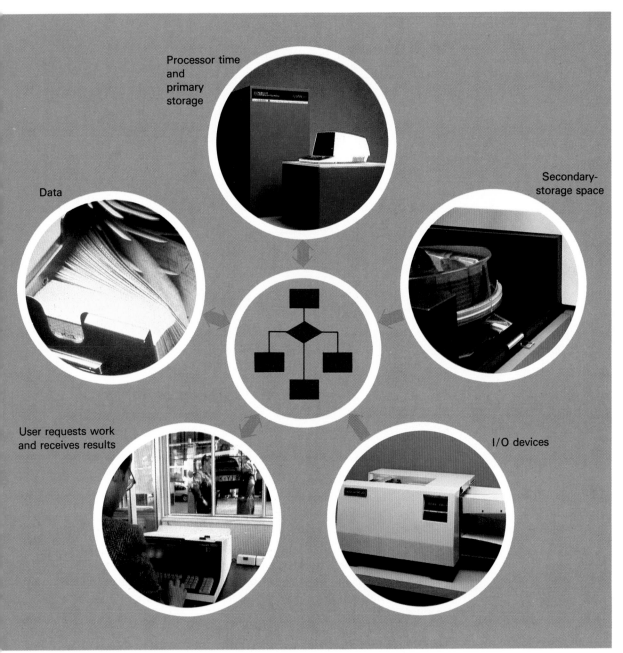

Processor time and primary storage

Data

Secondary-storage space

User requests work and receives results

I/O devices

FIGURE 14-5 Operating-system software performs a control function, allocating EDP-system resources to specific jobs during processing. (*Photos courtesy* [clockwise] *National Advanced Systems, IBM Corporation, National Computer Systems, TRW Inc., Recognition Equipment Incorporated*)

communication between the user and the computer is required. The user has to be able to tell the computer what kind of work (jobs and job steps) is to be done. *Job-control languages* (*JCL's*) were developed to serve this purpose. The job-control statements needed to define a job were punched into cards. The resulting job definitions were placed one behind another on the system input device to form a stack, or batch, of jobs. (See Figure 14-6.) An operating-system

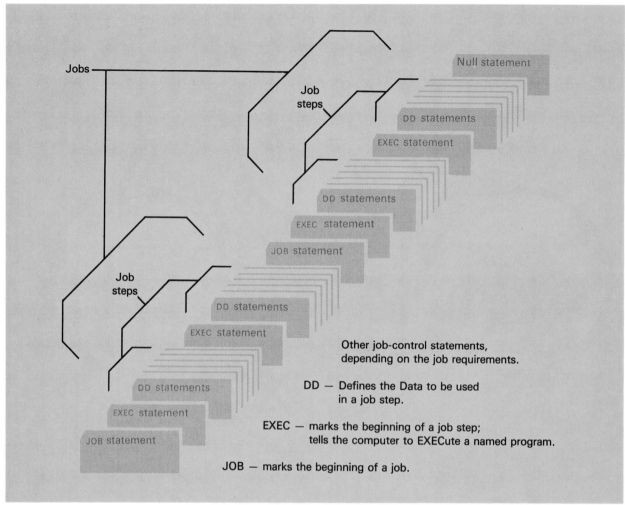

Jobs

Null statement

Job steps

DD statements

EXEC statement

DD statements

EXEC statement

JOB statement

Job steps

DD statements

EXEC statement

DD statements

EXEC statement

JOB statement

Other job-control statements, depending on the job requirements.

DD — Defines the Data to be used in a job step.

EXEC — marks the beginning of a job step; tells the computer to EXECute a named program.

JOB — marks the beginning of a job.

FIGURE 14-6 Some users place job-control statements, punched into cards, in a job input stream to be read by an operating-system program that controls batch processing.

job-control program read the cards and caused the continuous stream of jobs and job steps to be carried out with minimal operator intervention. This was the beginning of what we know today as *stacked-job processing, batched-job processing* or, more commonly, *batch processing.*

Batch processing is possible because the job-control program maintains a record of the names and locations of all programs stored in system libraries. The libraries are kept in online storage devices. With some operating systems, a user can place input data that is to be processed at the end of a job-step definition. The data can be any of several types. For example, it may be source statements to be translated by a language-processor program, machine-language instructions to be loaded into primary storage by a loader program, or data records to be sorted by a sort/merge program. Placing the data in the job input stream eliminates the need for an additional I/O device. However, in large EDP systems, this approach is seldom practical. The job input stream is usually entered from a terminal, a card reader, or a magnetic-tape or disk unit to which the job-control statements have been transferred during a special processing run. The programs and data files needed for the jobs are entered from other high-speed tape or disk devices.

One approach for increasing the speed of job-control and data input is based on a technique known as *spooling* (an acronym derived from *s*imultaneous *p*eripheral *o*perations *online*). Input that would ordinarily be entered directly from a terminal or card reader is actually entered from a virtual card reader—an area of a much faster disk storage unit on which the input has been stored previously and which has been defined to function in this way.

Another approach to system efficiency involves the use of *cataloged procedures*. Each procedure consists of the job-control statements for a particular sequence of job steps. The procedure is developed, placed in a system library, and cataloged (that is, its entry and location in the system library are recorded in a library catalog). When the particular job steps are to be executed, a single job-control statement containing the name of the cataloged procedure is included in the job input stream. When this statement is read by the job-control program, the cataloged procedure is referenced. Execution of the job steps proceeds accordingly.

ONLINE DIRECT-ACCESS SYSTEMS

The late 1950s and early 1960s were the heyday of second-generation computer systems. Small computers such as the IBM 1401 took over tasks formerly done by users at punched-card machines in many businesses. Much larger computers from IBM, Burroughs, RCA, General Electric, and Univac were installed by universities, government agencies, and large businesses.

The batch-processing techniques we just discussed worked well where large volumes of input data were involved—say the weekly time cards for all employees of a firm. They did not work well for small amounts of input generated randomly or for individual problem solving. Computer manufacturers addressed these needs by developing online direct-access systems.

In an online direct-access application, the computer communicates directly with both the source and the destination of the data it processes. The data can be sent to and received from local I/O devices, or to and from I/O devices at remote locations by way of communication channels. Therefore, input transactions can be processed as they are received. Master files can be read to produce up-to-date output information in the form of status reports, statistical summaries, invoices, and so on. As we learned earlier, this approach is called *transaction processing*. Because queries about master-file data are received in random order, the files are generally stored on direct-access storage devices.

The first online direct-access systems were typified by the early airline reservations systems. Perhaps best known of these was the Semi-Automatic Business Research Environment (SABRE) system developed jointly by IBM and American Airlines. Planning for the system was initiated by American in 1954; it became fully operational 10 years later. Master files containing seat inventory records for hundreds of scheduled flights were placed in secondary storage. Ticket and sales offices were equipped with I/O devices, known as *agent sets*, designed especially for airline use. Airline employees at widely separated locations were able to check the availability of space on particular flights, make or cancel reservations, and so on, within a few seconds. Crew assignments, maintenance requirements, freight and mail movements, and fuel and catering requirements were among other data stored and processed within the SABRE system. Sales data, cost data, return on investment (ROI) information, and inventory control figures were maintained for airline management.

These early online direct-access systems met many user needs, but they were far from perfect. Because the systems had to respond quickly to many individual transactions, it was neither possible nor desirable to collect the transactions into batches and then process the batches to query or update master files. Instead, the master files had to be updated continuously. The master-file updating was a time-consuming process, but it was essential. Otherwise, for example, a ticket agent at one location might sell airline space already sold by an agent at another location.

Furthermore, different types of transactions, such as inquiries, sales, and cancellations, required different programs to process them. These programs had to be kept in secondary storage and brought into primary storage when needed. Much time was spent in locating and gaining access to data and programs, rather than in processing transactions.

To add to the problem, transactions occurred irregularly. During peak periods of activity, hundreds of thousands of transactions had to be processed within minutes. At other times, the systems were relatively idle. It became apparent that, to use EDP-system resources as efficiently and effectively as possible, new techniques had to be developed.

MULTI-PROGRAMMING

Fortunately, during this same time period, system software and hardware developments were occurring elsewhere. In 1963, the Burroughs Corporation released its Master Control Program, or MCP, for use with Burroughs B5000 computer systems. MCP assumed greater control over system resources than its predecessors had. Input and output devices were activated by MCP rather than by individual application programs. This centralized control was possible because hardware interrupt conditions signaled to MCP when control of the EDP system should be passed to a special-purpose routine for I/O processing.

MCP could also assign memory areas to programs, determine the optimum sequence and mix of jobs, determine program priorities and system requirements, and provide for rescheduling if new jobs were introduced or job priorities changed. Of major significance was the fact that under MCP more than one user application program could be resident in primary storage at a time. Since the processor could only execute one instruction at a time, simultaneous execution of instructions from different programs was not possible. The processor could, however, execute instructions from one program, then instructions from another program, then those from the first program again, and so on. This type of processing is called *concurrent processing*. Program logic within MCP determined which system software routine or application program had control of the B5000 processor at any given time. Today, a system that provides these capabilities is said to support *multiprogramming*.

Concurrent execution of programs is desirable because I/O operations are much slower than internal processing operations. When only one program is being executed, the processor often must wait for an I/O operation to be completed before it can continue processing. Fortunately for the user, the design of modern computer systems permits overlapping of I/O and processing operations (recall Chapter 8). Even so, when only one program is resident in primary storage and being executed, the processor is idle much of the time.

Allocating Storage

When more than one program is to be loaded into primary storage, the storage area must be divided. In some systems, the area reserved for a particular program is called a *partition*. Each partition is fixed in size and location at the time the system is placed in operation. The size or location of a partition can be changed only by manual intervention; it cannot be changed by an operating-system control program during system operation. In other systems, the sizes and locations of reserved areas can be changed dynamically (that is, by a control program) during system operation. The term *region* rather than *partition* is often used for these areas to indicate the flexibility that's available. The control program allocates a portion of available primary storage to each job or job step as it is initiated. The use of storage reflects the requirements of the programs being executed at any given time.

In 1964, IBM introduced its major third-generation operating system, OS/360, for use with IBM System/360 computers. A System/360 user could select the version of OS/360 that included a control program called *Multiprogramming with a Fixed Number of Tasks (MFT)*. Each task was simply an independent unit of work, such as a program, subprogram, or subroutine, that needed system resources. As its name implies, OS/MFT could operate on a fixed number of tasks concurrently. Actually, it could read jobs from as many as three job input streams, handle up to 15 job steps, and record up to 36 streams of output concurrently. The System/370 operating system that performs similar functions is known as *OS/VS1*.

A System/360 user with extensive data-processing requirements could select another alternative: a version of OS/360 that included a control program called *Multiprogramming with a Variable Number of Tasks (MVT)*. As its name implies, OS/MVT could also control a variable number of tasks concurrently. It could change the number, size, and location of reserved storage areas to meet the data-processing requirements at any given time. Like OS/MFT, OS/MVT could handle as many as 15 job steps concurrently. Moreover, once a job step was initiated by OS/MVT, that job step could, in turn, initiate the processing of other tasks. There was not a one-to-one relationship between job steps and tasks (as existed under OS/MFT). The number of concurrent data-processing tasks was limited solely by the availability of the resources required to perform them. The System/370 operating system that performs similar functions, in an environment of even greater complexity, is known variously as *OS/VS2*, *OS/VS2 MVS*, or *MVS*.

Storage Protection and Priority

What does all this discussion mean, from a user's point of view? Two important considerations are that each primary-storage partition (or region) must be given protection and assigned priority. Fortunately for the user, storage protection is provided by the system as a part of its security features. Usually, both hardware and software are involved. In effect, each partition is "locked." An instruction must have the storage-protection key required to operate on instructions or data in a particular partition. If an instruction of one program attempts to operate on instructions or data stored in a partition reserved for another program, its storage-protection key will not be the required one and the instruction will not be executed. Thus, each program can modify only the primary-storage locations assigned to it. Each user is protected from other users and from certain errors that otherwise might go undetected for some time.

The user installation is directly involved in determining job priorities. Each user cares about those priorities; they play a significant role in determining the rate of service that can be expected for a particular job. Normally, jobs (and hence the programs making up the jobs) are assigned to user-specified job classes. In addition, each storage partition is reserved for jobs of a particular class. This plan insures that programs are loaded into specific partitions. The high-priority partitions are called *foreground areas;* programs loaded into these areas are called *foreground programs.* The lowest-priority partition is called the *background area;* programs loaded into this area are called *background programs.* In a batch-processing environment, the effects of job priorities are reflected in turnaround times. In an online direct-access environment, the priorities help to determine response times (how fast users receive information).

For simplicity, let's consider an environment in which two foreground programs and one background program can be executed concurrently. (See Figure 14-7.) The two foreground areas have different levels of priority and different storage-protection keys. The foreground-one area is used for a query program that provides responses to user entries from terminals. It has priority over any program that runs in foreground-two. The foreground-two program in turn has priority over any program that runs in the background area. These priorities determine which program receives attention first if more than one of the programs requires the processor—that is, is at a point where its next instruction should be executed—at any given time.

It's meaningful to note that the MCP and OS/360 operating systems were designed for medium-size and large computer systems. To some users, their multiprogramming capabilities were awesome. In succeeding years, however, similar capabilities have been developed for small machines. In Chapter 10, we learned that the Burroughs B1700, announced in 1972, was the first small computer with an operating system that supported multiprogramming. Today, there are microcomputer operating systems with equivalent or greater capabilities. Obviously, questions of storage protection and priority become complex as

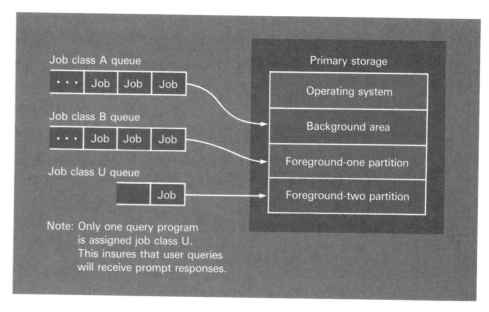

FIGURE 14-7
Programs may be loaded in primary-storage areas from specific job-class queues in a multiprogramming environment.

the number of programs to be executed concurrently increases. Fortunately for the user, operating systems are designed to handle the situation.

Selecting Programs

A program in which input/output time exceeds internal processing time is said to be *I/O bound*. A program in which internal processing time exceeds input/output time is said to be *process bound*. We learned earlier that when an I/O operation is taking place during program execution, both the program and the processor may be idle. In multiprogramming, however, whenever a foreground program is in an idle or wait state, the processor can execute the instructions of a program that has lower priority. Thus, when an I/O-bound program is run as a foreground program, processor time that would otherwise be wasted can be used to execute instructions of other programs.

Foreground programs usually have high I/O requirements and low internal processing requirements. Inquiry programs and file-to-file utility programs are in this category. Programs selected for use as background programs usually have low I/O requirements and high internal processing requirements. Thus, application programs that perform inventory control, payroll processing, accounts receivable, and the like, are run as background programs. System programs such as language processors and sort/merge programs are also run.

MULTIPROCESSING

Let's pause a moment to clarify some concepts and to relate some things we've learned. The terms *multiprogramming* and *multiprocessing* are sometimes used interchangeably, but they do not mean the same thing. Multiprogramming involves concurrent execution of instructions from two or more programs sharing one processor and controlled by one major operating-system control program. In multiprocessing, instructions are executed *simultaneously* (at the same time, in parallel) on two or more processors; the processors can execute different instructions from the same program or from different programs at a given time.

In a tightly coupled multiprocessing environment, some or all of the operations performed by each processor are controlled by a common operating-system program. Since this program resides in the internal storage unit of one of the processors, all processors must be able to refer to that storage unit. In a loosely coupled multiprocessing environment, two or more independently functioning processors are connected by means of a communication link. Each processor has its own operating system and primary storage. The processors can access each other's files. In some environments, tasks are assigned to processors dynamically to balance the over-all system workload.

Once again, Burroughs' MCP as released in 1963 merits attention. The MCP could control two identical processors operating in a master/slave relationship. The master processor was a general-purpose machine; the slave processor was used for selected computational processes. Control Data Corporation pioneered another approach with its 6000-series computer systems. A single 6000 system could include one or two large processors and up to 10 peripheral processors.

In today's basic multiprocessing system, one large processor handles all major processing functions. Smaller processors are integrated into the system to handle "housekeeping" chores such as opening and closing files, input validation and editing, and file maintenance.

More complex multiprocessing systems involve multiple large processors. In some current implementations, the processors are simply large computers of a type also used in single-processor configurations. For example, a UNIVAC 1100/84 may include up to four processors like the single processor used in a UNIVAC 1100/81. In other cases, a multiprocessing system consists of a single "computer," which is actually several processors linked together for purposes of communication and cooperation during processing. Each processor performs specific tasks. Control Data Corporation uses this approach in its most powerful computers.

Multiprocessing is not limited to mainframe environments. For example, in 1982 Tandy Corporation introduced a dual-processor desktop computer system, the TRS-80 Model 16. (See Figure 14-8.) The Model 16 unit houses a Motorola 68000 microprocessor that serves as the main processor and a Zilog Z80A microprocessor that handles I/O and housekeeping chores. The MC68000 accepts 16-bit units of data and processes them internally as 32-bit words. The Z80A is a well-known 8-bit microprocessor, also used in the TRS-80 Model II. The system design permits the Model 16 to have much more memory (up to 512K) and to process data at much higher speeds than typical 8-bit microcomputer systems. It can also operate as a TRS-80 Model II and use existing Model II software, which means that a large base of ready-to-run application programs is already available for it. Initially, the Model 16 was a single-user system only. However, TRS-XENIX, a multiple-user operating system derived from Bell Labs' well-known UNIX operating system, was soon to be available. Under this operating system, one remote terminal user can be entering inventory data, another remote terminal user can be accessing job-costing data stored previously, and a third user at the Model 16 can be running a utility program to copy the contents of a diskette for backup purposes. Opportunities to do work in parallel are

FIGURE 14-8
The TRS-80 Model 16 desktop computer is a multi-processor system, housing both a 16-bit and an 8-bit microprocessor. (*TRS-80 is a trademark of Radio Shack Division of Tandy Corporation*)

essential in today's office environments. (We say more about both XENIX and UNIX later.)

In general, multiprocessing support is dependent on enhancements to both hardware and software otherwise used in a uniprocessor mode. Multiprocessing systems are more complex and more costly than uniprocessor systems. However, some user needs can be satisfied only when such support is provided. System availability and system reliability are vital considerations (some installations must provide for 24 hours of uninterrupted processing daily). A multiprocessing system can be designed so that at least some work can continue even if one processor is down. Many of the problems now being addressed with computer help involve lots of data and lots of very fast computation and feedback – for example, monitoring and/or controlling the many variables that must be taken into account when journeys into space are initiated. With multiple processors, parallel work on different problems or on the same problem is possible. (See Figure 14-9.)

Through advances in microelectronics, hardware costs are declining rapidly. Increasingly powerful, yet relatively inexpensive microprocessors appear to be excellent building blocks for multiprocessors. We can expect that much attention will be focused in this area in the next several years. Much progress has been made in understanding the problems of processor-to-processor communication, resource contention, processor scheduling, the avoidance, detection, and resolution of deadlocks, and so on. Many of these problems can be handled by system software without involving users or user programs. Perhaps the biggest challenge that remains is to understand more fully the parallelism that can exist in solution algorithms. To exploit this parallelism, we need to think about solution steps in ways other than sequentially. Some progress has been made in providing features to support parallelism in programming languages (most notably, Pascal and Ada). Techniques are being pursued that will enable hardware, compilers, and operating systems – that is, the computer itelf – to detect opportunities for parallelism.

REAL-TIME SYSTEMS

As mentioned earlier in this chapter, an online direct-access system can accept input transactions as they are generated. A system that can also provide output fast enough to satisfy any user requirement can be further classified as a *real-time system*. Such a system makes output available quickly enough to control (not simply react to) real-life activity.

The concept of real time is closely related to immediacy; it is demonstrated as system response time, which we now define somewhat formally to be the interval of time between completion of input and start of output from an EDP system.

In actual operation, real time is a matter of degree, depending upon the application at hand. The customer-service representative of an insurance firm may be willing to wait from 3 to 10 seconds for details about the coverage of a policyholder. In a computer-controlled military defense system, responses within microseconds may be required. Variations in response time are due to differences in the system workload, internal processing requirements, frequency and type of access to computer files and/or databases, and so on. Both the hardware and the software must be capable of fast performance. In addition, the system must be tuned by system support personnel to fit the requirements

A

FIGURE 14-9
Online incident, reporting, dispatching, and real-time queries from a large, active municipal fleet of helicopters (A) are examples of data-processing tasks that can be handled in a timely manner by a system with multiprocessing capabilities (B). (*Photos courtesy Sperry Corporation*)

B

imposed on it. For example, system characteristics such as the number and size of I/O buffers may be set by means of installation-specifiable parameters at system startup time.

Although basic business applications such as order writing, inventory control, and payroll can be implemented as real-time systems, they are not likely to be. Increasing the costs of software, hardware, development, and ongoing support is more likely to be justified for specialized applications in industries such as transportation, manufacturing, banking, and distribution. Computer-controlled robotic systems on assembly lines, automated teller machines at banks, and point-of-sale terminals at retail department stores are components of real-time systems. In hospitals, patients' vital signs are monitored by real-time systems at their bedsides. Mobile police units gain access to vehicle registration data, missing person files, and case data via handheld terminals that are part of national and even international real-time computer networks.

TIME SHARING   *Time sharing* is a technique that allows several users of an online real-time system to use that system on what *appears* to be a simultaneous basis. The tremendous speeds of today's processors and the rapid data transfer rates of direct-access storage devices make it possible for many users, at a variety of terminals, to interact with the system. The speed at which the system components—both hardware and software—operate allows the system to switch from one active user to another, doing all or a part of each job until all work is completed. The speed may be so great that each user believes that he or she is the only one using the system. The purpose for which one person uses the system may be totally unrelated to that of others. The system resources are shared by all. (See Figure 14-10.)

Since the user is more concerned with the solution to a problem than with the techniques used to solve it, ease of use is an essential characteristic of any time-sharing system. In effect, the terminal (and therefore the computer) becomes a personal computing tool; it is used in much the same way that the slide rule, adding machine, and calculator have been used for years. In just a few hours, a manager, financial analyst, engineer, scientist, or student can learn a conversational (interactive) programming language such as BASIC or APL or a simple interactive query language. Then he or she can submit questions or problems directly to the computer and receive immediate responses. Time sharing's primary function is to make more computing power available to more users through facilities that support interactive processing—rapid, repeated alternation of user input and system response.

The capability of relatively fast two-way communication with the computer system is also valuable to data-processing professionals. A beginning programmer can request that a program be translated and executed, correct any errors detected during the translation, and then rerun the program immediately. An experienced programmer can test one or several programs without waiting for the output of complete processing runs, as is normally required in a batch-processing environment. Programs developed in this manner can be used in the time-sharing environment or become part of an integrated business application. Studies have shown that the most important factor in increasing the productivity of programmers is the availability of online interactive debugging and testing facilities.

Types of Time-Sharing Systems   Time-sharing systems were developed in the late 1950s and early 1960s at Carnegie Institute of Technology, Stanford University, and MIT. (The MIT system subsequently became Project MAC, an acronym for *multiple-access computer* or *machine-aided cognition*, with two shared IBM 7094 computers.) A fourth experimental configuration, the System Development Corporation time-sharing system, was similar to those developed at Stanford and MIT. Of major concern to all were the difficulties often experienced in programming.

Under a $300,000 grant from the National Science Foundation, two Dartmouth professors, John G. Kemeny and Thomas E. Kurtz, pioneered the development of time-sharing languages, applications, and teaching methods suitable for college students. Especially noteworthy are their efforts pertaining to BASIC, the widely used interactive programming language developed with support from General Electric. (We surveyed the major features of BASIC in Chapter 13.)

FIGURE 14-10 Many users at widely separated locations can interact with a computer at what appears to be the same time when time-sharing capabilities are available. (*Photos courtesy Tymshare, Inc.*)

The American Airlines' SABRE system, discussed earlier, is reputed to be the first prominent commercial example of shared computing. It can be described as a special-purpose time-sharing system.

These early systems illustrate, in part, the kinds of time-sharing systems in use today. There are:

- General-purpose systems, which support a variety of programming languages and allow users to create and run their own programs
- Systems in which a wide variety of application programs are available for execution but cannot be modified by users
- Systems in which all programs are related to one major application, and users merely provide input and request output

In practice, a time-sharing system may be a combination of these, with the major application having first priority. The distinguishing characteristic of the three systems is the degree of user independence provided.

System Software Like any EDP system, a time-sharing system is controlled by stored programs. It resembles a multiprogramming system in that several programs are processed concurrently. In fact, multiprogramming is usually the means of implementing time-shared operations. Fast processing of many user requests is rarely accomplished without having numerous programs in primary storage at the same time.

For efficient utilization of system resources, a system control program allocates exact primary-storage locations to programs and data at program execution times. It repositions programs in storage as necessary to maximize the amount of useful work that can be done. Storage-protection considerations are paramount. Insuring that each user accesses only the programs and data that he or she is authorized to access is in large part a system responsibility.

At any given moment, some users are entering programs or data into the computer, others are receiving output from the computer, and others are waiting for programs to be run. Since all users must share the available processor time, some method for distributing that time is required.

The simplest approach to distribution is called the *round-robin system.* Each user program is serviced for a predetermined period of time, known as a *time slice* or *quantum,* in the processing cycle. It is serviced again each time its turn comes, until its processing requirements are satisfied. An alternate method of distributing processor time is to switch from one program to another whenever the program being executed has to wait for a secondary storage or I/O operation. Since business-oriented applications commonly require frequent I/O operations, this method is most apt to be used in time-sharing systems designed especially for business data processing.

The system software of a time-sharing system must also handle accounting responsibilities. That is, the system itself must keep track of who uses what, for billing purposes. To insure fast response to users, the system should have performance-measurement facilities. At least some degree of automatic performance optimization should be provided. Provision for reconstruction of both programs and data files in case they are destroyed is another essential feature of a time-sharing system. Extensive logging of system activities may be required.

Approaches to Time Sharing

There are two basic approaches to the use of time-sharing facilities. One is internal to the user organization. The other involves dependencies on an external (outside) firm. An organization may use one or the other, or both.

In the first case, the user organization acquires a time-sharing system, including both hardware and software, for its own use (as did American Airlines, above). Such a system is called an *in-house time-sharing system*. It enables several departments or locations within a company to share one system. The hardware is purchased or leased. The software can be licensed for use from the manufacturer of the major hardware or from a software development firm. Real-time applications such as management inquiry, interactive problem solving, and engineering design are readily handled by this kind of system. Often, batch-processing applications such as accounts receivable or payroll are handled as background programs while time-sharing programs are executed as foreground programs on the same computer.

In the second approach to time sharing, computing service is purchased from another firm, which may be called a *computer service company*, a *service bureau*, or an *information utility*. The user organization pays for the computing service in much the same way that it pays for telephone service. An installation charge, basic monthly rental charges (for example, for terminals and communication equipment), and variable charges per transaction may be involved. The variable charges are based on the amount of time a particular terminal is connected to the computer, the amount of processor time actually used by each program whose execution is initiated from that terminal, and so on. Charges are frequently lower for evening and weekend use. Some service companies "bundle" charges into fixed fees for use of specific programs.

Most certainly, cost is one factor a user organization considers when determining whether to establish its own time-sharing system or purchase time-sharing services. From this viewpoint, an organization that needs the power of a large computer on an infrequent basis, or that requires a limited amount of computer resources on a regular basis, is a likely candidate for the second approach. New clients are sought at the $1000 to $2000 per month data-processing expenditure level. Established EDP users (including departments or functional units of large organizations with centralized computer facilities) that spend up to $7000 per month for data processing are also viewed by service companies as potential customers.

From the user organization's point of view, there are additional factors to consider. These may be more important than cost. Upper-level management may decide not to take on the headaches of an internal EDP installation. Managers of business operations may be reluctant to build a data-processing staff. They may view the task of finding employees with the technical, communication, and organization skills needed an extremely difficult one. The space and special environmental facilities needed may be serious obstacles. For multilocation organizations, facilities for data communication as well as for data processing must be taken into account.

VIRTUAL STORAGE

The desire to maximize the amount of useful work that an EDP system can do, which stimulated the development of both multiprogramming and multiprocessing, also stimulated the development of *virtual storage* (also called *virtual memory*). Through virtual-storage techniques, the high costs of primary-storage components and the constraints imposed by absolute limits of primary-storage capacity are eased or eliminated. The concept was not new when IBM announced virtual-storage operating systems for its System/370 computers in 1972. Virtual-storage techniques had been applied earlier (IBM's System/360 Models 85 and 195, the Burroughs B6500 and B1700, the CDC 7600, and others), but never before had the concept received such publicity. Many users first became aware of the potential benefits of virtual storage at this time.

The word *virtual* means "not in actual fact." It follows that *virtual memory* means memory that does not in actual fact exist. Fundamentally, virtual-storage capabilities give the user the illusion of a primary storage with characteristics different from those of the underlying physical storage. Usually, the significant difference is that the virtual storage is much larger. The EDP system itself maintains this illusion through a combination of hardware and software techniques. Each instruction of a program must be in primary storage (which we shall call *real storage* here, in contrast to virtual) before it can be executed, but not all parts of a program have to be in real storage at any given time. An operating-system control program keeps some portion of each executing program in real storage. Other unused portions of the program may be in virtual storage only. Such portions are loaded into real storage when (or if) the instructions or data they contain are referred to by other instructions executed within the program. Because only a portion of a program has to be in primary storage during its execution, a greater number of programs can be running at any given time.

Virtual-storage capabilities are implemented in various ways. The two principal methods are called *segmentation* and *paging*. Generally, both software and hardware are involved.

Under segmentation, each program's address space (range of storage locations referenced by the program) is split into variable-size blocks, or segments. (See Figure 14-11.) Each segment is a logically separable unit. For example, one segment may be an I/O routine; another may be a data area. An instruction or data item within the program is identified by a two-part address. The address tells the name of a segment and the relative location, or displacement, of the instruction or data item within the segment. The system constructs these addresses. It keeps track of the various segments in a segment table established for the program in real storage. If a program being executed tries to reference a segment that is not in real storage, the system intervenes and brings the segment into real storage. Burroughs' MCP and follow-on virtual-memory systems are examples of successful segmentation implementations.

Under paging, the physical-memory space is divided into fixed-size physical blocks, or page frames. Programs and data are divided into blocks (pages) of the same size. (See Figure 14-12.) The length of the pages is determined by the characteristics of the machine hardware rather than by program logic. The page size may be very small, say space for 256 characters, or very large, say 4K bytes. One page of information can be loaded into one page frame.

Each two-part address within a program specifies a page number and a displacement within that page. The system maintains a page frame table for all of real storage to keep track of page frame usage. In addition, it maintains a page table for each program executed. The page table contains a list of the pages that together compose the program, a flag for each page indicating whether it is

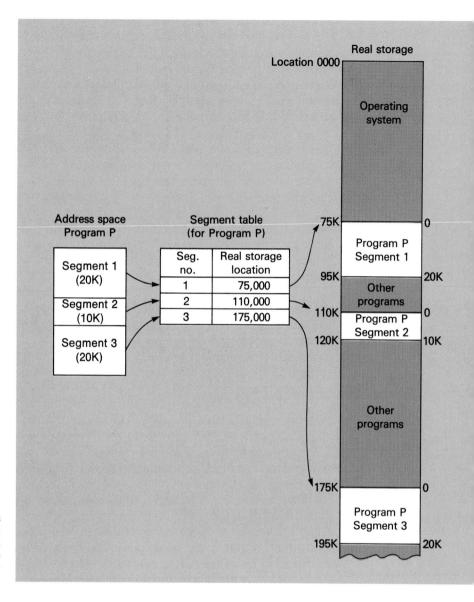

FIGURE 14-11
Segmentation techniques are used to load specific portions (segments) of a program into real storage as needed in one type of virtual-storage environment.

currently in real storage, and a pointer to where each page can be found. Because these tables are referenced frequently, they are kept in real storage.

A *segmentation and paging system* attempts to combine the best features of both segmentation and paging. Programs are first broken into logical segments by the operating system. Each segment that exceeds the uniform page size is in turn broken into pages for loading and execution on the computer. For each program, a segment table and a page table for each segment are needed. Addresses within the program have three parts: segment, page within segment, and displacement within page. *Dynamic address translation (DAT)* facilities are used to convert such an address to an absolute address each time an instruction or data item is referenced during program execution. (See Figure 14.13.) Generally, the DAT facilities are provided as special hardware—sequences of microcode instructions that can be carried out very quickly as often

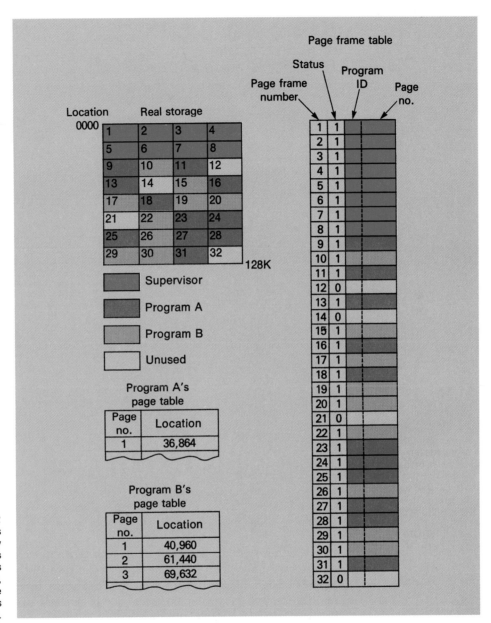

FIGURE 14-12
Virtual-storage capabilities may be implemented by means of paging techniques whereby real storage is divided into page frames, and program pages are loaded into those frames as needed during processing.

as required. The IBM virtual-storage operating systems mentioned above and the Multics operating system implemented on General Electric (and later, on Honeywell) computers are good examples of segmentation and paging implementations.

When a segment (or page, depending on the implementation) not in real storage is referenced during program execution, a *missing-item fault* occurs. Some paging systems attempt to minimize the number of faults by *prepaging* techniques. When one page is loaded into real storage, certain other pages are loaded as well, with the expectation that they are likely to be referenced. Only one *page-in operation* is needed for the entire group, whereas a separate page-in operation would be needed for each referenced page if they were brought in

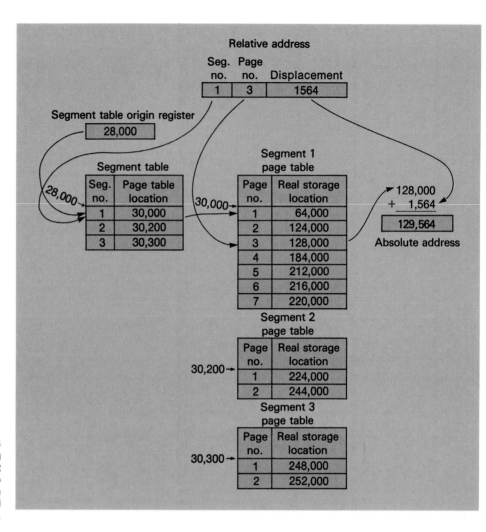

FIGURE 14-13
A segmentation and paging
system uses both a segment
table and page tables to
keep track of where program
pages are loaded into real
storage during processing.

singly. Other systems use *demand paging* techniques. Each page is loaded into real storage only when it is called for as the result of a missing-item fault. No page is loaded unless it is referenced. There may be more page-in operations, and the system may operate more slowly because of them, but no pages are brought into real storage unnecessarily.

Virtual storage cannot, of course, provide the user with an actual super-large real storage. If all portions of real storage are in use when another segment or page is referenced, a replacement operation is necessary. Numerous replacement policies have been proposed. In System/370 systems, for example, the least recently used (LRU) page in real storage is replaced. If that page was not modified while occupying real storage, it can simply be overlaid by the needed page, because a copy of the page being replaced exists in virtual storage. If the page was modified, however, a *page-out operation* must occur before replacement, to insure that a valid copy of the page will be available on virtual storage the next time it is referenced during program execution.

There is no concise, well-established rule for determining the amount of real storage that must be available to support a certain amount of virtual-storage space. We cannot say, for example, that there must be 1K of real storage for every 10K, 100K, or 1000K of virtual storage. We do know that if a program is not allocated enough real storage, many of the references to addresses within it are likely to generate missing-item faults. If a similar situation exists for numerous programs in execution, the system is forced to spend most or all of its time moving segments or pages between virtual and real storage—a phenomenon known as *thrashing*. When thrashing occurs, the system has very little time to perform useful work.

VIRTUAL MACHINES Some computer manufacturers have gone a step beyond the concept of virtual storage by offering an even more powerful capability: a *virtual-machine* environment. In a virtual-storage environment, each user is able to take advantage of internal storage that does not actually exist, but seems to. In a virtual-machine environment, each user is able to use a total computer system—both hardware and software—that does not actually exist, but seems to. The operating-system software and special hardware manage the real EDP-system resources (processor time, primary storage, I/O devices, and so on) and allocate them to currently active users.

The NCR Criterion series of computers are known for their support of the virtual-machine concept. Virtual machines are "constructed" through tailorable firmware (loadable control storage on flexible disks). Users are able to perform specific tasks more economically, to operate in a selected system environment more efficiently, and to exactly duplicate the processing characteristics of another, different computer. Putting it another way, users can tailor the computer to the type of problem to be solved, rather than try to adapt the problem to fit the machine.

Such capabilities are particularly attractive to existing NCR computer users who want to upgrade to the NCR Criterion series without having to rewrite all their existing application programs. For example, both programs and data files from an NCR Century 300 system can be moved to a Criterion virtual machine without any special user effort. The programs do not even have to be recompiled in the new environment.

NCR has exploited the virtual-machine concept further by developing firmware that can be used to set up a virtual machine especially tailored to translate and execute COBOL business application programs. Because of the special firmware, the NCR COBOL compiler can translate COBOL statements into an intermediate language that is interpreted directly and far more efficiently than COBOL programs are usually handled even on much larger computers.

IBM's support of the virtual-machine concept is available to users of its VM/370 operating system. Each virtual machine has, by definition, a certain amount of virtual storage, a virtual processor, and a virtual system console. Other virtual-machine resources include channels, control units, and I/O devices. These resources can be shared among users or alternately allocated to users for specified periods of time. The resources needed for a particular virtual machine are specified in its VM directory entry. When a user signs on to the EDP system from a terminal (his or her virtual console), a virtual machine is created, based upon that user's entry in the directory.

The VM operating system manages the setting up of virtual machines. Another operating system is needed to manage the resources and work flow within each virtual machine. After a user's virtual machine has been created, he or she issues a command to load the operating system for that machine. For example, a user who is moving from a System/370 Model 135 computer running under IBM's DOS/VS operating system to an IBM 3083 computer running under VM/370 may choose to define a DOS/VS virtual machine to run programs initially written to run under DOS/VS.

As another example, a user installation may choose to define an OS/VS2 MVS virtual machine. On this machine, fully checked-out business application programs (for example, general ledger) can be run on a regularly scheduled production basis—just as though they were running on an actual EDP system controlled by MVS. On other virtual machines, programmers can be writing new programs or making changes to other copies of the general-ledger programs without affecting the MVS production environment.

The conversational monitor system (CMS) is an IBM operating system that runs only under VM. It provides a user-oriented terminal environment suitable for interactive problem solving and program development. Several CMS virtual machines may be up and running under VM at any one time. It is CMS that makes the VM environment especially valuable for program development. Figure 14-14 shows five virtual machines executing programs concurrently on an IBM 3083 computer. One is doing production work—batch jobs running under the DOS/VSE operating system. A second is executing programs under a preceding release of DOS/VSE. The other three virtual machines are running under CMS. We can assume that the problem solvers or software developers are interacting directly with the computer via online terminals in these environments.

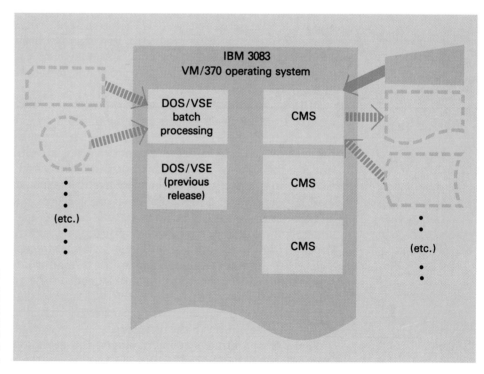

FIGURE 14-14
Execution of many unrelated, independent jobs can be happening in separate virtual machines when an operating system with virtual-machine capabilities controls processing.

PORTABLE OPERATING SYSTEMS

With the ever-decreasing costs of hardware and the exploding use of microcomputers in the early 1980s came a new demand from users and vendors alike – the demand for operating-system portability. In broad terms, a *portable operating system* is one that can easily be adapted to run on any computer having a particular architecture. From the common viewpoint of microcomputer users and vendors, on the other hand, a portable operating system is one that can be easily adapted to run on any computer based on a particular microprocessor. Functionally, a portable operating system is not very different from an operating system designed for a particular computer (referred to as a *proprietary operating system,* for purposes of distinction). Architecturally, the machine-dependent components of the operating system are well separated from the machine-independent components. This separation allows a user or vendor to (1) write a minimal amount of software that is unique to a particular computer system, and (2) take advantage of the machine-independent components of the portable operating system for the vast majority of system functions.

In the microcomputer arena especially, a few operating systems are appearing with increasing frequency. On 8-bit micros, Digital Research's CP/M operating system is the acknowledged leader. Some version of CP/M is likely to be available on any microcomputer system you encounter. Versions of the UNIX operating system initially developed at Bell Labs are gaining in popularity on 16-bit micros and on minis. These operating systems are quite different in design and in use. We discuss them briefly here as examples. There are many other operating systems supported on numerous vendors' systems.

A computer vendor whose system can be run under the control of one or more of these portable operating systems can point to the wide range of third-party-developed application software available to users of the system. An independent software vendor (i.e., third party) can afford to spend the time, talent, and other resources needed to develop high-quality application software when the potential customer set for the software includes users of many vendors' computers. A potential user who recognizes the importance of software and the lead time and resources needed to develop it is likely to choose a system for which portable operating system support is available.

For such reasons, we can expect the demand for portable operating systems to increase. We can expect the functions and range of vendor hardware supported by the systems to increase. We can definitely expect more of these systems in the future.

CP/M

CP/M (Control Program for Microcomputers) was initially written by one person – Gary Kindall, while employed as a consultant at Intel Corporation in the early 1970s. Intel chose not to market CP/M but it quickly evolved to become a general-purpose single-user operating system for the 8-bit Intel 8080 microprocessor. Now a product of Digital Research, Inc. (of which Kindall is president), CP/M is considered by many to be the de facto standard operating system for 8-bit microcomputer systems.

Architecturally, CP/M consists of three major subsystems: (1) the console command processor (CCP) interprets command lines entered by the user and provides responses; (2) the basic disk operating system (BDOS) manages system and user data files on from 1 to 16 disk drives of up to 8 megabytes capacity each;

and (3) the basic I/O system (BIOS) sends data to, and receives data and status information from, all devices other than disks—most notably, the user's console. (See Figure 14-15A.) The BIOS is the portion of CP/M that is subject to change; it consists of device drivers, or subroutines, coded to handle the I/O devices on a particular system configuration. Digital Research licenses CP/M for use by the purchaser; the firm supplies a source listing of a working BIOS that can serve as a model for the user or vendor developing a custom BIOS tailored to a specific environment.

The CP/M user interacting at a microcomputer sees an easy-to-use English-like command language, a general-purpose editor, a fast assembler, and an advanced debugger. Additional utilities, high-level-language processors, and application packages are available from Digital Research and a large number of independent software vendors. (See Figure 14-15B.)

The 8-bit version of CP/M now runs on Intel 8080, Intel 8085, and Zilog Z80 microprocessors. This code has been reworked, enhanced, and expanded to develop several alternative products. All are said to be *upward compatible* with CP/M. This means that users of systems running under CP/M can move to these products without having to rewrite all their existing application programs or buy new ones. In general, the alternative products offer additional capabilities.

MP/M II is a multiple-user, multitasking operating system that supports real-time multiprogramming at up to five terminals. We can think of it as a general-purpose time-sharing system. CP/M-86 and MP/M-86 are single-user and multiple-user operating systems for microcomputers based on the 16-bit Intel 8086 or 8088 microprocessor. Concurrent CP/M-86 supports single-user multitasking. CP/NET is a machine-independent microcomputer network

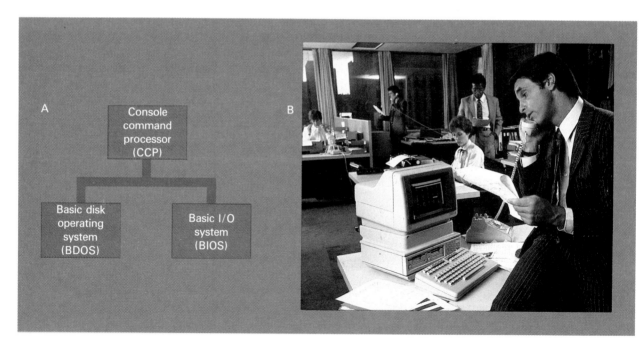

FIGURE 14-15 Designed with a basic structure that centralizes machine-dependent routines within its BIOS component (A), the CP/M operating system can be run on Hewlett-Packard's HP 120 desktop computer system (B) as well as on many other 8-bit microcomputers. (*Photo courtesy Hewlett-Packard Company*)

operating system. Microcomputers under control of MP/M II can operate as masters, and microcomputers under control of CP/M can operate as slaves within this network. I/O devices, programs, and data can be shared. In office environments, for example, users can share relatively expensive letter-quality and high-speed printers and transmission equipment in word-processing and electronic-mail applications.

With this expanded product line has come an expanded user base. In 1982, CP/M was said to be installed on more than 500,000 microcomputers. More than 100 hardware or system vendors and more than 500 independent software vendors were readily identifiable. Digital Research reinforced its commitment to 8-bit system software in late 1982 by announcing a new release of CP/M, called CP/M 3.0. Increased user friendliness, more efficient file accessing, and improved system performance were provided.

UNIX   The first version of the UNIX operating system was written in an assembler language by Ken Thompson at AT&T's Bell Labs in 1969. Dissatisfied with the computing facilities available to him, Thompson set out to create a friendlier environment for programming research and development. The system ran on a little-used DEC PDP-7 minicomputer. (DEC did not offer a proprietary operating system at the time.) Dennis Ritchie joined Ken as a co-designer. As interest grew, UNIX was rewritten in the C programming language for DEC PDP-11 machines. By 1973, it was made available for internal use by developers of the thousands of applications required at AT&T. (See Figure 14-16A.)

Word of UNIX spread to colleges and universities working in close assocation with Bell on various projects. Bell made UNIX available free to a few of these schools for use in their computer science departments. Commercial organizations could obtain a nonsupported copy of the system on tape from Western Electric (Bell's marketing arm at the time) for a $20,000 license fee. Interactive Systems Corporation was the first company to make UNIX commercially available. Like other companies that followed, it offered enhancements to the UNIX software and committed its support if problems arose.

UNIX is a multitasking, multiple-user (time-sharing) system designed for use in program development. It is unique in several ways. All system objects— including I/O channels, disk drives, and terminals—look like files to both system and application programs. Thus, a high degree of device independence is achieved. Communication between the system and its users is achieved by means of a command language interpreter called the *shell*. The interpreter accepts single command lines typed by a terminal user or previously typed sequences of commands stored within files as input. By design, the interpreter is simply an application program within the system. It can be changed or replaced with relative ease. Software vendors commonly incorporate customized shells to make interaction with the system easier for users who are not skilled programmers.

Each program starts out with a standard input unit (normally the console keyboard), a standard output unit (the console screen or printer), and a standard error output unit (the console screen or printer). The user can redirect any of these to any other file at program execution time. The standard output of one program can be directed to the standard input of another program without use of an intermediate file. The programs form a *pipeline*, or *pipe*. A program whose

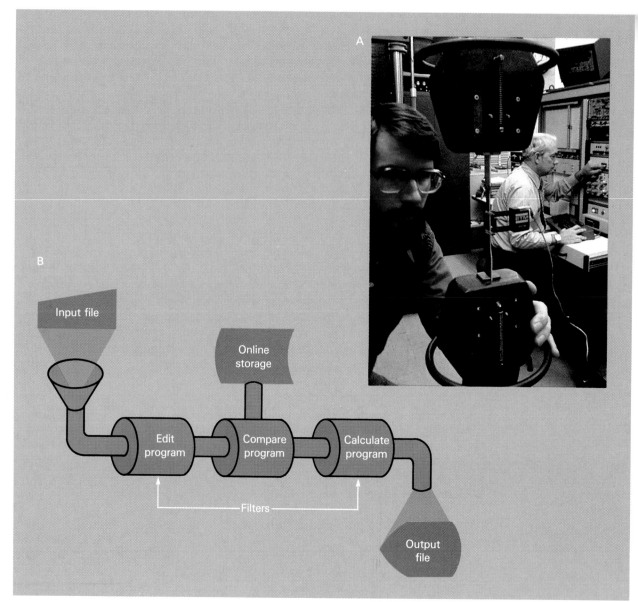

FIGURE 14-16 The UNIX operating system is widely used within Bell Labs (A) as well as on other manufacturers' 16-bit micros and minis; its internal pipeline structure (B) helps to provide the machine independence needed for portability. (*Photo courtesy Bell Laboratories*)

normal mode of operation is to accept input only from its standard input, to perform some operation on it, and to provide output only to its standard output is called a *filter*. The UNIX system itself is designed according to these constructs. For example, many UNIX utilities are filters that can be pipelined together to perform complex functions. (See Figure 14-16B.)

Several versions of UNIX have been developed by Bell Laboratories over the years. In addition, several UNIX-like operating systems and several UNIX-based operating systems now exist. Vendors offering the former have developed software patterned after UNIX, but are not marketing the code actually written at Bell. Vendors offering the latter have acquired Bell's UNIX code through contractual agreements with Western Electric. Most of them add features such as more high-level-language support, greater error detection and recovery capabilities, and ease-of-use characteristics. They also commit to provide ongoing assistance and maintenance. Charles River Data System's UNOS for MC68000-microprocessor-based machines is an example of the former. Microsoft's XENIX, which supports numerous 16-bit microprocessors, is an example of the latter. Western Electric is itself actively marketing UNIX System V, declared to be the "standard" base for all subsequent releases.

By 1982 well over 3000 UNIX systems existed worldwide: at least 1000 in the Bell System, close to 2000 at universities, and another 600 in commercial and government use. These numbers include many large mainframe and minicomputer implementations; they do not include microprocessor-based implementations, which are now appearing. Whether or not business users will find UNIX's features cost-justifiable at the microcomputer level remains to be seen. The demand appears to be increasing. Clearly, UNIX is currently supporting many key system development activities.

CHAPTER SUMMARY

1. Effective application of computers is heavily dependent on software. Both system programs and application programs are required.

2. Software has evolved through distinct generations just as hardware has. Initially, a small control program called a *monitor* took over the program load function formerly initiated by a human operator.

3. More sophisticated monitors and operating systems that could handle job-to-job transitions were developed. Job-control statements were used to tell the computer what to do next in batch, or stacked-job, processing.

4. Online direct-access systems were developed to process input transactions in random order as they were received and to assist individual users in problem solving.

5. In a multiprogramming system, more than one program resides in primary storage at a time. Programs with high I/O requirements and low internal processing requirements are loaded into foreground areas. Conversely, programs with low I/O requirements and high internal processing requirements are executed as background jobs.

6. In a multiprocessing system, instructions from the same program or from different programs are executed simultaneously on two or more processors. The processors may be large computers of a type also used in single-processor systems, a mix of large and small special-function processors, or microprocessors within a desktop computer system.

7. A real-time system provides output fast enough to satisfy any user requirements. It can be used to control real-life activity.

8. Time sharing allows several users to interact with a system on what appears to be a simultaneous basis. The system resources are shared among them.

9. Virtual-storage capabilities allow a system to be used as though more primary storage exists than is actually present. A greater number of programs can be running at any given time than would be possible otherwise.

10. In a virtual-machine environment, each user is able to use a total computer system—both hardware and software—that does not actually exist, but seems to. Many unrelated virtual machines running different jobs can be active on the system at a time.

11. A portable operating system can easily be adapted to run on any computer having a particular architecture. CP/M and UNIX are prominent examples.

DISCUSSION QUESTIONS

1. (a) List and discuss three broad categories of system software.
   (b) Give examples of programs in each category, based on a system available to you.

2. Choose any one of the industry categories illustrated in Figure 14-2. Suggest application programs for that industry that might be developed and marketed to users on a national or international basis.

3. Explain why operating systems are needed on today's computers.

4. Explain stacked-job processing.

5. Distinguish between an online system and a real-time system.

6. Distinguish between multiprogramming and multiprocessing.

7. Of what significance is priority in a multiprogramming environment?

8. Give examples of applications that can be computerized only if the system available can perform real-time processing.

9. Assume you are a member of a business firm that has decided to take advantage of time-sharing capabilities.
   (a) Suggest two approaches by which you can do so.
   (b) What are the advantages of each approach?

10. Distinguish between a virtual-storage environment and a virtual-machine environment. In doing so, emphasize the user's point of view.

11. Assume you are a computer manufacturer, an independent software vendor, or a user. From your chosen point of view, argue for or against operating-system portability.

15

MANAGING DATA

There's been an accident. Someone has been injured. An emergency medical helicopter flies to the scene, picks up the injured person, and rushes him to St. Anthony's Hospital for treatment. On the way, a computer on board the helicopter records data on the injury and provides assistance with diagnosis. At the same time, the computer records the data needed for patient admission to the hospital and signals what medication and equipment will be necessary upon arrival. Medicine has entered the Computer Age.

Hospitals are increasingly using computers for everything from admissions and discharges to diagnosis, treatment, and billing.

Courtesy St. Anthony's Hospital Systems

Courtesy St. Anthony's Hospital Systems

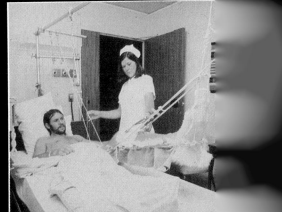
Courtesy Social Security Administration

Hospitals are using computers to predict factors leading to infant mortality. One computerized device uses ultrasound to create a picture of the unborn child in the womb. Other devices monitor fetal life, reveal the presence of tumors in adults, or provide full-color scan images of a person's brain, all without surgery. Another imaging device can be used to create 3-D, color-interpreted images, such as those of a woman's facial structure seen here.

A very important use of computers in medicine is in keeping track of diagnostic information. One medical computer application not only can speed preparation of diagnostic radiology reports, but can also provide information on workload, revealing staff efficiency. (National Computer Systems offers the appropriate materials for this application.) Reports on patients can be accessed from a number of terminals and printed out as needed.

Candler General Hospital, in Savannah, Georgia, uses a Hospital Communications Management System. With this system, doctors and nurses can update computerized records for patients from any of the hospital's internal telephones.

Used with permission of SCSS Inc.

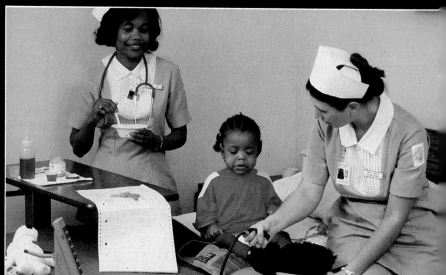
Courtesy IBM Corporation

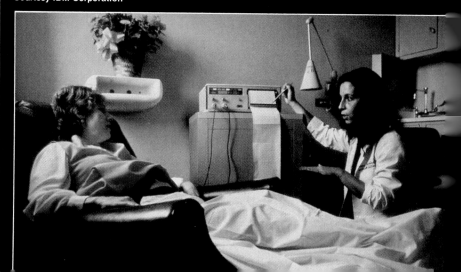

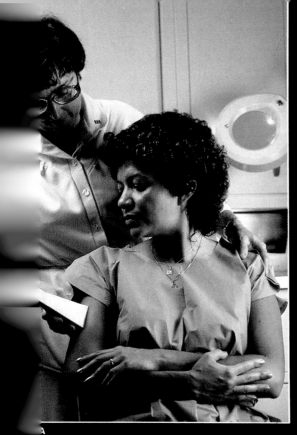

© **Dan McCoy/Rainbow**

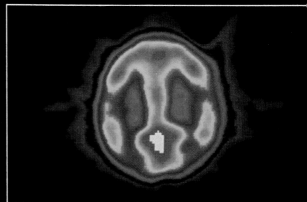

Courtesy Ramtek Corporation/UCLA Medical Center

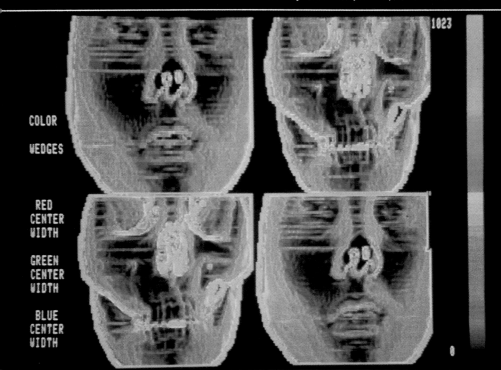

COLOR
WEDGES

RED
CENTER
WIDTH

GREEN
CENTER
WIDTH

BLUE
CENTER
WIDTH

1023

Two other areas in which prompt and correct information is important are the medical laboratory and the pharmacy. Computerized devices in the laboratory can speed the analysis of body fluids and tissue samples, providing more accurate results than earlier methods. Prescriptions can be entered as input at remote terminals and be displayed as output on the pharmacy's terminal. When the medication specified on the prescription has been picked up, that fact can be entered into the database as well.

Computers in hospitals and other medical facilities throughout the world are literally helping to save many human lives.

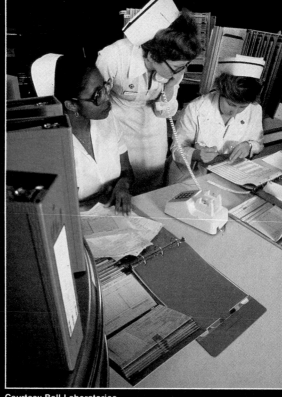

Courtesy Bell Laboratories

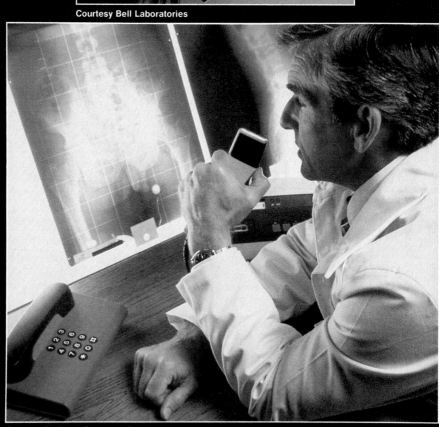

Courtesy National Computer Systems

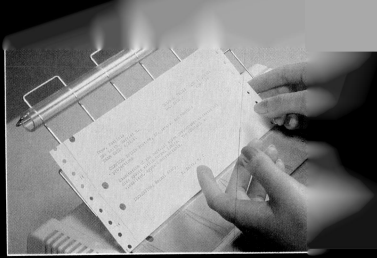

15 | MANAGING DATA

A computer system must be able to process data with speed and accuracy. Through microminiaturization techniques, the speeds of internal processing operations have increased steadily. The speeds of I/O operations have increased also. Because I/O operations involve the movement of physical components, they cannot be done as fast as internal processing operations.

In Chapter 8, we learned about techniques to minimize the inefficiencies caused by differences in speeds—buffering, overlapped processing, and asynchronous I/O, for example. For simplicity, we may want to read a single record, process the record, and then write the resulting record. However, to make efficient use of the computer system available to us, we usually need to do things differently.

In Chapter 6, we looked in some detail at both tape and disk devices. We learned that records can be written to and read from tape sequentially. With disk, either sequential or direct processing can be used. That may sound simple, but it isn't. How do we know where to write a record on a disk? How can we be sure there isn't another record already there?

How can we find a particular record written on a disk previously by our program or by another program? What will our program do if it tries to write to (or read from) a disk, but the disk isn't there?

If every microcomputer user had to know the number of tracks on a particular disk, how many records of a particular length can be fit on one track, how to move a read/write head from one track to another, what I/O operations really must occur to "close" a file, and so on, chances are there would be far fewer users of microcomputers!

Business application programs for payroll, accounts receivable, and inventory control have one characteristic in common: They involve a great deal of I/O activity. As we have seen, this activity includes not only initial entry of data and provision of output, but also creating, processing, and maintaining data stored in computer files. In fact, it is often said that if a user-programmer had to write all the coding necessary for I/O operations, he or she would spend 40 percent of the programming time on these operations alone. Clearly, then, both the productivity of the computer system and the productivity of user-programmers are directly related to the I/O programming required. In recognition of this fact, a number of programming aids have been developed by computer manufacturers and software development firms. Among them are input/output control systems, file systems, data management systems, and database management systems. All these aids are discussed in this chapter. We learn more about file organization and file access. Then we study the database approach. Finally, we discuss managers' information needs. We see how management information systems can be implemented to provide for these needs. Brief overviews of emerging database capabilities complete the chapter.

IOCS An *input/output control system* (*IOCS*) is a part of the basic I/O software of an EDP system. In early systems, the IOCS consisted of macro instructions provided as part of the computer's assembler language. When a program containing one or more of these macro instructions was translated into machine language, a sequence of machine-language instructions was inserted in place of each macro instruction. One or more of the inserted instructions were usually calls to still other sequences of instructions known as *I/O subroutines*. The I/O subroutines were also provided as part of the IOCS. They were held in primary storage or an online storage device. At program execution time, the subroutines were invoked by the inserted calls to do I/O processing.

When operating systems were developed, some IOCS routines were still embodied in programming languages. Others became integral parts of the operating systems. In these cases, the IOCS routines were either of two types: physical IOCS or logical IOCS.

Physical IOCS routines were usually included in the major system control program. A physical unit block (PUB) table associated the symbolic file or device name used by a program with the actual machine address of the device on which the user's data resided at program execution time. The concept of standard system file names was introduced as a means of providing some degree of device independence. The programmer could refer to SYSIN, for example, with the assurance that SYSIN would be associated with whatever device was being used as the standard *system input* unit. Similarly, SYSOUT would be associated with whatever device was being used as the standard *system output* unit.

Logical IOCS routines were the macro-instruction sequences needed to create, access, and maintain data files. As discussed above, these sequences were generally inserted in or called by programs coded by user-programmers.

To present specifics as to what IOCS routines were good for, from the user-programmer's point of view, some common features of IOCS routines provided by numerous vendors are described below. Since similar routines are also provided within system software today, these examples will help you understand what's really happening during I/O processing on any systems that you use.

Input/Output Scheduling

Some computers handle I/O in a serial, synchronous fashion. No internal processing can be done until an I/O operation is completed. Conversely, no I/O operation can take place while computation is being performed.

Other computers achieve simultaneous, asynchronous I/O and computing. The main processor can continue its processing while an I/O device locates data, reads data into primary storage, or writes data out. This simultaneous I/O and computing capability helps to prevent unnecessary delays. (See Chapter 8 to review these concepts.)

It is not easy to schedule card or tape I/O—which, because of the physical nature of the data-recording medium, must occur sequentially—in a way that maximizes system efficiency. When direct-access storage devices are used, proper scheduling becomes even more important and more difficult.

An IOCS allows the application programmer to make use of complex system-controlled synchronous or asynchronous I/O capabilities, both of which are designed to help the system operate efficiently.

Blocking and Deblocking Records

High-density tape and disk devices cannot be used efficiently if files contain only short blocks of data. For example, assume a parts master file contains 80-character records, and these records are written on magnetic tape. Less than one-tenth of the tape may contain useful data. The rest of the tape contains interblock gaps (IBG's). We learned in Chapter 6 that the gaps must be provided to allow for magnetic-tape-unit start/stop times. Using only one-tenth of the tape for data, however, is like putting nine blank cards in a deck for every one data card! We must look for a better alternative.

By grouping, or *blocking*, records, many IBG's can be eliminated. The number of records in each block is called the *blocking factor*. In Figure 15-1A, records are not blocked. An IBG follows every record. In Figure 15-1B, records are grouped with a blocking factor of 2. Only one IBG is needed for each pair of records. Half of the IBG's in the file have been eliminated. A given length of tape or area of disk containing blocked records holds several times the amount of data it could hold if the records were not blocked.

When there are fewer IBG's on a data-recording medium, less time is spent in passing over portions of the medium that contain no data. Thus, a magnetic-tape unit reading from a tape containing blocked records spends more of its time reading data and less of its time spacing over IBG's. The end result is a higher effective data transfer rate. When disk storage is used, the time required to move a piece of data is substantially less than the time required to find it. This also makes it advantageous to move data in large blocks. For example, it is much

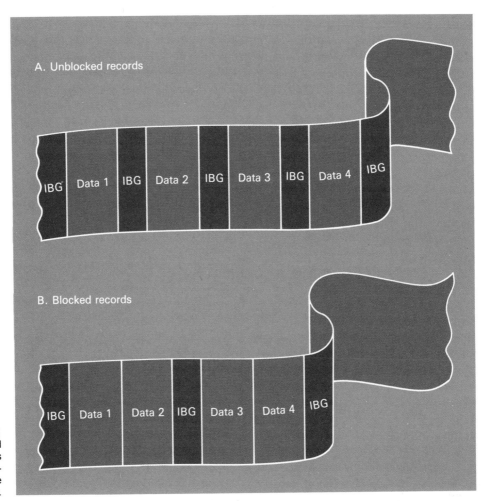

A. Unblocked records

| IBG | Data 1 | IBG | Data 2 | IBG | Data 3 | IBG | Data 4 | IBG |

B. Blocked records

| IBG | Data 1 | Data 2 | IBG | Data 3 | Data 4 | IBG |

FIGURE 15-1
When records are blocked on a storage medium, less space is needed for inter-block gaps and more space is available for data.

faster to retrieve 10 records stored sequentially on a disk during one access than to retrieve them one at a time by means of 10 accesses. For small blocks of data, the transfer time is negligible compared to seek time. (To review what actions must occur when moving data to or from a disk, see Chapter 6.)

When records are blocked, a single record in a block is called a *logical record*. The complete block is called a *physical record* because it is treated as a single physical entity for input or output. That is, it is read into or written from primary storage at one time. If records are not blocked, one logical record and one physical record are equivalent. If records are grouped with a blocking factor of 3, one physical record consists of three logical records.

An IOCS has the ability to read and write blocks of records. On output, it can accept single records that have been processed and hold them until a block has been accumulated. Conversely, on input, it can *deblock* a block of records read as input. That is, it can make single records available for processing as required by the application program. Thanks to the IOCS, the application programmer is free to treat all records to be read and written as single records. The application programmer need not be concerned with the mechanics of blocking and deblocking.

Standard
Error-Correction
Procedures

If transfer of data to or from an I/O device is not successful the first time it is tried, certain techniques can be used to correct the error and allow the execution of a program to continue without interruption.

If an IOCS is not available, error-correction routines must be included in application programs. For example, a program loop may be set up to cause backspace and reread operations to be executed if a read attempt fails. If necessary, the loop may be re-executed as many as, say, 10 times. If any one of the subsequent read attempts is successful, the program loop is exited immediately. If the record cannot be read in 10 attempts, the program must report the error. It may attempt to process another record, or it may terminate.

With an IOCS, such routines need not be written for each application program. A simple READ or WRITE statement (or its equivalent) causes an IOCS standard error-correction routine to be included in the program. In some EDP systems, if an uncorrectable I/O error occurs, it is documented via a message. Then, execution of the next program is initiated automatically. In the case of certain types of I/O errors, an IOCS need only inform the application program of the error condition. The program then determines how the condition should be handled.

End-of-Volume
and End-of-File
Processing

Two terms with related but very distinct meanings in electronic data processing are *volume* and *file*. Both deal with input and output. A *volume* is a physical entity used for storing data or instructions. Thus, one reel of tape is a volume; one disk or disk pack on a disk storage unit is a volume; and so on. In contrast, a *file* is a logical entity, a group of records whose contents are related. For example, customer names and addresses are often maintained on a master name and address (N/A) file.

A file need not be restricted by the physical limitations of volumes. As suggested in Figure 15-2, several files can be stored on one tape or disk volume. Conversely, one file may be stored on several tape or disk volumes.

When records are being read sequentially from a file on tape and all the records on a single reel have been processed, the tape is said to be at *end of volume* or, sometimes, at *end of reel*. Obviously, some special processing instructions are required to cause subsequent records to be read from another volume. Subroutines within an IOCS can control the required operations. The application program need not even be aware that end of volume has been reached. Generally, the nature of the particular volume from which data is read has no significant effect on the procedure needed to solve the problem.

When all data records from a particular file have been processed, the file is said to be at *end of file*. The programmer may not want to perform a test each time a record is to be read from the file to determine whether end of file has been reached. He or she may not be aware of certain standard system actions required at end of file. IOCS routines can make the test, perform end-of-file processing if appropriate, and then inform the application program that processing of the file is complete. The logic of the application program should be set up so that no instructions to read data from the file are executed thereafter.

FILE SYSTEMS

In the 1950s, when business data processing with computer help began, programs were relatively simple. In most cases, each program and the data it

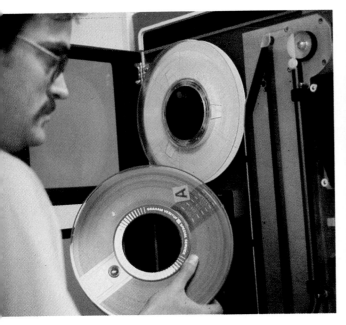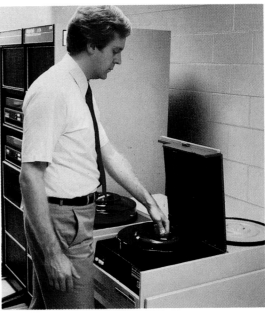

B

FIGURE 15-2 One volume may contain multiple files (A), or several volumes may be needed to hold one file (B). (*Courtesy* [A] *United Information Services, Inc.;* [B] *3M*)

processed were conceptually locked together. The data was, in effect, an extension of the program. For convenience, the data was usually grouped into records and files, kept on punched cards or on tape. Each file "belonged to" one program.

As programs became more comprehensive, they dealt with data in more than one file. The relationships between files were maintained within the program that processed them. In many cases, the file descriptions were also. This practice made the program larger and seemingly more complex.

Another layer of complexity was added when two or more programs were written to process the same data, but in different ways. Special sorting and merging steps were introduced to rearrange the data records as required for each program.

Soon, multiple copies of user data records began to exist, and yet additional files containing some or all of the same data were created. Perhaps the system analyst, designer, or programmer was not aware that the data was already being collected elsewhere. Perhaps the data was known to be available, but the format of the individual data records did not coincide well with the processing to be done by a new program. For example, a hospital using an EDP system might carry the name, address, and date of entry for each patient in an accounts-receivable master file, a patient master file, and a bed master file. The telephone number of the phone beside the patient's bed was likely to be in both the patient and bed master files, and so on. (See Figure 15-3.) This duplication of data led to the necessity for multiple updating (often overlooked) and the storage and processing of inconsistent data.

In the 1960s, both users and information system personnel saw the need to take a different approach. Programs that dealt with the same data began to be implemented as integrated application systems rather than as independent or

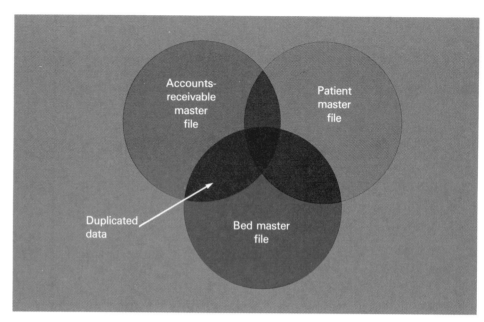

FIGURE 15-3
When master files are maintained for specific applications, user data is often duplicated in two or more files.

loosely related entities. The need for more care in file design and for recognizing the relationships between data within files began to be realized. To support this kind of application system development, computer manufacturers provided *file systems* as part of the operating systems for their computers. Most file systems were able to support direct processing as well as sequential processing of user data records. The file systems were also able to:

- Assist the user in creating, changing, and deleting files
- Provide a mapping from the symbolic names known in an application program to the physical addresses needed to access the files required
- Manage the allocation of physical space on tape or disk
- Keep account of the date of creation, the size, and the security characteristics of each file
- Move portions of files (that is, blocks of records) to and from primary storage
- Permit and control the sharing of files by multiple users
- Provide for backup and recovery of files to prevent loss of data
- Perform other I/O functions needed by programs in execution

In today's file systems, a distinction is made between the way a file is organized and how it is accessed. *File organizaton* is concerned with the techniques used in arranging the records in a file on the physical storage medium. *File access* is concerned with the manner in which the records in a file are written or read. We have discussed two types of reading and writing operations: sequential and direct. User data files to be accessed using either of these approaches may be organized in any one of several ways. Three common file organizations are shown schematically in Figures 15-4 through 15-6. They are:

- *Sequential*—Records are organized solely on the basis of their successive physical locations in the file. The "next" record is the record that physically follows the current one. (See Figure 15-4.) The records are usually – but not necessarily – sequenced according to a user-selected key that exists in all records. For example, the records in a student master file may be stored in student-number order. The 100th record in the file can be read only after reading the 99 records that precede it. Therefore, for practical purposes, a sequential file can only be processed sequentially. It is not reasonable to read 99 records to get the 100th one, or 145 records to get the 146th one, and so on. A sequential file may be stored on cards, tape, or disk (or on paper, as a simple list).

● *Direct* – Records are positioned in the file on the basis of an established relationship between the key of a record and the physical address of the location where the record should be stored. This relationship is established by logic within application programs. For example, suppose an 8-digit part-number field is declared to be the key field for records in an inventory master file. Further suppose the five rightmost digits of each record key are used as the address for the record containing the key. (See Figure 15-5.) The first three of these digits are the relative track number; the remaining two digits are a relative record number on that track. Unfortunately, this means that sensitivity to these device characteristics is built into application programs. If new high-speed disk storage devices are acquired and the inventory master file is moved to the new devices, all programs containing the physical addresses of locations on the old devices will have to be changed. An offsetting advantage of this approach is that, once the address of a desired record has been determined, direct processing can be used immediately to write the record as output (or read the record as input). In our example, this means that the records for parts in inventory can be processed in any order whenever the inventory changes. A direct file must be stored on a direct-access storage device (DASD).

● *Indexed sequential* – Records are positioned in a file in ascending or descending sequence on the basis of their record keys. In addition, one or more levels of indexes are maintained for the file. Each index entry contains the key of a record and an address that points to the location where the record is stored.

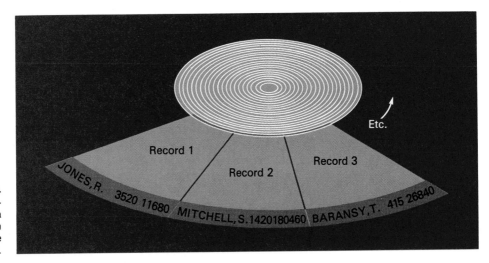

FIGURE 15-4
When sequential file organization is used, user data records are positioned in successive locations on the storage medium.

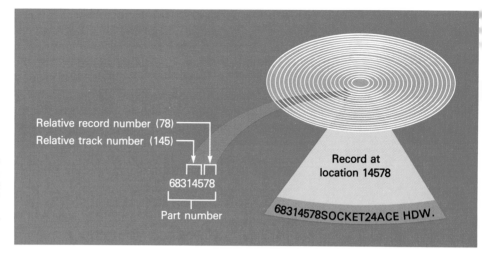

FIGURE 15-5
When direct file organization is used, user data records are positioned and accessed on the basis of their record keys; an 8-digit part number serves as the record key in this example.

(See Figure 15-6.) In a system that supports indexed sequential organization, the indexes are maintained automatically by system software; they do not have to be created or updated by application programs. Even more important, user data records in the file can be accessed sequentially or directly. In sequential processing, the records are simply retrieved in record-key order. In direct processing, the system software searches the index (or indexes) to find the index entry containing a key that matches or is the nearest key beyond the key of a desired record. Upon finding the entry, the system software then determines the location of the record. Next, it retrieves the record. A law firm's accounts-receivable records may be stored in an indexed sequential file, for example. Sequential processing can be used to read all the records in sequence and print monthly statements. Direct processing can be used to access individual records in response to customers' inquiries about their accounts.

DATA MANAGEMENT SYSTEMS

The term *data management* came into common usage in the late 1960s as users insisted that the costs of file storage and maintenance be reduced and the duplication of data within systems be eliminated. They wanted to be able to store their data in such a way that it could be accessed, retrieved, and manipulated in a variety of ways, by any of several programs, to meet constantly changing and ever-expanding information needs. A *data management system* included functions in addition to those normally found in a file system — functions that permitted the user to describe hierarchies of data and to name and use relationships between sets of data items. Many of the I/O subroutines formerly provided as part of an IOCS were incorporated in a variety of access-method routines. A macro instruction issued in an assembler-language program, or an I/O statement in a high-level-language program, was assembled or compiled as a branch or call to an appropriate access-method routine. Then, during program execution, the access-method routine performed the requested I/O operation at that point in processing.

The access-method routines needed by a particular program were determined by the way each file used by the program was organized and the methods of

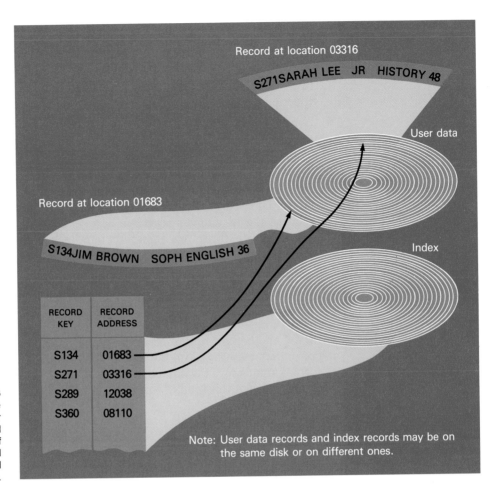

Record at location 03316

S271SARAH LEE JR HISTORY 48

User data

Record at location 01683

S134JIM BROWN SOPH ENGLISH 36

RECORD KEY	RECORD ADDRESS
S134	01683
S271	03316
S289	12038
S360	08110

Index

Note: User data records and index records may be on the same disk or on different ones.

FIGURE 15-6
When indexed sequential file organization is used, user data records are positioned nd accessed on the basis of their record keys, and tries in a system-maintained index point to them.

access desired. A sequential file was processed with the help of sequential access-method (SAM) routines. An indexed sequential file was processed by indexed sequential access-method (ISAM) routines. A direct file was processed by direct access-method (DAM) routines. Of these, the direct organization and DAM routines offered the greatest potential for fast response to input transactions keyed in by terminal users. These facilities were also needed for real-time processing. The sequential organization and SAM routines made the most efficient use of the storage medium and were suitable for batch-processing applications. The indexed sequential organization and ISAM routines offered flexibility. The user's data records could be processed sequentially for high-volume batch-processing applications or directly when volume was low but fast response was required.

In 1973, IBM responded further to users' data-handling needs by introducing two new file organizations and access-method routines to support them. Extensive software to assist users in defining and maintaining their files (usually called *data sets*) was also made available. Descriptions of user data sets and access information about them are kept in system-maintained catalogs. In 1975, a third data set organization was introduced. Collectively, all these data-handling facilities are referred to as the *virtual-storage access method*, or

VSAM. Today's VSAM organization and processing capabilities can be summarized as follows:

- *Entry-sequenced data set* – Records are stored in arrival-time order; each one physically follows the one that was written just before it. This organization is functionally equivalent to sequential organization on a DASD.
- *Key-sequenced data set* – Records are in ascending or descending order according to the keys of the records. This organization is functionally equivalent to indexed sequential organization on a DASD.
- *Relative record data set* – Records are stored in fixed-length slots identified by relative record numbers. When a record is to be written to the data set, it is assigned a relative record number that determines where it is stored. The relative record number serves as a key. This organization is functionally equivalent to direct organization but does not require that application programs be device-dependent to take advantage of its capabilities.

Today, software supporting sequential, indexed sequential, and direct file organizations is available for microcomputer systems as well as for minis, mainframes, and supercomputers. The term *file management* seems to be more common than *data management* – perhaps because it is less likely to be confused with yet another term, *database management* (discussed below). If you hear microcomputer users talking about an FMS program, for example, chances are that *FMS* stands for *file management system.* Few users can manage their data resources without this kind of software to help them.

THE DATABASE APPROACH

Even after users saw the need to design and implement programs as parts of integrated application systems, a typical approach was to set up separate files for each application. The employee master file was processed by the application programs that kept company personnel records; the payroll master file was used by the programs that prepared employee payrolls; the skills-inventory master file was maintained by the programs that kept track of in-house education class rosters; and so on. This approach still led to several files with duplicate data. If, for example, an employee changed jobs within the company or moved to a new home, every file that contained data pertaining to job status or home address had to be changed. The separate-file approach also made it difficult to extract data that was scattered throughout various files. For example, although the payroll master file contained the current pay rate of each employee, there was no easy way to extract the current pay rates of all employees hired after a particular date, or the average wage of all employees between the ages of 50 and 65.

To meet such information needs, the concept of a *database* was developed. Under this approach, a file is not treated as a separate entity. Master files are not set up for just one application. Instead, a system or database designer works with the current or prospective users of a system to identify (1) the information needs of those users, and (2) the data that must be stored and processed to satisfy them. The designer determines whether or not the data is already being collected and stored as part of the organization's data resource. The designer works to insure that the data is organized and structured in such a way that it can be accessed by the programs for all applications that use it. (See Figure 15-7.)

The database approach can be employed wherever storage and manipulation of data are required. It is most useful when relationships between data are numerous and complex, and where information requirements are subject to change. Common examples of databases are (1) a student database containing enrollment data for all students currently attending classes, and (2) a parts database established by a company for inventory-control purposes. A database for a commercial bank may contain, suitably linked together, all data about each customer's dealings with the bank—as a check writer, saver, borrower, safety-deposit-box holder, and so on.

Although we could say, for purposes of simplification, that a database is a lot of data, there's more to creating a database than just collecting data. In fact, certain characteristics are essential to a well-designed database:

- It is an organized, integrated collection of data.
- It can be referred to by all relevant applications with relative ease and with no (or, in practice, limited) duplication of data.
- It is a model of the natural relationships of the data that exist in the user's real-world environment.

To say that data is contained in a database does not imply that files no longer exist. They do, but the emphasis is changed. System designers do not direct their attention to collecting data for use by a particular program and in ways dictated by EDP-system hardware. Instead, they provide for collecting, organizing, and accessing data in ways that are natural and meaningful to users.

FIGURE 15-7
Under a database approach, integrated application programs such as IBM's MAPICS help users to achieve manufacturing, accounting, and production information control. (*Courtesy IBM Corporation*)

DATABASE DESIGN

Much software is being developed and marketed to support the database approach. A user organization cannot assume, however, that choosing appropriate software is all that it takes to establish database capabilities. The task of database design is prerequisite to successful database implementation. It must remain largely a responsibility of the user organization. The content and structure of the database must be tailored to the user's information needs. System or database designers must study, interview, and investigate to determine what data ought to be included in the database, what interrelationships among the data exist, what kinds of inquiries will be made against the database, and so on. This is a time-consuming, difficult task, but it is an essential and valuable one. It occurs during the system analysis phase of the system development cycle.

A simple example may give us some insight into the considerations involved. Assume a company's inventory data is organized by item number, as shown in Figure 15-8. Each type of item is identified by a unique item number. If all data entered into the database is associated with these item numbers, obtaining or changing data about a particular item whose number is known will be fairly straightforward.

The question is: Will a sales representative be able to determine how many items of a particular item class, say S1, are in stock? Will an accountant be able to determine what the current retail value of all in-stock items of another item class is? Suppose a product manager wants to know which items are obtained from supplier Z Company, whether orders for the items have been issued to that supplier, and whether it is possible to obtain the identified items from either of two other suppliers who are currently offering discounts.

To answer such questions, either (1) all data that may be needed for each item must be stored together with the item number, or (2) there must be additional data about, say, ordering or suppliers elsewhere in the database, and there must be multiple ways of getting at that data.

Often, a database approach is implemented in stages—first the inventory-control system, then the order-entry system, then the billing system, and so on. Obviously, such a task is not one to be undertaken lightly or to be redone easily whenever conditions change. Since user needs can be expected to change, however, the database itself must be designed so that it can be changed. The care (or lack of care) exercised in database design contributes substantially to the success (or failure) of the database approach and of the applications that depend on it.

LOGICAL DATA STRUCTURES

As with even a basic IOCS, a distinction is made here between the way data is stored on a data-recording medium (physical) and the way data is seen by users or application programs (logical). The logical view of data is the view that is meaningful to them. Various types of logical data structures are used to model real-world data relationships. The structures are called *data models.*

At the very simplest level, all units of data are independent and logically of equal significance. They may be either ordered or unordered. If ordered, they form a linear data structure. You may hear this type of structure referred to as a *flat file.* (Look back at Figure 15-4.)

Next in terms of complexity is the *inverted file.* Here data is modeled as one or more lists. Each list contains user data records with identical formats. Access to

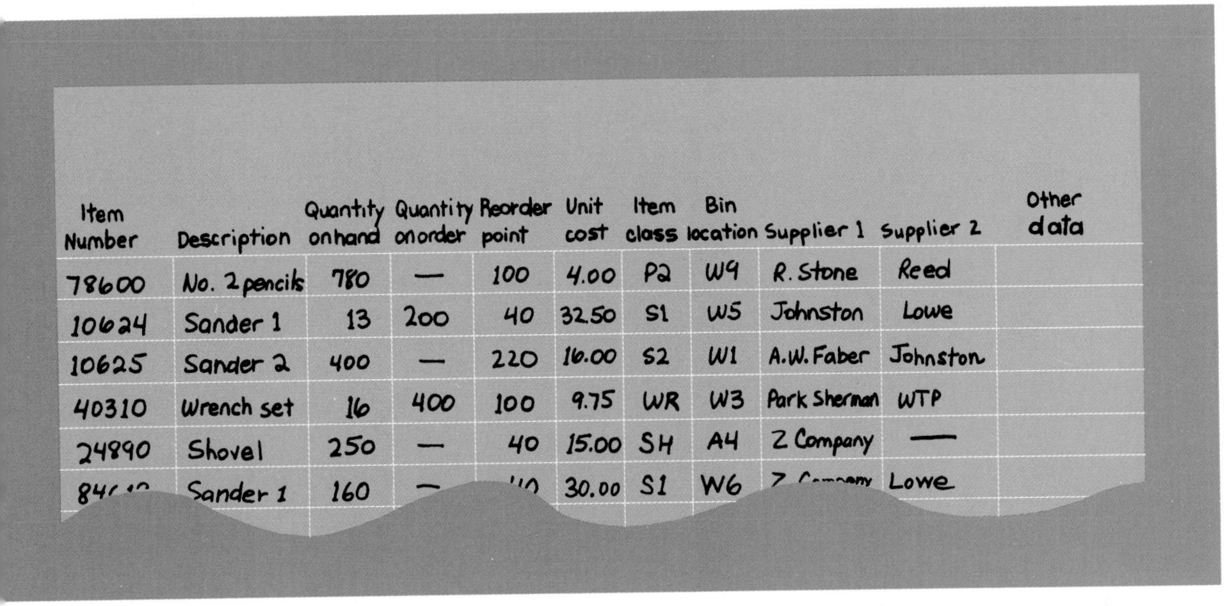

Item Number	Description	Quantity on hand	Quantity on order	Reorder point	Unit cost	Item class	Bin location	Supplier 1	Supplier 2	Other data
78600	No. 2 pencils	780	—	100	4.00	P2	W9	R. Stone	Reed	
10624	Sander 1	13	200	40	32.50	S1	W5	Johnston	Lowe	
10625	Sander 2	400	—	220	16.00	S2	W1	A.W. Faber	Johnston	
40310	Wrench set	16	400	100	9.75	WR	W3	Park Sherman	WTP	
24890	Shovel	250	—	40	15.00	SH	A4	Z Company	—	
84610	Sander 1	160	—	40	30.00	S1	W6	Z Company	Lowe	

FIGURE 15-8 Typical users have lots of data that must be collected, organized, and entered into online databases before database processing can occur.

the lists is achieved through an index, or inversion. Each index entry contains a key and pointers to records that contain that key value. If you're thinking that this type of data structure is similar in some respects to an indexed sequential file, you're right. (See Figure 15-6.) The system software that supports this type of data structure may also support the use of pointers, or links, in user data records. In this case, one or more levels of indexes are used to locate a particular user data record; that record in turn contains one or more pointers to other user data records. Those records can then be accessed without referring again to the indexes.

Since, in the real world, the user's data is often interrelated in many ways, there often exists a need for a more complex data model. When a *hierarchical model* is used, each data record is broken into logically related segments by system software. The segments are connected by logical pointers in a treelike arrangement. (See Figure 15-9.) The user's data is mapped onto this model when it is stored in the database.

As an example, assume the hierarchical data structure in Figure 15-9A is used to map data in an employee database. As with any hierarchical model, there is one root segment at the top level in the hierarchy. In this case, it's an employee-name segment. The root segment points to any number of dependent segments. In this case, each employee-name segment may point to several address segments, several experience segments, and several education segments for a particular employee.

The result of a data mapping—one *instance* of the hierarchical model in Figure 15-9A—is shown in Figure 15-9B. When applying for a job, employee J. Baker listed his current address and his immediately prior address; this data is stored in two address segments in the database. Since this employee has held positions as a sales representative and as a buyer, the database contains two experience segments for him. The three education segments for the employee reflect the formal education he has completed before or since taking the job.

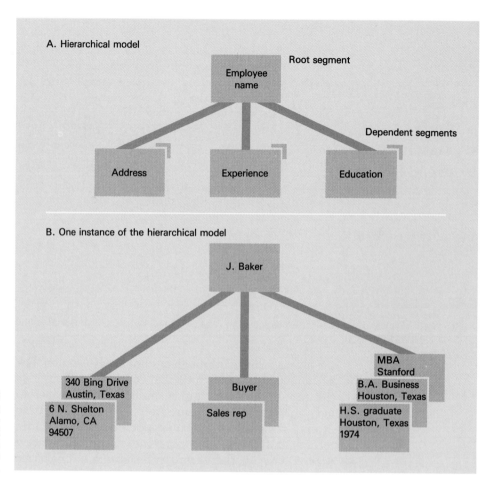

A. Hierarchical model

Root segment

Employee name

Dependent segments

Address

Experience

Education

B. One instance of the hierarchical model

J. Baker

340 Bing Drive
Austin, Texas

6 N. Shelton
Alamo, CA
94507

Buyer

Sales rep

MBA
Stanford

B.A. Business
Houston, Texas

H.S. graduate
Houston, Texas
1974

FIGURE 15-9
Data about employees can be mapped onto a hierarchical data structure that models the real-world relationships of employee data items.

Notice that, in Figure 15-9A, only one level of dependent segments exists below the top, or root, level in the hierarchical data model. There could be several levels. However, each dependent segment can be pointed to (owned) by one and only one segment in a level above it. We say that a parent segment can point to (own) any number of child segments, but each child segment can have one and only one parent segment.

Of course, there are real-world situations where this single-owner relationship of data elements does not apply. In such situations, a *network model* may provide a better representation of the user's data. (See Figure 15-10.) The general rules for the network model are that a parent segment may have any number of child segments, and a child segment may have any number of parent segments. Let's use Figure 15-10 to think this through for a particular application.

In this figure, a particular network model is applied to map the data collected by a community college. Notice that there are two types of segments at the top level in the model. There could be several. Notice also that each class segment at the second level in this model may be owned by one or more segments of either of two types: student-name segments and instructor-name segments. This reflects the real-world situation where a class may be taught by one or more instructors and may be attended by one or more students. In the particular data instance in Figure 15-10B, we see that instructor J. Turner teaches English I and English II,

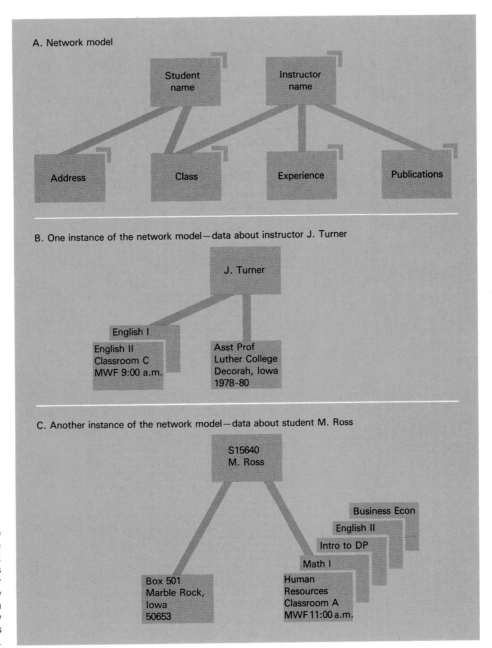

A. Network model

Student
name

Instructor
name

Address

Class

Experience

Publications

B. One instance of the network model—data about instructor J. Turner

J. Turner

English I

English II
Classroom C
MWF 9:00 a.m.

Asst Prof
Luther College
Decorah, Iowa
1978-80

C. Another instance of the network model—data about student M. Ross

S15640
M. Ross

Business Econ

English II

Intro to DP

Math I

Box 501
Marble Rock,
Iowa
50653

Human
Resources
Classroom A
MWF 11:00 a.m.

FIGURE 15-10
A college's data may be
mapped onto a network
model so that the classes
taught by a particular
professor (A) or attended by
a particular student (B) can
be determined easily
without storing the class
data several times.

that he was an Assistant Professor at Luther College from 1978 through 1980, and that he has no publications to his credit. In Figure 15-10C, we see that student M. Ross, from Marble Rock, Iowa, is currently taking five classes. One of the classes is English II. There is no need to store the data about the class English II in the database twice, because it can be accessed using either the instructor-name/class relationship or the student-name/class relationship provided for by the network model.

If you think from our discussions so far that designing a database is not an easy task, you're right. It's not, but recent developments have helped to simplify the task, at least for some applications. At the heart of these developments is the *relational model*. The most significant aspect of this data model is its simplicity. When the relational model is used, all data within a database is viewed as being in tables. (See Figure 15-11.) Each table is a model of real-world data relationships. At the same time, it is a logical data structure that we as users can readily understand and visualize. After all, we deal with tables daily.

Figure 15-11A shows the general structure of the relational model. Figure 15-11B shows instances of 2-, 3-, and 4-column relational models as they might occur in an inventory database. Relation SN shows the numbers and names of all suppliers. Relation SI shows the items supplied by each supplier and the delivery lead times for those items. Relation IQ contains data about each item.

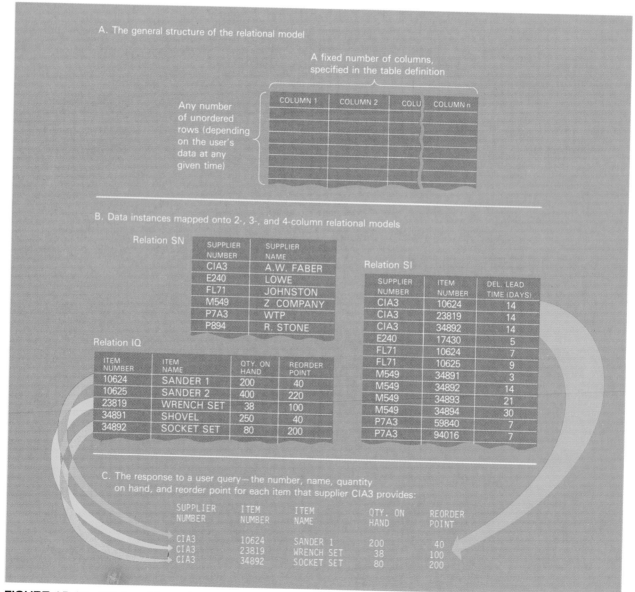

FIGURE 15-11 Inventory data can be stored in tables and retrieved from a number of those tables under system control when relational database processing capabilities are available.

Assume supplier CIA3, A. W. Faber, goes out of business. We may want to know immediately not only the number but also the name, quantity on hand, and reorder point for each item that supplier CIA3 provided. A system that supports the relational model can perform well-defined mathematical operations on the SI and IQ tables to obtain that information for us. We need not describe a specific access path to the data, as users often do when using a hierarchical or network model. The response to our query – also a relation – is shown in Figure 15-11C.

DBMS In simplest terms, a *database management system* (*DBMS*) is the system software that supports a database. Usually, it is supplied by a computer manufacturer or software development firm. It may be developed as an integral part of the operating system for a particular computer or family of computers. More often, it interfaces with the operating system, the database, and users or application programs.

Perhaps the best way to understand the value of a DBMS is to identify the major facilities that many of them provide. Some of the facilities have been mentioned earlier. Not all the facilities are available in all DBMS's. By thinking about why the items listed in Figure 15-12 are important, however, we may get a clearer picture of the kind of database support that's provided.

A file system or a data management system and a DBMS are not mutually exclusive system components. DBMS modules may invoke access-method routines for I/O processing just like application programs do for other than database processing. Because the DBMS does the interfacing with these file-oriented and, in many cases, device-oriented routines, users and application programs no longer need be concerned with them.

Users in turn may interact with a DBMS in various ways. The DBMS may allow INSERT, UPDATE, SELECT, and DELETE statements of a database language to be embedded in host-language (usually, COBOL) application programs. This means that host-language statements can be used to operate on data before it is entered into the database, or after it has been retrieved from the database, to format and print output. The DBMS may also allow query-language statements to be keyed directly into the system by terminal users. In this case, no user programming is required. Most DBMS vendors offer additional software – report writers, application development facilities, and data dictionaries, for example. User friendliness, ease of application development, and flexibility to meet ever-expanding and ever-changing user information needs are emphasized.

Most large and medium-size organizations that opt for the database approach set up a *database administration* (*DBA*) group within their information system staff. DBA personnel assist users in defining data elements, designing databases, estimating DASD requirements, and the like. If file (or data set) names and characteristics, underlying DASD device types, and other physical characteristics of the system must be specified at system installation or startup, the DBA group provides them. Establishing database recovery procedures, negotiating and enforcing data-handling standards, monitoring system performance, and administering system security mechanisms may also be DBA tasks. Notice that many of these tasks are required even in a small organization that uses a DBMS. If there is no DBA group, the user must assume the DBA role. It cannot be ignored.

- **Storage capability:** ability to store large volumes of data—enough to meet all user needs

- **Data integration:** a unified, common data storage designed to eliminate inefficiencies and inconsistencies stemming from duplicate data

- **Data independence:** separation of physical data storage characteristics from logical (user) views of the data, so that changes can be made to the database structure or underlying physical storage without widespread effects on existing programs

- **Data security:** protection mechanisms that prevent unauthorized or accidental disclosure, modification, or destruction of stored data; privacy controls that can be applied on a data-item basis where social and legal issues are potentially involved

- **Data integrity:** protection mechanisms to insure that security controls cannot be bypassed and to prevent corruption of stored data to the degree necessary to complement storage-protection features available in hardware, as well as standards and procedures within the user's operational environment

- **Physical data protection:** backup and recovery mechanisms that permit complete restoration of the database if a hardware or software failure occurs

- **Ease of use:** convenient means of modifying, retrieving, and analyzing data in a variety of ways; complete, accurate, and understandable documentation

- **Multiple-user:** support for concurrent use of the database by a number of users, none of whom need be aware of others; locking mechanisms and deadlock detection and resolution mechanisms that function automatically (without users or application programs having to invoke them)

- **Performance:** provides acceptable response times under the expected user workload; can be tuned to adjust to changes in the workload characteristics over time

- **Portability:** can be run on a range of computers within a particular manufacturer's product line, or across several manufacturers' machines; runs under CP/M, UNIX, PC DOS, . . . ; runs on Z80, 8086, 68000 . . . microprocessors

- **Compatibility:** interfaces with application programs written in COBOL and other available programming languages, and within existing system environments

- **Support:** ongoing support committed and readily available when questions or problems arise; report writers, application generators, and product updates and enhancements also provided

FIGURE 15-12
Managing user data is a major undertaking; a database management system can assist users by providing some or all of the facilities needed to do so.

THE MIS CONCEPT

It is sometimes claimed that every organization, whether or not it uses computers, has a *management information system (MIS)*. If the implication here is that any person in a position of authority or responsibility has a way of finding out at least something about what is going on in an organization, then this claim is valid. However, to increase our understanding of how computers can best be used, we must explore the MIS concept further.

As we saw in Chapter 1, when business personnel were first exposed to computers, they quickly recognized their data-processing value. EDP systems were established to automate what had been regarded as routine clerical (generally, manual or mechanical) functions. Basic business applications such as payroll, accounts receivable, and billing were computerized. In many cases, the applications were processed faster, more accurately, and at lower costs, but the end results, or outputs, were largely unchanged.

Gradually business personnel who used the outputs provided by EDP systems began to ask for modifications to those outputs, and for additional outputs. Management began to recognize the computer's potential—not only for data processing but also for generating information that could be used in decision making. In this context, an MIS can be defined as a computer-based system that is capable of both:

- Processing business transactions reflecting the day-to-day operations of an organization
- Providing to management useful information within the time frame necessary to assist in decision making

MANAGEMENT
Let's look at what the term *management* means. It includes both a process and the people who perform that process. As a process, the functions generally attributed to management are planning, organizing, staffing, directing, and controlling. First, a *plan* for what is to be done must be put in place. Then, an *organization* structure must be put in place to facilitate implementation of that plan. Next, the planned activity must be *staffed* with necessary personnel and they must be *directed* in the performance of the planned activity. Over-all *control* must be exercised so that the objectives of the plan are realized.

In terms of people, management is said to exist at three levels: strategic, tactical, and operational. (See Figure 15-13.) Examples of *strategic managers* are the chairman of the board, the company president, and the heads of major

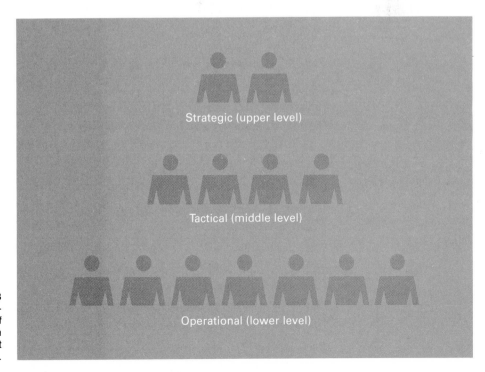

FIGURE 15-13
Several levels of management, with different levels of responsibility, exist within all but the very smallest organizations.

Strategic (upper level)

Tactical (middle level)

Operational (lower level)

divisions within the company. *Tactical managers* include directors of laboratories, plant managers, and regional managers. Supervisors and managers of administrative support groups are *operational managers.*

The managerial functions identified above are generally accepted as being performed at all management levels, but the managers at the top level of an organization have responsibilities different from those at the middle level. Similarly, middle-level managers have responsibilities different from those at the lower level. For example, top-level managers plan the organization's activities for five years or more into the future. Tactical managers plan what their area of responsibility will do within the next year or two. Operational managers put plans in place to achieve immediate goals. Strategic managers determine the over-all business organization—its divisions or regions, overseas network, subsidiaries, and so on. Tactical managers set up the organization within their particular manufacturing plant, sales territory, or the like. An operational manager has responsibility for the organization of a given department or group.

A successful MIS must respond to the information needs of each level of management. This means that:

- Input, or raw data, must be obtained from widely varying sources.
- Output, or information, must be presented in many forms.

Strategic managers depend heavily on data sources external to the organization—from its environment. Examples of external data sources are government legislation, economic trends and forecasts, and information about competitors available from common sources such as annual reports, product announcements, and public statements by company representatives. In contrast, operational managers depend heavily on internal data—how many trucks are available, what stock must be reordered, which employees can be freed to operate a particular machine, and so on.

Similarly, strategic managers need to see production data summarized by quarter or perhaps even by year. Tactical managers need reports that enable them to spot trends, to identify underutilized or overutilized resources, and so on. Operational managers need to determine planned performance versus actuals for a particular day, perhaps for a department, or perhaps for a single employee. (See Figure 15-14.)

CHARACTERISTICS OF INFORMATION

Information to be used in decision making must have certain characteristics. In particular, managers seeking to take effective action need information that is:

- *Accurate*—correct with respect to reality
- *Timely*—up to date
- *Available*—obtainable when needed, within acceptable response times
- *Concise*—summarized to the point of importance to the manager (information, not data, must be provided)
- *Relevant*—what the manager needs to know and can act upon
- *Complete*—all that is needed to make a decision

Perhaps the best way for us to appreciate the importance of these characteristics is to assume that one or more is missing in representative business

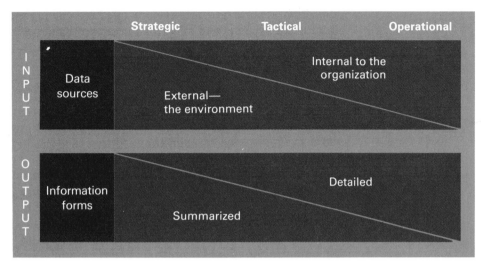

FIGURE 15-14
The managers at different levels within an organization impose different influences on MIS input and output.

situations. The product manager for a new line of jeans may set prices that are too low because the costs referred to when determining product markups are reported incorrectly. The chief executive officer of a toy manufacturer may conclude that long-term interest rates are going to fall, and thus may authorize additional borrowing for plant expansion, only to learn from a management briefing produced the preceding day that the converse has already occurred. The manager of an administrative support group needs to know which employees can key in data the fastest, which ones have the best attendance records, which ones work best under stress, and so on; the managers of interfacing departments have no need for this information. A shop-floor supervisor who receives vendor-quality statistics on a single-shipment basis cannot tell from the statistics whether the quality of vended parts is getting worse or improving.

Obviously, an MIS that provides high-quality information to all levels of management must produce several types of output. Generally, these include the following:

- *Periodic reports*, or regularly scheduled listings, showing routine business information in detailed or summarized form (e.g., weekly sales-by-item reports)

- *Exception reports*, signaling situations requiring management attention (e.g., an overdue-accounts-receivable report)

- *Demand reports*, generated in response to ad hoc queries submitted in batch mode or keyed in from a terminal; may be in printed form or on a display screen (e.g., a list of all warehouse locations having in stock more than 200 cases of the part identified by item number 17340)

- *Predictive reports*, created through statistical analyses or modeling techniques, often based on historical or parametric data (e.g., a monthly production forecast)

In the 1960s and 1970s, periodic reports generated as outputs of regularly scheduled batch-processing runs were commonplace. (Too often, instead of solving the paperwork problem with computer help, overenthusiastic users or information system staff created a worse one.) Over time, users learned that exception reports are often more effective management tools. Now, online interactive systems and microcomputers are being used increasingly to obtain on-demand and predictive information. (See Figure 15-15.)

THE MAKEUP OF AN MIS

From the user's point of view, an MIS is only as good as its output, and the output is only as good as its underlying database. In a very real sense, a comprehensive online database is the foundation of an MIS. (See Figure 15-16.) Generally, the database is accessed through the facilities of a database management system such as we have discussed.

Even after implementation, an MIS is not a physical entity that can be processed or manipulated. Generally, it is not even a set of specially created programs, packaged and documented as an MIS. Rather, a successful MIS is a fully integrated part of the user organization. It is developed around the functions to be managed. It has both computerized and noncomputerized parts. An organization cannot simply buy an MIS and install it.

Perhaps the best way to view an MIS is as a federation of information systems. It comprises a marketing information system, a manufacturing information system, and so on. (Look again at Figure 15-16.) These information systems are, in fact, subsystems of the MIS. Each information system has a functional identity. Within it are the bread-and-butter applications essential to the conduct of normal business activities. The system also meets the information needs of the managers of each function. The MIS draws upon and integrates information from an organization's functional-area information systems to provide a unified body of knowledge for use in decision making.

FIGURE 15-15
Systems with graphic capabilities provide information in a wide variety of forms to assist managers in decision making. (*Courtesy Westinghouse Electric Corporation*)

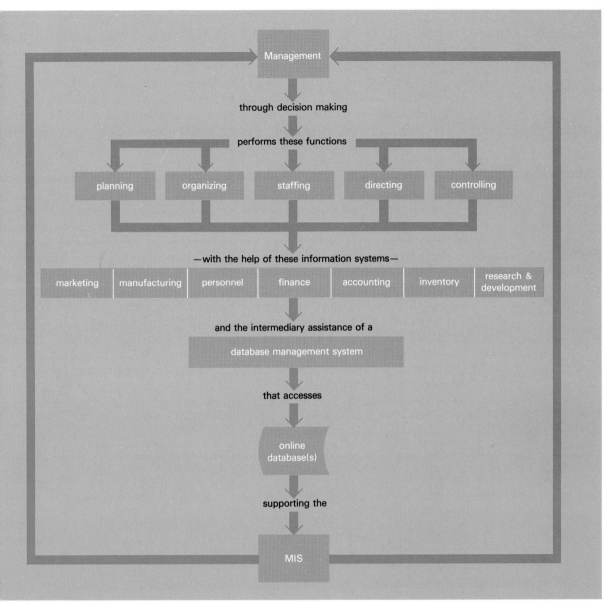

FIGURE 15-16 An organization's online databases and functional-area information systems are integral parts of its MIS.

Let's consider the personnel information system as an example. Employee paychecks are produced within this system. (It's hard to imagine a more bread-and-butter application than that!) This information system also provides for legislated reporting requirements such as Social Security payments, equal employment opportunity statistics, occupational safety and health items, and employee retirement security amounts. Inquiries such as how many employees have at least 15 years of service and which employees earn more than $800 per month can also be handled within the personnel information system. Managers need only request the information they want.

MIS IMPLEMENTATION

The actual implementation of an MIS extends over a long period of time. Some information systems of the type shown in Figure 15-16 may exist prior to an organizational decision to establish an MIS. A staged development and implementation plan can be established for the others.

Certain factors are key to the successful implementation of the MIS. Foremost among these is top-level management support. This support must go beyond allocation of resources. Top-level managers must be actively involved in the MIS effort. They must help to establish objectives and to define their own information needs. Other user personnel must be aware of their direct involvement in the MIS activity.

Communication about the MIS project is needed at all levels of the organization. Both those who will prepare inputs to the MIS and those who will receive outputs from it must be helped to understand it. Those who will be in direct contact with the hardware or software of the underlying information systems must be trained in their use.

The information system staff with technical responsibility for the MIS project must be trained to handle their responsibilities. They must understand the vital importance of user involvement throughout both development and implementation. They should also advise users of the 80/20 rule: Usually, 80 percent of the information that users think they need can be obtained with only 20 percent of the effort that would be required to obtain all of it. (See Figure 15-17.) By working together, the users and information system staff can identify the users' foremost information needs and prioritize the system development activities. Spending *five times* the effort required to attend to the top 80 percent of the users' needs is seldom warranted at the outset. As users gain experience with the

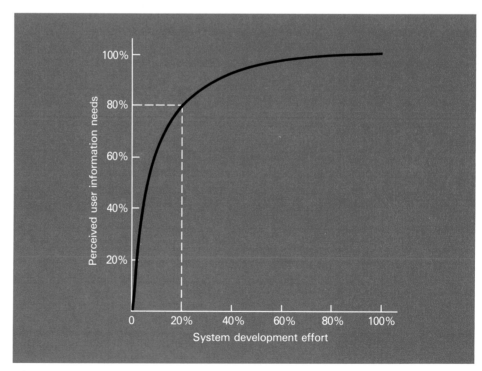

FIGURE 15-17
Eighty percent of the information that users think they need may be obtainable with only 20 percent of the system developmennt effort that would be required to obtain all of it.

MIS, they'll learn more about what information they really need. Follow-on MIS development can be planned accordingly.

No matter how sophisticated the MIS design is or how well the MIS operates, there is only one ultimate measure of success: Each user must accept the MIS as "his" or "hers" and use the information it can provide. Today, the manager with the greatest access to accurate, timely information has the greatest competitive advantage in the business world. Knowing how to put information to work has become critical to success, and perhaps even to survival.

DATABASE TRENDS

At a rate second only to microcomputers—and, indeed, in some cases together with them—the database approach is "coming on strong" in the 1980s. DBMS's for mainframes have been available since the late 1960s. Not until this decade, however, did most top-level executives and non-DP professionals really appreciate two factors: (1) the vital importance of data as an organizational resource, and (2) the facilities for organizing, storing, and accessing that data that a database approach can provide.

Perhaps best known of the proprietary DBMS's for mainframes are IBM's IMS/VS and Hewlett-Packard's IMAGE. Cincom's TOTAL and its follow-on TIS, Cullinet's IDMS, Intel's System 2000, and Software AG's ADABAS are popular DBMS's developed and marketed by independent software vendors. Some of these DBMS's can be run on DEC, CDC, Honeywell, NCR, and Sperry Univac machines as well as on IBM and IBM-compatible mainframes.

Relational and relational-like products are offered for supercomputers, mainframes, minis, and micros. Examples are ORACLE Corporation's ORACLE, Ingres from Relational Technology, and IBM's SQL/DS and DATABASE 2. Advocates of the relational approach point out that the applications for which it is best suited are not the high-volume, 24-hour-a-day, basic business operations of a company; they are the strategic planning, product forecasting, management decision-making ones. Such applications can help companies to be low-cost, high-quality producers in today's competitive business environment.

Advocates of DBMS's for micros usually point first to MDBS, a network-oriented DBMS offered by Micro Data Base Systems since the late 1970s. MDBS is used widely under CP/M operating systems on Z80-based and 8080-based microcomputers. Although some of the products currently marketed as DBMS's for micros do not have all the capabilities normally expected in a DBMS, more capabilities are coming. As microcomputer systems with one megabyte or more of primary storage become commonplace, comprehensive DBMS's for micros will also.

Decision Support Systems

We've discussed what an MIS is. Today, users are being encouraged to complement their MIS, or go a step beyond it, by implementing a *decision support system*, or *DSS*. An MIS provides information for managers, but much of that information is historical; it tells managers what has happened but not what may happen. The emphasis of a DSS is to provide "what-if" help directly to managers and other professionals. Such information can be used in shaping the future.

A word of caution applies here as well as with a DBMS or an MIS: An organization cannot simply buy a DSS and install it. Applications must be designed; the data required for those applications must be identified and collected; users must learn how to interact with the system; and so on. Nevertheless, in early 1983 over 100 products described as DSS's were being marketed. Some run only on large mainframes, but many run on micros. Their prices range from $200 to $300,000.

Many DSS's have evolved from either financial modeling systems or database management systems. In this process, the financial modeling systems have acquired database capabilities; the DBMS's have acquired statistical manipulation and modeling power. A full-scale DSS must have both. In addition, because users interact directly with the DSS to obtain information, extensive user-oriented display facilities, including graphics, are usually required.

Many people are frequent users of VisiCalc, Multiplan, SuperCalc, or any of several hundred other electronic spreadsheet programs available for micros. (See Figure 15-18.) If you haven't used at least one of them, you should try one. The major application areas for these spreadsheets include break-even analysis, ROI calculation, pricing strategy, loan amortization, cash flow analysis, merger and acquisition analysis, resource allocation, budget planning and control, financial statements, and intracompany, stockholder, and governmental record keeping and reporting. By experimenting with such packages, you'll get some feel for how full-scale DSS's can serve as analytical tools. You'll also see that DSS's do not make decisions. A good DSS does provide high-quality information, in a user-oriented way, so that managers of large corporations or of households can make good decisions.

FIGURE 15-18
Accurate, timely information in spreadsheet form is helpful when key business decisions must be made.
(*Courtesy Comshare, Inc.*)

Remote Databases   Not all the data needed to manage a business is generated within that business. Whether the "business" is a multinational conglomerate such as International Telephone and Telegraph or a single-family home in Omaha, Nebraska, this statement applies. Computer hardware and software can now support the collection and maintenance of seemingly infinite amounts of data. Decreasing communication costs and increasing demands have made it economically feasible to distribute that data via communication networks to users at widely separated locations. Telephones, TV sets, visual-display units, and microcomputers in homes and offices serve as terminals. (See Figure 15-19.) Companies such as CompuServe of Columbus, Ohio, Dialog Information Services of Palo Alto, California, and The Source of McLean, Virginia, are known for their remote database services. A subscriber to a particular Dialog service, for example, pays from $45 to $130 per online connect hour and from 15 cents to 70 cents per line for hard-copy output printed offline. Examples of the databases available are:

- *Insurance Abstracts*–Indexes more than 100 journals (much like two printed indexes, *Life Insurance Index* and *Property and Liability Insurance Index*) and provides extensive coverage of topics of broad interest, such as taxation, deferred compensation, health care costs, trusts, employee benefit plans, and retirement.

- *Labor Law*–Over 175,000 records providing summaries of court decisions related to labor relations, fair employment, wages and hours, occupational safety and health, mine safety and health cases, and National Labor Relations Board rulings; updated monthly with about 1500 records produced by the Bureau of National Affairs.

- *Books in Print*–Contains 650,000 records listing the entire current U.S. book publishing inventory, as well as books to be published within six months; from the R. R. Bowker Co.

- *Standard & Poor's News Daily*–Maintained (entered and accumulated) Monday through Friday, with daily financial news and financial reports, then transferred the next Monday to a companion database, the *Standard & Poor's News*. Interim and annual reports are entered line-for-line as reported by companies to their stockholders. Releases of stock exchanges and regulatory agencies as well as news releases issued by companies are also captured and made available.

AgriData Resources of Milwaukee offers its AgriData network as a nationwide, online, interactive information and communication service for U.S. farmers, ranchers, and others engaged in agriculture-related businesses. GTE has put drug, disease, socioeconomic bibliographic data, as well as medical procedures data supplied by the American Medical Association on its Telenet network to form AMA/Net. In summary, whatever your information needs are, chances are there's a computer service company eager to respond to them. (See Figure 15-20.)

Distributed Databases   In Chapter 16, we discuss data communications. We see how data-processing and data-communication technologies are being applied jointly to prove again that the whole of something–in this case, the user's total information system–can be bigger than the sum of its parts. Users who've begun to appreciate the

FIGURE 15-19
Online searches of hundreds of databases can be initiated from terminals at libraries nationwide that subscribe to available information services. (*Courtesy General Electric Research and Development Center*)

benefits of distributed data processing (discussed in Chapter 16) are also asking for distributed databases. Inventory-control personnel at St. Louis are best equipped to maintain the parts database for stock held at a St. Louis warehouse. Similar personnel at Memphis are best equipped to maintain parts data for stock at a warehouse there. Yet corporate management in Columbus or a sales representative seeking an expedited shipment of parts to a major customer in New York may need data and summaries of data from both locations.

As the term *distributed databases* implies, the data in a system with such capabilities is not all in one place. Under one approach, the data within a single database may be stored at any number of sites. Under another approach, all the data within a single database is stored at one site, but there may be many databases at many sites. In either case, authorized users and programs at any site in the network may need to access data at any other site. They should be able to do so. Furthermore, they should not have to know where the data is or what DBMS is controlling it.

Sound easy? The best minds in the computer field will tell you it's not. The system capabilities required to support database processing in such environments are extensive. Should the system ship each transaction (user request) as a message to wherever the necessary data is? If the data is at multiple sites, should the system ship functions, and yet bundle those functions somehow as a logical unit of work that either all completes or is all backed out (thereby restoring all

FIGURE 15-20
very large computer installation is needed at Dialog
Information Services to
upport its remote database
service offerings. (*Courtesy
Dialog Information Services,
Inc., Palo Alto, California*)

data to a prior consistent state)? Alternatively, should the system ship the necessary data to wherever the transaction invoking the functions is? Can or should the system store and maintain multiple copies of data at multiple sites? What if a communication link is down or (worse yet) goes down during transmission? What if two or more transactions become deadlocked, awaiting resources that cannot be made available to them? How can the system keep track of the effects of *every* transaction and insure that the effects of just *one* transaction can be backed out without invalidating the work or data of others? What if an entire system fails? How can the system know the current state of each and every resource within that system at the time of failure? How can the system absolutely guarantee to users that all data within the system will be restored to a consistent state, no matter what or when user errors, program errors, or system failures occur?

The need for distributed data clearly exists. Research in this area will continue. Some products offering limited distributed database support are appearing. Stay tuned for further developments!

Database Machines   Though both the internal processing speeds and the storage capacities of mainframes have increased significantly in recent years, user workloads have more than kept pace with them. Database machines are being proposed as a way to alleviate mainframe resource demands and, at the same time, improve system performance in database environments.

In simplest terms, a *database machine* is a processor that, by virtue of hardware and software, is specialized to perform database management. An early leader was Britton Lee's Intelligent Data Base Machine (IDBM) announced in 1980 and delivered commercially in 1981. The IDBM functions as a back-end processor, independently of the main processor, or host machine. It is a unique combination of relational database software and specialized hardware designed for high-speed database processing. Software AG's Data Base Machine (DBM) functions as a back-end processor to an IBM or IBM-compatible mainframe. It allows users to run ADABAS outside of their host machines. Intel's Data Base Processor (iDBP) is a microprocessor-based hardware/ software solution that provides file and database management services to other machines (hosts) as a back-end processor or as a database server at one node in a network.

To date, most users are taking a wait-and-see attitude with respect to database machines. Many are just learning what a DBMS is. In the interim, vendors can use the time to help users understand the advantages of database machines and to improve and enhance their offerings.

CHAPTER SUMMARY

1. IOCS routines perform I/O functions commonly needed by application programs. Examples are scheduling of synchronous or asynchronous I/O operations, blocking and deblocking records, I/O error correction, and end-of-volume and end-of-file processing.

2. File organization is concerned with the techniques used in arranging the records in a file; file access is concerned with the manner in which the records are written or read. Three common methods of organization are sequential, indexed sequential, and direct.

3. Under a database approach, the information needs of users are analyzed and the data that must be stored and processed to satisfy those needs is identified. Well-thought-out database design is prerequisite to successful database implementation.

4. Logical data structures known as *data models* are used to model real-world data relationships. The simplest data structure is a flat file. An inverted file supports indexed access to user data records.

5. More complex data relationships can be represented by mapping the user's data onto a hierarchical or network data model. The relational model, which deals with data in tables, is noted for its simplicity.

6. A DBMS provides many of the facilities needed to support the database approach. It interfaces with other system software, the database, and with users or application programs.

7. A computer-based management information system (MIS) processes business transactions reflecting the day-to-day operations of an organization and provides management with useful information for making decisions.

8. Managers are responsible for planning, organizing, staffing, directing, and controlling the activities of a business or other organization. Strategic,

tactical, and operational managers have different responsibilities and different information needs.

9. Information used in making decisions must be accurate, timely, available, concise, relevant, and complete. An MIS may produce periodic, exception, demand, and predictive reports to provide such information.

10. A decision support system (DSS) provides "what-if" help directly to managers and other professionals. Such information can be used in shaping the future.

11. Access to remote databases containing data on a wide variety of subjects, and facilities for distributing and maintaining data at multiple user sites, are two ways of helping to increase information availability.

12. A database machine is a processor that, by virtue of hardware and software, is specialized to perform database management. Today's database machines function as back-end processors to host machines or as database servers in network environments.

DISCUSSION QUESTIONS	1. (a) What is an IOCS? (b) What are some of the functions it can be expected to perform?

2. What are some of the functions performed by a file system?

3. Describe how an IOCS, file system, data management system, and DBMS are related. In doing so, explain how they are alike and how they differ.

4. What is a database?

5. Explain, by example, what it means to "model the relationships of data in the real world."

6. Are you aware of any computer files or databases in which personal data about you is stored? If so, name one and tell what you know about its contents and use.

7. (a) Describe a real-world situation in which multiple ways of getting at a particular data item are required.
(b) How might a database containing the data item be set up to provide for this requirement?

8. (a) What is a DBMS?
(b) What are some of the functions it can be expected to perform?

9. (a) List the five functions generally attributed to management.
(b) Show, by example, how an operational-level manager in a business organization of your choice performs each of these functions.

10. Show, by example, how the organizational level at which a manager operates affects his or her need for information.

11. Discuss the essential characteristics of information to be used in management decision making.

12. Why is user involvement from the outset critical to the success of an MIS?

13. (a) Distinguish between remote databases and distributed databases.
(b) Suggest situations where these kinds of databases are likely to be especially useful.

16
DATA COMMUNI-CATIONS

There is little doubt that technology is making our world smaller. With high-speed transportation, goods from all over the world have become available at our local stores. The world is becoming what design-science engineer R. Buckminster Fuller called a "one-town world."

What has happened to the distribution of goods is now also happening to the distribution of data.

Teleconferences can now be held, linking participants in different parts of the nation or of the world. Dish antennas of earth stations receive signals from and beam signals to orbiting satellites, relaying as many as 13,000 messages at one time. These messages are computer encoded and decoded.

Other uses of computerized data communications occur in banking. Automated teller machines (ATM's), linked by computers to bank-account databases, can be found at airports, in hotels, and on the street. Each time a customer attempts to use an ATM, the customer's identification code is checked before he or she is allowed to proceed.

Courtesy IBM Corporation

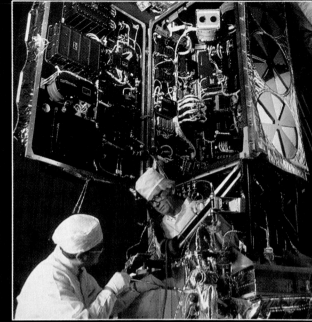
Courtesy RCA

Courtesy RCA

Courtesy Satellite Business Systems

Courtesy American Express Company

Data can be transmitted over public telephone lines or over private lines. A portable terminal or microcomputer may be connected to a large computer system from almost any telephone location.

Some public service agencies are taking advantage of high-speed data-communication capabilities. Fire-fighting forces at different locations can be coordinated and kept in communication via computer. The U.S. Postal Service offers eletronic mail services, made possible by a computerized telecommunications network. The U.S. Air Force's STAR TRACK network is a computerized defense-surveillance network that detects, tracks, and identifies objects in space. Computers are even used in the search for evidence of extra-terrestrial life. Weak radio signals from deep space are collected by a mammoth dish antenna, then amplified and clarified by computer, in search of meaningful patterns. This may be the first step in the emergence of a one-town universe!

Courtesy Lexicon Corporation

Reproduced with permission of AT&T

Courtesy Texas Instruments Incorporated

Courtesy Motorola Inc.

16 | DATA COMMUNICATIONS

The managers of today's complex and diversified businesses must have up-to-date knowledge of company operations in order to serve their customers and control their business activities. This need calls for rapid collection, processing, and distribution of large amounts of business data. Efficient, dependable data-collection and data-distribution capabilities are particularly important in cases where geographically separated facilities are controlled from one central facility, or where operations at one facility have a direct bearing on operations at another. For example, the corporate offices of a large grocery chain not only may maintain up-to-the-minute records of available inventory at all its supermarkets, but also may provide direction and control to its fleet of trucks on a nationwide or even international basis. As another example, the orders for parts received at remote warehouses of a manufacturer of large heating units may have a direct effect on the number of parts that must be produced at the manufacturer's central production facilities.

With the increased recognition of the potential of electronic data processing, more and more business applications have been computerized. Because data collection or distribution by mail, courier (runner or messenger), or carrier (motor freight line, bus company, or the like) is slow and subject to both traffic and weather conditions, other types of data transmission are needed. Initially, attention was directed to telephone and telegraph facilities. The latter offered one often-important advantage—printed copies of whatever was transmitted. The lines needed for transmission were rented from *common* (meaning *public*) *carriers*, such as the American Telephone and Telegraph Company (AT&T) and the Western Union Telegraph Company. We shall learn more about these carriers in this chapter.

Greater transmission speed was obtained through use of punched paper tape. Administrative correspondence was recorded on paper tape, transmitted in coded form over telegraph lines, then re-recorded on paper tape at the receiving location. Later, data from the field (orders, production costs, and so on) was punched into paper tape, transmitted over telegraph lines to the central computer site, and converted to a form usable as direct input to a computer there. The next step was the development of equipment that could transmit data directly from punched cards or magnetic tape, thus eliminating the initial paper-tape-conversion step as well. Finally, online direct-access systems came into use. We looked at the capabilities of such systems in Chapter 15.

For purposes of emphasis and clarity, let us define *communication* somewhat formally to be the transmission of information between points of origin and destination without altering the content or sequence of the information. We further define a special form of communication in which information is conveyed over long distances as *telecommunications*. Telephone, radio, and television are examples of modern telecommunications. *Teleprocessing* is a word formed by combining *telecommunications* and *data processing*. As we might expect, a *teleprocessing system* makes it possible to collect data at one or more points of origin, transmit that data to a designated location for processing, and distribute the results of processing to one or more points of use. In common practice, the term *data communication* refers to the transmission of data from one location to another, and a teleprocessing system is also called a *data-communication system*.

In this chapter, we look first at the basic components of a data-communication system and at the data-transmission options available. Since telecommunications (and data communication as one form of telecommunications) are subject to governmental regulations, we discuss the roles of the Federal Communications Commission and of state agencies in doing this regulating. You'll understand what common carriers are and why events like the breakup of AT&T come about. With this background, we then look at communication service offerings that are especially important to us as users. Distributed processing makes it possible for many users to enter data, process it, and receive results where they are, yet also access programs and data elsewhere if desired. Word processing—the manipulation of data in textual form—has been done for years. When word processing is done with the help of electronic equipment, and when the electronic equipment can be used for data-processing and data-communication functions as well, then office automation becomes a reality. Electronic mail and voice mail—a special form of electronic mail in which both input and output are in audio (voice) form—are doing much to speed user-to-user and office-to-office communication. Teleconferencing is designed to meet remote group communication needs. As an individual, you may already be taking advantage of videotex capabilities.

We conclude the chapter by summarizing the vast range of data-processing/data-communication capabilities that are currently available from computer service companies.

SYSTEM COMPONENTS

In its most basic form, communication generally involves at least four parts: (1) a sender, or data source, (2) a message, (3) a communication channel, or carrier, and (4) a receiver of the transmitted data. When information (feedback) is transmitted to tell the sender that the message has been received, or when the receiver initiates communication with the sender, the roles of sender and receiver are reversed.

The primary elements of a data-communication system can be viewed within the general framework that we have just described. Source data is converted into electrical signals (encoded) by a sending terminal. These signals are the message, in a transmission-code form. A transmitter, or modulator, impresses the signals on a communication channel (for example, a telephone line) to send the message to its destination. When it arrives there, a demodulator "undoes" the work of the modulator by reconstructing the signals for a receiving terminal. (See Figure 16-1.)

In an online direct-access system, there is no receiving terminal recognizable as a separate unit. A special *communication control unit* connected to the computer (or sometimes integrated within it) converts data in the transmission code used by the telecommunications equipment to a form acceptable as computer input. It then forwards the converted data to primary storage. Similarly, information written out from primary storage may be converted by such a control unit to a form suitable for transmission over telecommunications facilities.

Some vendors have developed sophisticated control units that can perform other functions besides code conversion, such as error detection and recovery when signals are lost or distorted during transmission, adding or deleting message headers or other control information used in routing, and so on. A *front-end processor* may serve as a communication control unit in a system that must support many terminals and/or heavy traffic on the data-communication network. In many ways a front-end processor is to data communication what a back-end processor is to database processing.

In a data-communication system, any I/O device at the end of a communication channel is called a *terminal*. More specifically, since the device is located at a point other than where the main computer is, it is called a *remote terminal*. In practice, almost any I/O device found in a main computer room can be taken out of that room and attached to a communication channel. Usually, however, a remote terminal is a user-oriented device designed to meet specific input/output needs in the user's ordinary environment. Many such devices were described in Chapters 4 and 5.

DATA TRANSMISSION

An organization that decides to take advantage of data-communication capabilities faces a seemingly overwhelming number of options. To determine what's best, a system analyst looks first at the organization's needs. Must data be

A

B

FIGURE 16-1
The user of a data-communication system enters source data, which is converted by the sending terminal and a modem to transmission-code form (A); the converted data travels over a communication channel and is then converted to a form acceptable to the computer at its destination (B). (*Courtesy* [A] *Sperry Corporation;* [B] *Motorola Inc.*)

transmitted between locations, or simply between points at a single location? Is speed of transmission especially important—say, to provide immediate responses to customers' inquiries about products or accounts? Is the volume of traffic fairly constant, or does it vary widely during the working day? Perhaps some data is to be batched and transmitted to the home office at night. The analyst evaluates available communication options against the identified requirements. We need to be aware of some of the options in order to understand representative data-processing/data-communication systems in use today. (See Figure 16-2.)

FIGURE 16-2 Online processing of reservations, guest registration, accounts, and inventory are managed with the help of data-processing/data-communication systems at hotels worldwide. (*Photos courtesy NCR Corporation*)

Analog or Digital Transmission

Source data can be transmitted over a communication channel in either of two forms: analog or digital. Initially, users' ordinary telephone lines served as communication channels in the vast majority of systems. *Analog transmission* was the major (if not the only) type of transmission available. When this type of transmission is used, the signals that constitute a message exhibit a continuous-wave form. (See Figure 16-3A.) At any point, the wave form has three major characteristics:

- *Amplitude*—the height of the wave, which is a reflection of the strength of the signal
- *Phase*—the duration in time of one complete cycle of the wave form
- *Frequency*—the number of times the wave form is repeated during a specified interval

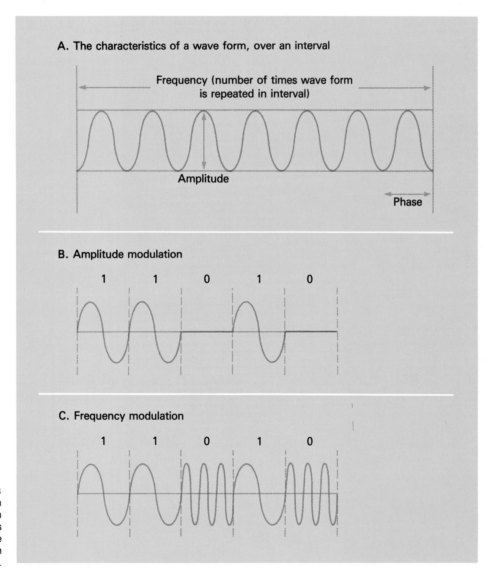

FIGURE 16-3
Either amplitude modulation (B) or frequency modulation (C) may be used to impress the signals of a message onto a continuous-wave form for analog transmission.

Changing any one of these three characteristics beyond specified limits changes the signal that is sent. For example, we can let the normal amplitude of the wave represent a 1 bit. We can alter it to represent a 0 bit. (See Figure 16-3B.) This way of impressing signals on a wave is called *amplitude modulation,* or *AM.* Alternatively, we can let the normal frequency of the wave represent a 1 bit. We can alter it to represent a 0 bit. (See Figure 16-3C.) This different way of impressing signals is called *frequency modulation,* or *FM.*

Are the terms *AM* and *FM* familiar to you? Yes, they identify techniques used to transmit the audible tones we hear on radio. We have just described how the techniques can be used to transmit data. Converting signals from a binary-digit pattern (pulse form) to a continuous-wave form is called *modulation.* The reverse—converting from wave form to pulse form, thereby reconstructing the signal—is called *demodulation.* When analog transmission is used, both are required.

With *digital transmission,* source data is not transmitted in wave form. Instead, it is transmitted as distinct pulses (on/off) in much the same way that it travels in the computer itself. (See Figure 16-4.) Hence, the special steps of modulation and demodulation are not needed. The elimination of these steps means less transmission time, less telecommunications equipment required, and so on. Digital transmission offers a substantially lower error rate and significantly better response time than analog transmission. The lower error rate (about 100 times lower) means users can transmit large amounts of data, even complete files, more reliably. The faster response time means better performance for the same amount of work, or the ability to handle more terminals or a larger volume of work and yet stay within existing response-time standards.

Since the advantages of digital transmission of data are significant, we might expect computer-using organizations to quickly take advantage of them. To date, that's not the case. Establishing analog-transmission capabilities is a relatively simple undertaking from the user's point of view. Ordinary telephone lines, coaxial cables, or microwave circuits already in place and in use for voice communication suffice in most cases. Establishing digital-transmission capabilities is a bigger step. However, as digital offerings become increasingly available, users are likely to take that step (with some encouragement).

Start/Stop (Asynchronous) or Synchronous Transmission

When electrical signals are sent over a communication channel by a transmitting unit, the receiving unit must be in synchronization with that unit so it can interpret the signals received. If the receiving unit does not start at the proper point, or does not maintain the same interval as the transmitting unit, it cannot interpret the signals correctly. Two techniques commonly used to keep sending and receiving units in step are start/stop synchronization and synchronous transmission.

When the *start/stop method* of synchronization is used, a start signal is transmitted at the beginning of a group of data bits (say, a character). A stop signal is transmitted at the end of the group. Upon receiving the start signal, the receiving unit sets up a timing mechanism to time the arrival of the bits in the group.

As an example, three 7-bit characters are transmitted under the start/stop method in Figure 16-5A. Each start signal prepares the receiving mechanism for the reception and recording of a character. Each stop signal brings the receiving

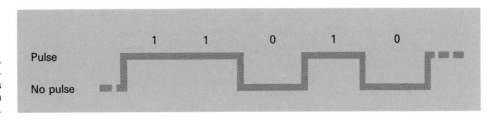

FIGURE 16-4
Message signals are transmitted as distinct pulses
when digital transmission
is used.

mechanism to rest. In effect, the sender and receiver are synchronized for the transmission of each character as an independent, single unit. Hence, the start/stop transmission mode is sometimes called *asynchronous transmission*.

Figure 16-5B shows what is known as *synchronous transmission*. The bits of one character are followed immediately by the bits of the next character. No start and stop signals are needed because the group of communication channels, or circuit, is sampled at regular intervals to receive and record data bits. The terminal equipment for a synchronous (also called *clocked*, or *fixed-rate*) system is more complex and usually more costly than that required for start/stop transmission. From the user's point of view, the potential for gains in both speed and efficiency may justify the additional expenditure. More data can be transmitted over a circuit per unit of time because no insertion, transmission, or reception of start and stop signals is necessary. During transmission, the receiving unit is kept in step with the sending unit by special timing circuitry.

When synchronization must be established by techniques within the system, it is accomplished by a *line discipline*, or *protocol*, which serves as a set of rules for the orderly transfer of data from one location to another. For example, binary synchronous communication (BSC) techniques were widely employed in early data-communication systems. Synchronous data link control (SDLC) is employed in IBM's Systems Network Architecture (SNA), designed to provide a uniform structure for computer-communication interfaces. NCR's Distributed Network Architecture (DNA), Digital Equipment Corporation's Digital Network Architecture (DNA), and Sperry Univac's Distributed Communications Architecture (DCA) serve similar purposes.

FIGURE 16-5
Either start/stop (asynchronous) transmission (A) or
synchronous transmission
(B) may be used to keep
sending and receiving units
in step during communica-
tion. Synchronous trans-
mission is dependent
on timing circuitry within
the network.

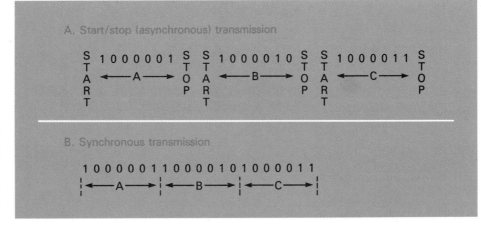

Simplex, Half-Duplex, or Full-Duplex Transmission

Yet another way to characterize communication is by allowable direction of transmission. If communication can occur in only one direction, the transmission is said to be *simplex*. A terminal that communicates via such a channel can either send or receive, but cannot do both. The involved user or program normally needs a return path for control information or error signals, even if data has to be transmitted in only one direction. Therefore, simplex transmission is rarely used for data collection or distribution in an EDP environment.

If communication can occur in only one direction at a time, but that direction can change, the transmission is said to be *half-duplex*. (See Figure 16-6A.) This type of transmission is used for most telephone service and for data transmitted via existing telephone networks. For example, source data can be entered from a terminal. *After* an entry has been received by the computer, a program in the computer can send an acknowledgment back to the terminal. *After* that acknowledgment has been received, the terminal user can enter more data.

If communication can occur in both directions at the same time, the transmission is said to be *full-duplex*. (See Figure 16-6B.) In systems supporting computer-to-computer communication, full-duplex capabilities are usually established. Without them, undesirable delays or bottlenecks are likely to occur.

A. Half-duplex transmission

B. Full-duplex transmission

FIGURE 16-6 Half-duplex transmission allows data to be transmitted in either of two directions at one time (A); a system supporting computer-to-computer communication usually has simultaneous, two-way, full-duplex transmission capabilities (B). (*Photos courtesy* [A] *Four-Phase Systems, Inc.;* [B] *Control Data Corporation*)

LINES AND CHANNELS When freight is shipped by train from, say, Detroit to Chicago, it travels along an established route–the railroad tracks. The rate at which the train travels determines how long it takes the freight to get to its destination.

In like manner, data in the form of signals travels between two points along one channel of a communication line. The *channel* is the data path. The *line* is the physical equipment, or transmission medium. The ability to combine several channels in one line materialized in 1874 with Jean Emile Baudot's *multiplexer system*. It enabled up to six signals from telegraph machines to be transmitted together over a single line. From the user's point of view, the messages appeared to be transmitted simultaneously.

Telephone lines were first constructed in the 1890s. Today, we depend on them. Their major use was, and still is, the transmission of sounds made by the human voice (hence the terminology, *voice-grade channels*). Some also carry data.

In 1918, the first *carrier system* was introduced. It enabled 12 voice-grade channels to be established over a single pair of wires. In the 1940s, coaxial cables were laid down; they could carry hundreds of voice-grade channels. This capacity was increased to thousands when microwave systems were built in the 1950s. The 1960s saw the development of communication satellites as relay stations in data-communication systems. High-speed fiber optics have also entered today's telecommunications picture. Many uses of pure-color light beams, or lasers, are being explored in laboratories. Communication uses are among them. (See Figure 16-7.)

In little more than 100 years, the information-carrying capacity of telecommunications lines has risen from 15 bits per second (bps) to about one billion (10^9) bps. In general, these increases in capacity have been achieved through increases in the range of frequencies used to transmit signals. Indeed, the quantity of information we can send over a channel is approximately proportional to its range of usable frequencies, or *bandwidth*. The frequencies are measured in cycles per second, which is really a means of describing the oscillation rates of particular wave forms. A voice-grade channel (say, a telephone line) capable of sending signals from 300 to 3300 cycles per second has a bandwidth of 3000 cycles per second. In communication terminology, 3000 cycles per second may be expressed in thousands of cycles per second as 3 kilohertz (kHz). The range of usable frequencies (bandwidth, remember) of microwave radio stretches from about 2000 to 12,000 millions of cycles per second, or 10,000 megahertz (MHz).

High-speed transmission media are capable of transmitting high-frequency waves. To take full advantage of these media, the high-frequency waves are made to carry lower-frequency waves as in the first carrier system. It is true that the various types of telecommunications have been assigned specific portions of the absolute frequency domains within the electromagnetic spectrum in our universe. This assignment is necessary to prevent undue interference and other difficulties in transmission. Of most interest to us as users, however, is the range of frequencies that can be sent over a medium, not the absolute frequency of operation. Wide ranges offer flexibility and capacity.

The terminals and computers in a data-communication system are connected in some type of line configuration. A *point-to-point line* is a direct connection between a terminal and a computer, two terminals, or two computers. (See Figure 16-8A.) Since a separate line is required for each connection, communication costs are high. When users must communicate with a computer on an almost continuous basis, or when fast response times are essential, the costs may

A

FIGURE 16-7
Researchers at Xerox'
Optical Science Lab are
studying the use of fiber-
optic components in
communication systems (A);
SEL, a German company, is
among the leaders in high-
speed fiber-optic data
transmission (B). (*Courtesy*
[A] *Xerox Corporation;*
[B] *ITT Corporation*)

B

be justified. For example, we might expect bedside patient-monitoring equipment connected to a main computer at a large hospital to communicate with that
computer via point-to-point lines.

A *multipoint*, or *multidrop, line* is a shared connection. Usually, several
terminals share the multipoint line. (See Figure 16-8B.) For example, several
visual-display units at a branch sales office may transmit sales data to a main
computer at corporate headquarters via a multipoint line. The company's
communication-line costs are significantly lower than they would be if an
analogous point-to-point configuration were used.

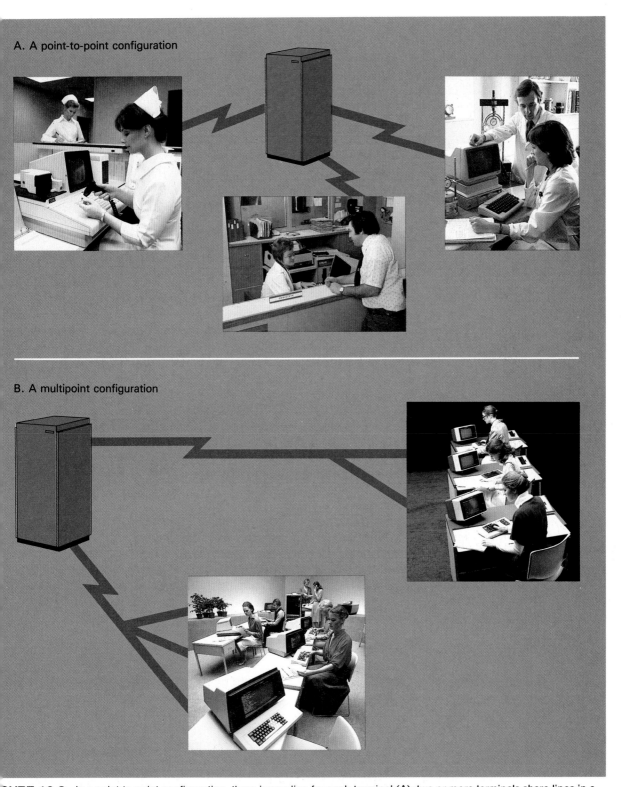

A. A point-to-point configuration

B. A multipoint configuration

FIGURE 16-8 In a point-to-point configuration, there is one line for each terminal (A); two or more terminals share lines in a multipoint configuration (B). (*Photos courtesy* [A, left to right] *NCR Corporation, Mohawk Data Sciences, Hewlett-Packard Company;* [B] *Sperry Corporation*)

MODEMS AND MUXES

As stated earlier, when analog transmission is used to transmit digital data, the signals in pulse form must be converted to wave form prior to transmission. The signals in wave form must be reconverted to pulse form at their destination. A *mo*dulator-*dem*odulator device (*modem*, for short) performs the conversion functions. Some modems are separate units (look back at Figure 16-1); some are integral parts of other network components.

Acoustic couplers are special modems that allow terminals to be connected to a data-communication system via standard telephones, no matter where those telephones are located. To gain access to the computer, a user simply goes to a telephone, dials the telephone number of the computer, places the telephone handset into the acoustic coupler, and begins sending or receiving data. The terminal itself may be a simple 10-key input device, a personal computer on a dining-room table, or one of several thousand other I/O devices now available. You may recall that we mentioned acoustic couplers when discussing how to sign on to a computer system in Chapter 2. We mentioned them again when discussing remote terminals in Chapter 4.

Many TRS-80, Apple II, or similar personal computer users want access to the latest stock market quotations, advice on what fertilizers to use—and when—in spring planting, a guide to prices of home furnishings, or whatever. Such a user can acquire a modem and software that allows communication with a supplier of the information via the personal computer and telephone lines.

In general, low-speed modems support asynchronous transmission, and high-speed modems support synchronous transmission. Some support both. Many vendors are dramatically increasing the speeds of their modems to allow users to take full advantage of the capabilities of today's high-speed I/O devices and transmission media. Of course, users wanting modems with special features and higher speeds often must pay more to get them.

Multiplexers, or *muxes*, are electronic devices that allow users to make efficient use of a line by combining data traffic from or to several low-speed communication lines onto a single, higher-speed line. The higher-speed line may be capable of transmitting data at 9600 or more bps, for example. In contrast, users at attached terminals may key in input or read and understand output at much slower rates. They may also spend time thinking.

Under *frequency-division multiplexing* (*FDM*), the higher-speed line is separated into several low-speed channels. Each channel covers a different frequency range. Electrical signals can be transmitted simultaneously to or from the feeder lines (and hence, to or from the terminals attached to them).

Under *time-division multiplexing* (*TDM*), separate time segments on a higher-speed line are reserved for each feeder line. Only a single signal from one terminal can be transmitted at one time. If a feeder line supplies no data during its time, no data is transmitted. A statistical TDM multiplexer, or stat mux, improves system efficiency by allocating line time on a dynamic basis. It takes into account which of the various terminals are active at a given moment. Recent stat muxes apply special protocols to label data sequences so that sending and receiving terminals can be identified. This procedure allows feeder lines to be multipoint lines. In contrast, though FDM muxes can be used in multipoint configurations, conventional TDM muxes cannot.

If a mux is used at one end of a high-speed communication line, another mux must be used at the other end of the line. That is, like modulation and demodulation, multiplexing and demultiplexing are complementary functions.

A modem and a mux are sometimes incorporated within one physical unit. Such units are especially useful in a data-communication system where all their functions are required. From a user organization's point of view, the combined unit also means one fewer "box" to find a place for.

COMMUNICATION SERVICE OFFERINGS

When you talk to a friend on the telephone, your communication passes through one or more *public exchanges,* or *switching facilities.* We now know that our ordinary telephone lines, sometimes called *switched,* or *dial-up, lines,* can also carry data. As mentioned earlier, the lines belong to firms known as *common carriers.* Under conventional public exchange service, a connection to a particular destination is made when a user at a terminal places a call to that destination. When data is to be transmitted, the user dials or presses the number of the destination (either a central computer facility or another user location), just as for an ordinary telephone call. The user must compete with other users for an available line. A busy signal may be encountered. The user or user organization is charged for the time used, with rates depending on the time of day, day of week, and distance traveled (plus a monthly service charge for right of access to the system). Switching facilities are often connected via *trunk lines* that can transmit many communications simultaneously. However, only half-duplex transmission is possible.

Alternatively, a user organization can acquire access to a *nonswitched line* on a full-time basis. Since the line is available at any time, dialing is not required to make a connection. The nonswitched line may be either leased or private. *Leased lines* are usually telephone or telegraph lines acquired via a fixed-term rental agreement from a common carrier. *Private lines* are privately owned and operated—by a user organization, a firm offering data-transmission facilities to subscribers, or an independent telecommunications equipment manufacturer. Full-duplex transmission may be provided. In common usage, the terms *leased* and *private* are used interchangeably to mean "other than public."

Leased or private lines can be connected through switching facilities to provide a private version of an exchange service. You'll hear such facilities referred to as a *private branch exchange,* or *PBX.* Telephone calls can be routed from callers to callees over any or all of the leased or private lines under control of the switching facilities. Calls can also be routed to outside lines for local or long-distance transmission. The leased or public lines can also be connected to a central computer facility for data-transmission purposes. The latest "third-generation" networks handle voice as well as data traffic in digital form. These networks are controlled by computer-based PBX's, or *CBX*'s, at various points. User costs generally consist of flat monthly rental charges based on length and type of lines. *Tie lines* are leased trunk connections acquired by a large user organization to connect its various locations.

Leased lines generally provide faster response and better-quality transmission than dial-up lines because of various techniques used to "condition" the lines. Privacy is more easily maintained with leased lines. Dial-up services provide greater access to the user's external environment because extensive interconnections are available through the public exchange facilities. In general, a user's choice between leasing a line and using public dial-up facilities is based on an analysis of over-all costs, message volume, and service requirements. The break-even point is a function of distance, average call time, and urgency. Low message volume favors dial-up facilities; heavy message volume favors leased facilities.

Few users today depend entirely on either leased lines or dial-up facilities. As suggested above, even users who lease lines often want to interconnect those lines to public networks. An organization dependent on communication between locations for its basic business operations may acquire leased lines to speed that communication but also maintain dial-up facilities as backup.

REGULATION AND COMMON CARRIERS

A telephone is a telephone. A computer is a computer. We wouldn't use a telephone to do what we need a computer to do. We wouldn't use a computer to do what we need a telephone to do. Well, maybe. In some systems that exist today it's difficult to determine where use of telephone facilities ends and use of computer facilities begins. So what, you may be thinking? Who cares?

Historically, at least, a telephone is a tool used in communicating. A computer is a tool used in processing. Data communication is subject to governmental regulation. Data processing is open to free enterprise. Let's start by understanding why.

Recall that, when communication occurs, signals travel in wave or pulse form in a certain frequency domain within the electromagnetic spectrum in our universe. No two communications can use the same part of the electromagnetic spectrum at the same time without interfering with each other. Specific portions of the spectrum must be allocated to specific users to prevent such interference. In the United States, the *Federal Communications Commission* (*FCC*) performs this allocation function. The seven-member FCC is an independent agency established by Congress through the Communications Act of 1934. It regulates both interstate and foreign communication facilities originating in the United States. Any organization intending to construct, operate, or acquire communication facilities must file a schedule, or *tariff*, giving details of the intended service, charges to users, classifications, regulations, and so on. The FCC may, if it chooses, grant the organization a *license*, thereby authorizing it to offer the service. The standard governing the granting of a license is "public interest, convenience, or necessity."

In most countries, the government owns and administers a nationwide telephone system. Often that system is allied with both postal and telegraphic services. In countries where the telephone system is provided by an organization independent of the government, as in Canada, a monopoly is usually granted to the organization. This approach avoids costly duplication of resources and insures coverage for the entire population. The monopoly is allowed and protected because it is deemed to be a public necessity.

The practice in the United States differs from this pattern. Not just one but several companies offer telephone services. However, they must be licensed to do so. The scope of "communication facilities" under the jurisdiction of the FCC includes terrestrial (land) lines as well as the electromagnetic spectrum. The FCC licenses and regulates radio, television, telephone, telegraph, facsimile (digitized imaging), and other transmission by wire, cable, and microwave. It also licenses communication services that use satellites as relay stations. In addition, each state has a *public utilities commission* (*PUC*) that regulates intrastate communication activities.

In most instances, the FCC and the PUC's act as complementary agencies. Together, they grant (or refuse to grant) and enforce monopoly rights in specific communication areas. They also regulate the prices charged for communication services in order to allow the providing organizations a fair rate of return on their investments and yet protect users from excessive rates.

Common carriers are organizations that have been authorized by the FCC and/or state agencies to provide communication services to the public. Typically, the organizations are investor-owned and privately operated. Today there are about 3000 common carriers. Most of us have heard of American Telephone and Telegraph (AT&T). We know it as (1) Ma Bell, the parent company of the Bell System – a vast communication network – and of Bell Laboratories; (2) the owner of Western Electric, a subsidiary that manufactures, purchases, distributes, and installs equipment to meet needs of the Bell System; and (3) the owner of all or part of the stock of 22 independent telephone companies often referred to as the Bell operating companies or BOC's. (See Figure 16-9.) Many of us also know something about Western Union and about General Telephone and Electronics (GTE). Initially, computer-using organizations that wanted to acquire data-communication capabilities turned to their common carriers for support. Over time, other options have opened to them.

The "winds of change" started in 1968 when the FCC, by its Carterfone decision, opened the public switched telephone network to independent (non-Bell System) equipment. Prior to that time, only the common carrier's equipment was allowed to be directly attached to the network. The transmission of data was dependent on Teletypes, which are inherently slow, or on remote batch terminals whose throughput was severely impaired by the lack of high-speed modems. The FCC's decision prompted the development of high-speed modems. It sparked American ingenuity and enterprise to pursue new business opportunities in the field of telecommunications.

B

FIGURE 16-9 A regional switching center within the Bell System handles hundreds of thousands of messages daily (A); at the same time, researchers at Bell Laboratories in Murray Hill, New Jersey, pursue further advances in communications (B). [A] *Reproduced with permission of AT&T;* [B] *courtesy Bell Laboratories)*

In 1971, the FCC allowed firms other than the authorized monopoly common carriers to construct and offer terrestrial communication services. In 1972, it permitted the launching of communication satellites by new common carriers intending to offer services that could compete directly with terrestrial communication systems. Known as the "open skies policy," this decision encouraged organizations to compete in applying satellite technology to a wide variety of domestic private-line services.

Specialized common carriers, then, are firms other than the authorized (albeit regulated) monopoly common carriers, which have received approval from the FCC or state agencies to offer communication services. Among the leaders are MCI Telecommunications and Southern Pacific Communications (SPC). Both are authorized to offer terrestrial private-line services for voice and data transmission. Both are meeting AT&T head-on in an area where AT&T is strong—namely, long-distance phone service—and doing it very successfully. You have probably seen ads for SPC's Sprint on TV. You may even be an MCI or SPC subscriber. So far, however, neither firm appears to have focused on the data-transmission needs of users.

GTE's Telenet and Tymshare's Tymnet are examples of *value-added networks* or *VAN*'s. These firms and other *value-added carriers* are not competing directly with the established common carriers. Instead, they improve (add value to) the common-carrier offerings. In doing so, they use leased common-carrier communication channels—typically, those underutilized at all but peak hours or overutilized during peak hours (and therefore not capable of handling the workload). They apply specialized data-handling techniques to decrease costs for users subscribing to their services. VAN switching facilities provide economical, low-error, fast-response communication services especially designed to meet the needs of computer users. An organization whose terminals and computers communicate through a VAN pays only for data transmitted and not for idle, unused capacity. The network handles daily and seasonal fluctuations without degradation and can absorb long-term growth in traffic.

The era of commercial use of satellites for telecommunications began when the Communications Satellite Corporation, or COMSAT, was set up by Congress in 1962, not as a government agency, but as a shareholder corporation. It was to be the "carrier's carrier," responsible for the launching and operation of communication satellites to serve as relay stations in telecommunications networks providing worldwide coverage. Since 1964 COMSAT has represented the United States in the International Telecommunications Satellite Consortium, or INTELSAT. About 100 countries, the members of INTELSAT, have signed international agreements whereby they share in the financing and owning of satellites within one global satellite communication system.

As mentioned above, in the early 1970s the FCC determined that essentially any qualified firm could own and operate domestic communication satellites. Western Union launched its Westar I and Westar II satellites in 1974 as part of the first domestic telecommunications system using satellites as relay stations. In 1977, Satellite Business Systems, or SBS, a partnership of subsidiaries of The Aetna Casualty & Surety Company, COMSAT, and IBM, received approval from the FCC to develop and operate a domestic satellite communication system. Voice, data, teleconferencing, and electronic document distribution are offered to subscribers who communicate via SBS satellites and earth stations located at or near customer premises. In late 1980, the FCC gave nine companies the go-ahead to build and launch more than two dozen satellites in the 1980–85 time frame, thus tripling the available channel capacity. In 1982, the FCC relaxed its restrictions on COMSAT, allowing them to lease satellite circuits to noncarriers (i.e., directly to users) as well as to authorized carriers.

Not surprisingly, AT&T wants to move into data-processing areas just as other firms are moving into communications. Until recently, an AT&T vs. the U.S. Justice Department antitrust settlement (the 1956 consent decree) prohibited it from doing so. AT&T could enter no business that was not regulated by the FCC. In December 1980, the FCC ruled that AT&T could expand into new areas, provided it did so through a separate subsidiary. This ruling has since been affirmed by a U.S. District Court. AT&T is proceeding with a divestiture plan whereby the 22 BOC's are grouped within seven regional holding companies. Western Electric has become AT&T Technologies, Inc. A separate subsidiary, AT&T Information Systems, offers value-added networking services (AIS/Net 1000) and customer-premises equipment such as phones, terminals, and PBX's. AT&T forecasts that AIS/Net 1000 "will do for data communications what the switchboard did for telephone service." Computers, terminals, and related I/O equipment from almost any vendor can communicate via the network; intelligence within the network makes such communication possible.

DISTRIBUTED PROCESSING

Since its introduction about three decades ago, the business computer system has occupied an "inner sanctum" of corporate America. Giant mainframes have crunched away on numbers, in air-conditioned, glass-walled isolation. All that is gradually changing, as we've seen throughout this book. Yes, there are still giant mainframes. Yes, there are still some tasks that can only be accomplished with the help of these mainframes. On the other hand, you're likely to find a computer at work wherever you find (or may expect to find) a desk, a typewriter, or a telephone.

In recent years, many geographically dispersed, nationwide, and even multinational organizations have evolved. Initially, the management of these organizations saw a need for tight-fisted, centralized control, particularly with respect to profit and loss accountability. Large, fast, accurate, centralized computer systems served as important tools in achieving this control.

Yet, counter to this move toward centralization, management techniques favoring decentralization of control have also been developing. Management by objectives has been stressed. Profit centers have been created at various organizational levels. Managers of geographical locations and/or functional areas are being given opportunities to control their own destinies. They, in turn, are demanding control of the organizational resources for which they are held accountable. They are also demanding better information, so they can exercise control more effectively.

There may have been a time when organizations were forced to centralize their EDP-system resources to achieve economy of operation at low cost. That time has passed for most organizations. The declining costs of minicomputers, microcomputers, and intelligent terminals are forcing organizations to take another look at their approach to EDP. Organizations that have considered EDP capabilities beyond their reach are also taking another look. Technological advancements are paving the way for techniques of *distributed processing*.

What is distributed processing? There is no universally accepted definition. Perhaps its one basic characteristic is a dispersion of the processing power, or intelligence, within an EDP system among geographically separated locations. (See Figure 16-10.) The functional groups or site locations within an organization can do most of their data processing locally. In addition, an executive may dial the large central computer, or host, at the beginning of the business day (to get the latest corporate-wide directives or management information). At the end of the day, a shop supervisor may dial the central computer to get the totals of production activities at a particular plant. Because less data is transmitted to and from the central computer, communication costs are lower. Since the mainframe workload is reduced, expensive large-computer upgrades may be postponed or avoided. Users whose data is processed locally experience faster job turnaround. Routine business documents can often be produced where they are needed as byproducts of ongoing activities. For example, customer invoices may be generated at the same time that sales-order data is entered from visual-display units at various sites.

System availability may be improved in a distributed-processing environment. Even if a central computer or some or all of the data-communication facilities are inoperable, a local data-processing system may be able to function independently. Tandem Corporation is an industry leader in this area, offering its totally fault-tolerant NonStop network. If a component fails, intelligence within the network selects an alternate component. Under a recent marketing agreement with American Satellite Corporation (ASC), earth stations can

FIGURE 16-10
Intelligent terminals or small computers at widely separated locations perform some processing locally and communicate with other locations when necessary in a distributed-processing environment. (*Courtesy Aetna Life and Casualty, Hartford, Conn.*)

receive and transmit data over two parallel paths—thus extending the nonstop concept to long-distance satellite communications.

An organization that elects to move to EDP using a distributed-processing approach can do so gradually at its own pace. In effect, the user can do top-down planning but bottom-up implementation by, say, first establishing a minicomputer-controlled production system at a manufacturing facility, then an order-processing system at each of several warehouses, and so on. The marriage of word processing and data processing is perhaps most readily achieved under the umbrella of distributed processing.

WORD PROCESSING

Just what is all the excitement about word processing? What is it anyway? In simplest terms, the basic appeal of word processing can be understood by anyone who's had to use White Out to correct a mistake on a letter, retype several pages of a report because somebody wants to add or change one paragraph, or type a zillion copies of a form letter just so that every recipient of the letter gets "an original."

In Chapter 1, we learned that *data* is raw material—facts and figures generated from one or more sources. *Data processing* is the manipulation of data to achieve a desired result. The finished product of data processing is *information.* *Word processing* is a term coined to emphasize the manipulation of certain types of data—characters combined to form words, sentences, paragraphs, memos, letters, reports. A *word-processing system* includes hardware, software, procedures, and people whereby ideas are expressed and distributed in hard-copy form (usually, paper) and/or soft-copy form (e.g., displayable on a CRT screen). The term *text processing* is synonymous with word processing, and a word-processing system may also be referred to as a *text-processing system.*

The initial impetus to develop word-processing equipment arose from a desire to automate certain office functions. Word-processing techniques were developed as a means of raising office productivity. Consider a simple example. In a conventional office, a secretary receives a handwritten or dictated piece of correspondence. He or she types a rough draft; returns it to the writer for approval, changes, or corrections; and corrects the revised draft until the writer is satisfied. Each revision usually means a complete retyping of one or more pages of the document. While typing, the secretary is interrupted frequently— to answer the telephone, find a memo in a file, escort a visitor from the lobby to an executive's office, schedule a conference room for an unanticipated afternoon meeting, and so on. Finally, a retyped version of the document is accepted as satisfactory. The secretary makes as many copies as needed, using a photocopying machine. Each copy is readied for mailing, addressed, and routed to a central mailroom. Communicating with someone in the same building may take from one to four days. Going through the U.S. postal system takes two days under the best of circumstances—sometimes much longer!

Suppose an electronic device with word-processing capabilities is available. Initially, someone keys in a document. As the person types, the characters are displayed on the screen. If the device has a page-size screen, the format of each "electronic paper page" can be manipulated until it looks exactly as it should in printed form. Text can be centered on a line or on a page; margins can be changed; lines can be justified on the right (as well as on the left); words, sentences, and paragraphs can be moved from one part of a page to another, even from one page to another; and so forth. If the typist is not the writer, or if people other than the writer need to review the document as it evolves, printouts can be generated. Corrections can be made to the stored form of the document. Only when it is exactly right need it be committed to a final, hard-copy form. (See Figure 16-11.)

The earliest word processors had very limited amounts of internal memory. For example, IBM's Magnetic Tape/Selectric Typewriter (MT/ST) and Magnetic Card/Selectric Typewriter (MC/ST) used small magnetic tapes and magnetic-powder-coated plastic cards as recording media. Today's word processors have larger internal memories. In addition, many can write to and read from flexible disks like the ones we discussed in Chapter 6. Such disks can hold from 60 to 150 pages. Some devices or clusters of devices allow access to hard-disk units. A user can "call up" to the screen a previously typed document or page of a document to make revisions. Key paragraphs of text can be stored for quick insertion into standard documents such as contracts. Form letters can be merged with names and addresses, then printed to produce any number of personalized originals. Some systems allow graphic-image and text files to be combined on output. (See Figure 16-12.)

According to recent surveys, U.S. businesses now deal with more than 300 billion documents. That number is increasing by billions annually. Some documents are "one-time shots," but even routine intracompany memos are often retained for reference or as proof of commitments that have been made.

FIGURE 16-11
Word processors with page-size screens allow users to view text material exactly as it would appear if printed as hard-copy output. (*Courtesy Xerox Corporation*)

Paper is the most expensive medium a business can use for storing such information. Office systems with electronic storage and retrieval capabilities can serve as electronic filing cabinets as well as word processors. Most companies find that electronic files give them 50 to 90 percent better access to stored documents than traditional filing methods—and at lower costs.

FIGURE 16-12
Text and graphics can be intermixed on outputs of today's electronic printing subsystems, which include numerous word-processing devices. (*Photos courtesy Xerox Corporation*)

In many business environments, the tasks we've discussed so far are performed by secretaries and other support personnel. In terms of over-all cost, it's the productivity of managers and other highly paid professionals that businesses need to be most concerned about. Managers, analysts, accountants, and sales representatives are likely to be more productive if their support staffs are more productive. Still, if some of the tasks they perform can be automated, and if they learn to use today's office systems, even greater productivity gains may be achieved. White-collar workers now make up more than 50 percent of the U.S. labor force. Their needs are worth looking at.

To meet these broader objectives, the manufacturers of word-processing equipment have added data-processing capabilities to their systems. Software is now available to support business planning, financial modeling, and basic business operations such as accounts payable, accounts receivable, and inventory control. The manufacturers of conventional data-processing equipment have emphasized ease of use and environmental concerns in their product developments. Word-processing software, graphics packages, a wide variety of application packages, and "user friendliness" via menus, prompts, detachable keyboards, and nonglare tiltable screens are marketed. Communication capabilities have been added to many of these expanded office systems so that the systems can function as standalone units or as parts of larger shared-resource distributed-processing groupings. (See Figure 16-13.)

LOCAL AREA NETWORKS

With the desire to distribute some data-entry and data-processing functions out to users, and the increased emphasis on office automation and productivity, have come increased demands for faster, more efficient, more dependable means of user-to-user, office-to-office, and machine-to-machine communication. *Local area networks*, or *LAN's*, are a response to these demands. A LAN can be defined as a system for transmitting data from one point to two or more other points simultaneously, within a relatively small area. Typically, it interconnects devices in the same room, building, or group of buildings. Supporters of LAN's point out that from 80 to 90 percent of all business communications occur between users within a mile of each other. (See Figure 16-14.)

From the user's point of view, a LAN should support communication between any of a wide variety of devices—those the user already has when the network is installed and those acquired later, whether they be computers, data-entry terminals, word processors, electronic copiers, ordinary telephones, or whatever. Manufacturers and vendors want to offer devices that can be interconnected in any network; otherwise, the network users may not buy the devices.

Xerox, DEC, and Intel were early leaders in promoting standardization of LAN interfaces. In 1980, they united behind Ethernet, a network architecture providing a single channel (1 to 50 megabits per second transmission rate) for digital transmission. There is no switching logic within the network. Active components contend for use of a coaxial cable transmission bus through "listen before talk" and "listen while talk" protocols. Wang Laboratories has developed WangNet, an analog transmission system that takes advantage of the huge bandwidth available with cable television networks to support simultaneous voice, data, and video transmission. Areas of up to 20 square miles can be covered. Ungerman-Bass and Sytex are among firms marketing general-purpose LAN's; existing telephone lines and CBX's rather than coaxial cables serve as the basic components of these offerings.

FIGURE 16-13
Many user needs can be handled by a multipurpose configuration such as Burroughs' Office Information System, which has both word-processing and data-processing capabilities. (*Courtesy Burroughs Corporation*)

A Online electronic file/retrieval system
B Multipurpose user workstation
C Desktop printer
D Word processor
E Shared printer with cut forms feeder

F Executive inquiry/display station
G Page reader input station
H Facsimile station
I Communication/control processor

An organization that acquires a private LAN often uses a small computer, known as a *gateway processor*, to interconnect that network with public transmission facilities. Assume, for example, that an insurance firm has LAN's at office buildings in five major cities. Gateway processors may interconnect the LAN's to a public value-added network such as Telenet or Tymnet. Software and switching logic within the gateway processors must route outgoing messages to the appropriate destination LAN; they must direct incoming messages to the appropriate destination node within the LAN they service. Some vendors and users are suggesting that gateway processors can and should perform many of the communication functions performed by front-end processors (thereby eliminating the need for them in some environments).

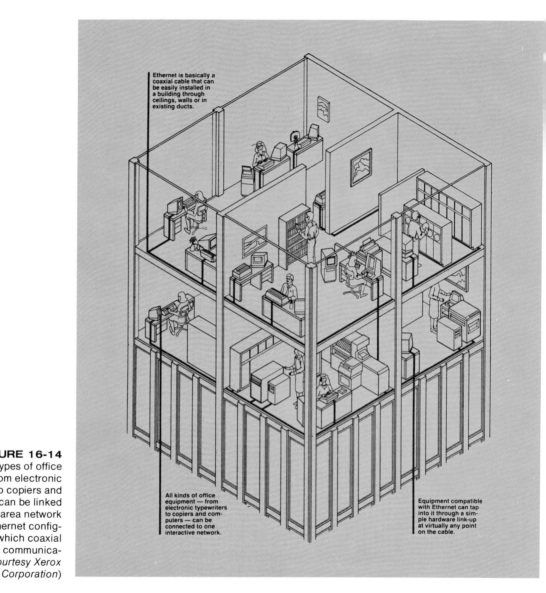

Ethernet is basically a coaxial cable that can be easily installed in a building through ceilings, walls or in existing ducts.

All kinds of office equipment — from electronic typewriters to copiers and computers — can be connected to one interactive network.

Equipment compatible with Ethernet can tap into it through a simple hardware link-up at virtually any point on the cable.

FIGURE 16-14
Many types of office equipment—from electronic typewriters to copiers and computers—can be linked within a local area network such as this Ethernet config-uration in which coaxial cables serve as communica-tion lines. (*Courtesy Xerox Corporation*)

ELECTRONIC MAIL

Remember the last time you tried repeatedly, and unsuccessfully, to telephone to a friend or business associate? Chances are you finally resorted to leaving a message. Likewise, chances are you were out when the other person returned your call.

Remember the business, church, or school meeting notice you received the day *after* the meeting? The package you had to go after, because the delivery person wouldn't leave it when you were out? The letter or report that somehow got lost in transit and never did arrive?

Eliminating problems like these is what *electronic mail* is all about. It is the delivery, by electronic means, of messages that otherwise would be transmitted physically through intracompany mailrooms or external postal systems, or verbally via telephones. Each message may be a short one-liner, a copy of one page of text, or a several-hundred-page document.

Electronic mail offers the speed and convenience of a phone call without the frustration of "telephone tag" and with the option of creating any number of hard copies of the message. At 50 to 75 cents per message, electronic mail still costs more than a postage stamp. However, when somewhat less tangible benefits such as timeliness and increased efficiency are taken into account, the arguments for electronic mail become more convincing. For example, electronic mail gets rid of the "information float" of ordinary mail: About 10 pages of information can pass from sender to receiver in one minute (instead of two or more days later as mentioned above). If you're still looking for alternatives, contrast the cost of 50 to 75 cents per message – plus relatively low increments as message lengths increase – with the cost of your most recent long-distance phone call.

Strictly speaking, electronic mail is not new. The telegraph and Morse code, Western Union's TWX/Telex and Mailgram services, and low-cost, low-speed Teletypes and similar machines have been around for some time. Facsimile (fax) equipment can provide a hard-copy duplicate at the receiving end of an original message that exists in hard-copy form at the sending end. Signatures and line drawings or other graphics as well as text can be transmitted. For most purposes, a fax machine functions as a copier at the end of a telephone line. In the middle 1970s, electronic mail became synonymous with computer-based message systems. Word processors that could transmit results to be printed out or displayed at distant word processors became available; they were marketed as communicating word processors. Electronic document distribution became a practical reality.

Now, electronic mail is taking on an enhanced role. Vendors are developing hardware and software to allow managers and other communicators to actually create their own correspondence. They can change it, send it to one or more colleagues, file it, and destroy it at their convenience. Of course, managers can't become skilled typists overnight, and some are reluctant to use keyboards. To appeal to them, vendors are continuing to emphasize user friendliness. Some systems simulate the in-basket, pending, and out-basket functions with which managers are familiar. Many provide extensive full-screen forms guidance and menus. Managers simply fill in blank areas, or press one key or touch one area on a screen to choose from a variety of message-handling alternatives.

Today's computer-based message systems are available from several sources. Some are subscription services. For example, Telenet's Telemail and Tymnet's OnTyme II enable users to send, receive, and file messages electronically anywhere in the United States at any time. Each authorized user has an electronic mailbox that can be accessed from office, home, or out-of-town using a desktop, portable, or handheld terminal coupled to a telephone. The Source and CompuServe offer similar capabilities. Alternatively, an organization may acquire electronic mail software, such as Wang's Mailway or Hewlett-Packard's HPMAIL, to use on a LAN or CBX. Finally, both the hardware and the software needed to run electronic mail can be installed as a *turnkey system* at user locations. Ideally, the user need only "turn the key" on such a system to make the system work. Vendor personnel install the system, get the electronic mail application up and running, and provide whatever maintenance support may be necessary.

The potential impact of electronic mail becomes particularly exciting where the underlying network is widespread. Many U.S. Congressmen send and receive messages from constituents via electronic mail. K-Mart and J. C. Penney are among leading retailers who communicate electronically with hundreds of suppliers; they are experiencing significant reductions in order lead time, as well as increased accuracy and reduced clerical costs. The electronic funds transfer (EFT) systems that many of us take advantage of are special forms of electronic mail. The U.S. Postal Service is competing for a piece of the action with its E-COM system, intended for high-volume *electronic* *computer-originated* *m*ail. (See Figure 16-15.) Messages sent to any of 25 service post offices are guaranteed to be printed, enveloped, and delivered anywhere in the 48 contiguous states within two days. The service is being used for direct mail by financial institutions, insurance carriers, airlines, retailers, federal agencies, professional sports groups, and other large organizations. Since the electronic messages sent to a service post office are converted to hard copy for final delivery, E-COM is not a totally electronic mail system. It is, however, a communication offering you are likely to hear about.

VOICE MAIL Voice mail can be regarded as a particular kind of electronic mail—one in which both input and output are in audio form. Typically, to access a voice mail system, a user dials the system's extension on a telephone, then states a user identification and password (the equivalent of signing on to a terminal by keying those

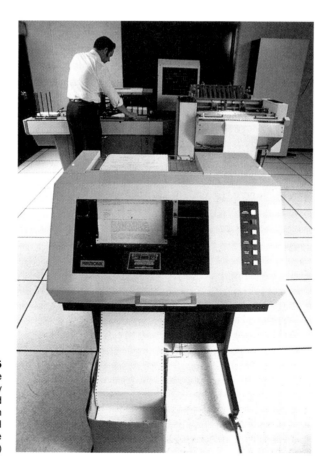

FIGURE 16-15
The U.S. Postal Service guarantees that a hard-copy form of computer-originated mail will reach its destination within 2 days after the mail arrives at an E-COM service post office. (*Courtesy RCA*)

items). Once they are validated, the user may then listen to any new messages, listen again to any old messages (received and saved previously), delete messages, save messages, forward messages, or create and send new messages to one, some, or all other system users. Since each user has an assigned voice mailbox, messages are simply stored in those mailboxes until the addressed recipients "get their mail." (See Figure 16-16.)

All voice mail (also called *voice store-and-forward*) systems are alike in that words spoken into a telephone or audio terminal are converted from analog to digital form. Once digitized, voice messages can be manipulated like typed messages in computer-based message systems. Turnkey voice mail systems for rental or purchase come in several varieties. For example, a standalone minicomputer-based voice mail system may be accessed from the caller's telephone to leave a voice message if an attempted direct call to another system user cannot be completed successfully. A voice mail system that is an integral part of an organization's LAN or CBX may be able to switch automatically to a callee's voice mailbox if a call is not answered or a busy signal is received. The system may also notify the callee, via a flashing light on the phone or similar method, that a message is waiting. Organizations wanting to evaluate the usefulness of voice mail technology before committing heavy investments to it can do so by subscribing to vendors' voice mail services. Such services are similar to the vended electronic mail services mentioned above.

TELE-CONFERENCING

Teleconferencing is group communication achieved in spite of the fact that the source of a message to be communicated and the intended recipients of that message are at geographically distant locations. Satellite carriers and licensed vendors of communication services using satellites as relay stations are marketing teleconferencing as a means of eliminating travel time and expense,

FIGURE 16-16
Users of IBM's Audio Distribution System use ordinary telephones to communicate via voice messages with other system users.
(*Courtesy IBM Corporation*)

improving and personalizing communications, and increasing productivity. Suggested uses of teleconferencing include company stockholder, sales, and product information meetings, personnel training, continuing education programs, corporate staff communications with regional counterparts, and joint planning, consultation, and decision making in ongoing business activities. (See Figure 16-17.)

The participants in a teleconference communicate with those presenting information through two-way audio, one-way video, or two-way video. In most

A

B

C

FIGURE 16-17 At Hewlett-Packard, new products may be introduced at a company briefing (A), which is transmitted from a control room via satellite (B), to teleconference sessions at sales sites nationwide (C). (*Photos courtesy Hewlett-Packard Company*)

cases, the viewers can see and hear the presenters but are not on camera themselves, though their questions and comments may be heard. The viewing screen may present moving pictures (full motion) or static images (freeze frame). Color and high-resolution graphics may be offered as options. Screen sizes vary widely.

Western Union, AT&T, SBS, and ASC now offer teleconferencing services. Holiday Inn was the first hotel chain to offer teleconferencing. Its subsidiary, Holiday Inn Video Network (Hi-Net), held its first teleconference for TRW on June 4, 1980. Marriott, Hilton, Sheraton, and several large independent hotels have contracted with VideoStar Connections, Inc., an Atlanta-based firm, to offer teleconferencing at selected locations. The extent to which these offerings are used will help determine the future application of this technology.

VIDEOTEX What teleconferencing is to remote group communications, *videotex* is to remote communications with individuals in homes and offices. It is the delivery of information from computerized files and databases over cable or telephone lines for display on the screen of a TV set. The information may be in the form of text, line drawings, and simple graphics.

The simplest videotex systems are broadcast videotex, or *teletext*. These systems support one-way noninteractive communication. Hundreds of individually numbered pages of information are sent repetitively every minute or two over unused portions of a TV channel. A special decoder added to a standard TV set is all that is needed to allow a subscriber to punch certain codes and thereby "grab" a page and display it on the screen of the set the next time it is sent. The more advanced videotex systems are interactive. They use two-way cables or telephone lines and allow users to call for the specific information they want. Some allow users to make reservations, purchase items, and the like from their own homes and offices.

Until now, U.S. firms have lagged behind their counterparts in Britain, France, and Canada in offering TV-based information services. Britain's Post Office led the pack when it began trials of its videotex services, then known as *Viewdata* (now *Prestel*), in 1976. However, the broad potential of this technology is such that it cannot be ignored. Even conservatives estimate that as many as 7 percent of all U.S. households—some 8 million homes—will have videotex systems by 1990. Estimates of as many as 45 million videotex-using households by 1990 are not uncommon. Videotex was initially aimed at users in homes, but businesses are also spending at an accelerating rate to obtain access to remote computerized information.

Though we have not used the term *videotex* in earlier discussions, the information access offered by The Source, CompuServe, and Dialog Information Services can be classified as videotex. Telephone companies, cable TV operators, broadcasters, publishers, retailers, bankers, and equipment manufacturers are all increasing their videotex efforts. Many firms face the prospect of significant changes in the way they do business if or when videotex really takes off. At-home banking, nonstore retailing, and advertising via these information services may become commonplace. You may select the categories of news you want rather than see or hear whatever news is presented. As individuals, and as members of businesses and other organizations, we are, in fact, a nation of information users and information providers.

COMPUTING SERVICES

To complete our discussion of data-processing/data-communication alternatives, we now summarize the vendor offerings referred to collectively as *computing services*. Through these offerings, the computing power of large mainframes is made available to, and shared by, many users. Personal computers often play vital roles as both remote terminals and processors. Vendors direct their attention to the tasks that users want to accomplish, as well as to the tools needed to accomplish them. (See Figure 16-18.)

Generally, the basic offering of a computer service company is the capability to handle *remote batch* work. Here, an organization submits its data for batch processing via remote batch terminals linked in a communication network with the vendor's service center. Each terminal must have a storage area, or buffer, where the data can be collected prior to transmission. The buffer can be high-speed (semiconductor or bubble memory) or low-speed (magnetic-tape cassette or flexible disk). Some vendors accept batched data transported to their centers via regular mail or courier facilities.

To understand the magnitude of such processing, consider Automatic Data Processing of Santa Clara, California, as an example. This firm, commonly known as ADP, performs computerized payroll processing for more than 6000 companies and prepares paychecks for one of every 12 people in the country. On a cost-comparison basis, manual preparation of payroll, including record-keeping and filing quarterly reports with the government, costs about $3 per check. A company can process its own payroll with computer help at about $1.20 per check. ADP can do it for about 42¢ per check. Computer service companies can handle applications such as payroll processing more cheaply because they have enough work to keep their computers busy full time and because the cost of software updating and maintenance can be spread over a huge customer base.

Remote job entry (*RJE*) capabilities are a step beyond remote batch. Here, an organization's terminal can be used to initiate the execution of an application program as well as to supply some or all of the input to it. In effect, the remote location is job-oriented rather than data-oriented. The user's terminal serves much like a remote system console. It may be part of an RJE station that also includes a printer; the printer can accept and print the output of application programs executed at the service center. Some stations include disk units that provide local data-storage capabilities. A complete minicomputer or microcomputer system may also function as an RJE station.

As explained in Chapter 14, users may acquire interactive problem-solving capabilities through access to an outside (vendor-supplied) time-sharing system. Because the marketing of time-sharing systems is highly competitive, many vendors offer application packages consisting of programs specialized for an industry (e.g., electric power) or a discipline (e.g., accounting). Graphics packages that run on everything from Apples to Sperry Univac 1180s and that do everything from business charts to 35-mm slides are prevalent here as elsewhere.

Vendors such as General Electric Information Services Co. (GEISCO) develop application systems under contract in far less time (and with far less impact on users' resources) than would be required if the systems were developed in-house. Boeing Computer Services offers development assistance and remote computing services to The Boeing Company and to other organizations worldwide. (See Figure 16-19.)

As another feature, many vendors are establishing large databases, or *data banks*, for commercial use. Examples of the kinds of data available are (1) lists,

A

B

FIGURE 16-18

Programmers at the Anacomp development center in Sarasota, Florida, work on enhancements to a real-time banking application that can handle most of a bank's retail business (A). Banks and credit unions that do not have their own data-processing installations can use the facilities of an Anacomp financial data center (B). Automated teller machines can be linked into regional or national networks controlled by Anacomp switching facilities that route user transactions to home banks for account processing (C). The end users of Anacomp services are bank customers (D). (*Photos courtesy Anacomp, Inc.*)

C

D

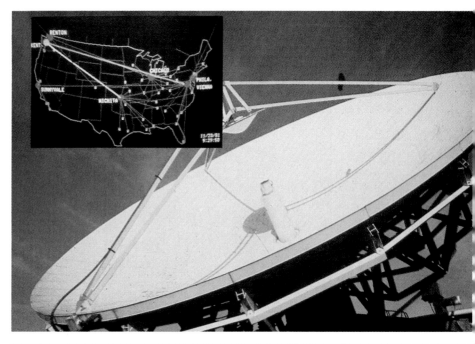

FIGURE 16-19
Organizations throughout the world depend on remote facilities at Boeing Computer Services, Seattle, to carry out many of their basic business activities. (*Photos courtesy Boeing Computer Services Company*)

updated daily, of stolen or lost credit cards issued by membership firms; and (2) regularly updated reports on stocks, bonds, commodities, futures, options, gold and other precious metals, money markets, mutual funds, foreign exchange, and Treasury rates. In Chapters 1 and 15, as well as here, we identified The Source, CompuServe, and Dialog Information Services as leading suppliers of remote databases on a seemingly unlimited variety of subjects.

Plummeting hardware costs, increasingly powerful minis and micros, and stable or rising communication costs have made in-house systems formidable alternatives to remote service offerings. In response, some vendors are marketing turnkey systems. Both system and application software are optimized to run on a particular computer configuration and provide a complete solution to specific user needs. For example, McAuto, headquartered at St. Louis, Missouri, offers Unigraphics ADS-100, a fully integrated CAD/CAM system. Turnkey electronic mail and voice mail systems were mentioned earlier in this chapter. In some cases, the user is advised *what* to do as well as *how* to do it. Such offerings are a recognition of the fact that users want help in solving their total business problems – not just a convenient way of electronically processing data.

CHAPTER SUMMARY

1. A data-communication system provides for the transfer of information from one location to another without altering the content or sequence of the information.

2. When analog transmission is used, the signals that constitute a message are transmitted in wave form. In digital transmission, the signals are transmitted as distinct pulses in much the same way that data is moved about in the computer.

3. Sending and receiving units are kept in step during the communication process through either start/stop synchronization or synchronous transmission facilities.

4. Signals travel between two points along one data path, or channel, on a communication line. The line may be a direct point-to-point connection or a shared multipoint, or multidrop, line.

5. Modems are needed to convert digital data in pulse form to wave form prior to analog transmission, and to reconvert the data to pulse form at its destination.

6. Multiplexers allow users to make efficient use of a line by combining data traffic from and to several low-speed communication lines into a single higher-speed line.

7. When a user places a call to send voice or data traffic over a switched, or dial-up, line, a connection to the call destination is established through one or more public exchanges, or switching facilities.

8. A user organization with heavy message volume may acquire leased or private lines, then connect them through a PBX or CBX for better-quality transmission and flexibility.

9. Common carriers are organizations authorized by the Federal Communications Commission (FCC) and/or state public utilities commissions (PUC's) to offer communication services. MCI Telecommunications and Southern Pacific Communications (the owner of Sprint) are prominent specialized common carriers. GTE's Telenet and Tymshare's Tymnet are examples of value-added networks.

10. Distributed processing is characterized by a dispersion of the processing power, or intelligence, within an EDP system among geographically separated locations.

11. Word, or text, processing is the manipulation of character data to form words, sentences, paragraphs, memos, letters, and reports. Electronic mail and voice mail systems are additional aids to office productivity.

12. Teleconferencing provides for group communications between persons at geographically distant locations. Satellite carriers, vendors of services using satellites, and large hotel chains are marketing teleconferencing as a means of eliminating travel expenses, improving communications, and increasing productivity.

13. Videotex is the delivery of information from computerized files and databases over cable or telephone lines for display on a TV screen. The simplest videotex systems (teletext) support one-way communication only. More advanced systems allow users to make reservations, purchase items, and the like from their homes and offices.

14. Computer service companies offer remote batch, remote job entry, time sharing, application packages, application system development, access to data banks, and turnkey systems—all tailored to user needs.

DISCUSSION QUESTIONS

1. Show, by example, the difference between data processing and data communication.

2. List and explain the basic elements of a data-communication system, giving the primary functions of each.

3. (a) List three sets of characteristics of data transmission from which a user organization must select appropriate options to suit its telecommunication needs.
(b) Explain in detail one of the sets of characteristics that you named.

4. Assume you are the president of a tri-state trucking firm, specializing in long hauls of perishable goods.
(a) What telecommunication needs might your firm have?
(b) Distinguish between public and private (leased) lines. Suggest factors your firm should consider in choosing between them in order to meet the needs you've identified, and develop recommendations accordingly.

5. What is the role of the FCC in telecommunications?

6. (a) Why and how is the breakup of AT&T occurring?
(b) Discuss its potential ramifications.

7. Suggest advantages and disadvantages of distributed processing from the point of view of a large brokerage firm such as Dean Witter or E. F. Hutton.

8. Show how word processing and data processing are alike, and how they differ.

9. Discuss electronic mail systems. In doing so, point out the capabilities they have that are not available with conventional mail or telephone services.

10. Describe user situations where teleconferencing may be appropriate, pointing out why.

11. (a) What is videotex?
    (b) What capabilities of videotex offerings are of most interest to you as a user or potential user?

12. Show how a savings and loan, real estate agency, or community college might take advantage of remote computing services.

Courtesy Aetna Life and Casualty, Hartford, Conn.

Courtesy Anne Arundel Community College/Rob Hendry

21
COMPUTING ISSUES AND IMPACTS

At Anne Arundel Community College's 21st commencement ceremony, the guest "speaker" was Robot Redford, a battery-powered, robotlike device remotely operated by William Bakaleinikoff, its creator. "Tomorrow is the future," Redford said, "and you, and what I represent, will be there together." If it were not for emergency repairs, the 4-foot-high robot would have delivered its address with a stiff neck. In other words, the man behind the machine is what makes it work. Although computer technology is here now, it ultimately depends on human beings for its maintenance and use.

Few people at the commencement ceremony reacted to the device with much enthusiasm. Kathleen L. Hammac, the class valedictorian, told her fellow graduates that "our primary challenge is to retain our humanity in this technological world." Many people have expressed anxiety over the future effects of computerization on our society. Most concerns about the future stem from a deep-rooted fear that we may not be able to cope with

change. Perhaps we need to take a closer look at how our Computer Age is progressing.

One of the primary concerns some people have about a computerized society is the vulnerability they see resulting from information and information-processing capabilities in the hands of the wrong people. Already, various security procedures are being used to limit the access to data and data processing. Key-operated terminals and bar-code identification badges are two of the security tools used to assure that only authorized personnel can have access to programs and data that have been placed under a computer's control. Again, it is the humans behind the machines who determine the rules. The necessity for such security measures, and how restrictive our "Information Society" must become, is largely determined by how much integrity there is in our society as a whole. The more integrity we have, the less restrictive things need to be.

Meanwhile, the Computer Age continues to emerge. Computer fairs have sprung up around the country. At the fairs, computer enthusiasts can view the latest hardware, see exotic software applications, and buy, sell, and trade computers and computer-related products. They may see demonstrations of such things as computerized holography scanning.

© 1983 Luz Bueno Graphics, Berkeley, California

Courtesy National Advanced Systems

Courtesy Intermec

Another use of computerized imagery is in architectural modeling. A proposed model of an office can be viewed at many angles and from many distances with the help of a computer. Space planning and facility management can also be done with the aid of a computer.

Computers have also entered, unobtrusively, the entertainment industry. Elektra/Asylum Records uses computers to design and record digital video disks of popular musical groups. Many computerized video games combine entertainment with educational materials.

Another use to which computers are being put is interplanetary exploration. A United States Geological Survey satellite sent back pictures of a Martian volcano called Olympus Mons. This volcano rises 26 kilometers above the surrounding plateau. It's approximately 15 miles, or 75,000 feet high! Digital picture reconstruction allows us to see the lava flows (in red).

The future lies in the present, in the form of every undeveloped capability and every possible happening. No one really knows how the Computer Age will evolve. We can only be assured that the traditional forms of our society will continually be replaced by new forms, as our adjustment to the needs and opportunities of the times continues. We might simply rest in the faith that our forward and upward development is assured by forces much greater than us all.

Courtesy Intergraph Corporation

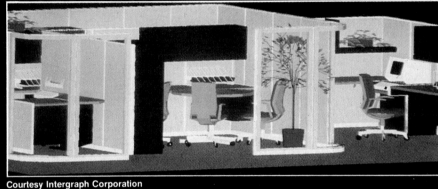

Courtesy Intergraph Corporation

Courtesy Intergraph Corporation

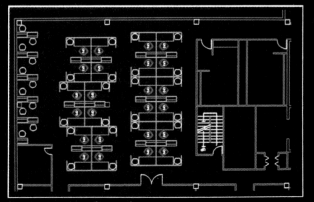

en/Capital Records, Inc.

Courtesy RCA

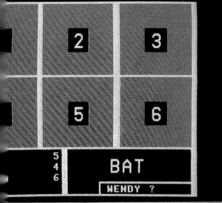

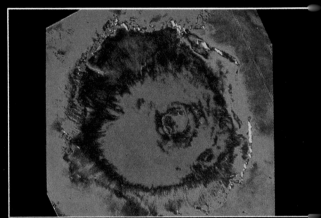

rporation

Courtesy United States Department of the Interior, Geological Survey

From *Sunstone,* a computer animation videotape by Ed Emshwiller,
computer program by Alvin Ray Smith, made at New York Institute of Technology, 1979

17 | COMPUTING ISSUES AND IMPACTS

COMPUTING AND ORGANIZATIONS
COMPUTING AND JOBS
ROBOTIC SYSTEMS
ARTIFICIAL INTELLIGENCE
INDIVIDUALISM AND THE RIGHT OF PRIVACY
COMPUTER CRIME
PROTECTION MECHANISMS
SOCIAL DEPENDENCY AND VULNERABILITY
WHAT CAN BE DONE?

In 1927, *Time* magazine named its first "man of the year": Charles A. Lindbergh. The following year, *Time* chose Walter P. Chrysler. In 1950, *Time* chose a group: G.I. Joes. For more than half a century, key individuals and groups have been honored similarly. In 1982, computer scientists and computer kids alike were startled when *Time* altered its long-standing tradition by naming, not a man or a group, but a machine of the year. That machine was the computer.

As we have learned throughout this book, no one person invented computers. No one person is responsible for computer applications. Every year computers are getting faster, smaller, and cheaper. Few if any persons would debate the fact that the Computer Age is here.

Since computers are so powerful and so prevalent, it's appropriate for us to step back a moment as we study them. What effects are these machines having on organizations, and on us as members of those organizations? On society, and on us as members of society? On each of us as individuals? What do those effects imply and what, if anything, should we be doing about them? In the years ahead, you can expect to face such questions, and they will not be easy to answer. The purpose of this chapter is to help you think about computers from several different perspectives. The need to do so is increasingly urgent.

In this chapter we look first at the impact of computing on organizations. Then we look more closely at the impact of mechanization, automation, and computers on jobs, and we discuss job attitudes. Both current and potential applications of two rapidly emerging technologies – robotic systems and artificial intelligence – are described. Much has been said about the computer's ability to destroy our individualism and to invade our privacy, so we examine the dangers and safeguards in

514

these areas. The threats of computer crime and other natural and man-made disasters are with us daily. The chapter closes with a look at the extent of our exposure to such threats and suggests some security mechanisms.

COMPUTING AND ORGANIZATIONS

Computers are impacting organizations, first and foremost, because computers are used by organizations. In the 1960s and 1970s, the typical business computer was a large mainframe, enclosed in a special environment-controlled room at a central site. Data was transported to that site; processing was done there; and a centralized DP group did whatever needed to be done computerwise. Some persons argue that the centralized DP function simply mirrored the corporate structure of user organizations of the time. Other persons suggest that the centralized nature of these computing systems not only supported but also fostered large, centralized organizations.

Today, that picture has changed. To be sure, there are still large mainframes and there are still large organizations. There are many more small computer systems, however, and they are appearing in organizations of all types and sizes—from elementary schools to government-funded research labs; from "mom and pop" grocery stores to Fortune 500 companies. Computing power is migrating from mainframe-based data centers to manufacturing floors, executive offices, and even briefcases. About a million desktop computers were shipped to users in 1982 alone; this number is expected to reach 5 million by 1986 (and remember, the "desktop" category doesn't include many handheld, portable, and home models). Administrators who cannot purchase computers via capital equipment budgets are resorting to petty cash vouchers. "Keeping up with the Joneses" doesn't mean having faster, bigger (or smaller), more expensive (or less costly) computers than other organizations in the sales territory, district, or service area. It does mean having the computing tools needed to be competitive and successful.

An obvious impact of computing on organizations is the direct economic impact. Computers cost money; computer programs cost money; computer talent is expensive; and so on. (See Figure 17-1.) A survey of the 1983 DP budgets of 50 U.S. corporations showed that the average DP budget accounts for 2 percent of a firm's annual gross revenues, regardless of the firm's size.* Conversely, computers save money—the carrying costs of inventory are lower because stock levels better match demands; customer payments are received sooner because bills are generated and mailed sooner; fewer employees are needed in the payroll department because the computer can do many of the routine, repetitive tasks of payroll preparation; and so on.

Computers also have an indirect economic impact on organizations. For example, they can compute and display trends in customer buying habits that enable managers to anticipate and respond to customer wants in a timely fashion. The computer-using firm can thereby outsell competitors who have not had access to the trend data. As another example, a computer can produce reports monthly, weekly, or even daily, showing actual schedules and costs of product development versus planned schedules and costs. On the basis of these reports, the responsible managers can initiate corrective action immediately instead of discovering too late that schedule and cost overruns have occurred.

---

*Susan Blakeney, "Making Do," *Computerworld* XVII, 1 (Jan. 3, 1983): 4-6.

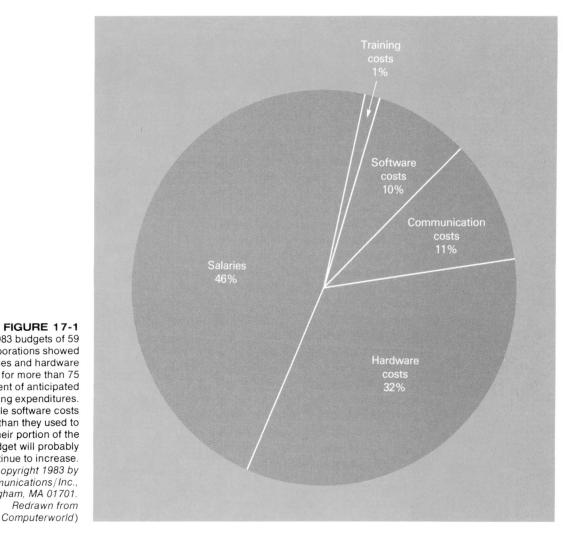

Computers may also impact organizational structure and individual behavior. The management and control of an organization may be centralized. Alternatively, a geographically or functionally diverse organization may be managed as several independent business units. Each unit can be supported by computing systems that meet its particular needs. The units can stand alone, just as their systems can stand alone, for some purposes. The units can interact or communicate, just as their systems can communicate, when it's appropriate to do so. There is no conclusive empirical proof that computers cause centralization or decentralization; we can see that computers facilitate either. They also support a management style in which policies and directives are set at a corporate level, but where authority and accountability for day-to-day operations rest with lower-level line managers.

If knowledge is power, and if information is a source of knowledge, then we can assume that information is also a source of power. The individual or department that controls an organization's computing systems—or even one of its several computing systems—controls at the very least a potential source of power. The individual or department determines not only its own use of the organization's information resource, but also who else has access to the information and with what priority. The individual may be the president of the organization, the head of MIS, the head of administrative services, or whatever. The department may be a central DP department, an information system staff, or one of several user divisions or departments.

An individual or department with information power may view the proposed acquisition of 15, 100, or even 1000 microcomputer systems as a threat to that power. Persons knowledgeable in the computing field are quick to advise cooperation rather than resistance to such a proposal. In most organizations, the backlog of users' computing requirements is very large. Information system staffs commonly point to three years' worth of application development work ahead of them. Multiple approaches to such backlogs are warranted. Some vendors are suggesting that organizations establish *information centers*— in-house departments chartered to promote and support end-user computing.

COMPUTING AND JOBS

The *mechanization* of work is not new. It's been going on for centuries. Stated simply, it's the use of a machine or group of machines to carry out a process under the direction of a human operator. *Automation* is not new either. It's the performance of a specific combination of actions by a machine or group of machines "automatically"—without the aid of a human operator. Most of us tend to think of automation as something that's happening in manufacturing plants and warehouses, but it's not limited to that. Remember, for example, office automation.

The effects of mechanization and automation on, say, the U.S. labor force warrant examination. In 1850, farmers made up 64 percent of that labor force. Today, only 3.1 percent of American workers are engaged in agriculture. (See Figure 17-2.) In 1850 the average farm worker supplied food and fiber for 4

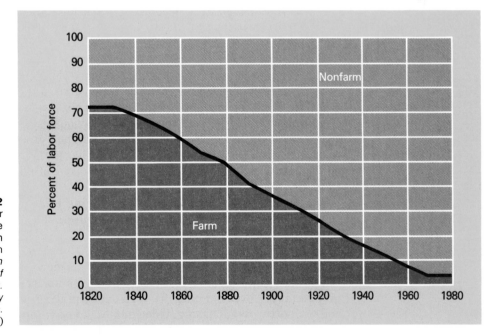

FIGURE 17-2
The portion of the U.S. labor force engaged in agriculture reflects, over time, the high degree of mechanization achieved in farming. (*Graph from "The Mechanization of Work," by Eli Ginzberg. Copyright © 1982 by Scientific American, Inc. All rights reserved.*)

people; today the average output of each farm worker provides for 78 people! Of wage and salaried workers not engaged in agriculture, more than 70 percent are employed in service industries. Fewer than 30 percent are employed in the basic goods-producing industries (manufacturing, mining, and construction).

In 1940, white-collar workers, blue-collar workers, and service-industry workers (narrowly defined, as in Figure 17-3, to include just those workers who provide services primarily to consumers) constituted 31, 57, and 12 percent, respectively, of the U.S. labor force. Forty years later, they constituted 54, 34, and 12 percent. The truly impressive growth in white-collar workers occurred primarily in two U.S. Bureau of Labor groupings: (1) professional, scientific, and technical workers, and (2) managerial and administrative workers. Consider General Electric Company as an example. The firm manufactures thousands of different items, from night lights to huge turbine engines. Yet not more than 40 percent of its employees are directly engaged in production; the rest work in in-house producer services, ranging from planning to personnel to marketing.

In a major way, computers have facilitated this redistribution of labor. More often than not, a machine or group of machines not under the direction of a human operator is under the direction of a computer. In many cases, the machine itself is a computer. Although computers have not *caused* mechanization or automation, they have dramatically increased both the rate at which firms are automating their processes and the speed and extent of that automation.

Some persons are concerned that computers and microelectronics may cause a shift in the American workplace as fundamental as the move from an agricultural to an industrial economy. If there are fewer jobs, what happens in a society in which a job not only defines a person (he's a dentist, she's a housewife. . .) but often provides much of the person's meaning in life? Where is the "social cement," or togetherness, that work has long provided?

In response to such concerns, other experts point out that the traditional work ethic is changing. Many Americans do not need a job classification to have an identity. "Success" is not measured in terms of the size of one's annual income or one's position on the corporate ladder. For the most part, American workers have had a positive attitude toward technological advancements; they view such advancements as making jobs less tedious and easier to accomplish, rather than as threats to their livelihood. Data-entry operators in industries such as banking may feel under more time pressure and more closely supervised because their rates of keystroking can be monitored by computers and reported exactly to management. Financial analysts who like to work with numbers may get bored if the computer does all the "tough stuff." Obviously, computers have had a more direct effect on lower-level jobs than on higher ones. However, there is no conclusive research showing that this effect has led to a more negative attitude on the part of workers in those lower-level jobs. Here, as elsewhere, individuals react differently.

In any case, persons who have been studying this problem point out that the time for contemplating whether or not computers should be allowed to enter and impact the workplace has long since passed. We've grown too accustomed to the benefits of having them there—more goods to choose from, lower prices than would be possible otherwise, and so on. Furthermore, as we've seen throughout this book, computers and related technologies are creating new jobs even as they're taking over old ones. They're even creating new industries—semiconductors, software publishing, video games, home information, and space explo-

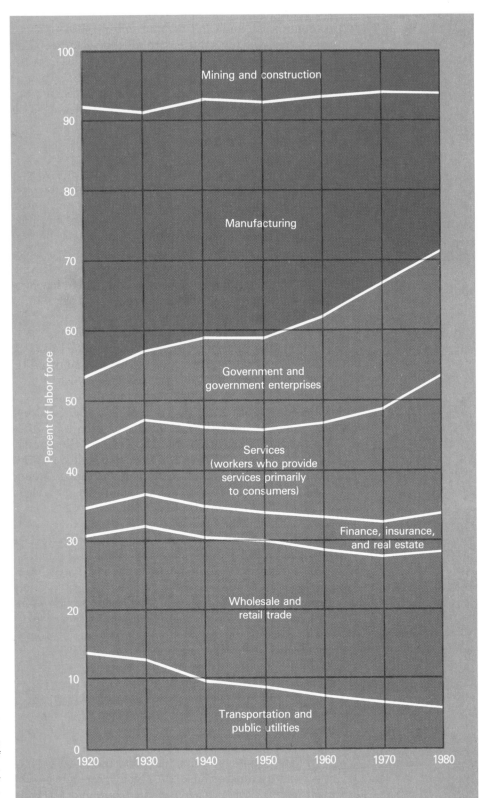

FIGURE 17-3
The jobs in nonfarm segments of the U.S. economy, over a 60-year period, reflect significant growth in the service sector; fewer and fewer employees are needed to produce a given amount of goods in the goods-producing (mining and construction, manufacturing sector. (*Graph from "The Mechanization of Work," by Eli Ginzberg. Copyright © 1982 by Scientific American, Inc. All rights reserved.*)

ration, to name a few. Our approach, then, should be to understand just what computers can and can't do, and to capitalize on this knowledge. There are no easy, wand-waving solutions to fill the vacuum created when vast numbers of jobs for which the current labor force has been trained disappear. Perhaps a computer can help these workers decide what other jobs (or nonjob activities) they'd like to do. Perhaps it can retrain them. By looking directly at the challenges presented in this Computer Age, we can better equip ourselves, our organizations, and our society to deal with them.

ROBOTIC SYSTEMS

According to the Robot Institute of America (a Michigan-based association of suppliers and users of robotic equipment), a *robot* is "a reprogrammable multifunctional manipulator designed to move materials, parts, tools, or specialized devices through variable programmed motions for the performance of a variety of tasks." Stated simply, a robot is a general-purpose programmable machine that can do any of several tasks under stored-program control. At the present time, the United States is second to Japan in the production and use of robotic systems. In Japan, nonprogrammable machines capable of performing fixed sequences of actions are also classified as robotic systems. Even excluding this category, Japan still leads.

Industrial robotic systems are undergoing a virtual population explosion. Their numbers have increased from about 200 in 1970, to 3500 in 1980, to 8000 in 1983. General Motors, the first auto maker to install a robotic system, plans to have about 14,000 of these systems by 1990. At Chrysler's Detroit and Newark, Delaware, assembly plants, the Plymouth Reliant and Dodge Aries K-cars come to life in a framing fixture called a *Robogate*. The Robogate locks the two body sides and the underbody assembly of each car into position and welds them together into a car body. (See Figure 17-4.) Similar robotic systems are used to produce Chrysler LeBaron and Dodge 400 midsize cars at St. Louis. High product quality, uniformity, and increased production efficiency are being achieved.

Many robotic systems look like giant cranes. Cables run along their mechanical arms to computers that transmit instructions as pulses to their clamps or claws. The most advanced robotic systems have feedback mechanisms—touch sensors and optical scanners that enable them to adapt to changing conditions. For example, if a parts-feeder tray is empty, a robotic system may bypass it and go on to the next tray. If a part is mispositioned, the system may jiggle it into place. A robotic system works untiringly, first, second, and third shifts, without complaining. Moreover, since the system is computer-based, it generates data for management reports and for diagnostic purposes.

The costs of robotic systems vary widely—from $8000 for pneumatically driven ones, from $24,000 to $140,000 for hydraulic ones, and from $80,000 to $170,000 for electrical ones. Such costs are easy to justify. Simple arithmetic shows that a $70,000 industrial robotic system used in a two-shift automatic subassembly spot-welding routine pays for itself within two years. (Four "person-years" of work are accomplished at $17,500 per year.) It may have an 8- to 10-year lifespan. During or after that period, it may be upgraded or replaced with new technologies.

To date, robotic systems have had the greatest impacts on the automobile, steel, and aerospace industries. Now, large farm-equipment and truck-equipment manufacturers such as John Deere and International Harvester are also

FIGURE 17-4
Chrysler Corporations'
Robogate and other auto-
matic welding systems apply
nearly 3000 welds to each
-car body, thus maintaining
a uniform computer-
controlled standard of
quality in production. (*Photos
courtesy Chrysler Corporation*)

going into robotics in a big way. Robotic systems can work near blast furnaces, radioactive materials, or noxious fumes. In addition to heavy work, they can perform very fine work such as inserting lipsticks into cosmetic cases, assembling printer chains with 80 or more different character slugs per chain, or putting together music boxes. They can inspect finished work and discard defectives.

Without doubt, some workers—autoworkers in spot welding and body painting, for example—feel that robotic systems have taken away their jobs. Many of these workers have been retrained, but the total number of employees needed within their companies is likely to be lower than it would be without the robotic systems. Nevertheless, we should realize that industries that are unable to modernize, or companies that are unable to meet or exceed the productivity levels of their competitors, may fail entirely. In that event, there would be no jobs at all.

Robotics enthusiasts contrast the $1.75 to $4.75 per hour needed to maintain a robotic system, to the $12 to $15 per hour paid to skilled laborers. According to classical economists, productivity is determined by three factors: labor, capital investment, and technological advancement. In practice, whether or not a proper blend of (and commitment to) these factors has been achieved is determined by one common measure: output per labor-hour worked. Robotics enthusiasts further argue that robotic systems improve the quality of worklife by reducing the number of dull, dirty, and dangerous tasks that must be performed by humans. They point out that many of the tasks performed by robotic systems are done in unpleasant and even unsafe surroundings.

ARTIFICIAL INTELLIGENCE

As humans, we perceive the world around us. Through our senses, we distinguish or "make sense" of the barrage of signals confronting us. We set goals and strive to attain them. We fail, and we learn from our failures. We make and break habits. We build up a background of experiences. We view old and new things in light of those experiences. We adapt to our surroundings. In doing so, we communicate with one another in our natural language (English, French, Spanish, or whatever). We both produce and understand utterances in that language. We reason. We draw conclusions on the basis of our findings.

These capabilities are said to make us different from other creatures. We don't understand very well *how* we think, but we know we *do*. Since the 1950s, a few leading artificial intelligence (AI) researchers have been trying to develop hardware and software so computers can do likewise.

Early successes—machines that could beat humans at checkers, prove mathematical theorems, and make logical deductions—led to extravagant predictions of fantastic accomplishments to come. Leading corporations established AI labs, only to back off in the 1960s when the task of building machines that could think proved to be far more difficult than many had anticipated.

Let's first look at why we might want machines to think. Your first reaction may be that perhaps we don't. Letting computers do manual labor for us is one thing. Letting them do our thinking for us is another. The following are positive examples of thinking-machine applications.

- *Expert systems:* Knowledge-based systems, in which the computer sorts through masses of data (knowledge) about a particular subject in order to detect patterns, then determines which rules apply on the basis of its findings, then applies them to generate new data and identify new patterns, and so on—thereby bringing "intelligence" to bear on fuzzy, nonnumerical problems. In medicine, for example, Stanford University's *Mycin* system can diagnose certain blood infections; *Puff* helps doctors at Pacific Medical Center in San Francisco diagnose lung problems; and *Caduceus* at the University of Pittsburgh can diagnose any of a wide variety of adult illnesses. Take the mining industry. SRI International's *Prospector* helps locate mineral deposits. At Schlumberger Ltd., an expert system called *Dipmeter Advisor* interprets down-hole data collected from oil-drilling sites and advises where to drill. Expert systems that design circuit chips, give financial advice, and determine how fabric designs can be woven are operational in test environments.

- *Natural language understanding:* Programs that allow English-speaking people to use ordinary English (not just an English-like query language) to ask questions about data stored in a database. Artificial Intelligence Corporation's *Intellect*, one of the few real AI products available, can respond to typed questions such as "How many employees are paid weekly?" and "Who works in Accounting?" It runs on numerous mainframes and interfaces with numerous DBMS's. As computer use spreads, programs that interface directly with users at terminals may have to support several human (natural) languages. The natural language of French-speaking Canadians, for example, differs significantly from the natural language of Italians.

- *Vision systems:* The "eyes" of robotic systems, enabling them to recognize silhouettes (whether a sedan or a station wagon is next on the assembly line). Some advanced vision systems can distinguish among three-dimensional objects. Some can provide complete graphic representations of objects on a CRT, even when not all parts of the objects are within the observing machine's "view."

- *Continuous speech recognition:* Programs that accept and understand ordinary conversational speech unpunctuated by deliberate silences, such as are required by conventional voice-input units. (For review, see "Remote Terminals" in Chapter 4.) With truly continuous speech recognition, widespread direct use of computers by busy executives, computer-assisted instruction (CAI) on almost any subject and at almost any level, and verbal programming may become realities.

AI computers that play games are a popular application of expert systems. These systems have progressed from checkers to backgammon and chess. A computerized backgammon program developed by Hans Berliner, a senior research computer scientist at Carnegie-Mellon, has been beating human backgammon grand masters since 1979. A $100,000 Fredkin Foundation grant was earmarked by Edward Fredkin of MIT in 1980 to go to the first person designing an unbeatable chess program. It is as yet unclaimed. Though high-speed computers can ponder up to 130,000 moves per second, today's best chess programs play roughly at the expert level—one notch below master and two notches below grand master. (See Figure 17-5.)

Why, you might ask, are the best minds at Duke, Northwestern, Bell Labs, and elsewhere trying to develop an unbeatable chess program? Well, certainly $100,000 would be nice, but they were trying before that inducement was offered. In attempting to teach the computer to think, these researchers are

FIGURE 17-5
Only confident chess players
take on Belle, one of the
world's leading chess-
playing computer systems.
(*Courtesy Bell Laboratories*)

understanding more and more about the way we think. When selecting a chess move, for example, a human player does not identify every possible move and then plow through those moves in a brute-force trial-and-error fashion until he or she finds one that's acceptable. Rather, most chess players try to control the center of the board—an elementary rule of thumb—and focus their attention accordingly. When AI designers began taking advantage of similar, seemingly acquired learning (that is, began using *heuristics*) they started to achieve success in game playing and theorem proving. Some AI researchers will tell you that mimicking the way an expert thinks about a topic is easy; figuring out how or why a child reacts to certain stimuli is something else.

The goal of AI researchers is not to develop machines that *think* for us, but rather machines that *help* us. Some of these AI machines are doing or will do work formerly done by humans. However, many researchers caution that people in business may again be expecting too much too soon. Attention must be directed to the potential impact of AI technology. What work can justly be done by machines? What work should be done by people? If 900 persons are doing a particular kind of job, and 100 other persons who also can do the job are looking for work, should the work be shared among them? Or should the pay? Should overtime be eliminated? Suppose a 4-day workweek, or even a 3-day one, becomes a widespread reality! Much research, development, and testing remains to be done.

INDIVIDUALISM AND THE RIGHT OF PRIVACY

Computers work primarily with numbers. The numbers are data. Much of the data is about us. When we're at school, the computer keeps records of courses taken, grades obtained, fees due, and so forth. When we've got a job, the computer keeps records of educational background, prior experience, rate of pay, taxes withheld, vacation, and lots more. The computer must track separately each person's data. (Joe's travel expense check mustn't go to Mary.) That means each person's data must be identifiable. Names won't do as identifiers; there may be several J. P. Yukies. An alternative is to make sure that each person the computer keeps data on is assigned a unique number.

Following this line of reasoning, as computer use spread, many people began to worry about depersonalization. Soon we would no longer need to have names; we would be known by numbers.

That hasn't happened. We *do* have student numbers, employee numbers, credit-card numbers, course numbers, trip numbers, even numbers for numbers. We *do* get mad when the computer sends us the same bill 3 months in a row, even after its been paid (there's been a program or data mixup.) We *do* become frustrated when a customer service representative fails to address our problem and instead (1) says that a computer is at fault, or (2) challenges us to prove the computer is wrong before action will be initiated. On the other hand, computers *can* deal with letters as well as numbers. Our bills still are addressed to us by name. Our paychecks are made out to us by name. We give our names when applying for jobs. We sign our names on the checks we write.

As employees of a computer-using firm understand more how to communicate with computers and with the information system staff, they are less prone to hide behind them. As computer hardware and data-communication costs come down, terminals become prevalent. As we've seen, sometimes we're expected to interact with them in order to do business. We may get the computer's attention more quickly than we would get that of a teller or sales clerk. On the other hand, we may feel that a computer-generated telephone response is too impersonal. We all bear the responsibility to help determine where person-to-person communication is needed, and where a computer interface is acceptable.

Another concern related to the computer's use of numbers as identifiers is the fear that some day all the data about each of us may be related by a unique universal identifier. Our Social Security numbers—which by definition must be unique, with or without computers—are pointed to as likely candidates. The real concern here is our individual right of privacy and whether or not that right is seriously endangered because of computers.

As used here, the term *privacy* refers to the rights of each individual regarding the collection, processing, storage, release, and use of data concerning the activities and characteristics of the individual. In this context, privacy is therefore a social and legal issue. It involves questions such as how and what data will be collected, how and by whom it will be used, and how and by whom it can be reviewed or changed. Such questions are not new. The issue of how much control individuals should have over data about themselves is not new. It is rooted in a fundamental, persistent dilemma of social organization: Individuals rightly desire to withhold certain personal information from others, yet numerous public and private organizations need (or think they need) certain personal information to carry out their agreed-to social or business responsibilities.

The trend toward the establishment of large, centralized data banks was started by the federal government. By 1980, it had about 7000 data banks, containing an average of 18 files for every American. The Internal Revenue Service, Social Security Administration, Veterans Administration, Secret Service, FBI, Department of Labor, Department of Justice, Department of Transportation, Department of Housing and Urban Development, and Department of Health and Human Services are among groups using them. State and local governments maintain data banks for a variety of uses also. These include tax collection, welfare programs, motor vehicle registration, law enforcement and criminal justice. It's safe to say both the number and the size of government-controlled data banks are still growing. (See Figure 17-6.)

Private business has not lagged far behind government. To see this, we need only discuss a couple of examples.

Today, the personal data collected by private organizations is manipulated within a vast information network. At the switchboard of this network are a few nationwide credit bureaus. Each credit bureau relies primarily on credit-card companies, financial institutions, department stores, and local governments for data. With the aid of high-speed data-communication facilities and computers, they provide information to credit-card companies, financial institutions, department stores, employers, landlords, lawyers, academic researchers, mailing list companies, insurance companies, government agencies, and other credit bureaus.

Suppose you live in Omaha, Nebraska. Concerned because of increasing family responsibilities, you decide to apply for life insurance. You are doing business not with one company in Omaha, but with the whole life insurance industry. About 700 life insurance companies—accounting for more than 90 percent of the life insurance coverage in the United States—exchange personal medical information via a computerized data bank in Boston called the *Medical Information Bureau*. This bureau holds the health histories of 11 million individuals.

FIGURE 17-6
Computer systems collect and maintain personal data about hundreds of thousands of licensed drivers and motor vehicle registrants nationwide. These expanding databases are used for many purposes. (*Courtesy Mohawk Data Sciences*)

Fortunately, out of concern comes action — albeit sometimes slowly. The first federal legislation aimed directly at computerized personal data collection was the Fair Credit Reporting Act, passed in 1971. It pertains to credit-reporting systems and the extensive information network mentioned above. The act insures to you the right of access to credit information collected about yourself. You can also find out the sources of that information. If you dispute the information, the credit bureau with whom you are dealing must either verify it or delete it.

Few Americans have not heard of the Nixon Administration and Watergate. A very unfortunate incident, some say. Others say Watergate was good for us. It alerted us anew to the dangers of wiretapping, snooping, and surveillance. Out of the resultant political climate came amendments to the Freedom of Information Act (initially passed in 1970) and the Privacy Act of 1974. Under these acts you can write for copies of personal records about yourself that have been collected by federal agencies. You can correct inaccuracies in those records. You can, to a great extent, control the disclosure of those records to other agencies. Unfair practices (i.e., invasions of privacy) are subject to criminal and civil penalties. The Family Educational Rights and Privacy Act, also passed in 1974, applies to universities and public school systems in much the same manner as the Privacy Act governs federal agencies.

The Privacy Act also established a Privacy Protection Study Commission. Its charter was to study the effects of the act and to recommend to the President the extent to which provisions and principles of the act should be applied to the private sector. The Commission's final report* was presented to President Carter and Congress on July 12, 1977. Its general thrust was toward openness and fairness in record keeping. When a person establishes a relationship with a private organization, he or she is to be fully informed about such factors as what data will be collected, what records will be kept, what role the records will have in decisions about him or her, with what organizations the records will be shared, by what organizations the records or portions thereof will be verified, his or her right to see, copy, and correct the records, and an assurance that they will be protected as confidential material.

Even while the final report was being prepared, additional privacy legislation was being discussed in Congress. The Right to Financial Privacy Act was passed in 1978. This act spells out the procedures that federal authorities must follow to obtain records of an individual or small-partnership customer of financial institutions (such as bank institutions, savings and loan institutions, and credit unions). If you are such a customer and the government wants to obtain records about you, it must notify you. It must also outline your right to block the action. Access may be authorized by you, or under administrative or judicial subpoena, search warrant, or formal written request. Any records obtained under this procedure cannot be transferred to another government agency or department unless related "to a legitimate law enforcement inquiry."

Also passed in 1978 was the Electronic Funds Transfer Act. This act requires financial institutions to make available written documentation of each transfer of funds (even though such transfer can be accomplished without it). The act protects your resources as a consumer by limiting your liability for unauthorized

---

Personal Privacy in an Information Society, U.S. Government Printing Office (Superintendent of Documents, Washington, D.C. 20402), July 1977, Stock No. 052-003-00395.

transfers to $50 per transfer and to $500 for multiple transfers. It protects your privacy by requiring financial institutions to notify you if any data about you or your transactions is released to a third party. A financial institution that fails to abide by this law may be directed to pay triple damages.

Lest we become complacent, it's appropriate to pause a minute. In 1935, President Roosevelt pledged confidentiality of the Social Security Administration records. Yet in 1982 the Selective Service System of our federal government persuaded Congress to allow it to use data obtained through Social Security applications to identify American men who had not yet registered for the draft. The list of names so obtained was to be matched against Department of Defense and Department of Transportation files to delete the names of those currently serving in the military services and the Coast Guard. The culled list was then to be matched against IRS files to find the current addresses of these persons. (About 525,000 or 7 percent of all draft-age men were claimed to be still unaccounted for.) In the late 1970s and early 1980s, computer matching of files was used by the federal government to search for welfare recipients who were also on federal or District of Columbia payrolls. The Reagan Administration initiated computer matching of files to check veterans with loans and other benefits, food stamp recipients, Medicare users, students with federal loans, housing beneficiaries, and others. The justification given for these computerized searches was an all-out war against waste and fraud.

The FBI's National Crime Information Center, or NCIC, was discussed in Chapter 1 of this book. Recall that it contains millions of records about persons who have been *officially accused* of crimes. In late 1982, Attorney General W. F. Smith approved a plan that would allow the Secret Service to enter into the NCIC the names of persons it decides *may pose a threat* to the President, Vice President, presidential candidates, visiting heads of state, and others for whom the Secret Service is responsible. Some members of Congress objected immediately. In their minds, the plan was—at least potentially—a dangerous precedent for wholesale surveillance. "Officially accused" differs significantly from "may pose a threat." In neither case must the individuals about whom data is entered ever be proved guilty.

We should ask ourselves several questions: Do ends justify means? For what purposes might other, more extensive searches be used? The focus of what we've discussed thus far has been on massive databases and the dangers associated with them. These dangers still exist. In the 1980s, however, the technical emphasis in many cases has shifted to widely distributed databases, electronic mail, home information systems, and interactive computing. About 25 percent of American households (and about 25 million viewers) were estimated to be wired for cable TV by yearend 1982. About 96 percent of American households had telephones. Computers and terminals selling for less than $100 apiece were readily available. Both cable TV and telephone-based systems were being used to test-market a wide array of two-way communication (videotex) services to consumers. Your home thus becomes a data source. You become not only an information receiver but also a data generator. Since these interactive systems operate in real time, eavesdroppers can learn about your actions as they occur, not simply after the fact. The difference can be compared to learning from your credit records that you traveled to, say, Chicago last month versus learning that you are in Chicago attempting to make a purchase right now. Such information may be useful for many purposes. It's not just coincidence either that firms with much experience in direct marketing have acquired major interests in the cable business; it seems to have great potential as a marketing tool. Time, Inc., Fingerhut, and American Express are noteworthy examples. (See Figure 17-7.)

In 1981, Illinois became the first state to enact legislation to protect individuals from invasions of privacy in the operation of cable TV systems. Its Cable Television Privacy Act prohibits the installation of equipment that can be used to monitor a subscriber's set or viewing habits except for service purposes. In October 1981, Warner Amex, operator of the Qube system in Columbus, Ohio, published its own voluntary, comprehensive code of privacy. This was the first such code to be promulgated by an operator of an interactive consumer service offering. At this writing, several states have created state cable commissions, but statewide subscriber privacy rules are yet to be formulated in most instances. The FCC has taken the position that cable privacy is not yet an issue calling for federal action.

Free-market advocates argue that decisions about secondary uses of personal data should be left to individuals, not dictated by privacy advocates. The core of the privacy issue is each individual's right to choose what he or she reveals to others.

COMPUTER CRIME   The subject of privacy, and more specifically, the computer-assisted invasion of privacy, leads us to a somewhat broader issue of computing. That issue is computer crime. Here, too, there are many questions without tidy textbook answers. What is computer crime? What causes it? How can we as individuals, organizations, or society prevent it? How can we detect it? Are there computer

FIGURE 17-7
Viewdata began offering Viewtron, its two-way communication service, to households in three counties of southern Florida in late 1983. Available items include government reports on products; reference and education materials; recreational information, such as airline schedules, menus, and concert guides; classified ads; games; electronic shopping, banking, and message service; and gateways to other databases.
(*Courtesy Bell Laboratories*)

criminals and, if so, how should they be punished? Are computers altering work patterns and other social activities in such a way that they actually lead people to crime? Are computers causing us to think differently about what is right and what is wrong? Are they, in fact, changing the moral behavior of our society?

At this writing, there is no widely accepted definition of the term *computer crime*. To prod our thinking about the topic, Jay Bloombecker, as Director of the National Center for Computer Crime Data, Los Angeles, proposed several scenarios. (See Figure 17-8.) He named each scenario in such a way as to provoke mental pictures that serve as memory joggers. Each of us needs to be ever mindful of the situations depicted.

The possibilities for theft, or *larceny*, in an EDP-system environment are limited only by the imaginations of all who directly or indirectly come in contact with the system. Diskettes, terminals, microcomputer chips, and even complete computer systems may be taken from inventory. Software—say the backup copy of a program that does marketing analysis—may be removed from a tape library. In 1982, FBI agents and sheriff's deputies recovered $3.2 million worth of integrated circuits stolen six months earlier from Monolithic Memories, Inc., the largest chip theft in California's Silicon Valley history. About that same time many loyal Apple users were stunned to learn than an in-house theft ring had

The Playpen: An act is committed as the result of an experiment, out of mischief, by a person or persons knowledgeable about computers—e.g., a student finds and accesses files containing course grades.

The War Zone: The computer serves as a tool of revenge—e.g., a disgruntled employee modifies a program so that it lowers customer account balances in a firm's accounts-receivable master file.

The Cookie Jar: Someone who is in need of money (or thinks so) has access to a computer system handling financial accounts and uses that access for personal gain.

The Land of Opportunity: Even when there is no financial need, someone knowledgeable about computers or computer-related procedures is tempted by the ease with which he or she can obtain funds by accessing the computer for personal gain.

The Toolbox: The computer serves as a tool in carrying out non-computer-related illegal operations—e.g., a sophisticated crime syndicate uses a computer as a means to more efficient and less easily detectable law breaking, as in interstate gambling or drug traffic.

Fantasyland: A person unknowingly assists others in committing a crime, not realizing the consequences of his or her actions—e.g., an employee discards company-confidential computer output into a waste bin that can be searched by others during off-hours.

The Soapbox: A person or group desiring the attention of an individual, organization, or society at large uses the computer as a means of getting that attention—e.g., a terrorist organization sabotages a computer installation.

FIGURE 17-8
Computer crimes of many kinds are being committed daily; these scenarios show common examples of such crimes, for which prevention and detection procedures are now being developed.

successfully diverted scores of Apple II and Apple III computers from the company's shipping and receiving department for illicit sale on the open market.

Fraud is, in legal terms, intentional deception to cause another to give up property or some lawful right. In an EDP-system environment, it is reflected most often as data manipulation or program modification. It may also occur as unauthorized access to computer-controlled funds. For example, one member of a household may use another member's Versateller card to withdraw cash without authorization to do so.

Embezzlement is the theft or fraudulent appropriation of money or other substance entrusted to one's care. It is a crime that has probably existed since the practice of having someone else do work began. A trusted employee may write or modify a program to calculate compound interest amounts, truncate them to the nearest dollar, and keep track of the truncated amounts. Over a large computer run, the accumulated sum of the truncated amounts can be sizable – a tidy nest egg to be routed to the account of a cooperating friend or relative. (See Figure 17-9.)

Computer files containing proprietary (company-owned) data, programs, product designs or specifications, and marketing plans can be copied, and the copies sold to a competitor, all with the help of the rightful owner's computer. Yet the original files may remain in place. If the competitor uses the files discreetly, no one may be the wiser.

An organization may purchase or lease a software product, then make copies of that software to run on computers in several departments. User groups often band together to buy a program, and then make and distribute copies of the program as though each member had purchased it. School kids make copies of copyrighted games stored on diskettes, trading for opportunities to do so among themselves with the same casualness they exhibit when trading baseball cards. Yet such acts are thefts, known as *software piracy*. Where is the concern for right and wrong?

An instructor or student may use computer time and storage space available on campus or via a time-sharing network for non-school-related purposes. Similarly, an employee may use a firm's computer system to write and debug programs, then sell those programs to small businesses via a software publishing firm. These persons may see computer time as an intangible asset, something that cannot be stolen physically, and therefore something that cannot be a proven loss to the computer system's owner. If other instructors, students, or employees ignore and therefore seemingly condone the usage, are they not also involved?

By 1982, estimates of the costs of reported computer crimes ranged from one hundred to several hundred million dollars per year. Experts who've been studying this issue for some time are quick to point out that even these estimates are but the tip of the iceberg – say from 5 to 15 percent of the computer crimes that occur. No official statistics on computer-related crimes are available because even those that are reported are tabulated under categories of larceny, fraud, and other "white-collar crimes." Of more significance is the fact that a vast number of detected computer crimes are not reported. The victims of the crimes knowingly absorb the losses, perhaps fearing even greater losses because of bad publicity if the crimes were made known. Are you and I likely to buy stock in a firm whose Vice President of Development has just been charged with siphoning more than $400,000 (the *average* payoff in a white-collar

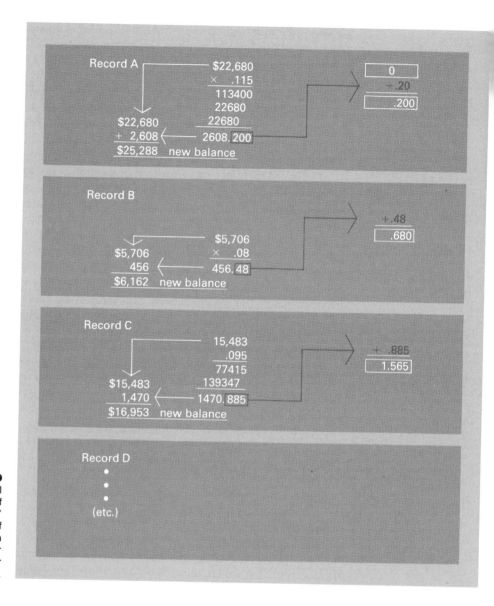

FIGURE 17-9
Because computers deal
with such large volumes of
data, a "salami attack,"
siphoning off the results of
truncation or rounding, can
yield significant funds. Their
loss may go unnoticed for
some time.

computer crime) from the firm's operating funds to a bogus vendor account? Are we likely to use a bank's automated teller machine if we are fully aware that fraud losses involving the bank's ATM's are doubling or even tripling each year? By law, banks now have to report when their computer systems have been compromised, but they are not likely to publicize it. Other businesses are not bound by such a requirement.

In the early 1980s, 18 states passed laws dealing specifically with computer crime. Many other states are considering such legislation. Montana law is representative. It prohibits four main types of computer crime: the placing of fraudulent information into a computer system; using the computer without the consent of the owner; altering or destroying computer files or data; and stealing computer-related property or services or using the computer to steal other types of property such as money or commercial documents. The law addresses the difficulty of detecting computer crimes by allowing the statute of limitations to extend until one year after a computer crime is discovered, rather than one year after a crime is committed, as is normally the case. A penalty of 2.5 times the value of the property damage may be imposed on convicted offenders.

Since the late 1970s, numerous bills dealing with computer crime have also been proposed at the federal level. Opponents of such legislation argue that the flexibility of the nation's legal structure makes specific laws aimed at computer crime unnecessary (40 federal statutes already in existence are claimed to cover all aspects of computer crime). They also argue that computer crime is neither as prevalent nor as costly as some experts indicate (and in many cases the computer is said to play only an incidental role).

Those who favor the legislation counter with specific examples to the contrary. In one well-known case, a conviction was obtained only because the offender had used a telephone line to penetrate the computer system of a federal contractor across state lines. If the telephone had been used only within the state, the wire fraud statute under which the indictment was brought might have been inadequate. In another case, the government failed to obtain a conviction because of definitional difficulties in establishing whether or not checks issued by a computer on the basis of fraudulent or manipulated data were forgeries. In a third case, two programmers had used nearly $250,000 of their employer's computer time to rescore music for a private business. They were convicted—not of stealing, but of mail fraud. After assessing the situation, the prosecutor had determined that focusing on the programmers' ancillary, or subordinate, actions rather than on their theft of computer time was the only road to conviction.

PROTECTION MECHANISMS

Since many computer crimes go undetected, preventing computer crimes before they occur is the best approach. At the organizational level, many steps can be taken. Most of them are just good business practices. They include:

- Carefully screening all job applicants, and making sure all employees are fully aware of organizational procedures and policies.

- Separation of functions so that, for example, the same employee is not writing a program, running the program during normal production use, and retrieving its output.

- Physical security mechanisms, such as cardkey locks that control parking lot entrances and exits, exterior and interior doors, and the use of equipment such as copy machines; closed-circuit television (CCTV) systems; and premise alarms that can be activated during off-hours. (See Figure 17-10.)

- Programmed controls, invoked within the computer system, such as user identification and password verification, input edit routines that check values for consistency or reasonableness, record counts or other control totals that are accumulated and balanced from run to run, and software locks designed to prevent users from copying certain programs and data files.

- Encryption of proprietary and sensitive data, programs, and other computer-related information

- Systematic and complete auditing procedures, conducted by both internal and external auditors, around, through, and with the help of the computer. For example, audit trails can and should be included in all programs at design

FIGURE 17-10
Electronic security systems
are helping to prevent
unauthorized access at
Boeing's Bellevue Data
Center and many similar
computer facilities.
(*Courtesy Boeing Computer
Services Company*)

time; the contents of changed master-file records can be compared with activity logs at periodic intervals to verify complete and accurate processing; and both normal and exception-handling procedures for operators, data center librarians, and other DP personnel must be documented, well understood, and followed at all times.

Individuals, organizations, and society at large can also employ legal mechanisms to protect computer-related and computer-controlled assets. Many of these mechanisms can act as deterrents to would-be offenders if they are applied with consistency. All too often, they are not. Nowhere is inconsistency, confusion, and disagreement better demonstrated than in the case of attempts to protect—or not protect—computer software. Among the mechanisms that organizations and individuals are using are trademarks, trade secrets, copyrights, and patents. In addition, almost all vendors use licensing agreements—specific terms and conditions regarding the use of software, hardware, or systems agreed to by all parties involved.

Organizations and individuals who are using trademarks are doing so primarily to protect selected names as unique identifiers. For example, Teletype is a registered trademark of Teletype Corporation; ECLIPSE is a trademark of Data General Corporation; and UNIX is a trademark of Bell Labs. These names cannot be used by others for similar products or for other purposes.

A trade secret gives its owner exclusive rights to use the technology, so long as the technology remains secret. The holder of the trade secret must go all out to keep the proprietary information secret. If the holder attempts to recover damages for the use of that information by another, say in a competitive process or product, the holder must be able to prove in court that all reasonable and prudent precautions were taken to protect the information.

The basic law of copyrighting in the United States is set forth in the Copyright Act of 1976, which took effect on January 1, 1978. This law was further clarified with respect to computer programs by the Computer Software Copyright Act of 1980. Of course, copyrighting as a protection mechanism precedes either of these dates. The rules of copyrighting are, by law, examined periodically.

Basically, copyrighting gives the owner of the copyright the right to prevent others from making copies of more than insubstantial portions of the copyrighted work; from making modifications, translations, and other derivatives of the work; and from displaying the work without the owner's permission. A work is copyrighted *automatically* when it is first fixed in a tangible medium of expression. Based on common history, we tend to think of copyrighting as a way of protecting printed documents. The fact that copyrights are also being used to protect software makes them especially interesting to the computer community.

When a computer program is created by an employee as a part of his or her job, the employer owns the copyright. A program created by a consultant belongs to the consultant, however, not to the client. The employer or the consultant may, of course, sign over the ownership of the copyright to another organization or individual. The program or other copyrighted work may be either unpublished (kept close to the vest through restrictive licensing) or published (marked with a prescribed form of copyright notice and distributed widely). Where the owner is not a single individual, the copyright is effective for 75 years in the case of published works, and 100 years in the case of unpublished works. Where the owner is a single individual, the copyright is effective for the life of that individual plus 50 years.

The essence of copyrights as a protection mechanism is that they are easy to obtain, are not broad in coverage since they guard only the form of expression and not the concept being expressed, and leave the burden of proof of infringement on the owner of the copyright, who must show that copying has occurred.

Patenting is an attractive protective measure to many because it provides such broad protection: a government-granted monopoly. The owner of a patent may prevent all others from making, using, or selling the invention covered by the patent during the 17 years of the life of the patent. These rights apply even if another inventor comes up with the same invention *independently* of the patented work after the date of the initial invention. Patents have been used to protect the creative works of scientists, engineers, and other designers for some time. Now the question arises: Can patenting also be used to protect creative work embodied in software?

Many software developers favor patent protection for software, but the U.S. Patent and Trademark Office (PTO) and some firms developing and/or marketing software and EDP systems oppose it. The PTO may be overwhelmed by the prospect of having to search prior work in the course of handling many, many patent applications. Opposing firms argue that allowing patent protection for software forces programmers to "reinvent the wheel" rather than build on technological progress, and that it places serious impediments on the spread of computer use so vital to our society and our nation. The U.S. Supreme Court has taken various positions on software patentability. Initially, programs were seen to be unpatentable on the grounds that they were simply implementations of mathematical algorithms. However, a 1981 ruling indicates that inventions using software or firmware cannot be denied patents solely because they contain such software or firmware. Since that ruling, numerous software patents have been granted. Moreover, literally thousands of applications for software patents have been filed and are awaiting action by the PTO at this time.

SOCIAL DEPENDENCY AND VULNERABILITY

In this section we examine the broad concerns of how computing affects certain aspects of our lives, namely, our *social dependency* on technology and our *social vulnerability* as a result of that dependency. Notice, first, the scope of activities we are considering. In recent years, we've seen rapid expansion of computer use. We know that more and more individuals, businesses, governments, and other organizations are directly and indirectly using computers. More and more kinds of activities are being done or controlled by computers. In terms of the actual volume of work accomplished, computer use is increasing at a phenomenal rate. Do we actually realize the scope of these computer-related activities? Let's consider some examples.

It's obvious that a hospital patient whose respiratory system functions as a result of computer-directed, life-sustaining equipment is dependent on that equipment. In a similar fashion, the "life" of the hospital as an organization is likely to depend on not just one but several computer systems. (Recall the many uses of computers in hospitals we identified in Chapter 1. You may also want to review the group of photographs at the opening of Chapter 15.) Furthermore, each person who lives in the vicinity of the hospital lives with the expectation that if he or she needs a service provided by the hospital, the service will be available.

A leading banking executive said recently: "If our computer installation is down for an hour, our bottom line is directly impacted. If we're down for 24 hours, the state's business revenue is impacted. If we're down for 48 hours or more, the GNP [gross national product] of our nation suffers."

To the extent that computer crimes prevent or impede the correct functioning of an EDP system, they are a major threat to that system. Acts of sabotage and vandalism are man-made disasters to which a computer system, hence an organization, and hence society, may be vulnerable.

Fires, floods, rainstorms and lightning, spillage of industrial chemicals or gases, and explosions are environmental disasters that can and do destroy computer systems. Perhaps because fire is often an aftereffect of other types of disasters, such as earthquakes, tornadoes, hurricanes, strikes, or riots, fire is the most widely feared threat, and also the most common one. The tons of paper and many other materials stored near computers are highly combustible. Moreover, once a fire starts, heat, smoke, and toxic fumes as well as flames may do extensive damage.

Only very small, battery-operated, handheld, and portable computers are immune to electrical power failures. What air is to humans, electricity is to most computers. As noted earlier, a loss of power may do more damage than simply stopping operations. In a system with storage components that are volatile, a loss of power is a loss of stored data and instructions. Furthermore, power surges can be as damaging to some types of equipment as power failures. Mainframe systems commonly require special air-conditioning facilities. If the air conditioning fails for an extended period of time, serious damage to system components may occur. Even systems that do not require special facilities may be damaged by excessive heat, humidity, dirt, dust, and other contaminants.

The most common software losses are attributable to program errors, or bugs. The greatest danger here is the program that appears to work but doesn't—the output that is "almost right." Designers, programmers, and/or testers may be at fault. Another consideration here is that the software may not have been developed in-house. Errors in acquired software are often hard to detect, isolate, and report (or correct), especially if in-house personnel are not familiar with the software or do not have access to related documentation.

Computer operators can damage equipment by, for example, dropping or mishandling disk packs or diskettes. They may also mount the wrong input tapes, or mount the right tapes on the wrong drives, and thus cause valuable data to be destroyed. The hazard of accidental modification of data is perhaps best exemplified by such everyday occurrences as keying errors made by users or data-entry personnel. We all make mistakes. Are such mistakes likely to be serious? A prominent security analyst puts it this way: "The crooks will never catch up with the incompetents."

WHAT CAN BE DONE? Whether an organization's EDP system consists of six IBM 3081s housed in a gigantic central computer facility, a network of DEC VAX machines distributed nationwide in ordinary office environments, or one desktop microcomputer, computer security should be a part of the organization's over-all security program. Management should consider: What assets do we want to protect? What are the risks and hazards to which the assets are exposed? What is the potential cost and the likelihood of each hazard's occurring? Then items should be prioritized and a risk-management plan established. For each asset, management may decide to (1) do nothing, (2) lower the dollar impact in case an identified problem does occur, or (3) lower the probability or possibility of the problem's occurring.

The EDP-system components housed in a main computer room can be safeguarded by a number of environmental protection mechanisms. (See Figure 17-11.) Such mechanisms are readily available from many vendors. The mechanisms must be complemented by well-designed security procedures. The procedures must be well understood and adhered to by all system users. Just as application programs must be tested, an organization's security mechanisms and procedures should be tested regularly. All too often, for example, personnel who work in an output distribution center do not know where the handheld fire extinguishers are, much less how to use them.

Whether distributing computing power throughout an organization lessens or increases that organization's security exposure is a topic that can be debated from several viewpoints. Since system components are positioned at various locations rather than at a central site, a single environmental disaster should be less devastating, at least from an equipment-cost point of view. On the other hand, office personnel may not realize that a wealth of proprietary information can be accessed by means of the desktop terminals or microcomputers at their disposal. Their lack of awareness may prove to be costly. Security analysts

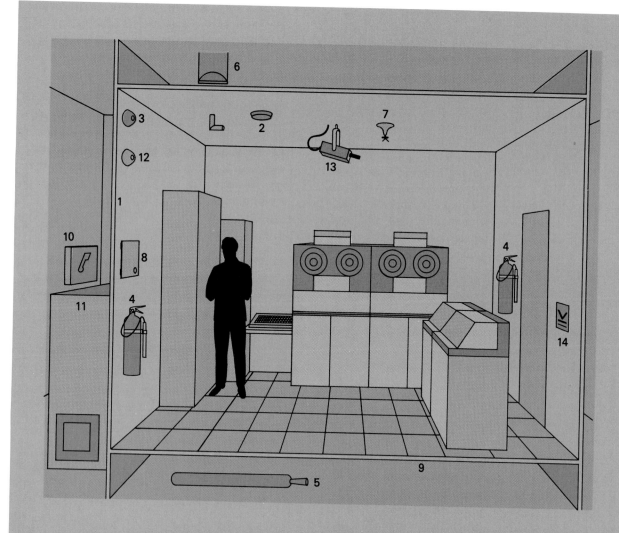

1. Fire wall
2. Automatic smoke, heat, and fire detection systems
3. Audible alarm (bell) for automatic detection systems
4. Handheld fire extinguisher
5. Carbon dioxide fire prevention system with cylinder under raised flooring
6. Halon fire prevention system with cylinder above ceiling
7. Automatic sprinkler equipment
8. Power distribution panel
9. Raised flooring; structural floors with positive drainage
10. Main switch for choice among public utility, standby power generator, or uninterruptible power system (UPS)
11. UPS
12. Premise alarm
13. CCTV to guard station
14. Identification card reader

FIGURE 17-11 The facilities of a main computer room can be safeguarded by a wide variety of environmental protection mechanisms, some of which are shown here.

sometimes point out that sending messages over public telecommunications networks is tantamount to posting the messages in neon lights in, say, downtown Houston. In any case, the security of a computer system is as strong as its weakest link, but no stronger.

Because not all security problems and disasters will be prevented, an organization's approach to security must include provisions for backup, that is, the means to recover when a problem or disaster occurs. Even a microcomputer user learns early to make duplicate copies of diskettes containing important programs or data files, for example. To fail to do so is to learn the hard way, when a diskette becomes unreadable or is written over by mistake. In like manner, the DP operations staff of a large organization may make daily or weekly backup copies of master files, accumulate log data sets reflecting all changes made to the master files between copy runs, and then re-apply the changes to a particular master file if it becomes necessary to do so. For greatest security, the backup files must be kept off-premises. Consider for a moment the vast databases of the Social Security Administration, the IRS, or the FBI. The contents of these databases are irreplaceable; many day-to-day functions of society are dependent on them. Plainly, there is no room for error in designing, implementing, and adhering to backup and recovery procedures for these files.

Site evacuation, damage assessment, emergency processing, salvage operations, permanent-site restoration, and methods of keeping system users and perhaps stockholders and the general public informed about developments are considerations that must be addressed as a part of contingency planning. An organization with similar processing facilities at multiple locations may have an easier time planning for emergencies than an organization with one large centralized data center. Reciprocal emergency-processing agreements and group mutual aid pacts agreed to by multiple organizations are other alternatives. Some service companies offer backup processing facilities as a major part of their businesses. Of course, an online order-entry system that normally runs under IBM's MVS operating system on an IBM 3084 can't be moved to a Burroughs 7900 merely because that happens to be the nearest computer system on which processing time and storage space are available!

Social dependency becomes social vulnerability when the technologies that we are dependent on are in themselves dependent on conditions that we cannot control, or cannot control without massive disruption to the normal functioning of our society. The computer is not one large machine that provides for all the needs of a utopian society, but many socially important things are dependent on computing—military systems, airlines, banks, telephones, to name a few. (See Figure 17-12.) Concerns about such dependencies are not based on the assumption that all these computer-assisted activities will fail at once, but on the recognition that a sizable failure in any one of them can cause major problems. To what extent is it reasonable and safe to depend on highly automated, complex computer systems for management and monitoring of critical functions?

The impacts of computers have raised many questions that have not yet been answered. For some questions, there may be no answers in the foreseeable future. For others, the answers may be set before we face the questions. The point at issue may really be whether computing is under human control. Most of us tend to believe that it should be. In support of this belief and to keep pace with the spread of computer technology, we must continue to develop system safeguards that are designed to protect the privacy of our personal affairs, the integrity of our organizations, and the very foundations of our society.

A   B

FIGURE 17-12 Real-time computer systems are helping law enforcement agencies to insure public safety in both the United States (A) and Canada (B). ([A] © *Stacy Pick 1982/Stock, Boston;* [B] *Phototheque, National Film Board of Canada*)

CHAPTER SUMMARY

1. Computers are having both direct and indirect economic impacts on organizations.

2. Computers may also impact organizational structure (for example, by facilitating centralization or decentralization, or a blend of both). The individual or department that controls an organization's computing systems controls a source of power within the organization.

3. Automation is the performance of a specific combination of actions by a machine or group of machines "automatically"—without human intervention. Computers are increasing both the rate at which firms are automating and the extent of that automation.

4. A robot is a general-purpose programmable machine that can do any of several tasks under stored-program control. In the United States, the greatest impacts of robotic systems have occurred in the automobile, steel, and aerospace industries. A virtual population explosion of industrial robotic systems is occurring at this time.

5. Artificial intelligence researchers are trying to understand how we think and, accordingly, to develop machines that help us in machine-thinking applications.

6. Concerns about depersonalization—even to the extent of replacing our names with numbers—have not materialized. Each of us has a responsibility to help determine what kind of, and where, a computer interface is acceptable to us.

7. Privacy is a social and legal issue involving questions such as how and what data will be collected about an individual, how and by whom it will be used, and how and by whom it can be changed. Both federal and state legislation has been passed to help protect an individual's rights in this regard.

8. Computer crimes involving larceny, fraud, piracy, and so on are prevalent, costly, hard to detect, and often go unreported (even when detected). Some laws dealing specifically with this problem have been passed. Good business practices can help to prevent computer crimes from occurring.

9. To protect their software assets, individuals and organizations developing and/or marketing software are using trademarks, trade secrets, copyrights, patents, and licensing agreements.

10. As more organizations use computers, as more kinds of activities are done or controlled by computers, and as the actual volume of work done by computers increases, our social dependency on computers increases also.

11. The threats to EDP systems include sabotage, vandalism, fires, floods, rainstorms and lightning, industrial chemicals and gases, explosions, electrical power failures or surges, and human errors reflected as operational mistakes or program bugs.

12. EDP systems can be protected by environmental protection mechanisms and well-designed security procedures. Backup and recovery procedures for system resources must be designed, implemented, and adhered to before disasters occur.

13. Social dependency becomes social vulnerability when the technologies that we are dependent on are in themselves dependent on conditions that we cannot control, or cannot control without massive disruption to the normal functioning of our society. As members of society, we must help determine the extent to which it is reasonable and safe to depend on highly automated, complex computer systems for management and monitoring of critical functions.

DISCUSSION QUESTIONS

1. (a) Show, by example, key differences between centralized and decentralized organizations in the way tasks are accomplished.
   (b) Point out how computers can support either method of organizational structure.

2. Discuss the implications of the following statement: "If knowledge is power, and if information is a source of knowledge, then we can assume that information is also a source of power."

3. Show, by specific examples, how the computer is changing the nature of jobs.

4. What is a robotic system?

5. (a) Why might robotic systems be viewed unfavorably by American workers?
   (b) How might workers benefit from them?

6. Describe some current practical applications of artificial intelligence?

7. (a) Suggest some concerns that might lead an individual, organization, or society to decide against further research or application of artificial intelligence.
   (b) How might these concerns be dealt with?

8. What constitutes invasion of privacy?

9. Choose any one of the computer crime scenarios in Figure 17-8.
   (a) Give specific examples of that scenario as they might occur in your home or business environment.
   (b) How can each crime that you named in part (a) be detected?
   (c) How might it be prevented from occurring in the first place?

10. (a) Show, by specific examples, what software piracy is.
    (b) What preventive or punitive actions do you think are warranted for these examples of piracy?

11. Distinguish between social dependency and social vulnerability with respect to computers.

12. In what ways are you addressing the issues and impacts of computing in your ongoing activities?

Glossary and Index

assembler program: a computer program that assembles programs written in an assembler language to produce machine-language programs: 368–70, 392

assembly listing: a printed output of an assembly run, showing both the source-program (assembler-language statements) and the object program (machine-language instructions) created from them, as well as other information that is useful to the programmer: 368–70

asynchronous operations: events occurring without regular time relationship. Hence, as applied to program execution, unexpected or unpredictable events with respect to instruction sequence. *Contrast with* synchronous operations: 218, 420

asynchronous transmission: a method of electrical transfer of data in which the sending and receiving units are synchronized on each character, or small block of characters, usually by the use of start and stop signals. *Synonymous with* start/stop transmission. *Contrast with* synchronous transmission: 480–81, 486

Atanasoff-Berry Computer (ABC): 8

AT&T: 429, 489–91

audio response: *See* voice output.

auditing: 533–34

automated teller machine: an unattended (self-service) banking device designed for direct use by customers: 31, 105–7, 416, 505, 532

automatic data processing: data processing performed largely by a machine, without intervention by a human operator; when that machine is an electronic digital computer, the sequence of operations may be referred to specifically as electronic data processing: 8, 40, 45

automation: the performance of a specific combination of actions by a machine or group of machines without the aid of a human operator (i.e., "automatically"). *Contrast with* mechanization: 7–10, 40, 45, 517–20. *See also* industrial automation; office automation.

auxiliary storage: storage that supplements primary storage. *Synonymous with* secondary storage: 48–49, 157–75, 245

background program: in a multiprogramming environment, a program that can be executed whenever the facilities of the EDP system are not required by a program having higher priority. *Contrast with* foreground program: 412–13, 420

backup: alternative files, equipment, or procedures available for temporary or emergency use in case of total or partial system failure: 159, 165–66, 414, 539

band printer: 121–23

bandwidth: the range of usable frequencies available for signaling; that is, the difference expressed in cycles per second between the highest and lowest frequencies available on a channel: 483

bar code: a machine-printed data representation consisting of lines that can be read by an optical reader: 64–66, 100–2

BASIC (Beginners' All-purpose Symbolic Instruction Code): a high-level programming language designed primarily for use in interactive problem solving by engineers, scientists, and others who may not be professional programmers: 45–46, 53–56, 330–32, 381–83, 392, 417

batch processing: a technique in which data to be processed or programs to be executed are collected into groups to permit convenient, efficient, serial processing. *Also called* stacked-job processing. *Contrast with* transaction processing: 12–13, 87, 407–9

belt printer: 122

beltbed plotter: 130–31

binary component: an element that can be in either of two possible conditions at any given time: 67–68

binary notation: 68

binary number system: a numeration system using the digits 0 and 1 and having a base of 2. For example, the binary numeral 1001 means $(1 \times 2^3) + (0 \times 2^2) + (0 \times 2^1) + (1 \times 2^0)$, which is equivalent to the decimal numeral 9: 69–70, 222–23

binary state: one of two possible conditions of a component. Most digital-computer components (for example, vacuum tubes, magnetic cores, transistors, and logic gates) are essentially binary in that they have two stable states: 67–68

bit: an acronym for *b*inary dig*it*; the smallest unit of data in the representation of a value in binary notation. A bit can be either a 0 or a 1: 68, 163, 168

block: (1) a group of words, characters, or digits handled as a unit and read into or written from primary storage in one I/O operation. In common usage, synonymous with physical record: 214; (2) in block-structured programming languages, a section of program coding treated as a unit, largely for purposes of storage allocation and transfer of control; for example, a PL/I procedure or begin block: 380, 384

blocking: handling two or more data units (such as records) as a single unit, or block, usually to increase the efficiency of EDP-system I/O operations. *Contrast with* deblocking: 440–41

block multiplex mode: the interleaved execution of channel programs to transfer, consecutively, single blocks of data to or from various high-speed devices to or from primary storage over a single channel interface. *Contrast with* selector mode: 214

branch: to pass control to other than the next sequential instruction in storage. *Also called* jump: 194. *See also* conditional branch; unconditional branch.

break-even analysis: 305–7, 464

bubble memory: storage constructed of tiny cylinder-shaped magnetic domains contained in a thin, crystalline magnetic film: 153–55, 247

buffer: a storage area used to collect data in order to compensate for differences in rates of data flow or times of occurrence of events when transmitting data from one device to another: 211, 216–18, 268

buffering: 216–18

bug: an error in a design or in program coding or an equipment fault: 56, 315–18, 329–30, 537

data, and supplying the results of these operations. In data processing, the device is usually a stored-program computer, which performs these operations without the intervention of a human operator: 8–10. *See also* analog computer; digital computer.

computer-aided design/computer-aided manufacturing (CAD/CAM): 19–22, 130, 258

computer-assisted instruction (CAI): 27

computer literacy: 5

computer-managed instruction (CMI): 27

computer store: 15, 32, 259–60

computer, uses of: 10, 18–31, 255–58, 270–74

computer word: a sequence of bits or characters moved, used in operations, and stored as a unit: 74, 148–49, 189, 199, 222–23

COMSAT: 490–91

concurrent processing: 410–13

conditional branch: an instruction that may or may not cause a transfer from the normal sequence of instruction execution, depending upon the result of some operation, the content of some register, or the setting of some indicator. *Contrast with* unconditional branch: 194

consistency check: a test of the relation of two or more values for control purposes: 533

console: the part of the computer used for manual control and observation of an EDP system: 51–52, 504

constant: a value that does not change during processing. *Contrast with* variable: 232, 331

control field: a fixed portion of a data item or record where information for control purposes is placed; for example, account numbers used for sequencing or transaction codes used for identifying the types of operations to be performed on input data. *Also called* a key: 159

control section: the part of a processor that effects the retrieval of instructions in proper sequence, the interpretation of each instruction, and the application of the proper signals to the arithmetic/logic unit and other parts of the computer system in accordance with this interpretation: 47–48, 184–86

control total: a sum of the numbers in a specified field of a group of records, determined repetitively during processing steps; any discrepancy from the total indicates that an error has occurred: 233–34, 533

control unit: a device functioning between the central processing unit and one or more input/output devices to perform error checking, buffering, code conversion, and similar functions during input/output operations. *Also called* a controller: 210, 212–16, 476

conversational computing: *Synonymous with* interactive computing.

conversion, data: changing from one form of representation to another; for example, from decimal to binary: 75–79, 90

    binary to decimal: 75
    binary to hexadecimal: 78
    binary to octal: 76
    decimal to binary: 75

    decimal to hexadecimal: 78–79
    decimal to octal: 77
    division-multiplication method: 75, 77, 78–79
    expanded notation: 75, 77, 79
    hexadecimal to binary: 78
    hexadecimal to decimal: 79
    octal to binary: 76–77
    octal to decimal: 77

copyrighting (to protect software): 535

core storage: an internal storage unit consisting of magnetic cores: 150–52

courseware: computer programs for instructional use: 26–28

CP/M (Control Program for Microcomputers): a well-known portable operating system especially common on 8-bit microcomputer systems: 258, 381, 427–29

CPU: *See* central processing unit.

crime, computer: 529–33, 536

CRT: *See* cathode-ray tube.

cursor: an indicator that shows the current position on a visual-display screen; not uncommonly, the indicator is an underscore character: 54–55

cycle time: the time the computer takes to get ready to process a request: 150

cylinder: all tracks accessible at one setting of the access mechanism of a direct-access storage device: 169

daisywheel teleprinter terminal: 124–25

DASD: *See* direct-access storage device.

data: any representation of a fact or an idea that can be manipulated and to which meaning can be assigned. *Related to* information: 6, 443–44, 493. *See also* database.

data bank: (1) a comprehensive collection of libraries of data (in inventory control, for example, one line of an invoice constitutes an item, a complete invoice constitutes a record, the complete set of such records constitutes a file, a collection of inventory-control files forms a library, and the libraries used by an organization are known as its data bank); (2) loosely, a database: 504–5, 525–26, 528

database: a comprehensive, integrated collection of data organized to avoid duplication of data, yet permit retrieval of information to satisfy a wide variety of user information needs: 273, 448–55, 460–61, 463, 465–67

database administration (DBA): 32, 455

database machine: a processor specialized by hardware and software to perform database management: 467–68

database management system (DBMS): software that handles the organizing, cataloging, locating, storing, retrieving, and maintaining of data in a database: 273, 455–56, 460–61, 463

data-collection device: 105–8

data communications: the electrical transfer of data from one point to another: 474–507

data communication system: *Synonymous with* teleprocessing system: 475–76

data element dictionary: 313

EBCDIC (Extended Binary Coded Decimal Interchange Code): an eight-bit code used to represent specific data characters in many current computer systems: 70–72, 90, 163, 167

E-COM: 500

EDSAC: 10

eighty-twenty rule: 462

electronic data processing (EDP): data processing performed largely by electronic equipment, such as electronic digital computers, rather than by manual, mechanical, or electromechanical techniques. *Related to* automatic data processing: 40–52

electronic digital computer: *See* digital computer.

electronic funds transfer: a communication between computer systems or within a computer system to transfer monetary values from one account to another electronically: 31, 500, 527–28

electronic mail: automated communication through electronic transmission facilities and devices: 24, 31, 257, 429, 475, 498–500

electronic security system: 533–34, 537–38

electrostatic plotter: 130–31

electrostatic printer: 127

embezzlement (with computer help): 531

employee security: 533

employment (in computing): 31–34

emulation: a process by which one computer system is made to function like another, in order to accept the same kind of data, execute the same programs, and achieve the same kind of results: 186

encryption: 533

end-of-file: *Also called* end-of-input: 233–34, 343–44, 442–43

end-of-volume: 442–43

ENIAC: 8–9, 145

Ethernet: 496–98

E13B type font: 98

E-time (execution time): the time required to perform the operation specified by an instruction. *Contrast with* I-time: 194–96

excess-64 arithmetic: 226

executive: *See* supervisor.

expert system: *Also called* knowledge-based system: 522–24

external data transfer: 212

facsimile equipment: digitized imaging devices often used as terminals in communication systems. *Also called* fax machines: 488, 499

feasibility report: 298

feasibility study: 296–98

Federal Communications Commission (FCC): 488–91, 529

fiber optics: 483–84

file: (1) a collection of related records (in inventory control, for example, one line of an invoice constitutes an item, a complete invoice constitutes a record, and the complete set of such records constitutes a file). *Also*

called a data set: 157–58, 442–48. *See also* master file; transaction file; (2) a logical entity operated on by an EDP system. *Contrast with* volume: 442–43

file maintenance: the process of updating master files by adding, changing, or deleting data to reflect the effects of nonperiodic changes; for example, the addition of new-product records to an inventory-control master file: 387

file management system: 448. *See also* data management system.

file organization: the techniques used to arrange the records in a file on a physical storage medium: 444–48

file system: software that manages physical space allocation on storage media, the creation and manipulation of files, and similar I/O-related functions: 442–46

firmware: *See* microcode.

first-generation computer: an electronic computer characterized by the use of vacuum tubes as basic components: 14, 404

fixed-length operation: pertaining to an operation in which operands always have the same number of bits or characters. *Contrast with* variable-length operation: 197–98, 222, 226

fixed-length word: 74, 198

fixed-point operations: pertaining to a numeration system in which each number is represented by a single set of digits and the position of the base point is implied by the manner in which the numbers are used. *Contrast with* floating-point operations: 222, 224, 227

flatbed plotter: 130–31

flat file: 450

flexible disk: a single thin manipulatable disk with one or two magnetic recording surfaces. *Synonymous with* diskette; floppy disk: 95–97, 146, 167, 170–71

floating-point operations: pertaining to a numeration system in which the base point is not held at a given position with respect to a given end of all numerals; each number is represented by two sets of digits, one of which represents the significant digits (the fraction) and the other indicates the position of the base point (the exponent). The number represented is equal to the fraction multiplied by the base raised to the power of the exponent. *Contrast with* fixed-point operations: 224–28, 235

floppy disk: *Synonymous with* flexible disk.

flowchart: a pictorial representation of the types and sequence of operations within a program (program flowchart) or the data, flow of work, and work stations within a system (system flowchart): 332–35. *See also* program flowchart; system flowchart.

flowcharting:
    cross-referencing: 329–30
    striping convention: 334–35
    symbols: 333, 345
    template: 332–34
    worksheet: 332–34

foreground program: in a multiprogramming environment, a program that has a high priority and therefore

simplex transmission: 482

simulation: (1) representation of the functioning of one system by another; for example, representing a computer or a physical system by the execution of a computer program, or a biological system by a mathematical model: 21–22, 27, 279–80; (2) same as desk checking: 330

small business system: 40, 156–57, 255–57, 271–73

snapshot: a dynamic dump of the contents of selected storage locations and registers performed at specified points or times during the execution of a program: 349

social dependency: 536–39

social vulnerability: 536–39

soft copy: a temporary, or nonpermanent, record of machine output; for example, a CRT display. *Contrast with* hard copy: 118

software: (1) a collection of programs, routines, and subroutines that facilitate the programming and operation of a computer; (2) as in (1), but also including documentation and operational procedures. *Contrast with* hardware: 46, 245, 258–59, 400–1, 534–36

software piracy: 531

solid character: 120

source data automation: the capture of data in a machine-readable form at the place where it is generated: 87–88. *See also* magnetic-ink character recognition; optical character recognition; voice input.

source document: 87

source program: a program written in a programming language such as COBOL, FORTRAN, or PL/I for input to a language processor (such as an assembler or compiler). *Contrast with* object program: 368–70, 372–74

source-program listing: a printed output of a compilation, showing the source-program statements as they were provided as input and other information useful to the programmer: 372–74

specialized common carrier: a company that furnishes communication services under the regulation of local, state, or federal agencies, generally by providing enhancements or special features to tailor common-carrier communication offerings to specific user needs: 490

spooling (simultaneous peripheral operations online): techniques that permit input to be transcribed from a slow-speed device (say, a card reader) to a high-speed data-recording medium (say, tape or disk) for subsequent entry into the computer, or that permit output to be written to a high-speed medium from where it can be transcribed to final form (say, a printed report) at a later time: 409

spreadsheet program: software developed to aid users in break-even analysis, budget planning and control, cash flow analysis, loan amortization, and other common business application areas. Examples are VisiCalc and Multiplan: 464

stacked-job processing: *Synonymous with* batch processing.

standardization: 73, 332–33, 372, 375, 378, 381, 383, 385

start/stop transmission: *Synonymous with* asynchronous transmission.

storage: pertaining to a device into which data can be entered and retained, and from which data can be retrieved at a later time: 144–76. *See also* primary storage; secondary storage.

storage capacity: 148–49, 267, 275, 279

storage printout: 347–49, 370

storage protection: a technique applied to prevent unauthorized reading or writing of data in a particular area of storage: 411–13, 419

storage register: a register to which an instruction is moved (from primary storage) when the instruction is to be interpreted and executed by the computer. *Also called* an input/output buffer or a data register: 187–88, 194–96, 198–99

stored-program computer: a digital computer that, under control of an initial sequence of stored instructions, can synthesize, interpret, alter, and store instructions as though they were data, and can execute these new instructions as though they were the initial instructions; in electronic digital computers, the instructions are generally stored internally in high-speed storage so they are readily accessible: 10, 41–46, 364–65

structure chart: a pictorial representation of the logical structure of a program or system; a tree diagram: 315–16, 336

structured design: *See* top-down design.

structured programming: a top-down, modular approach to program development that emphasizes certain basic patterns and control structures, and short one-entry-point/one-exit-point modules: 338–45, 375, 378, 380

structured walkthrough: a formalized defect removal technique in which reviewers go step-by-step through design or code; a formal design review or formal code inspection: 318, 347

supercomputer: 283–85

supervisor: the primary control program of an operating system; a program designed to organize and regulate the flow of work in a computer system by initiating and controlling the execution of other programs. In common usage, synonymous with executive and monitor: 46

synchronous operations: events occurring at regular, timed intervals. *Contrast with* asynchronous operations: 218, 440

synchronous transmission: a method of electrical transfer in which a constant time interval is maintained between successive bits or characters. Equipment within the system is kept in step on the basis of this timing. *Contrast with* asynchronous transmission: 480–81, 486

system: a set of interrelated elements that work together to perform a specific task or function: 291–92

system analysis: the study of an existing task or function in order to understand it and to find better ways to accomplish it: 293–309, 326–28